Understanding Youth Justice in Canada

Edited by Kathryn M. Campbell
University of Ottawa

PEARSON
Prentice
Hall

Toronto

This book is dedicated to all of the children and youth
I have worked with over the years:
For teaching me a great deal and in hopes of finding a better way.

And for Kathleen Darney, who showed me the true meaning of compassion.

Library and Archives Canada Cataloguing in Publication

Understanding youth justice in Canada / edited by Kathryn M. Campbell.

Includes index.
ISBN 0-13-121749-6

1. Juvenile justice, Administration of—Canada. 2. Juvenile
delinquency—Canada. I. Campbell, Kathryn M. (Kathryn Maria), 1960– II. Title.

HV9108.U54 2005   345.71'08   C2004-903977-6

ISBN 0-13-121749-6

Vice-President, Editorial Director: Michael J. Young
Acquisitions Editor: Ky Pruesse
Executive Marketing Manager: Judith Allen
Associate Editor: Patti Altridge
Production Editor: Charlotte Morrison-Reed
Copy Editor: Kelli Howey
Proofreader: Audrey Dorsch
Senior Production Coordinator: Peggy Brown
Page Layout: Janet Zanette
Art Director: Mary Opper
Cover Design: Michelle Bellemare
Cover Image: Getty Images

Statistics Canada information is used with the permission of the Minister of Industry, as Minister responsible for
Statistics Canada. Information on the availability of the wide range of data from Statistics Canada can be obtained from Statistics Canada's Regional Offices, its World Wide Web site at http://www.statcan.ca, and its toll-
free access number 1-800-263-1136.

3 4 5 DPC 09 08 07

Printed and bound in Canada.

Contents

Part Four LEGAL RESPONSES TO YOUNG OFFENDERS   156

Part Six **ISSUES OF SOCIAL JUSTICE**   289

Chapter Fourteen Understanding Girls' Delinquency: Looking Beyond Their Behaviour   289

Sibylle Artz, Diana Nicholson and *Carmen Rodriguez*

Chapter Fifteen Aboriginal Youth and the Criminal Justice System   313

Larry N. Chartrand

Chapter Sixteen Voices of Youth   334

Compiled by Kathryn M. Campbell

Preface

My interest in juvenile justice stems from my time as a youth worker during the early 1980s, which began following completion of an undergraduate degree in psychology. While I had little to no practical experience, I was hired at a large custody facility for young offenders and shortly thereafter was dealing directly with groups of young persons in open and secure placements. With no specific training, I quickly learned that the role of youth worker demanded that I was at times parent, caregiver, teacher, disciplinarian, and nemesis. Within the confines of policy regulations, and through an attempt to provide some sort of guidance to the youth I worked with, I engaged in supervision, recreation, counselling, and discipline. Five years as a frontline worker opened my eyes to several disturbing realities about how intervention for young offenders was practised and about youth justice in general: that there appeared to be little thought given to what was done with incarcerated youth, aside from straightforward containment and incapacitation; that living in a youth custody facility can be a harsh and terrifying experience for many young persons, where bullying and victimization occur frequently; that some young persons commit serious acts of violence at a young age, but are in the minority; and that young offender legislation falls very short of addressing the myriad social issues and family problems that are the reality for many youth and greatly influence their involvement in the system. My experiences dealing with young persons in custody fostered a desire to further explore these issues, which in turn influenced my graduate work and current research direction.

In this book, I have compiled a series of chapters that I believe cover the seminal issues in youth justice today. Having taught an upper-level university course in Youth Justice for the previous six years, I am cognizant of many of the critical issues and recent developments in this field. Given that no existing book appeared to cover in sufficient detail what I considered to be all of the significant issues, I decided to compile one myself. While my initial intention was to have a book that addressed my teaching needs, I had also hoped that by bringing together contributions from eminent scholars in the field of youth justice in Canada I would develop a book that would be of use to researchers as well. Furthermore, the introduction of the *Youth Criminal Justice Act* (YCJA) has opened up various new avenues for researchers to explore the current and future impact of this law on youth, on how legal professionals will interpret its new provisions, and on how young persons will be processed by the police, by the courts, and by correctional institutions.

While there are many existing books on the topic of youth justice, with the recent introduction of the *Youth Criminal Justice Act* there will be many new Canadian books on this topic. However, this book is aimed at filling a gap in the literature as it attempts to present a variety of perspectives on youth law, on how youth crime is perceived, and on the operation of the youth justice system. A book of this nature is not limited to a singular focus and brings together many noted scholars in the field of youth justice. Thus, it represents an attempt to marry a variety of approaches and provide an overview of differing philosophies, positions, and beliefs with respect to understanding youth justice in Canada. This book also contains several unique features that distinguish it from other books in the field of youth justice. For the most part, the contributions to this edition are original and written specifically for this publication. Each chapter covering a specific issue, theme, or problem about youth justice links the discussion with the *Youth Criminal Justice Act*.

Further, while each chapter is unique in its own right, this book tackles other topic areas not usually covered in a youth justice book. In particular, this book addresses the force of the United Nations *Convention on the Rights of the Child* on Canadian youth justice legislation (Chapter 4); the roles of legal professionals from the perspective of a Crown attorney and a youth court justice on the *Youth Criminal Justice Act* (Chapter 10); the issue of restorative justice and its role with respect to youth crime in Canada (Chapter 12); the changing nature of rehabilitation in juvenile justice (Chapter 13); and provides an experiential chapter from the perspective of youths in conflict with the law (Chapter 16).

A book of this nature would be useful for upper-level courses that examine youth justice and youth law in a variety of fields, such as criminology, psychology, sociology, social work, and law. It could also be used as a text for advanced college courses that examine perspectives on youth justice. Individuals working in the field of youth justice, such as probation officers, police officers, social workers, teachers, and professionals working in the mental health arena—or similarly, those who have an interest in this area—could also benefit from this book.

This book has been organized into six parts, based on similarly themed chapters grouped together. In Part 1, Introduction, Kathryn M. Campbell presents a theoretical framework to situate the remaining chapters of the book. Through an historical and contemporary overview of criminological and sociological theories, a format and context is provided for understanding the discourses about youth justice, youth crime, and youth law that follow. Part 2, Historical-Legal Perspectives on Youth Justice, contains four chapters focusing on the history and evolution of youth justice and youth rights legislation. Chapter 2, written by Bryan Hogeveen, presents a historical overview of youth justice, particularly how children were understood and regulated during the nineteenth century. Specific developments related to youth justice, such as the creation of institutions for delinquents, and the enactment of the *Juvenile Delinquents Act* and a separate youth court, are located within the context of the reform movement. In Chapter 3, Nicholas Bala provides a more recent historical analysis of youth law through an examination of the short life of the *Young Offenders Act* and problems in implementation that led to the enactment of the *Youth Criminal Justice Act*. Bala presents an overview of the youth justice court process, the limited powers of a youth court judge, and the role of the youth justice system in responding to youth crime, and clarifies how decisions will be made under this law. A recent decision by the Quebec Court of Appeal, which has great significance regarding how the YCJA will be implemented, is noted in detail.

Chapter 4, focusing on children's rights and written by Myriam S. Denov, presents the evolution of children's rights internationally and outlines the historical development of the United Nations *Convention on the Rights of the Child*. In explaining how the Convention applies in the national context, Denov examines the strengths and weaknesses of Canada's compliance with children's rights as recognized under the Convention. Further, Denov then presents an overview of the manner in which the terms of the *Youth Criminal Justice Act* comply with Canada's international commitment to children's rights. In the final chapter in this part, written by Susan A. Reid and Justice Marvin Zuker, juvenile justice procedure is used as a context for examining various conceptual frameworks. Reid and Zuker outline how these frameworks emanate from differing political and ideological perspectives and have been represented in legislation for young offenders over the last century. Recent case law illustrates how the *Youth Criminal Justice Act* reflects aspects of these models and demonstrates a movement away from incarceration for youth.

Part 3, The Nature and Extent of Youth Crime, comprises two chapters and focuses on how youth crime is measured, and then further interpreted via the media. The first chapter, by Jane B. Sprott and Anthony N. Doob, investigates trends in youth crime occurring over the previous two decades. Sprott and Doob explore various sources used to measure crime, specifically self-report and victimization surveys, police arrest data, and court statistics, and demonstrate the difficulties that occur when attempting to assess levels of youth crime. Their chapter provides statistics and information on trends in specific types of youth crime—homicides, violence, minor offending behaviour—and demonstrates provincial and regional variation for some of these data, as well as gender differences. The next chapter in this part, written by Susan A. Reid, focuses on the role of the media in perpetuating myths about the nature and extent of youth crime. Specifically, Reid explores the history of the issue of confidentiality of youth justice proceedings within the context of a young person's right to privacy when accused of criminal offences, as well as a consideration of the social implications of the existing provisions under the YCJA. Reid examines myths about youth crime, as advanced by the media, within the framework of a "moral panic." She then provides examples from several media content analyses, including her own recent research, that demonstrate how myths regarding youth and youth crime are developed, disseminated, and perpetuated.

Part 4, Legal Responses to Young Offenders, is comprised of four chapters, all examining various aspects of the application of criminal justice legislation. In the first chapter in this section, written by Peter J. Carrington and Jennifer Schulenberg, the role of the police is examined with respect to decision-making; specifically, the authority to arrest, search, and question, the decision whether to lay a charge, and the decision regarding the means used to compel court attendance. Through reference to the *Youth Criminal Justice Act,* they also demonstrate how the experience of youth in this regard differs from that of adults. Carrington and Schulenberg, by referring to their own data collected from police officers, outline those factors that police officers believe influence their decision-making when charging a young person.

The following chapter, by Nicholas Bala, examines the use of community dispositions from both historical and contemporary perspectives. In this chapter, Bala provides a rationale for the use of diversion and reviews its development historically, illustrated by examples of diversion programs, such as alternative measures under the *Young Offenders Act* and extrajudicial sanctions under the *Youth Criminal Justice Act.* Bala describes recent innovations in community-based programs in Canadian youth justice legislation, including youth justice committees and youth justice conferences, which both emphasize restorative justice principles. The roles and rights of youth with respect to extrajudicial sanctions are examined, as well as the consequences for youth of participating in these programs.

Chapter 10, by Crown Attorney Miriam Bloomenfeld and Justice David Cole, presents a unique perspective on the roles of prosecutors, defence counsel, duty counsel, and judges when dealing with young persons in youth justice court. By means of a fictional case study, Bloomenfeld and Cole illustrate how provisions of the *Youth Criminal Justice Act* are enacted with respect to extrajudicial measures, bail, charge screening, plea resolutions and sentencing, conferencing, and judicial pretrials. The final chapter in this part, written by Anthony N. Doob and Jane B. Sprott, traces the development of sentencing of young offenders. They provide an overview of the evolution of sentencing for young offenders through the previous century culminating with the YCJA, which contains specific sentencing principles. Statistics are used to illustrate trends in sentencing, as well as provincial variations. In this chapter, Doob and Sprott outline the contentious area of adult sentencing for young persons and demonstrate that this sentencing option was little used in the past and will likely remain so.

Part 5, Methods of Intervention, is comprised of two chapters that focus on traditional and non-traditional means of intervening with young persons who have been found guilty of crimes. In Chapter 12, Liz Elliott examines the history of restorative justice practice, particularly its Aboriginal roots, and describes many current programs based on this model of justice. Elliott outlines the difficulty of instituting restorative justice initiatives within the existing retributive framework of the Canadian criminal justice system, particularly the fate of victims and communities. Elliott then examines specific provisions within the *Youth Criminal Justice Act* that show promise with respect to restorative justice. The second chapter in this part, written by Kathryn M. Campbell, tackles the contentious issue of intervention. Campbell provides a framework for understanding how programs of reform have been aimed at troubled youth both historically and through legislation. Campbell introduces some of the larger debates in criminology around the provision of rehabilitation, particularly arguments over efficacy, the notion of treatment/intervention as a form of punishment, and how issues of race and culture impact on how programs are offered. Campbell discusses new sentencing options for judges available under the *Youth Criminal Justice Act* and provides examples of existing programs, both institutional and community based.

The final part of the book introduces issues of social justice. Each of these chapters illustrates the experiences of individuals who have been traditionally marginalized within the mainstream youth justice system. The first chapter in this part, by Sibylle Artz, Diana Nicholson, and Carmen Rodriguez, provides an overview of how the juvenile justice system in Canada interprets, labels, and responds to girls' delinquency. Artz, Nicholson, and Rodriguez provide statistics that demonstrate the degree of the problem and underline the difficulty in trying to get a clear picture of the nature and extent of girls' offending behaviour. Artz et al. are sensitive to how these issues are exacerbated for minority youth, and discuss the issue of "racialized justice" encountered by Aboriginal girls and African American girls. Further, they underscore how girls' behaviour in institutional settings is viewed in a stereotypical manner and provide examples of some promising intervention strategies for girls in custody that acknowledge the importance of gender differences. In Chapter 15, Larry Chartrand examines the experiences of Aboriginal youth involved in the criminal justice system. Chartrand presents an overview of some characteristics and causes of Aboriginal youth crime and victimization, as well as some disturbing facts about Fetal Alcohol Spectrum Disorder and its prevalence in Aboriginal communities. Chartrand compares traditional Aboriginal approaches to justice with more mainstream approaches. Finally, Chartrand examines aspects of the *Youth Criminal Justice Act* that are consistent with Aboriginal approaches to justice, such as conferences and youth justice committees. A case illustration provides an example of how the YCJA, when used creatively, can be implemented in a manner consistent with Aboriginal justice.

The final chapter in this book is an experiential presentation of interviews with two young persons. Both of these youth have been involved with the criminal justice and social service systems for extensive periods of time. Both come from troubled home environments and both have served custody in open, secure, and group home facilities. These two young persons provide, from their own perspective, a frank description of their dealings with police, lawyers, social workers, and the court system, as well as what it is like to live in custodial facilities. They offer accounts of the difficulties they experienced in their home environments that brought them into the system in the first place. Their stories present the opportunity to understand the effects of the youth justice system in a way that none of the other chapters in this book can. Ultimately, their voices remind us that we need to continue to undertake research in this area in order to develop a better system for young persons—one that is more just, more humane, and that acknowledges their voice in the process.

Acknowledgments

Primarily, I wish to thank all of the contributors who provided, for the most part, original work for this book. Given our short time frame, I appreciate the dedication evident in their contributions and for sharing their insight and expertise with others.

Several people were helpful to me in compiling and writing my own contributions to this book. First of all, I want to thank Chris Bruckert for her helpful comments on critical theory in the introduction. I would also like to thank Julian Roberts for comments on Chapter 13. Further, thanks go to Myriam Denov for reviewing Chapter 13, as well as being a sounding board for many ideas about this edition. Given the special nature of Chapter 16, I want to thank Loco, James, and Jewel for taking the time to meet with me and for sharing their stories. I would also like to thank Sandy Campbell for his invaluable assistance in compiling Chapter 16. Moreover, I want to extend my gratitude to Joanne Proulx and Sam Barile for facilitating my access to the young persons interviewed for Chapter 16. Finally, I want to thank Craig Norman, whose love and support, as always, keeps me grounded.

This book would not have been completed if it were not for the contributions of several people at Pearson Education. I want to thank acquisitions editor Jessica Mosher for her initial interest in the subject, and Ky Pruesse for following through where Jessica left off. Special thanks go out to Patti Altridge, associate editor, for her kindness, support, and patience throughout the entire process. Finally the comments of the anonymous reviewers at an earlier stage of development were particularly helpful in shaping the overall book.

Kathryn Campbell
Department of Criminology
University of Ottawa
Ottawa, Ontario

chapter one

Introduction: Theoretical Overview

Kathryn M. Campbell

Department of Criminology
University of Ottawa

INTRODUCTION

With the introduction of the *Youth Criminal Justice Act* (YCJA) in April of 2003, a new era of youth justice in Canada began. Any new legislation—especially youth law, which raises many legal, ethical, and moral questions—will respond in part to particular dissatisfactions with the old legislation, and at the same time will also foster new and different debates. Created in part as an attempt to address the overuse of custody for young offenders, the YCJA is meant to offer a compromise of sorts, blending the varying philosophies and approaches to youth justice in a more coherent fashion than its predecessor, the *Young Offenders Act* (YOA). At the same time, it is a lengthy, complex piece of legislation and it will take many years before its full impact is understood and the extent to which its provisions are meeting their stated intent is known. However, with respect to implementation, the law contains specific principles to guide police, prosecutor, judges, and others at various stages of the process (Tustin & Lutes, 2003).

There are a variety of approaches from which to examine the issue of youth justice, including but not limited to the following: from the perspective of youth justice law and its application, from varying theoretical frameworks regarding youth crime, from the perspective of youth justice policy (both contemporary and historical), as a historical examination of socio-political developments related to youth justice, or through an examination of intervention strategies aimed at young offenders. This book attempts to tackle the issue of youth justice from many of these perspectives, which are interrelated and to a large degree affect how youth justice is understood. Naturally, with the introduction of new legislation, other changes in both policy and practice will follow. Consequently, it is important to provide both a format and a context for understanding those changes. This involves an examination of issues surrounding the differing perspectives on crime causation, or rather theories and perspectives on why youth commit crimes. Criminological theories attempt to address questions of context, causation, motivation, and explanation for crime and delinquency. Emerging from a variety of epistemological traditions and philosophical premises, the various theories provide different frameworks for understanding crime more generally, and youth crime specifically.

Over the years, and in particular in the last century, a variety of theories have emerged to explain adult and youth criminality. While many have fallen into disfavour, some are still considered credible and offer certain insights. This brief overview will examine those theories that have emerged from the late nineteenth century up until the present day. This discussion of theories will be broken down into specific areas: historical theories including biological/pathological theories, psychological theories, sociological theories, and more contemporary approaches including other sociological and critical perspectives. Recently, various researchers have begun to develop a more integrative approach to understanding youth crime. This integrative perspective reflects the notion that theories that focus solely on single-factor explanations are insufficient in explaining criminality, and integrative approaches, which include complementary propositions from a number of traditionally distinct theories, are beginning to emerge (Smandych, 2001). While the framework for this introduction simplifies an understanding of youth crime causation, it nonetheless provides a comprehensive scope for situating similarly based conceptual perspectives.

Further, an overview of theories provides a framework for understanding the chapters that follow. This introduction ends with a brief discussion of how theory is interspersed throughout this text, as well as a short commentary on how the YCJA is understood as representing new liberal strategies of governance.

THEORIES: HISTORICALLY

Classical Perspective

The classical perspective encompasses the first recorded scientific perspective about crime in the Western world. Classical theorizing holds that individuals possess free will and are therefore responsible for their own actions. Thus, through human reasoning, individuals make choices regarding their behaviour that are premised on maximizing pleasure and minimizing pain. This perspective emerged from an era when demonic possession was considered the cause of much criminal or deviant activity. In essence, from the time of antiquity to eighteenth-century Enlightenment, the causes and cures of deviant activity were sought in the world of the supernatural (Pfohl, 1985). During that time, individuals who committed deviant acts were considered to be evil, as a result of either demonic temptation or possession. Thus, if possessed by the devil, an individual could still be punished but was not held responsible for his/her actions. The seventeenth-century example of the Salem witch trials illustrates one manifestation of this perspective. The control of so-called demonic deviants was publicly meted in the hands of religious authorities, and took the form of public executions and other rituals such as public shaming.

Thus, it was during the period of Enlightenment that the first "modern" perspectives of deviance and social control emerged. The Italian philosopher Cesare Beccaria's influential work *An Essay on Crimes and Punishments* reflected the dominant thinking during that period, which called for a movement away from super-natural accounts of deviance and toward the primacy of reason and the role of calculated rational choice (Pfohl, 1985). His essay emphasized the presumption of innocence and the need for a written code of criminal laws. Beccaria believed that the guilty deserved to be punished, that the punishment should fit the crime, and that those who commit crimes must be held responsible for their actions (Bell, 2003, p. 141). He and other Enlightenment thinkers emphasized the notion of the "social contract," whereby society itself represented a legalistic contract among consenting individuals. During the same period in England, Jeremy Bentham advocated for rational legal reform similar to Beccaria. Both scholars believed that those who committed crimes were rational actors and would be susceptible to state efforts to deter crime. The objective of classical state control was the deterrence of future deviance through the rational application of calculated punishment in the form of the state prison (Pfohl, 1985, p. 63).

Deviance as Biology/Pathology

The next period of theorizing regarding crime and deviance can be described as positivism and emerged during the late nineteenth century. This type of thinking seeks reasons for deviance in the biological or pathological makeup of the individual. Those who share this perspective hold a belief in determinism; deviance was considered to be the product of natural causes. Furthermore, knowledge regarding how pathology causes deviance was obtained only through positivistic science; that is, through controlled observation and scientific experimentation (Pfohl, 1985, p. 87). One of the first to theorize about criminals in this way was Cesare Lombroso, as evidenced in his publication of *The Criminal Man*. Through an autopsy of a known criminal, Lombroso explained the presence of unusual depressions in the skull as evidence that this individual was an atavist, or born criminal: an evolutionary throwback. By studying a group of Italian prisoners, Lombroso attempted to prove that criminals were somehow biologically different and had more "atavistic" anomalies. Another nineteenth-century positivist, Dugdale, sought to prove that deviance was hereditary and studied an entire "criminal" family. Tracing the Jukes family history, Dugdale (1877) found a preponderance of social and criminal problems, which he took as evidence for the heredity of crime. Later, feeblemindedness (Goddard, 1912) and "tainted life blood" (Weinberg, Rubington, & Hammersmith, 1981) were also scientifically studied in order to demonstrate causality with respect to deviance and criminality.

The notion that organic pathology was responsible for criminal behaviour was alive and well at the turn of the twentieth century. In a study in the United States, Hooton (1939) compared a large sample of incarcerated criminals with a control group over a 12-year period. He found that the criminal group possessed more "organic weaknesses," and classified types of criminals according to their body types. Not long after Hooton's work, Sheldon (1949) undertook research that suggested a certain body type or soma-type predisposed individuals to certain types of criminal or deviant behaviour. For Sheldon, an individual's soma-type was thought to affect temperament and personality, which in turn influenced criminal behaviour. The soma-types *endomorph* (soft and round), *mesomorph* (muscular and lean), and *ectomorph* (thin and frail) were each thought to engage in particular delinquent or deviant behaviour. His conclusions were later supported by the Gluecks (1956), who found the mesomorph soma-type most frequently amongst delinquent youth.

More recently, studies of twins and adoptees have been used to bolster the "deviance as pathology" arguments. Studies have involved comparing identical twins to fraternal twins, as well as studying identical twins who are separated at birth and adopted, to ascertain the extent to which parental criminality affects children. Early twin research indicated higher concordance in criminality among identical twins, and some parent criminality studies indicated a small trend suggesting that some adopted children reproduce the criminality of their biological parents (Pfohl, 1985, p. 95). Chromosome research has also been put forward as evidence for the heredity of deviance. In particular, early research supported the notion that chromosomal abnormalities, such as cases of Klinefelter's syndrome, where males possess an extra X chromosome, or cases of XYY, where males possess an extra Y

chromosome (Taylor, 1984), could be linked to deviance. However, the links between chromosomal abnormalities and violent crime or deviance are particularly weak, as such abnormalities are found in equally small numbers amongst the general population (Sarvin & Miller, 1970).

Further research has attempted to demonstrate links between intelligence and delinquency. A great deal of this work has consistently shown that the lower a person's IQ, the greater the chance they will become involved in delinquency (Gordon, 1987), or rather that a relationship exists between incarceration and a low IQ score (Pfohl, 1985). Such results should not be interpreted as demonstrating a causal relationship, given that it is difficult on such tests to separate out the effects of race and living in disadvantaged life circumstance from intelligence. However, it has also been consistently found that youth who commit crimes have a higher incidence of both learning problems, or problems in school achievement, and attentional difficulties (Loeber et al., 1998). Again, the findings do not demonstrate a causal relationship, but rather point to the importance of examining the impact of factors such as race, poverty, prenatal environment, and other life circumstances on later learning and attentional problems.

One main difficulty with this perspective is necessarily dictated by its response: if deviance is determined by biology, then the social control of deviance would likely require a biological or medical component. Thus, repressive biological control in the name of "treatment" has taken a variety of forms over the years. At the turn of the twentieth century, the eugenics movement sought to eliminate "undesirables" (criminals, mentally ill persons, and epileptics) through involuntary sterilization (Lilly, Cullen, & Ball, 1995). It is only very recently that such practices have been abolished. The de-institutionalization movement of the 1960s also resulted in a reliance on pharmaceutical medication to control the behaviour of so-called deviants, including those with psychiatric disorders and those who commit crimes. The increasing use in recent years of stimulant medication to manage the behaviour of young persons diagnosed with attentional problems, such as attention deficit hyperactivity disorder, is a clear example of the pathologizing of deviant behaviour and the control of that behaviour through psychopharmacology (cf. Diller, 1996; Olfson et al., 2003).

As with much of the pathologically oriented research, positive results may be more indicative of flawed research methods than actual genetic disposition (Pfohl, 1985, p. 95). A great deal of the research seeking evidence for pathological origins of deviance was methodologically flawed as it failed to account for the impact of environmental influences on criminal behaviour. Furthermore, restricting the sampling to mainly prisoners as representative of all who commit crimes is erroneous, as criminals are simply those who have been unsuccessful in crime and have been caught. Also, when control groups have actually been used for comparison purposes, their non-random nature negates their purpose. A great deal of value judgment occurs with this type of theorizing, as does defining what in fact constitutes delinquent or deviant behaviour. Recent theorizing of this nature is much more modest, as such theorists now believe that biology may have an effect on criminality, but does so by interacting with the social and physical environment (Bell, 2003, p. 148).

Psychological Explanations

Psychoanalytic Theory Psychological explanations for criminality are similar to biological ones; they are positivistic, but rather than focusing on physical attributes as causative, they point to the importance of the mind, or the psyche, on criminal behaviour. The first of these is psychoanalytic theory. Originally introduced by Freud in the nineteenth century, the psychoanalytic perspective viewed deviance as emanating from various ego deficits or ego failures (Lester & Van Voorhis, 2000, p. 119). According to this perspective, deviance is reflective of an imbalance among the three aspects of personality: the *id*, the *ego*, and the *superego*. In particular, an overdeveloped id, or pleasure-seeking aspect of the personality, would cause problems, as would an underdeveloped superego, the parenting part of the personality. An underdeveloped superego would be unable to harness the desires of the overdeveloped id, and thus individual desires would take precedence over societal ones and result in deviant or antisocial behaviour (Redl & Toch, 1979).

From a psychoanalytic perspective, deviance could also occur due to disruptions in childhood development. If unresolved conflicts occur during the developing years, when a child must successfully pass through various stages of development, then an abnormal personality may likely develop.

Deviance at this point may assume a symbolic relationship to some aspect of the unresolved developmental crisis, which could likely manifest in criminal behaviour. Psychoanalytic explanations for criminality also emphasize the importance of childhood experiences on later adult choices. Unconscious motives are also proffered as explanatory for a variety of anti-social acts. Erikson (1968) further developed psychoanalytic theory and identified eight stages of development through which individuals must progress, each representing an opportunity for conflict and crisis. Identity crises are thought to occur when individuals do not successfully progress through each stage of development. As explanatory models, psychoanalytic explanations are somewhat circular in reasoning, are virtually impossible to measure and prove, and are thought to overemphasize the importance of childhood experiences (Pfohl, 1985, p. 100).

Personality Theory   The second type of psychological explanation for criminal behaviour is personality theory. This type of theorizing proposes that particular personality traits or variables can be linked to criminal or deviant behaviour. Early research tended to point to clusters of specific types of traits, such as jealousy, inadequacy, and impulsiveness, as being more commonly found in the backgrounds of criminals (Eysenck, 1964). Various personality inventories developed in recent years are thought to be objective and capable of ascertaining particular personality traits in individuals. The Minnesota Multi-Phasic Personality Inventory (MMPI) has been used extensively and contains a scale that measures "psychopathic deviation," which is said to differentiate criminals from non-offenders (Pfohl, 1985, p. 100). Early tests of the MMPI indicated that prisoners scored high on asocial, amoral, and psychopathic scales (Hathaway & Monachesi, 1953). More recently, the *Diagnostic and Statistical Manual of Mental Disorders* (DSM-IV-TR), 4th edition (American Psychiatric Association, 2000), contains descriptions of several personality disorders thought to be located extensively within criminological populations. For example, conduct disorder has been diagnosed amongst young offenders, and anti-social personality disorder and borderline personality disorder diagnoses often are found in adult prisoner populations. A variety of symptoms must be present over a specific period of time in order for a definitive diagnosis to be made. As with psychoanalytic theorizing, it is difficult to objectively and accurately measure the existence of personality traits linked to criminal behaviour. Furthermore, not all those who possess such traits will ultimately engage in criminal behaviour.

Behavioural Theory/Behaviourism/ Social Learning Theory   Behaviour theory posits that all behaviour is learned, whether it is considered problematic or normal. It is only through societal labelling that some learned behaviours are considered deviant. Behaviour theory is less concerned with childhood experiences and more focused on the "here and now." Behavioural approaches tend to ignore the emotional sources of problematic behaviour and focus on increasing or decreasing target behaviour by identifying the conditions that maintain or discourage it

(Lester, Braswell, & Van Voorhis, 2000, p. 129). Watson (1916), one of the first to write from this perspective, believed that human behaviour could be learned in the same way that animals learned behaviour in the laboratory. He emphasized the notion that newborn babies represented a *tabula rasa,* a blank slate, from which they are capable of learning anything. Radical behaviourism, of which classical conditioning is an example, involves the association between a stimulus and a response as it changes behaviour. A conditioned response can be learned through a conditioned stimulus. In the famous example of Pavlov's dog, food (an unconditioned stimulus) could stimulate an unconditioned response—salivation (Pavlov, 1927). Over time, and by pairing a bell (conditioned stimulus) with the food, salivation would happen when the bell occurred alone, thus becoming a conditioned response.

More recently, B. F. Skinner, the father of operant conditioning, posited that all behaviour is influenced by reinforcers (1953). Thus, behaviour that is followed by positive reinforcement will likely be repeated, whereas behaviour that is followed by a punisher or negative reinforcer will likely desist. Finally, social learning theory takes behaviour theory somewhat further by instituting a cognitive component. Learning is said to occur through observation and imitation and is shaped by the reinforcement of role models (Bandura, 1977). From this premise, if all behaviour is learned then it also can be unlearned, and many existing programs in adult and youth correctional facilities are based on this principle. Many cognitive behavioural interventions, premised on social learn-

ing theory, attempt to alter cognitive strategies that reinforce negative or anti-social behaviour by replacing them with pro-social skills. While some positive results have been found with these strategies in terms of reducing anti-social behaviour, behaviour and learning theory is somewhat limited in application in that it is difficult to generalize beyond institutional environments.

Sociological Explanations

Sociological explanations differ from psychological explanations of crime in that they seek to understand crime and delinquency by examining the social environment and are not concerned with individual pathology. However, early sociological perspectives were more positivistic in nature. In essence, they attempted to seek out the causes of delinquency by discerning what aspects of environment affect behaviour and by examining the differences between delinquents and non-delinquents (Bell, 2003, p. 153).

Social Disorganization and Strain Theory
This sociological perspective, which has also been described as an ecologically oriented theory of crime, emerged from the University of Chicago in the 1920s–30s, a time of rapid social change resulting in a breakdown of normative social control (Pfohl, 1985, p. 152). Here, explanations for crime causation were sought in the environment of the delinquent, and not in rational choice or individual pathology. Accordingly, early researchers from this school, such as Shaw and McKay (1931, 1942), describe deviance and crime

as emerging from situations of social disorganization. Certain types of social environments or neighbourhoods, characterized by higher rates of poverty, adult crime, unemployment, and social assistance, were considered more "disorganized." Deviance and criminality were said to emerge when less dominant values and norms conflict with the more dominant ones (Winterdyk, 2000, p. 40). Through studying crime in the neighbourhoods where it occurred, Chicago researchers were able to develop statistical maps of "naturally" delinquent areas within cities. Where social disorganization theorizing breaks down is by defining disorganization in a very narrow manner; its failure to account for white-collar crime; and its portrayal of all forms of social disorganization in a negative manner. Finally, social disorganization neglects the determining effects of social stratification, or the unequal distribution of material resources (Pfohl, 1985, p. 168).

Anomie This sociological perspective emerged from functionalism, which considers deviance to be constructive in that it strengthens the bonds of existing social order. Anomie, Durkheim's original conception, simply refers to a state of normlessness where moral convictions and compliance with social controls are absent. In such instances, crime, delinquency, suicide, and other social problems increase. Merton (1938) extended and refined this notion of anomie in describing how discrepancies between cultural goals and the means to achieve them are created and reinforced by a class system of reward distribution (Bell, 2003, p. 155). These conditions create "strain," where other means, some

illegal, may be sought to achieve success. Merton identified forms of adaptation to strain, or explanations of different types of deviance, which include conformity, ritualism, innovation, retreatism, and rebellion (Winterdyk, 2000, p. 42). Conformity refers to the extent that one adopts mainstream values and strives to achieve these goals by conventional means, while each further adaptation contrasts with the path of conformity. Ritualism involves the rejection of cultural goals and focuses on the means of goal achievement. Innovation occurs when a person adopts social goals but creates new means of attaining them as he or she is unable to use legitimate means. Retreatism occurs when individuals do not participate in society as they reject the goals and means of attaining them, whereas rebellion results when individuals reject both culturally defined goals and the institutional means to achieve these goals. Thus, in reaction to "strain," individuals find creative means of adapting and/or succeeding in society.

Delinquent Subculture In a further extension of Merton's *anomie* perspective, Cohen (1955) developed the idea that the delinquent subculture or gang is a psychologically based reaction to the frustration associated with the inaccessibility of middle-class goals for working-class youth. Gang involvement has a psychological component in that it is a collective "reaction formation" against the unreachable, yet valued status of middle-class culture (Pfohl, 1985, p. 218). In this instance, youth are able to achieve status or success in their own right, through the many delinquent activities that accompany gang involvement. According to this perspective, it is through a breakdown in the home and school environments that working-class youth are blocked from aspiring to middle-class values. These youth are considered vulnerable to the lure of gang involvement and the frustration-relieving rewards that are needed to sustain involvement in gangs.

Differential Opportunity One final extension of Merton's *anomie* perspective is that of Cloward and Ohlin (1960), who situated the sociological cause of strains toward deviance in blocked opportunities to achieve socially valued goals. For them, this produces discontent and results in frustration and a search for alternative means of achieving aspirations. The subcultures that develop in response to this are produced by the same blocked opportunities, but vary in terms of deviant adaptation. In their study of juvenile offenders, Cloward and Ohlin were able to identify three forms of subculture involvement: the criminal subculture, the conflict subculture, and the retreatist subculture. The *criminal* subculture represents a highly organized criminal authority, allowing youth the opportunity for structured, profitable involvement in delinquency. The *conflict* subculture is less organized and offers the opportunity for expressing anger and frustration through violence. Finally, the *retreatist* subculture contains failures from the other groups; unable to achieve cultural goals, youth involved in this subculture are often detached and engage in alcohol and drug abuse.

The *anomie* perspective was widely accepted in the 1960s–70s and greatly influenced thinking about deviance and social control in spite of the fact that there was little empirical research supporting its central concepts (Pfohl, 1985). This may be due in part to the significant rise of the welfare state following the Second World War, which had a large impact on the growth of professional sociology. However, this perspective has been criticized for its overemphasis on social class (Bell, 2003, p. 157) and its portrayal of society as being overly homogeneous, with shared cultural goals and aspirations (Pfohl, 1985, p. 233).

Culture and Learning Theory

Learning theory has roots in both psychology and sociology. The central theme for sociology is that deviance or criminality is learned behaviour. Learning deviance is not a result of pathology of the individual, but occurs in larger society, although society is not considered the cause of deviance per se. Rather, deviance in this instance is thought to emerge from the interactions that occur between individuals in society. A French social theorist from the nineteenth century, Tarde (1912), was the first to speculate about the effects of learning on delinquency. He discussed how the origins of deviance were governed by imitation and suggestion, concepts that were later adopted by more contemporary sociological theorists.

Differential Association The concept of learning theory was further elaborated on by Sutherland (1939), who believed that delinquent behaviour was learned, particularly through interacting or associating with those who commit crime. For Sutherland, social disorganization does not foster crime, but rather crime occurs through differential social organization, based on different subgroups or subcultures within society. From this perspective, deviant behaviour will likely occur when criminal acts are viewed more favourably than non-criminal acts. However, the type of behaviour engaged in is dependent on the frequency, intensity, duration, and priority of contacts with criminals (Winterdyk, 2000, p. 43). Nonetheless, those who commit crimes must also possess the requisite skills, attitudes, and motivations to follow through on their criminal acts. Whether or not criminal behaviour becomes permanent is dependent on what types of reinforcements the young person receives; if positive, criminal behaviour will likely increase, if negative, it may cease.

Drift and Delinquency Matza's (1964) theory of delinquency and drift further incorporates learning models and suggests that deviance is partly chosen and partly determined. From this perspective, deviants drift in and out of conventional society and do not differ significantly from non-delinquents in terms of their value system (Pfohl, 1985, p. 273). For Matza, delinquent behaviour is situational and not learned, thus it is based on the situational factors presented at a given time, dependent on the circumstances and opportunities available. Involvement in delinquent activity is thought to occur over a period of time, whereby an individual is slowly drawn in through mutual support from others. Attraction or experimentation with deviance involves a drift toward deviance, but later becomes learned when experimentation with deviance proves successful. The idea of drift toward a deviant lifestyle is supported by what has been described as a "subterranean" American tradition that favours risk, excitement, and adventure (Pfohl, 1985, p. 274).

Most social learning theorists do not elaborate on why certain types of behaviours are thought of as deviant. This perspective emerges from a social–psychological framework and thus downplays the role of conflicting social interests. While this type of theorizing is practical and continues to garner support in explaining youth engagement in crime, it falls short in that it is difficult to test empirically and does not acknowledge the role of less tangible factors such as intelligence, different personality traits, or environmental conditions on the commission of crime (Winterdyk, 2000, p. 44).

Social Control Theories

There are many social control theories and they share a common assumption that deviance does not have to be explained (Williams & McShane, 1998). They question the concept of conformity and seek to understand what makes some conform, since deviance is thought to occur when socialization breaks down. Following from earlier theories of social disorganization and strain theory, control theory examines the way in which people become insulated from pressures to deviate, or how social bonds that tie people to conventional society protect them from delinquency (Pfohl, 1985, p. 163). In other words, control theories examine those factors that serve to control behaviour for some individuals.

Techniques of Neutralization Furthering Sutherland's notion of differential association, Sykes and Matza (1957) suggest that in learning deviance one also learns a set of rationalizations that protect the self against the moral claims of the conventional world (Pfohl, 1985,

p. 249). These learned techniques of neutralization are used to face moral challenges that allow for the rationalization and justification of deviant choices, protect individuals from self-blame, and allow them to blame others (Sykes & Matza, 1957). Accordingly, there are five techniques of neutralization. The first, the denial of responsibility, happens when a young person denies responsibility for deviance and blames others. Through the second technique of neutralization, denial of injury, a young person would admit responsibility for deviance but deny that any injury occurred. The third technique, denial of the victim, acknowledges responsibility for the act and for the injury but conveys the victim as the deserving target. The fourth technique, condemning the condemners, focuses on the authority figures, who are blamed for targeting the youth and are then ridiculed. The final technique of neutralization, appeal to higher loyalties, involves an admission of deviance, but the motivation is considered unselfish or honourable—for example, to help friends, family, gang, or political causes (Sykes & Matza, 1957).

Control Theory–Containment, Social Bond Reckless (1973) theorized about how social structural factors, such as disorganization, can have a mediating effect on crime through social psychological factors, such as containments. These containments or constraints serve to inhibit criminal activity and emerge from the self: there are "inner" containments of self-control or "outer" containments such as a strong supportive environment. When these containments are weakened, criminal activity or non-conformity is more likely to result. Hirschi's (1969) control theory, a slight variation on Reckless', states that delinquency results when an individual's bond to society is weakened or broken. For Hirschi, the inner dimension of social bonding is based on the extent to which one is committed to a conventional belief system, thus preventing involvement in delinquent activity. However, the outer dimension of social bonding is based on attachment, commitment, and involvement.

Attachment refers to a person's bond or ties to others, *commitment* refers to the degree to which a person is tied to conventional ways of behaving, while *involvement* refers to the level to which a person is engaged in the pursuit of conventional activities. Hirschi's social bond theory, an extension of the themes involved in the disorganizational perspective, focuses on those forces that work to constrain people to stay within the bounds of established normative order (Pfohl, 1985, p. 164). While social control theory has been an influential theory with respect to youth crime, it does not account for "maturational reform," where youth naturally move away from criminal involvement as they age (Bohm, 1997).

CONTEMPORARY THEORIES
Societal Reaction Perspective

The societal reaction perspective works within the tradition of interpretive sociology, which emphasizes the importance of the subjective meaning in the social organization of everyday living (Pfohl, 1985, p. 287). Hence, this perspective is less concerned with the "causes" of deviance per se or with statistical probabilities and official data for understanding crime. The focus of inquiry is no longer on the criminal but rather poses questions about crime itself. Theoretical underpinnings of the societal reaction perspective on deviance are found in labelling theory, the interactionist or the social constructionist perspective. This perspective is concerned with power as the driving force behind labelling and the consequences of the labelling process.

Labelling Theory Societal reaction perspectives on crime and delinquency can be first traced to Tannenbaum (1938). Tannenbaum believed that once a youth admitted to committing delinquency it was difficult for him or her to escape criminal stereotypes, and he or she would begin to accept the criminal label (Winterdyk, 2000, p. 43). Tannenbaum described this process as the "dramatization of evil"; the label of deviant becomes the consequence of the act, once the young person is sanctioned by the authorities. The premise of Tannenbaum's theorizing was expanded upon significantly in the 1960s–70s by sociologists Becker (1963), Goffman (1963), Kituse (1975), and Schur (1973). These labelling theorists were also influenced by symbolic interactionism (Blumer, 1966), which posits that humans interpret or define—and do not simply react to—the actions of others.

However, labelling theory appeared a decade earlier, when Lemert (1951) examined how certain individuals or things become labelled deviant in the first instance, as well as the later effects on individuals of being labelled as deviant. There are, then, two types of deviance: *primary deviance* occurs through the commission of a deviant act, whereas *secondary deviance* refers to all the behaviours a person develops as a result of societal responses to the primary deviance, or the reactions to others' reactions (Bell, 2003, p. 166). In other words, through a lengthy process of socialization a person begins to develop a self-concept as a deviant, which is further reinforced by official reactions to the deviant acts. The social context and circumstances greatly influence whether or not a particular behaviour becomes labelled as deviant and whether an individual retains the deviant label. Becker (1963) expanded on Lemert's ideas and hypothesized that the deviant nature of an act emanates from societal responses to that act. In essence, deviance becomes the "master status" of the individual—all other defining characteristics of the individual disappear, and only the deviant status remains. A further aspect of the labelling process, as defined by Schur (1973), is "retrospective interpretation," which means that once a deviant label is inferred all previous behaviour is understood within the context of that label. Further, Goffman (1963) describes how labelling occurs when people are forced to take on roles whereby they are stigmatized not only for how they appear, but also for how they act.

Labelling theory had a significant impact on social policy for young offenders in the early 1970s, as it greatly influenced the growth and development of community-based sanctions. Such sanctions were considered preferable to incarceration, from a labelling perspective, as young persons could thus avoid the stigma associated with being imprisoned. The emergence of labelling theory also paralleled the decarceration movement for adult prisoners and the deinstitutionalization movement for mental patients during that same era. However, one resultant effect of this movement for young persons was "net widening" (Cohen, 1985), which meant there was a large increase in the numbers of young persons who remained in the community but were under the social control of the criminal justice system—youth who previously would have been dealt with far more informally. Furthermore, labelling theory falls short as reaction or labelling theorists tend to disregard the relationship between labelling and the social, political, and economic organization of society as a whole.

Social Construction This perspective has also been referred to as *phenomenological sociology,* which involves the study of society as it appears within the consciousness of its members (Pfohl, 1985, p. 292). Social realities are understood only as they are constructed by members of society. Berger and Luckmann (1967) posit that language is used to symbolically communicate and create social order. Within this social order are social constructs of what society has deemed to be deviant or criminal behaviour. *Objectification* is the term used by Berger and Luckmann to describe the process whereby symbols are experientially transformed into external social realities and become natural realities. Thus, the label of criminal or deviant is in itself a social construction, and is not questioned by society but rather accepted as part of the natural order.

Critical Perspective

The critical perspective in sociological and criminological theorizing rejects the traditional approaches of the past and turns its attention to power relationships and issues of social control. Theorists from this perspective suggest that in hierarchically structured societies, such as ours, the social control of deviance is shaped by the interests of those in positions of power (Pfohl, 1985, p. 334) and functions to reproduce social inequality. Accordingly, acts of resistance by those who threaten the status quo are defined as deviant or criminal, while the harmful acts committed by elites are not addressed. This process results in the behaviour of differing groups of marginalized persons becoming stereotyped as deviant. The critical perspective gained prominence from the 1970s onward, empowered in part by movements toward the recognition of the rights of groups previously discriminated against in society: women, racial minorities, prisoners, and youth.

Conflict Theory

Conflict theories are concerned with the struggles between various factions in a society: religious, social, political, ethnic, and economic. This perspective differs from most other consensual approaches, as conflict theorists object to the notion that social order is based on public consensus and believe that the law is operating in the interests of particular segments of society. From this perspective, how rules and laws are created and applied is of particular significance. Here, the notion of power is central, and conflict theorists view law as a tool of power. Radical conflict theory, which emanates from Marxist thinking, focuses on how material existence and its regulation to a large extent determine the content of social control (Pfohl, 1985, p. 347). In order to understand why specific behaviours, actions, and actors are considered deviant, they must be situated within the system of economic relations, in the fundamental struggles to control capital.

While Marx was not particularly concerned with the application of his theory to crime and criminals, since the 1970s various criminology and social theorists have incorporated some basic Marxian premises into their thinking. In particular, Quinney (1977) presents a Marxist critique of crime, criminology, and crime control where he links capitalist structures to the organization of crime control by the state. Platt (1969) presents a critical analysis of the political and economic origins of the youth justice movement in the United States. Finally, Taylor, Walton, and Young (1973) present a left idealist perspective that recognizes that structural inequalities in power and interest underpin the processes by which laws are created and enforced. From the perspective of new criminology, capitalism creates relationships of exploitation, inequalities become institutionalized, and crime is a rational response to this social order, in essence a by-product of the political economy (Lilly, Cullen, & Ball, 1995, p. 190).

Left Realism

This perspective emerged out of existing radical criminological circles in the United Kingdom of the late 1970s and early 1980s. Left realism attempted to marry the critical sense of conflict theory (or what came to be known as *left idealism*) with an acknowledgment of the "real" aspects of crime. In particular, this included the origins, nature, and impact of crime in the working classes (Lilly, Cullen, & Ball, 1995,

p. 194). Left realism differed from the new criminology and accused it of placing too much emphasis on the state and neglecting issues of crime causation (Young, 1986). Not surprisingly, left realists were concerned with the study of victimology, as it was perceived up until that time that victims had been neglected from the more radical perspectives. This perspective is concerned with researching and developing social and criminal justice policies to address the harms caused by crime and examining explanations of crime through social policy.

Governmentality Theory

Governmentality theory emerged from the latter work of Michel Foucault and takes as its focus issues of government (Dean, 1999). Government, in this sense, is concerned with acting on or directing human conduct, which is perceived as something that can be fashioned toward specific ends. In dealing with how we think about governing, governmentality focuses on rationalities, which are broad frameworks that shape how we should govern, what we govern, and with what means (O'Malley, 1996). Studies of governmentality are concerned with how thought operates within organized ways of doing things, with regimes of practice, and with its ambitions and effects (Foucault, 1977).

The governmentality framework attempts to understand how policies and practices of governance create blueprints of what constitutes good, moral, and responsible conduct. It also examines how these policies and practices of governance ensure that citizens are regulated through coercive tactics, and at the same time are encouraged to become self-regulating actors through subtle discourses of responsibilization. This particular perspective does not provide an explanation or understanding of crime causation or responses to deviance per se. Instead, governmentality approaches seek to understand how broader criminal justice discourses become enacted, and in turn how such practices act on individuals.

Feminist Perspectives

Many of the psychological and sociological theories previously discussed do not acknowledge gender differences; nor do many recognize women's or girls' criminal behaviour as criminal. Historically, the criminal behaviour of women and girls was often pathologized as "sickness," and the manner in which they were processed through the criminal justice system reflected existing patriarchal attitudes. Furthermore, early theories about the crime of women and girls emphasized female biology and sexuality as explanatory factors. Thus, women and girls were marginalized or ignored in much of psychological and sociological theorizing up until the mid twentieth century. The women's movement, which emphasizes the centrality of gender and power in social relationships, emerged in part from the emancipation movement of the mid nineteenth century United States (Miles, 1989). Second-wave feminism, which surfaced during the women's movement of the 1960s–70s, furthered these notions by examining the role of women in society as affected by existing patriarchy (Daly & Chesney-Lind, 1988). However, there are many types of feminist theories, including radical, phenomenological, and liberal, that place differing emphases on the effects of patriarchal structures as they affect women. Feminist criminology examines those factors that impact on how women and girls become involved in the criminal justice system and the discriminatory treatment they receive once they enter the system (Gelsthorpe, 1988; Smart, 1976). Some feminist theorists explore the experience of women as criminals, while others examine women's experiences as victims of crime.

Integrative Theories

In recent years, theorizing in criminology has moved away from singularly focusing on one theoretical perspective to more integrative approaches, combining the strengths of various theories into one approach. While most of the integrative approaches have emerged from a particular discipline, in some cases theories have even bridged different disciplines.

Opportunity Theory This particular approach focuses on the criminal event itself, as dependent on situational and social factors. Here, the emphasis is on the notion of rational choice and that there may be many different explanations for criminal activity, given the complexity of crime itself (Bell, 2003). *Routine activity theory,* advocated by Cohen and Felson (1979), is a lifestyle theory that is concerned with the availability of opportunities to commit crimes. Crimes would occur only when suitable targets were available, controls to deter crime were absent, and individuals were motivated to commit crime. *Rational choice theory* further expands on routine activity theory by integrating all parts of a criminal event (targets, motivation, situation) and then adding the notion of rational choice (Clarke & Felson, 1993). The idea is that a potential criminal will assess all available information before engaging in a criminal act, including the consequences of that act, and then make a rational choice whether or not to act.

Differential Association and Learning Theory Combining tenets of Sutherland's theory of differential association with that of learning theory, Burgess and Akers (1966) developed a theory they term *differential association–reinforcement theory*. This perspective posits that delinquent and criminal behaviour is learned through association with more criminal or delinquent peers. This theory was later reformulated by Akers (1994) and renamed *social learning theory*. Here, borrowing from Bandura (1977) as well as Sutherland, Akers explains the development of delinquent and criminal behaviour through principles of differential association and learning theory. He hypothesizes that in order for delinquent and criminal behaviour to occur, one must be exposed to criminal norms; criminal behaviour must be further rationalized as acceptable and must be imitated and rewarded.

Social Control and Social Learning Theory A variety of theoretical approaches that integrate a diverse number of theories can be subsumed under this heading, including social learning theory, control theory, strain theory, labelling theory, social bond theory, and radical conflict theories (Bell, 2003). Self-derogation theory, introduced by Kaplan (1975), posits that self-esteem motivates many of our actions, and our ability to conform is minimized by interactions with family, school, and peers that devalue our self-esteem. Interactional theory developed by Thornberry et al. (1991) focuses on how social structures affect social bond and social learning. Weakened social bonds will produce delinquent behaviour, but it also must be learned and reinforced. Colvin and Pauly (1987) incorporate aspects of radical conflict theory, social control, and social learning theory and believe that coercive aspects of social control in the home and school, which impact on the development of delinquent behaviour, are in turn influenced by class structures in society.

THEORY IN RELATION TO UNDERSTANDING YOUTH JUSTICE IN CANADA

Theories that attempt to explain causation with respect to crime and delinquency are many and varied for both adult and youthful offenders, and this chapter has discussed only some of them. Many theories are no longer relevant, but provide a historical understanding of how modern-day theorizing has evolved. Several theories, particularly the sociological ones, are similar or complementary and are only slight variations on other theories. Nonetheless, theory is particularly significant in understanding youth justice, both historically and today. In criminology, theory provides a foundation, or context, for situating not only the practice of justice, but also how justice is conceptualized and understood. Theory is of particular importance with respect to youth crime, as understanding crime causation allows us to explain the frequency, perceived seriousness, and social impact of youth crime, which in turn allows us to better control, deter, or prevent such behaviour (Winterdyk, 2000, p. 36).

Not all of the chapters in this text have a theoretical orientation per se; nor do they attempt to situate aspects of youth justice and youth law within the framework of theory. Rather, these chapters provide an understanding of aspects of youth law from a more practical position, in terms of how the law or youth justice policy is applied, or present an overview of existing policy considerations with respect to youth justice. They provide explanatory indications of how the YCJA is currently being implemented, as well as how existing social structures affect its implementation. This book is broken down into five specific parts and contains 16 chapters, many of which nonetheless emphasize theory with respect to youth justice. In Chapter 2, "History, Development, and Transformations in Canadian Juvenile Justice, 1800–1984," Bryan Hogeveen draws attention to how children were conceived of and regulated by those in positions of power in the nineteenth century. Within a conflict theory perspective, Hogeveen outlines how efforts on behalf of the reform movement and child savers of that century, while ostensibly motivated by concerns for the welfare of the working classes, also disguised paternalistic attempts by the ruling classes to control their behaviour. In addition, in Chapter 5, "Conceptual Frameworks for Understanding Youth Justice in Canada: From the *Juvenile Delinquents Act* to the *Youth Criminal Justice Act*," Susan Reid and Marvin Zuker situate youth justice within models of juvenile justice procedure. These models, while not concerned with causation directly, reflect differing ideological perspectives regarding the importance of the "protection of society" versus the "needs of young persons" in responding to youth crime. Here, the authors demonstrate how juvenile justice procedure reflects these differing ideologies, which have evolved significantly over time and have been affected by larger socio-political developments.

In Chapter 7, "Youth Crime and the Media," Susan Reid provides an overview of how collectively popular images of young offenders have been socially constructed through myth making by the media. Through the lenses of both labelling theory and social constructionism, the processes employed by the media to "interpret reality" and sell the news convey youth and youth criminal activity in a distorted and exaggerated manner. In Chapter 12, "Restorative Justice in Canadian Approaches to Youth Crime: Origins, Practices, and Retributive Frameworks," Liz Elliott situates her discussion of restorative justice by contrasting it with retributive justice practices. Accordingly, she demonstrates how the theoretical premises inherent in a retributive approach, such as utilitarian beliefs and the argument that crime can be deterred by the threat of punishment, are inconsistent within a restorative framework. In Chapter 13, "Rehabilitation Revisited: The Changing Nature of 'Intervention' in Juvenile Justice," Kathryn Campbell explores how the concept of rehabilitation has been construed historically, which in turn impacts on strategies of intervention. Here, through an overview of youth legislation, Campbell describes how conceptions of youth crime causation have in turn affected policy positions from rehabilitation to punishment, from strategies in the "best interests of the child," to overriding concerns of proportional punishment. Finally, in Chapter 14, "Understanding Girls' Delinquency: Looking Beyond Their Behaviour," Sibylle Artz, Diana Nicholson, and Carmen Rodriguez explore responses to girls' offending behaviour, through feminist theory. By examining gender differences in the pathways to delinquency and violence, Artz, Nicholson, and Rodriguez illustrate how societal structures that discriminate against women impact on young girls in conflict with the law and how the criminal justice system to a large extent fails in its attempts to address the problems presented by these youth.

THE *YOUTH CRIMINAL JUSTICE ACT:* ADVANCED LIBERAL STRATEGIES OF GOVERNANCE?

The YCJA, as did its predecessor, the *Young Offenders Act,* attempts to be many things to many people. At the same time, the YCJA appears to present a more coherent sentencing philosophy than did the YOA, within the context of proportionality considerations. However, certain aspects of the YCJA can be understood within the framework of governance, within those broader discourses about youth and youth crime and how those have become enacted in practice. The evolving political climate from which the YCJA emerged reflects existing socio-political structures; in particular, the neo-liberal political climate existing in late twentieth- and early twenty-first-century Canadian society. Evident within certain provisions of the law are aspects of these new liberal political rationalities, which in turn reflect the notion that the individual must be responsibilized; that is, made responsible for his or her own state or situation. This is consistent with "rights"-based legislation for youth. Thus, the fact that a young person commits a crime is regarded as the result of his or her own actions, for which he or she is held responsible. In the case of youth under criminal law, this "responsibilization" is also broadened to include his or her parents. While the notion of holding parents directly responsible for the crimes committed by their children did not exist under the YOA, various provincial statutes contain provisions that hold parents financially liable for damages their children incur. This issue re-emerged for the drafters of the YCJA through the inclusion of section 25(10), a provision that allows provincial governments to seek reimbursement from parents for their children's legal costs.

The YCJA represents a return to a less formal, more privatized, and more paternalistic approach—or, in neo-liberal terms, a minimal state. This minimal state can be understood as involving less direct government in the provision of the law. The role of government agents has been drastically reduced; in extreme instances, state involvement becomes limited to organizing and contracting out services. For example, under the YCJA there is much greater emphasis on the use of community sanctions for youth who commit minor offences. In particular, the federal government has tied several funding initiatives to the provision of community-based, community-supported programs. Ostensibly, a decreased emphasis on custody, firmly entrenched in provisions of the YCJA, should naturally result in an increased use of community-based sanctions. However, it is likely that community-supervised sentences do not receive the same attention or the same formal supervision as institutional programs. This in turn could result in less accountability and a great deal less uniformity of approach, as well as the potential for abuse. Given the difficulty for existing provincial social and community services to handle the current number of community-based sanctions, an increase in these numbers will likely result in a greater reliance on privatized services provided by the market.

The introduction of the *Youth Criminal Justice Act* and developments surrounding its implementation can be understood as typical "advanced liberal" strategies of governance. In particular, under the YCJA, there is evidence that the new law is attempting to "define deviance down." What is occurring is that minor offending is effectively being decriminalized and becomes the purview of an equally minor response; for example a trespass notice, caution, or extrajudicial sanction. Minor offences, including first-time offences, are less and less subject to formal sanctioning under the YCJA. At the same time, youth who commit minor offences are deemed worthy of the investment of time and resources on the part of the state. Minor offenders become re-

sponsibilized, as it is believed that such offenders have the potential to be saved; to be transformed; to become good, self-regulating, self-governing citizens. Moreover, at the same time, minor offenders become further bifurcated from so-called serious offenders. The YCJA reserves more and more serious sanctions for those who commit more serious offences. For example, the YCJA has lowered the age of eligibility for a presumptive adult sanction from 16 years to 14. Similarly, it has also extended the reach of a presumptive adult sentence to those individuals who have committed a third serious violent offence.[1] These more violent offenders are thus excluded from society; they are perceived as beyond help and are warehoused by the state as a means of protecting its citizens. This bifurcation of offences was also evident in the last set of amendments to the YOA in 1995, which were an attempt to institute a similar strategy (Campbell, Dufresne, & Maclure, 2001). In effect, this conceptual bifurcation of young offenders into two groups of serious and minor also underlies an assumed division of responsibility between the state and the community in managing them.

CONCLUSION

Theorizing about crime and delinquency has evolved considerably over the last century. While pathological theories are no longer relevant, some psychological or positivist accounts still influence thinking in certain circles. It would appear that a number of the later sociological theories, integrative perspectives and critical approaches continue to influence thinking in the study of youth justice with respect to

understanding how youth become involved in criminal activity. However, the
myriad different perspectives demonstrate
that no single one dominates—that there
are many ways of conceiving of youth
crime, and that further research is welcomed and necessary.

Theoretical perspectives about youth
crime causation provide the opportunity,
context, and framework for further understanding youth crime and ultimately
youth justice. By beginning a text on youth

justice from the perspective of its origins—
from the perspective of theory—the
groundwork has been laid for a more rigorous and thoughtful study of this topic.
In reading the following chapters, this
foundation in theory will likely aid in a
more critical analysis of youth research,
youth policy, and youth law. It is hoped
that this particular overview will provide
the context for a greater, more reflective
understanding of youth justice in general.

References

Akers, R. (1994). *Criminological theories: Introduction and evaluation.* Los Angeles, CA: Roxbury Publishing.

American Psychiatric Association. (2000). *Diagnostic and statistical manual of mental disorders* (4th ed.), Text Revision. Washington, DC: Author.

Bandura, A. (1977). *Social learning theory.* Englewood Cliffs, NJ: Prentice-Hall.

Becker, H. (1963). *Outsiders: Studies in the sociology of deviance.* New York: Free Press.

Bell, S. J. (2003). *Young offenders and juvenile justice: A century after the fact.* Scarborough, ON: Nelson, Thomson Canada Limited.

Berger, P., & Luckmann, T. (1967). *The social construction of reality.* Garden City, NJ: Anchor Books, Doubleday.

Blumer, H. (1966). *Symbolic interactionism.* Englewood Cliffs, NJ: Prentice-Hall.

Bohm, R. M. (1997). *A primer on crime and delinquency.* Belmont, CA: Wadsworth Publishing.

Burgess, R. L., & Akers, R. (1966). A differential association-reinforcement theory of criminal behaviour. *Social Problems, 14,* 128–147.

Campbell, K. M., Dufresne, M., & Maclure, R. (2001). Amending youth justice policy in Canada: Discourse, mediation and ambiguity. *The Howard Journal of Criminal Justice, 40*(3), 272–284.

Clarke, R., & Felson, M. (1993). *Routine activity and rational choice.* New Brunswick, NJ: Free Press.

Cloward, R. A., & Ohlin, L. E. (1960). *Delinquency and opportunity: A theory of delinquent gangs.* New York: Free Press.

Cohen, A. J. (1955). *Delinquent boys: The culture of the gang.* New York: Free Press.

Cohen, L., & Felson, M. (1979). Social change and crime rate trends: A routine activity approach. *American Sociological Review, 44,* 588–608.

Cohen, S. (1985). *Visions of social control: Crime, punishment and classification.* Cambridge, UK: Polity Press.

Colvin, M., & Pauly, J. (1987). A critique of criminology. *American Journal of Sociology, 89,* 513–551.

Daly, K., & Chesney-Lind, M. (1988). Feminism and criminology. *Justice Quarterly, 5,* 497–535.

Diller, L. (1996). The run on Ritalin: Attention deficit disorder and stimulant treatment in the 1990s. *Hastings Center Report, 26*(2), 12–18.

Dean, M. (1999). *Governmentality.* London: Sage Publications.

Dugdale, R. L. (1877). *The Jukes: A study in crime pauperism and heredity.* New York: Putnam.

Erikson, E. (1968). *Identity: youth and crisis.* New York: Norton.

Eysenck, H. J. (1964). *Crime and personality.* Boston, MA: Houghton Mifflin.

Foucault, M. (1977). *Discipline and punish.* Paris: Gallimard.

Gelsthorpe, L. (1988). Feminism and criminology in Britain. *British Journal of Criminology, 28,* 93–110.

Glueck, S., & Gleuck, E. (1956). *Physique and delinquency.* New York: Harper.

Goddard, H. (1912). *The Kallikak family.* New York: Macmillan

Goffman, E. (1963). *Stigma: Notes on the management of spoiled identity.* Englewood Cliffs, NJ: Prentice-Hall.

Gordon, R. A. (1987). SES versus IQ in the race-IQ delinquency model. *International Journal of Sociology and Social Policy, 7,* 29–96.

Hathaway, S., & Monachesi, E. (1953). *Analyzing and predicting juvenile delinquency with the MMPI.* Minneapolis, MN: University of Minnesota Press.

Hirschi, T. (1969). *Causes of delinquency.* Berkeley, CA: University of California Press.

Hooton, E. A. (1939). *The American criminal: An anthropological study.* Cambridge, MA: Harvard University Press.

Kaplan, H. B. (1975). *Self-attitudes and deviant behaviour.* Pacific Palisades, CA: Goodyear.

Kituse, J. (1975). The "new" conception of deviance and its critics. In W. Gove (Ed.), *The labelling of deviance: Evaluating a perspective.* New York: Halstead.

Lemert, E. (1951). *Social pathology.* New York: McGraw-Hill.

Lester, D., Braswell, M., & Van Voorhis, P. (2000). Radical behavior interventions. In P. Van Voorhis, M. Braswell, & D. Lester (Eds.), *Correctional counselling and rehabilitation* (4th ed.), pp. 129–148. Cincinnati, OH: Anderson Publishing Co.

Lester, D., & Van Voorhis, P. (2000). Psychoanalytic therapy. In P. Van Voorhis, M.

Braswell, & D. Lester (Eds.), *Correctional counselling and rehabilitation* (4th ed.), pp. 111–128. Cincinnati, OH: Anderson Publishing Co.

Lilly, J., Cullen F., & Ball, R. (1995). *Criminological theory: Context and consequences* (2nd ed.). Thousand Oaks, CA: Sage Publications.

Loeber, R., Farrington, D. P., Stouthamer-Loeber, M., & Van Kammen, W. B. (1998). *Antisocial behaviour and mental health problems.* Mahwah, NJ: Lawrence Erlbaum.

Matza, D. (1964). *Delinquency and drift.* New York: Free Press.

Merton, R. K. (1938). Social structure and anomie. *American Sociological Review, 3,* 672–682.

Miles, R. (1989). *The women's history of the world.* London: Paladin.

Olfson, M., Gameroff, M., Marcus, S., & Jensen, P. (2003). National trends in the treatment of attention deficit hyperactivity disorder. *The American Journal of Psychiatry, 160,* 1071–1077.

O'Malley, P. (1996). *Criminology and the new liberalism.* Centre of Criminology, University of Toronto. Online at http://www.library.utoronto.ca/librairies_crim/centre/lecture/htm.

Pavlov, I. (1927). *Conditioned reflexes: An investigation of the physiological activity of the cerebral cortex.* G. Anrep (trans.). London, UK: Lawrence and Wishart.

Platt, A. (1969). *The child savers.* Chicago: University of Chicago Press.

Pfohl, S. J. (1985). *Images of deviance and social control: A sociological history.* New York: McGraw-Hill Publishing Company.

Quinney, R. (1977). *Class, state and crime.* Boston, MA: Little.

Reckless, W. (1973). *The crime problem* (5th ed.). Englewood Cliffs, NJ: Prentice Hall.

Redl, F., & Toch, H. (1979). The psychoanalytic perspective. In H. Toch (Ed.), *Psychology of crime and criminal justice.* New York: Holt, Rinehart & Winston.

Sarvin, T. R., & Miller, J. E. (1970). Demonism revisited: The XYY chromosomal anomaly. *Issues in Criminology, 5*(2), 199–207.

Schur, E. (1973). *Radical non-intervention: Rethinking the delinquency problem.* Englewood Cliffs, NJ: Prentice-Hall.

Shaw, C., & McKay, H. (1931). *Social factors in juvenile delinquency.* Chicago: University of Chicago Press.

Shaw, C., & McKay, H. (1942). *Juvenile delinquency and urban areas.* Chicago: University of Chicago Press.

Sheldon, W. (1949). *Varieties of delinquent youth: An introduction to constitutional psychiatry.* New York: Harper.

Skinner, B. F. (1953). *The behavior of organisms.* New York: Appleton.

Smandych, R. C. (2001). *Youth crime: Varieties, theories and prevention.* Toronto: Harcourt Canada.

Smart, C. (1976). *Women, crime and criminology: A feminist critique.* London: Routledge and Kegan Paul.

Sutherland, E. (1939). *Principles of criminology* (3rd ed.). Philadelphia, PA: Lipincott.

Sykes, G. M., & Matza, D. (1957). Techniques of neutralization: A theory of delinquency. *American Sociological Review, 22,* 664–670.

Tannenbaum, F. (1938). *Crime and the community.* Boston: Ginn.

Tarde, G. (1912). *Penal philosophy.* Boston: Little, Brown.

Taylor, I., Walton, P., & Young, J. (1973). *The new criminology: For a social theory of deviance.* London: Routledge and Kegan Paul.

Taylor, L. (1984). *Born to crime: The genetic causes of criminal behavior.* Westport, CN: Greenwood.

Thornberry, T., Lizotte, A., Krohm, M., Farnworth, M., & Jang, S. (1991). Testing interactional theory: An examination of reciprocal causal relationships among family, school, and delinquency. *Journal of Criminal Law and Criminology, 82*(1), 3–33.

Tustin, L., & Lutes, R. E. (2003). *A guide to the Youth Criminal Justice Act.* Toronto: Butterworths Canada Ltd.

Watson, J. (1916). The place of the conditioned reflex in psychology. *Psychological Review, 23,* 89–116.

Weinberg, M. E., Rubington, E., & Hammersmith, S. (1981). *The solution of social problems.* New York: Oxford University Press.

Williams, F. P., & McShane, M. D. (1998). *Criminological theory: Selected classic readings* (2nd ed.). Cincinnati, OH: Anderson Publishing Company.

Winterdyk, J. A. (2000). Explaining delinquent behaviour. In J. A. Winderdyk (Ed.). *Issues and perspectives on young offenders in Canada* (2nd ed.), pp. 35–60. Toronto: Harcourt Canada.

Young, J. (1986). The failure of criminology: The need for a radical realism. In J. Young and R. Matthews (Eds.), *Confronting crime* (pp. 4–30). London: Sage Publications.

Cases Cited

Quebec (Ministre de la Justice) v. Canada (Ministre de la Justice) (2003), 10 C.R. (5th) 281, [2003] Q.J. 2850 (C.A.)

Note

1. Under the YOA, a presumptive adult sentence was applicable to 16- to 17-year-olds who had committed one of the following offences: murder, attempted murder, manslaughter, or aggravated sexual assault. That now includes a third conviction for a serious violent offence. However, a recent decision by the Quebec Court of Appeal has rendered the presumptive aspect of this type of sentencing unconstitutional and the federal government has stated it will not appeal this decision and will enact legislation to this effect (10 C.R. (5th) 281, [2003] Q.J. 2850 (C.A.)).

chapter two

History, Development, and Transformations in Canadian Juvenile Justice, 1800-1984

Bryan R. Hogeveen

Department of Sociology
University of Alberta

INTRODUCTION

Although the importance of a separate juvenile justice system is rarely questioned today, the Juvenile Court in Canada has a relatively short history. Prior to the passage of Canada's first youth justice legislation, the *Juvenile Delinquents Act* (JDA), youthful deviants—with some limited exceptions—were governed in much the same way as adults. They came before the same judges, were sentenced to the same jails, and received much the same punishments as did adults. This generalized system of governance was continuously eroded throughout the nineteenth century as interested reformers questioned the wisdom of governing and adjudicating youth in this way. Reformers were convinced that youth, in contrast to their older counterparts, were infinitely malleable and should therefore be separated from adults for fear that those more mature in crime would set them on a path to habitual criminality.

The belief that juvenile offenders should be managed according to a separate law, a distinct set of institutions, and a divergent philosophy culminated in the JDA's implementation. When introduced in 1908, the philosophy underlying the JDA pronounced that rebellious and delinquent youth were products of their environment who could be reformed through intervention strategies situated in the community (i.e., through probation). Detention was a last resort, and then only as incentive to behave well while supervised by probation officers. Early twentieth-century juvenile justice officials were convinced that deviant youth were the product of cumulative exposure to such offensive and deprecating influences as the street, idleness, the working-class family, delinquent peers, and a lack of contact with the normalizing pressures of church attendance and classroom instruction. As such, the JDA was predicated on the understanding that youth crime was caused by injurious life circumstances and corrupting role models. Moreover, Juvenile Court officials believed that individually tailored probations strategies could reverse the effects of these deleterious influences.

The 1960s–70s was a volatile period in Canadian history. During this time, many societal institutions that once seemed firmly entrenched in society were held up to scrutiny. The JDA did not escape notice, as the informality of the court process, indeterminate sentences, and the inconsistent age jurisdictions across the country were called into question. Heightened awareness of human rights that followed in the wake of various social movements (i.e., women's rights, Aboriginal rights, African-American rights, gay and lesbian rights) created an environment whereby indeterminate sentences and abuse of children's due-process rights—all intrinsic to the JDA—became increasingly difficult to justify (Hogeveen & Smandych, 2001). At the same time, the belief in a "reformable young offender" was increasingly called into question. When the very foundation upon which juvenile justice was built—that youth deviants could be reformed—was challenged, philosophical and legislative change became critical. In Canada, that change came in the form of the *Young Offenders Act* (YOA).

This chapter provides a brief history of juvenile justice until the enactment of the YOA in 1984. Specifically, the understanding and regulation of childhood during the nineteenth century will be explored, as well as an overview of how youth were treated in the adult system.

This is followed by an examination of nineteenth-century reform movements, the creation of carceral institutions for youth (reformatories and industrial schools), and legislative change that resulted in the enactment of the JDA. The last section highlights the limitations juvenile justice officials in the 1980s argued curtailed the JDA's efficacy and prompted calls among the public and politicians for new youth justice legislation—the YOA.

EARLY PERSPECTIVES

The fundamental idea that juvenile offenders ought to be governed by separate legislation and according to distinct legal principles emerged over a period of many years. However, the ancestry of juvenile justice can be traced to much earlier legal perspectives on children and the creation of separate institutions to govern youth. Socio-legal forces that had an impact on these developments included the formation of the first reformatories at Penetanguishene, Ontario, and Isle aux Noix, Québec; the emergence of industrial schools; a burgeoning anti-institutional discourse; and the pioneering work of such prominent social reformers as J. J. Kelso and W. L. Scott.

Prior to the creation of separate institutions for juvenile offenders, legal doctrine held that all suspected criminals were acting rationally when they committed their crimes and should therefore be held to account for their conduct. Given that youth and adults were, under law, thought to be acting with the same level of intent while engaged in crime and deviance, they were consequently held responsible for their criminality and punished in much the same way. While some authors, such as Anthony Platt (1969), suggest that jurors were much more sympathetic when sentencing youthful offenders than they were with their adult counterparts, in most cases juvenile and more mature offenders were handed very similar sentences. D. Owen Carrigan (1998) illustrates this point by documenting how a young child was sentenced to death in eighteenth-century Montréal for stealing a cow. The rationality embedded in the administration of law held that the majority of offenders, young and old, calculated the risks and benefits associated with their deviant conduct prior to the act and should for that reason be held to account for their contraventions.

While this mentality of law certainly held true in the preponderance of cases appearing before nineteenth-century magistrates, there was one critical exception. For a crime to have occurred in the legal sense, two fundamental conditions must be met. First, an act that violates criminal law statutes must have occurred *(actus reus)*. Second, the individual who contravened the law must fully appreciate the consequence of his or her conduct and possess the mental capacity to form the necessary intent *(mens rea)*. While the majority of adult offenders possess a level of maturity that allows them to comprehend the seriousness and nature of their actions, this line of reasoning does not apply in the same way to all children and youth. The immaturity and seeming inability of this group to comprehend the seriousness of their conduct meant that the legal requirement of *mens rea* remained unfulfilled. A recognition of this lack of maturity on the part of juvenile offenders was manifest in the legal doctrine of *doli incapax*.

Doli Incapax

Under Canadian law during the nineteenth century, children under the age of seven were presumed too immature to form the requisite intent to satisfy criteria for criminality; therefore, these children were immune from prosecution. The law considered youth over the age of 14, however, mature enough to understand the consequences of their criminal behaviour and to stand trial for their contraventions in the same manner as adults. Thus, children between 7 and 14 years, by contrast, were assumed to be *doli incapax*, which literally translated means incapable of wrong (Bala, 1988). Nevertheless, if the court could demonstrate that the accused possessed the discretion to determine right and wrong, could differentiate good from evil, was competent to understand the consequences of his/her conduct, and could appreciate the nature of his/her wrongdoing, the presumption of *doli incapax* was rebutted and the accused was ordered to stand trial. If convicted, the young offender was invariably subjected to the same punishments as adult criminals.

CHILDREN IN ADULT INSTITUTIONS

From the mid to late nineteenth century, existing prisons and penitentiaries were subject to increasing attack from politicians and reformers for (among many other reasons) abusing inmates, hiring poorly trained staff, housing inmates in dilapidated facilities, and intermixing offender categories. Moreover, prison reform groups, such as the Prisoners' Aid Association (PAA),[1] were convinced that housing adults with young offenders had a deleterious effect on their potential for a future law-abiding existence. Reform-minded philanthropic groups like the PAA commissioned reports and lobbied the colonial government for reformatory institutions for juveniles. For example, when the Brown Commission explored the conditions of life in Upper Canada's prisons and penitentiary in 1849, the investigators found that offenders were "consigned together to the unutterable contamination of the common gaol; and by the lessons there learnt, soon become inmates of the Penitentiary" (Brown Commission, 1849, p. 112). In this second of two reports into problems evident in the Kingston Penitentiary, the investigators criticized the practice of confining children in the same facilities as adults. Brown argued that it was "distressing to think that no distinction is now made between the child who has strayed for the first time from the path of honesty, or who perhaps has never been taught the meaning of sin, and the hardened offender of mature years." Novices in crime were "placed with the most depraved, even the murderer" (p. 286). Prison reformers were convinced that facilities modelled on reformatory institutions operating in the United States and Europe would eliminate these conditions and have a positive influence on a vulnerable population.

Of the issues raised by the Commission's report, none was more urgent than the recommendation for "immediate action [to] be taken on behalf of the juvenile delinquent" (p. 576). Although Brown claimed that the history of Canadian prisons did not furnish the same tales of horror as their European counterparts, he was certain little "progress"

had been made toward introducing reforms other countries had tested and approved. More importantly, while countries such as Britain were moving forward with separate carceral facilities for juvenile offenders, the Canadas' efforts were postponed as juvenile offenders continued to be incarcerated together with, in Brown's terms, the "hoary-headed evil doer." Toward ameliorating the deplorable conditions juvenile offenders experienced in jails and lockups, Brown's report recommended "the immediate erection of one or more Houses of Refuge for the reformation of juvenile delinquents" similar in scope to American and European institutions (pp. 71–72).

Prison inspectors and religious officials during the 1850s used Brown's report to push Upper and Lower Canadian governors for the creation of separate reform institutions for juvenile offenders. The second report of the Brown Commission and the influence of the European reformatory movement marked the beginning of separate Canadian juvenile justice initiatives. In subsequent years, the Commission's report had a fundamental impact on how youth were adjudicated, reformed, and punished in Canada under nineteenth-century law.

REFORMATORIES

In 1857, two statutes were enacted toward establishing juvenile reformatories in the Canadas. The legislation mirrored the emerging sentiment expressed in Brown's report that legal regulation of deviant youth should be separate from adults. The first, *An Act for the More Speedy Trial and Punishment of Young Offenders,* was intended to accelerate the trial process for deviant youth. The second, *An Act for Establishing Prisons for Young Offenders,* provided for the construction of "reformatory prisons" in Upper and Lower Canada. The intent of this legislation was for boys to be sent to these facilities to "be detained and corrected, and receive such instruction and be subject to such discipline as shall appear most conducive to their reformation and the repression of crime" (Canada, 1857). Taken together, the Acts reflected a burgeoning mid nineteenth-century mentality concerning juvenile justice—a concern that adjudication of deviant youth should be distinct from adults and have a purpose beyond incapacitation, retribution, or deterrence.

As a result of the legislation, two reformatories were erected. The first was built in Québec at Isle aux Noix, and the second saw boys move into a derelict army barracks in Penetanguishene, Ontario. Almost as soon as the Penetanguishene Reformatory opened its doors to the province's youth it was subject to damaging criticism (Jones, 1978). Although the outward façade of the reformatory resembled a military barracks, the program, inner architecture, and discipline found within the institution's concrete walls reflected that of an ordinary prison. Not only did the infrastructure mirror the prison, but also few reformatory staff made a practical separation between the treatment of juvenile and adult offenders. As a result, the early history of the reformatory was marred by a close practical and administrative connection to adult corrections—punishment, restraint, and exclusion. In the evening, for example, inmates were locked up in their cells behind

doors made of iron bars with fastenings that were intended to deter. A very high fence confined activities when boys were allowed out of their cells during the day, with guards stationed around the institution. In 1891, Prison Inspector J. W. Langmuir observed, "In those days the prevailing idea respecting reformatories was that they should be little else than prisons, in which juveniles, while receiving some education and industrial training, should be strictly confined" (Ontario, 1891, p. 8).

In addition to mirroring adult prisons in operation and management, several other problems afflicted the reformatory. For example, Penetanguishene was located at a great distance from the centres of population (e.g., 150 km from Toronto). Without modern modes of transportation, moving boys sentenced to the institution from Toronto was a significant undertaking. Moreover, magistrates were reluctant to send convicted boys to the institution when the municipality was footing the bill. When confronted with the price tag and inconvenience of shipping boys to Penetanguishene, many magistrates chose to maintain the status quo by sentencing young offenders to local gaols.

Rothman (1980) has argued that smooth links between actual institutional operation and rhetoric can seldom be found. This certainly rang true at Penetanguishene, as several other problems effectively hindered the reformation of young boys. Difficulties that plagued the institution included forcing inmates to build the facility; mixing younger, more malleable boys with older, hardened offenders; and the use of a system of fixed sentences. However, that the institution resembled the prison was Penetanguishene's most objectionable quality.

As the 1880s came to a close, any enthusiasm that initially surrounded the Reformatory program quickly descended into disdain. W. L. Scott, later the author of the *Juvenile Delinquents Act* of 1908, referred to reformatories as "schools for crime" (1913). According to critics such as Vancouver juvenile court judge Helen Gregory MacGill, more innovative alternatives were required to "prevent further wrong doing" (1943, p. 3). A scathing report by the Commissioners Appointed to Enquire into the Prison and Reformatory System of Ontario, chaired by J. W. Langmuir, sealed the institution's fate. Langmuir articulated his obvious dissatisfaction when he regretted that he could not "point to that institution as one in all respects worthy of the name [reformatory]" (Ontario, 1891, p. 10).

ROOTS OF NINETEENTH-CENTURY YOUTH DEVIANCE

During the nineteenth century, waves of immigrants from Western Europe and migrants from the rural parts of the province descended on cities in search of employment. While increased wages and opportunities to find employment may have meant greater economic certainty for the working classes, it also meant increased scrutiny of their children's conduct by upper-class reformers concerned with how the ballooning population would affect their own socio-economic standing (Chunn, 1992; Valverde, 1991).

Reformers and child savers were economically and socially privileged groups that attempted to alter existing justice practices to more adequately meet the unique conditions of youth. They considered working-class parents to be at the root of the city's youth deviance problem. They were convinced that working-class parents were frequently negligent in their duty as parents by failing to raise law-abiding children, by neglecting to attach primary importance to education, and by allowing their children to aimlessly wander city streets. However, distress felt among the social and economic elite was shortsighted and did not attend to working-class families' lived reality or youths' love of adventure. Indeed, countless working-class families were recent immigrants who struggled to maintain even a modest standard of existence. Children's economic help was never a supplement to keep working-class parents in luxury, but was required for the family to survive the harsh economic reality of pre–social welfare Canada. Moreover, innumerable children shirked their school responsibilities, which they inevitably found tedious, in favour of excitement found on the street; a situation where blame could not be placed solely on their working-class parents.

Influential social reformer and child saver J. J. Kelso was dismayed throughout his long and prominent career by working-class parents thrusting their children into the world of work as newsboys or to beg on the street in an effort to earn money for, in his estimation, the negligent family. When building trades were suspended during the winter months, a great number of men were suddenly unemployed. Kelso suggested that sending children to the street to earn money for the family at the expense of school attendance was an example of the evil influence of wicked parents. Similarly, and reflecting on his considerable experience with deviant youth, an Assize Court Judge argued that, "parental authority is the greatest evil to which these poor children are exposed" (Anon., 1868, n.p.).

The child savers have been criticized by commentators as being naïve and overly indulgent in their identification with offenders, rather than being concerned about the protection of victims (Shireman & Reamer, 1986). Moreover, Platt (1969) notes that the benevolence of these reformers also disguised the paternalism of the elite classes to control the behaviour of the proletariat. Nonetheless, in spite of their motives, their impact on the treatment of juvenile offenders resulted in the provision of much-needed specialized services.

INDUSTRIAL SCHOOLS

Nineteenth-century reformers considered the shirking of school attendance in favour of excitement or work troubling and campaigned for measures to compel working-class children's attendance at school and reform their deviant ways (Houston, 1982). While reformers tinkered with several different strategies to regulate unruly working-class children—which included a missionary approach that would have seen children attend school during the day and return to the familial home at night to disseminate "respectable" lessons to derelict parents—by the 1860s industrial schools modelled (once again) on the European and American experience had become the magic potion to counter working-class youths' deviance. Enabling provincial legislation in Ontario passed in 1871 (*Act to Improve the Common and Grammar Schools of the Province of Ontario*) and 1874 (*Industrial Schools Act*) empowered school boards to establish industrial schools. According to the 1874 Act, the Ontario government would be responsible for periodic inspections of the institution but would not provide direct financial aid (Morrison, 1971). Lack of provincial funding on the one hand, and assigning responsibility for establishing institutions to school boards on the other, contributed to the Act's cool reception (Neff, 1999).

Because provincial funding was not immediately obtainable, 12 years would pass before an industrial school was erected. In 1887 the Victoria Industrial School, one of the first industrial schools in Canada, opened among much anticipation and promise. The school was built on 20 hectares of land less than a kilometre west of Mimico, Ontario, where two substantial brick buildings modelled on the Gothic style immediately greeted inmates. Unlike the reformatory, which architecturally resembled the prison, an observer commented, placed anywhere else, the industrial school's buildings might have been mistaken for "handsome private residences" (Anon., 1887). Throughout the late nineteenth century, the industrial school program spread all through the country as groups in Québec, Manitoba, and the Maritime provinces established institutions that promised to create respectable working-class citizens out of errant boys and girls.

Industrial schools functioned and managed their deviant charges in direct opposition to the reformatory. The industrial school was separated from the reformatory not only by the architecture but also by lessons in self-control and how to avoid potentially deviant situations. This involved schooling, instruction in the habits of industry, training in drill, religious lessons, and participation in recreation and athletics. Theoretically, the institution was intended to instill an ideal of appropriate working-class character and help prepare youth for life in the late nineteenth and early twentieth centuries. In essence, industrial training was aimed at creating a breadwinner and encouraged the values of obedience, respect, and self-discipline (Hogeveen, 2003).

Problems with Industrial Schools

Despite their initial enthusiasm for the industrial schools, critics charged that the industrial school program seldom reformed youth, suggested that building facilities were inadequate, and disapproved of the relative lack of parole provisions. A further objection held that the environment found within carceral institutions was artificial. Such environments could thus promote institutionalization, whereby the training and education received in industrial schools fostered adherence to institutional rules but was not transferable once an individual was released. Moreover, serious questions began to surface during the late nineteenth century regarding the efficacy of carceral institutions as a strategy to govern juvenile deviance, as well as concerns regarding children being abused at the hands of institutional officials (Hogeveen, 2003). A major criticism of the practice from the perspective of social reformers was that institutionalization

brought youth who may be teetering on the verge of a criminal career in contact with hardened and repeat offenders.

However, opinions were divided regarding the criminalizing effects of industrial schools. The longest-serving superintendent of the Victoria Industrial School, Chester Ferrier, viewed the industrial school walls as dividing deviant boys from street influences. Kelso, by contrast, was certain that the industrial school environment amplified negative street influences. Overall, rather than promote reclamation and reformation, carceral institutions such as industrial schools were thus thought to contribute to the juvenile delinquency problem (Ontario, Sessional Papers, 1899, p. 12). To many late nineteenth- and early twentieth-century observers, industrial schools were simply "schools for crime" (Scott, 1913).

Since industrial schools seldom reformed, spread the contagion of criminality, and created "institutionalized" youth, a shift away from institutional structures of reform was increasingly evident throughout the late nineteenth and early twentieth centuries. For reformers like Kelso, incarcerating large numbers of deviants seemed no "credit to any country" (Ontario, Sessional Papers, 1895, p. 11). If institutionalization was ineffective at eliminating youth delinquency, at this juncture few options remained.

PROBATION AND ANTI-INSTITUTIONAL DISCOURSE

Rampant dissatisfaction with carceral institutionalization was at the heart of reformers' pursuit of alternatives to the working-class juvenile crime problem. By the early twentieth century, probation as a non-institutional alternative was promoted as a viable substitute to this form of discipline. At this time, probation involved a variety of agents (i.e., probation officers, church officials, social workers, parents, teachers, etc.) supervising young offenders and reforming their conduct in the community through strategies tailored to their individual needs. By moving surveillance and regulation away from institutional walls and into the larger society, probation represented a radical departure from previous modes of managing deviant youth (Chunn, 1992). Moreover, Kelso reasoned, probation as a mode of training and surveillance was more "natural," since offenders remained in the community and among family (1903).

As a regulatory strategy, probation was not only a "natural" alternative to custody, but also offered additional benefits. First, probation was flexible. Whereas youth detained in carceral facilities were subjected to a standardized round of life, probation could be tailored to the unique needs of each and every individual. By studying the underlying reasons why youth appeared before the court, officials were empowered to assemble a reformative strategy designed specifically to the individual's character. Second, probation was reflexive. If weekly updates of youths' progress toward acceptable working-class conduct were deemed unacceptable, probation officers could, without excessive difficulty, alter the reformative strategy. Although changing an individual treatment program to achieve the optimum combination of reformative influences was rather effortless, changing an institutional program

necessitated a complete overhaul of the carceral structure. From all accounts, probation was a radical and important departure from contemporary custodial modes of regulation.

SEPARATE LEGISLATION AND SEPARATE COURTS FOR JUVENILE OFFENDERS

The anti-institutional discourse and probation movement were not the only catalysts toward establishing separate courts for juvenile offenders. Beliefs that cases involving rebellious youth should be heard in a separate court from adults and adjudicated on a distinct philosophical plane were similarly fundamental to the creation and dissemination of Canada's juvenile court movement. The enactment of the *Juvenile Delinquents Act* in 1908 did not mark the first occasion that divergent legislation was created to divide juvenile criminals from their adult counterparts under law and for the purposes of governance. When the JDA was penned in 1906, the province of Ontario already had a history with separate courts for youthful offenders. Thus, it is not surprising that the movement to develop the JDA had its greatest supporters in the province of Ontario (Leschied et al., 1992).

LEGISLATIVE PRECURSORS TO THE *JUVENILE DELINQUENTS ACT*

Legislation enacted in 1893 *(Ontario Children's Protection Act)* was supported through various philanthropic and charitable organizations subsumed under the rubric of the Children's Aid Society. The most important element of the changes ushered in by the legislation with respect to the administration of youth justice was the manner in which deviant children were regulated and adjudicated by the criminal law. In particular, the *Ontario Children's Protection Act* of 1893 drew attention to the need for complete separation of adult and children's courts. Despite the innovation in juvenile justice accomplished by the Act, as a provincial statute, the legislation was still very limited in application. Since criminal law under the *British North America Act* is the exclusive jurisdiction of the federal government, the 1893 statute applied only to the relatively unimportant offences committed against provincial statutes (Scott, 1931). This omission was later addressed by the enactment of legislation the following year *(Respecting the Arrest, Trial and Imprisonment of Youthful Offenders)*, which allowed for the prosecution of children in special children's courts. This legislation contained conditions for the private detention of children under the age of 16, and introduced special provisions whereby when boys under 12 and girls under 13 were charged with an offence, the court should give notice to the Children's Aid Society (Leon, 1977; Hogeveen, 2001; Anand, 1998/9).

Under the auspices of the 1894 Act, Toronto inaugurated the Children's Court, which, according to Toronto's first Juvenile Court Judge, John Edward Starr, was "the first to be established upon this continent" (1913, p. 195). Nevertheless, the Children's Court, according to Colonel Denison, "was not really a separate court, but a small room in the lower part of the City Hall"

(1920, p. 252). Notwithstanding the break from traditional jurisprudence that the Children's Court represented, this initial step in establishing separate Courts resulted in a mere spatial shift in juvenile justice rather than a philosophical one. Put simply, the court proceedings against children were moved from the main court to a room "with a table and a few chairs, [and Denison] was accustomed to go down to that room to try all charges against children, in order to keep them out of the public court" (p. 254). This alteration in the spatial distribution of justice made no special provision for children in law, but recognized the impressionable nature of children and physically separated them for the purposes of prosecution. The 1894 legislation, then, did not noticeably alter the spirit of the law, nor did it replace those responsible for hearing cases. Children's cases continued to be presided over by magistrates, whose typical caseload involved older and habitual criminals.

Traditionally, courts did little to take into account individuals' conditions of life. Many problems of a social and domestic character were involved in a child's delinquency, and "to expect the ordinary magistrate and police authorities in a large city to deal with it [was] simply to invite failure" (Kelso, 1903, p. 2). Quite simply, the ordinary court did not recognize the youth's "mental condition, education, social environment or bodily health." The legal condition of "guilty or not guilty [was] the only problem up for consideration, and action [was] based on that and that alone" (p. 8). By contrast, juvenile court advocates, such as Kelso and Scott, argued that such youth should never be regarded as criminal, but as "victims of crime," the product of injurious life circumstances and dubious role models.

In contrast to Denison's Children's Court, Juvenile Court reformers advocated the creation of separate judicial milieux that not only were set apart philosophically from the adult court and offered probation, but also were staffed by experts in social work and mental sciences. Professionals in these areas were trained to study the offender in all of his or her manifestations (in the home, at school, with friends, in sports, etc.) in order to understand the reason(s) for the appearance before the Court. When the causes and conditions of delinquency were understood, experts and Juvenile Court officials reasoned, a reformative program could then be assembled to reclaim the individual to ordinary citizenship.

THE *JUVENILE DELINQUENTS ACT*

The enactment of the JDA ushered in a new era of Canadian juvenile justice. No longer were youth to be governed in the same manner as their elders and judged according to adult legal principles. From 1908 to 1984, the period of time when the JDA was Canada's youth justice legislation, youth were considered infinitely malleable provided their lives were studied in detail, the causes of their delinquency were uncovered, and a reformative probationary program was put into effect. No distinction; was made between neglected and delinquent children under this legislation, considerations of their "best interests" were paramount, and juvenile delinquents were thought to be in need of "guidance and assistance."

The JDA defined a delinquent as "any child who violates any provision of the *Criminal Code* or of any federal or provincial statute, or of any by-law or ordinance of any municipality, or who is guilty of sexual immorality or any similar form of vice, or who is liable by reason of any other act to be committed to an industrial school or juvenile reformatory under any federal or provincial statute" (sec. 2[1]; see Appendix 1). Following this rather broad definition of delinquency was an equally broad array of sentences or dispositions available to judges, including adjournment, fine ($10), placing the child in a foster home, placing the child in the care of the Children's Aid Society, imposing probation, or sending the child to a reformatory or industrial school (Bell, 2003, p. 44).

In addition to creating separate juvenile courts and establishing probation programs, the JDA introduced status offences. Status offences involved conduct that if undertaken by an adult would not incite legal action, which included such things as drinking, gambling, truancy, and promiscuity. Proceedings were held *in camera* (in private), and the names of offenders could not be published. The traditional rules of courtroom decorum were suspended and lawyers were initially discouraged from representing youthful offenders. To ensure that delinquent youth did not remain a threat to the community, sentences under the JDA were indeterminate and officials could return youth to the Court to review their sentences at any time until they reached the age of 21. Judges were granted wide discretionary powers and could conceivably commit a youth to an indeterminate sentence served in detention for minor forms of theft if he or she was convinced the sentence was absolutely necessary for the offender's rehabilitation.

For the greater part of the twentieth century the Act's greatest impact was felt in larger urban communities, while smaller centres continued to govern youth as in the past. Rather than declaring the JDA in effect for the country as a whole, the Canadian House of Commons realized that many cities and towns could not afford to launch a fully functional court. Therefore, one of the Act's provisions was that municipalities were responsible for proclaiming the JDA to be in effect. Some cities could not initially afford the expense associated with implementing the new youth justice legislation—for example, Guelph, Ontario was without a juvenile court until 1964. Nevertheless, larger urban centres like Winnipeg committed to the legislation almost immediately (in 1909), and Charlottetown, Halifax, Montréal, Victoria, Toronto, and Vancouver soon followed. By 1933, 32 juvenile courts were in operation throughout the country, with at least one court in every province except New Brunswick (Carrigan, 1998). In comparison to the United States, where juvenile courts were quickly diffused throughout the nation, Canadian development in this regard was severely protracted (Platt, 1969).

For the reformers, Juvenile Courts were revolutionary and stood in stark contrast to the established criminal law. Under the JDA juvenile offences were, employing Jacques Donzelot's terminology, dematerialized and the conditions of deviance became the focus of investigation and amelioration (1979). That is, the JDA was underpinned by a social welfare orientation toward managing juvenile deviance. Juvenile Court officials were less concerned with criminal conduct and more concerned with the underlying social causes that manifest themselves in juvenile law breaking and deviance. When the JDA was passed in 1908, this discourse was clearly reflected and embedded in the JDA's justice philosophy and definition of delinquency. For example, section 38 of the Act states:

> [T]he care and custody and discipline of a juvenile delinquent shall approximate as nearly as may be that which should be given by his *parents,* and that as far as practicable every juvenile delinquent shall be treated, not as criminal, but as a misdirected and misguided child, and one needing aid, encouragement, help and assistance. (emphasis added)

Inclusion of the term *parent* conveys the standard of discipline to which juvenile court officials adhered and underscores the Act's spirit. Judicial decision making under the JDA was guided by the ancient doctrine of *parens patriae,* which literally translated means "parent of the country." Originating in medieval England, where it ensured the king's right to control the property of orphaned heirs, the doctrine was expanded in the eighteenth century to include a "best interest" clause intended to safeguard children's well being (Bell, 1999). This legal doctrine provided the king, in his presumed role as "father" of his country, with the legal authority to take care of "his" people, especially those who, for whatever reason, were unable to care for themselves (Chesney-Lind & Sheldon, 1992). Over time, *parens patriae* evolved into the state's practice of assuming legal guardianship over children in need of protection or those without parents. By the nineteenth century the doctrine of *parens patriae* that rationalized intervention into children's lives (when the state determined it was in their best interest) had become firmly entrenched within youth justice legislation and practice (Bell, 1999; Reitsma-Street, 1989/90).

Criticisms of the *Juvenile Delinquents Act*

The JDA remained relatively unchanged for many years. This does not mean, however, that the legislation escaped criticism. Two of the many censures of juvenile justice administration under the JDA centred on the informality that governed the Juvenile Courts' day-to-day operations and the indeterminacy of Juvenile Court sentences. In 1967, for example, the Department of Justice's Committee on Juvenile Delinquency submitted its report on the nature and extent of juvenile crime in Canada. Given the increase in the prison population and the impending maturation of the baby boom generation, the report concluded that "Canadians knew that there was a problem of juvenile delinquency in Canada" (1967, p. 12). In addition to the 1967 investigation, several other reports and inquiries were launched to ensure that the Canadian model of juvenile justice remained at the cutting edge of global young offender policy and practice. For example, between 1970 and 1984 a bill (1970) to replace the JDA was introduced in Parliament that ultimately died on the order paper (1972), a federal government report containing recommendations for revised legislation was tabled in 1975, and a set of legislative proposals were suggested in 1979 (Doob & Sprott, forthcoming). Finally, in 1981 the bill that would ultimately replace the JDA was introduced in Parliament.

Throughout the 1970s and 1980s, criticism about existing Canadian juvenile justice centred on several fundamental issues. The JDA was criticized for the informality that dominated the court process, for its lack of due-process guarantees, for its reliance on indeterminate sentences, for being too "soft" on some offenders, for the inconsistent application of law across the country, and for the tensions that existed between social/child welfare concerns and legal principles. In addition, the provision that allowed provinces to set the maximum age jurisdiction created inconsistencies across the country. For example, Manitoba set the upper age at 18, while Ontario had an upper age limit of 16. Therefore, a 17-year-old youth convicted of robbery would conceivably receive a lighter sentence in Manitoba than the same offender in Ontario, since the latter would automatically be subjected to an adult sentence. Moreover, the inclusion of status offences in this legislation meant that the definition of delinquency was far too sweeping, thus undermining the seriousness of some offences and exaggerating the seriousness of others. In this way, a young female convicted of sexual immorality for being out late with her boyfriend could be handed an indeterminate reformatory sentence (as often happened). While no one issue dominated debate regarding the JDA's continued efficacy, the lack of due-process rights for young offenders and rehabilitation as the fundamental principle upon which juvenile justice was based were of particular importance.

During the same period of time, a rights discourse was taken up by many traditionally disenfranchised groups—

Aboriginal people, women, African-Americans, gay and lesbian groups—who demanded and eventually achieved legal and constitutional recognition (Bala et al., 2002; Ignatieff, 2000). The spread of rights discourse to juvenile justice became particularly evident in the oft-cited *Gault* (1967) case, where the U.S. Supreme Court ruled that juvenile offenders were entitled to state-provided counsel and due-process guarantees. International developments in rights discourse challenged the fundamental tenets of the JDA and prompted a shift in the philosophy of Canadian juvenile justice. The informality of the court process and inconsistent age jurisdictions across the country were criticized in this light by juvenile justice officials with a heightened awareness of human rights. A discourse on rights diffused throughout the social and political sphere and created an environment whereby indeterminate sentences and the abuse of children's rights that were fundamental to contemporary juvenile justice became increasingly difficult to justify (Hogeveen & Smandych, 2001). When Canada enacted the *Charter of Rights and Freedoms* in 1982, the same year the *Young Offenders Act* was passed by Parliament, the rights of young offenders (e.g., access to legal counsel) were finally enshrined in juvenile justice legislation (Bala et al., 2002).

Furthermore, it was also during the late 1960s and early 1970s that faith in the efficacy of rehabilitation in both adult and youth corrections began to wane. Martinson's conclusion in his seminal article (1974) that "nothing works"—although later retracted by Martinson himself—brought the rehabilitative ideal to a crashing halt. In light of a perceived failure of rehabilitation to have an impact on recidivism, juvenile justice officials and politicians alike were keen to refocus the intent of justice programs and the philosophical underpinnings of young offender legislation.

When the YOA was enacted in 1984, it signalled a new spirit of governing juvenile offenders, whereby delinquent youth ceased to be "reformable subjects" and the causes of their criminality were no longer the focus of intervention. Whereas juvenile delinquents were once considered amenable to reform, with the emergence of the YOA, young offenders were now considered "responsible for their actions" and "should be held accountable" for their criminality *(Young Offenders Act*, sec. 3; see Appendix B).

CONCLUSION

The nineteenth century saw tremendous change in the governance of juvenile offenders. Youth were no longer governed and judged according to adult legal principles. Rather, new and innovative institutions (i.e., industrial schools and reformatories) borrowed from Europe and the United States became the response to youthful offending. Legislation and these carceral institutions not only recognized "youth" as a unique stage of life, but also suggested that this group was infinitely malleable.

By the beginning of the twentieth century, however, the privileged place reformatories and industrial schools occupied as Canada's response to delinquent youth was superseded by an anti-institutional discourse that was intrinsic to the JDA. Juvenile justice reformers like Kelso and

Scott were certain that carceral solutions to youth crime were artificial and had the effect of amplifying—rather than eradicating—the negative influences of the street, felonious peers, and the derelict family. Supported by community-based probation strategies, Juvenile Courts fundamentally departed from all previous modes of regulation in both philosophy and practice. Juvenile court supporters were convinced that probation, by moving surveillance and control of youth into the community, was the panacea to juvenile offending.

During the 1960s and 1970s, when rehabilitation programs "failed" and youth crime rates continued to climb, juvenile justice officials and politicians alike were keen to adjust young offender legislation. In addition, the Juvenile Court's informality, inclusion of status offences, lack of due process guarantees, and uneven implementation across the country (among other factors) contributed to its demise. As a result, the *Young Offenders Act* was enacted in 1984. However, after only 10 years of implementation and amendment, criticisms were once again voiced about the inadequacies of Canada's legislative approach to youth crime. Justice officials, politicians, police officers, and victims' rights groups argued that the YOA was soft on crime, silenced victims of crime, and failed to protect the public from the serious violent offender. On April 1, 2003 the YOA was replaced by what Canadians are told is new and improved legislation (the *Youth Criminal Justice Act;* see Chapter 3). Clearly, juvenile justice legislation and youth governance strategies are in perpetual motion, where no one strategy or philosophy is ever dominant for an extended period of time.

References

Anand, S. (1998/1999). Catalyst for change: The history of Canadian juvenile justice reform. *Queen's Law Journal, 24,* 515–559.

Anon. (1868). Preventative measures against crime. *Journal of Education for Upper Canada, 21,* 51–52.

Anon. (1887, April 12). Boys' industrial school. *Globe,* n.p.

Bala, N., Hornick, J., Snyder, N., & Paetsch, J. (2002). *Juvenile justice systems: An international comparison of problems and solutions.* Toronto: Thompson Publishing.

Bala, N. (1988). *Young Offenders Act:* A legal framework. In J. Hudson, J. B. Hornick, & B. Burrows (Eds.), *Justice and the young offender in Canada.* Toronto: Wall and Thompson.

Bell, S. (1999). *Young offenders and juvenile justice: A century after the fact.* Toronto: Nelson.

Bell, S. (2003). *Young offenders and juvenile justice: A century after the fact* (2nd ed.). Toronto: Nelson.

Brown Commission. (1849). Appendix to the Journals of the Legislative Assembly of the Province of Canada. *Second report of the Royal Commission on the Provincial Penitentiary in Kingston, Appendix bbbbb.* Ottawa: King's Printer.

Canada. (1857). Consolidated statutes. *An Act for Establishing Prisons for Young Offenders, for the Better Government of Public Asylums, Hospitals and Prisons, and for the Better Construction of Common Goals.*

Canada. Department of Justice. (1967). *Juvenile delinquency in Canada: The report of the Department of Justice Committee on Juvenile Delinquency.* Canada: Queen's Printer.

Carrigan, D. (1998). *Juvenile delinquency in Canada: A History.* Toronto: Irwin Publishing.

Chesney-Lind, M. & Sheldon, R. (1992). *Girls: Delinquency and juvenile justice.* California: Brooks/Cole.

Chunn, D. (1992). *From punishment to doing good: Family courts and socialized justice in Ontario, 1880–1940.* Toronto: University of Toronto Press.

Denison, G. T. (1920). *Recollections of a police magistrate.* Toronto: Musson Book Company.

Donzelot, J. (1979). *The policing of families.* New York: Pantheon Books.

Doob, A., & Sprott, J. (forthcoming). Changing models of youth justice in Canada. *Youth Justice Systems* (special issue volume of *Crime and Justice: A Review of Research).*

Hogeveen, B. (2003). *"Can't you be a man?" Rebuilding wayward masculinities and regulating juvenile deviance in Ontario, 1860–1930.* Unpublished doctoral thesis, University of Toronto.

Hogeveen, B. (2001). Winning deviant youth over by friendly helpfulness: Transformations in the legal governance of deviant children, 1857–1908. In R. Smandych (Ed.), *Youth justice: History, legislation, and reform.* Toronto: Brace/Harcourt.

Hogeveen, B., & Smandych, R. (2001). Origins of the newly proposed *Youth Criminal Justice Act:* Political discourse and the perceived crisis in youth crime in the 1990s. In R. Smandych (Ed.), *Youth justice: History, legislation, and reform.* Toronto: Brace/Harcourt.

Houston, S. (1982). The "Waifs and Strays" of a late Victorian city: Juvenile delinquents in Toronto. In Joy Parr (Ed.), *Childhood and family in Canadian history.* Toronto: McMillan-Stewart.

Ignatieff, M. (2000). *The rights revolution.* Toronto: Ananasi.

Jones, A. (1978). Closing Penetanguishene Reformatory: An attempt to deinstitutionalise treatment of juvenile offenders in early 20th century Ontario. *Ontario History, 70,* 227–.

Kelso, J. J. (1903). Reforming delinquent children: Address delivered at the 13th national conference of Charities and Correction. CIHM/CHIM collection 87454.

Leschied, A. W., Jaffe, P.G., Andrews, D., & Gendreau, P. (1992). Treatment issues and young offenders: An empirically derived vision of juvenile justice policy. In R.R. Corrado, N. Bala, R. Linden, & M. LeBlanc (Eds). *Juvenile justice in Canada: A theoretical and analytical assessment.* Toronto: Butterworths.

Leon, J. (1977). The development of Canadian juvenile justice: A background for reform. *Osgoode Law Journal, 15,* 71–106.

MacGill, H. G. (1943). *The work of the Juvenile Court and how to secure such a court in a Canadian community.* Vancouver: n.p.

Martinson, R. (1974). What works? Questions and answers about prison reform. *The Public Interest, 35,* 22–54.

Morrison, T. R. (1971). *The child and urban social reform in late 19th century Ontario.* Unpublished doctoral thesis. University of Toronto.

Neff, C. (1999). The *Ontario Industrial Schools Act* of 1874. *Canadian Journal of Family Law, 12,* 171–189.

Ontario. (1891). *Report of the Commissioners appointed to enquire into the prison and reformatory system of Ontario, 1891.* Toronto: Warwick & Sons.

Ontario. Sessional Papers. (1899). *Annual report of the Superintendent of Neglected Children.* Toronto: King's Printer.

Ontario. Sessional Papers. (1895). *Annual report of the work done under the Children's Protection Act.* Toronto: King's Printer.

Platt, A. (1969). *The child savers: The invention of delinquency.* Chicago: University of Chicago Press.

Reitsma-Street, M. (1989/90). More control than care: A critique of historical and contemporary laws for delinquency and neglect of children in Ontario. *Canadian Journal of Women and the Law, 3,* 510–530.

Rothman, D. (1980). *Conscience and convenience: The asylum and its alternatives in progressive era*. Boston: Little Brown.

Scott, W. L. (1931). *The genesis of the Juvenile Delinquents Act*. Unpublished notes and letters.

Scott, W. L. (1913). *Juvenile court and probation system for children*. Unpublished pamphlet.

Shireman, C. H., & Reamer, F. G. (1986). *Rehabilitating juvenile justice*. New York: Columbia University Press.

Starr, J. E. (1913). First annual report of the Juvenile Court. *Public Health Journal, 4*, 201–212.

Valverde, M. (1991). *In the age of light, soap and water: Moral reform in English Canada, 1885–1925*. Toronto: McClelland & Stewart.

Note

1. The PAA is the forerunner of the modern-day John Howard Society.

chapter three

The Development of Canada's Youth Justice Law

Nicholas Bala

Faculty of Law
Queen's University

INTRODUCTION: A CENTURY OF CHANGE IN YOUTH JUSTICE

As discussed in Chapter 2, the common law and later Canada's *Juvenile Delinquents Act* (JDA)[1] recognized that children and youth are different from adults and should not be held accountable for violations of the criminal law in the same fashion as adults. While there is widespread recognition that children and adolescents—having special needs and limited capacities—require distinctive, or at least separate, treatment from adults, the nature of the special legal treatment for youth has dramatically evolved over the course of history and remains controversial today.

Historically, the rationale for establishing a juvenile justice system that was separate from the adult criminal justice system was the belief that youths are not only more vulnerable than adults but also more amenable to rehabilitation. It was believed that long-term social protection could best be achieved by concentrating resources on the rehabilitation of youth and by protecting them from the full glare of public accountability. At the very least, concerns about the corruption or abuse of youths placed in correctional facilities with adult offenders offer a justification for their separate confinement. However, concerns about the special needs and rehabilitation of youth did not always translate into more lenient treatment. Under the *Juvenile Delinquents Act,* the desire to promote rehabilitation and the "best interests" of the child offender often resulted in an intrusive approach to youth crime. Not infrequently, child and adolescent offenders, especially those who were from marginalized backgrounds, were placed in custody facilities for much longer periods than were adults who committed the same offences. The rationale for the longer detention was that the youth needed the benefit of

---

*Portions of this chapter are a revised version of Nicholas Bala, *Youth Criminal Justice Law* (Toronto: Irwin Law, 2003), chapter 5.

a longer period in a rehabilitative environment or a longer period away from a corrupting situation at home. Despite the rehabilitative aspirations, these juveniles inevitably felt that they were being punished, and it is now known that all too often youths placed in custody under the JDA not only were denied their legal rights, but also were subjected to abuse or exploitation by staff or by other youths.

In 1984, the *Juvenile Delinquents Act* was repealed and replaced by the *Young Offenders Act* (YOA).[2] The introduction of the YOA represented a dramatic change in Canada's response to youth offending, moving from a discretionary welfare-oriented regime that—in theory at least—promoted the "best interests" of juvenile offenders to a regime that was clearly criminal law. The YOA emphasized "due process" for young persons and provided that young offenders were to be held accountable for their crimes—albeit not as accountable as adults.

The YOA was in turn replaced by the *Youth Criminal Justice Act* (YCJA) in 2003.[3] While there are significant differences between these two most recent statutes, the change in 2003 was "more evolutionary than revolutionary,"[4] and both statutes share some important characteristics, emphasizing respect for legal rights and the accountability of young offenders. The YCJA makes clear that youth court sentences are not to be a vehicle for imposing child welfare, mental health, or other treatment services if this type of response is more intrusive than warranted by the offence and the youth's record. The YCJA also provides that a youth should not receive a greater punishment than an adult convicted of the same offence in similar

circumstances (sec.38(2)(a)). And, in most cases, a concern with rehabilitation and the principle of limited accountability of adolescents will result in a less serious sanction than an adult would receive for the same offence. However, rehabilitation programs are not suitable for all young offenders, as some youth do not want to participate in such programs or may not benefit from participation. In spite of these concerns, rehabilitation clearly remains more central to the youth justice system than to the criminal justice system for adults.

This chapter explores the development of Canada's youth justice system over the past three decades, examining the *Young Offenders Act* and the problems under that statute that led to the enactment of the *Youth Criminal Justice Act*. The chapter further summarizes the principles and most important provisions of the YCJA.

ENACTING THE *YOUNG OFFENDERS ACT*

The deficiencies of the *Juvenile Delinquents Act* were becoming clear by the mid-1960s. The release of the federally commissioned report *Juvenile Delinquency in Canada* (Canada, 1965) began a lengthy period of debate about how to reform Canada's juvenile justice system. By the 1970s some provinces, most notably Quebec, were starting to take steps to change their juvenile justice system—by, for example, ensuring that youths charged with serious offences had access to lawyers. Other provinces continued to maintain informal juvenile courts with little recognition of legal rights. At the federal level, discussion papers and draft legislation were released, though it was not until February 1981 that the bill that would finally be enacted as the *Young Offenders Act* (R.S.C. 1985, c. Y-1) was tabled in Parliament.

A strong impetus to federal action was the constitutional entrenchment of the *Canadian Charter of Rights and Freedoms* in 1982. The informality and lack of legal rights for youths in the JDA were inconsistent with the legal protections recognized in the *Charter,* while the interprovincial variation allowed by the JDA was inconsistent with the equal protection of the law guaranteed by section 15 of the *Charter*.[5] The YOA was enacted in 1982 and came into force on April 1, 1984.

The YOA provided greater recognition of legal rights than the *Juvenile Delinquents Act* as well as establishing a uniform national age jurisdiction, developments consistent with the emphasis in the *Charter* on due process of law and equal treatment under the law.[6] The YOA tried to balance a concern for the special needs of youth with the protection of the public. It abolished the indeterminate sentences of the JDA, which were premised on providing involuntary treatment as long as this was consistent with the best interests of a delinquent youth. The YOA used determinate (fixed) custodial dispositions, subject to judicially controlled early release, premised on the notion that holding a youth accountable—rather than rehabilitation— was the dominant objective of the Act (see Appendix B, Declaration of Principle of the YOA). The YOA was also a much more detailed piece of legislation than the JDA, regulating every stage of the youth justice process, including arrest and police questioning, diversion to alternatives to youth court, access to legal counsel, public dis-

closure of information, and the sentencing process. The YOA moved away from the child-welfare philosophy of the JDA, abolishing the vague status offence of "sexual immorality" and focusing on federal criminal offences.

At the same time that the YOA came into force in 1984, several provinces transferred some or all of the responsibility for young offenders from their social services ministry to the adult corrections ministry, although this was not required by the new federal Act. Québec, however, has maintained youth justice and corrections systems that are closely linked to its child-welfare system.

AMENDING THE *YOUNG OFFENDERS ACT:* CANADIAN POLITICS AND YOUTH CRIME

In 1986 minor amendments were made to the YOA in response to concerns raised by police and provincial governments about difficulties implementing that law and to "toughen" some parts of the Act (R.S.C. 1985 (2d Supp.), c. 24). Provisions were added to facilitate charges for breach of probation orders and to allow publication of information about the identity of dangerous young persons at large in a community.

By the late 1980s the YOA had become subject to much public criticism. Concerns were raised about the perceived inadequacy of its maximum three-year sentence for violent young offenders, especially those convicted of murder, and about the difficulties encountered in transferring youths to adult court—where they might face much longer sentences in adult prisons. Moreover, the

1990s in particular was a decade when governments began to use crime—including youth crime—as an election platform issue. In 1992, the Progressive Conservative federal government enacted further amendments to the Act, lengthening the maximum sentence for murder in youth court from three years to five years less a day, and amending the transfer provisions to stipulate that the "protection of the public" (YOA, sec. 16) was to be the paramount consideration (Bala, 1990).

In 1995 the Liberal Party in power enacted another set of amendments, again primarily intended to demonstrate to the public that it was getting tougher, in particular on the most violent offenders. These amendments lengthened to 10 years the maximum youth court sentence for murder; created a presumption that 16- and 17-year-olds charged with the most serious offences would be transferred to adult court, where longer sentences could be imposed; and facilitated information-sharing with professionals in the community, for example, teachers (Bala, 1994a). Other amendments were also introduced to address concerns about the treatment of less serious offenders, including some rather vague provisions that attempted to emphasize the rehabilitative themes of the YOA and, in particular, to increase the use of community-based dispositions for youths who did not pose a risk of serious harm to the community. However, these latter amendments had little impact on the provision of community-based dispositions, and were considered by many in the field to be without substance (Campbell, Dufresne, & Maclure, 2001).

Interestingly, when it was enacted by Parliament in 1982, the YOA was supported by all federal political parties and was hailed as ushering in a new era in juvenile justice. Ironically, following such unanimous parliamentary support, the Act became the focus of enormous public controversy and was ultimately attacked by both federal and provincial politicians across a broad political spectrum for being too lenient with young offenders and failing to protect society adequately. In 1993, for the first time in Canadian history, federal politicians made juvenile justice itself an election issue, with all parties taking a stand concerning—typically against—the YOA. The four national parties (at that time Liberal, Reform, Progressive Conservative, and New Democratic) all played to growing public fears of youth crime and pledged to toughen the Act again (see Bala, 1994a). The Bloc Québécois, prepared to "speak out against law-and-order rhetoric" (Bala, 1994b), supported the Act, taking an approach consistent with the provincial policies in Québec, which were more oriented toward child-welfare concerns. These attacks on the Act continued in the 1997 and 2000 federal election campaigns (as well as in some provincial elections, even though criminal law is an area of federal responsibility).

Although it is not clear that youth crime actually became an increasingly serious problem in Canada after the YOA came into force in 1984, political concerns about youth crime and media reporting about youth offending increased dramatically in the late 1980s. The police reports of youth crime in Canada increased in the late 1980s, and the reported rate of youth crime peaked in the early 1990s. The rise in police reports reflected, at least in part, changes in police charging patterns and in reporting practices; for example, during this period "zero-tolerance" policies were introduced in many school systems across the country, requiring school officials to report to the police about minor assaults that previously would have been resolved informally (Carrington, 1999). While *police and court-based statistics* reported significant increases in youth crime in the years after the YOA came into force, certain key indicators of serious youthful criminality, such as the youth homicide rate, have remained relatively constant for years,[7] as have measures of youth offending based on self-reports by adolescents (LeBlanc & Girard, 1997). Furthermore, as media reporting about youth crime increased amidst growing political concerns about the YOA during the mid and late 1990s, the actual rate of youth crime reported by police was slowly falling for much of the decade. In spite of the fact that the latter half of the 1990s saw a drop in reported youth crime rates, media reports of youth violence and public anxiety about the problem of youth crime continued to escalate in Canada and elsewhere (Estrada, 2001; Sprott, 1996).

DISSATISFACTION WITH THE *YOUNG OFFENDERS ACT*

There was a public misperception that the YOA contributed to, or at least was associated with, a substantial increase in youth crime (Bala, 1994b). Ironically, there was even a vague sense among the public that the old regime under the *Juvenile Delinquents Act* provided for a greater degree of accountability and social protec-

tion than the YOA, in spite of the welfare-oriented philosophy of the JDA. Further, while the real youth crime rate may not have increased after the YOA came into force, that Act resulted in a more punitive approach with much higher rates of custody use for adolescent offenders (Markwart & Corrado, 1989).

Public perceptions about the inadequacy of police and court responses to youth crime are affected more by the fear of crime than by actual experience as a victim (Sprott & Doob, 1997). The media, by focusing on relatively rare instances of serious youth violence, may contribute to a distorted public perception of youth crime. Fears about youth crime may also be fuelled by the aging demographic makeup of the population, and by the insecurity felt by many Canadians in the face of accelerating social and economic change. Canada's population has a relatively high proportion of youth from visible minority and Aboriginal backgrounds, due in part to differences in birth rates in various ethnic communities. As a result, some of the public fear about youth crime may derive from unarticulated elements of racism, as reflected in certain expressions of concern about crimes committed by visible minority or immigrant youth.[8]

Political and public criticisms of the YOA also held an element of anti-youth sentiment. The perception of many adults that youth are more rebellious and less respectful than when they themselves were younger is a common assertion. Nevertheless, the level of anti-youth rhetoric may be more intense today, as reflected in political campaigning. For example, during the 1999 Ontario election campaign, Progressive Conservative premier Mike Harris argued in favour of lowering the maximum age of youth court jurisdiction to 15, and complained that the YOA was "too soft ... too lenient, it does not teach respect and responsibility and it's got to be toughened up." At the same time, the Premier suggested that teenagers' "lack of respect" might be improved by introducing a provincewide common code for schools of student behaviour and dress (Canadian Press, 1999). This campaign rhetoric clearly played to the sentiments of many older members of the public that teenagers are increasingly out of control.

FEDERAL-PROVINCIAL TENSIONS

In Canada, an important element of political and administrative concern about youth justice issues relates to the division of responsibilities among the federal and provincial governments.[9] Under the *Constitution Act, 1867*, sec. 91(27), the federal government has jurisdiction over "Criminal Law ... [and] Procedure," while the provinces have jurisdiction under sec. 92(14) for the "Administration of Justice," as well as responsibility for such important related services as education, health, and child welfare. The federal legislative power in this area has been interpreted by the courts "in its widest sense," to permit Parliament to enact laws "intended to prevent ... juveniles [from becoming] prospective criminals and to assist them to be law-abiding citizens."[10] The courts consistently rejected challenges under the *Constitution Act, 1867* to the juvenile justice legislation, accepting that the federal

government can enact laws to deal with prevention of youth crime, the control of youth corrections facilities, and diversion from the court system without interfering with provincial jurisdiction.[11]

The federal government has a broad power to enact legislation dealing with young offenders and may enact laws to deal with such issues as protection of the privacy of proceedings[12] and the establishment of non-court alternative measures.[13] Provincial governments are obliged to implement these laws, including paying for the legal, judicial, correctional, and social services required for youths. The federal government transfers money to the provinces for some of the expenses associated with the administration of juvenile justice, but the level of federal financial support for such services declined after the YOA came into force in 1984 as a result of efforts to reduce the federal deficit. For financial and philosophical reasons, some provincial governments disagreed with various provisions of the YOA.

In a federal system it is understandable that provincial politicians will criticize federal politicians for imposing costs and obligations on provincial governments. The federal government consults extensively with provincial governments about law reform in the youth justice field, and the provinces played a significant role in the development of the *Youth Criminal Justice Act*. However, the provinces do not always agree among themselves about the directions that they would like the federal government to take. Furthermore, in regard to some issues, the federal government was not prepared to adopt the consensus position of the provinces, although the YCJA gives the provinces significantly more flexibility to shape youth justice policies than they had under the YOA. While increasing provincial control over juvenile justice policy has given the new law a degree of provincial support, it has also increased concerns that youths in different provinces may receive different treatment.

By the end of the 1990s the decline in the level of federal financial support for provincial spending on youth justice ended. The YCJA is part of a federal strategy that includes some additional support for provincial spending on youth justice, although the federal government imposed conditions on how this increased funding was to be spent, with an emphasis on community-based programs and alternatives to custody. While increased federal funding may help to reduce some of the tensions created by funding cuts in the early 1990s, the provinces are concerned about increased federal controls on their spending.

There was another dimension to some of the provincial critiques of the youth justice system, given increasing public concern over youth crime. The YOA was an easy target for provincial politicians responsible for many of the expensive services that most directly affect crime levels and public safety, such as policing, as well as those that have an indirect effect, such as social services. It may be easier for provincial politicians to attack the federal legislation for not being tough enough than to take responsibility for improving police services to increase community protection or to make the changes to the health, education, and social service systems that may in the long term produce a less violent society.

THE POLITICAL CLIMATE FOR THE ENACTMENT OF THE *YOUTH CRIMINAL JUSTICE ACT*

Demands for politicians to get tough on youth crime grew louder in the late 1990s as Canadian politics became more conservative. With its law-and-order agenda, the conservative Reform Party (now merged into the Conservative Party of Canada) pressed for major changes in many criminal laws, including those governing the youth justice system. This included demands from some Reform Party members for the total repeal of the YOA, although even the advocates of this position recognized the value of both separate correctional facilities for most young offenders and special treatment for less serious offences committed by adolescents (Howard, 1996). While these "get tough" demands were occurring, there was also an increasing awareness of the high costs associated with the use of expensive custody facilities. In spite of the large increase in the numbers of youth in custody following the enactment of the YOA, more than three-quarters of youth receiving custodial sentences under that Act had not committed violent offences (Canada, 1998).

In comparison with other countries at that time, Canada relied excessively on court- and custody-based responses to non-violent youth crime, responses that are relatively expensive and ineffective (Canada, 1998). In many other countries, youth who are convicted of less serious offences are diverted from the court system, and greater use is made of community-based dispositions for those who are sent to court. For example, the United

States has a more serious youth crime problem than Canada—including a youth homicide rate that is six times higher—but under the YOA, Canada was sending youth into custody at twice the rate of American courts (Canada, 1996; Hornick, Bala, & Hudson, 1995).

ENACTING THE *YOUTH CRIMINAL JUSTICE ACT*: 1996-2002

In response to public and political pressures to deal with youth crime during the late 1990s, the federal, provincial, and territorial governments established a task force of senior bureaucrats to review the YOA and propose amendments. In 1996, this task force delivered its report (Canada, 1996). This was followed by Parliamentary Committee hearings held across Canada by the federal government to gather opinions and ideas about responses to youth crime and propose amendments to the YOA. The final report of this Committee, released in the spring of 1997, reflected many of the political tensions over youth justice issues (Canada, 1997). Each party had a differing perspective as to what should be a priority for new youth justice legislation. The Liberal majority on the Committee wrote a report that tried to place greater emphasis on crime prevention and rehabilitation, while toughening some of the provisions of the YOA. The report recommended, for example, increased federal spending on crime prevention and greater use of such alternatives to youth court as family-group conferencing. It recommended explicit recognition of the principle that the protection of society is the main goal of criminal law,

but also recognized that the protection of society, crime prevention, and rehabilitation are mutually reinforcing strategies in reference to young offenders.

The Bloc Québécois members of the Parliamentary Committee criticized the majority report for its lack of understanding of the problem of youth crime and opposed any amendments to the YOA. The Bloc also opposed any efforts by the federal government to change provincial spending priorities for youth justice. At the same time, the Reform Party criticized the Liberal majority for its recommendations about spending on crime prevention, an area of primarily provincial jurisdiction. However, the Reform members advocated sweeping changes to the YOA, including establishing an age jurisdiction from the tenth to the sixteenth birthdays, providing automatic transfer to adult court for 14- and 15-year-olds charged with violent offences, imposing longer sentences in youth court, and allowing publication of identifying information about any violent young offenders.

As the discussions proceeded and public pressure for a response to the Parliamentary Committee report increased, the federal government developed a strategy for reform that included but was not limited to legislative reform. The May 1998 document, entitled *Strategy for the Renewal of Youth Justice,* set out the general themes the federal government was adopting (Canada, 1998). After further consultation, mostly with provincial officials, the Liberal government introduced to Parliament the *Youth Criminal Justice Act* (Bill C-68) in March 1999.

The proposed law was the subject of lengthy Parliamentary Committee hearings, during which it was criticized by conservative politicians for being too soft on young offenders, while the Bloc Québécois continued to argue that no changes were needed in the YOA, expressing concern that the new law would result in more youths being treated as adult offenders. The Bloc had strong support from youth advocates in Québec and delayed the progress of the original bill through Parliament. The Progressive Conservative Ontario government made public calls for amendments that would "finally get tough on youth crime" (Ontario, 2001). Some relatively minor amendments were made in the course of the Parliamentary hearings, and the Act received royal assent on February 19, 2002. In response to pressure from the provinces, the federal government delayed proclaiming the new law into force until April 1, 2003, to allow time for provincial governments to introduce the new programs and policies required by the new Act.

The federal youth justice reform strategy was intended to respond to the belief that there had been a "disturbing decline in public confidence in the youth justice system" in Canada (McLellan, 1999). The most prominently publicized aspect of the strategy, accordingly, was the stated intention "to respond more firmly and effectively to the small number of the most serious, violent young offenders" (McLellan, 1999). But there was also an important recognition by the federal government that Canada had made too much use of expensive and often ineffective court-based responses and custody for the majority of young offenders who are not committing serious violent offences. The federal strategy also called for more use

of community-based alternatives to court and custody, and for more resources for crime prevention. The strategy aimed to achieve these objectives by changing the law and working with the provincial governments and various professional groups to change the way in which the youth justice and corrections systems operate.

The main area of federal authority in this area under the *Constitution Act, 1867,* is for the enactment of legislation, and this is where much of the government's efforts have focused. The federal government also committed more than $200 million to provincial governments, principally to increase community-based alternatives, and more than $30 million to initiatives to prevent youth crime, mainly directed to local groups. One significant development in youth justice has been the federal initiative to give provincial governments greater flexibility in how they deal with youth justice and youth corrections. While greater provincial flexibility increased the support of provincial governments for the federal strategy, it also tends to increase disparities in the ways in which different provinces deal with youth offenders.

Initial federal government planning in 1997 had called for the amendment of the YOA rather than enactment of an entirely new statute. Significant changes were contemplated to the YOA, but not the type of radical reforms that the YOA had produced when it replaced the *Juvenile Delinquents Act* in 1984. However, as discussions with the provinces about altering the Act continued, the changes grew in number and complexity. It also became apparent that an entirely new statute would be easier to understand and use than one with a large number of amendments. Politically, the repeal of the YOA and its replacement by a new statute enabled the federal government to claim that it had put "a new youth justice regime in place" (McLellan, 1999). Institutionally, the enactment of a new statute signalled to police, prosecutors, judges, probation officers, and others that some fundamental changes were expected in the administration of youth justice.

THE *YOUTH CRIMINAL JUSTICE ACT:* A SUMMARY

The YCJA is a complex and lengthy piece of legislation. Below is a summary of its most salient features, in contrast to the YOA. The YCJA:

- states in its Preamble[14] that Canada should have a youth justice system that "reserves its most serious intervention for the most serious crimes and reduces the over-reliance [under the YOA] on incarceration for non-violent young persons";

- in its Declaration of Principle (see Appendix C) places a clearer emphasis on the long-term protection of the public, meaningful consequences for offenders, and reparation to victims, while continuing to recognize that, compared to adults, there should be a lesser degree of accountability and more emphasis on rehabilitation;

- sets "fair and proportionate accountability" (sec. 3.(1)(c)) as the central sentencing principle, making clear that custodial sentences are not justified solely for achieving child welfare or rehabilitative objectives;

- includes statements of principle and specific provisions that are intended to encourage police and prosecutors to divert more young persons from the court process and to encourage more use by judges of non-custodial sentences for youths not convicted of serious violent offences;

- encourages the involvement of victims, parents, and members of the community in the youth court process, for example, through conferences that may advise the court or meet to deal with youth outside the court system;

- gives courts limited authority to admit statements made to police even if there has been a technical irregularity in the way in which a youth has been fully advised of his/her legal rights;

- introduces new community-based sentencing options such as "intensive community supervision" (sec. 42(2)(l)) and "attendance centres" (sec. 42(2)(m));

- restricts the use of custody to cases where a youth has:

  (1) committed a violent offence; or

  (2) has committed a non-violent offence and has a history of non-compliance with community-based sentences; or

  (3) has committed a non-violent offence and has a "history that indicates a pattern of findings of guilt"; or

  (4) has committed a non-violent offence in "exceptional circumstances" (sec. 39);

- requires that young offenders receiving custodial sentences ordinarily serve the last third of their sentence on community supervision, thereby promoting a planned reintegration of the youth into the community (sec. 42(2)(n));

- introduces a new treatment-oriented sentencing option for youth found guilty of the most serious offences, "intensive rehabilitative custody and supervision" (sec. 42(2)(r));
- gives provinces greater authority to establish youth justice policies, for example, by permitting provinces to determine whether judges or correctional officials will decide the level of custody—open or secure;[15]
- facilitates the imposition of adult sentences on the relatively small number of young offenders 14 years and older who commit the most serious violent offences;
- permits the publication of the names of young offenders convicted of the most serious violent offences in specified circumstances.

The new legislation in many respects represented a political compromise. It was an attempt to find a better, or at least a more politically popular, balance on youth justice issues. To appease the vocal law-and-order critics of Canada's youth justice system, a number of provisions of the YCJA place an emphasis on accountability, especially for serious violent offenders, and address some concerns of victims for greater participation in the justice process. Some provisions of the YCJA were intended to result in a relatively small number of the most serious offenders serving longer sentences, sometimes in adult prisons, and in the publication of identifying information about young offenders who committed very serious offences. While the new statute continues to recognize that young persons have the right to due process of law, there is some weakening compared to the YOA in the protection of legal rights—a further reflection of a law-and-order agenda.[16]

To address the concerns of child-advocacy groups and politicians who wanted a more supportive and preventive approach to youth offending, the YCJA was intended to move youths charged with less serious offences out of custody facilities and the youth courts, and to have more effective community-based responses to youth offending. It is, however, the responsibility of each province to determine whether more community-based services will be made available.

DECISIONS UNDER THE *YOUTH CRIMINAL JUSTICE ACT*

The *Youth Criminal Justice Act* came into force April 1, 2003 and substantially changed Canada's youth justice system. As intended by its drafters, the Act resulted in an increase in community-based responses to youth crime. While there continues to be significant variation across the country, populations in youth custody facilities declined by 20 to 50 percent in the first months that the Act was in force.[17] This decline in the use of youth custody was a result of several factors:[18]

- diversion of youth from the courts by increasing police use of warnings, conferencing, and extrajudicial measures;
- a decrease in the use of pretrial detention due to police and Crowns seeking detention less frequently as well as judges and justices of the peace releasing more youth on supervision;
- judges making less use of custodial sentences and greater use of community-based sentences;

- the fact that the last third of almost all custodial sentences are to be served in the community under supervision.

Although there has been substantial variation in the interpretation of the YCJA, police, prosecutors, and judges have in general responded to the admonition in the Preamble that the Act is intended to "reduce the over-reliance on the incarceration of ... young persons" (Bala & Anand, 2004).

In most parts of Canada, a great number of youth court judges have accepted the principle that a youth sentence must be a "fair and proportionate" response to youth crime, and are not using pretrial detention or custodial sentencing to achieve child-welfare objectives (YCJA secs. 3(1)(c) and 3(1)(b)(ii)). Further, in fashioning a proportionate response, youth courts have generally emphasized the limited accountability of youth in comparison to adults and focused on the need to impose community-based sentences that "promote ... rehabilitation and reintegration into society" (YCJA sec. 38(1)). In cases involving more serious offences or youths with lengthy records who clearly are not responding to community-based options, youth courts have generally continued to impose custodial sentences.

THE QUÉBEC COURT OF APPEAL IN *REFERENCE RE BILL C-7*

While the YCJA has, at least initially, had the intended effect of reducing the use of courts and custody for less serious offenders, the intended impact of the Act for the most serious violent offenders was lessened by the Québec Court of Appeal

decision in *Reference Re Bill C-7*[19] and by the response of the federal government to that decision.

When the YCJA was being debated in Parliament, politicians and youth justice professionals from Québec expressed concerns that the Act's focus on accountability would undermine the more welfare-oriented approach to youth justice in that province (Bala & Anand, 2003). Prior to the Act coming into force, the Québec government launched a reference case[20] before the Court of Appeal in that province, challenging the constitutional validity of many of the provisions of the YCJA. The Québec Court of Appeal rejected most of the arguments of the provincial government, but it did rule unconstitutional some of the provisions of the YCJA that deal with young persons aged 14 and older found guilty of the most serious violent offences.

As enacted, the YCJA has extensive provisions to deal with youths convicted of the most serious offences, facilitating the process by which adult sentences could be imposed and allowing in certain circumstances for the publication of their identity even if a youth sentence were imposed. The Act created a presumption that an adult sentence would be imposed on youths 14 years of age and older and found guilty of murder, attempted murder, manslaughter, aggravated sexual assault, or a third serious violent offence.[21] The Québec Court of Appeal decision in the *Reference* case held that it is a violation of the *Charter of Rights* to have any offences for which there is a *presumption* that an adult sentence will be imposed and to allow for the publication of identifying information about a youth who is not subject to an adult sanction. The federal government announced that it would not appeal this decision, and that it would enact legislation consistent with this decision. While it is still possible for a youth who is found guilty of a very serious offence to receive an adult sentence, in all cases the onus will be on the Crown to justify this; identifying publicity will still be permitted, but only if an adult sentence is imposed. The effect of the *Reference* decision and the federal government's reaction is that the specific provisions of the YCJA that were most directly aimed at "toughening" the responses to serious youth crime were ruled unconstitutional.

The Court of Appeal indicated that it is constitutionally acceptable for Parliament to permit judges to impose adult sentences and to allow for the publication of identifying information in regard to adolescents found guilty of the most serious offences, such as murder, provided that each case is individually assessed and the Crown satisfies the onus of justifying this response to a young person's criminal behaviour. It was the provisions in the YCJA that created a class of offences for which there is a *presumption* that there will be an adult sentence and publication of identifying information that the Court ruled unconstitutional. In the spring of 2003, the federal government announced that it planned to enact amendments to the YCJA that are consistent with the Québec Court of Appeal decision. However, at the time of writing (June 2004) it had not done so.

The Québec Court of Appeal decision rested on its interpretation of sec. 7[22] of the *Charter,* and its articulation of previously unrecognized "principles of fundamental justice" that are applicable to cases involving adolescents who are being prosecuted for violations of the criminal law. The Court based its approach to sec. 7 of the *Charter* on the fact that for nearly one hundred years the Canadian justice system has accepted the need to protect one of the most vulnerable groups in society, adolescents, and to treat them separately and differently from adults in the criminal justice system. The Court accepted that the principles of fundamental justice include the requirement that (para. 215–231):

(1) Young offenders in the criminal justice system must be kept separate and treated differently than adults;

(2) Rehabilitation, not repression and deterrence, must be the basis of legislative and judicial intervention involving young offenders;

(3) The youth justice system must restrict disclosure of the identity of minors in order to prevent stigmatization, which could limit rehabilitation; and

(4) The youth justice system must consider the best interests of the child.

These principles may seem very broad, though the Court limited their effect by stating that they must be applied so as to strike a "certain balance" between, on the one hand, the public's right to be informed and protected and, on the other hand, the right of young people to be treated differently from adults and their right to have rehabilitation and their "best interests" as the main focus of decisions taken concerning them. Despite this "balancing," the articulation by the Court of Appeal of these principles may constrain future legislative reform. For example, establishing a young offender sentencing philosophy that totally ignores rehabilitative and welfare concerns would violate these principles. Legislation removing all restrictions on the publication of identifying information and protection of the privacy of young offenders would also violate these principles. Although the outcomes mandated by these constitutional imperatives may be welcomed by many advocates for youth, they may constrain how future, more "law and order"-oriented governments may choose to "reform" youth justice legislation.

The Court also considered whether the provisions of the YCJA are consistent with international law. The Court noted that it is an established principle of statutory interpretation that, in the case of ambiguity, "domestic legislation," like the YCJA, is expected to comply with international law, including Canada's obligations under international treaties. The Court examined each provision of the YCJA that the Québec government argued was inconsistent with international law; it found an interpretation of each section that is consistent with international law, and concluded that these were the interpretations that should be applied by youth court judges. In doing so, however, the Court of Appeal may have interpreted the YCJA in a manner that places less emphasis on the principles of proportionality and accountability than Parliament intended.

One issue in the *Reference* decision was how to interpret section 38 of the YCJA, which establishes the principles that are to govern sentencing. The generally accepted view of politicians and academic commentators before the Act came into force was that sec. 38 establishes proportionality as the central sentencing principle of the YCJA, though also requiring youth courts to consider rehabilitative concerns in fashioning an appropriate sentence. The Court of Appeal considered how sec. 38 should be interpreted in light of the United Nations *Convention on the Rights of the Child,* which requires that state actions in regard to those under the age of 18 are to be guided by a concern with the "best interests of the child" (Art, 3). The Court further observed that the United Nations *Standard Minimum Rules for the Administration of Juvenile Justice* provides that state reactions to crime should always be in proportion not only to the circumstances and gravity of the offence but also to the needs of young people, and that the well-being of the young person must be the guiding factor. The Court concluded:

> The Attorney General of Québec sees in that provision [sec. 38] the legislator's intention to make proportionality *the primary objective* of the sentencing regime. He believes that, by thus subjecting one of the main purposes ... pursued by the YOA to the achievement of the other, the legislator fundamentally upsets the delicate balance previously sought [under the YOA] between *the protection of the public and the needs of young persons.*

> The Court does not share that point of view. Section 38 [of the YCJA] must not be considered in isolation from the other provisions of the Act; a proper reading of the Act suggests that *neither guiding principle must take precedence over the other.* A court to which the case of a young person is referred *must necessarily seek a balance between the two* in imposing a youth sentence. (*Reference*, para. 146–147. Emphasis added)

In taking this "balancing" approach, the Québec Court of Appeal allows youth justice courts to impose custodial sentences that may be disproportionately long, if considered necessary to promote the best interests of an adolescent. While this approach may be consistent with the words of international treaties, it seems inconsistent with the intent of the federal politicians who enacted the new law—and with the explicit words of the YCJA, which make proportionality the dominant principle, and which appear to preclude a disproportionate response that is intended to meet the needs of youth. The statements in the *Reference* decision about the balancing of proportionality and rehabilitative concerns, and the rejection of proportionality as the dominant sentencing principle, do not seem consistent with the words of the YCJA or the intent of Parliament. However, this interpretation of the law may not be followed outside of Québec. The approach of the Québec Court of Appeal on this issue reflects the concerns of the Québec-based opponents of the YCJA who wanted to retain the more welfare-oriented approach to youth justice that prevailed in that province under the YOA. Such an approach allowed youth courts to impose sentences that were disproportionate to the offence (i.e., generally longer than warranted given the nature of the offence) in the hope of achieving welfare or rehabilitative objectives. Thus, that part of the *Reference* decision[23] may well affect youth courts in Québec, which have long taken a more welfare-oriented approach than youth courts elsewhere in Canada. It seems unlikely to affect courts outside of Québec, which have generally accepted that the YCJA does not allow for disproportionately intrusive responses that are intended to meet welfare objectives. If this approach to the broad interpretation of the YCJA is

followed in Québec, which seems likely, but rejected elsewhere is Canada, which also seems likely, very significant interprovincial disparities in how the new youth justice statute is interpreted will continue.

OVERVIEW OF THE YOUTH JUSTICE COURT PROCESS IN CANADA

Before beginning a detailed study of the application and provisions of the YCJA—the focus of much of the rest of this book—it is useful to have an overview of the youth court process and of salient issues that typically arise in youth cases.

A significant proportion of offences committed by youths, especially minor ones, are resolved informally by victims or are not reported to the police. When cases are reported, a police investigation follows and will involve the questioning of the victim and any witnesses, and possibly some forensic work (i.e., the taking of fingerprints from a crime scene, or, in a sexual assault case, having a medical exam performed on the victim). Assuming that the investigation identifies a suspected perpetrator of the offence, the police will usually attempt to interview him or her. All the protections of the *Charter* apply to youths who are suspects of criminal offences, and sec. 146 of the YCJA requires that the police take special measures to protect the rights of young persons who are being questioned, including advising the youth of the right to consult with a parent and a lawyer before making a statement.

In some cases, the police may decide not to take any official action against a youth whom they believe committed a less serious offence. The YCJA encourages the police to consider "extrajudicial measures" (YCJA, sec. 4)—an informal response to less serious offences—by cautioning a youth; the police may warn the youth about not committing any further offences, perhaps speaking to the parents as well. The youth, and possibly the parents, may also be referred to a social agency or some other source for assistance on a voluntary basis. If, however, the police have reasonable grounds to believe that a youth has committed an offence, the police may lay charges and commence the youth justice court process. Before or after a charge is laid, a youth may still be diverted to a program of "extrajudicial sanctions" (YCJA, sec. 10) instead of proceeding through court. These programs are intended to provide a relatively expeditious, informal resolution for less serious cases and may, for example, involve restitution, an apology to a victim, or community service.

In more serious cases that are proceeding through the court system, the Crown prosecutor, in consultation with the police, may decide to seek detention of the youth in a custody facility pending trial. The decision about whether to detain a youth is made by a judge at a pretrial detention (bail) hearing. A youth should not be detained before trial if an adult in a similar situation would be released. Further, a youth generally should not be detained before trial if a custodial sentence would not be imposed if there is a conviction (YCJA secs. 28–31). The judge may decide not to detain the youth pending trial but may impose conditions on release. It is not uncommon for youths to be released into the care of their parents, provided that the parents are willing and able to supervise their child.

As soon as a youth is arrested, the police must inform the youth of the right to consult a lawyer (YCJA sec. 25). If the youth's parents have the means to pay for a lawyer, they may decide to privately retain counsel for their child. If, however, the parents are unable or unwilling to pay for a lawyer, the YCJA provides that a youth has the right to have a government-paid or legal aid lawyer. This is a significantly broader right than what is afforded an adult in the criminal justice system. While an adult always has the right to privately retain counsel, under the terms of legal aid plan regulations, adults facing criminal charges can have a government-paid lawyer only if they have very limited income *and* are facing serious criminal charges. The provisions of the YCJA that provide for greater access to counsel for youths reflect not only the desire to ensure that their rights are protected but also the belief that they may lack the capacity to meaningfully participate in the criminal justice process without legal representation.

The lawyer may provide assistance at the time of pretrial questioning by the police, at a pretrial bail hearing, at trial, and at a sentencing or review hearing. After an initial appearance before a judge, a youth will decide whether to plead guilty or not guilty, often acting with the advice of a lawyer. In practice, most youths decide to plead guilty, often as a result of a plea bargain with the Crown prosecutor. Except for those very serious cases that may result in an adult-length sentence, trials in youth justice court are almost always resolved by a judge sitting without a jury, with special rules to limit the public disclosure of information about the youth before the court. After a trial, a youth may be found not guilty and be acquitted, or may be found guilty of the offence.

If there is a finding of guilt, the youth court judge imposes a sentence; in some cases, this will happen immediately. In more serious situations, the case is likely to be adjourned so that a pre-sentence report may be prepared; sometimes a medical or psychological assessment may also be conducted before the sentencing hearing. The YCJA gives judges a range of sentencing alternatives, from a verbal reprimand to three years in youth custody; except for a conviction of murder in youth justice court, the maximum sentence is 10 years. There is no direct equivalent to parole for young offenders. However, if a youth justice court imposes a custodial sentence under the YCJA, normally the last third of the total sentence is to be served under community supervision. The period of community supervision is intended to allow for the reintegration of the young offender into the community while being followed by social or probation services. There is a narrow discretion for a youth justice court to decide later that, if the youth will likely re-offend, he or she will not be released for the last third of the custodial sentence.

The youth justice court retains jurisdiction to review sentences; that is, to lessen their severity. For example, a young offender may be released from custody by a youth justice court judge at a review hearing even before two-thirds of the sentence has been served if there has been sufficient progress toward rehabilitation. Unless a youth is in breach of a term of an original order, a more severe sentence cannot be imposed as part of the review process, but a youth on supervision after release from custody may be returned to custody if any term of the release is breached.

Several provisions of the YCJA are intended to protect the privacy of young offenders. These provisions reflect notions of the limited accountability of youth and are intended to promote rehabilitation and reintegration into society. They include:

- restrictions on the disclosure of information from the records of police and the courts about young offenders
- a prohibition on the publication of information that might identify a young person involved in the youth justice process
- a narrow judicial discretion to allow publication when a youth who is at large poses a serious risk to the public.

Youth court proceedings are presumptively open to the public, though the judge has the discretion to exclude specific witnesses or members of the public.

The YCJA provides that young persons aged 14 and older may receive adult sentences for the most serious offences. In these cases, before the youth decides how to plead, he or she must be informed of the possibility that an adult sentence may be sought. The youth then has the right to have a jury trial, although, even if there is a jury trial, the provisions of the YCJA concerning issues such as pretrial detention, admissibility of statements, and prohibitions on public disclosure of identifying information apply to the proceedings until the completion of the trial. If the youth is found guilty, the court proceeds to hold a hearing to determine whether the sentencing options of the YCJA are adequate to hold the youth accountable for the offence. If the Act is considered adequate, the youth will receive a youth sentence. If the provisions of the Act are not considered adequate to hold the youth accountable, the youth will receive an adult-length sentence and may then be identified in the media. The court may determine that part of an adult sentence be served in youth-custody facilities. In most situations a youth receiving an adult sentence will be eligible for parole under the adult rules—although, in the case of murder, youths may be eligible for earlier parole.

THE LIMITED POWERS OF THE YOUTH COURT JUDGE

Those who work in the youth justice system in Canada are frequently faced with the stark reality that the appropriate rehabilitative resources are not available to help a young offender who has significant problems related to his or her offending behaviour. While there are some excellent programs and facilities for rehabilitating young offenders, in many places justice system professionals are often confronted by cases where there is a lack of real options. There may be no appropriate treatment available in the youth's community, and the only available custody facilities may offer little more than security, accommodation, and access to educational programming, or may not have treatment resources that can help the youth deal with his or her specific problems (Ontario Social Development Council, 1994). There is, for example, a lack of programming available for young offenders who suffer from drug addiction or fetal alcohol spectrum disorders, and few services are available for young offender females.

The absence of such services means that the needs of individual youths may not be addressed in the youth justice system, which is a cause of profound concern not only for the youth themselves but also for society as a whole, which may be subjected to further offending. Both the YOA and the YCJA have general statements in their Declarations of Principle (section 3 in both Acts; see Appendices B and C) about the need to address the "underlying causes" of offending behaviour and to recognize the "special" needs of individual young offenders. In some cases under the YOA, youth court judges dealing with young offenders relied on sec. 3 of the YOA to give them the authority to develop treatment-oriented dispositional plans to meet the needs of youth and ordered provincial governments to pay for these plans. In *R. v. L.E.K.*, the youth court judge—Judge Turpel-Lafond, one of Canada's few Aboriginal judges—had ordered that provincial officials develop a treatment and education plan to meet the special needs of an Aboriginal female offender suffering from fetal alcohol syndrome, citing the general statements in sec. 3 as giving her the authority to do this in order to address the youth's special needs. The Saskatchewan Court of Appeal held that the trial judge had exceeded her authority under the YOA, ruling that a youth court judge cannot require a provincial government to supply specific services. The Court of Appeal stated that

> the general principles of the Act in sec. 3 do *not* … confer jurisdiction on the youth court that has not specifically been conferred elsewhere. The Act carefully defines the powers and duties of the youth court judge, the provincial director, the offender

and the Attorney General. It is the responsibility of the province to provide the programs and facilities necessary to enable the terms of the statute to be carried out, but sec. 3(1) does *not* impose a mandatory duty on the director to create a specific kind of program. The youth court's jurisdiction is limited not only by the terms of the statute which created it but also by fundamental constitutional principles relating to the separation of powers between the judiciary, whose role it is to impose sanctions, and the executive, whose role it is to administer the sanctions.[24]

While sec. 3 and the Preamble of the YCJA recognize the value of crime-prevention strategies that address the underlying causes of youth crime, there is nothing in the principles or provisions of the Act to require or compel provincial spending on preventive, social, or educational programs that could actually prevent youth offending from occurring. Furthermore, there is nothing in the YCJA to allow a youth court judge to order any particular type of rehabilitative program or service to be provided to a young offender as part of a sentence imposed by the court. The judge can impose a community-based sentence that requires a youth to attend an *available* counselling or treatment program, or that requires the youth to be confined to a place of custody where it is expected that such services will be provided, but the judge cannot require that the government actually provide any specific services to the youth as this is the responsibility of provincial correctional authorities.

The statements in the Declaration of Principle of the YCJA about the importance of crime prevention and rehabilitation require a youth court judge to consider the rehabilitative value of different sentences that might be imposed in accordance with the principles of "fair and proportionate accountability." Rehabilitative concerns might, for example, result in a youth court judge deciding that a term of probation should be imposed rather than a custodial sentence that would be warranted on purely accountability-based principles. This could be justifiable in light of the rehabilitative potential of an *available* community-based treatment program that could help reduce the likelihood of a young offender committing further offences. However, the proportionality principles of sentencing and provisions like sec. 39(5) of the YCJA make clear that a youth court cannot impose a longer custody sentence than would be justified by the nature and circumstances of the offence if the objective is to provide rehabilitative or social services to the youth.

Judges are critical decision makers in the youth criminal justice system. Their attitudes, demeanour, and decisions profoundly affect the treatment of individual youths. However, judges cannot effect rehabilitation or prevent crime. Rehabilitation and crime prevention are missions of the entire youth justice and corrections system. Judges can make orders that may allow various professionals and agencies to work toward the objectives of rehabilitation and reintegration; however, their role in this regard is limited.

CONCLUSION: THE ROLE OF THE YOUTH JUSTICE SYSTEM IN RESPONDING TO YOUTH CRIME

In every society there are real limits to the potential of criminal laws and the youth justice system to protect society and reduce youth crime. Public policies related to health, education, child welfare, law enforcement, and gun control, as well as a range of cultural and social factors, are much more important than its youth justice system in determining a country's youth crime rate. It is clear from the American experience that merely enacting juvenile justice laws that require longer sentences or greater numbers of adolescents to be treated as adults does not reduce youth crime.

In Canada, the appropriate role of the youth justice system and the principles that are to guide that system have been subjects of long-running debates. The *Juvenile Delinquents Act* of 1908 established a highly discretionary regime with little regard for the rights of children and, at least in theory, with a focus on the welfare of the juvenile offender. The *Young Offenders Act,* which came into force in 1984, had a clearer criminal law orientation and placed greater emphasis on due process. However, the YOA continued to give judges a significant degree of discretion, and, perhaps not surprisingly, resulted in a regime with substantial variation throughout the country in how the Act was applied, especially in terms of the use of court and custody.

The *Youth Criminal Justice Act* has a number of statements of principle and specific provisions that are intended to establish a new set of principles to direct the youth justice system. Although these provisions could have been drafted in a more elegant and concise fashion, when read together they offer a more coherent set of principles than those in the YOA. While the Preamble of the YCJA clearly recognizes the value of a range of social, educational, and health programs to address the underlying causes of youth crime and prevent youth crime, the YCJA itself is premised on a narrower, more focused role for the youth justice system. The youth justice system is intended to respond to adolescent offending that has already occurred. A central principle of the YCJA is that there is to be fair and proportionate accountability, which, for many adolescents, may mean an informal response by means of a police warning or some form of extrajudicial measures. The Preamble of the YCJA makes clear that an objective of the Act is to reduce the reliance on custody, especially for non-violent offenders. The YCJA continues to recognize the importance of attempting to rehabilitate young offenders, and thereby prevent future offending, but the attainment of this objective cannot be used to justify a longer custodial sentence than the offence merits. Those responsible for the implementation and interpretation of the Act will continue to face challenges in making decisions on both a systemic and individual case basis. The application of the Act to individual young persons will continue to require professional judgment and a balancing of principles and concerns, made in the context of the resources available.

The more coherent message of the YCJA has resulted in less use of custody for youths. However, the Act continues to allow for substantial variation among provinces and territories in terms of policies and resources available to deal with young offenders. The principles in the YCJA are important, but their significance will depend on the actions of justice system officials. In individual cases, these principles will be applied by police officers, prosecutors, judges, and youth court workers exercising their individual professional judgment. As under the YOA, judges dealing with individual young offenders are constrained by what resources and programs are available. Moreover, the policy and resource decisions of provincial governments will continue to have a profound effect on Canada's youth justice system and on how principles are applied

in individual cases. Ultimately, it will be the cumulative effect of these decisions by provincial and territorial governments and by individual professionals that determines whether the hopes of Justice Canada for the new Act are achieved, namely, the aspiration that "the YCJA will correct fundamental weaknesses of the YOA and result in a fairer and more effective youth justice system" (Canada, 2001).

References

Bala, N. (1990). Dealing with violent young offenders: Transfer to adult court and Bill C-58. *Canadian Journal of Family Law, 9*(1), 11–37.

Bala, N. (1994a). The 1995 *Young Offenders Act* amendments: Compromise or confusion? *Ottawa Law Review, 26,* 643–676.

Bala, N. (1994b). What's wrong with YOA bashing? What's wrong with the YOA? Recognizing the limits of the law. *Canadian Journal of Criminology, 36,* 247–270.

Bala, N., & Anand, S. (2004). The first months under the *Youth Criminal Justice Act:* Survey and analysis of case law. *Canadian Journal of Criminology.*

Campbell, K., Dufresne, M., & Maclure, R. (2001). Amending youth justice policy in Canada: Discourse, mediation and ambiguity. *Howard Journal, 40,* 272–284.

Canada. Department of Justice. (1965). *Report of the Committee on Juvenile Delinquency, juvenile delinquency in Canada.* Ottawa: Queen's Printer.

Canada. Department of Justice. (1998). *A strategy for youth justice renewal.* Ottawa: Ministry of Supply and Services. (Available online at time of writing at http://canada.justice.gc.ca)

Canada. Department of Justice. (2001, February). Why new youth justice legislation?

Canada. Federal-Provincial-Territorial Task Force on Youth Justice. (1996). *Review of the Young Offenders Act and the youth justice system in Canada.* Ottawa: Ministry of Supply and Services.

Canada. House of Commons. (1997). *Thirteenth report of the Standing Committee on Justice and Legal Affairs: Renewing youth justice.* Ottawa: Ministry of Supply and Services.

Canadian Press. (1999, March 2). Teenagers still a hot topic: Premier renews call for tougher *Young Offenders Act.*

Carrington, P. J. (1999). Trends in youth crime in Canada, 1977–1996. *Canadian Journal of Criminology, 41*(1), 1–32.

Estrada, F. (2001). Juvenile violence as a social problem: Trends, media attention, and social response. *British Journal of Criminology, 41,* 639–55.

Hackler, J. (2001). An impressionistic view of Canadian juvenile justice: 1965 to 1999. *Canadian Journal of Community Mental Health, 20,* 17–.

Hornick, J. P., Hudson, J., & Bala, N. (1995). *American responses to juvenile crime: A Canadian perspective.* Department of Justice Canada and Canadian Research Institute for Law & Family, 94 pp.

Howard, R. (1996, June 8). Reform's grassroots dig in on tough ground: Party would scrap *Young Offenders Act,* new gun-control law. *The Globe and Mail,* p. A4.

LeBlanc, M., & Girard, S. E. C. (1997). The generality of deviance: Replication over two decades with a Canadian sample of adjudicated boys. *Canadian Journal of Criminology, 39(2),* 171–183.

Markwart, A., & Corrado, R. (1989). Is the *Young Offenders Act* more punitive? In L. Beaulieu (Ed.), *Young offender dispositions: Perspectives on principles and practice.* Toronto: Wall and Thompson.

McLellan, A. (1999, May 12). [Press Release]. Remarks by (then) federal Justice Minister, Department of Justice.

Ontario Ministry of the Attorney General. (2001, June 12). No more free ride for the *Young Offenders Act.*

Ontario Social Development Council. (1994). Myths, facts, and the potential of the treatment option. In *Youth justice in crisis.* Toronto: Author.

Sprott, J. (1996). Understanding public views of youth crime and the youth justice system. *Canadian Journal of Criminology, 38(3),* 271–290.

Sprott, J., & Doob, A. (1997). Fear, victimization and attitudes to sentencing, the courts and police. *Canadian Journal of Criminology, 93(3),* 275–291.

Cases Cited

B.C. (A.G.) v. S., [1967] S.C.R. 702.

Québec (Ministre de la Justice) v. Canada (Ministre de la Justice) (2003), 10 C.R. (5th) 281 (Que. C.A.).

R. v. L.E.K., [2000] S.J. No. 844 (Sask. C.A.).

R. v. M.(.B), [2003] S.J. 377(Sask.), and [2003] S.J. 602.

R. v. R.J.H., [2000] A.J. No. 396 (C.A.).

R. v. S.(S.), [1990] 2 S.C.R. 254.

Southam Inc. v. R. (1984), 48 O.R. (2d) 678 (H.C.J.), aff'd. (1986), 53 O.R. (2d) 663 (C.A.).

Notes

1. *Juvenile Delinquents Act,* first enacted as S.C. 1908, c. 40; subject to minor amendments over the years, finally as *Juvenile Delinquents Act,* R.S.C. 1970, c. J-3.

2. *Young Offenders Act,* R.S.C. 1985, c. Y-1, enacted as S.C. 1980-81-82-83, c. 110.

3. *Youth Criminal Justice Act,* S.C. 2002, c. 1, received royal assent February 19, 2002; was in force April 1, 2003.

4. The enactment of the YOA in 1984 was characterized as "revolutionary." See, for example, Leschied, A., Jaffe, P., & Willis, W. (Eds.). (1991). *The Young Offenders Act revolution: Changing the face of Canadian justice.* Toronto: University of Toronto Press.

5. *Canadian Charter of Rights and Freedoms,* enacted as Part I of the *Constitution Act, 1982,* being Schedule B to the *Canada Act, 1982* (U.K.), 1982, c. 11 (subsequently referred to as the *Charter*).

6. Some critics have decried the increased emphasis on due process and legal rights at the expense of other needs; see, for example, Hackler (2001).

7. For example, for the years 1968 through 2002 the numbers of youth named as suspects for homicide offences have ranged from as few as 30 (2001) up to 68 (1975 and 1995) (Sprott & Doob, 2004).

8. During the 1999 Ontario election campaign, the Toronto Police Association sponsored a controversial advertisement urging voters to support "law and order" candidates. The ad pictured five obviously Latino young men, who were actually in Los Angeles when the picture was taken. Group wants apology for police poster. (1999, June 1). *The Globe and Mail*, p. A13.

9. Territorial governments have essentially the same responsibilities as provincial governments with regard to youth justice, although their jurisdiction derives from federal statutes. For the sake of simplicity, most references in this text are only to provincial governments.

10. *B.C. (A.G.) v. S.*, [1967] S.C.R. 702 at 710.

11. See, for example, *Québec (Ministre de la Justice) v. Canada (Ministre de la Justice)* (2003), 10 C.R. (5th) 281 (Que. C.A.).

12. *Southam Inc. v. R.* (1984), 48 O.R. (2d) 678 (H.C.J.), aff'd. (1986), 53 O.R. (2d) 663 (C.A.).

13. *R. v. S.(S.)*, [1990] 2 S.C.R. 254.

14. The Preamble to the YCJA is meant to provide an explanation of the social context and policy concerns that are the Parliamentary intentions of this law (Bala, 2003, p. 76).

15. Despite the request of several provinces for this provision (sec. 88 of the YCJA), all provinces chose to let judges make this decision.

16. For example, sec. 146 of the YCJA allows for the admission of the confession of a youth to police even if there is not full compliance with the cautioning requirements of the Act. Sec. 25(10) allows provinces to seek reimbursement from parents for the costs of paying a lawyer to represent their children; at the time of writing, no province has chosen to implement this provision, but if it is implemented, parents are likely to discourage their children from exercising their right to have legal counsel.

17. See, for example, Fewer youths jailed under new law. (2003, July 18). *National Post*, p. A1, reporting a 20- to 25-percent decline in the use of custody in Ontario and Alberta.

18. While Statistics Canada data for the first full year under YJCA implementation are not currently available, unpublished reports from both Ontario and British Columbia indicate significant changes. During the first year of implementation of the YCJA, police charges for youth were down 13 percent in Ontario, while in B.C., there was a 29-percent decline in police referrals of youth cases to the Crown. Similarly, pretrial detention populations were down 11 percent in Ontario and 10 percent in B.C. For the same time period in Ontario, secure custody populations were down 37 percent and open custody was down 40 percent, while in B.C. the overall youth custody populations were down more than 25 percent in the first year the YCJA was in effect (Glenn Semple, Ontario Ministry of Children and Youth Services, personal communication; Alan Markwart, B.C. Ministry of Children and Family Development, personal communication).

19. The *Reference* decision is officially known as *Québec (Ministre de la Justice) v. Canada (Ministre de la Justice)* (2003), 10 C.R. (5th) 281, [2003] Q.J. 2850 (C.A.). For a detailed discussion, see Anand & Bala (2003).

20. Unlike an ordinary appeal that arises out of an actual case, such as a conviction in youth court, and requires a decision that affects a specific youth, a reference case is placed before an appeal court based on the government asking the court for its opinion on one or more stated, general questions. In this case, the government of Québec asked the Court of Appeal in that province a series of questions about the constitutional validity of the YCJA.

21. Under sec. 61 of the YCJA, provinces or territories could elect to have 16 years as the

age for the presumption of an adult sentence after a finding of guilt for murder, attempted murder, manslaughter, aggravated sexual assault, or a third serious violent offence. Only Québec and Newfoundland and Labrador chose the age of 16.

22. Section 7 of the *Charter* provides that no person shall be deprived of "liberty or security of the person … except in accordance with the principles of fundamental justice."

23. The portion of the Court of Appeal decision that dealt with the interpretation of the sentencing provisions of the YCJA was *obiter dicta* (Latin for "things said in passing") and not strictly part of the court's ruling about the constitutional invalidity of the parts of the YCJA.

24. *R. v. L.E.K.*, [2000] S.J. No. 844 (Sask C.A.), para 20. Emphasis added. The same conclusion was reached in *R. v. R.J.H.*, [2000] A.J. No. 396 (C.A.). For another disturbing case involving a fetal-alcohol disordered young offender under the YCJA and the lack of adequate resources in the youth justice system for dealing with the problems of this youth, see *R v. M.(.B)*, [2003] S.J. 377 (Sask.), and [2003] S.J. 602, per Turpel-Lafond Prov. J.

chapter four

Children's Rights, Juvenile Justice, and the UN *Convention on the Rights of the Child:* Implications for Canada

Myriam S. Denov

Department of Criminology
University of Ottawa

INTRODUCTION

Although many may assume that the notion of children's rights is a new or novel concept that has recently emerged in the West, the children's rights movement has had a long history. Efforts to recognize children's rights, particularly their right to survival, development, protection from abuse and exploitation, as well as full participation in family, cultural, and social life, can be traced back to the 1870s and were in fact part of larger international efforts to recognize human rights (Todres, 1998). This movement arose principally in reaction to historical beliefs and practices where children[1] were not accorded either dignity or respect and were instead reified, treated as objects of intervention rather than legal subjects, often reduced to being seen as property (Freeman, 1992). Although more recent views have transcended the notion of children as property, perceptions of children as passive beneficiaries of assistance and objects of compassion rather than as active participants in their own development have prevailed.

As a general rule, children are afforded the same human rights as adults. However, children's rights advocates argue that because of children's vulnerability and level of maturity, they require special protections to meet their unique needs. Under a rights-based approach, children are not viewed as the objects of compassion or pity, but as the subjects of human rights under international law. From this perspective, children are seen as protagonists, even agents of social transformation, and their individual experiences, voices, and participation are to be actively sought out and promoted.

Although a progressive notion for some, for others the idea of specific rights for children may evoke discomfort and, at times, conflict. As Minow aptly notes:

> Children's rights make adults uncomfortable because they represent new ideas or old ideas in new forms, and signal that adults and existing practices have to change (cited in Toope, 1996, p. 41).

Indeed, ensuring that children have internationally recognized rights may pose specific challenges to governments, particularly when such rights are called into question. Moreover, when the rights of children are acknowledged, it enables children to make legitimate claims and confront authority. Ensuring children's rights may incite other controversial issues. For example, under a rights-based approach in the realm of juvenile justice, young persons may exercise choices, ask questions, challenge procedures, and have the opportunity to be heard in proceedings. The emphasis on guaranteeing the rights of children in conflict with the law may be perceived as a direct or indirect threat to the rights of victims or to the protection of society as a whole. Conceiving of children's rights may thus require significant changes in social attitudes in almost all nations of the world, including Canada (Toope, 1996). The potential doubts and fears that accompany discourses on children's rights continue to prevail. Price Cohen (1996)

notes that in the context of the United States there have been well-organized and vocal national nongovernmental organizations that fundamentally object to the notion of children's rights and are working to ensure that the U.S. never becomes a party to the United Nations *Convention on the Rights of the Child*.

Despite protracted debate on the issue, significant international developments have been made within the realm of children's rights, particularly over the last 30 years. This chapter traces the evolution of children's rights in Canada and explores the development and creation of the United Nations *Convention on the Rights of the Child* (hereafter referred to as the Convention).[2] The significance of this Convention and its implications for Canada are highlighted. While the chapter addresses the issue of children's rights generally, specific attention is given to the rights of children in conflict with the law. In particular, the chapter assesses the extent to which the *Youth Criminal Justice Act* (YCJA) complies with the provisions set out in the Convention. In doing so, the chapter considers Canada's commitment to the principles of the Convention in relation to juvenile justice and to children's rights more generally.

THE EVOLUTION OF CHILDREN'S RIGHTS

Although movements to promote the unique rights of children have existed for centuries, the direct implementation of children's rights into both public policy and law is quite new, both in Canada and abroad. Recent developments reflect current perceptions of children as subjects and individuals with distinct human rights. However, this view of children has not always prevailed. According to Covell and Howe (2001), Canadian perceptions of children have altered and evolved through three unique stages. The first stage, which was apparent from colonial times to the nineteenth century, reflected a social laissez-faire philosophy where children were viewed largely as possessions or objects of parental authority. Although parents were required by common law to provide their children with the necessities of life, they were given free rein in child rearing. As such, parents had the parental right of "reasonable chastisement," leaving them with considerable leeway in discipline. Reflecting the view of children as objects rather than individuals with fundamental rights, protective legislation against child abuse or neglect was nonexistent and there was no separate system of juvenile justice. Young offenders who were over age 13 were treated much the same as adult offenders. These laws and practices left children vulnerable to various forms of abuse, neglect, exploitation, and brutality.

The second phase occurred from the time of Confederation to the mid twentieth century, when views and perceptions of children altered dramatically, influenced by a humanitarianism and newfound sentimentality toward children. Children began to be considered not as parental property or as possessions but as a separate and special class of immature persons. The overarching theme at that time was the perceived *vulnerability* of children and their need for state protection. It was argued that the state had a duty to prevent child cruelty and maltreatment, and if parents failed in the protection and welfare of their children the state must intervene. While the new philosophy was clearly progressive in some respects, children continued to be viewed as objects in need of care either by their parents or by the paternalistic state. As Covell and Howe (2001) argue, children were regarded as "not-yets"—individuals in need of care rather than individuals with inherent rights. While parents now had obligations to their children under the law, children had no right to demand anything from their parents. Moreover, state intervention in cases of child maltreatment occurred not because children were perceived to hold inherent rights, but because their parents had failed. It is important to note, however, that despite a dominant view of children as objects in need of care, significant yet sporadic efforts were made to establish international standards on the rights of the child. For example, in 1924, the *Declaration of the Rights of the Child* (known as the Declaration of Geneva) was adopted by the League of Nations. This early initiative, however, was largely paternalistic and welfare-oriented, and, reflecting the period, its conceptualization of the child stressed vulnerability and emphasized protective strategies (Fottrell, 2000).

Following the Second World War, state paternalism gradually gave rise to a third and new perception of children as individuals with inherent rights. This perspective focused on the empowerment of children in political, civil, and social contexts (Fottrell, 2000). In Canada, as elsewhere, children were no longer viewed as objects in need of state protection, but as subjects—existing persons with dignity and basic rights of their own (Freeman, 1997; Hart, 1991). Given this recognition that children held inherent rights, both parents and the state had concurrent obligations to provide for these rights. Several declarations were brought forth that both reflected and further cemented the notion of children's rights. In 1959, the United Nations officially recognized the human rights of children by adopting the UN *Declaration of the Rights of the Child.* The essential theme underlying this non-binding declaration was that children are entitled to special protections and that "the best interest of the child shall be considered paramount" (Todres, 1998). Twenty years later, to commemorate the twentieth anniversary of the UN Declaration, the year 1979 was recognized as the year of the child. It was at this point that Poland began to press that the principles set forth in the 1959 Declaration be turned into a legally binding convention.[3] In its 1978 submission to the UN Commission on Human Rights, the Polish delegation claimed that there was a need to further strengthen the comprehensive care and well-being of children all over the world. However, not all were in agreement that a convention on children's rights was necessary. Some argued that it was dangerous or unwarranted to identify children as a special or separate category of human beings (Detrick, 1992). Other opponents believed that the rights of children were adequately covered by existing human rights instruments (LeBlanc, 1995).

Despite ongoing dissent, a working group was formed to begin to draft a convention. The working group included members of government, intergovernmental organizations, and non-government organizations[4] (NGOs). The hesitation that characterized some governments' reactions to the proposal for a convention was reflected in the level of participation. According to Detrick (1992), during the early years of the drafting never more than 30 countries took part in the meetings of the working group; this number rose to 40 in the mid 1980s, with an overrepresentation of industrialized countries. While there were legitimate concerns that the outcome would be a text that reflected primarily the beliefs and practices of the First World, this was attenuated to some degree by active participation on the part of developing countries such as Algeria, Argentina, Senegal, and Venezuela, as well as a last-minute surge of delegates from states with Islamic law (Detrick, 1992).

The proposal was redrafted several times as particular controversies emerged regarding the inclusion of certain rights. Throughout the drafting process a central tension existed between a desire for consensus and efforts to create an effective legal document. As Fottrell (2000) notes, the drafting process was "generally hampered by the need to strike a balance between traditional attitudes, cultural peculiarities and radical proposals for empowerment of children, while at the same time ensuring the rights of the child were adequately protected and the document had as wide appeal as possible" (p. 3).

In spite of many protracted debates on specific articles within the document, on November 20, 1989 the *Convention on the Rights of the Child* was unanimously adopted by the UN. The Convention entered into force within 10 months of its adoption—no other specialized UN human rights treaty has entered into force so quickly and been ratified[5] by so many states in such a short period of time. Some suggest that the rapid acceptance of the Convention is likely a result of its subject matter—children. Most states do not want to be perceived as neglecting children. Others have suggested that the Convention's popularity stems from the belief that children are vulnerable to the most serious forms of human rights abuse and therefore a treaty that aims to protect children is not as controversial as some of the other more specialized conventions (Todres, 1998). Today, 191 states are parties to the Convention, making it the most widely ratified human rights treaty (Melton, 1991). The creation of the Convention, whereby children are acknowledged as being full beneficiaries of human rights, marked a significant grounding of children's rights internationally.

STRENGTHENING CHILDREN'S RIGHTS INTERNATIONALLY: HALLMARKS OF THE CONVENTION

The major innovation of the Convention is that it is the first of any globally applicable human rights convention to integrate the two broad classifications of rights—(1) civil and political and (2) economic, social, and cultural. Examples of civil and political rights include the rights to self-determination and to being protected from arbitrary arrest or torture and compulsory labour. Economic, social, and cultural rights include basic economic welfare, health care, education, and freedom of religion. Toope (1996) notes

that nations have tended to favour the implementation of civil and political rights, arguing that economic, social, and cultural rights could be postponed to a time when resources were less scarce. Importantly, the Convention advances the argument that economic, social, and cultural rights are full rights and deserve the same degree of commitment and promotion as accorded to civil and political rights.

Hammarberg (1990) has suggested that the range of human rights protections addressed in the Convention may be divided into three categories, or what is often referred to as the *3 Ps:* provisions, protection, and participation. Under the category of *provisions,* the Convention ensures that children are provided with basic welfare and nurturance. These include children's right to survival and development (Article 6), basic economic welfare (Article 27), health care (Article 24), education (Article 28), play and recreation (Article 31), and the right to a name, a nationality, and to be cared for by parents (Article 7). Under Article 3 the best interests of the child are a primary consideration in all matters concerning the child. The articles that fall under the category of *protections* ensure that children are protected from harmful practices such as abuse and neglect (Article 19), economic exploitation (Article 32), sexual exploitation (Article 34), discrimination (Article 2), and that children are entitled to a separate juvenile justice system (Articles 37 and 40). Finally, several articles fall under the rubric of *participation,* which seeks to enhance the autonomy of children and ensure that children participate in decision-making that affects their lives, with more weight being given according to the age and maturity of the child. These include freedom of expression and information (Article 13), freedom of thought and religion (Article 14), and freedom of association and peaceful assembly (Article 15). Significantly, references to child participation have not been made in any previous international document on children's rights. While the articles provided for in the Convention apply to all children, the Convention provides for children in special circumstances. These children include orphans (Article 20), children with disabilities (Article 23), refugee children (Article 22), and minority and indigenous children (Article 30).

To provide an overarching philosophical framework, the Convention's working group set out four fundamental principles to be used in interpreting all articles of the Convention. These include:

- the best interests of the child must be the primary consideration in all actions concerning children;
- all children have the right to non-discrimination;
- all children have the right to life, survival, and development; and
- all children have the right to participation.

Although state parties are responsible for implementing the children's rights contained in the Convention, reservations may be made to particular provisions. When a state party enters a "reservation," it simply means that the state is not bound by a provision of the convention for some specific reason, although the state agrees with the provision in principle. State parties may declare a reservation as long as it does not violate the overall purpose and spirit of the Convention and is agreed to by the UN. It is consistently recommended that state parties review their reservations with a view toward withdrawing them.

To ensure compliance to the Convention, a monitoring mechanism in the form of the *Committee on the Rights of the Child*[6] (hereafter referred to as the Committee) has been established, to which state parties are accountable. The task of the Committee is to "examine the progress made by state parties in achieving the realization of the obligations undertaken in the present convention." State parties are required to submit a report to the Committee within two years of ratification, and thereafter every five years. As is outlined in Article 44, these reports must detail the "measures they have adopted which give effect to the rights recognized [in the convention] and on the progress made on the enjoyment of those rights." State parties must also "indicate factors and difficulties, if any, affecting the degree of fulfillment of the obligations under the present Convention." Upon reviewing reports, the Committee makes recommendations for changes in policy and practice. State parties are expected to consider the recommendations and to report back on progress in the next report. However, no formal measures exist to enforce the Convention or the Committee's suggestions.

There are obvious limitations to this monitoring mechanism. Importantly, the monitoring process does not allow for state-to-state complaints, nor does it provide any avenue for individuals to bring complaints against a state, which is in stark contrast to some of the other international human rights instruments (Fottrell, 2000). Without its own system for handling complaints, the Committee relies exclusively on the courts of the various state parties to interpret and implement the provisions of the Convention (Todres, 1998). This presents a potentially thorny situation where state parties become both judge and jury in their own cause, ultimately limiting the efficacy of the Convention (Verhellen, 1996).

Another problem lies in the sheer scale of the Committee's task. The Committee meets three times a year for sessions of four weeks, and there is some concern about its capacity to contend with its burgeoning workload. According to Fottrell (2000), the Committee is running four years behind in its assessments, and is saved only by the fact that so many states are also behind in their submission of reports. Writing in 2000, Fottrell conveyed that 57 states were overdue in their submission of initial reports and an alarming one hundred periodic reports were overdue.

Although state parties are accountable to the Committee, in the absence of international policing and a strict method of legal enforcement, compliance can be perceived as ultimately voluntary. However, one cannot discount the power of international peer pressure, invoking a moral obligation to comply (Covell & Howe, 2001).

THE UN CONVENTION AND ITS IMPLICATIONS FOR CANADA

As a signatory of the Convention in 1991, the Canadian government pledged its commitment to meeting the needs and assigning and respecting the rights of Canadian children regarding their physi-cal, psychological, social, and educational well-being. However, it should be noted that the Convention does not have the same legal status as a Canadian statute or other constitutional instruments such as the *Charter of Rights and Freedoms*. As such, only if Parliament itself enacted legislation to explicitly adopt the Convention as having the force of law could it be used to negate or override a Canadian statute. In this sense, the Convention can currently be seen as an "interpretive guide" for situations where legislation is ambiguous or silent rather than an independent source of legal rights (Bala, 2003). Where Canadian laws are found not be in accord with the standards of the Convention, Canada has agreed to amend its laws over time and harmonize them with the Convention.

When ratifying the Convention, Canada made reservations to Articles 37 and 21. Under Article 37, children held in custody must be held separately from adults unless this is not in their best interests. Canada has reserved the right not to be bound by this provision, thus enabling children to be held in adult remand or correctional facilities. Canada's reservation to this provision, as well as its implications, will be discussed later in the chapter.

Article 21 addresses the adoption system and aims to ensure that the best interests of the child remain paramount during the adoption process. In making its reservation to this article, Canada declared that out of respect for Aboriginal cultural traditions and practices it could not apply a section that called for state regulation of adoption. Instead, it intended to leave room for Aboriginal control over the adoption process. The reasons for this reservation relate to the many historical abuses of adoption laws that facilitated the removal of Aboriginal children from their homes.

In addition to these reservations, the Canadian government entered a "statement of understanding" concerning the Convention's impact upon Aboriginal communities (Article 30). This statement of understanding constitutes an interpretive guideline, giving great weight to Article 30 in interpreting the government's duties toward Aboriginal children. In essence, it is an attempt to address the complex and deeply rooted history of colonization and domination that has characterized the relationship between Aboriginal peoples and the Canadian government.

It is the understanding of the Government of Canada that, in matters relating to Aboriginal peoples of Canada, the fulfillment of its responsibilities under Article 4 (with respect to ensuring the implementation of all rights) of the Convention must take into account the provisions of Article 30. In particular, in assessing what measures are appropriate in implementing the rights recognized in the Convention for Aboriginal children, due regard must be paid to not denying their right, in community with other members of their group, to enjoy their own culture, to profess and practise their own religion, and to use their own language.

The Canadian government completed two reports, in 1994 and in 1999, outlining how the country and each specific province and territory has attempted to meet the needs and rights of children through various practices, policies, and federal and provincial legislation. While a lack of space prevents an in-depth discus-sion of Canada's reports to the UN and the subsequent responses of the Committee, it is possible to highlight the Committee's primary comments and recommendations. Following Canada's first report submitted in 1994, the UN Committee raised a principal concern that insufficient attention had been paid to the establishment of a permanent monitoring mechanism allowing effective and equal implementation of the Convention in all parts of the country. Moreover, the Committee recommended that Canada reconsider its reservations to Articles 21 and 37, and address federal legislation relating to basic provisions of the Convention regarding non-discrimination, the best interests of the child, and respecting the views of the child. The Committee also suggested that the Canadian government address the growing issues of child poverty, immigration practices, legislative measures to combat corporal punishment, the increasing incidence of suicide among young people (particularly Aboriginal children), its approach to vulnerable and disadvantaged children (particularly Aboriginal, migrant, and refugee children), and the fundamental right to education and housing (International Save the Children Alliance, 1999).

Many of these concerns continue to resonate today. While Canada has addressed the Committee's response in some areas,[7] it has failed in others. Although the principles of non-discrimination and best interests of the child have been incorporated into legislation and policy to varying degrees, as noted earlier, the Convention is not fully embedded in ongoing legislation and judicial developments relating to the

Canadian Charter of Rights and Freedoms. The government still faces three areas of primary concern. First, there is a need to coordinate and disseminate information and programs that protect children's rights across provincial, territorial, regional, and local jurisdictions. Second, Canada has been encouraged to strengthen its commitment to children's rights by devoting resources to long-term programs that address economic disparity, child poverty, discrimination, and relations with First Nations peoples. Finally, more legislation and programs need to be developed that include the voices and participation of young people in the systems of justice, policy-making, and family and community life (International Save the Children Alliance, 1999).

Although there are many challenges to effectively implementing children's rights and the principles of the Convention in Canada, the process of implementation may be facilitated when revising and amending new legislation. When laws are created or amended, Canada has the opportunity to incorporate the distinct guidelines of the Convention to successfully protect and promote the rights of Canadian children. On April 1, 2003, the *Youth Criminal Justice Act*[8] (YCJA) came into force, replacing the *Young Offenders Act* (YOA). According to the Department of Justice, the YCJA "builds on the strengths of the YOA and introduces significant reforms that address weaknesses in the YOA. The YCJA provides the legislative framework for a fairer and more effective youth justice system" (Canada, Department of Justice, website). While the government has hailed the YCJA as an improvement over its predecessor, few have

assessed the degree to which the YCJA complies with the principles of the Convention. The following section explores the degree of harmonization and compliance of the YCJA with the Convention. In doing so, we can begin to explore more fully Canada's level of commitment to the principles of the Convention and to children's rights more generally.

HOW DOES CANADA MEASURE UP? ASSESSING THE *YOUTH CRIMINAL JUSTICE ACT* AND ITS COMPLIANCE WITH THE CONVENTION

The YCJA, which was developed long after Canada ratified the Convention, has been declared by the Canadian government as "more consistent with national and international human rights in protecting the interests of children" (Canada, Department of Justice, website). Given the recent implementation of the YCJA, few have appraised whether this in fact holds true. This section highlights the terms of the YCJA that strongly comply as well as those that fail to comply with the provisions of Convention, particularly those provisions that deal with children in conflict with the law.

Compliance with the Convention

An examination of the provisions of the YCJA reveals many instances of strong compliance with the principles of the Convention. These include ensuring that a variety of dispositions are available for young offenders; ensuring an increased focus on a child's dignity, worth, rehabilitation, and reintegration; ensuring a child's right to life and maximum survival and development; ensuring provisions that promote child participation in the youth justice system; and special considerations for Aboriginal youth.

Ensuring a Variety of Dispositions for Young Offenders

When considering the circumstances of children in conflict with the law, Article 40(4) of the Convention requires that a variety of dispositions be available to young people "such as care, guidance, supervision orders, counseling, probation, foster care, education and vocational training programs and other alternatives to institutional care." In compliance with Article 40(4) of the Convention, the YCJA stipulates that while custody may be imposed for a violent offence, section 39(1) "places restrictions on the use of custody for non-violent offences, requiring a history of failing to comply with non-custodial sentences, a pattern of non-violent offending or exceptional circumstances" (Bala, 2003, p. 411). Moreover, if custody is an option, the court must consider all alternatives to custody that are reasonable prior to giving a custodial disposition (sec. 39(2)). The increase in the scope of alternatives to judicial proceedings and in the variety of dispositions and alternatives to custody clearly harmonizes the YCJA with the principles of the Convention. Moreover, the federal government has promised an increase in funding to the provinces and territories to ensure the im-

plementation and availability of community-based dispositions (Bala, 2003).

Ensuring an Increased Focus on a Child's Dignity, Worth, Rehabilitation, and Reintegration

Article 40(1) of the Convention highlights the need for children in conflict with the law to be "treated in a manner consistent with the promotion of the child's dignity and self worth … promoting the child's reintegration and the child's assuming a constructive role in society." The Society for Children and Youth of British Columbia (1998) has noted that as compared to the previous law the YCJA has an increased focus on the concepts of rehabilitation and reintegration that is consistent with Article 40(1). The following sections of the YCJA illustrate this emphasis:

> The youth criminal justice system is intended to rehabilitate … and reintegrate (sec. 3(1)(a));

> The criminal justice system for young persons must … emphasize the following: rehabilitation and reintegration … enhanced procedural protection … and timely intervention (sec. 3(1)(b)).

While the YOA contained similar principles, the YCJA has other, more practical, provisions that promote rehabilitation and reintegration differently than the YOA. For example, in the past children tended to serve the entirety of their custodial sentence in residential facilities. With the new law, there is a presumption that the last third of the sentence will be served on conditional supervision in the community. Additionally, the YCJA emphasizes custody as a last resort and provides for a variety of non-custodial means for dealing with young offenders.

Ensuring a Child's Right to Life and Maximum Survival and Development

Article 6 of the Convention guarantees the right to life and to survival and development to the maximum extent possible. The YCJA, if properly implemented, could contribute to the survival and development of young people in conflict with the law given the repeated references to rehabilitation and reintegration and the increased focus on non-judicial options and alternatives to custody. However, the degree to which these goals will be met will depend on the extent to which these aspects of the law will be implemented. Given the social, political, and economic differences across the country, there is likely to be a great deal of provincial variation in implementation.

Ensuring Provisions to Promote a Child's Participation in the Youth Justice System

Article 12 of the Convention puts forward that "the child shall in particular be provided the opportunity to be heard in any judicial or administrative proceedings affecting the child, either directly, or through a representative or an appropriate body, in a manner consistent with the procedural rules of national law." The YOA (sec. 3(1)(e)) had provisions that offered the potential for the voices of young people to be heard, and this has been reiterated in the YCJA. Section 3(1)(d)(i) of the YCJA recognizes the young person's "right to be heard in the course of and to participate in the processes, other than the decision to prosecute, that lead to decisions that affect them." While the YCJA should be commended for requiring that young persons be given an opportunity to be heard in proceedings that affect them,[9] there is no concurrent obligation for the young person's views to be taken into account in the decision-making process. Compliance with Article 12 of the Convention could be improved if this were addressed through a statutory regulation or obligation to incorporate children's views in a pre-disposition report or in sentencing considerations.

It is clear that the YCJA has addressed the issue of child participation in the youth justice system through some of its provisions. Nonetheless, the extent to which a child is actively involved in the process remains questionable. In her study of youth hearings in Australia, Naffine (1992) has demonstrated that in practice it is passivity rather than participation that characterizes the young defendant. Naffine argues that despite the ideological presence of the Convention and the seeming promotion of children's rights, children's hearings in Australia continue to be the preserve of experts. It is the lawyers who provide the "voice" of their clients and whose very presence implies that the child's rights have been protected. However, it is unclear as to whether children truly participate in hearings affecting them. As Naffine notes:

> Rarely do children speak in court.... Typical of proceedings is speed, routine and the appearance of efficiency. Cases are often dealt with in a matter of minutes. As more than one lawyer has described the process: "it is not unlike a sausage machine: child in child out".... The overwhelming impression one gains of children's criminal proceedings ... is that of administrative efficiency. This is not to say that children are not treated with dignity, nor that some magistrates do not make a conscious

endeavour at times to extract words from the defendant.... But still the compelling feeling is that there is need for haste and that there is little time to spell out the details of the matter for the benefit of defendants nor seek to involve them in their own legal matter. (Naffine, 1992, pp. 89–90)

While the YCJA contains provisions that offer the potential for the voices of young people to be heard, time will tell whether they will provide for truly meaningful youth participation in everyday practice and not simply symbolic, empty rhetoric.

Ensuring Special Considerations for Aboriginal Youth

Article 2 of the Convention asserts that "State Parties shall respect and ensure the rights set forth in the present Convention to each child within their jurisdiction without discrimination of any kind, irrespective of the child's ... race, colour, sex, language, religion, political or other opinion, national, ethnic or social origin, property, disability, birth or other status." When examining the youth justice system, the issue of race is of critical importance. In Canada, Aboriginal youth and youth from certain immigrant and visible minority groups are overrepresented in the justice system.[10] For example, Aboriginal youth are overrepresented at every stage of the criminal justice process, including arrests, convictions, and populations in youth detention facilities (Fisher & Jantti, 2000; Royal Commission on Aboriginal Peoples, 1993). A paper by the National Indian Brotherhood, Assembly of First Nations, clearly illustrates the problems facing Aboriginal youth:

A study entitled *Locking Up Indians in Saskatchewan* concluded that a treaty Indian boy turning 16 in 1976 had a 76% chance of at least one stay in prison by the age of 25. The corresponding figure for a non-Indian was 8%. Put into context, in Saskatchewan, prison for young treaty Indians had become the equivalent to the promise of a just society which high school and college represented to the rest of Canada. (Canada, Department of Justice, 1991, p. 2)

Although the causes of this overrepresentation are complex and include factors such as colonization, assimilation, poverty, and social and cultural upheaval, the potential role that conscious or unconscious racism may play in charging and detention practices and even in judicial decision-making must be considered (Bala, 1999). While Section 3(1)(c)(iv) of the YCJA states that "measures taken against young persons who commit offences ... should respect gender, ethnic, cultural and linguistic differences and respond to the needs of Aboriginal young persons," this is only a guideline and is not operative as are other legal requirements in the law. However, during readings of the YCJA in 2002, the Canadian Senate objected to the new law's lack of attention to the special needs of Aboriginal youth. In response, the law was changed to include a sentencing principle, similar to section 718(2)(e)[11] of the *Criminal Code* of Canada. This section of the *Criminal Code* requires judges to consider alternatives to incarceration for Aboriginal adult offenders at the time of sentencing.[12] Not only has this section been incorporated into the YCJA for consideration when sentencing Aboriginal young offenders (sec. 50(1)), but section 38(2)(d) also addresses this issue and directs judges when sentencing young offenders to consider:

(**d**) all available sanctions other than custody that are reasonable in the circumstances … for all young persons, with particular attention to the circumstances of aboriginal young persons.

It is likely that the inclusion of this sentencing principle and reference to section 718(2)(e) of the *Criminal Code* may address the recommendation of the Committee on the Rights of the Child that the Canadian government "pursue its efforts to address the gap in life chances between Aboriginal and non-Aboriginal children" (2003, p. 13). However, the extent to which judges will incorporate these principles into their sentencing decisions for Aboriginal youth remains to be seen.

Non-compliance with the Convention

Despite the above-noted examples of compliance, there are several areas in which the YCJA fails to meet with the standards of the Convention. These include the Act's emphasis on punishment, the emphasis on custody and detention, the practice of detaining youth in adult correctional facilities, the practice of administering adult sentences to youth, inadequate accommodation of the special needs of youth in custody, restrictions on a child's right to privacy, a lack of consideration of social and economic disadvantages in sentencing, inadequate consideration of the best interests of the child, and inadequate consideration of regional disparities.

Emphasis on Punishment In the face of growing evidence that punishment does little to lessen recidivism and is destructive to youth development (Seagram,

Pyke, & Mack, 1997; Doherty & de Souza, 1995), in Canada a growing trend among politicians and members of the public has been to "get tough" on youth crime. Recent surveys clearly demonstrate that the overwhelming majority of the Canadian public (82–90%) believe youth should be treated more harshly and should be tried in adult court since youth court is too lenient (Hartnagel & Baron, 1995; Lithwick & Lithwick, 1995; Covell & Howe, 1996). In response, all federal political parties, except for the Bloc Québécois, now favour a more punitive response to young offenders (Tanner, 2001). This punitive approach is also reflected in parts of the YCJA. The use of language provides an example of this trend. For example, the term "disposition" used in the YOA has now been replaced in the YCJA with the more criminal sounding term "sentence." Furthermore, although the Act includes several sections that encourage rehabilitation and reintegration, this step forward is countered by the Act's focus on "accountability"—a word that is typically intended to project a get-tough approach to criminal justice and places the interests of society over those of the young person. For example, the term "accountability" appears twice in the YCJA's Declaration of Principle and once in the Preamble, yet the notion of the "best interests" of the child is entirely absent. Moreover, in its overview of the Act's core principles, the Department of Justice notes that the "protection of society is the paramount objective of the youth justice system" (1999). This approach to youth justice is in sharp contrast to the Convention, which clearly instructs that the emphasis should be placed not on punishment or the protection of society, but on rehabilitation and reintegration programs (Article 40), and that the best interests of the child be of primary consideration (Article 3). As a member of the Committee on the Rights of the Child stated, "the rehabilitation of offenders should be the primary objective, not the third, following the protection of society and the punishment of the child in the interest of society" (UNICEF, 1998, p. 545).

It has been argued by many that the Canadian government's increased focus on punishment has been a political response to public pressure (Bala, 1999; Tanner, 2001). However, a significant problem with following the lead of the public, apart from putting political interests before the Convention, is that the public perception of increasing youth crime is inaccurate (Covell & Howe, 2001). Despite high-profile media stories about youth crime, particularly violent youth crime, since the mid 1990s the number of both violent and property crimes committed by youth in Canada has decreased (Alvi, 2002).

While the YCJA does include several statements consistent with the child's best interest (see Declaration of Principle, Appendix C), this step forward is ultimately countered by the Act's focus on "accountability." Strict compliance with the Convention would require a more protective rather than punitive approach to youth justice.

Emphasis on Custody and Detention
In the past the Committee had called into question Canada's overuse of custodial dispositions for young offenders. According to the Convention, detention

and imprisonment are to be used "only as a measure of last resort and for the shortest appropriate period of time" (Article 37). Nonetheless, since 1987, the rate of incarceration for young offenders has increased by 26 percent (Canadian Centre for Justice Statistics, 1997, in Alvi, 2002, p. 193). In fact, Canada's rate of juvenile incarceration has been one of the highest in the world, higher than the rates in both the U.S. and Britain (Alvi, 2002; Covell & Howe, 2001). While the YCJA will attempt to address this trend by limiting the use of custody for less serious offences, in other areas, custody remains an option for those convicted of more serious offences. Additionally, custody can also be imposed in cases where a youth has failed to comply with two previous non-custodial dispositions, such as probation. Although several sections of the YCJA appear to encourage reducing the use of custody for youth, the Act nevertheless fails to have rehabilitation as its priority. True compliance with the spirit of the Convention would mean the establishment of youth justice policy and legislation that shifts from incarceration to rehabilitation. Also, greater emphasis would need to be placed on creating long-term measures for the prevention of youth crime.

Detaining Youth in Adult Correctional Facilities
An important contribution of the Convention has been its emphasis on ensuring that young offenders are treated differently from adult offenders. In sharp contrast, there are current movements in Canada to treat young and adult offenders in a similar manner (Covell & Howe, 1996). For example, Article 37 of the Convention stipulates

that "every child deprived of liberty shall be separated from adults unless it is considered in the child's best interest not to do so." However, as a result of Canada's reservation to Article 37, Canadian authorities continue to remand or hold children in adult correctional facilities. Many child advocates believe that Canada's reservation has less to do with the lack of available detention facilities in close proximity or to children's issues as a whole than with economic policy and budget limitations. It has been argued that the government has wanted to avoid having to build more youth detention centres (Society for Children and Youth of British Columbia, 1998).

To comply with the Convention and ensure that the best interests of the child are of primary consideration would mean the removal of Canada's reservation on the requirement that young offenders be kept separate from adults. In assessing Canada's record in 1995, the Committee on the Rights of the Child noted this reservation and suggested that Canada consider withdrawing it; to date, Canada has not.

Administering Adult Sentences for Youth The contentious issue of adult sentencing for youth reflects another example of the law's failure to treat young and adult offenders in a different manner. Under the YCJA, young offenders can now receive an adult sentence, post adjudication, whereas under the YOA the process was more complex, involving a transfer hearing prior to a finding of guilt. Moreover, the list of offences for which a youth can receive an adult sentence has expanded. While under the *Young Offenders Act* youth could conceivably have

been transferred to an adult facility at age 14, the YCJA has lowered the age of presumptive transfer from 16 to 14.[13] In such instances, under section 61, young persons who commit certain serious offences (murder, attempted murder, manslaughter, aggravated sexual assault, or repeat violent offences) can receive an adult sentence when they are as young as 14 years old. This expansion of the use of adult sentences for young offenders erodes the boundaries between the youth and adult criminal justice systems and is contrary to the spirit of the Convention.

Inadequate Accommodation of the Special Needs of Youth in Custody Within the YCJA there are a lack of provisions that specifically address the importance of accommodating the special health or other needs of young persons in custody or under supervision. While the law introduces a new sentencing provision entitled "intensive rehabilitative custody," it is directed toward a very select group of youth who have committed a serious violent offence and/or are suffering from a mental illness or emotional disturbance (sec. 42(7)). Moreover, the imposition of this sentence is also contingent on the existence and availability of such programming in the provinces. To date, few provinces have such facilities in existence for adolescents. Additionally, it is unclear how the system will deal with a possible increase in the numbers of young offenders serving their sentences in adult correctional facilities. A correctional officer has noted that "overcrowded institutions and continued budget reductions make special treatment of young offenders within adult facilities unlikely" (Cuddington, 1995,

p. 2). Given the Convention's emphasis on the protection of minority and indigenous children, it will be particularly important to monitor the application of adult sentences for Aboriginal, visible minority, and female offenders.

Restrictions on a Child's Right to Privacy The YCJA falls short of a child's right to privacy as indicated in the Convention. According to Article 16 of the Convention, "no child shall be subject to arbitrary or unlawful interference with his or her privacy, family, home or correspondence, nor to unlawful attacks on his or her honour or reputation. The child has the right to protection of the law against such interference or attacks." It could be argued that the YCJA is remiss in regard to this Article by permitting the publication of the names of all youth convicted of a crime who receive an adult sentence.

The YCJA also allows potentially harmful disclosure of information to victims and other individuals deemed acceptable by the court. Moreover, there is no requirement that the court consider the young person's best interests in having such information disclosed. These practices, which allow for the possibility of harmful stigmatization, fail to comply with Article 16 of the Convention.

Lack of Consideration of Social and Economic Disadvantages in Sentencing The governing principles of the YCJA could further be improved if they included consideration of other disadvantages faced by young persons in conflict with the law, particularly those faced with social and economic disadvantages.

This would be further support for the principle set out in the Preamble to the Convention, which states that "in all countries in the world, there are children living in exceptionally difficult conditions, and that such children need special consideration." By failing to address this principle in the YCJA, certain areas of the Act, such as those that consider the importance of family stability when considering community alternatives to sentencing or custody, could discriminate against socially disadvantaged youth who have not had access to the same social supports as other youth. For example, family stability and school attendance are factors taken into consideration in pre-sentence reports and in sentencing. However, the impact of social disadvantage is not sufficiently addressed within the provisions of the YCJA.

Inadequate Consideration of the Best Interests of the Child The best interests of the child is one of the overarching principles of the Convention. Article 3(1) states that "in all actions concerning children, whether undertaken by public or private social welfare institutions, courts of law, administrative authorities or legislative bodies, the best interests of the child shall be a primary consideration." Despite the recognition of the Convention in the Preamble to the YCJA, the Act neglects to mention "best interest" in its Declaration of Principle in section 3. While the federal government has argued that the YCJA is "more consistent with national and international human rights in protecting the interests of children while, at the same time, protecting public safety" (Canada, Department of Justice, website), the emphasis is clearly on the latter. The fact that the YCJA does not have the child's best interests[14] as one of its guiding principles and that it continues to erode the boundaries between the youth and adult criminal justice systems demonstrates inadequate compliance to the Convention. In 1995, Canada was informed by the Committee on the Rights of the Child that "principles relating to the best interests of the child and prohibition of discrimination in relation to children should be incorporated into domestic law and it should be possible to invoke them before the courts" (UNICEF, 1998, p. 43). This has yet to be fully realized.

Inadequate Consideration of Regional Disparities Given the diverse political, social, and economic makeup of this country, it is not surprising that a great deal of disparity exists with respect to equal treatment of youth under the law in Canada. The law itself contains many provisions where the provinces can apply specific sections as they wish. For example, section 61 of the YCJA permits each province/territory to set an age for which young persons between the ages of 14 and 16 can be sentenced as adults for certain offences. As such, a 14-year-old from one province could be subjected to an adult sentence, whereas a 14-year-old from another province who committed the same offence could have the benefit of being sentenced as a young offender. In essence this allows for discrimination based on both age and location and contravenes Article 2 of the Convention.[15]

Sections 7, 18, 19, 86, 87, and 157 of the YCJA all address programs and procedures for dealing with youth involved with the criminal justice system. Each section states that provinces "may" (except for sections 86 and 87, which state that provinces "shall") establish such programs, thus allowing for disparity in application. Furthermore, there is no requirement for consistency among provinces. As such, custody and reintegration decisions, as well as the quality of care or protection that young people receive, could vary greatly depending on which provincial jurisdiction they fall under. For instance, Québec historically provides alternatives to detention that emphasize rehabilitation, whereas Ontario, Manitoba, and Alberta have developed youth detention centres modelled on military boot camps.

Importantly, the Committee on the Rights of the Child had admonished Canada for the "disparities between provincial or territorial legislation and practices which affect the implementation of the Convention" (UNICEF, 1998, p. 27). Given that both provincial and federal governments were made aware of this contravention to Article 2 prior to the development of the YCJA, the continued disparity found in Canada's youth justice system is particularly disconcerting.

DISCUSSION

While the YCJA takes many commendable and progressive steps to protect and promote the rights of children in conflict with the law, these steps forward are countered by an apparent disregard for key elements of the Convention. This highlights the contradictory nature of several principles and provisions of the YCJA that appear to simultaneously emphasize both rehabilitation and punishment/accountability. To meet the standards of the Convention, regional disparities in the treatment of young offenders need to be addressed, as do issues relating to discrimination, privacy, the erosion of the boundaries between young and adult offenders, and ensuring that the "best interests of the child" are of equal importance to the "protection of society." The Committee on the Rights of the Child recently expressed its concern about the YCJA's compliance with the principles of the Convention:

> The Committee is encouraged by the enactment of the new legislation in April 2003. The Committee further welcomes crime prevention initiatives and alternatives to judicial processes. However, the Committee is concerned at the expanded use of adult sentences for children as young as 14, that youth custody is among the highest in the industrialized world, that mixing of juvenile and adult offenders in detention facilities continues to be legal, and that access to youth records and public identification is permitted. (2003, p. 12)

The inability of the YCJA to wholly comply with the Convention casts doubt on the Canadian government's commitment to fully implementing children's rights. It also throws into question the ability of the Convention to successfully protect the rights of children in everyday practice. One danger of an instrument such as the Convention is that its value becomes solely a symbolic one. Despite the many proclamations, legal provisions, and well-meaning program initiatives, these do not always filter down as practical assistance, protection, and empowerment to children. This may be further complicated by the imperfect monitoring mechanisms in place. For children deprived of their rights, safeguards provided through the Convention may be somewhat limited. This issue becomes even

more apparent in countries that have ratified the Convention and yet continue not only to passively ignore children's rights but also to actively perpetrate human rights violations against children, further highlighting the limited role of such international agreements.

Politics obviously played a large role in the implementation of the principles of the Convention into the YCJA. In an era where the protection of society and punitive responses to youth crime are the accepted norm, ensuring the rights and best interests of young offenders does not appear to be high on the political agenda of recent governments. Direct pressure on governments to better implement the provisions of the Convention is an important step to ensuring full implementation. However, given that many politicians follow an approach to youth crime based on the so-called "three Rs"—retribution, revenge, and re-election (Bala, 1999)—better education and sensitization to the issues may be needed for both politicians and the general public. Within the realm of juvenile justice, there is evidence that a better-informed public is a less punitive public (Covell & Howe, 1996). Given that harshness of attitudes may be lessened with the provision of more information, child advocates may need to devote greater attention to public education regarding the realities of juvenile offending. In particular, this would involve a greater understanding of the unique experiences and circumstances of youth in conflict with the law, youth crime rates, the growing evidence that punishment does little to reduce recidivism and is destructive to youth development, and a recognition that the YCJA's focus on "accountability" and the "protection of society" at the expense of the "best interests of the child" contravenes the principles of the Convention. If the status quo is maintained, Canada will continue to fail to meet the standards of the Convention.

Another important challenge to the implementation of the Convention within the YCJA is a lack of economic resources. Assuming that Canadians are in support of the implementation of children's rights in general and in support of the rights of children in conflict with the law under the YCJA in particular, the cost of implementation is considerable. Funds need to be directed toward long-term programs and structures that effectively address the recommendations made by the Committee on the Rights of the Child regarding Canada's progress and commitment to children's rights. To be in full compliance with the Convention, formulas for funding the youth justice system should emphasize the need for preventive, restorative, and rehabilitative programs. As MacDonald (cited in Toope, 1996, p. 45) notes, the governments of Canada "must be pressured into allocating their expenditures toward providing the necessary services, or higher taxes must be imposed." However, Toope (1996) argues that there is little evidence that Canadians are interested in seeing a shift in the allocation of resources away from current social spending programs, nor is there evidence of a willingness to bear higher taxes in order to better promote children's rights. If Canada is to meet its commitment under the Convention, substantial reallocation of resources must follow these commitments.

A final challenge to ensuring that the YCJA is in compliance with the rights set out in the Convention has to do with a child's right to participate in decisions affecting him or her. A corollary to this right is a child's ability to fully understand those rights. Within the context of the juvenile justice system, the complexities of the court process are such that it is unclear whether children sufficiently understand their rights.[16] In their study of Canadian young offenders, Dufresne, Maclure, and Campbell (2003) argue that a child's understanding of legal rights and procedures may be more of an illusion than a reality. As the youth in their study reveal, many do not meet their lawyers until the day of trial and, with little understanding of the implications, are encouraged to plead guilty to expedite the court process. Rather than awareness and insight into the legal process, confusion and misunderstanding appear the norm, as the following quotes illustrate:

> [In court] I did not understand what was going on and my lawyer was just doing everything. "Tell me what is going on" I used to say. While we were in court, I had no clue what was going on and when [my lawyer] came out he was telling me things he should have told me before we went to court. (pp. 17–18)

> Whenever I'd go there, I'd talk to legal aid and he would tell me all this stuff that I didn't understand and I'd go inside the court room. ... They didn't explain nothing. (p. 11)

The implications of this are highly significant. The successful implementation of children's rights, both in theory and in practice, may ultimately mean very little if children are not properly informed of these rights and if they fail to fully understand them. In Article 42 of the Convention, state parties are called on to "make the provisions of the Convention widely known, by appropriate and active means, to adults and children alike."

Clearly, more needs to be done to educate and sensitize both adults and children regarding rights and their meaning, as well as their implications.

CONCLUSION

Over the years, children's rights in Canada have evolved and been transformed, and with the development of the Convention on the Rights of the Child these rights are increasingly being implemented into both public policy and law. The importance of the Convention as a legal document cannot be understated—it has been heralded as a historic achievement of the UN in the promotion and protection of human rights. Its scope, its content, and its very existence make it a landmark effort on behalf of children. It not only serves as an important child advocacy tool, but also encourages uniformity by providing international standards on meeting the rights of children. Nonetheless, the Convention does not exist within a political vacuum, and many significant problems have been noted at the implementation stage. Without sufficient monitoring and without meaningful consequences to state parties who significantly breach the provisions of the Convention, its efficacy is ultimately limited. Despite these limitations, the Convention provides guidelines and principles that can assist in solidifying children's rights in emerging legislation such as the YCJA.

Although the YCJA has made important steps forward from the YOA, several areas beg reconsideration for it to be in full compliance with the Convention. In particular, the government needs to reconsider the Act's emphasis on punishment, the emphasis on custody and

detention, the practice of detaining youth in adult correctional facilities, the practice of administering adult sentences to youth, inadequate accommodation of the special needs of youth in custody, restrictions on a child's right to privacy, a lack of consideration of social and economic disadvantages in sentencing, inadequate consideration of the best interests of the child, and inadequate consideration of regional disparities. To address these issues, greater financial resources are essential to ensure appropriate and equal programming, implementation, and monitoring across provincial and territorial jurisdictions. However, in an era of growing government cuts to social programs, and where support for children's issues appears to take the back burner to support for tax cuts, this may prove to be difficult. Perhaps more importantly, ensuring that the provisions of the Convention are taken seriously requires government commitment and strong public support for the implementation of children's rights. Within a climate of increasing punitiveness and an emphasis on the protection of society at the expense of the best interests of the child, this remains a significant challenge. As long as the public is misinformed about the causes, seriousness, and frequency of youth crime, we can expect that rights for children in conflict with the law will continue to be eroded.

Throughout the world, political rhetoric has increasingly emphasized the need to put children first. In reality, however, the needs and best interests of children are frequently neglected or actively undermined by mainstream models that fail to recognize specific effects of laws and policies on children. Moreover, children are rarely consulted on policy or program design. Significant political will and adequate resources must follow this alleged commitment to children if it is meant to represent real action and not simply a reiteration of more meaningless promises.

References

Alvi, S. (2002). A criminal justice history of children and youth in Canada. In B. Schissel & C. Brooks (Eds.), *Marginality and condemnation.* Halifax: Fernwood.

Bala, N. (1999). Juvenile justice: International themes and a Canadian perspective. In A. Trahan, (Ed.), Proceedings of the 4th biennial international conference of the international association of women judges. A new vision for a non-violent world: Justice for each child (pp. 305–313). Quebec: Les editions Yvon Blais Inc.

Bala, N. (2003). *Youth criminal justice law.* Toronto: Irwin Law.

Committee on the Rights of the Child. (2003). *Concluding observations of the Committee on the Rights of the Child: Canada.* CRC/C/15/Add.215.

Covell, K., & Howe, B. (1996). Public attitudes and juvenile justice in Canada. *The International Journal of Children's Rights, 4,* 343–355.

Covell, K., & Howe, B. (2001). *The challenge of children's rights for Canada.* Waterloo, ON: Wilfrid Laurier University Press.

Cuddington, L. (1995). Young offenders: A correctional policy perspective. *Forum, 7*(1), 43. Retrieved from http:198.103.98.138/crd/forum/e07/e071m.htm.

Canada. Department of Justice. (1991). *Aboriginal people and justice administration: A discussion paper.* Ottawa: Department of Justice.

Canada. Department of Justice. (1999). *Canada's Youth Criminal Justice Act: A new law, a new approach.* Ottawa: Minister of Public Works and Government Services Canada.

Canada. Department of Justice. Retrieved from http://canada.justice.gc.ca/en/ps/yj/repository/2overvw/2010001a.html.

Detrick, S. (1992). The origins, development and significance of the United Nations Convention on the Rights of the Child. In S. Detrick (Ed.). *The United Nations Convention on the Rights of the Child: A guide to the "travaux preparatoires."* London: Martinus Nijhoff Publishers.

Doherty, G., & de Souza. (1995). Recidivism in youth courts, 1993–1994. *Juristat 15,* Statistics Canada.

Dufresne, M., Maclure, R., & Campbell, K. (2003). *The rights of young offenders.* Unpublished manuscript.

Fisher, L., & Jantti, H. (2000). In J. Winterdyk (Ed.), *Issues and perspectives on young offenders in Canada* (2nd ed.). Toronto: Harcourt Canada.

Fottrell, D. (2000). One step forward or two steps sideways? Assessing the first decade of the children's convention on the rights of the child. In D. Fottrell (Ed.). *Revisiting children's rights.* London: Kluwer Law International.

Freeman, M. (1992). Taking children's rights more seriously. In P. Alston, S. Parker, & J. Seymour (Eds.), *Children's rights and the law.* Oxford: Clarendon Press.

Freeman, M. (1997). *The moral status of children.* The Hague: Martinus Nijhoff.

Hammarberg, T. (1990). The UN Convention on the Rights of the Child—And how to make it work. *Human Rights Quarterly, 12,* 97.

Hart, S. (1991). From property to person status: Historical perspectives on children's rights. *American Psychologist, 46*(1), 53–59.

Hartnagel, T., & Baron, S. (1995). It's time to get serious: Public attitudes toward juvenile justice in Canada. In J. Creechan, & R. Silverman (Eds.). *Canadian delinquency.* Scarborough, ON: Prentice Hall.

International Save the Children Alliance. (1999). *Children's rights: Reality or rhetoric? The UN Convention on the Rights of the Child: The first ten years.* London: author.

LeBlanc, L. (1995). Origins and background. *The Convention on the Rights of the Child.* Lincoln & London: University of Nebraska Press.

Lithwick, N., & Lithwick, D. (1995). The "liberal" treatment of young offenders. *How Ottawa Spends.* Carleton Public Policy Papers #16, 287–322.

Melton, G. B. (1991). Preserving the dignity of children around the world: The UN Convention on the Rights of the Child. *Child Abuse & Neglect, 15,* 342–350.

Naffine, N. (1992). Children in the children's court: Can there be rights without a remedy? In P. Alston, S. Parker, & J. Seymour (Eds.), *Children's rights and the law.* Oxford: Clarendon Press.

Price Cohen, C. (1996). Monitoring the United Nations Convention on the Rights of the Child in a non-party state: The United States. In E. Verhellen (Ed.), *Monitoring children's rights.* London: Martinus Nijhoff Publishers.

Roach, K., & Rudin, J. (2000). *Gladue:* The judicial and political reception of a promising decision. *Canadian Journal of Criminology, 42,* 355–388.

Royal Commission on Aboriginal Peoples. (1993). *Aboriginal peoples and the criminal justice system.* Report of the National Round Table on Justice Issues. Ottawa: Canada Communications Group.

Seagram, B., Pyke, S., & Mack, J. (1997). Solution-focused therapy and young offenders: Does it work? Paper presented to the Annual Meeting of the Canadian Psychological Association: Toronto.

Society for Children and Youth of British Columbia, Canada. (1998). *The UN Convention on the Rights of the Child: Does domestic legislation measure up?* Vancouver, BC: Author.

Stenning, P., & Roberts, J. (2001). Empty promises: Parliament, the Supreme Court, and the sentencing of Aboriginal offenders. *Saskatchewan Law Review, 64,* 137–168.

Tanner, J. (2001). From delinquency to youth crime: The Young Offenders Act and the response to juvenile offenders in Canada. *Teenage troubles: Youth and deviance in Canada.* Toronto: Nelson Thomson Learning.

Todres, J. (1998). Emerging limitations on the rights of the child: The U.N. convention on the rights of the child and its early case law. *Columbia Human Rights Law Review, 30,* 159–200.

Toope, S. J. (1996). The Convention on the Rights of the Child: Implications for Canada. In M. Freeman (Ed.), *Children's rights: A comparative perspective.* Aldershot: Dartmouth Publishing Co. Ltd.

UNICEF. (1998). *Implementation handbook for the Convention on the Rights of the Child.* New York: author.

Verhellen, E. (1996). Monitoring children's rights. In E. Verhellen (Ed.), *Monitoring children's rights.* London: Martinus Nijhoff Publishers.

Cases Cited

Québec (Ministre de la Justice) v. Canada (Ministre de la Justice) (2003), 10 C.R. (5th) 281 (Que. C.A.).

Notes

1. For this chapter, the definition of a child will coincide with the definition set out in the United Nations *Convention on the Rights of the Child*. According to the Convention, a child is defined as "every human being below eighteen years" (Article 1). "Children" refers equally to both boys and girls. The terms "children" and "youth" will be used interchangeably throughout this chapter to refer to those under age 18.

2. The Convention is available online at www.unhchr.ch/html/menu3/b/k2crc.htm.

3. Poland's interest in protecting children can be dated back to the Second World War (LeBlanc, 1995). During the war, more than two million Polish children were killed and many others were subjected to Nazi persecution and medical experimentation. The Polish delegation to the UN pressed the Commission on Human Rights to deal with the many child-related problems that arose as a result of the war, and in 1978 the Polish delegation submitted a proposal to the UN that advocated the adoption of a convention.

4. It has generally been acknowledged in the international community that NGOs had both a direct and an indirect impact on the creation of the Convention. The level of NGO involvement in developing the Convention is said to be unparalleled in the history of drafting international instruments (Detrick, 1992).

5. When a country ratifies an international treaty such as the Convention, that country is obligated to observe the treaty's norms and regulations and must adjust its laws to meet the provisions of the international document.

6. The Convention stipulates in Article 43(2) that the Committee should be made up of "ten experts of high moral ground" and "recognized competence in the field covered by the Convention," "who shall serve in their personal capacity."

7. The Committee has been "encouraged by numerous initiatives undertaken by the State party," including the National Children Agenda; the National Child Benefit; the establishment of a Secretary of State for Children and Youth; the Federal-Provincial-Territorial Council of Ministers on Social Policy Renewal; the Social Union Framework Agreement; the enactment of Bill C-27 amending the *Criminal Code*; Canada School Net; Gathering Strength: Canada's Aboriginal Action Plan; and the constructive role played by CIDA to assist developing countries in fulfilling the rights of children (Committee on the Rights of the Child, 2003, p. 1).

8. The provisions of the YCJA apply to young persons between the ages of 12 and 17 who are in conflict with the law.

9. There are many other examples where the YCJA provides for the participation of young

people, including sections 25, 34, 39(6), 42(1), 48, 56, 59(1), 63(1) and others.

10. While various groups of immigrant and visible-minority youth are discriminated against by the youth criminal justice system, more evidence has been documented to date about the situation of Aboriginal youth and will be examined in this section.

11. *Criminal Code*, R.S.C. 1985, c. C-46, s. 718.2(e).

12. It is important to note that the creation of section 718 (2)(e) is not without its critics. Roach and Rudin (2000) and Stenning and Roberts (2001) have argued that the new provision will not significantly reduce Aboriginal overrepresentation in the Canadian prison system.

13. The Quebec Court of Appeal decision in *Reference Re. Bill C-7* has since ruled that the presumptive nature of such sentencing is unconstitutional. In addition, it ruled that it is also a violation of the *Charter of Rights* to allow for the publication of any information about a youth who is not subject to an adult sanction. The federal government, in turn, has decided to enact legislation to comply with this ruling (see *Québec (Ministre de la Justice) v. Canada (Ministre de la Justice)* (2003), 10 C.R. (5th) 281, [2003] Q.J. 2850 (C.A.)).

14. The notion of a "best interests" provision in youth justice legislation is not foreign to Canadian legal discourses. Under the Juvenile Delinquents Act (1908–1984) the "best interests of the child" was considered to be an overriding theme in adjudicating young persons before the courts. However, this resulted in a great deal of discrepant sentencing across the country and many children served disproportionately long sentences in correctional facilities for relatively minor offences. Subsequent youth criminal justice legislation (YOA and YCJA) appears to have avoided using such "best interests" terminology.

15. While provinces and territories have the choice of deciding the minimum age for an adult sentence for certain offences, only Quebec and Newfoundland and Labrador have chosen the age of 16.

16. In Canada, recognition of due-process rights under the law for children emerged only with the YOA in 1984. While children now have much better legal representation in front of the courts, research indicates that they feel alienated during court proceedings and have little knowledge as to what is actually occurring (Dufresne, Maclure, & Campbell, 2003).

chapter five

Conceptual Frameworks for Understanding Youth Justice in Canada: From the *Juvenile Delinquents Act* to the *Youth Criminal Justice Act*

Susan A. Reid, Ph.D.

Associate Professor, Criminology and Criminal Justice
Director, Centre for Research on Youth at Risk
St. Thomas University
and

Marvin A. Zuker, Justice

Ontario Court of Justice
Associate Professor, Theory and Policy Studies
Ontario Institute for Studies in Education

INTRODUCTION

In an analysis of the conceptual frameworks underlying youth justice, it becomes apparent that the issue of youth imprisonment has been a significant concern in the debates of parliamentarians. In recent years, debates have centred around the overuse of custody as a sanction for young offenders. Prior to the implementation of the *Youth Criminal Justice Act*, Judge Heino Lilles argued in *R. v. J.K.E.* (1999) that the high rate of youth incarceration in Canada was a "national disgrace." According to Mallea (1999), Canada has "one of the harshest regimes for young offenders in the Western world" (p. 3). In her introduction of the *Youth Criminal Justice Act* to Parliament in 1999, Justice Minister Anne McLellan spoke directly to the issue of youth incarceration:

> We incarcerate youth at a rate four times that of adults and twice that of many U.S. states. We incarcerate youth despite the fact that we knowingly run the risk that they will come out more hardened criminals and we incarcerate them knowing that alternatives to custody can do a better job of ensuring that youth learn from their mistakes.

Clearly, this overreliance on youth custody as a costly and fundamentally ineffective response to youth crime has negative ramifications for young persons. Furthermore, the deliberations regarding the overuse of youth custody exemplify many of the larger debates about the role and function of the youth justice system itself, reflective of varying political ideologies and differing theoretical perspectives. Unfortunately, this continuing struggle between socio-political ideologies has meant that ultimately the youth justice system, in its attempts to be all things to all people, has not been effective in managing the needs of young people who engage in risky behaviour.

This chapter will provide an overview of the main conceptual frameworks or ideological perspectives for understanding youth justice based on four models of juvenile justice procedure (Reid-MacNevin, 1986). The development of these models emanates from political and ideological preferences regarding the most suitable means of intervening with young people who commit offences, reflective of an ongoing conflict between concerns about the

"protection of society" versus the "needs of young persons." Thus, the chapter will present an overview of the influence of ideology on juvenile justice procedure, within the conceptual framework of a series of models. The models will then be examined within the context of Canadian youth justice legislation. The last section of the chapter examines the extent to which the *Youth Criminal Justice Act* reflects these models in its early stages of implementation, as illustrated through current case law.

YOUTH JUSTICE LEGISLATION IN CANADA: A CENTURY OF CHANGE

The *Juvenile Delinquents Act,* first enacted in 1908, was based on the doctrine of *parens patriae,* its main purpose allowing the state to intervene in the lives of children and youth. This law not only permitted state intervention for cases of youth delinquency but also allowed the state to intervene in situations where children were living in circumstances of poverty, abuse, and neglect. This legislation did not recognize the legal rights of due process for young persons, and many injustices occurred as a result. For example, under the *Juvenile Delinquents Act* young people could be "treated" for offences that would not yield significant sanctions if they were adults. Further, the juvenile court judges controlled the movements and decision-making of young persons until such time as they were no longer "delinquent." Providing treatment and rehabilitation to these "wayward" youth often meant that they spent long periods of custody in training schools, industrial schools, or reformatories. Such sanctions were imposed on children and youth who may not have committed any criminal offence, but had been seen to be incorrigible, truant, or otherwise disruptive to the maintenance of an orderly community. The fact that juvenile courts treated all youths in the same manner, regardless of what circumstances brought them to the court, was widely criticized. Nonetheless, the JDA remained relatively unchanged for more than 70 years. It was only during the 1960s, and up to the enactment of the *Young Offenders Act* in 1984, that extensive consultation and discussion regarding the nature and purpose of the juvenile justice system began to emerge.[1]

Once enacted, the *Young Offenders Act* maintained, to a lesser extent, the *parens patriae* doctrine of the *Juvenile Delinquents Act*. However, the YOA also attempted to meet the competing interests of the youth, the larger society, and the professionals entrusted to "care" for and "control" youth who came under their jurisdiction. In the 1982 government publication providing the rationale for the new legislation, the then Solicitor General, Robert Kaplan, gave the following summary of the principles:

> The Act balances the rights of society, the responsibility that young offenders must bear for their actions, and the special needs and rights of our young people. (Solicitor General Canada, 1982, p. 1)

Section 3(1) of the YOA, Declaration of Principle (see Appendix B), reflected the competing principles applicable to youth justice, and this has been held to have the weight of substantive law in the courts (*R. v. T. (V.)*, [1992]; *R. v. M. (J.J.)* [1993]).

This combination of philosophical perspectives was applauded by a number of commentators as being a more balanced system of juvenile justice than the former *Juvenile Delinquents Act* (Archambault, 1983; Kaplan, 1982; Lilles, 1983; Nasmith, 1983). However, others were more guarded in their analysis of the potential benefits (Reid & Reitsma-Street, 1984), as the conflicting philosophies of the YOA were seen to be much too ambiguous and overly reliant upon judicial interpretation. This inclusion of a variety of ideological perspectives without any direction regarding priority was seen to create even more tension and conflict between and among juvenile justice practitioners. While the combined ideological orientation of the legislation called for a "delicate balancing act by the court" (Nasmith, 1983, p. 10), a lack of stated priority within the principles was seen to further enhance the discretion, influence, and power already held by juvenile justice practitioners (Reid & Reitsma-Street, 1984).

Since its implementation in 1984, the YOA evinced three major legislative reforms in response to public pressure to "get tough" on youth crime.[2] In the 14 years following the enactment of the YOA, the maximum sentence for murder for those young offenders who remained in youth court was increased twice. The YOA retained the provision to transfer serious young offenders to adult court so that upon conviction they would be subject to adult sentences. Again, as a result of public pressure to respond to the perceived "youth crime crisis," parliamentarians amended the provisions regarding the test for transfer of youth to the adult court system in 1992 and 1995, with each new amendment reducing the burden of proof necessary to allow for youth to become enmeshed within the adult criminal justice system (Reid-MacNevin, Stewart, & Hill, 1994; Stewart, Leonard, and Reid-MacNevin, 1995).

A nationwide review of the implementation of the *Young Offenders Act* by members of the Standing Committee on Justice and Legal Affairs, in 1996 resulted in plans to completely overhaul and eventually replace the YOA with the *Youth Criminal Justice Act*. In the announcement of the *Strategy for the Renewal of Youth Justice* (the precursor to the YCJA) by the Minister of Justice in 1998, one of the most prominent reasons given for reform was that "the public believes that the *Young Offenders Act* and youth court judges are too lenient on youth" (Department of Justice, 1998, p. 5). Clearly, history repeats itself once again.

THE INFLUENCE OF IDEOLOGY ON JUVENILE JUSTICE

As the youth justice system in Canada has evolved over the years, external socio-political events and circumstances have clearly influenced the direction of those changes. It is beyond the scope of this chapter to examine the myriad ways that larger social and political events and circumstances have influenced justice policy. What is clearer is how juvenile justice, more generally conceived, reflects particular ideological perspectives or standpoints at different moments in history (Elrod & Kelley, 1995).

One perspective that is helpful in understanding juvenile justice emanates from beliefs about human nature and social order as they relate to criminal behaviour (Marchak, 1989). These two contrasting views can be seen as polar opposites, as either collectivists or individualists. On one side, the extreme individualists suggest that society has absolutely no claims on the individual and there should be no rules, government, or constraints on individual actions. On the other hand, extreme collectivists argue that society always has precedence over individuals and the right to demand conformity through enforcing rules for the public good (Marchak, 1989, p. 62). When these differing world views clash, "ideological conflict" occurs (Miller, 1973, p. 142). These arguments can also be understood within the context of juvenile justice procedure, as extreme ideological positions about the most appropriate means for dealing with youthful offenders can be understood to fall on either the left or the right of the political spectrum, with more moderate positions lying at various points in between.

Reid and Reitsma-Street (1984) proposed these ideological perspectives within youth justice could be explained in terms of four theoretical models of juvenile justice procedure. These include the *crime control model* (Packer, 1964; Horton, 1981), the *justice model* (Packer, 1964; Catton, 1975), the *welfare model* (Griffiths, 1970), and the *community change model* (Miller, 1973). These four models can also be viewed as falling on a continuum with polar dichotomies; the community-change model falls on the radical or extreme left ideological position, while the crime control model falls at the conservative or extreme right position. The welfare model lies more to the political left and the justice model more to the right (see Figure 5.1).

Crime control, at the extreme right of the continuum, is largely concerned with

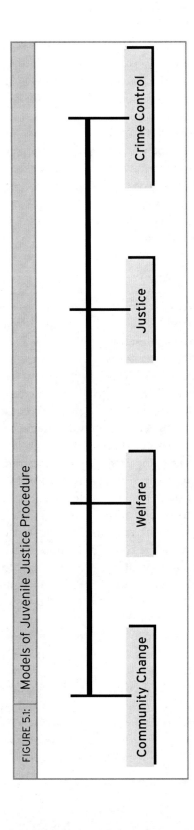

FIGURE 5.1: Models of Juvenile Justice Procedure

Community Change   Welfare   Justice   Crime Control

the protection of society through the assurance to the public that crime will not be tolerated. From this perspective once crime has been discovered, it will be severely punished. Closer to the other end of the continuum is the welfare model. This orientation is more concerned with the needs of the offender in order to ensure that the problems that he/she presents are treated so that crime will not reoccur in the future. The crime control model is based on the philosophy of deterrence, while the welfare model is premised on a medical model of treatment or intervention.

The justice model also focuses on the protection of society through deterrence principles, but suggests that there may be human errors in the discovery and subsequent finding of guilt for those accused of criminal conduct. Advocates of the justice model argue that young people, like adults, should be afforded the same rights to legal protection and have their cases defended by legal counsel. Concerns regarding legal protections for young people in the juvenile courts were raised during the 1960s, leading a number of individuals to question why juvenile offenders did not receive the same protections as adults. This rallying for the rights of young people coincided, in Canada, with the proclamation of the *Canadian Charter of Rights and Freedoms* in 1982. Around this time, some critics of the juvenile justice system's reliance on the welfare model argued for the need to get tougher on those young people who come before the youth justice system. The return to the basic tenets of crime control was contrary to the emerging literature on effective treatments for young offenders. This literature argued, convincingly, that placing low-risk, low-need

offenders in intensive "rehabilitation" programs could do more harm than good (Andrews et al., 1990; Antonowicz & Ross, 1994; Gendreau, 1996; Dowden & Andrews, 1999). It was believed that intensive treatments should be reserved for those young people who commit more serious offences. This led some advocates to propose a system of radical non-intervention based on the notion of "net widening" (Austin & Krisberg, 1981). In this approach, the critics argued that doing nothing at all is sometimes superior to using the machinery of the criminal justice system (Moyer, 1980). The more contact that low-risk offenders have with the system, the more likely it is that the net will be widened, and ultimately the more youth will enter the system.

A great deal of work in the criminological literature has pointed to the strong positive correlation among the roots of disadvantage, poverty, and crime (Polk & White, 1999; Weatherburn & Lind, 2001). Within a framework of social justice, a number of critics have pointed to the need to consider the impact of external socio-demographic factors, sometimes referred to as the "root causes of crime" (Reiss, 1986; Muncie, Coventry, & Walters, 1995; Muncie, 1999; White, 2003). The community change model suggests that disadvantage and the lack of access to resources by some members of society form the basis for the underlying factors leading to the commission of crime. From this perspective, all who live, work, and play within a community have a responsibility for the ongoing prevention and rehabilitation of young people who come in conflict with the law.

Restorative justice initiatives can also be understood to exist within the framework of the community change model. As will be discussed further in Chapter 12, restorative justice does not focus on punishment, but rather emphasizes healing relationships that have been broken by conflict and crime. Viewed through this lens, crime is understood as a violation of people and relationships and a disruption of the peace of the community, and not an offence against the state. Restorative justice encourages the participation of victims, offenders, and the community affected by the crime in finding solutions that will achieve reconciliation and restore harmony.

The models discussed above are not the only means of conceptualizing juvenile justice procedures or responses to youth crime. Two other models are the *modified justice model* and the *corporatist model*. Proponents of the modified justice model have argued that while there are provisions within youth legislation that provide for the legal protection of young people, these protections are further supported by a degree of limited or mitigated accountability on the part of the young person in comparison to his or her adult counterparts (Corrado, 1992). In describing the "modified justice model," Corrado argues that there must be further guarantees of the young person's rights, not only to ensure due process of law but also to ensure that the young person understands the nature and extent of the proceedings that he or she faces.

In response to this continuing debate on the merits of treatment vs. punishment, Pratt (1989) proposed a corporatist model of juvenile justice procedure. He argues that criminal justice officials familiar with

the adult criminal courts did not necessarily have the appropriate knowledge base for understanding the tumultuous period of adolescence that many young offenders experience. Pratt proposes a model that takes into account the youth's developmental level with the principles of both punishment and treatment. Pratt further argues that focusing solely on the rehabilitation of offenders under the welfare approach did not go far enough in terms of balancing both the right of society to be protected and the need of the offender for treatment. The main tenets of each of these models are outlined in Table 5.1.

Variations on the four main models of juvenile justice procedure are shown in Figure 5.2; a number of aspects apply equally to other models. Still focusing on a left–right dichotomy, restorative justice and radical non-intervention models share some elements of the community change, welfare, and justice models. Similarly, while the corporatist and modified justice models are more predominantly placed between justice and crime control, there are also elements within these models that focus on the welfare of the young person.

Juvenile justice systems may be categorized according to their adherence to the various aspects of these models; however, most systems are a combination of philosophical rationales. No juvenile justice system exists as reflecting only one form of any given model; there are always tenets of other models that overlap, creating further tension (Urban, St. Cyr, & Decker, 2003). The models are useful in understanding complex legislation and allow for comparisons between and among a set of essential principles underlying the legislative

TABLE 5.1	Models of Juvenile Justice

Crime Control
- main tenet is that it is the responsibility of the state and the courts to maintain order in society;
- youth behaviour is seen as freely determined; youth choose to commit offences;
- focus is on the repression of criminal conduct through punishment;
- focus on a screening process that diverts the innocent out of the courts (i.e., only the guilty go to court);
- offences are specified and defined prior to their occurrence;
- conservative, right-wing, law-and-order position.

Justice
- main tenet is that interference with individual's freedom is limited and procedures for criminal justice matters are based on consent by all parties as much as possible;
- youth behaviour is seen as freely determined;
- focus is on the repression of crime with a qualification that there is a high probability of error in informal fact-finding (i.e., need to have legal safeguards that protect individual liberty and rights);
- focus on formal adversarial system of justice; offences clearly specified prior to occurrence and formal system of legal intervention;
- key is the protection of rights of the public and the accused, legal safeguards, due process rights, right to a lawyer, right to appeal, right to legal representation at all stages of proceedings.

Modified Justice Model*
- main tenet is that youth offending does not fit conveniently into either a justice or a welfare perspective, so the components of each model are more suitable;
- focus is on criminal offending behaviour but with the recognition of diminished responsibility for the actions of young persons;
- in coming to a decision about the most appropriate intervention, the focus is on diverting minor offenders and punishing serious offenders. Similarly, there are dual roles under this model for both child care/social workers and legal experts who will be able to ensure that individual needs are respected as well as individual rights;
- focus is on providing treatment through diagnosis for those who require it, while sanctioning through punishment those young people who are seen as "hard" offenders.

Corporatism**
- main tenet is to focus on the implementation of social policy that has been developed by administrative decision making;
- youth behaviour is seen as being determined by outside factors influencing the young person, in particular a lack of socialization;
- focus on interagency cooperation and the ability of juvenile justice specialists to intervene, retrain, and socialize young offenders;
- the juvenile justice system is to operate through diversion programs and alternatives to care and custody programs which are run by specialized juvenile justice practitioners.

Welfare***
- main tenet is that the needs of the young person and his or her family must be addressed;
- youth behaviour is seen as being determined by social/psychological forces;
- focus on criminal conduct as being part of other social events impacting on young person (family dysfunction, low income, single parents, alcohol/substance abuse, victim of family violence, etc.);
- focus on evaluation of youth and his/her life circumstances;
- offences are unspecified prior to occurrence and young person is brought to court to be aided and assisted (state intervention to rescue youth from social problems);
- primary ideology of the former *Juvenile Delinquents Act,* youth not seen as committing a specific offence but rather in a "state of delinquency".

Community Change
- main tenet is that society is responsible for the promotion of the welfare of its citizens and must work to prevent crime and delinquency;

TABLE 5.1	Models of Juvenile Justice (continued)

- youth behaviour is seen as being determined by life circumstances;
- focus is on collective society rather than the individual youth as being responsible for criminal conduct (social structural explanation);
- focus is on changing social processes that lead young people to engage in criminal conduct and to improve the quality of life.

Restorative Justice**
- main tenet is that crime impacts not only on the victim and the offender, but also on the wider community;
- all citizens have a role to play in the prevention and repair of the harm done when a crime is committed;
- families, victims, and the community are involved to the greatest extent possible in rehabilitation, community safety initiatives, and holding offenders accountable;
- youth are required to face the personal harm that their offending behaviour has done to the victim and the wider community;
- restitution, victim offender mediation, and community service form part of the restoration of the victim, the offender, and the community.

Notes:
* Corrado, R. R. (1992). Introduction. In R. R. Corrado et al., *Juvenile justice in Canada: A theoretical and analytical assessment*. Toronto: Butterworths.
** Pratt, J. (1989). Corporatism: The third model of juvenile justice. *British Journal of Criminology, 29*(3), 236-53.
*** Reid-MacNevin, S. A. (1991). A theoretical understanding of current Canadian juvenile justice policy. In Leschied, A. et al, *Young Offenders Act: A revolution in Canadian juvenile justice policy*. Toronto: University of Toronto Press, p. 28.
**** Van Ness, D. W., & K. H. Strong. (2002). *Restoring justice* (2nd ed.), Cincinnati, OH: Anderson; Stewart, E. A. et al. (2002). Beyond the interactional relationship between delinquency and parenting practices. *Journal of Research in Crime and Delinquency 38;* Prashaw, R. (2001). Restorative justice: Lessons in empathy and connecting people. *Canadian Journal of Community Mental Health (20),* 23.

provisions (Corrado, 1992). The following section describes how youth justice legislation in Canada reflects various aspects of the models.

APPLYING MODELS OF JUSTICE TO THE CANADIAN EXPERIENCE

The *Juvenile Delinquents Act*

As stated earlier, the *Juvenile Delinquents Act* primarily focused on intervening with youth who were found to be in a "state of delinquency," thus emphasizing the welfare model of juvenile justice procedure. Many of its provisions involved considerations regarding the "best interests" of the child, sentences were indeterminate to allow treatment to occur, and children were denied due process rights (see Appendix A). At the same time, the JDA also discussed the separation of the "control" and "welfare" or treatment components of the legislation. For example, under sec. 20(3) of the JDA a child found to be "delinquent" could have been held under the supervision of the court from the age of 7 to the age of 21. The "supervision" by a juvenile court judge included the provision of "help, guidance and assistance" as well as the control of the young person's movements (Reid & Reitsma-Street, 1984). In fact, under the JDA there were no "offences" per se, and young persons could be found to be in a

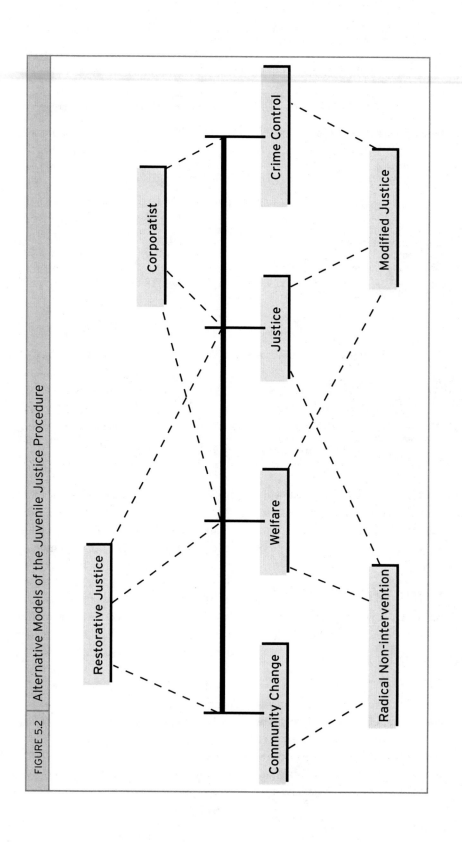

FIGURE 5.2   Alternative Models of the Juvenile Justice Procedure

"state of delinquency." Furthermore, children and youth could be apprehended for behaviour that was not determined to be criminal if committed by an adult. Status offences, as they were called at that time, included truancy, sexual precocity, and a generic term, incorrigibility, which meant that the youth was "beyond the care and control" of his or her parents.

In the era of the JDA, from 1908 to 1982, the majority of children who appeared in youth court were not represented by legal counsel (Wilson, 2003). The lack of procedural and legal safeguards under the JDA was soundly criticized, and between 95 and 99 percent of the children charged entered guilty pleas (Chapman, 1971, p. 92). A retrospective examination of many of these cases revealed that if the young people had obtained "even a modicum of counsel from a lawyer," a large majority of them would have been counselled to enter a not-guilty plea (Little, 1970; Wilson, 1978).

Clearly, the primary model represented in the philosophy of the JDA is that of the welfare perspective. However, given the lengthy "dispositions" meted out in the name of treatment, some have argued that there was more "control" than "care" under the first Canadian juvenile justice legislation (Leschied & Jaffe, 1991; Hogeveen, 2001) (see Figure 5.3).

The *Young Offenders Act*

In response to the many criticisms leveled at the JDA, the *Young Offenders Act* was an attempt to balance the varied perspectives regarding youth justice within its Declaration of Principle (see Appendix B). This involved acknowledging that young persons must bear responsibility for their criminal conduct against society (sec. 3(1)(b),(c),(d)), a consideration of their special needs (sec. 3(1)(a),(c),(f)), and a recognition of the rights of individual youth (sec. 3(1)(a),(d),(f),(g)). Further, the *Young Offenders Act* acknowledged the responsibility of the community to take reasonable measures in the prevention and control of youthful crime (sec. 3(1)(b)).[3] The *Young Offenders Act* marked a shift from the historical child welfare model of the *Juvenile Delinquents Act* toward a more adult criminal law model. Figure 5.4 presents an overview of the models and their emphasis within the *Young Offenders Act*.

As indicated in Figure 5.4, the predominant trend under the YOA was the protection of society (crime control). At the same time, the substantial improvements in terms of the legal rights of young people and due process provisions were indicative of an emphasis on the justice perspective. While the YOA maintained some provisions related to the welfare perspective, overall rehabilitation received much less emphasis under this law. The community change perspective, most notably reflected in the provision of restorative justice practices in some parts of the country, was limited in application under this law (sec. 3(j)). Some critics have argued that the YOA focused almost entirely on a modified justice perspective (Corrado, 1992). However, the implementation of the Act, with its focus on an expanding role for probation officers and the proliferation of intensive probation programs to more actively supervise youth in the community, also suggests a focus on the corporatist model. The idea of need for specialized knowledge on the part of youth practitioners under the YOA was spelled out in *R. v. L.E.K.* (2000). In this

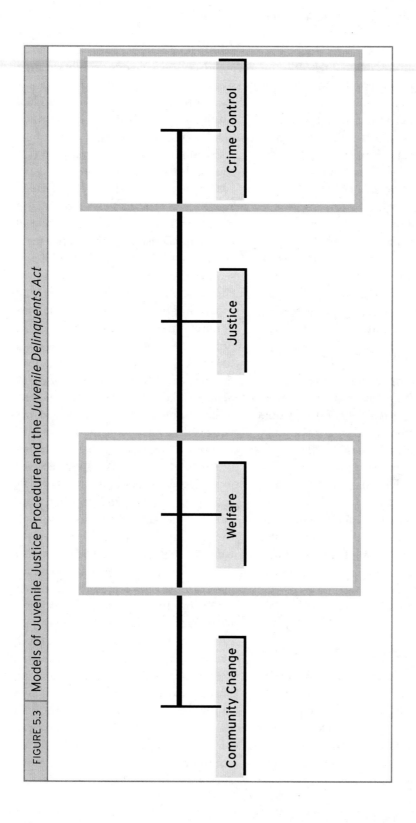

FIGURE 5.3 Models of Juvenile Justice Procedure and the *Juvenile Delinquents Act*

Community Change

Welfare

Justice

Crime Control

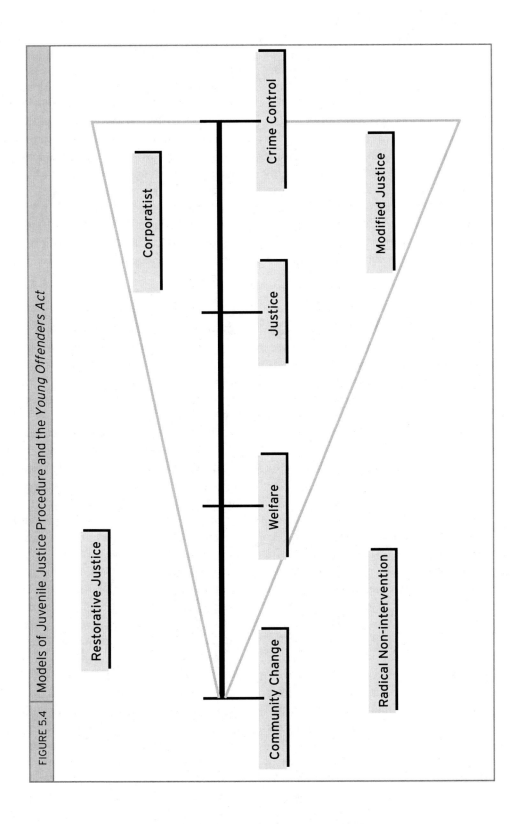

FIGURE 5.4 | Models of Juvenile Justice Procedure and the *Young Offenders Act*

Restorative Justice

Corporatist

Crime Control

Justice

Modified Justice

Welfare

Community Change

Radical Non-intervention

case, the youth court judge directed that a "youth court worker with special training and understanding in the organic brain impairment" be assigned to the "file."

The overriding philosophy of the YOA did attempt to provide something for everyone and all occasions (Reid & Reitsma-Street, 1984). However, the implementation of this legislation led to an overarching focus on the protection of society, as was evidenced in the increased use of youth custody over, and at the expense of, more rehabilitative models such as welfare and community change.

The *Youth Criminal Justice Act*

One of the most significant changes to the philosophy of the new *Youth Criminal Justice Act* is that the Declaration of Principle (see Appendix C) includes four ranked and interlinked statements. They emphasize not only the long-term protection of public (sec. 3(1)), but also the importance of a separate system of justice for young persons (sec. 3(2)). Furthermore, these principles also highlight that responses to young offenders should reinforce respect, encourage the reparation of harm, and be meaningful and respect differences and special needs (sec. 3(3)). The final principle focuses on special considerations for youth, victims, and parents (sec. 3(4)).

The YCJA addresses one of the main criticisms of the former YOA by providing a statement of purpose and principles for sentencing young offenders. Central to this latest reform in juvenile justice is an emphasis on proportional sentencing that, as Roberts (2003, p. 421) suggests, is the fundamental principle of adult sentencing. The YOA made no mention of the principle of proportionality in the determination of appropriate dispositions (now called sentences under the YCJA[4]). However, as Roberts and Bala (2003) argue, the statutory provisions within the new legislation will ensure that the sentencing of youth under the YCJA is to be conceptualized as something quite distinct from adult sentencing practices. In retaining the principle of rehabilitation from the former YOA and JDA, and avoiding the use of any language related to deterrence or denunciation as found in the adult sentencing principles under sec. 718 of the *Criminal Code,* the conceptualization of sentencing for young persons is promoted as distinct from adults. In fact, sec. 50(1) of the YCJA states that the principles of sentencing under Part XXIII of the *Criminal Code* do not apply in respect to proceedings under this Act.

The statement of purpose and principle found in sec. 38(1) states that the overall purpose of sentencing in youth justice courts is to contribute to the "long term protection of society" by holding "a young person accountable for an offence through the imposition of just sanctions that have meaningful consequences for the young person and that promote his or her rehabilitation and reintegration into society." The principle of proportionality is found in sec. 38(2)(c), which states that youth sentences "must be proportionate to the seriousness of the offence and the degree of responsibility for the offence." Bala (2003, pp. 411–412) suggests that section 3 and section 38 of the YCJA require youth justice courts to begin the sentencing process by considering accountability and proportionality. After these considerations, he argues, the court should then determine whether there are rehabilitative concerns and services that would justify changing the nature and mitigating the severity of a sentence that would otherwise be imposed.

As was outlined earlier, the *Juvenile Delinquents Act* primarily focused on the welfare model, whereas the *Young Offenders Act* was a blending of conceptual perspectives with the balance in favour of the protection of society through punitive measures inherent to the crime control perspective. The Youth Criminal Justice Act contains a number of provisions that are related to a variety of diverse ideological perspectives. While it is difficult to determine a unique conceptual orientation, there appears to be a shift toward the liberal left (see Figure 5.5).

The Declaration of Principle in the YCJA (see Appendix C) clearly outlines the role of the community in responding to youth crime, as exemplified by the community change model. However, there is also a strong emphasis in this legislation on using alternatives to the youth justice system through police warnings and cautions (sec. 6(1)) as well as extrajudicial measures and sanctions (secs. 4,5,10). These provisions are in keeping with the notion of "radical non-intervention" (Schur, 1973). Furthermore, the provisions within the legislation for restorative justice such as conferences (sec.19) at all stages of the proceedings and an inherent recognition of the role of victims in the youth justice system (sec. 5) suggest a much stronger emphasis on repairing the harm than has been seen in the past. Recognition of the role of families (sec. 5) and a desire to strengthen family relationships is also contained within the law, which is in keeping with the tenets of a welfare orienta-

tion. While due process rights for youth are retained under the YCJA (secs. 25, 86), it can be argued that the strong influence of "extrajudicial measures" and "extrajudicial sanctions" may require the inclusion of alternative "experts" in youth justice to implement policies that would be consistent with the corporatist perspective. Further, the mitigated accountability in terms of proportional sentencing for young persons would provide evidence for the modified justice model. The very narrow band in Figure 5.5 dealing with crime control is indicative of the provisions within the legislation aimed at the small number of youth who are repeat (sec. 38) and serious violent offenders (secs. 2(1), 68).

As emphasized in the YCJA, the majority of young people in conflict with the law should be dealt with outside of custodial facilities, thereby reserving custody for the relatively few young persons who commit serious offences. Doob & Cesaroni (2001) suggest that the focus in this legislation on "repeat violent" offending by youth is part of current political rhetoric. Given that the public generally overestimates the amount of crime that involves violence (Doob, 2000), the inclusion of "harsh sentences" for a very small group of youthful offenders can be viewed as a politically motivated symbolic gesture.

EARLY STAGES OF *YOUTH CRIMINAL JUSTICE ACT* IMPLEMENTATION: CASE LAW EXAMPLES

In these early stages, it appears that the courts have been implementing the YCJA as it was initially intended. There are clearly marked differences in how the YOA legislation was initially interpreted in

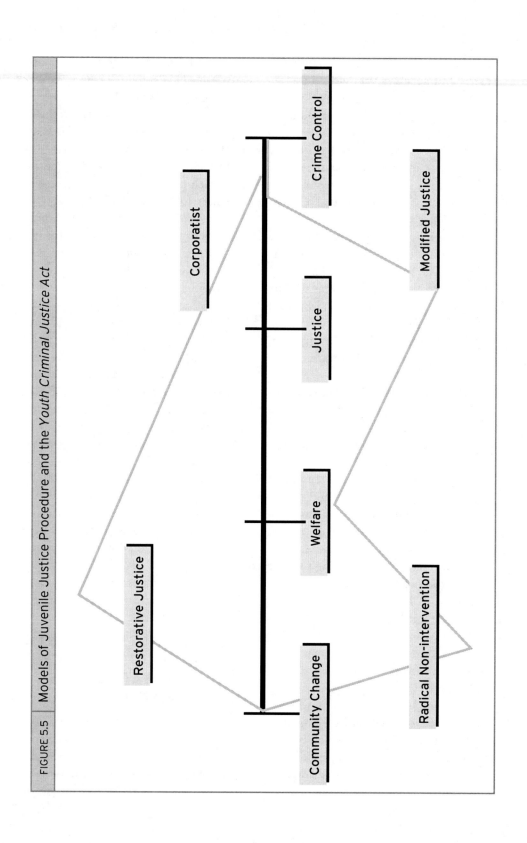

FIGURE 5.5   Models of Juvenile Justice Procedure and the *Youth Criminal Justice Act*

comparison to the recent proclamation of the YCJA. For example, under the YOA, the Declaration of Principle made explicit reference to the value of "taking no measures" (sec. 3(1)(d) YOA) and set up a legislative framework for the creation of diversion programs known as alternative measures (sec. 4 YOA). However, soon after the proclamation of the Act, there was a dramatic increase in the use of formal court responses to youth crime (Markwart & Corrado, 1989), and as time progressed, more youth not only were being processed through the youth courts, but also were being sentenced to periods of custody. In 1998 in Canada, only 25 percent of youth who came in contact with the police were diverted to alternative measures, as compared to 53 percent in the United States and 57 percent in Great Britain (Department of Justice, 1998, p. 20). Unlike the YOA, the YCJA specifically directs police to consider whether to deal with a youth outside the court system (secs. 7, 8, YCJA). As Bala (2003) suggests, this may have a direct influence on police practice, depending on the level of training and the bureaucratic policies of individual police forces. Considerable funding has been provided to train police officers across Canada and to establish police screening and caution programs that will likely encourage police departments to embrace the provisions within the YCJA.[5]

Early case law exchanges illustrate that judges are considering a variety of sentencing options, given the circumstances of specific cases and the needs of the young person, as emphasized in the YCJA. These include considerations of restorative justice, restrictions on the use of custody, special sentencing provisions for serious violent offences and considerations of special needs.

Restorative Justice

In terms of the use of restorative justice practices, the recent case of *R. v. M.B.* illustrates an attempt on the part of the youth justice court judge to follow the spirit of the law. In this case, the young person pleaded guilty to two robberies; a joint submission from the Crown and defence for a two-year custody and supervision order was rejected by the court in order that two conferences could be convened, as outlined under sec. 41 of the YCJA. The judge in this case suggested that "Conferencing under the YCJA is a tool for Youth Courts to delve into the reasons for offending and the best measure available to reduce offending behavior and rehabilitate young people" (*R. v. M.(B.)* 2003 at para. 48). The result of the conference allowed for a complete assessment of the young person, which provided evidence that the youth suffered from fetal alcohol spectrum disorder. This information, coupled with the ability to discuss the offending behaviour within the conference, allowed the court to give good reasons as to why a non-custodial sentence should be imposed.[6]

Restrictions on the Use of Custody

It would appear that the courts are responding to the new provisions regarding restrictions on sentencing youth to custody in accordance with the YCJA. Under the YOA, the provisions regarding restrictions on youth custody were far less explicit. A legislative amendment in 1992 to the YOA created sec. 24(1.1), aimed at limiting the use of custody. Furthermore, there was also a directive that stated that custody should be imposed only "when all available alternatives to custody" have been considered (sec. 24(1.1)(c)). A subsequent amendment to that law in 1995 required judges to state reasons why a non-custodial option would not have been appropriate (sec. 24(4)). Under the YCJA, the early indications of court decisions indicate compliance with the new sentencing regime, and examples from case law illustrate these new trends.

Under the YOA as recently as 2001, the majority of the Manitoba Court of Appeal took no issue in the sentencing by the trial judge of a first-time offender to six months' open custody and 18 months' probation for a number of property offences (*R.v. A.J.G.N.* (2001)). More recent decisions indicate a reticence to impose custody in similar circumstances. On October 24, 2003, the British Columbia Court of Appeal found that the trial judge failed to consider the sentencing provisions of the YCJA in sentencing a young person to six months' custody for aggravated assault. The Court of Appeal found the trial judge did not give sufficient weight to the "repeated mandatory directions not to sentence young persons to time in custody if there is any other available alternative." The Court argued that the "trial judge erred in law and in principle" and stated emphatically that "it is incumbent on trial judges to adhere to the direction in the statute and state the reasons for not imposing a custodial sentence" (*R. v. S.L.* 2003 at para.59). The Court varied the sentence to time served plus one year of probation. Similarly, in a Nova Scotia Court of Appeal decision in December 2003, the Court dismissed an appeal from the Crown to vary a young person's sentence from one year's probation and time served in remand to three months' custody followed by 18 months' probation. The Court stated that even if there had been the determination by the court that the offences in question were violent, custody is not mandatory and concluded that the sentencing judge had applied the appropriate principles of sentencing, which included the "emphasis on rehabilitation and the de-emphasis of custodial sentencing except in special circumstances" (*R. v. T.M.D.* [2003] at para.43).

Serious Violent Offences

Even in the case of a serious violent offence (sec. 39(4)), the courts have been reluctant to impose long terms of custody. In a recent decision of the Ontario Court of Justice, an 18-year-old first-time offender pled guilty to the second-degree murder of his father. In accepting the plea of second-degree murder, the sentencing judge recognized the admission by the young person that he had intended to kill his father and, therefore, the sentence to be meted out needed to reflect the severity of the crime. Considering the principle and purpose of sentencing under the YCJA, the sentencing judge said there were significant mitigating circumstances. She pointed to this being his first offence, his low risk to re-offend, his lack of mental illness, and his strong family support as factors that justified a sentence of three years in closed custody followed by conditional supervision for four and a half years (*R. v. J.C.* [2004]).

In the Court of Appeal for British Columbia, a 17-year-old youth attended a party and consumed alcohol to the point of intoxication and then engaged in a drag race in a high-powered BMW, which led to the death of the passenger. He was convicted of criminal negligence causing death and impaired driving causing death that would have exposed him to a maximum penalty of life imprisonment if he had been five months older. The Crown did not seek an adult sentence, preferring the maximum sentence under the YCJA of a three-year custody and supervision order. Defence Council for the young person sought a non-custodial sentence of two years' probation. The case before the B.C. Court of Appeal was an appeal by the young person of the sentence imposed by the trial judge of a custody and supervision order of one year with the first eight months to be served in open custody and the final four months under intensive supervision in the community. The reasons stated by the sentencing judge concluded that "without imposing a custodial sentence, there was no reasonable hope of achieving the purpose ... of holding the person accountable for his offence through the imposition of just sanctions which might have meaningful consequences for him" (*R. v. S.S.* (2004) at para. 9). In the trial judge's conclusion before sentencing, he pointed out to the young person the serious nature of the offences of which he had been convicted but also restrained the use of the most onerous sentence by recognizing that the young person was a first-time offender. In dismissing the appeal, the Court pointed out that had the appellant reached his eighteenth birthday the appropriate sentence would not be a conditional sentence as proposed by the defence counsel: "Had this appellant been over the age of 18, it can be safely assumed that a fit sentence would have been well

into the penitentiary range" (*R. v. S.S.* (2004) at para. 18). This decision clearly reflects the intent of Parliament with regard not only to the purposes and principles of the Act and sentencing under the YCJA but also to the distinctiveness of the youth court from the adult court.

Special Needs

A recent decision of the Nova Scotia Supreme Court of January 20, 2004 involved a 14-year-old girl charged in December 2002 with the theft of pepperoni; subsequent to the initial charge, a number of breaches were laid related to curfew, failing to live where directed, and failing to attend school. The young person had been remanded in pretrial detention for approximately one month prior to her sentencing hearing, and despite both Crown and defence counsel recommending a non-custodial sentence, the sentencing judge went on to impose a period of custody for 90 days. The Court of Appeal quashed the custodial sentence by the sentencing judge and insisted that there be no additional sentence imposed because it would "simply be repeating the errors of the Youth Court Judge by imposing a sentence that is disproportionate to the offences" (*R. v. M.J.S.* [2004] at para.27). In reviewing the sentencing judge's decision, it was clear that there were a number of errors in law and the Nova Scotia Supreme Court went so far as to say that the sentencing judge "misinterpreted or misapplied each of the sections she referred to" (at para.12).

The issue before the sentencing court was that the young person was a troubled 14-year-old who was not able to return home to live with her parents, and it was believed that she was living on the streets. In reading the submissions and the sentencing judge's remarks it was clear that the issues presented by the young person were more child-welfare matters, and the use of custody as a substitute for child protection, mental health, or other social measures is in violation of sec. 39(5) of the YCJA. This decision clearly underscores and corrects many of the problems under the YOA, where young people who would have been better served through social services were often incarcerated due to the lack of appropriate child-welfare services. Further, in the Supreme Court reasons, the sentencing judge erred in ordering a custodial sentence based on the proportionality principle within the YCJA. The judge remarked that "the entire series of events started with the primary offence where this troubled young person took a piece of pepperoni" (at para. 24). Further, "a young person who has committed a relatively minor offence but has serious psychological needs that seem to have contributed to the behaviour should receive a sentence that reflects the seriousness of the offence, not the seriousness of the psychological needs" (at para.15). This clearly underscores the move away from the welfare model reminiscent of the *Juvenile Delinquents Act*.

From this recent case law, it appears that the appellate courts are ensuring that the principle and purpose of the new legislation are being addressed. One can expect that there will consequently be a dramatic decrease in the use of custody as time goes on. The YCJA has ensured that the high rate of incarceration for property offenders[7] will no longer be tolerated. It is also to be expected that there will be a demonstrated reduction in the number of young people who are serving terms of custody for breach of conditions of a non-custodial sentence, as the YCJA requires that the young person must have violated at least two "previous" non-custodial dispositions in order to receive a custodial sentence (sec. 39(1)(b)).[8]

These recent sentencing decisions demonstrate an effort on the part of appellate courts to reduce the numbers of youth receiving custodial sentences. The data on youth in custody also demonstrate these trends. The province of Ontario in December 2003 showed a decrease in the average count of young persons in secure custody of 44.2 percent from the previous year and a 49.7-percent reduction in the average count of youth in open custody facilities (Ontario Ministry of Correctional Services, 2004). Also within the province of Ontario, the much-debated boot camp (Reid-MacNevin, 1997) "Project Turnaround" dropped its occupancy to zero in November 2003 and officially closed in January 2004. Other facilities within the province are also reducing their capacity by closing as many as 20 or more beds (Ontario Ministry of Correctional Services, 2004). In British Columbia, there has been a 34-percent decrease in the number of secure custody placements as of November 2003 compared to the previous year, as well as the closure of four youth custody facilities. In February 2004, the Nova Scotia government announced it would close the Shelburne Youth Centre, which housed 120 young people at a cost of $2.8 million per year (Cox, 2004). From these data, it is clear that we are currently experiencing an effort to consider alternatives to secure custody for the majority of young people who come before the courts.

CONCLUSION

It has been argued throughout this paper that the overarching theme during the last century in Canada has been a commitment, through policy and legislation, to maintain a separate system of justice for young offenders. However, the shifts in political rhetoric and ideological debates in the latter part of the twentieth century reflect calls for a more repressive system, characteristic of adult criminal justice processes. Nonetheless, the implementation of the YCJA, when compared with developments in the United States, indicates that Canada is now moving in a different direction. Various states in America continue to implement strategies that facilitate the transfer of youth to adult facilities and make use of mandatory punitive sentences for youth coupled with funds to assist communities to follow stricter regimes. At the same time, Canada has taken a strong position in reaffirming the importance of a separate juvenile justice system and reducing the number of young people who are held in custody. This appears consistent with some of the more progressive policies seen in some European countries. For example, both the Netherlands and Spain have recently implemented policies that provide for the increased use of community-based alternatives to the formal justice system, as well as a greater emphasis on diversion practices such as police cautioning (Alberola & Molina, 2003; Wittebrood, 2003).

The Declaration of Principle of the YCJA represents a hopeful step forward. Maintaining a clear distinction between adult and youth sentences, as well as the increasing sentencing options for youth court judges and reduced accountability of young persons based on their age and stage of development, will help to ensure the continuation of a separate system of youth justice. A further focus of the YCJA incorporates the victim, the offender, and the wider community, while emphasizing the reparation of harm caused by youth criminal conduct. Clearly, the models or ideological perspectives described earlier do not manifest themselves in a straightforward manner through the YCJA. However, as early case law has illustrated judges appear to be sentencing within the framework of a modified justice perspective: diverting youth who commit minor offences while reserving harsher sanctions for those committing more serious offences.

Perhaps the most striking promise of the new legislation is evident in the Quebec Court of Appeal Reference.[9] This ruling draws attention to the nature and focus of the new legislation, which will make it very difficult to return to a "get tough" regime for young offenders in the future (Anand & Bala, 2003, p. 397). The Reference has effectively eliminated the presumptive nature of some adult sentences for young persons. In essence, this decision further emphasizes the need to treat youth differently than adults, where there is a clearer focus on rehabilitation (Anand & Bala, 2003). Furthermore, developments such as these can be understood as "glimmers of hope" within what Junger-Tas (2003) refers to as a beginning reaction in the Western World to the existing repressive penal climate for youth:

> In a number of countries, there is a renewed emphasis on (early) crime prevention and a continuous search for innovative and effective rehabilitative

community interventions, which may push custody to a marginal measure for very serious offenders only (Junger-Tas, 2003, p. 383).

The YCJA may prove to be that glimmer of hope for Canadian youth.

References

Alberola, C. R., & E. F. Molina. (2003). Juvenile justice in Spain. *Journal of Contemporary Criminal Justice, 19*(4), 384–412.

Anand, S., & Bala, N. (2003). "The Québec Court of Appeal *Youth Justice References*: Striking down the toughest part of the new act." 10 C.R. (6th), 397–418.

Andrews, D. A., Zinger, I., Hoge, R. D., Bonta, J., Gendreau, P., & Allen, F. T. (1990). Does correctional treatment work? A clinically relevant and psychologically informed meta-analysis. *Criminology, 28*(3), 369–404.

Antonowicz, D., & Ross, R. (1994). Essential components of successful rehabilitation programs for offenders. *International Journal of Offender Therapy and Comparative Criminology, 38*, 97–104.

Archambault, O. (1983). *Young Offenders Act*: Philosophy and principles. *Provincial Judges Journal, 7*(2), 1–20.

Austin, J., & Krisberg, B. (1981). Wider, stronger and different nets: The dialectics of criminal justice reform. *Journal of Research in Crime and Delinquency, 18*(1), 165–196.

Bala, N. (2003). Diversion, conferencing and extrajudicial measures for adolescent offenders. *Alberta Law Review, 40*(4), 991–1027.

Canada. Solicitor General. (1982). *The Young Offenders Act, 1982: Highlights.* Ottawa: Supply and Services Canada.

Catton, K. (1975). Models of procedure and the juvenile courts. *Criminal Law Quarterly, 18*, 181–201.

Chapman, P. B. (1971). The lawyer in juvenile court: A Gulliver among Lilliputians. *Western Ontario Law Review, 10*, 88–92.

Corrado, R. R. (1992). Introduction. In R. R. Corrado et al. (Eds.), *Juvenile justice in Canada: A theoretical and analytical assessment.* Toronto: Butterworths.

Cox, K. (2004, February 14). New law prompting provinces to close jail. *The Globe and Mail,* p. A7.

Canada. Department of Justice. (1998). *A strategy for the renewal of youth justice.* Ottawa: Queen's Printer.

Doob, A. N. (2000). Transforming the punishment environment: Understanding public views of what should be accomplished at sentencing. *Canadian Journal of Criminology, 42*, 323–340.

Doob, A. N., & C. Cesaroni. (2001). Mandatory minimum sentences: Law and policy, the political attractiveness of mandatory minimum sentences. *Osgoode Hall Law Journal, 39*, 287–304.

Dowden, C., & Andrews, D. A. (1999). What works in young offender treatment: A meta-analysis. *Forum on Correctional Research, 11*(2), 21–24.

Elrod, P., & Kelley, D. (1995). The ideological context of changing juvenile justice. *Journal of Sociology and Social Welfare, 22*(2), 57–75.

Gendreau, P. (1996). The principles of effective intervention with offenders. In A. T. Harland (Ed.), *Choosing correctional options that work: Defining the demand and evaluating the supply.* Thousand Oaks, CA: Sage.

Griffiths, J. (1970). Ideology in criminal procedure or a third model of the criminal process. *Yale Law Journal, 79*, 359.

Hogeveen, B. (2001). Winning deviant youth over by friendly helpfulness: Transformations in the legal governance of deviant children in Canada, 1857–1908. In R. C. Smandych (Ed.), *Youth justice: History, legislation and reform.* Toronto: Harcourt.

Horton, J. (1981). The rise of the right. *Crime and Social Justice, 15*, 7–17.

Junger-Tas, J. (2003). Editorial. *Journal of Contemporary Criminal Justice, 19*(4), 380–383.

Kaplan, R. (1982). *Highlights of the Young Offenders Act.* Ottawa: Ministry of the Solicitor General, Canada.

Leschied, A. W., & Jaffe, P. G. (1991). Dispositions as indicators of conflicting social purposes under the JDA and YOA. In A. W. Leschied, P. G. Jaffe, & W. Willis (Eds.), *Young Offenders Act: A revolution in Canadian juvenile justice.* Toronto: University of Toronto Press.

Leon, J. (1977). The development of Canadian juvenile justice: A background for reform. *Osgoode Hall Law Journal, 15,* 71–106.

Lilles, H. (1983). Beginning a new era. *Provincial Judges Journal, 7*(3), 21–26.

Little, W. T. (1970). A guarantee of the legal rights of children through legal aid. *Gazette, 4,* 217–230.

Mallea, P. (1999). *Getting tough on kids: Young offenders and the "law and order" agenda.* Winnipeg, MB: Canadian Centre for Policy Alternatives.

Marchak, P. (1989). Ideology and social organization. In H. B. McCullough (Ed.), *Political ideologies and political philosophies.* Toronto: Thompson.

Marinelli, J. (2002). Youth custody and community services in Canada, 2000–01. *Juristat, 22*(8).

Markwart, A., & Corrado, R. (1989). Is the *Young Offenders Act* more punitive? In L. Beaulieu (Ed.), *Young offender dispositions: Perspectives on principles and practice.* Toronto: Law and Thompson.

Miller, W. B. (1973). Ideology and criminal justice policy. *Journal of Criminal Law and Criminology, 64,* 141–162.

Moyer, S. (1980). *Diversion from the juvenile justice system.* Ottawa: Department of Justice.

Muncie, J., Coventry, G., & Walters, R. (1995). The politics of youth crime prevention. In L. Noaks, M. Maguire, & M. Levi (Eds.), *Contemporary issues in criminology.* Cardiff: University of Wales Press.

Muncie, J. (1999). *Youth and crime: A critical introduction.* London: Sage.

Nasmith, A. P. (1983). Paternalism circumscribed. *Provincial Judges Journal, 7*(3), 16–20.

Ontario Ministry of Correctional Services. (2004). *Statistical highlights: Custodial populations December 2003.* Program Effectiveness, Statistical Services and Applied Research Unit.

Packer, H. (1964). Two models of the criminal process. *University of Pennsylvania Law Review, 113,* 1–69.

Polk, K., & White, K. (1999). Economic adversity and criminal behaviour: Rethinking youth unemployment and crime. *Australian and New Zealand Journal of Criminology, 32*(3), 284–302.

Prashaw, R. (2001). Restorative justice: Lessons in empathy and connecting people. *Canadian Journal of Community Mental Health, 20,* 23.

Pratt, J. (1989). Corporatism: The third model of juvenile justice. *British Journal of Criminology, 29*(3), 236–53.

Reid, S. A., & Reitsma-Street, M. (1984). Assumptions and implications of new Canadian legislation for young offenders. *Canadian Criminology Forum, 7,* 1–19.

Reid-MacNevin, S. A. (1986). The juvenile justice revolution in Canada: The creation and development of new legislation for young offenders. *Canadian Criminology Forum, 8*(1), 1–14.

Reid-MacNevin, S. A. (1991). A theoretical understanding of current Canadian juvenile justice policy. In A. Leschied, et al. (Eds.), *Young Offenders Act: A revolution in Canadian juvenile justice policy.* Toronto: University of Toronto Press.

Reid-MacNevin, S. A. (1997). Boot camps for young offenders: A politically acceptable punishment. *Journal of Contemporary Criminal Justice 13*(2), 155–171.

Reid-MacNevin, S. A. (2002). Forging a new beginning for young offenders in New Brunswick police training: *Youth Criminal Justice Act:* Police training. New Brunswick, Department of Public Safety. Available online at www.jhsnb.ca/policeycja.pdf.

Reid-MacNevin, S. A., Sauvageau, J., & Fitch, L. (2000). *Considerations for a national RCMP youth strategy.* Ottawa: RCMP. Available online at www.rcmp.ca/gazette/gazette-youth-e.pdf.

Reid-MacNevin, S. A., Stewart, G., & Hill, B. (1994). *Brief submitted to the standing committee on justice and legal affairs on bill C-37, The Young Offenders Act* (written for the John Howard Society of Canada).

Reiss, A. (1986). Why are communities important in understanding crime? In A. Reiss & M. Tonry (Eds.), *Communities and crime.* Chicago: University of Chicago Press.

Roberts, J. V. (2003). Sentencing juvenile offenders in Canada: An analysis of recent reform legislation. *Journal of Contemporary Criminal Justice, 19*(4), 413–434.

Roberts, J. V., & Bala, N. (2003). Understanding sentencing under the *Youth Criminal Justice Act. Alberta Law Review, 41*(2), 394–423.

Schur, E. M. (1973). *Radical nonintervention: Rethinking the delinquency problem.* Englewood Cliffs, NJ: Prentice Hall.

Statistics Canada. (2000). *Youth court statistics 1998–1999.* Ottawa: Canadian Centre for Justice Statistics

Stewart, G., Leonard, C., & Reid-MacNevin, S. (1995). *Brief submitted to the Standing Committee on Justice and Legal Affairs regarding the Phase II Review of the Young Offenders Act* (written for John Howard Society Canada in conjunction with John Howard Society Ontario and John Howard Society Alberta). Available online at http://www.johnhoward.ca/document/brief/Jhsdoc.htm.

Stewart, E. A., Simons, R. L., Conger, R. D., & Scaramella, L. V. (2002). Beyond the interactional relationship between delinquency and practices: The contribution of legal sanctions. *Journal of Research in Crime and Delinquency, 39*(1), 36–59.

Urban, L. S., St. Cyr, J. L., & Decker, S. H. (2003). Goal conflict in the juvenile court. *Journal of Contemporary Criminal Justice, 19*(4), 454–479.

Van Ness, D. W., & Strong, K. H. (2002). *Restoring justice* (2nd ed.). Cincinnati, OH: Anderson.

Weatherburn, D., & Lind, B. (2001). *Delinquent prone communities.* Cambridge: Cambridge University Press.

White, R. (2003). Communities, conferences and restorative social justice. *Criminal Justice, 3*(2), 139–160.

Wilson, L. C. (1978). *Children and the law.* Toronto: Butterworths.

Wilson, L. C. (2003). The role of counsel in the *Youth Criminal Justice Act. Alberta Law Review, 40*(4), 1029–1040.

Wittebrood, K. (2003). Juvenile crime and sanctions in the Netherlands. *Journal of Contemporary Criminal Justice, 19*(4), 435–453.

Cases Cited

R. v. J.K.E., [1999] Y.J. No.119 (Yukon Ter. Ct.—Youth Ct.) at paragraph 61.

R. v. D.L.C., [2003] N.J. No. 94 (Newfoundland and Labrador Prov. Ct.) at paragraph 32.

R. v. T.(V.), [1992] 1 S.C.R. 749.

R. v. M.(J.J.), [1993] 2 S.C.R. 421.

R. v. L.E.K., [2000] S.J. No.844 (QL) at paragraph 25.

R. v. R.P.B., [2003] A.J. No 925 (Alta. Prov. Ct.).

R. v. A.J.G.N., [2001], Y.O.S. 01-042 (Man. C.A.).

R. v. S.L., [2003] B.C.C.A. 563.

R. v. M.B., [2003] S.J. Nos. 377 and 602.

R. v. T.M.D., [2003] N.S.J. No. 488 (N.S.C.A.).

R. v. S.S., [2004] B.C.C.A. 94.

R. v. M.J.S., [2004] N.S.J. No.64 (N.S.S.C.).

R. v. J.C., [2004] O.J. No. 281, B.Y.O.U./2004-022; Ont. Ct. of Justice, January 29, 2004.

Québec (Ministre de la Justice) v. Canada (Ministre de la Justice) (2003), 10 C.R. (5th) 281 (Que. C.A.)

Notes

1. See, for example, Leon, 1977.

2. Refer to: Bill C-32, *An Act to Amend the Young Offenders Act, the Criminal Code, the Penitentiary Act and the Prisons and Reformatories Act* (1986); Bill C-11, *An Act to Amend the Young Offenders Act and the Criminal Code* (1992); and Bill C-19, *An Act to Amend the Young Offenders Act and the Criminal Code* (1995).

3. Reid & Reitsma-Street (1984) conducted a content analysis of the phrases within each subsection of the Declaration of Principle of the *Young Offenders Act*. This involved breaking down the eight subsections into 13 phrases, due in part to the fact that the subsections themselves often appeared to reflect more than one model of juvenile justice.

4. *R. v. R.P.B.*, [2003] A.J. No 925 (Alta. Prov. Ct.).

5. See, for example, Reid-MacNevin, et al., 2000; Reid-MacNevin, 2002.

6. The youth then received a sentence of 18 months' probation, which was later overturned by the Saskatchewan Court of Appeal.

7. In 2001, three-quarters of the admissions to custody were for property offences (Marinelli, 2002).

8. In 1998 –99, 31 percent of youth sentenced to custody were incarcerated for failing to appear in youth court or breaching their original disposition (Statistics Canada, 2000).

9. Quebec Court of Appeal (Reference re: Bill C-7, 2003 paras. 244–252).

chapter six

Trends in Youth Crime in Canada

*Jane B. Sprott**

Department of Sociology and Anthropology
University of Guelph
and

Anthony N. Doob

Centre of Criminology
University of Toronto

INTRODUCTION

This chapter investigates issues around trends in youth crime in Canada that have occurred over the past few decades. After a brief discussion of the complexities involved in measuring youth crime, certain trends will be investigated. Specifically, self-reported offending and victimization surveys will be explored, along with police arrests and court processing of both violent and property offending. In addition, provincial variation in rates of offending and court processing will be presented. Finally, a more detailed investigation of the nature and types of violent offences Canada has witnessed over the past decade will be provided, as well as an examination of the involvement of girls in youth crime and violence specifically.

MEASURING YOUTH CRIME

When investigating youth crime trends over time, the general starting point for many people might be to examine arrests for offences identified in the *Criminal Code*. However, it is important to keep in mind that offending does not begin at the age of criminal re-

*© Jane B. Sprott and Anthony N. Doob

sponsibility (12 years old), when police can officially arrest youths. Indeed, it may be useful to think more generally about the development of deviance or criminal behaviour when exploring youth crime. For example, most youths engage in aggressive behaviours in infancy and steadily *decrease* their involvement in such acts as they mature. Using information on involvement in aggressive acts from a national sample of Canadian children, Tremblay et al. (1996) found that:

> The age at which the largest proportion of children were reported by parents to "sometimes" or "often" "hit, bite or kick" was at 28–29 months. The frequency of this aggression then decreased steadily with age for both boys and girls.... These results suggest that the majority of children in Canada benefit from the socializing impact of their families and other socialization agents in their environment. (pp. 129–130)

Thus, while we do not bring youths under the age of 12 into the youth justice system, it is important to remember that youths, by the time they enter adolescence, are less aggressive than they were earlier in their lives. In addition, acts that we consider "criminal" (e.g., pushing, shoving, hitting, etc.) do not emerge anew at age 12. Typically, those behaviours are thought of as part of normal development—behaviours that all children engage in to some extent and then grow out of later. Our decision to label them as "criminal" at age 12, then, is somewhat arbitrary.

HOW TO MEASURE YOUTH CRIME

When thinking about how to measure youth "crime," clearly the justice system (arrests, number of cases brought to court, etc.) cannot provide an adequate description of the extent of these events. For example, in order for an event to be recorded as an arrest we first need an incident (e.g., a fight) to occur that involves a youth age 12 or older. Someone must next notice the incident and see it as an "offence." The fact that an "offence" has taken place does not necessarily mean that it will be reported to anyone. A youth might start a fight with another youth; however, this fight will never be recorded as an "assault" if the fight ends and nobody does anything about it. Similarly, if a youth were to steal something from a store and not be caught, this "theft" will not be recorded. It goes without saying, then, that an incident cannot become a crime unless someone decides that the police should get involved. If the incident were to be reported to the police, the police must make a decision: Is the incident a crime, and is there any value in officially recording it as such? Many rather insignificant offences, like a fight, minor vandalism, or a minor theft, may be dealt with completely informally and not recorded.

Depending on the type of crime (e.g., theft, vandalism, etc.), the next step would be to identify the suspect. In many cases the police are unable to find a suspect. Victimization data suggest that only about 62 percent of break-ins to houses in Canada are reported to the police (Besserer & Trainor, 2000). Police statistics (Canadian Centre for Justice Statistics, 2002) suggest that only about 17 percent of these are "cleared" by the police (i.e., that a suspect is identified and a person is either charged or a decision is made not to charge the offender). Taking these two figures together, it would seem that of the household burglaries identified by victims, only about 11 percent end up with a suspect being identified by the police. Furthermore, it is well known that the police screen out many cases (see Doob & Chan, 1982; Doob & Cesaroni, 2004). Thus, there are many youths who may be identified by the police but not officially charged for a variety of reasons (e.g., too minor an offence, etc.).

If one is looking at rates of youths taken to court, it is clear that changes in policy at the stage of police charging can have a large impact on crime "trends." If, for example, there is a new policy in a police division to officially charge all youths and not divert any from the system, we would see an "increase" in youths charged and in the number of youths entering the youth court system. This clearly would not be an indication that youth crime is "increasing"—it is due in fact to a change in policy—however, many would see it as an increase. Such a change appeared to have occurred in many provinces soon after the *Young Offenders Act* became law. Carrington (1998, 1999) demonstrated that much of the apparent increase in "youth crime" in the latter part of the 1980s reflected not a change in the behaviour of youths, but rather a change in the behaviour of the police. A higher proportion of apprehended youths were charged than had been the case previously. Hence, while it appeared that "youth crime" was increasing if one looked at youth court statistics, the changes were really the responsibility of the police, not Canadian youths.

Following the decision to charge a young person, the case will typically go on to youth court. However, depending on the jurisdiction, at this stage the case may be screened out of the system and instead go into Alternative Measures (as they were called under the *Young Offenders Act*) or Extrajudicial Sanctions (as they are now called under the *Youth Criminal Justice Act*). Cases referred to some sort of extrajudicial sanctions program may or may not remain in our youth court statistics. If the youth successfully completes the program, there is no finding of guilt. If, however, the case stays in youth court, the youth may or may not be found guilty. In addition, depending on the types of charges against the youth, the "guilty" finding may or may not be for the most serious offence the youth had been charged with as the case entered youth court.

Clearly, then, one could argue that arrest and court data are more measures of the policy decisions of adults than of the offending behaviour of young people. This leads many researchers to examine crime by youths through self-reported behaviours and victimization surveys in order to obtain information on offending. Given that many crimes may or may not be brought to the attention of police, and subsequent charges may or may not be laid, self-reported behaviours are likely to more accurately capture offending then police arrest statistics.

TRENDS IN YOUTH CRIME
Self-Reported Behaviours

Self-report studies of delinquency differ dramatically in the specificity of questions that are asked. Doob and Cesaroni (2004) note that

> if a youth is asked whether he or she damaged anyone's property, a certain portion

will admit to damaging property. If, on the other hand, they are asked a set of specific questions about property damage (e.g. broken windows, scratched or otherwise damaged cars, broken limbs off trees, written graffiti on public or private property) a high number of incidents will be reported. (p. 61)

Many self-report studies, however, reveal that it is quite common for youths to do things that, if officially recognized, would be called "criminal." In one study on vandalism, for example, it was found that 90 percent of elementary-school students and 89 percent of high-school students admitted to engaging in some sort of vandalism over the past year (Task Force on Vandalism, 1981). In a more recent study of more than 3,000 Toronto high-school students, slightly more than half of males and more than 40 percent of females surveyed admitting to committing minor thefts in their lifetime (Tanner & Wortley, 2002). Within a one-year period, almost a third of males and a quarter of females admitted to using the transit system without paying (Tanner & Wortley, 2002). Thus, all available self-report data indicate that a majority of adolescents will, at some point, engage in some minor offending. Only a small proportion of those behaviours will ever be officially recognized and recorded in arrest and youth court statistics.

Unfortunately, there have been no long-term surveys carried out in Canada that have asked youths about their involvement in offending. Thus, is it not possible to examine long-term trends using self-report data. However, we have a small amount of data from the Canadian National Longitudinal Survey of Children and Youth. This is a longitudinal study in which a nationally representative cohort of children (chosen initially to represent Canadian children under age 11) are being studied every two years until they reach the age of 25. For the younger children (age 9 and under), data are collected from the person in the household most knowledgeable about the child (referred to as the "person most knowledgeable" or "PMK"—typically the mother). At age 10 and older, the youths themselves answer questions as well. The first cycle of data was collected in 1994/95. Examination of self-reported offending from this representative sample of 10- and 11-year-olds does not reveal an escalation in serious offending as these youths age over a two-year period (Sprott, Doob, & Jenkins, 2001). Roughly 83 percent of 10- and 11-year-olds reported no property offending, while two years later, at ages 12 and 13, 78 percent of these youths reported no property offending (see Table 6.1). With respect to violence, 63 percent of 10- and 11-year-olds reported no violent offending, and two years later 71 percent were reporting no violent behaviour.

These data are useful for another purpose; they can be used to show the level of stability of offending within an individual over time (see Table 6.2). The data in Table 6.2 show two related phenomena quite clearly. First, consistent with previous literature, there is a relationship in the level of offending across the two-year period (from when the youths were 10–11 to when they were 12–13). For example, of those who reported a lot of aggressive behaviour when they were 10 or 11 years old, almost a quarter (24%) reported a similarly high level of aggressive behaviour two years later. In contrast, only a very small

TABLE 6.1	Level of Offending of Youths at Age 10-11 and Two Years Later at Age 12 and 13 (longitudinal comparison)

			Level of offending*		
Offence type	Age	None	Some	A lot	Total
Property offending	10-11	83%	10%	7%	100% (n=1528)
	12-13	78%	15%	7%	100% (n=1528)
Violent offending	10-11	63%	24%	13%	100% (n=1625)
	12-13	71%	18%	11%	100% (n=1625)

*The property offending questions asked of both 10-11 and 12-13-year-olds inquired about the frequency (never, sometimes, often) of stealing at home, stealing outside the home, destroying other people's things, and vandalizing. These four questions produced a scale that was then recoded into "none," "some," or "a lot" of property offending. There were only two violence questions asked of both 10-11 and 12-13-year-olds: frequency (never, sometimes, often) of getting in fights, and physically attacking people. Again, these two questions produced a scale that was recoded into "none," "some," or "a lot" of violent offending. For all of these questions there was no specific reference period (i.e., during past year or in lifetime).
Source: Adapted from the Statistics Canada publication *Juristat*, Catalogue 85-002, Vol. 21, No. 4, Problem Behaviour and Delinquency in Children and Youth.

TABLE 6.2	Relationship Between Level of Self-reported Aggressive Behaviour at Age 10-11 and Age 12-13

Level of aggressive behaviour at age 10-11	Level of aggressive behaviour at age 12-13*			
	None	Some	A lot	Total
None	82%	12%	5%	100% (n=1006)
Some	55%	28%	17%	100%(n=386)
A lot	45%	31%	24%	100%(n=233)

*There were only two violence questions asked of both 10-11 and 12-13-year-olds: frequency (never, sometimes, often) of getting in fights, and physically attacking people. These two questions produced a scale that was recoded into "none," "some," or "a lot" of violent offending. For all of these questions there was no specific reference period (i.e., during the past year or in lifetime).
Source: Adapted from the Statistics Canada publication *Juristat*, Catalogue 85-002, Vol. 21, No. 4, Problem Behaviour and Delinquency in Children and Youth.

minority (5%) of youths who reported no aggressive behaviour when they were 10–11 reported high levels of aggressive behaviour when they were 12–13. Clearly, then, to some extent those who were aggressive at age 10–11 were more likely (than the initially non-aggressive children) to be aggressive at age 12–13. However, the other side of this coin should also be noted: many of the youths changed dramatically. Almost half (45%) of the initially relatively aggressive 10- to

11-year-olds were reporting no aggression two years later.

Victimization Surveys

There are also some data on victimizations over time in Canada. Statistics Canada carried out victimization surveys in 1988, 1993, and 1999 that asked a representative group of respondents whether they had experienced each of a number of different kinds of victimizations. For the crimes where comparisons could be made (i.e., those with identical questions through all three surveys), there was no evidence of increased victimizations (see Gartner & Doob, 1994; Besserer & Trainor, 2000; Doob & Cesaroni, 2004). Of course, a survey such as this cannot, in many cases, identify whether an offender is a youth. However, given that there were no substantial changes across this 11-year period overall, if there were an increase in youthful offending it would have to be accompanied by a decrease in offending in other age groups in order to achieve the finding of no overall change in victimization rates.

Homicides

Many agree that homicides are the least likely offences to suffer from the various problems involved in using arrest or court data to measure crime. That is, homicides are unlikely to go unreported or misreported in any significant way. Many Canadians, apparently, think that homicides involving youthful offenders are increasing. In 1997, 79 percent of Ontario residents reported, in a public opinion poll, that they believed the number of youths named as suspects in homicides was increasing (Doob, Sprott, Marinos, & Varma, 1998). However, the data indicate otherwise. When looking at the number of youths named as suspects[1] in homicide offences (murder, manslaughter, and attempted murder), one sees considerable variability over the years (Figure 6.1). There have been as many as 68 youths named as suspects (in 1975 and again in 1995), and as few as 30 (in 2001) or 42 (in 2002). Generally, however, there does not appear to be any clear increase in the number of youths named as suspects in homicide offences. Indeed, given the roughly

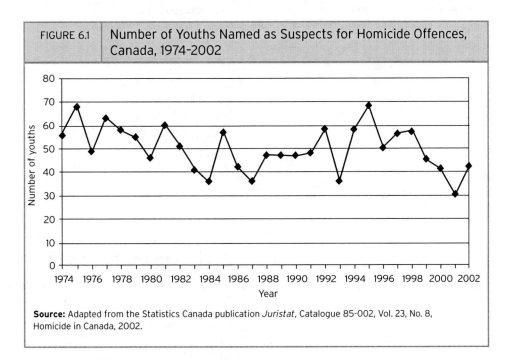

FIGURE 6.1 Number of Youths Named as Suspects for Homicide Offences, Canada, 1974-2002

Source: Adapted from the Statistics Canada publication *Juristat*, Catalogue 85-002, Vol. 23, No. 8, Homicide in Canada, 2002.

2.4 million young offender age (12 to 17) children in Canada currently, having an average of about 50 involved in homicide offences in the past 10 years may appear surprisingly low to many people.

Police Recorded Arrests and Youth Court Data

In an examination of the number of crimes (involving youths and adults) reported to the police over the past 20 years, increases are evident until about 1992. Over the past 10 years, however, there has been a relatively steady decline in the overall rate of reported crime to the police (Figure 6.2). One can also see from Figure 6.2 that violent crime contributes relatively little to the overall crime rate.

More specifically for youths, we have data on police charging since 1986.[2] Figure 6.3 shows the rate of charging youths for all violent offences and the three levels of

assault. The overall rate of charging for violent offences indicates a rather substantial increase that occurred until the mid 1990s, at which point charging began to level off. As noted earlier, while people often cite this trend as evidence of an "increase" in youth violence, Carrington (1995, 1998, 1999) suggested that much of the apparent increase in youth crime or youth violence during the 1980s was illusory. His analysis suggests that the police, under the new law at that time (i.e., the *Young Offenders Act,* which came into effect in 1984), tended to charge youth whom previously they would have cautioned or dealt with informally. Thus, increased youth crime—as measured by changes in the number of youths charged by police—appeared to have had less to do with changes in the behaviour of youth and more to with changes in police decision making. Any "youth crime increase," then, was likely police induced.[3]

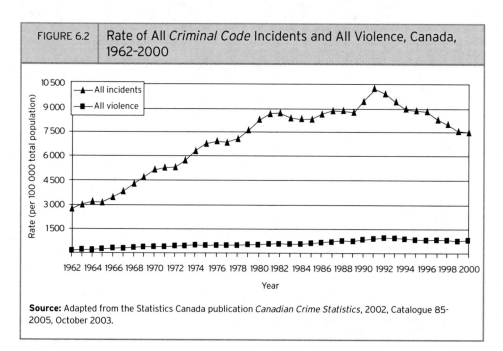

| FIGURE 6.2 | Rate of All *Criminal Code* Incidents and All Violence, Canada, 1962-2000 |

Source: Adapted from the Statistics Canada publication *Canadian Crime Statistics,* 2002, Catalogue 85-2005, October 2003.

To understand any "increase" in youth violence it is also important to examine the type of violence that is, apparently, increasing. An examination of the three levels of assault (Figure 6.3) indicates that the increase is disproportionately driven by minor assaults (assault level 1). Indeed, a large portion of youth violence is comprised of minor assaults (pushing, shoving; no injuries beyond minor bruising). The rates of the other two levels of assaults (level 2: assault causing bodily harm/assault with a weapon; level 3: aggravated assault) are lower by comparison and more stable over the past decade or so.

Overall, then, there is no clear evidence of an "increase" in youth crime generally, or youth violence specifically. Increases appear more likely to be due to a change in police charging rather than a change in

youths' behaviour. Further support for that idea is the fact that most "increases" are seen in the more minor forms of crime or violence—minor assaults, for example.

Contrary to public perception, serious youth violence is, in fact, relatively rare. As Figure 6.1 demonstrates, there are few youths named as suspects in homicide offences each year. An examination of more general "serious" violence—defined as murder, manslaughter, attempted murder, aggravated sexual assault, and aggravated assault—indicates that there are few cases involving that level of violence. Table 6.3 shows how there are very few serious violence cases in youth courts in Canada. Out of our 2.45 million youths (age 12 to 17), we had 102 061 youth court cases,[4] 22 937 of which involved violence. However, of the 22 937 violence cases, only 553 were

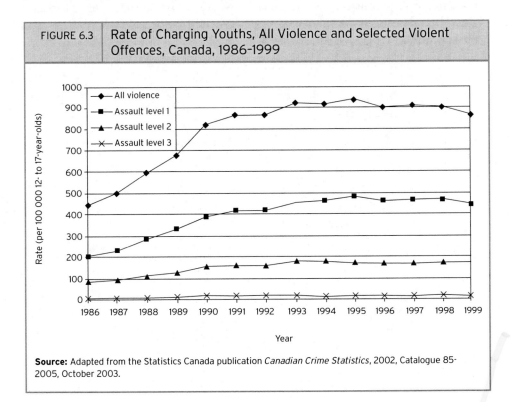

| FIGURE 6.3 | Rate of Charging Youths, All Violence and Selected Violent Offences, Canada, 1986-1999 |

Source: Adapted from the Statistics Canada publication *Canadian Crime Statistics*, 2002, Catalogue 85-2005, October 2003.

TABLE 6.3	Serious Violence in Canada, 1999-2000

Total number of youth (age 12-17) in Canada	2.45 million
Cases entering court	102 061
Violent cases to court	22 937
"Serious violent"* cases to court	553
"Serious violent"* transferred to adult court or found guilty in youth court	236
Murder and manslaughter to court	67
Murder and manslaughter transferred to adult court or found guilty in youth court	38

*"Serious violence" includes murder, manslaughter, attempted murder, aggravated sexual assault, and aggravated assault.

Source: Adapted from the Statistics Canada publication *Juristat*, Catalogue 85-002, Vol. 22, No. 3, Youth Statistics, 2000/01.

"serious violence"—even fewer (236) ended up being found guilty or transferred to adult court. Thus, while serious violence obviously happens, it appears to be relatively rare.

Another way of exploring the minor nature of youth crime is to examine the cases that fill the courtrooms. Table 6.4 shows that close to half (43%) of what we see in youth court involves the four offences of theft under $5,000, possession of stolen property, failure to appear, and failure to comply with a disposition. Adding in other thefts, mischief/damage, break and enter, and minor assaults accounts for 73 percent of cases in youth court. Similar proportions of cases are seen when looking at the types of cases sentenced to custody (Doob & Cesaroni, 2004).

TABLE 6.4	Majority of Cases (Principal Charge) in Youth Court, Canada, 1999-2000

	Total number of cases	Percentage
Theft under $5000	14 514	14%
Possession of stolen property	4738	5%
Failure to appear	11 078	11%
Failure to comply with a disposition	13 517	13%
Subtotal of minor offences	**43 847**	**43%**
Other thefts	4536	4%
Mischief/damage	5103	5%
Break and enter	10 285	10%
Minor assault	10 235	10%
Subtotal: Sum of eight less serious offences	**74 006**	**73%**
All other violence	12 702	12%
Drug possession	3779	4%
All other drug offences	1615	2%
All other offences	9959	10%
All cases	102 061	100%

Source: Adapted from the Statistics Canada publication *Juristat*, Catalogue 85-002, Vol. 22, No. 3, Youth Statistics, 2000/01.

Provincial Variation

Interestingly, while youth justice legislation is federal—and, therefore, the same law is administered in each province—there is considerable provincial variation in the use of youth court, though the eight offences shown in Table 6.4 generally account for the majority of the cases in youth court in every province (Doob & Sprott, 1996). As Table 6.5 shows, in Québec, Ontario, and Manitoba those eight offences generally account for the majority of cases in youth court. However, it is clear that Québec uses youth court considerably less than either Ontario or Manitoba. Indeed, Québec uses youth court less than any other province (Doob & Sprott, 1996). Thus, it makes sense that fewer of Québec's youth court cases would involve minor offences. This reflects, un-

doubtedly, the Québec policy of attempting to screen out of the court system many of the minor cases that in other provinces would end up in youth court.

Table 6.6 shows the overall rate in Canada, and the rate in all the provinces and territories, of bringing cases into youth court as well as the overall crime and violent crime rate. In 1999–2000 the overall rate of bringing youths into youth court in Canada was 4.17 per 100 youths. A more dramatic way of stating this rate is that for every 24 youths in Canada, there is, each year, one youth court case. The rates of the eastern provinces tend to be somewhat lower than the overall Canadian rate of bringing youths to court—ranging from 2.71 in PEI to 4.12 in Nova Scotia. Québec clearly stands out as the province that brings the fewest cases to court—1.96 per 100 youths in the

TABLE 6.5	Majority of Cases (Principal Charge) in Youth Court, Québec, Ontario, and Manitoba, 1999–2000		
Most serious charge in the case	**Cases in Québec court, 1999-00**	**Cases in Ontario court, 1999-00**	**Cases in Manitoba court, 1999-00**
	Percentage (and number) of cases to court	Percentage (and number) of cases to court	Percentage (and number) of cases to court
Theft under $5000	14%(1449)	13%(5203)	11%(767)
Possession of stolen property	2%(178)	6%(2249)	3%(210)
Failure to appear	3%(359)	10%(3908)	19%(1279)
Failure to comply with a disposition	11%(1207)	10%(3792)	15%(1004)
Subtotal	**30% (3193)**	**39% (15 152)**	**46% (3260)**
Other thefts	3%(309)	5%(1945)	6%(436)
Mischief/damage	4%(377)	5%(1834)	4%(308)
Break and enter	13%(1376)	5%(3460)	11%(738)
Minor assault	10%(1050)	12%(4813)	7%(504)
Total: Sum of eight offences	**59% (6305)**	**70% (27 204)**	**76% (5246)**
All cases	100%(10 768)	100%(39 096)	100%(6878)

Source: Adapted from the Statistics Canada publication *Juristat*, Catalogue 85-002, Vol. 22, No. 3, Youth Statistics, 2000/01.

population. Ontario brings in cases at a rate of 4.28, and the Prairies tend to bring in more cases—ranging from 6.14 in Alberta to 9.41 in Saskatchewan. British Columbia brings in cases at a rate that is similar to Newfoundland and Labrador (3.64 per 100 youths). The Yukon and Northwest Territories are considerably higher than all the other jurisdictions, but Nunavut is closer to the Ontario rate. Another way of expressing these data is that in Québec there is one youth court case each year for every 51 youths, while in Saskatchewan there is one youth court case each year for every 11 youths.

There is a tendency for the provinces with the higher police recorded crime rates to also have higher rates of bringing cases into court (Table 6.6). For example, the Prairies generally have higher crime rates and also bring in more cases. However, this relationship does not hold perfectly in all instances. For example, B.C. has the second highest overall *provincial* crime rate but brings in cases at a rate that is similar to Newfoundland and Labrador, which has the lowest overall crime rate. Québec has an overall crime rate similar to Ontario, but brings youth to court at a rate that is less than half that of Ontario (1.96 compared to 4.28). Therefore, it appears that the variation that exists in the numbers of youth brought to court cannot be explained solely in terms of variation in crime rates in each province.

When examining self-reported delinquency across the provinces, we again see variation (Sprott et al., 2001). For 12- to 13-year-old youths, for both property and violent offending, the Prairies appear to be relatively high (Table 6.7), whereas Québec reports the lowest level of violent offending for this age group. Youths from the Atlantic provinces, Québec, and B.C. were most likely to report no involvement in property offending. Comparisons of

TABLE 6.6	Variation in Use of Youth Court: Bringing Cases into Youth Court and the Overall Crime Rate and Violent Crime Rate, 1999–2000		
Jurisdiction	Youth court cases per 100 youths	Overall *Criminal Code* crime rate* (per 100 000)	Overall violent crime rate* (per 100 000)
Canada	4.17	7655	982
Newfoundland and Labrador	3.64	5711	900
Prince Edward Island	2.71	6686	719
Nova Scotia	4.12	7571	990
New Brunswick	3.73	6519	937
Québec	1.96	6027	718
Ontario	4.28	6421	887
Manitoba	7.00	10 723	1638
Saskatchewan	9.41	12 730	1663
Alberta	6.14	8822	1062
British Columbia	3.64	11 253	1251
Yukon	13.81	23 540	3326
Northwest Territories	10.09	27 389	4722
Nunavut	4.29	21 190	6074

Note: Excludes *Criminal Code* traffic, other federal statutes.

TABLE 6.7	Regional Variation in Self-report Offending Among 12- to 13-year-olds			
		Level of offending*		
		None	**Some**	**A lot**	**Total**
Violent offending	Atlantic	60%	28%	12%	100% (469)
	Québec	68%	23%	9%	100% (378)
	Ontario	55%	32%	12%	100% (499)
	Prairies	47%	39%	14%	100% (462)
	B.C.	60%	31%	9%	100% (144)
Property offending	Atlantic	68%	23%	8%	100% (461)
	Québec	68%	19%	13%	100% (373)
	Ontario	63%	28%	9%	100% (494)
	Prairies	61%	27%	12%	100% (456)
	B.C.	69%	24%	8%	100% (144)

*When using only cycle two data (12- and 13-year-olds), the property offending measure consisted of the following eight questions: past year stolen something from a store, stolen something from school, taken money from parents, broken into a house, sold something you knew was stolen, damaged something, taken a purse or wallet, and taken a car. The violence measure included the addition of the following nine questions: past year threatened to beat someone up, in a fight but no serious injuries, in a fight with serious injuries, in a fight and used a weapon, used knife for attack, threatened to get money, attempted sexual touching, forced sex, and set fire to something. With both scales, the questions were added together and then recoded into "none," "some," or "a lot" of violence or property offending.

Source: Adapted from the Statistics Canada publication *Juristat*, Catalogue 85-002, Vol. 21, No. 4, Problem Behaviour and Delinquency in Children and Youth.

these data to criminal justice indicators (e.g., police reports of crime or youth court data) are problematic, since these latter measures reflect criminal justice decision making and citizen reporting as well as youth behaviour. However, the general pattern of variation appears somewhat similar—the Prairies have higher self-reported delinquency and more arrests and court usage. However, the variation across provinces in self-reported delinquency does not come close to the variation seen in arrests or the use of courts.

Quality of Youth Violence

During the early 1990s some scholars claimed that, although official measures of youth violence did not necessarily show any increases, the "quality" of violence that youth were engaging in was becoming more serious (see, for example, Gabor, 1999). How might one assess the quality of violence, then, with the measures available? If the quality of violence were becoming more serious, one might expect that police would be laying more serious charges against youth. So, for example, instead of "minor assaults" the violence might be "aggravated assaults," which consist of more serious harm to the victim. However, as shown in Figure 6.3, there does not appear to be a substantial change in police charging youths for the more serious levels of assaults.

Using youth court data, Doob and Sprott (1998) examined the "quality" of violence. The argument was a simple one: If those involved in the process of charging youths (i.e., the police) were coming across violence of a more serious nature, this should show up in higher charging rates for the most serious forms of violence. An analysis of the data for the period when these assertions of increasingly violent youths were being expressed (i.e., the early 1990s) found no support that the nature of violence was changing. While the proportion of cases in youth court that involved violence increased somewhat from 1991 to 1995, that increase was concentrated in minor assaults. Table 6.8 shows a 31.3-percent increase in the number of minor assault cases (column 1). When viewed as a rate per population (per 100 000 12- to 17-year-olds), there was a 20.7-percent increase (column 4). The figures for other, more serious violence indicate that there was not such a large increase (columns 2 and 3). Indeed, once corrected for the number of youths in Canada (expressed as rates—columns 5 and 6), there was, in fact, an overall slight decrease in the rate of bringing serious-violence offences into youth court in Canada.

Understanding any increase in minor assaults is difficult because it is not clear whether that increase is due to a change in youth behaviour, or whether that increase is the result of policy changes (e.g., "zero-tolerance" school policies that mandate police be called and a charge be laid). Generally, however, during the early to mid 1990s there were few cases of serious violence, and while there was year-to-year variation, there was no clear evidence of an increase or change in the quality of violence (Doob & Sprott, 1998; for an opposing view see Gabor, 1999, and then Doob & Sprott, 1999).

TABLE 6.8	Changes in the Distribution of Youth Court Cases, Three Levels of Assault, Canada, 1991-1996					
	Column 1: Number of minor assault cases (level 1)	Column 2: Number of cases of assault with a weapon or causing bodily harm (level 2)	Column 3: Number of aggravated assault cases (level 3)	Column 4: Cases of minor assault per 100 000 YO-age youths (level 1)	Column 5: Cases of assault with a weapon or causing bodily harm per 100 000 YO-age youths (level 2)	Column 6: Cases of aggravated assaults per 100 000 YO-age youths (level 3)
1991-1992	8594	3431	308	392	156	14.0
1992-1993	9717	3685	311	420	159	13.5
1993-1994	10 854	3836	309	465	165	13.3
1994-1995	10 906	3745	317	462	159	13.4
1995-1996	11 280	3695	312	473	155	13.1
Change from 1991-2 to 1995-6	+2686 +31.3%	+264 +7.7%	+4 +1.3%	+81 +20.7%	-1.0 -0.64%	-0.9 -6.4%

Looking at more recent youth court data, we see that the findings from earlier in the 1990s still hold. Figure 6.4 shows the rate of violence overall and for specific levels of violence in youth court until 2000. Again, the rates of the most serious levels of assaults in youth court are low, and stable. Any slight overall increase appears to be driven solely by minor assaults. This change in minor assaults, as mentioned above, is difficult to interpret. It may reflect changes in youth behaviour or it may be more reflective of our policy changes and decisions.

Girls' Involvement in Youth Crime

On occasion, concerns are raised regarding the increasing involvement of girls in youth crime—often, specifically, violence. Self-report data, however, reveal that girls are typically less involved in offending,

particularly violent offending, when compared to boys (Sprott et al., 2001). Self-report data from the National Longitudinal Survey of Children and Youth show that roughly 70 percent of girls reported no property or violent offending, while 60 percent of boys reported no property offending and only 44 percent reported no violent offending (Table 6.9).

Previous analyses investigating the quality of youth violence found no evidence of an increased involvement in serious violence by girls (Doob & Sprott, 1998). Similar to the trends presented overall (Table 6.8), when looking at girls only (Table 6.10) we see that increases are concentrated in minor assaults. Table 6.10 shows, generally, that there has been both an increase in the number of cases involving girl violence (column 1) and the rate of bringing violence cases into youth court (column 5). The largest increase (in both number and rate) is in minor assaults

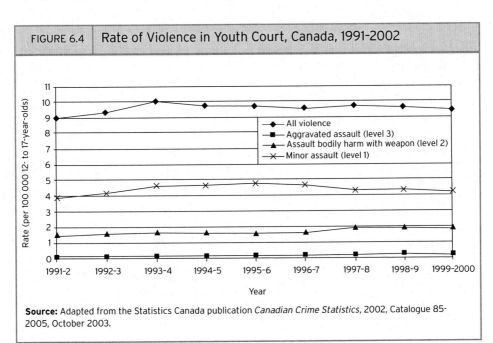

| FIGURE 6.4 | Rate of Violence in Youth Court, Canada, 1991-2002 |

Source: Adapted from the Statistics Canada publication *Canadian Crime Statistics*, 2002, Catalogue 85-2005, October 2003.

| TABLE 6.9 | Gender Differences in Self-report Offending at Age 12-13 | | | | |

Type of offending	Gender	Level of offending*			Total
		None	Some	Alot	
Property offending	Females	70%	23%	7%	100% (967)
	Males	60%	27%	13%	100% (964)
Violent offending	Females	71%	22%	7%	100% (981)
	Males	44%	40%	16%	100% (974)

*When using only cycle two data (12- and 13-year-olds), the property offending measure consisted of the following eight questions: past year stolen something from a store, stolen something from school, taken money from parents, broken into a house, sold something you knew was stolen, damaged something, taken a purse or wallet, and taken a car. The violence measure included the addition of the following nine questions: past year threatened to beat someone up, was in a fight but no serious injuries, in a fight with serious injuries, in a fight and used a weapon, used knife for attack, threatened to get money, attempted sexual touching, forced sex, and set fire to something. With both scales, the questions were added together and then recoded into "none," "some," or "a lot" of violence or property offending.
Source: Adapted from the Statistics Canada publication *Juristat*, Catalogue 85-002, Vol. 21, No. 4, Problem Behaviour and Delinquency in Children and Youth.

(columns 2 and 6). As one moves toward the more serious violence, one sees either a smaller increase or a slight decrease in both the number and rate of cases involving girls (columns 3, 4, 7, and 8).

Girls are generally more likely to be involved in the less serious forms of violence. In Doob and Sprott's (1996) analysis, they found, for example, roughly 29 percent of common assault cases involved girls as defendants, while only 4.5 percent of homicide cases involved girls as defendants.

More recent analyses have found that, on the whole, the proportion of youth court cases involving girls has been increasing (Sprott & Doob, 2003). Figure 6.5 documents this increase overall, and for violence specifically. Overall, it appears that girls were involved in about 17 percent of cases brought into youth court in 1991, and 21 percent in 2000. This could be described as a 25-percent increase (in the proportion of youth court cases involving girls). Similar trends appear when looking at violence. Figure 6.5 could, therefore, be seen as suggesting that girls

are increasingly involved in violence over the period covered by this figure (the 1990s). This would, however, be a risky conclusion to draw.

It is unclear from this figure alone whether the upward slopes of the percentage of youth court cases involving girls reflect changes for girls, boys, or both. When one looks at the *rate* of guilty cases involving girls and boys, a very different picture emerges. Figure 6.6 shows the rate of bringing boys and girls into youth court. Overall, the rate of bringing boys into youth court has decreased from roughly 85 per 1000 in 1991 to 64 per 1000 in 2000. Girls have remained relatively stable, at a rate of roughly 19 per 1000 in 1991 to 18 per 1000 in 2000. Thus, it appears that girls are accounting for larger proportions of guilty findings not because they are being brought into youth court (or found guilty) at substantially higher rates than in the past, but rather because boys are being found guilty at substantially lower rates (Sprott & Doob, 2003). For most offences, the rate of bringing

TABLE 6.10 Changes in the Distribution of Youth Court Cases (Girls Only), Three Levels of Assault, Canada, 1991-1996

	Column 1: Number of cases with principal charge of violence	Column 2: Number of cases of minor assault (level 1)	Column 3: Number of cases of assault with a weapon or causing bodily harm (level 2)	Column 4: Number of cases of aggravated assault (level 3)	Column 5: Cases involving violence per 100 000 YO-age girls	Column 6: Cases of minor assault per 100 000 YO-age girls (level 1)	Column 7: Cases of assault with a weapon or causing bodily harm per 100 000 YO-age girls (level 2)	Column 8: Cases of aggravated assault per 100 000 YO-age girls (level 3)
1991-1992	3547	2354	532	44	332	220	49.8	4.12
1992-1993	3947	2774	573	41	350	246	50.9	3.64
1993-1994	4688	3277	706	48	412	288	62.1	4.22
1994-1995	4484	3127	659	43	390	272	57.3	3.74
1995-1996	4684	3272	658	35	403	281	56.6	3.01
Change from	+1137	+918	+126	-9	+71	+61	+6.8	-1.11
1991-2 to 1995-6	+32.1%	+39.0%	+23.7%	-20.5%	+21.4%	+27.7%	+13.7%	-26.9%

Source: Doob & Sprott. (1998). Canadian Journal of Criminology, 40(2), 185-194. Reproduced by permission of the Canadian Journal of Criminology and Criminal Justice. Copyright by the Canadian Criminal Justice Association.

FIGURE 6.5	Percentage of Youth Cases Involving Female Youths, Canada, 1991-2000

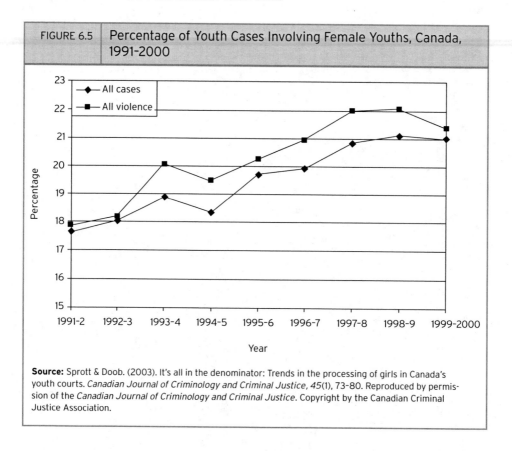

Source: Sprott & Doob. (2003). It's all in the denominator: Trends in the processing of girls in Canada's youth courts. *Canadian Journal of Criminology and Criminal Justice, 45*(1), 73-80. Reproduced by permission of the *Canadian Journal of Criminology and Criminal Justice*. Copyright by the Canadian Criminal Justice Association.

girls into youth court, or of finding them guilty, has remained relatively stable over the past decade (see Sprott & Doob, 2003 for a detailed analysis).

When looking at the rate of finding girls and boys guilty in all offence categories, we see that the only clear increase is in YOA offences. YOA offences involve failure to comply with a disposition, failure to comply with an undertaking, and contempt against youth court. However, the majority of offences are failure to comply with a disposition—accounting for roughly 98 percent of the offences in this category. Figure 6.7 shows the rate (per 10 000 girls) of finding girls guilty in youth court for violence, property, drug, and YOA offences;

Figure 6.8 shows the rate (per 10 000 boys) of finding boys guilty in youth court in those same four offence categories.

Figure 6.7 shows slight fluctuations in the overall rates of finding girls guilty in youth court—a low of about 109 in 1994/5 to a high of 120 in 1997/8. More recently, in 2000, the rate has dropped back down to roughly 112 per 10 000. The rate of finding girls guilty of offences involving violence has increased slightly (from a rate of roughly 20 to 25—though more detailed analyses found that this increase was concentrated in minor assaults: see Sprott & Doob, 2003). The rate of finding girls guilty of property offences, however, has been decreasing. The largest increase in

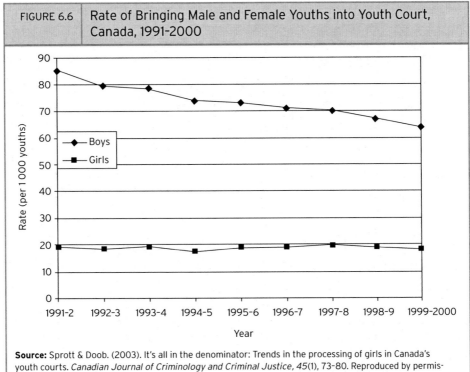

FIGURE 6.6 Rate of Bringing Male and Female Youths into Youth Court, Canada, 1991–2000

Source: Sprott & Doob. (2003). It's all in the denominator: Trends in the processing of girls in Canada's youth courts. *Canadian Journal of Criminology and Criminal Justice, 45*(1), 73–80. Reproduced by permission of the *Canadian Journal of Criminology and Criminal Justice*. Copyright by the Canadian Criminal Justice Association.

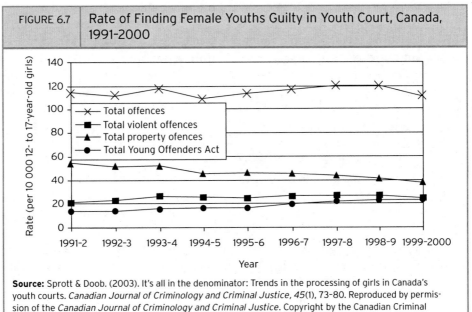

FIGURE 6.7 Rate of Finding Female Youths Guilty in Youth Court, Canada, 1991–2000

Source: Sprott & Doob. (2003). It's all in the denominator: Trends in the processing of girls in Canada's youth courts. *Canadian Journal of Criminology and Criminal Justice, 45*(1), 73–80. Reproduced by permission of the *Canadian Journal of Criminology and Criminal Justice*. Copyright by the Canadian Criminal Justice Association.

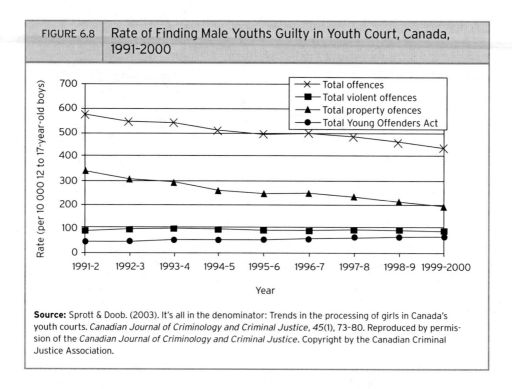

| FIGURE 6.8 | Rate of Finding Male Youths Guilty in Youth Court, Canada, 1991–2000 |

Source: Sprott & Doob. (2003). It's all in the denominator: Trends in the processing of girls in Canada's youth courts. *Canadian Journal of Criminology and Criminal Justice, 45*(1), 73–80. Reproduced by permission of the *Canadian Journal of Criminology and Criminal Justice*. Copyright by the Canadian Criminal Justice Association.

the rate of finding girls guilty is in YOA offences—that has increased from about 14 per 10 000 to 23 per 10 000.

Figure 6.8 shows the rate (per 10 000 12- to 17-year-olds) of finding boys guilty in the same offence categories. Finding boys guilty of violence offences has remained stable, while finding them guilty of property offences has decreased. The only increase in finding boys guilty is in YOA offences. Looking at rate changes in finding boys and girls guilty of YOA offences reveals that girls saw a rate increase of 9.3 (14.1 to 23.4) in YOA offences from 1991 to 2000 while boys saw a rate increase of 19.1 (45.2 to 64.3). It is not clear why there has been this increase in YOA offences (predominantly, failure to comply with a disposition). There are, obviously, numerous possible explanations ranging from a change in youths' behaviour to a change in policing or judicial policy. The most plausible explanation likely relates to a change in policy; however, more research needs to be conducted before a definitive explanation can be provided. Overall, then, the decrease in the past decade of finding boys guilty is due largely to a decrease in finding them guilty of property offences.

CONCLUSION

In general, self-report surveys reveal that youths are most violent in the early years of life and typically grow out of violence as they age through adolescence. In addition, most younger youths commit acts that, if taken seriously at the age of 12, could be considered criminal offences. However, all available data—whether self-report, victimization, or official arrest and court data—suggest that the majority of youth crime is relatively minor.

In addition to the nature of youth crime, it appears that there have been no significant changes in either the quality of violence or the amount of youth crime over the past decade. Where there have been increases, it is difficult to interpret what those increases mean. When we see increases (or decreases) in offences like minor assaults, it may be more a change in policy (either to charge or deal with informally) as opposed to a change in youths' behaviour. For the more serious offences—offences where police have always been likely to officially record (e.g., homicide offences or serious violence)—there is no clear evidence of either a change in the quality or in the rate of involvement by both boys or girls.

References

Besserer S., & Trainor, C. (2000). Criminal victimization in Canada, 1999. *Juristat, 20*(10). Ottawa: Canadian Centre for Justice Statistics, Statistics Canada.

Canadian Centre for Justice Statistics. (2002). *Canadian crime statistics, 2001*. Ottawa, Ontario: Statistics Canada. Catalogue No: 85-205-XIE.

Carrington, P. J. (1995). "Has violent crime increased? Comment on Corrado and Markwart. *Canadian Journal of Criminology, 37*, 61–73.

Carrington, P. J. (1998). Changes of police charging of young offenders in Ontario and Saskatchewan after 1984. *Canadian Journal of Criminology, 40*, 153–164.

Carrington, P. J. (1999). Trends in youth crime in Canada 1977–1996. *Canadian Journal of Criminology, 41*, 1–32.

Corrado, R. R., & Markwart, A. (1994). The need to reform the YOA in response to violent young offenders: Confusion, reality or myth? *Canadian Journal of Criminology, 36*, 343–378.

DeSouza, P. (2000). Youth court statistics, 2000–01. *Juristat, 22*(3). Ottawa, Ontario: Statistics Canada. Catalogue No: 85-002 XIE.

Doob A. N., & Cesaroni, C. (2004). *Responding to youth crime in Canada*. Toronto: University of Toronto Press.

Doob, A. N., & Chan, J. B. (1982). Factors affecting police decisions to take juveniles to court. *Canadian Journal of Criminology, 24(1)*, 25–37.

Doob, A. N., & Sprott, J. B. (1996). Interprovincial variation in the use of youth courts. *Canadian Journal of Criminology, 38(4)*, 401–412.

Doob, A. N., & Sprott, J. B. (1998). Is the "quality" of youth violence becoming more serious? *Canadian Journal of Criminology, 40(2)*, 185–194.

Doob, A. N., & Sprott, J. B. (1999). The pitfalls of determining validity by consensus. *Canadian Journal of Criminology, 41(4)*, 535–543.

Doob, A. N., Sprott, J. B., Marinos, V., & Varma, K. (1998). *An exploration of Ontario residents' views of crime and the criminal justice system*. Toronto: Centre of Criminology, University of Toronto.

Gabor, T. (1999). Trends in youth crime: Some evidence pointing to increases in the severity and volume of violence on the part of youth people. *Canadian Journal of Criminology, 41(3)*, 385–392.

Gartner R., & Doob, A. N. (1994). Trends in criminal victimizations: 1988–1993. *Juristat 14*(13). Ottawa: Canadian Centre for Justice Statistics, Statistics Canada.

Markwart, A., & Corrado, R. R. (1995). A response to Carrington. *Canadian Journal of Criminology, 37,* 74–87.

Sprott, J. B., & Doob, A. N. (2003). It's all in the denominator: Trends in the processing of girls in Canada's youth courts. *Canadian Journal of Criminology and Criminal Justice, 45(1),* 73–80.

Sprott, J. B., Doob, A. N., & Jenkins, J. M. (2001). Problem behaviour and delinquency in children and youth. *Juristat, 21*(4). Ottawa: Canadian Centre for Justice Statistics, Statistics Canada.

Tanner J., & Wortley, S. (2002). *The Toronto youth crime and victimization survey: Overview report.* Toronto: Centre of Criminology, University of Toronto.

Task Force on Vandalism. (1981). *Vandalism: Responses and responsibilities.* Toronto: Queen's Printer for Ontario.

Tremblay, R. E., Boulerice, B., Harden, P. W., McDuff, P., Pérusse, D., Pihl, R. O., & Zoccolillo, M. (1996). Do children in Canada become more aggressive as they approach adolescence? In *Growing up in Canada— National Longitudinal Survey of Children and Youth* (pp. 127–137). Ottawa: Human Resources Development Canada, Statistics Canada. Catalogue No. 89-550-MPE, No.1.

Notes

1. "Named as suspects" means that these youths were believed to be involved in homicides but were not yet officially charged.

2. This is the first available year of data after the full implementation of the YOA, which came into effect in 1984.

3. This interpretation is not universally accepted; see, for example, Corrado and Markwart (1994) and Markwart and Corrado (1995).

4. Youth court data are collected through the Youth Court Survey. This is a joint venture between CCJS and Canadian courts. CCJS provides the raw number of cases, and we then calculate rates based on population estimates. For more information, see DeSouza, (2000). *Youth court statistics, 2000–01. Juristat, 22*(3). Ottawa, Ontario: Statistics Canada. Catalogue No: 85-002 XIE.

chapter seven

Youth Crime and the Media

Susan A. Reid, Ph.D.

Associate Professor of Criminology and Criminal Justice
Director, Centre for Research on Youth at Risk
St. Thomas University

Traditionally, most children have been in the news only when they've done something bad or when others have done bad things to them. Even though most kids don't fit into either category, this coverage can adversely—and unfairly—influence public perceptions and public policies that affect children, especially teenagers *

INTRODUCTION

When members of the general public pick up a newspaper on any given day, they are confronted with a variety of images both from the pictures and the printed word that are stored in their "mental data bank for instant playback" (Reynolds, 1996, p. 12). As newspapers continue to be the "literature of the people," it is important to recognize that the storytelling of journalists can have a profound impact on the way in which people interpret their world. In the area of juvenile justice policy, many images from the news media convey the notion that youth crime is out of control and youth are increasingly violent; the youth justice system doesn't work and is too lenient to deal with today's "super-predators" and violent youth; and the remedy to the current "youth crime crisis" is found in longer and harsher punishments. When youth crime news coverage dramatically increases while actual youth crime is decreasing, the public's perception of how safe they feel from victimization by young people becomes somewhat skewed. In particular, for the uneducated consumer of crime news who relies on the media for information about the issues affecting young people, the "regular diet of unusual over time, seems usual" (Dorfman & Schiraldi, 2001, p. 31).

---

* Shaw, D. (2000, July 11). Kids are people too, papers decide. *Los Angeles Times*, p. A1.

Another issue presented in the news media as problematic is the inability of journalists to name young offenders, which is often understood within the rhetoric of "outdated" youth justice laws. However, it has been argued that journalists may use the publication ban on the identity of the young person to their own advantage. Unlike the adult system, where journalists may be restricted in the number of times they are able to report on the same case, as it may be prejudicial to a case that has not come before the courts, journalists are free to repeat stories about current or past young offenders, provided that they do not identify the young person or any youth victims. This may account for the seeming overrepresentation of more sensational stories in the news media about young offenders.

Seskus and Mofina (2000) suggest that "it is not the newspaper's job to tell people what to think, but rather to tell people what to think about" (p. 140). They argue, "It is a reader's responsibility to use the information as a stepping stone to further participate in the democratic process" (p. 141). However, one must question the extent to which readers actually critically evaluate the information being presented in the newspapers they read. When one considers that very few people have had any direct experience with the youth justice system or with young people who commit criminal offences, it becomes clear that there is often no basis for comparison beyond what is reported in the newspaper.

This chapter will explore the historical roots of the confidentiality of juvenile justice proceedings and analyze the development in law of the right to privacy for young persons accused of criminal of-

fences. Following an overview of the provisions that ban the publication of the identity of young offenders, this chapter will consider the larger social implications of the current provisions in law that allow the media to publish all the details of a case except the identity of the offender. A discussion of the perpetuation of myths about youth crime in the media and the media portrayal of youth generally will be examined within the framework of a "moral panic." A number of media content analyses have been conducted that provide clear evidence of the perpetuation of myths about youth generally and young offenders in particular. Suggestions regarding the need for journalists to understand the ethical concerns surrounding reporting on events involving children and youth will be discussed. The media have been credited for being the public's most important and immediate source of information about youth crime (Seskus & Mofina, 2000). It will be argued that the media have a social responsibility to inform the public about the context of the lives of young people and not merely present sensational accounts that further exacerbate tensions about a perceived "youth crime crisis."

RIGHT TO PRIVACY IN YOUTH JUSTICE PROCEEDINGS: LEGISLATIVE PROVISIONS

One of the cornerstones of youth justice in Canada is that, as a general rule, the identity of a young person should be protected. This is considered important as the publication of the name of the young person is thought to impede rehabilitation efforts and could conceivably detrimentally affect the young person. In the end, the result of such damaging effects for young persons is that public safety, in the longer term, would be compromised.

THE *JUVENILE DELINQUENTS ACT*

The *Juvenile Delinquents Act* provided that all juvenile court hearings were to be held "without publicity" and without the public in attendance. Despite some criticism that juvenile court hearings were not open to the public in the late 1970s,[1] the Supreme Court of Canada in *C.B. v. R (1981)* concluded that "without publicity" in sec. 12(1) of the *JDA* meant *in camera*.[2] The *JDA* also banned the publication of the identity of young persons. This meant that the media would not be entitled to report on charges against juveniles or on their trials unless "special leave of the court" were granted. Keeping with the welfare philosophy of the JDA, the court would have to be satisfied that the observation and subsequent publication of details of a juvenile justice proceeding by the media (see Appendix A (sec. 12(3)) would be in the "best interests of the child." In practice, rarely would the publication of such details be seen to be of benefit to the juvenile before the court. In other words, to a large extent the public did not receive any information about youth crime in the newspapers prior to the mid 1980s.

With the advent of the *Charter of Rights and Freedoms* in 1982, there were some successful challenges to exclusion of the media and the public in Ontario appellate courts. The Supreme Court of Ontario[3] ruled that any legislative provision that prohibits the press and the public from attending criminal proceedings involving juveniles was unconstitutional and violated the provision of freedom of the press under the *Charter*. The court stated, "The State has not satisfied me that a blanket denial of a public hearing without any cause being shown other than social purposes, can be justified."[4]

The *Young Offenders Act*

In the period leading up to the proclamation of the *Young Offenders Act*, a compromise of sorts was created that continued the ban on the publication of the identity of the young person before the court while allowing a more open and accountable process through inclusion of the public and the media within the courtroom. Public accountability and media scrutiny under the provisions of the new legislation meant that for the first time in history, the public would learn details about youth crime in Canada. However, Wilson and Tomlinson (1986) suggest that under sections 38 and 39 of the *Young Offenders Act* there was a "cure for the constitutional problem of blanket prohibition" (p. 388). In the case of *Southam Inc. v. R. (1984)*, the court stated:

> In my view,… the protection and rehabilitation of young people involved in the criminal justice system is a social value of "super-ordinate importance" which justifies the abrogation of the fundamental freedom of expression, including freedom of the press to the extent effected by s.38(1) of the YOA…. Section 39(1)(a) is in my view, a reasonable limitation on freedom of expression, including freedom of the press.

While opening the courtroom to the media and the public had the potential of informing the public of some of the causes of youth crime and the contexts in which youth crime took place, the media did not capitalize on this opportunity in this manner. Through the presentation of sensational crimes and relying on "expert" sources such as the police, the voice of youth was not heard in the stories that were being told about them. The media were used as a platform for political debate, and as Bala (2003) argues, "For some politicians, youth justice law had become a symbol of what was wrong with Canadian society and a metaphorical starting point for ideological change" (p. 71).

During the latter part of the 1990s, despite national statistics showing a decrease in youth crime, there was a lack of public confidence with the youth justice legislation as reported in the news media. Despite some excellent commentary by journalists that a "get tough" mentality among the public for the reform of youth justice would not prove to be effective,[5] there was also extensive coverage during this period that encouraged the public to be more fearful. Ultimately, the only way to deal with that sense of fear was through "harsher punishment" for the "serious problem" of youth crime (Wente, 2000). Politicians, eager to fuel their popularity by responding to the public's perceptions, were often cited in news reports. In 1998, the then Ontario Premier, Mike Harris, told a reporter that "the *Young Offenders Act* is so permissive that it actually seems to condone criminal behavior."[6]

In the 2000 federal election, the Liberals used the media to promote their "youth justice strategy,"[7] developed around the bill defeated just prior to the election.[8] The Conservatives also used the media to promote the message that their party would not allow any new legislation to be "too soft on crime."[9] After the federal Liberals were re-elected, the Conservative province of Ontario continued to be highly critical of the proposed youth justice legislation and advocated not only for the imposition of longer sentences for young offenders, but also for the publication of names of youth who were charged with serious offences. In the provincial brief regarding the proposed *Youth Criminal Justice Act,* their calls for amendments would "finally get tough on youth crime."[10]

The "get tough" rhetoric on youth crime is not unique to Canada and was indeed being promoted across the globe at that time, as evidenced in a case of child murder in England (the James Bulger case). In this case, the names of the young offenders were released in the courts and hit the national news wires almost immediately (Bromwich, 2002). During the same time period that these legislative changes were being proposed in Canada, the United States was also discussing a series of crime bills aimed at transferring more youth to adult court and providing "harsher penalties" for young offenders (We Interrupt This Message, 2001).

The *Youth Criminal Justice Act*

In the *Youth Criminal Justice Act* (YCJA), youth court proceedings are open to the public and to the press as they were under the YOA. The provision to exclude persons if the court believes that it would impede the administration of justice, found in sec. 39 of the YOA, has also been retained in sec. 132 of the YCJA. Perhaps one of the most important changes to the section on publication under the *Youth Criminal Justice Act* was to clearly define what was meant by the term "publication." Under sec. 2(1), publication is described as "the communication of information by making it known or accessible to the general public through any means, including print, radio or television broadcast, telecommunication or electronic means," which clearly outlines the meaning of publication as it relates to the media. Further, sec.110(1) summarizes the general provision that "no person shall publish the name of a young person, or any other information related to a young person, if it would identify the young person as a young person dealt with under this Act." There are other provisions within the YCJA (sec.111) to ban the publication of the identity of a young victim or witness to a youth crime. These are considered necessary in order to protect the young person testifying on sensitive issues, with the intention of protecting them from feeling threatened and intimidated by the public attention that such testimony might attract.

With respect to the ban on publication of the identity of young persons, there are exceptions that can be found in both the YOA and the YCJA. Under the former YOA, if a youth was transferred to adult court, revealing the identity of the young person was permitted even though the young person had not been found guilty of any offence. The YCJA has remedied this situation by eliminating the transfer provisions. As it now stands, youth are to be tried in youth court and upon conviction the Crown can then seek an adult sentence

(sec.73). In such cases, the identification of the young person cannot be published until the youth justice court finds the young person guilty and the person has received an adult sentence. There are also provisions to allow for the publication of the names of young persons if they are found guilty in youth court and receive a youth sentence for a series of presumptive offences (sec. 100(2)(b)). However, the court can decide not to allow publication of a young person's name, taking into account the importance of rehabilitating the young person and the public interest (sec. 75(3)). A recent decision by the Quebec Court of Appeal has ruled that provisions regarding the publication of the identities of young persons who are not subject to adult sanctions under sec. 110(2)(b) are unconstitutional because they violate the principles of fundamental justice under the *Charter*.[11]

International Agreements

Several international agreements that apply in the Canadian context also contain provisions that recognize the importance of the right to privacy. There are a series of rules and provisions contained in various conventions from the United Nations that establish exemplary standards to which all states can refer.[12] Courts cite international human rights agreements as an aid to help in the interpretation of legislation specifically as it relates to confidentiality and privacy issues in youth justice cases (Bromwich, 2002). In particular, with respect to confidentiality and privacy in dealing with young persons before the court, the "Beijing Rules" have been valuable. Rule 8 states:

(8.1) The juvenile's right to privacy shall be respected at all stages in order to avoid harm being caused to her or him by undue publicity or by the process of labeling;

In principle, no information that may lead to the identification of a juvenile offender shall be published

The United Nations *Convention on the Rights of the Child,* to which Canada is a signatory, is based on the recognition that during the period of childhood, a person is entitled to special care and assistance. The Convention provides that "every" child accused of having infringed the criminal law is entitled to a guarantee to "have his or her privacy fully respected at all stages of the proceedings."[13] As discussed in Chapter 4, while the Convention does not have the force of law in Canada, it is important to note that in the Preamble to the YCJA reference is made to the fact that Canada is a party to the Convention.

RIGHT TO PRIVACY: RATIONALE

Proponents of the publication of young offenders' identities argue that the protection of society would be better served in identifying young offenders (Seskus & Mofina, 2000). However, this line of reasoning is based on the assumption that the media would publish the identities of all such young persons and the public would then become aware of this information in order to be protected from the risk that a particular youth poses. Even if all violent crimes were published in the newspaper, it is unrealistic to expect that the public would avail themselves of the information necessary to be protected from the apparent risk posed by these so-named violent young offenders. Furthermore, it is im-

portant to recognize that the majority of youth crime cases reported in the media generally focus on aspects of the young person's arrest, trial, or sentencing. Thus, if the young person were seen to pose such a risk to the community, then the public would have to follow the case through until the completion of the sentence—presumably when the young offender is released from custody. Most members of the general public do not have the time, interest, or inclination to inform themselves of criminal events to this degree. Therefore, arguments that information on youth crime is of value in ensuring public protection is premised on faulty logic.

Another argument in favour of the identification of young offenders in the newspapers is that there would be an enhanced deterrent effect on youth by shaming those young persons who have their identities published in the newspaper (Federal-Provincial-Territorial Task Force, 1996, p. 404). However, research has shown that deterrence is ineffective for young offenders (Baron & Kennedy, 1988; Doob, Marinos, & Varma, 1995). The assumptions required for a deterrent effect in and of itself are not likely to have much impact on young persons who come before the courts. In order for deterrence to be effective, youth must understand the consequences and possible punishments of an act prior to committing the act and be discouraged from committing a crime by those potential consequences. In some cases, having a young offender's identity published in the newspaper may have the opposite effect and reinforce the criminal propensities of youth who are seeking the attention and "notoriety" that their name and identity in the newspaper would provide (Federal-Provincial-Territorial Task Force, 1996, p. 416).

It is important to question the extent to which the inclusion of a young person's identity actually helps the public to have a greater understanding of the youth justice system in Canada. It is also possible that the inclusion of identities of young people before the courts further entrenches already existing myths and misperceptions about youth crime in Canada. If the desired aim is to have public confidence in the youth justice system and to understand the nature and circumstances leading to the unfortunate situation of young people being tried in youth justice courts, it is imperative that the messages that are being reported in the media are not reinforcing the myths already circulating about crime and criminal behaviour.

MYTHS ABOUT CRIME: IMPACT ON PUBLIC OPINION AND POLICY

The media are perhaps the most important source of common misconceptions and myths of crime, criminals, and crime control policy. Crime myths can be seen as distorted conceptions of issues related to crime and criminal justice policy that, while false, have come to be accepted as truths because they have been consistently reiterated in public forums, debates, and individual private conversations (Pepinsky & Jesilow, 1984; Kappeler, Blumberg, & Potter, 1996). Surette (1992) argues that crime constitutes a constant and significant portion of the total news portrayed on radio, television, and in the print media. When significant attention is paid to infrequently occurring events, such as

serial killings, these events appear to be commonplace. This practice serves to underline the lack of realistic information on crime and justice and misleads the public regarding the true rate of violent crime, also fostering an unrealistic fear of being victimized by violent crime.

Factors that influence crime news selection include the seriousness of the offence, "whimsical" or unusual elements of the crime, sentimental or dramatic aspects of the offence or the criminal, and the involvement of famous or high-status individuals (Roshier, 1973; Sheley & Ashkins, 1981; Ericson, Baranek, & Chan, 1987, 1989). Media reporting reinforces the "validity of law" as purported through crime myths and further delineates for the general public who is considered to be criminal and what is considered to be a crime (Robinson, 2000, p. 139). Gorelick (1989) suggests that the media present criminality as a choice of the individual offender, thus implying that other social, economic, or structural explanations of the crime phenomenon are irrelevant. Further, the frequent use of a "vocabulary of force"—such as police as "crime fighters" or the "war on crime"—leaves the public with a clear message that crime must be "fought" rather than "solved," "eliminated," or "prevented" (p. 429). The message that the public receives is that the best solution to crime is through the expansion of the present criminal justice system, through harsher punishments and greater law enforcement.

In studies of newspapers and television, the most consistent finding over time has been the higher likelihood of reporting and publicizing a criminal act if it is unusual in some manner. Chermak (1998) found that the number of victims left as a result of a violent crime was the strongest predictor of whether a crime would be covered by the media. Similarly, multiple offenders; an unusual method of committing homicide; murder victims that were children, elderly, or female; and the occurrence of homicide in an affluent neighbourhood were all factors that increased the likelihood of a story being published (Johnstone, Hawkins, & Michener, 1994; Sorenson, Manz, & Berk, 1998). Dorfman and Schiraldi (2001) found that despite a continuing drop in the crime rates over the period they studied, the rate of crime coverage in the news media increased. In a study of *Time* newsmagazine from 1975 through 1982, there was a 55-percent increase in reporting of crime from 1979 through 1982, when the actual U.S. crime rate for this period increased by only one percent (Barlow, Barlow, & Chiricos, 1995).

The media are replete with sensationalized crime stories depicting rising crime rates and, in particular, rising rates of violent crime (Graber, 1980; Garofalo, 1981; Gorelick, 1989; Marsh, 1991). As has been suggested by others, the media have the ability to manipulate the fear of crime (Doob, 1982; Heath, 1984; Tunnell, 1992; Williams & Dickinson, 1993; Heath & Gilbert, 1996). This media hype creates an elevated fear through "crime-time news" (Cohen & Solomon, 1994). Fear reinforces crime mythology and has myriad other effects. This fear leads the public to avoid certain "dangerous" people and encourages the police to apprehend people who are posing the greatest threats to our societal well being. It further places pressure on policy makers to "do something" about

the crime problem (Garofalo & Laub, 1978; Rome, 1998).

MORAL PANICS

The concept of "moral panic," as coined by the sociologist Stanley Cohen (1972, 2001), represents the process of creating societal outrage against certain groups within a society through the repeated presentation of negative images of them in the media. These negative representations in turn can create a public outcry, leading to a justification for harsher and more oppressive treatment for those groups of targeted individuals. Bell (2002) suggests that a moral panic about youth crime is produced through "continual and sensationalized" crime reporting, which is reinforced through the "selective reporting" of public outrage toward not only "out of control youth" but also the legislation that is supposed to control crime as the cause of the problem (p. 32).

In his research, Cohen (1972) looked at the role of the media in shaping public discourse around youth crime and youth justice by showing how random groups of young people came to be defined as "deviant." Through sensationalist newspaper representation in Britain during the 1960s of two groups of young people, the "mods" and the "rockers," a moral panic occurred. Cohen (1972, p. 29ff) recounts the story of how groups of young people, gathered at a seaside resort one weekend, ended up in a street scuffle over a rumour that a local bartender had refused to serve some of the young people. The police, in turn, overreacted by arresting more than 100 young people. The major newspapers ran headlines such as "Youngsters Beat Up Town,"

"Wild Ones Invade Seaside," and "Day of Terror by Scooter Groups." The *Daily Express* presented the following story:

> There was Dad asleep in a deckchair and Mum making sandcastles with the children, when the 1964 boys took over the beaches at Margate and Brighton yesterday and smeared the traditional postcard scene with blood and violence.[14]

This sensational media reporting was also picked up by international newspapers. Youth disturbances continued to rank high in terms of their "newsworthiness" for the next three years. Given that nothing particularly newsworthy was happening nationally or internationally during that weekend in 1964, the events surrounding the "mods" and the "rockers" were equally not particularly newsworthy in the context of being new or unfamiliar. However, they were presented in the news media as "new" to justify their creation as "news." Cohen (1972) used the term "folk devils" to describe these youth and to draw attention to the idea that they were conceived of similarly to the witches of seventeenth century New England. In England, "mods" and "rockers" came to be seen as a potential threat to adults and to the traditional values and beliefs of broader society. The interpretation of these events as a moral panic illustrates how a new and potentially threatening phenomenon can impact on certain "positions, interests, ideologies and values" (p. 191).

Goode and Ben-Yehuda (1996) underscore the distinction between a moral panic and other "seemingly threatening new phenomenon" (p. 30). In the case of a "moral panic," a societal reaction occurs that is out of proportion to the threat of the new phenomenon, as evidenced by five specific indicators. The first criterion is that there must be a heightened level of *concern* over the behaviour of the group and the consequences of the behaviour for the rest of society. Second, there must be an increased level of *hostility* toward the group responsible for engaging in the behaviour in question, and third, that there is a widespread *consensus* that the threat from this group's behaviour is serious. Fourth, the public concern about the behaviour is *disproportionate* (in excess) to the objective harm. Another way of speaking about this fourth dimension of disproportionality has been quoted by Jones and his colleagues (1989) that "objective molehills have been made into subjective mountains" (p. 4). The final dimension is that moral panics are *volatile* and relatively short-lived; some simply subside, while other become institutionalized and routinized.

In his book *Blaming Children: Youth Crime, Moral Panic and the Politics of Hate*, Schissel (1997) implies that the "logic and rhetoric of politics and news is so flawed and poorly struck that malicious intentions cannot be dismissed" (p. 99). From a more radical perspective, Schissel argues that media reporting of crime does more than sensationalize events—he believes that it presents "hateful, stereotypical views of youth misconduct" and that media crime reporting borders on "hate literature" (pp. 49, 51). The result is the "continuing scapegoating of youth for political purposes" and the likelihood of an even more "disenfranchised, disaffiliated and uncompromising" youth population (Schissel, 2001, p. 85).

Similarly, Tanner (1996) suggests that youth are seen as threatening to adult society and viewed as continually "troubled" or "troubling" (p. 17). Consequently, media coverage, which does not provide a context for the events that precipitate youth involvement in criminal activity, is selective in its desire to print "sensational" events in order to sell newspapers and at the same time arouse the general public's fear and sense of moral indignation.

A less extreme perspective views panics as being a product of the media, not so much as a conspiracy against young people, but through "institutional pressures and failures which then take on a life of their own and compound the problem" (Simpson, 1997, p. 13). Bortner (1988) suggests that what appear to be "crime waves" may in fact be "media waves." In his classic study of three daily newspapers in New York City, Fishman (1978) examined the statistics surrounding an alleged dramatic increase in violent youth crimes against the elderly. In the media reports, the police were active spokesmen for the news and promoted the further entrenchment of this crime wave by responding with more police efforts to "crack down" on youth crime. When Fishman compared the media reports with the police statistics during this so-called "crime wave," he found that in fact there had actually been a 19-percent decrease in violent criminal activity in the areas of the city where the escalating crime rates had purportedly occurred. Fishman concluded that much of what is reported in the media as "crime waves" could be seen to be ideologically based and not necessarily a reflection of the actual incidents of crime.

As outlined earlier, myths about crime are so entrenched within the psyche of the general public that there is usually sufficient community support to help legitimize the moral crusade, perpetuated in part by the media. However, the community is made up of all of its members: those who commit crimes, those who are victimized, and those who fear crime victimization. Murray (1996) suggests by way of example that when members of the "community" report acts of youth graffiti or vandalism, they are doing so without considering that the young people who are committing these anti-social acts are part of what they refer to as "the community" (p. 80). As Simpson (1997) suggests, it is another aspect of the moral panic that the perpetrators and those who would support them are cast outside "the community" who scorn them (p. 4).

These "public panics" are more focused on the social, economic, and political contexts occurring at a given time, and often ignore the "criminogenic reality" of young offenders' lives (Schissel, 2001, p. 86). Media provide "de-contextualized" accounts of youth crime, thus exaggerating the seriousness of the "problem" of youth crime. Moreover, there is an almost complete absence of the complex range of circumstances within young offenders' lives that often lead them toward conflict with the law. The ideological underpinnings and myths about young criminals "originate with fictionalized, distorted and stereotypical accounts of young offenders and their socio-economic affiliations" (p. 94). Thus, those who present these negative, de-contextualized images of youth and young criminals have an inherent ideological bias, while ignoring the social and economic reality of these youths' lives.

The lack of an overall contextual base to the reporting of individual cases of crime has been reported in numerous studies (Dorfman, Woodruff, Chavez, & Wallack, 1997; Perrone & Chesney-Lind,

1997). In particular, Dorfman and Schiraldi (2001, p. 12) concluded from their analysis of studies on news reporting that the most frequent type of reporting on crime was comprised of a series of individual, episodic events that appeared in isolation from the larger social, historical, or environmental contexts in which they occurred. As noted by the Youth Media Council (2002):

> The distance between the experiences and conditions of youth and the news stories about us is a landscape of media bias in which myths become public opinion and lies become public policy. (p. 7)

We Interrupt This Message is an American non-profit organization that has conducted a variety of media analyses related to stereotypes perpetuated by the media. They suggest that the news coverage of youth crime "paints the landscape" from within which juvenile justice policy debates occur. Information regarding juvenile justice policy is presented to the public via articles that relate to arrest rates, pending legislation, and other policy initiatives, but equally through themes reported in individual articles on crimes committed by youth. From their perspective the themes promoted by these individual youth crime articles "provide the context in which the policy debate happens" (2001, p. 21). Moreover, media representations of youth crime do not address the real context of the lives of young people, but rather reinforce myths about youth generally, and youth crime in particular. Young people become easy targets for moral panic because when they engage in risky behaviour, they do so under the scrutiny of adult supervision and in the public sphere.

THEMES INHERENT TO MEDIA PORTRAYALS OF YOUTH CRIME

Given that juvenile justice proceedings were held *in camera* under the *Juvenile Delinquents Act,* there were very few articles written about youth crime during the 76-year period of its enactment. It was only following 1982, after the proclamation of the *Young Offenders Act,* that reporters were allowed to enter youth justice courtrooms and begin actually reporting on youth crime. However, they were limited in reporting only about the event per se, and could not under any circumstances identify the young person. Similarly, throughout the United States, juvenile justice hearings in most states were confidential prior to the 1990s. As a result, there were few articles about youth crime to analyze in this respect, and fewer media analyses.

More recently, Dorfman and Schiraldi (2001) conducted a content analysis of youth crime in the news by reviewing 146 scholarly articles on crime news reporting. They concluded that the studies taken together indicate that depictions of crime in the news do not reflect the rate of crime generally and tend to exaggerate the proportion of crime when it is violent, when committed by people of colour, and when committed by youth. Of the 146 studies examined, only 16 investigated whether and how youth were portrayed on television news or in newspapers. Many of these studies indicated that youth were often portrayed in violent contexts, and young people of colour were more often presented as perpetrators of crime (Stensaas, 1961; Humphries, 1981; Males, 2000).

In an analysis of 1500 news articles, op-eds, editorials, and letters to the editor in five major California newspapers from January 1999 to March 2000, media coverage of juvenile justice was dominated by the idea that youth crime is out of control and increasingly violent. The most common solution conveyed in the media for dealing with "out-of-control" youth crime was the imposition of harsher penalties. The clear message was that the present juvenile justice system did not work and was considered "out of date" and much "too lenient" to deal with today's violent youth (We Interrupt This Message, 2001, p. 21).

A study of three major Ontario newspapers[15] conducted over a two-month period found that 94 percent of the articles about youth crime involved youth violence. However, provincial statistics for that year showed that violent youth crime accounted for less than one-quarter of all crimes committed by young people (Sprott, 1996). The majority of these articles focused on the police and youth courts as sources of information. Furthermore, many of the stories focused on charges, arrests, and the impact of the crime on the victim, while very few outlined youth court sentences. In addition, when surveying Toronto residents about their knowledge related to youth crime, Sprott found that many individuals indicated the newspaper as their primary source of information about youth crime. Interestingly, while the three major newspapers in this study published very little information about young offender dispositions, most people surveyed felt that young offender sentences were too lenient (p. 272). This is not surprising, given that the ultimate goal of the press is to sell newspapers, while journalists "interpret reality" and tell stories rather than "reflect reality" (p. 287).

In a study undertaken by Reid-MacNevin (1996), newspaper articles were analyzed from four daily newspapers[16] in Ontario between May and August 1996, yielding a sample of 716 articles related to youth. From these four newspapers, articles were sought that involved individuals from 12 to 17 years of age. Also included were articles that involved individuals slightly younger or older if the individuals were referred to by the author as "youth." The location of the article in the newspaper,[17] the newshole space,[18] the percentage of headline space for total article size, the percentage of the total page for the article, and the total number of advertisements surrounding the article were all systematically collected and coded (Poremner, 1997).

Youth crime–related articles accounted for slightly more than half of all the articles collected (56.7%). Like previous research, violent crime was the most frequent type of crime reported (52%), while property offences accounted for only seven percent of the articles on youth crime. In the same year that the study was conducted, official statistics on youth crime in Canada reported almost the exact reversal of the news reporting with respect to property offences: they accounted for almost one-half of the case load, whereas violent offences counted for 18 percent of all young offender cases processed (Doherty & De Souza, 1996). This dramatic difference in violent crime statistics, compared to the number of articles that are published about youth committing violent crimes, further reinforces crime myths and strengthens stereotypes and mispercep-tions about youth crime.

Similar to previous research, 42 per-cent of the news articles on youth crime were police occurrence reports, with the majority of these articles promoting a law-and-order ideology. In terms of the pro-posed solution to youth crime, the most predominant suggestion was "more inter-vention" and "stricter punishments" (58%), while 32 percent of the articles fo-cused on more community-based solu-tions. Also found was a statistically significant relationship indicating that ar-ticles that were youth crime–related were more likely to fall within the first 15 pages of the newspaper.[19] Similarly, those arti-cles that were youth crime–related occu-pied significantly more newshole space[20] and had larger headlines[21] than articles not related to youth crime.

In the months of June, July, and August 2002, a similar media analysis was con-ducted by Reid-MacNevin (2003) follow-ing news stories that were distributed through internet news sources. These ar-ticles were found using common search engines and yielded a total of 238 news stories on the broad category of youth and the narrower category of youth crime. Unlike the print news study conducted in 1996, only 30 percent of the articles col-lected through Internet search engines were related to youth crime. However, of those articles that were youth crime–re-lated, an even more exaggerated view of violent youth crime was presented, with 64 percent of all youth crime–related ar-ticles depicting violent crime. Further, the most likely sources quoted were the po-lice or court reports in almost 60 percent of the youth crime–related articles.

In 95 percent of all youth articles found in this three-month period, there were only 12 articles (6%) that were writ-ten from the perspective of a young per-son. All of the other articles—whether youth crime–related or general interest ar-ticles about young people—were written in the voice of adults. In a content analy-sis of words commonly found within all the articles it is interesting to note that the slang term "kids" was used as often as the word "youth." The predominant term in all youth-related articles was "child" for depicting young people between the ages of 10 and 13, and "youth" for those over the age of 14 up to and including age 21 or 22. While youth justice legislation has carved out specific ages of young persons to include those between 12 and 18 years, in the *Globe and Mail Style Book* (a guide for newspaper writers and editors) it is suggested that "the term youths may be taken to include a few members who are slightly younger or older" (McFarlane & Clements, 1998, p. 409). This may partially account for the variation in the terminol-ogy utilized in the news stories.

Among the words used to describe young people in these articles, there are a number of phrases that Schissel (1997) refers to as a further de-contextualization of the crime through the promotion of im-ages that are tied to youth culture. These words provoke powerful images of the young people described: "belligerent teenagers," "brats," "punks," "rowdies," "thugs," and "troublemakers." Also discon-certing was the terminology used to de-scribe youth that appears to provide mixed messages: "peak physical aggression," "soft-spoken Christian punk," "freshmen children," and "soother-sucking youth." As suggested by Neil Reynolds (1996), former editor in chief of the *New Brunswick Telegraph Journal*, "…almost every headline, in almost every newspaper, makes a public statement of some kind on moral conduct" (p. 12). A sample of the headlines that were gathered during the summer of 2002 provides more mental images of the depiction of youth generally and young offenders in particular:

Table of Headlines:
Researcher Finds Gene that Makes Bad Boys Bad
Kids Get Fighting Chance to Grow
Vandalism Spells End of Skateboard Park
Youth a Prime Candidate for Repeat Court Visits
The Ugliness of Hockey: Boy Sues Coach
Watch Out, Kids About
Canadian Teen Blamed
Two Teens Stabbed in Huge Pub Brawl

Many of these headlines and the content of the news stories represent alarmist reactions to crime. Such reactions are significant because they are emotionally driven, they frighten the public, and they remain instrumental in generating fear of crime. Alarmist reactions are both the cause and the effect of moral panics, and, when pronounced by politicians and law enforcement officials, often take the form of "demagoguery" (Welch, Fenwick, & Roberts, 1997, p. 484). The following example from Welch and his colleagues' analysis of quotes in feature news reports in the *New York Times* demonstrates this assertion:

> Our streets are being stained with the blood of our children, and it's going to stop. Damn it. It has got to stop. (Pete Wilson, California Governor, *New York Times*, 1994)[22]

When alarmist reactions are delivered by seemingly credible "moral entrepreneurs,"[23] the dominant ideology is advanced. Welch, Fenwick, and Roberts (1997) suggest that these moral panics further contribute to what they refer to as the "escalating vocabulary of punitive motives," which are used to justify inappropriate strategies for dealing with crime (p. 486). Other headlines gathered in the 2002 Internet study of Canadian news sources further exemplify this point: "No Jail for Student Killer Called Travesty"; "Youth Crime Leads to Town Curfew"; and "Girls' Cruelty Can be Deadly."

By attempting to evoke passionate images in this type of news reporting, the details of a case become secondary to the metaphors of "law abiding" victims. A murder case, extensively reported by the news media, illustrates this point. As part of its ongoing coverage of the story, the *Toronto Sun* ran an article about the victim's family being left out of the notification process by the court, and upon arrival at the courtroom the family learned that the case had been put over for another date. This was the "news" content of the story, but the article went on to describe the incident and the sense of injustice that would evoke passion in the reader where a young man who was "doing everything he should be doing" ended up dead. The article goes on to describe that "he [the victim] was at the subway station to take his girlfriend home for her 11:30 p.m. curfew…. The two sweethearts never missed a curfew."[24] Such a presentation, ostensibly intended at discussing the court trial notification process, instead draws attention to the murdered victim as not only an innocent bystander, but also a "good son" and boyfriend.

On occasion, there are opinion editorials and letters to the editor in newspapers that point out the de-contextualization of events in news reporting. From time to time, the general public does react to how such cases are presented in the media, and some opinion pieces are very critical of news reporting. Such letters, while reflecting a sense of outrage at the sensationalist nature of some news reporting on youth crime, are the exception. More commonly, a steady dose of headlines and sensationalistic case reporting in the news has greater, detrimental consequences with respect to misleading public perceptions about the nature and extent of youth crime. The resultant effect is an overreliance on the media for images of youth crime, which in turn also reflects the dominant ideology of punishment and harsher sentences. Part of the responsibility for the de-contextualization of news reporting lies with the available sources of information sought for such reporting. It is important to also consider what alternatives are available to enable the news media to gather the necessary facts, in order to better reflect the reality of youth crime as opposed to interpreting reality from their respective vantage points.

MISSING VOICES IN THE MEDIA PORTRAYAL OF YOUTH CRIME

What appears to be missing from a great deal of news reporting on issues of youth crime, in spite of issues of confidentiality and privacy, are further details that would provide a context for a better understanding of the life circumstances of these youth in conflict with the law. In other areas of news reporting, such as sports, business, or entertainment, general information is integrated with the news story and events are placed within a larger context, often within the same article. Stevens (1998) suggests that with every other topic, newspapers are including information that depicts the status of issues as well as the "unusual events," and it is time that these same processes be integrated into the reporting of youth crime.

As outlined by the Federal-Provincial-Territorial Task Force on Youth Justice (1996), the purpose of an open youth process is not to punish offenders by publicly identifying them (p. 407). Rather, the openness of the court and media scrutiny of the court process is meant to promote public understanding of the youth criminal justice system and ensure that the "state acts fairly and within the law, without political or social bias." However, this overreliance on the police, politicians, and courts as the main source of information about youth crime results in many voices being silenced, and if heard could ostensibly help in educating the public about youth crime. Perhaps one of the most predominant groups in this regard is that of academics and researchers.

Welch, Fenwick, and Roberts's (1997) analysis of quotes in feature news articles compared those from primary definers of crime (law enforcement and political spokespersons) and those from "intellectuals" and found that there was a significant overreliance on the primary definers of crime. They suggest that the "dominant ideology continues to be reproduced because the voice of dissent is minimal"

(p. 482). Despite a tendency to rely mainly on law enforcement officials, there is an "emerging window of opportunity for intellectuals to educate the public about crime." The concept that researchers have a role in contributing to a better understanding of media reporting has also been noted elsewhere (Greek, 1994; Barak, 1994). One quote from the Welch study is an example of a criminal justice professor commenting in the *Los Angeles Times* about the moral panic related to youth crime:

> It'll go away. It's called a moral panic. Moral panic is almost completely unrelated to underlying reality. I've seen them come and go. There was carjacking. Hate crime. Gold chain snatching. Remember gold chains?[25]

Listening to the voices of educated others who can provide evidence that harsher penalties for youth do not make our communities safer is important. Researchers can also provide examples of programs that work in preventing youth crime at the community level.

Another voice missing from the debates about youth crime in the media is that of those who advocate for youth. Very rarely are young people's lawyers asked to comment on the cases before the courts. Further, child-care workers, youth workers, and social workers who advocate for the rights of youth are virtually silent in news reports. These individuals are in a unique position to speak about the realities that youth face in the system. Youth advocates can provide information about what happens to young persons once they have been tried, convicted, and sentenced and must serve time in open or closed youth custody institutions, information that is rarely reported by the media. Susan

McClelland (2003), writing in *Maclean's* magazine shortly after the proclamation of the *Youth Criminal Justice Act,* provided an interesting overview of the problems faced by young people confined to youth custody. In discussing the rituals for new inmates at a youth custody centre in Toronto, the gruesome details of life behind bars were spelled out:

> Sometimes, inmates tie another kid's hands, feet and neck to one of the metal bed frames with sheets and then beat his exposed torso, or they force their peers to stick their heads in toilets filled with urine and feces and blow bubbles. (at para 6)

Further in the article, she provides an overview of family group conferencing, group homes, and other forms of "correction" that are available to young persons convicted of offences. This article provides a perspective on the violence within institutions and draws attention to one of the main purposes of the new Act: "and it's a problem the newly minted *Youth Criminal Justice Act* aims to solve, by sending fewer kids to prison" (at para. 20).

Messages promoting the reality of life in youth custody facilities have appeared more frequently since the proclamation of the YCJA. Another example is a story recently written by Rosie DiManno in the *Toronto Star* (2004). In a report on the suicide of a 16-year-old youth at the Toronto Youth Assessment Centre, DiManno begins the article with, "God forgive us for the harm we do to our children simply because we can." She goes on to point out that the young man who took his life was among 140 other young people who had been convicted of nothing but, having been denied bail, were awaiting trial in locked detention. The realities of life for youth sentenced to adult prisons are also absent in most media accounts of youth crime. One recent exception illustrates the harsh living conditions for youth in adult jails:

> At a rally Tuesday, hand lettered signs flanked the speakers. One said, "Children in adult prisons are 500 percent more likely to be sexually assaulted, 200 percent more likely to be beaten by staff, 50 percent more likely to be attacked with a weapon than youth in a juvenile facility."[26]

When covering a story that may contain sensitive content, journalists are not bound to report all of the gruesome details of an event. As Merrill (1989) suggests, "the journalist can, from time to time, refrain from publishing a story, thus going against the principle of the people's right to know, on the ethical grounds that the evil consequences of publication would outweigh the good" (p. 201). Further, "the journalist can in certain cases withhold information from a story while still being basically dedicated to an ethics of full disclosure." William Thorsell, the former editor in chief of *The Globe and Mail,* suggested that investigative journalism must move beyond the formula taught in journalism school:

> The five W's of reporting (what, who, where, when and why) are heavy on description. I believe that the five Ws must be supplemented by the capital-H of How and the capital-SW of So What. How do things work? How do things happen? Why does it matter? Print reporting must go beyond detailed descriptions of what happened to what we might call "adult education." (cited in Reynolds, 1996, p. 14)

CONCLUSION

While some journalists argue that audiences want news about violence, this may be more of a reflection of their own ideological preferences and pressures from media ownership to sell the news. Reporters, producers, and editors have learned to choose the news they believe will draw the most attractive audience for advertisers. As Dorfman and Schiraldi (2001) suggest, individual news workers make decisions about what to include in the news of the day based on whether they personally care about the story, in essence reflecting their own personal values and emotional responses as to what is most appropriate for inclusion in the news (p. 25). However, Merrill underscores the subjectivity of this type of reporting:

> We must as journalists, recognize that we are making mere scratches on the slate of history, that these scratches are largely reflective of our own backgrounds and ideologies, and that they are only the briefest and most unreliable pictures of reality around us (Merrill, 1989, p. 240).

In telling the story, journalists must give the audiences some guideposts for understanding the crime (Dorfman & Schiraldi, 2001). Advocates for youth, including those who work in the media, can challenge the messages used to scapegoat youth, and can promote more balanced reporting of youth criminal activity.

> It is mean spirited and just plain wrong to portray youth as criminals. Scapegoating youth doesn't make us safer and it doesn't help our youth. It only blinds us to the poverty and abuse facing today's youth. (We Interrupt This Message, 2001, p. 21)

By consistently ignoring the myriad social problems that are often a large part of the background of many youth in conflict with the law, the picture remains incomplete. In reporting youth crime, the inclusion of factors relating to context would likely enlighten the public to the difficult realities that many youth face—whereas a commitment to more honesty in reporting in an attempt to provide greater truths would likely sell fewer newspapers, it may also have the effect of a more realistic portrayal of young persons in conflict with the law.

References

Bala, N. (2003). *Youth Criminal Justice Law.* Toronto: Irwin Law.

Barak, G. (1994). *Varieties in criminology: Readings from a dynamic discipline.* Westport, CN: Praeger.

Baron, S., & Kennedy, L. (1998). Deterrence and homeless male street youths. *Canadian Journal of Criminology, 40*(1), 27–59.

Barlow, M. H., Barlow, D. E., & Chiricos, T. G. (1995). Economic conditions and ideologies of crime in the media: A content analysis of crime news. *Crime and Delinquency, 4,* 3–19.

Bell, S. (2002). *Young offenders and juvenile justice: A century after the fact* (2nd ed.). Toronto: Nelson Thomson Learning.

Bortner, M. (1988). *Delinquency and Justice: An age of crisis.* Toronto: McGraw Hill.

Bremmer, M. (1997). *Youth and youth crime: A moral panic, a content analysis* of four Ontario Newspapers. M.A. Dissertation, Department of Sociology, University of Guelph.

Bromwich, R. J. (2002). Compassion, human rights and adult sentencing under the YCJA. *Windsor Review of Legal and Social Issues 14,* 71.

Canada. Department of Justice. (1998). *A strategy for the renewal of youth justice.* Ottawa: Queen's Printer.

Chermak, S. (1998). Predicting crime story salience: The effects of crime, victim and defendant characteristics. *Journal of Criminal Justice, 26,* 61–70.

Cohen, J., & Solomon, N. (1994). Crime time news exploits fears. *Indianapolis Business Journal, 15*(13), 6.

Cohen, S. (1972). *Folk devils and moral panics: The creation of the mods and rockers.* London: MacGibbon & Kee.

Cohen, S. (2001). Youth deviance and moral panics (reprinted). In R. Smandych (Ed.), *Youth justice: History, education and reform.* Toronto: Harcourt.

DiManno, R. (2004, February 11). Tough love proved terribly, tragically wrong for youth. *Toronto Star.*

Doherty G., & deSouza P., (1996). "Youth court statistics, 1994–95". Highlights. Canadian Centre for Justice Statistics, *Juristat, 16*(4).

Doob, A. (1982). The role of mass media in creating exaggerated levels of fear of being the victim of a violent crime. In P. Stringer (Ed.), *Confronting social issues: Applications of social psychology.* Toronto: Academic Press.

Doob, A., Marinos, V., & Varma, K. N. (1995). *Youth crime and the youth justice system in Canada.* Centre of Criminology. Toronto: University of Toronto Press.

Dorfman, L., & Schiraldi, V. (2001). *Off balance: Youth, race and crime in the news.* Office of Juvenile Justice and Delinquency Prevention, U.S. Department of Justice. Available online at www.buildingblocksforyouth.org.

Dorfman, L., Woodruff, K., Chavez, V., & Wallack, L. (1997). Youth and violence on local television news in California. *American Journal of Public Health, 87,* 1311–1316.

Ericson, R. V., Baranek, P. M., & Chan, J. B. L. (1987). *Visualizing deviance: A study of news organizations.* Toronto: University of Toronto Press.

Ericson, R. V., Baranek, P. M., & Chan, J. B. L. (1989). *Negotiating control: A study of news sources.* Toronto: University of Toronto Press.

Federal-Provincial-Territorial Task Force Report. (1996). *A review of the Young Offenders Act and the Youth Justice System in Canada.* Ottawa: Queen's Printer.

Fishman, M. (1978). Crime waves as ideology. *Social Problems, 25,* 531–543.

Garofalo, J. (1981). Crime and the mass media: A selective review of the research. *Journal of Research in Crime and Delinquency, 18,* 319–350.

Garofalo, J., & Laub, J. (1978). The fear of crime: Broadening our perspective. *Victimology, 3,* 242–253.

Goode, E., & Ben-Yehuda, N. (1996). *Moral panics: The social construction of deviance.* Oxford: Blackwell.

Gorelick, S. (1989). Join our war: The construction of ideology in a newspaper crime-fighting campaign. *Crime and Delinquency, 35,* 421–436.

Graber, D. (1980). *Crime news and the public.* New York: Praeger.

Greek, C. (1994). Becoming a media criminologist: Is "newsmaking criminology" possible? In G. Barak (Ed.), *Media, Process and the Social Construction of Crime: Studies in Newsmaking Criminology.* New York: Garland Press.

Heath, L., & Gilbert, K. (1996). Mass media and fear of crime. *American Behavioral Scientist, 39*(4), 379–384.

Heath, L. (1984). Impact of newspaper crime reports on fear of crime: Multimethodological investigation. *Journal of Personality and Social Psychology, 47*(2), 263–276.

Humphries, D. (1981). Serious crime, news coverage and ideology: A content analysis of crime coverage in a metropolitan paper. *Crime and Delinquency, 27,* 191–205.

Johnstone, J. W. C., Hawkins, D. F., & Michener, A. (1994). Homicide reporting in Chicago dailies. *Journalism Quarterly, 71,* 860–872.

Jones, B.J. Gallagher, B.J., & McFalls, J.A. (1989). Toward a unified model for social problems theory. *Journal for the Theory of Social Behaviour, 19,* 337–356.

Kappeler, V., Blumberg, M., & Potter, G. (1996). *The mythology of crime and criminal justice.* Prospect Heights: Waveland.

Liska, A., & Baccaglini, W. (1990). Feeling safe by comparison: Crime in the newspapers. *Social Problems, 37*(3), 360–374.

MacFarlane, J.A., & Clements, W. (1998). *The Globe and Mail Style Book: A guide to language and usage.* Toronto: McCelland & Stewart.

Males, M. A. (2000). Kids and guns: How politicians, experts and the press fabricate fear of youth. Monroe, ME: Common Courage Press.

Marsh, H. (1991). A comparative analysis of crime coverage in newspapers in the United States and other countries from 1960–1989: A review of the literature. *Journal of Criminal Justice, 19*(4), 67–79.

McClelland, S. (2003, June 9). Institutional correction: A new youth crime act aims to fix a broken system. *Maclean's.*

Merrill, John C. (1989). *The dialectic in journalism: Toward a responsible use of press freedom.* Baton Rouge: Louisiana State University.

Murray, G. (1996). Public spaces. *Alternative Law Journal, 22,* 80–81.

Online Dictionary of the Social Sciences. (2001). Nelson Thomson Learning. Available online at http://socialsciencedictionary.nelson.com.

Ontario Ministry of the Attorney General. (2001, June 12). *No more free ride for the Young Offenders Act.* Toronto: Author.

Orlando Sentinel. (2003). Newshole space. Pocket Definition Glossary of Marketing and Advertising Terms. Available online at www.orlandosentinel.com.

Orstod, K. (1997, March). What are we: The myth of youth crime. *Saturday Night.*

Pepinsky, H.E., Jesilow, P. (1984). *Myths that cause crime.* Cabin John, MD: Seven Locks.

Perrone, P. A., & Chesney-Lind, M. (1997). Representations of gangs and delinquency: Wild in the street? *Social Justice, 24,* 6–11.

Reid-MacNevin, S.A. (1996). *The media portrayal of troubled youth.* Unpublished manuscript, University of Guelph.

Reid-MacNevin, S.A. (2003). *Bad, bad… youth: The media portrayal of youth.* Paper presented at the Crime and Media Symposium, October 2003, St. Thomas University.

Reynolds, N. (1996). Foreword to P. Lee, *Home pool: The fight to save the Atlantic salmon.* Fredericton: Goose Lane Editions, New Brunswick Publishing Co.

Robinson, M. (2000). The construction and reinforcement of myths of race and crime. *Journal of Contemporary Criminal Justice, 16*(2), 133–156.

Rome, D. (1998). Stereotyping by the media: Murderers, rapists and drug addicts. In C. R. Mann & M. Zatz (Eds.), *Images of color, Images of crime.* Los Angeles, CA: Roxbury.

Roshier, B. (1973). The selection of crime news by the press. In S. Cohen & J. Young (Eds.), *The manufacture of the news.* Beverly Hills, CA: Sage.

Schissel, B. (1997). *Blaming children: Youth crime, moral panics and the politics of hate.* Halifax: Fernwood.

Schissel, B. (2001). Youth crime, moral panics and the news: The conspiracy against the marginalised in Canada. In R. Smandych (Ed.), *Youth justice: History, education and reform.* Toronto: Harcourt.

Seskus, T., & Mofina, R. (2000). Young offenders and the press. In J. Winterdyk (Ed.), *Issues and perspectives on young offenders in Canada* (2nd ed.). Toronto: Harcourt.

Sheley, J. F., & Ashkins, C. D. (1981). Crime, crime news and crime views. *Public Opinion Quarterly, 45,* 492–506.

Simpson, B. (1997). Youth crime, the media and moral panic. In J. Bessant & R.

Hill (Eds.), *Youth, crime and media.* Australia: National Clearinghouse for Youth Studies.

Sorenson, S. B., Manz, J. B., & Berk, R. A. (1998). News media coverage and the epidemiology of homicide. *American Journal of Public Health, 88,* 1510–1514.

Sprott, J. B. (1996). Understanding public views of youth crime and the youth justice system. *Canadian Journal of Criminology, 38*(3), 271–290.

Stensaas, H. S. (1961). The front-page teenager: How 11 dailies treat him. *Journalism Quarterly, 38,* 373–4.

Stevens, J. E. (1998, winter). Integrating the public health perspective into reporting on violence. *Nieman Reports,* 38–41.

Surette, R. (1992). *Media, crime and criminal justice: Images and realities.* Pacific Grove, CA: Brooks/Cole.

Tanner, J. (1996). *Teenage troubles: Youth and deviance in Canada.* Toronto: Nelson Canada.

Tunnell, K. (1992). Film at eleven: Recent developments in the commodification of crime. *Sociological Spectrum, 12,* 293–313.

United Nations. (1976). *International Covenant on Civil and Political Rights.* General Assembly Resolution 2200 A (XXI).

United Nations. (1985). *United Nations Standard Minimum Rules for the Administration of Justice (The Bejiing Rules).* U.N. Document 40/33.

United Nations. (1989). *United Nations Convention on the Rights of the Child.* U.N. Document A/44/736.

United Nations. (1990). *United Nations Standard Minimum Rules for Non-Custodial Measures (The Tokyo Rules)* U.N. Document 45/110.

Welch, M., Fenwick, M., & Roberts, M. (1997). Primary definitions of crime and moral panic: A content analysis of experts' quotes in feature newspaper articles on crime. *Journal of Research in Crime and Delinquency, 34*(4), 474–494.

We Interrupt this Message. (2001). *Soundbites and cellblocks: Analysis of the juvenile justice media debate and a case study of California's Proposition 21.* San Francisco, CA. Available online at www.interrupt.org.

Wente, M. (2000, February 1). The kids aren't all right. *Globe and Mail.*

Williams, P., & Dickinson, J. (1993). Fear of crime: Read all about it? *British Journal of Criminology, 33*(1), 33–52.

Wilson, J., & Tomlinson, M. (1986). *Children and the law* (2nd ed.). Toronto: Butterworths.

Youth Media Council. (2002). *Speaking for ourselves: A youth assessment of local news coverage.* New York. Available online at www.interrupt.org.

Cases Cited

R. v. N. (1979) 10 C.R. (3d) 68 (B.C.C.A.).

N. v. MacDonald, [1979] 4 W.W.R. 621, 634 (B.C.S.C.).

C.B. v. R. (1981), 62 C.C.C. (2d) 107 (S.C.C.).

R. v. R.J. (1982) 37 O.R. (2d) 173 (Ont. H.C.).

Québec (Ministre de la Justice) v. Canada (Ministre de la Justice)(2003), 10 C.R. (5th) 281, [2003] Q.J. 2850 (C.A.).

Southam Inc. v. R. (1984), 48 O.R. (2d) 678.

Notes

1. See, for example, *R. v. N.* (1979) 10 C.R. (3d) 68 (B.C.C.A.); *N. v. MacDonald*, [1979] 4 W.W.R. 621, 634 (B.C.S.C.).

2. *In camera* refers to the courtroom being closed to anyone who was not directly participating in the hearing.

3. *R. v. R.J.* (1982) 37 O.R. (2d) 173 (Ont. H.C.).

4. Ibid at p. 184.

5. K. Orstod. (1997, March). What are we: The myth of youth crime. *Saturday Night.*

6. Tories say new act "wishy-washy." *The Globe and Mail*, September 19, 1998.

7. Department of Justice, *A strategy for the renewal of youth justice, Ottawa: 1998.*

8. Bill C-68, First Session 36th Parliament, First reading March 11, 1999.

9. Day unveils law and order message. *The Globe and Mail*, July 19, 2000.

10. Ontario Ministry of the Attorney General (2001), *No more free ride for the Young Offenders Act.* June 12, 2001.

11. Reference Decision [2003] Q.J. no 2850 (C.A.).

12. United Nations Standard Minimum Rules for the Administration of Justice (1986); United Nations Standard Minimum Rules for Non-Custodial Measures (Article 3.11) (1990); and International Covenant on Civil and Political Rights (Article 14(1)) (1976).

13. United Nations *Convention on the Rights of the Child*: Article 40(1)(b)(vii).

14. From the *Daily Express,* May 19, 1964 as cited in Cohen (2001) at page 77

15. The papers included the *Globe and Mail, Toronto Star, Toronto Sun.*

16. The four newspapers included the *Toronto Star, Toronto Sun, Guelph Mercury,* and *Kitchener Waterloo Record.*

17. This follows Liska and Baccaglini's categorization (1990), who suggest that placement in the first 15 pages of the newspaper is significant and would likely impact on readership.

18. Newshole space refers to the portion of a newspaper available for editorial matter (*Orlando Sentinel,* 2003).

19. (χ^2=150.36, p =.000, p<.001, d.f. 20).

20. χ^2=157.57, p =0.0142, p<.05, d.f. 120.

21. χ^2=61.14, p =.000, p<.001, d.f. 18.

22. Pete Wilson, *The New York Times,* January 24, 1994, p. A-14, cited in Welch et al., 1997, 484

23. Moral entrepreneurs are considered to be in the business of persuading society to make policy from particular moral viewpoints (Online Dictionary, 2001).

24. Mix-up leaves stab victim's kin in limbo. *The Toronto Sun,* June 11, 1996: News 4.

25. Dan Lewis, Criminologist, Northwestern University, *Los Angeles Times,* February 13, 1994, P. A-16, quoted in Welch et al, 1997, 491.

26. "Hallinana, youth rally against Prop. 21." Associate Press of California, 12/7/99, as cited in We Interrupt This Message, 2001, 16.

chapter eight

Police Decision-Making with Young Offenders: Arrest, Questioning, and Dispositions*

Peter J. Carrington

Department of Sociology
University of Waterloo

and

Jennifer L. Schulenberg

Department of Sociology
University of Waterloo

INTRODUCTION

Police are the gatekeepers of the youth justice system, since they have discretion to decide whether to deal informally with an apprehended young offender, whether to refer to a diversion program, or whether to lay a charge. The laying of a charge initiates court proceedings, which may result in a conviction and sentence and an official record; informal action precludes these outcomes. In this chapter, we examine three major aspects of police decision-making in relation to youth: the authority to arrest, search, and question; the decision whether to lay a charge; and the decision concerning the method to be used to compel the attendance of the youth in court if a charge is laid. We also discuss the factors that appear to influence police in their decision-making with apprehended youth.

---

*Preparation of this chapter was supported by Social Sciences and Humanities Research Council of Canada Standard Research Grant No. 410-2000-0361 and Doctoral Fellowship No. 752-2002-1071.

INITIAL CONTACT WITH THE POLICE

Police can become aware of youth crime as a result of either proactive or reactive policing. However, research has found that most police work is reactive; that is, the police respond, or react, to reports of crime or requests for help or service from the public or other agencies. Black and Reiss (1970) found that 72 percent of police encounters with youth resulted from requests by citizens. Webster (1970) found that fewer than 20 percent of encounters with suspects were a result of proactive police work, such as police-initiated patrols of crime "hot spots," traffic stops, stopping youth on the street, or other police-initiated investigations. More recent studies such as those by Cordner (1989) and Ericson (1982) found that approximately 50 percent of encounters were reactive, but a large proportion of the rest involved administrative work.

Thus, most youth crime is not detected by police working alone, or on their own initiative, but in response to a report by a member of the public. After receiving a report of an apparent crime, either in progress or completed, a police dispatcher will decide whether to send a patrol car. From here, the process of dealing with an incident can be broken down into five stages, or decision points (Klinger, 1996). The first stage is gathering initial information and making a decision as to whether further investigation is warranted; that is, deciding whether the incident involves a criminal violation (is founded or unfounded). In the second stage, investigation results in the identification of the offender(s), or "clearing" the incident. The third stage involves the choice of disposition for each apprehended offender. This can entail the police laying a charge (or referring a recommendation to the Crown to charge in some provinces), with or without a recommendation for post-charge extrajudicial sanctions;[1] referring the youth to a pre-charge extrajudicial measures program; or taking informal action. The next decision is whether to make a police (occurrence) report. If the suspect is charged or referred to extrajudicial sanctions, a report must always be completed. However, if an officer chooses to use informal measures to handle the incident, it is up to the officer's discretion or departmental policy whether a report is completed. Finally, if charges are (to be) laid, an officer makes a decision concerning the mode of compelling the youth's attendance at court: whether the youth is to be given an appearance notice, summonsed, or taken into custody (arrested); and, if arrested, whether to be released or held for a judicial interim release hearing (JIR).

ARREST, SEARCH, AND QUESTIONING OF YOUNG PERSONS

The legal authority of police to arrest, search, and question anyone, whether adult or youth, and the constraints on that authority, are set out primarily in the *Criminal Code*. The applicability of *Criminal Code* provisions to young persons is explicitly acknowledged in sec. 140 of the *Youth Criminal Justice Act*. The YCJA also contains provisions that modify the police authority to arrest and question in relation to young persons, due to their presumed level of maturity. In addition, the *Charter of Rights and Freedoms* contains provisions relevant to these police powers. In each of the following sections, we begin by reviewing the law as it applies to all persons, and then show how it is modified by the YCJA and/or case law developed under the *Young Offenders Act.*

Arrest

The term "arrest" is used repeatedly, but never defined, in the *Criminal Code*. Its meaning has become established by case law as the constraint of a person's freedom by physical coercion or the implication of possible coercion. The most obvious form of arrest occurs when an officer physically takes someone into his or her custody. However, an arrest also occurs if the officer, without using physical force, orders someone to stand still, or not to leave, or to get into the police car, and the subject believes that the officer would enforce the demand physically if necessary (Arcaro, 2003a, p. 16).

To *lay a charge* means to make a formal accusation of law-breaking against someone. To lay a charge, an officer completes a form called an *information,* takes it to a justice of the peace, and swears on oath that the information is accurate. A date is then set for the youth to appear in court to answer the charge; that is, to make a plea and possibly to undergo a trial. Arrest and the laying of charges are distinct and independent actions, but both require that the officer have reasonable grounds to believe that the youth has committed an offence. An officer may arrest a youth and then release him or her without laying a charge, and an officer may lay a charge without arresting the youth.

Freedom of movement is a fundamental right, so the authority of the police to suspend it by arrest is carefully defined and regulated by the *Criminal Code* (sections 493–525). Arrest may be with or without an arrest warrant. To arrest a person *with* a warrant, the officer must first lay a charge against the person before a justice of the peace or a judge. A warrant is issued to arrest the accused person by a judge or justice of the peace only if he or she is satisfied that it is in the public interest, and only if other less intrusive methods of apprehending the accused person would not be satisfactory (*Criminal Code*, sec. 507). Typical public-interest considerations that might require arrest are when the alleged offence is very serious, or when there is reason to believe that the accused might not appear in court unless held in custody, might interfere with evidence or witnesses, or might commit other crimes. Thus, before arresting with a warrant, an officer must persuade a judicial official that there are reasonable grounds to believe that the person has committed an offence and that arrest is the most appropriate means of apprehension (Mewett, 1996, p. 51).

Section 495(1) of the *Criminal Code* authorizes police officers to arrest *without* a warrant in certain circumstances:

- a person who he believes, on reasonable grounds, has committed or is about to commit an indictable offence;
- a person whom he finds committing a criminal offence; or
- a person who is the subject of an outstanding arrest warrant.

Thus, if the suspect is caught in the act ("found committing") by the officer while committing *any* criminal offence, arrest without a warrant is lawful. However, the first criterion applies only to the more serious (indictable) offences. Even in circumstances where arrest without a warrant is authorized by sec. 495(1), sec. 495(2) provides that the officer "shall not" arrest without a warrant in cases of many types of less serious offences unless the public interest requires it.

The police authority to arrest is further limited by certain provisions of the *Charter of Rights and Freedoms,* the applicability of which to young persons is explicitly noted in the Preamble to the YCJA. The sections of the *Charter* that are most directly relevant to the arrest of young persons (and adults) are:

(7) Everyone has the right to life, liberty and security of the person and the right not to be deprived thereof except in accordance with the principles of fundamental justice.

(9) Everyone has the right not to be arbitrarily detained or imprisoned.

(10) Everyone has the right on arrest or detention

a. to be informed promptly of the reason therefore;

b. to retain and instruct counsel without delay and to be informed of that right; and

c. to have the validity of the detention determined by way of *habeas corpus* and to be released if the detention is not lawful.

These *Charter* rights put considerable limits on the discretion that police may exercise with suspects or accused persons, whether youth or adults (Greenspan & Rosenberg, 2001, ch. 4–39).

The police authority to arrest applies in the same manner with young persons as it does with adults, but the YCJA creates an additional duty for police, and protection for youth, that does not apply to adults. When a young person is arrested, the police must notify a parent, orally or in writing, that the arrest has occurred, and state the reason for the arrest and the place of detention of the youth (YCJA, sec. 26). The YCJA also reiterates the *Charter* right of a young person (like an adult) who is arrested to retain and instruct a lawyer prior to making a statement, and to be given a reasonable and effective opportunity to obtain a lawyer (sec. 25). The young person must also be advised of the existence and availability of duty counsel, free preliminary legal advice, and legal aid in the jurisdiction (Tuck-Jackson, 2003, p. 2070). The right to counsel "belongs to the young person"—that is, the lawyer represents the young person, not the parents or guardian (Canada, Department of Justice, 2003).

Search

Like the arrest of a person, the search of a residence or person is considered such an intrusion upon fundamental rights that it is permissible only if it is explicitly authorized, and regulated, by law. This principle is stated in the *Charter of Rights and Freedoms*:

(8) Everyone has the right to be secure against unreasonable search or seizure.

The main statutory authority for police to search *dwelling places* is found in sec. 487 of the *Criminal Code*, which provides that police may search a "building, receptacle or place" if authorized to do so by a search warrant. As with the arrest warrant, the officer applies to a justice of the peace or judge for a search warrant after laying a charge, and the justice may issue the warrant only if there are reasonable grounds to believe that specified evidence relevant to the charge is present in the specified place(s). Thus, this form of warrant cannot be used for a "fishing expedition" or to obtain evidence that is needed to lay the charge, since it cannot be issued until *after* the charge is laid (Mewett, 1996, pp. 40–42).

Police may search a dwelling place without a search warrant under certain limited circumstances. A warrant-less search is permitted under common law when a police officer is doing so to protect him/herself or to prevent destruction of evidence (Mewett, 1996, p. 43). It is permitted under *Criminal Code* sec. 487.11, when the conditions to obtain a sec. 487 warrant (see above) are present, but it "would be impracticable to obtain a warrant" due to "exigent circumstances," such as the likelihood of the destruction of evidence; under *Criminal Code* sec. 117.04 when the officer has reasonable grounds to believe that a weapon is present in the place that presents an immediate danger to someone, and there is not time to obtain a warrant; and if an officer has reasonable grounds to believe that an illegal drug ("controlled substance") is present and there is not time to obtain a warrant (*Controlled Drugs and Substances Act*, sec. 11(7)).[2]

The search of a *person* is lawful in very few circumstances. Police may lawfully search persons for their own protection when making an arrest (e.g., to seize a concealed weapon) or when, in the course of a search of a place under sec. 11 of the *Controlled Drugs and Substances Act*, they have reasonable grounds to believe that an occupant has the named substance "on their person." However, search warrants may *not* authorize the search of a person, except under sec. 11 of the CDSA as noted

above, or when taking samples of hair, blood, or saliva for forensic DNA analysis under sec. 487.04 of the *Criminal Code*.

The YCJA does not modify the law of search in relation to young persons. However, case law under the YOA has interpreted the law of search in relation to the special circumstances of young persons. The Supreme Court has held that school officials are not subject to the same constraints as police officers and may make reasonable searches of students in furtherance of school rules and discipline. However, if the school official is acting to enforce criminal law, not school rules, or is acting on behalf of the police, then the official is subject to the same constraints as a police officer (Bala, 2003, pp. 195–199). The case law on the search of the room of a youth who is not "in control of" his or her dwelling place (e.g., because he or she is living in the parents' home) is somewhat contradictory: some decisions have held that consent of a parent is sufficient to authorize a police search without a warrant, while others have held that it is not (pp. 190–192).

Questioning

The law governing the questioning of suspects—whether youth or adults—is complex, but can be summarized as follows. A confession made to a person in a position of legal authority, such as a police officer, is inadmissible in court if

- it is not proven beyond a reasonable doubt by the Crown to be voluntary; or

- it was obtained in a manner that denied or infringed on any of the rights or freedoms specified in the *Charter of Rights and Freedoms,* and its admission would bring the administration of justice into disrepute (Arcaro, 2003b).

The issue of the "voluntariness" of a statement is especially significant in respect to young persons. According to Bala (2003), young persons "may lack the sophistication and maturity" to understand and exercise their legal rights or to understand the roles of legal professionals (pp. 210–216). Thus, they may be more open to the influence of authority figures such as police officers and make false confessions under police questioning. In recognition of the vulnerability of young persons to police questioning, sec. 146 of the YCJA provides that no oral or written statement made by a young person is admissible in court unless the following conditions are met:

- Before the statement was made, the person in authority explained that

  - the young person had the right to remain silent

  - the statement may be used in evidence against the young person

  - the young person has the right to consult counsel and a parent, and

  - the statement must be made in the presence of counsel or other person consulted by the young person

- Before the statement was made, the young person was provided with a reasonable opportunity to consult with counsel or other person chosen by the youth

- If the young person consulted counsel or another person, that the young person was given the opportunity to make

the statement in that person's presence (Canada, Department of Justice, 2003).

Furthermore, these cautions must be given in "language clearly appropriate to his or her age and understanding" (YCJA, sec. 146(2)(b)). These provisions provide young persons with several protections that adults do not have: they must be informed of their right to silence, they must not be questioned in the absence of counsel (or other adviser), and they must be informed of their rights in appropriate language. Nevertheless, according to Bala (2003), young persons are more likely than adults to make confessions, and the admissibility of their statements is "one of the issues most likely to be litigated" at trial (p. 203).

Although these provisions of the YCJA, in addition to the safeguards contained in the *Charter,* the *Criminal Code,* and case law, appear to provide strong protection to young persons when questioned by police, there are two additional provisions of the YCJA that may undercut their effectiveness (Tustin & Lutes, 2003, p. 194). First, a young person may waive his or her right to counsel or advice from another person. This waiver must be videotaped, audio-taped, or "must be in writing and contain a statement signed by the young person that he or she has been informed of the right being waived" (YCJA sec. 146(4)). Second, a judge may admit a statement where there has been a "technical irregularity" in cautioning a young person, if the judge is satisfied that the "admission of the statement would not bring into disrepute the principle that young persons are entitled to enhanced procedural protection to ensure that they are treated fairly and their rights are protected" (YCJA, sec. 146(6)).

POLICE DISPOSITIONS FOR YOUNG OFFENDERS

The YCJA provides several options for police to deal with a young person who they believe on reasonable grounds has committed a criminal offence. These possible dispositions fall into three categories: informal action, diversion to a program, and laying a charge. The following discussion of police dispositions and the factors affecting the decision to charge summarizes the existing literature and also integrates new findings by the authors (Carrington & Schulenberg, 2003). In 2002, the authors carried out more than 200 interviews with more than 300 police officers in 95 police services across Canada, in order to learn more about their exercise of discretion with young offenders.[3] The sample was representative of all types of police services in Canada and included those in all of the largest cities, and many in the smallest towns and the most remote rural areas of the country. The various factors are reviewed in the order of importance that our interviewees assigned to them.

Informal Action

When police decide not to lay (or recommend) a charge, or to recommend diversion to a program, they have a choice among several kinds of informal action. Under the *Youth Criminal Justice Act*, these informal actions are called "extrajudicial measures": that is, measures applied outside the court, or judicial, process. Police may give an informal or formal warning, involve the parents and/or social services, arrest and question the youth at the police station and release him or her, make an informal referral to a community-based intervention program, or simply take no action, except possibly to file an occurrence report (Bala et al., 1994).

Officers in 78 percent of the police services in our sample indicated that they would usually or always consider using informal action with young persons. The least intrusive kind of informal action is the informal warning, which generally involves a police officer discussing the young person's behaviour with him or her and the parents, warning them that further law-breaking will result in formal action. Whether this informal warning is recorded varies considerably. A "formal" warning, as the phrase was used by our respondents, and used by 32 percent of them, involves not only the warning being issued but also a record being kept of the warning. The nature of the formal warning varies considerably and ranges from a warning letter signed by youth and parents to the Crown issuing a caution letter to notations in the police information system.

Diversion to a Program

Rather than using informal action or laying (or recommending) charges, police may choose to refer or to recommend diversion of the youth to a program.[4] Typically, diversion is considered appropriate for less serious offences and first-time offenders. The eligibility criteria for diversion are set by provincial authorities, and vary from province to province (Kowalski, 1999). Diversion may take place without the officer laying a charge ("precharge" diversion), or the officer may lay a charge but recommend to the Crown that the youth be considered for diversion ("post-charge" diversion).

Officers in 99 percent of the police agencies in our sample said that they use or recommend either pre- or post-charge diversion for youth. Just under one-half (48%) of the police agencies we spoke to indicated that they used some form of pre-charge diversion with youth-related incidents. Police forces in our sample referred to several different types of diversion programs, including police-run pre-charge programs (4%); external non-governmental organizations, such as the John Howard Society (15%); government ministry programs (9%); community-based restorative justice forums (25%); and community-based restorative justice conferences (12%). Almost all (91%) of the police in our sample indicated that youths could also be diverted post-charge to alternative measures in their jurisdiction.[5] By far the greatest source of dissatisfaction with diversion programs, for our interviewees, was their unavailability. In many communities, the range of programs is inadequate; in many others, there are no programs at all.

Factors Affecting the Decision to Charge

The literature on factors affecting police decision-making with youth is voluminous.[6] Researchers have observed police–suspect encounters, interviewed police officers (and, occasionally, youth), and analyzed arrest and charge statistics. Possible influences on police decisions fall into two groups: the nature and circumstances of the incident and characteristics of the young person. Examples of the nature and circumstances of the incident include the seriousness of the (alleged) offence,

whether there was a victim and if the victim expressed a preference as to the disposition of the incident, and whether the young person acted alone or in a group. Characteristics of the offender include, among others, the history of prior contacts with the police or prior court convictions and his or her age, gender, and race.

In our research, we presented officers with a list of factors that have been identified in the literature and asked them to indicate for each whether it was a major factor, a factor, a minor factor, or not a factor in their decisions to charge a youth, to take informal action, or to divert him or her. We also used statistical data from the Incident-based Uniform Crime Reporting Survey (UCR2),[7] provided by the Canadian Centre for Justice Statistics, on 38 727 youths apprehended by police in 2001. These data indicated whether the youth was charged and various characteristics of the youth and of the offence. We analyzed these data statistically to determine the relative weight of these characteristics in the decision to charge. The factors that we analyzed, using interview data and/or statistical data, are discussed below, in the order of the importance our interviewees assigned to them.

Seriousness of the Offence There is a consensus in the literature on police discretion that the seriousness of the (alleged) offence is the most important factor affecting the exercise of police discretion with youth (Black & Reiss, 1970; Carrington, 1998; Doob, 1983; Doob & Chan, 1982; Fisher & Mawby, 1982; Gaines et al., 1994; Krisberg & Austin, 1978; Landau, 1981; Lundman et al., 1978; Piliavin & Briar, 1964; Terry, 1967;

Werthman & Piliavin, 1967). As the seriousness of the offence increases, the likelihood of the exercise of discretion tends to decrease. Police officers appear to agree that many youth involved in minor crimes should be dealt with informally or referred to a pre-charge diversion program (Caputo & Kelly, 1997). However, police perceptions of "minor" and "major" crime may vary across police services and among individual officers. Apart from the *Criminal Code* classification of the offence, police perceptions of the seriousness of an offence have been found to be related to the use or presence of a weapon and the degree of harm done, whether to the person or property of a victim. The presence of a weapon in a violent incident usually results in the incident being classified as involving an indictable, rather than a (less serious) summary or hybrid, offence.

We asked officers whether the seriousness of the offence, the presence or use of a weapon, and the extent of harm done to person or property play a role in their use of discretion with young persons. Our respondents answered almost unanimously (98%) that they take the seriousness of the offence into account every time they deal with a youth-related incident, and it is usually the first factor they consider in their decision-making. In some cases, *all* other factors are considered secondary to the seriousness of the offence. They were also virtually unanimous that the presence of a weapon in the commission of the crime was taken very seriously and had a major effect on their decision-making with young persons. The extent of harm done to person or property also has a substantial effect on police decision-making with youth-related incidents. All of

our respondents indicated that they feel the extent of harm done is a major factor (88%) or a factor (12%) in their decision to charge, divert, or proceed with informal action. The more harm that is done, either physically or psychologically, the less likely officers are to divert to a program or deal with the incident informally.

Statistical data confirm the importance of the seriousness of the offence in police decision-making. Table 8.1 shows that low proportions of youth apprehended for minor crimes are charged (e.g., 38% of cases of property damage/mischief, 52% of common [minor] assaults), whereas high proportions are charged in serious cases (e.g., 87% of robberies). However, there are exceptions to the general pattern. Most people would consider sexual assault to be a major crime, but only 68 percent of youth apprehended for sexual assault were charged. Administrative offences, such as failure to attend court or breach of conditions of bail or probation, are non-violent and cause no harm (other than expense and inconvenience to court officials), but they are subject to charges in higher proportions than any other offence except murder and attempted murder.

Statistical data from the UCR2 Survey for 2001 also confirm the importance of weapons and of harm done as factors in police decision-making. Police laid a charge in 84 percent of cases of offences against the person in which a firearm was involved (which were rare), in 64 percent of cases involving another type of weapon, and in only 47 percent of cases where no weapon was present. In cases involving an offence against the person that resulted in major injury or death to a victim, police laid a charge against 89 percent of the ac-

TABLE 8.1	Proportion of Apprehended Youth Charged, by Offence, Canada, 2000

Offence category	Percentage charged %
Homicide and related	100
Attempted murder	100
Offences against the administration of justice	96
Kidnapping	95
Robbery	87
Possession stolen property	84
Abduction	80
Criminal Code traffic	80
Major assault	79
Traffic/import drugs	77
Other federal statutes (primarily YOA)	76
Impaired driving	76
Break and enter	71
Sexual assault	68
Fraud and related	65
Weapons and explosives	62
Sexual abuse	55
Other *Criminal Code* offences	54
Theft	53
Common assault	52
Possession of drugs	47
Morals–sexual	46
Arson	45
Morals–gaming/betting	40
Property damage/mischief	38
Public order offences	29
Total violent crimes	63
Total property crimes	56
Total other crimes	64
Total *Criminal Code*	59

Source: Canadian Centre for Justice Statistics, Uniform Crime Reporting Survey. Data in electronic format licensed to the University of Waterloo Library.

cused youth; in cases involving minor injury or no injury, a charge was laid against 61 percent of apprehended youth.

Prior Contacts with the Police A record of prior convictions or prior contacts with the police has been found by many researchers to be strongly associated with the likelihood of being charged (Cicourel, 1968; Cohen & Kluegel, 1978; Conly, 1978; Doob, 1983; Doob & Chan, 1982; Ericson, 1982; Fisher & Mawby, 1982; Landau, 1981; Lattimore et al., 1995; Morash, 1984; Piliavin & Briar, 1964; Terry, 1967). Whether or not it led to charges or a conviction, contact with police labels a youth as a likely delinquent, increasing the probability of formal treatment on subsequent contact. Doob & Chan's (1982) statistical analysis of police dispositions found that prior contacts was one of the strongest, if not *the* strongest, correlate of the decision to charge.

In our study we asked respondents to consider the effects on their decision-making with apprehended youth of prior contacts with police, prior referrals to alternative measures, prior charges, and prior convictions. However, none was inclined to differentiate among these. Almost all (96%) of our respondents said that prior record (in any and all forms) is a major factor (87%) or a factor (9%) in their decision-making process with youth-related incidents. Officers repeatedly emphasized that they consider a youth's prior record as important as the seriousness of the offence. They consider both of these factors together, and invariably they are the first and principal factors that officers say they take into consideration. Statistical data from the UCR2 Survey for 2001 support these claims. Only 40 percent of apprehended youth with no prior contacts with police were charged, compared with 59 percent of youth with one prior contact, 69 percent of those with two prior contacts, 76 percent of those with three or four contacts, and 85 percent of those with five or more prior contacts.

Demeanour Previous research in the United States and Britain has found that the demeanour of the apprehended youth is an important influence on how an officer deals with a youth. An officer is more likely to arrest a juvenile suspect who is hostile, uncooperative, or disrespectful—partly because of the necessity of establishing and maintaining control of the situation in the street; partly because officers and young people, especially males,

place great weight on maintaining "respect"; and partly because in many cases the officer depends on the cooperation of the suspect to learn what happened and what the suspect's role was. On the other hand, some researchers have found that "unusually respectful" juvenile suspects are also more likely to be arrested, as their demeanour invites suspicion (Black & Reiss, 1970; Lundman, 1994, 1996a, 1996b). Piliavin & Briar (1964) found that demeanour was the *most* important factor in police discretion with juveniles, and Fisher and Mawby's (1982) research in Britain found that an attitude of remorse, or lack thereof, was the most important factor in police decisions regarding cautioning of 10- to 13-year-olds. Doob (1983) found that police dispositions of cases coming to the youth bureau of an Ontario police force were significantly affected by the youth's attitude and "action he took when he came in contact with the police"; for example, whether he or she admitted the offence (p. 161; see also Doob & Chan, 1982).

Almost three-quarters (71%) of the respondents in our study consider the demeanour of the young person to be a factor or a major factor in decision-making. The majority of respondents indicated they have no choice but to take the demeanour of the young person into account in order to make a referral to alternative measures (AM). A young person must take responsibility for his or her actions in order to qualify for AM, and many officers indicated that those with a "bad attitude" tend to deny their involvement in the crime. However, the notion that young people should accept responsibility for their actions, and preferably feel some remorse, was linked by officers not just to eligibility for AM but also to the intent of the *Young Offenders Act,* which is that young persons should be held responsible for their actions.[8] Thus, if the apprehended youth showed that he or she held himself or herself responsible, this made intervention by the police or courts less necessary, in the eyes of some of our respondents.

The Victim's Preference Black & Reiss's (1970) analysis of police–suspect encounters found that if there is a victim present, and he or she expresses a preference, the officer will take it very seriously (see also Ericson, 1982; Hohenstein, 1969; Lundman et al., 1978; Smith & Visher, 1981). Doob's research (1983) is ambivalent concerning the impact of the victim's preference: on the one hand, "victims seemed to have an important part in the process of bringing the juvenile to the attention of the Youth Bureau and perhaps in the disposition finally decided on by the bureau," and the victim's request was found by multiple regression analysis to be a significant correlate of the disposition (pp. 159–161). On the other hand, "the police were polite in dealing with [victims], but explained that the decision on appropriate disposition was one that they alone would make…. The victim does not play an important part *because* of the nature of the decision process" (pp. 160–161; emphasis in the original).

In our study, 56 percent of respondents said that victim preference was a factor or major factor in decision-making. However, according to many officers, difficulties arise when a victim would like a young person charged for a relatively minor offence, but the officer feels that using informal action or alternative measures would be much more appropriate, given the nature of the offence and the characteristics of the young person. The majority of officers who rated victim preference as only a minor factor cited their belief that they must balance the rights of the victim with the best course of action for the administration of justice and for the young person.

The Youth's Home and School Situation and Parental Involvement There is very little research on the role of parents in police decision-making. According to Bynum and Thompson (2002), "When parents can be easily contacted by the police and show an active interest in their children and an apparent willingness to cooperate with the police, the likelihood [of informal treatment] is much greater" (p. 374; see also Conly, 1978, Goldman, 1963). On the other hand, if the youth appears to lack responsible adult supervision, he or she is seen as a poor candidate for informal action. Doob (1983) found that when a parent was the victim or complainant, the youth was more likely to be charged, because the complaint to police was seen as an indicator that "one traditional socialization agent, the family, had failed" (pp. 158–160).

In our interviews, slightly less than half (42%) of the respondents indicated that they consider a young person's home and school environments to be a factor or major factor in their decision-making. These officers generally understood questions concerning parental involvement to refer to "positive" involvement—that is, to the level of interest exhibited in the proceedings and the level of support provided to the youth, although some officers volunteered that "the parents can be worse to deal with than the young person." Many officers indicated that they are more willing to use alternative measures (diversion) if "the parents are on board." Further, these officers were much more likely to release a young person on an appearance notice or summons when they felt there were high levels of parental involvement. If the offence was more serious, then instead of holding the young person for a judicial interim release ("bail") hearing, they would release the young person on a promise to appear (see "Compelling Attendance" below).

However, there were a few examples given in which the converse had a negative effect on police decision-making. If a youth was arrested and the parents (1) wanted nothing to do with the young person, (2) minimized the seriousness of the situation, or (3) denied that their son or daughter could have committed the crime, officers were more likely to lay a charge and, if the circumstances warranted, release on stringent conditions or hold in detention until a judicial interim release hearing.

Gang-related Crime/Gang-affiliated Youth

Youth gangs and crimes committed by youth are currently a subject of much concern for the public and police. However, we could find no research on the impact of gang-related crime on police decision-making. Among our respondents, 39 percent said that whether the crime was gang-related was a factor or major factor in their decision-making. Officers' views on this subject were, not surprisingly, related to the prevalence of youth gangs in their community: 78 percent of officers who felt that there was a problem with youth gangs in their community identified gang-related crime as a factor or major factor in their decision-making, compared with only 21 percent of officers in communities with no perceived gang problem.

Youth who perceive themselves, or are perceived by police, to be gang members may behave differently and be treated differently by police when they are apprehended. Involvement in a delinquent peer group or "youth gang" may result in elevated risk of both victimization and commission of crime (Hornick et al., 1996). Those youths who are male and belong to a predominantly male delinquent peer group have a much higher chance of arrest (Morash, 1984). Only 22 percent of our respondents said that they would consider a youth's gang affiliation to be a factor (21%) or a major factor (1%) in their decision-making. As with gang-related crime, officers in communities with a perceived youth gang problem were much more likely to take gang affiliation into account.

The Youth's Age

Previous research has found that police tend to treat younger juveniles more leniently than older juveniles: younger youth are seen as immature and out to test limits; older youth may be virtually indistinguishable from adult offenders (Carrington, 1996, 1998; Conly, 1978; Ericson, 1982; Fisher & Mawby, 1982; Goldman, 1963; Hornick et al., 1996; Landau, 1981; McEachern & Bauzer, 1967; Morash, 1984; Terry, 1967). Only a small percentage of our respondents (27%) considered the age of the youth to be a factor or major factor in their decision-making. Statistical data from the UCR2 Survey for

2001 show that only 28 percent of apprehended 12-year-olds were charged, compared with 52 percent of 15-year-olds, and 65 percent of 17-year-olds.

Race While many American and British researchers have found that a youth's race has an impact on police decision-making (e.g., Goldman, 1963; Krisberg & Austin, 1993; Landau, 1981; Lundman, 1996a; Piliavin & Briar, 1964; Smith & Visher, 1981), Canadian research on this subject is inconclusive. While it is well-established that Aboriginal Canadians, for example, are overrepresented in the criminal and juvenile justice systems, researchers have been unable to disentangle the various related factors and processes that contribute

to this overrepresentation. None of the officers whom we interviewed felt that the race of the suspect was a factor in their decisions or those of their colleagues.

Other Factors Other factors that have been identified as influences on police decision-making—such as whether the crime was committed by a lone offender or a group, the location and time of day, whether the youth was intoxicated, any relationship between the youth and victim, whether an adult co-offender was involved, whether the victim was a person or business, and the gender of the young person—were also found to play little or no role in their decision-making, according to our respondents (Table 8.2).

TABLE 8.2	Overall Ranking of Factors Affecting Police Decision-making with Youth	
Factor		Percentage of interviewees who identified it as "a major factor" or "a factor" %
The seriousness of the offence		100
The amount of harm done		100
Whether or not a weapon was involved		98
The youth's history of prior contacts with police		97
The youth's demeanour		71
The victim's preference		56
The level and nature of parental involvement		48
The youth's home and/or school situation		42
Whether the crime was gang-related		39
The youth's age		28
Whether the youth was a gang member		22
Whether the crime was committed by one or more persons		14
The location or time of day of the crime		13
Whether the youth was under the influence of alcohol or drugs		11
Any relationship between the youth and the victim(s)		10
Whether there was an adult co-offender		9
Whether the victim was a person or a business		3
The gender of the youth		1
The race of the youth		0

Source: Interviews conducted by the authors.

COMPELLING ATTENDANCE AT COURT

If police have laid a charge, or intend to lay a charge, against a youth (or adult), then the accused person must appear in court to answer the charge. There are various methods available to police to require or compel the youth's attendance in court. They are governed by Part XVI (sec. 493 to 529) of the *Criminal Code,* which applies equally to youth and adults. The surest method is to detain the youth; that is, lock him or her up in a secure facility prior to the court date. Youth (and adults) who are detained by police must be brought before a judge or justice of the peace, normally within 24 hours of being detained, for a judicial interim release hearing, commonly called a bail hearing. The judge or justice of the peace will decide whether there is justification to detain the youth until his or her court appearance, whether he or she should be released, and whether to apply conditions on the release. Other methods of compelling appearance in court all rely on the youth to appear voluntarily; that is, there is no physical compulsion. These other methods include the appearance notice, the summons, and the promise to appear.

Summons and Appearance Notice

The summons and appearance notices are forms that specify the alleged offence and the date and place of the court hearing of the charge(s) and are the only methods of compelling appearance that do not require arresting the young person and bringing him or her back to the police station. Therefore, their use would appear to be particularly appropriate with young persons, consistent with the principle of the YCJA of "least possible interference with freedom." However, they are rarely used in Canada with young offenders. Officers in 62 percent of the police services in our study said they never use summonses with young persons, and those in 63 percent of the police services said that appearance notices are rarely used or used only for very minor offences.

Release on a Promise to Appear

Many police agencies rely on a form called a *promise to appear* (PTA) to compel the attendance at court of young persons who have been arrested and taken to the police station. As its name implies, by signing this form the youth promises to appear at the specified court hearing. Officers in 60 percent of police agencies interviewed said that they release on a PTA whenever they have taken a youth into custody temporarily but continued detention is unnecessary. A major reason for this is the use of a PTA in conjunction with an *officer in charge* (OIC) *undertaking* (discussed below), which specifies conditions of release on the accused, and which cannot be used with release on a summons or appearance notice. By signing it, the youth "undertakes" to obey the conditions. Breach of any of the conditions is a *Criminal Code* offence ("failure to comply with conditions").

Various conditions may accompany an undertaking. The *no go* condition prohibits a youth from going to a certain place or area (e.g., schools, neighbourhoods, or shopping malls). The *no association* condition prohibits the youth from coming in contact with certain specified individuals. The meaning of the condition *keep the peace and be of good behaviour* was somewhat unclear to many of our interviewees. Certainly if the youth committed another crime, he or she would be in breach of this condition. However, youths who did not go to school or obey their parents might also be considered to be in breach of this clause. The *no alcohol or drugs* condition is meant to control a young person's substance abuse and is commonly attached when the young person committed the crime under the influence of either alcohol or drugs. The condition prohibiting *possession of a weapon* is used rarely with youth and is much more common with adults. A *curfew* condition is usually set with specific starting and stopping times, such as dawn to dusk or 7:00 p.m. to 7:00 a.m.

Detention for a Judicial Interim Release Hearing

The final, and most intrusive, option for compelling appearance is detention for a *judicial interim release* (JIR) hearing, also known as a bail hearing. This is a hearing before a justice of the peace or a judge to determine whether the youth should be held in detention or released until his or her first appearance in court. In considering whether detention of a youth (or adult) is appropriate, the *Criminal Code* requires the police officer to assess whether detention is required to

   (i) establish the identity of the person,
   (ii) secure or preserve evidence of or relating to the offence,
   (iii) prevent the continuation or repetition of the offence or the commission of another offence,
   or because the officer has reason to believe...
   (b) that, if the person is released from custody, the person will fail to attend court....

According to Bala et al. (1994), in making this assessment the police typically consider the personal history of the accused (any prior breaches of release conditions or failures to appear for court, education, family, and employment), the circumstances of the specific charge, and the victim's reaction.

When we asked police officers why they held youth in detention rather than releasing them, 82 percent of the officers interviewed said that they *follow the law* when determining whether a young person will be detained or released. They tended to characterize the decision to detain or release as relatively non-discretionary, determined by the provisions of the *Criminal Code*. Officers were more likely to detain youth who were repeat offenders (46%); if there was a record of *multiple breaches* (36%) including breaches of probation, undertakings, or bail conditions; or in cases where a youth had committed an offence while on release in connection with another offence (26%). Other considerations included detaining youth for their "best interests" (20%), where no responsible adult or social services could take custody of the youth, to remove them from prostitution (3%), detaining them because of their attitude (3%), if they were intoxicated or under the influence of drugs (24%), or if the incident they were charged with was gang-related (6%).

The reasons given by police officers for detaining youth appear to fall into three broad categories. The first includes reasons related to law enforcement and crime detection, narrowly defined—for example, protection of the public, to ensure the youth would appear in court, and to protect evidence. The second group of reasons could be summarized as "detention for the good of the youth." These include detaining youth who are intoxicated, who do not have a safe or secure home to be released to and whom social services will not or cannot accommodate, or who are prostitutes. In these circumstances, police find themselves acting not as law enforcement officials, but as staff of the "only 24-hour emergency service in town." The third type of rationale treats detention as another kind of police disposition—that is, as another in the repertoire of measures police can take in order to administer a sanction or "meaningful consequence" for a youth's illegal behaviour.

CONCLUSION

In dealing with young persons who are believed to have committed criminal offences, police have certain objectives and powers and work within certain constraints. Their main objective is to enforce the law: to investigate the incident, identify and apprehend the perpetrator(s), and assemble the necessary evidence if there is to be a prosecution. However, they sometimes have subsidiary objectives: to deliver an appropriate sanction, or "consequence," semi-independently of the courts and correctional system; or to address the perceived needs of the youth—whether these needs are directly related to the crime, or are seen as problems with which the youth needs assistance.

To achieve these objectives, police draw on a range of legal powers, but their exercise of these powers is limited by law. Their authority to arrest and question suspects and to conduct searches for evidence is broad, yet carefully circumscribed by statutes and case law—and, above all, by the requirement in most cases to obtain judicial approval in advance, in the form of warrants. Their ability to obtain statements from apprehended youth is severely limited by the numerous protections that have been legislated to protect all persons, but especially young persons, from making confessions that are not truly voluntary.

One area in which police have a great deal of discretion is the decision concerning the disposition of an apprehended young offender. Police may initiate formal court action by laying a charge, or they may choose not to proceed formally but rather to use informal action or divert the youth to a program—that is, to use "extrajudicial measures," in the language of the YCJA. The YCJA encourages police to use extrajudicial measures wherever possible, but does not require any particular disposition in any particular circumstances.

Research on the factors affecting police discretion has found that the main factors police take into account are the seriousness of the offence, including the amount of harm and the use of a weapon; any history of prior contacts with the police; the youth's demeanour when confronted by the police; and any preference stated by the victim of the crime. Other less important but substantial factors include the youth's home and school situations and the level of parental involvement, whether the crime was gang-related or the youth was affiliated with a gang, and the youth's age.

If police charge a young person with an offence, they must decide how to compel his or her attendance at court. The surest method is to hold the youth in detention, but this is discouraged by the *Criminal Code* and the YCJA since it represents a very serious infringement on the liberty of a person who is presumed innocent. Alternatives to pretrial detention include the summons, the appearance notice, and the promise to appear, which is often accompanied by an undertaking to abide by certain conditions (often called "bail conditions"). As with the decision whether to charge, officers' reasons for choosing a method of compelling attendance at court appear to include traditional law enforcement considerations, as well as a desire to impose an appropriate sanction, and reflect concern for the young person's welfare.

References

Arcaro, G. (2003a). *Basic police powers: Arrest and search procedures* (3rd ed.). Toronto: Nelson.

Arcaro, G. (2003b). *Criminal investigation: Forming reasonable grounds* (4th ed.). Toronto: Nelson.

Bala, N. (2003). *Youth criminal justice law*. Toronto: Irwin Law.

Bala, N., Weiler, R., Copple, P., Smith, R. B., Hornick, J. P., & Paetsch, J. J. (1994). *A police reference manual on youth and violence*. Ottawa: Canadian Research Institute for Law and the Family and the Solicitor General of Canada.

Black, D., & Reiss, A. J. Jr. (1970). Police control of juveniles. *American Sociological Review 35*, 63–77.

Bynum, J. E., & Thompson, W. E. (2002). *Juvenile delinquency: A sociological approach* (5th ed.). Boston: Allyn & Bacon.

Canada. Department of Justice. (2003). *YCJA explained*. Accessed on January 24, 2004 at http://canada.justice.gc.ca/en/ps/yj/repository/index.html.

Canadian Centre for Justice Statistics. (2003). *Canadian crime statistics 2002*. Catalogue No. 85-205. Ottawa: Canadian Centre for Justice Statistics, Statistics Canada.

Caputo, T., & Kelly, K. (1997). *Police perceptions of current responses to youth crime*. Catalogue No. JS4-1/1997-3. Ottawa: Ministry of the Solicitor General of Canada.

Carrington, P. J. (1996). *Age and youth crime in Canada*. Working Document No. 1996-1e. 2 vols. Ottawa: Department of Justice Canada.

Carrington, P. J. (1998). Factors affecting police diversion of young offenders: A statistical analysis. Ottawa: Solicitor General of Canada.

Carrington, P. J., & Schulenberg, J. L., with Brunelle, A., Jacob, J., & Pickles, I. (2003). *Police discretion with young offenders*. Ottawa: Department of Justice Canada.

Cicourel, A. V. (1968). *The social organization of juvenile justice*. New York: John Wiley & Sons, Inc.

Cohen, L. E., & J. R. Kluegel. (1978). Determinants of juvenile court dispositions: Ascriptive and achieved factors in two metropolitan courts. *American Sociological Review 43*, 162–176.

Conly, D. (1978). Patterns of delinquency and police action in the major metropolitan areas of Canada, during the month of December, 1976. Ottawa: Ministry of the Solicitor General.

Cordner, G. W. (1989). The police on patrol. In D. J. Kenny (Ed.), *Police and policing*. New York: Praeger Publishers.

Doob, A. N. (1983). Turning decisions into nondecisions. In R. R. Corrado, M. LeBlanc, & J. Trépanier (Eds.), *Current issues in juvenile justice*. Toronto: Butterworths.

Doob, A. N., & Chan, J. B. L. (1982). Factors affecting police decisions to take juveniles to court. *Canadian Journal of Criminology, 24*, 25–37.

Ericson, R. V. (1982). *Reproducing order: A study of police patrol work*. Toronto: University of Toronto Press.

Fisher, C. J., & Mawby, R. I. (1982). Juvenile delinquency and police discretion in an inner city area. *British Journal of Criminology 22*(1), 63–75.

Gaines, L. K., Kappeler, V. E., & Vaughn, J. B. (1994). *Policing in America.* Cincinnati, OH: Anderson.

Goldman, N. (1963). *The differential selection of juvenile offenders for court appearance.* New York: National Research and Information Center, National Council on Crime and Delinquency.

Greenspan, E. L., & Rosenberg, M. (2001). *Martin's annual Criminal Code 2001.* Aurora, ON: Canada Law Book.

Hohenstein, W. F. (1969). Factors influencing the police disposition of juvenile offenders. In T. Sellin & M. E. Wolfgang (Eds.), *Delinquency: Selected studies.* New York: Wiley.

Hornick, J. P., Caputo, T., Hastings, R., Knoll, P. J., Bertrand, L. D., Paetsch, J. J., Stroeder, L., & Maguire, A. O. (1996). *A police reference manual on crime prevention and diversion with youth.* Catalogue No. JS42-75/1996E. Ottawa: Canadian Research Institute of Law and the Family and the Solicitor General Canada.

Klinger, D. A. (1996). Quantifying law in police–citizen encounters. *Journal of Quantitative Criminology 12*(4), 391–415.

Kowalski, M. (1999). Alternative measures for youth in Canada. *Juristat 19*(8). Ottawa: Canadian Centre for Justice Statistics, Statistics Canada. Catalogue No. 85-002.

Krisberg, G., & Austin, J. (1978). The children of Ishmael: Critical perspectives on juvenile justice. Palo Alto, CA: Mayfield.

Krisberg, G., & Austin, J. (1993). *Reinventing juvenile justice.* Newbury Park, CA: Sage.

Landau, S. F. (1981). Juveniles and the police. *British Journal of Criminology 21*(1), 27–46.

Lattimore, P. K., Visher, C. A., & Linster, R. L. (1995). Predicting rearrest for violence among serious youthful offenders. *Journal of Research in Crime and Delinquency 32,* 54–83.

Lundman, R. J. (1994). Demeanor or crime? The Midwest City police–citizen encounters study. *Criminology 32,* 631–653.

Lundman, R. J. (1996a). Demeanor and arrest: Additional evidence from previously unpublished data. *Journal of Research in Crime and Delinquency 33*(3), 306–323.

Lundman, R. J. (1996b). Extralegal variables and arrest. *Journal of Research in Crime and Delinquency 33*(3), 349–353.

Lundman, R. J., Sykes, R. E., & Clark, J. P. (1978). Police control of juveniles: A replication. *Journal of Research in Crime and Delinquency 15*(1), 74–91.

McEachern, A. W., & Bauzer, R. (1967). Factors related to dispositions in juvenile police encounters. In M. W. Kline (Ed.), *Juvenile gangs in context: Theory, research and action.* Englewood Cliffs, NJ: Prentice-Hall.

Mewett, A. (1996). *An introduction to the criminal process in Canada* (3rd ed.). Toronto: Carswell.

Morash, M. (1984). Establishment of a juvenile police record. *Criminology 22*(1), 97–111.

Piliavin, I., & Briar, S. (1964, Sept.). Police encounters with juveniles. *American Journal of Sociology 70,* 206–214.

Smith, D. A., & Visher, C. A. (1981). Street-level justice: Situational determinants of police arrest decision. *Social Problems 29*(2), 167–177.

Terry, R. M. (1967). Discrimination in the handling of juvenile offenders by social control agencies. *Journal of Research in Crime and Delinquency 4,* 218–230.

Tuck-Jackson, A. (Ed.). (2003). *Annotated Youth Criminal Justice Act service.* Markham, ON: LexisNexis.

Tustin, L., & Lutes, R. E. (2003). *A guide to the Youth Criminal Justice Act.* 2004 ed. Toronto: Butterworths.

Webster, J. (1970). Police task and time study. *Journal of Criminal Law, Criminology, and Police Science 61,* 94–100.

Werthman, C., & Piliavin, I. (1967). Gang members and the police. In Bordua, D. J. (Ed.), *The police: Six sociological essays*. New York: John Wiley and Sons, Inc.

Whitehead, J. T., & Lab, S. P. (1999). *Juvenile justice: An introduction* (3rd ed.). Cincinnati, OH: Anderson.

Notes

1. Extrajudicial measures and sanctions under the *Youth Criminal Justice Act* are discussed in the following chapter.

2. Places other than dwellings, such as cars and business premises, are also protected against unauthorized entry by police, but "there are so many exceptions … that the same measure of protection by no means applies" (Mewett, 1996, p. 44).

3. Most of the interviews were conducted and analyzed by Schulenberg as part of her doctoral dissertation at the University of Waterloo.

4. Diversion to programs is discussed in detail in the following chapter.

5. At the time of the interviews, youth crime was governed in Canada by the *Young Offenders Act* (YOA), which was replaced in April, 2003 by the *Youth Criminal Justice Act* (YCJA). Diversion programs could be designated by provincial authorities as official alternative measures programs under the YOA if they met certain criteria. Alternative measures programs have been renamed *extrajudicial sanctions* programs under the YCJA.

6. See Bynum and Thompson (2002, pp. 366–375) and Whitehead and Lab (1999, pp. 190–194) for recent reviews of the American literature, which deals primarily with the decision whether to arrest or not to charge.

7. For more information on the Uniform Crime Reporting Survey (UCR) and the Incident-based Uniform Crime Reporting Survey (UCR2), see Canadian Centre for Justice Statistics, 2003.

8. These considerations are similar to those found under the new *Youth Criminal Justice Act*, which has changed alternative measures to extrajudicial sanctions.

chapter nine

Community-Based Responses to Youth Crime: Cautioning, Conferencing, and Extrajudicial Measures

*Nicholas Bala**

Faculty of Law
Queen's University

INTRODUCTION

Community-based, informal measures have long been available for dealing with less serious youthful offending. For a variety of reasons, in the 1990s in Canada there was a trend to make greater use of a formal court-based response to youth crime. The *Youth Criminal Justice Act,* which came into force in 2003, encouraged greater use of a range of informal community-based responses to the formal youth justice system, which included police cautioning, conferencing, and what are referred to as "extrajudicial measures" under the YCJA. These responses are forms of diversion from the formal youth justice system. Diversionary responses to youth crime are generally used for less serious offences, involve a voluntary admission of responsibility, and result in no permanent criminal record. These responses are more expeditious and less expensive than going to court, and may allow for greater engagement of both victims and offenders than the formal court process, facilitating a "restorative justice" approach to certain types of offences.

This chapter begins with a discussion of the rationale for diversion and a review of its historical development. A major focus is the range of diversionary responses that are available under the YCJA. Conferencing and youth justice committees are also considered;

---

*Portions of this chapter are a revised version of Nicholas Bala, *Youth Criminal Justice Law* (Toronto: Irwin Law, 2003), chapter 5.

these innovations have elements of both a court-based and a community-based response. The chapter ends with a discussion of the rights of youth who are being diverted and with the consequences for youth of participating in diversion programs.

THE HISTORY AND RATIONALE FOR JUVENILE DIVERSION IN CANADA

Under the *Juvenile Delinquents Act,* Canada's first youth justice legislation, alternatives to formal charging were widely used. Most frequently, diversion was handled informally; although the Act had no expressed provisions dealing with diversion, it was common practice for police who apprehended juveniles for minor offences to release them after issuing a warning to the youth, and perhaps to the parents, that if there was further offending the case would be taken to juvenile court. It was also common for school officials and parents to deal with less serious youthful offending, including most of the assaults that occurred in schools, though often resorting to corporal punishment.

By the early 1970s the first few formal diversion programs were being established by various social agencies in Canada; referrals were received from police and prosecutors, who sent cases that would otherwise have gone to juvenile court. "Labelling theory" was one of the rationales offered for the first juvenile diversion programs. This theory posits that youths who are referred to by police and other authority figures as "delinquents" will come to label themselves as offenders. It is argued that the adoption of this deviant self-identity will lead to future offending, or "secondary deviance" (Moyer, 1980, pp. 67–74). Proponents of labelling theory argue that some youths may be unnecessarily harmed by being labelled as "young offenders" through the formal court process and that they may be less likely to reoffend if they are diverted to an informal process. However, empirical research is equivocal about whether identifying and describing a youth as an "offender" actually increases the likelihood of reoffending. Several studies from Australia and New Zealand have reported that *some types* of diversion programs may reduce recidivism. Specifically, programs that involve both victims and offenders and have significant "restorative justice"[1] components may result in lower recidivism rates than court-based responses for comparable groups of young offenders (Morris & Maxwell, 2001; Daly, 2001).

There is only one reported Canadian study that compared the outcomes for youths randomly assigned to court with the outcomes for youths assigned to a community diversion program involving an informal meeting with offenders, parents, and victims (Morton & West, 1983). That study reported no significant difference between use of court and use of diversion in terms of future recidivism, though victims and youths reported that they were more engaged in the informal diversion process and cases were resolved more quickly through diversion. Another Canadian study of police charge decisions found that youths who were not charged but rather dealt with by means of an informal police caution were no more likely to reoffend than a comparable group of youths who were charged and sent to court (Kijewski, 1983).

Assessing the effectiveness of diversion programs through recidivism rates is not the only way to measure their impact. The fact that diversion does not necessarily reduce reoffending does not mean that diversion programs are without value. Diversionary responses can resolve less serious cases in more expeditious and less expensive ways than court-based responses, leaving the formal justice system with more resources to deal with serious cases. Further, in comparison to the formal and adversarial nature of youth court—a forum that tends to preclude open discussion by the individuals concerned with a crime—a properly designed diversion program can offer youths, parents, and victims an opportunity to engage actively in achieving a resolution that may prove more satisfactory to all involved. There may also be an important role for members of the community in diversion programs. Such community involvement may, for example, be especially important for Aboriginal communities, and appropriate in others as well. Further, some programs may have access to counselling resources and an ability to engage youth in a way that is not possible in the court system.

ALTERNATIVE MEASURES UNDER THE *YOUNG OFFENDERS ACT*

The drafters of the YOA wanted to encourage the practice of diversion as it developed under the JDA and to regulate certain aspects of it to prevent overly intrusive diversionary reponses. The Declaration of Principle in sec. 3(1)(d) of the YOA (see Appendix B) expressly recognized that

"where it is not inconsistent with the protection of society, taking no measures or taking measures other than judicial proceedings should be considered for dealing with young persons who have committed offences." Section 4 of the YOA created a legislative framework for the establishment of alternative measures programs.

Alternative measures programs were a form of diversion generally used with youths who committed the least serious offences and who did not have a history of offending. However, some provinces took a more expansive approach and permitted youths facing more serious charges and with a prior record of offending to be considered for alternative measures. The YOA was intended to increase the use of various informal alternatives to the formal youth justice system. Paradoxically, it was actually the use of court-based responses to youth crime that increased under the YOA.

The reasons for the increase in the use of formal responses to youth crime under the YOA are complex, and this general trend to make greater use of courts rather than informal responses was not uniform across Canada. Notably, the Quebec government established alternative measures programs and policies that encouraged police and Crown prosecutors to divert less serious offenders from the youth court system to community-based alternatives or the child-welfare system. In most provinces, however, the introduction of the YOA was accompanied by a phenomenon known as "net widening." Alternative measures programs were established, but frequently the police did not actually divert youths who would otherwise have been charged in court to these programs.

Rather, young persons who committed minor offences who would have received an informal police warning under the JDA were sent to the new programs, while charge rates in court remained the same or increased.

The YOA came into force around the same time as the *Charter of Rights and Freedoms,* and together these two legal instruments created a more formal and rights-oriented response to dealing with youth offending. While the YOA was intended by the federal Parliament in Ottawa to encourage diversionary responses, the police and prosecutors (who are generally answerable to the provincial rather than federal government) were influenced by the more formal approach to youth justice. More significantly, the increased use of court following the enactment of the YOA may in part have been a response to growing public pressure to "do something" about youth crime. Arresting youths who in the past may have been dealt with informally was one police response to community demands to "get tough" with young offenders. In some provinces the use of court-based responses was also encouraged by provincial policies that restricted the use of alternative measures or, for a time, precluded it altogether.

Under the JDA, while juvenile diversion was widely used it received little or no attention from most provincial governments. Local programs, police forces, and Crown prosecutors could exercise their discretion to divert a broad range of cases. When the YOA came into force, provincial governments began to develop formal referral policies for alternative measures that were often more restrictive than the practices of police, prosecutors, and operators of diversion programs under the JDA. For example, under the YOA, Ontario's opposition to alternative measures reflected a general political resistance by the provincial government to the federally enacted statute. The Ontario government argued that research into the effectiveness of diversion in terms of reducing recidivism was "ambiguous and conflicting," and it expressed concern about the potential for the abuse of the rights of youths in these programs as well as about "net widening" (Ontario Social Development Council, 1988, p. 16). Ontario initially provided no new funding for the establishment of diversion programs and refused to implement sec. 4 of the YOA. Section 4(1)(a) provided that "[a]lternative measures may be used ... *only* if ... the measures are part of a program authorized" (emphasis added) by the provincial government, and the Ontario government decided not to authorize any programs.

Since all the other provinces and territories established programs to give adolescents access to alternative measures, Ontario's decision not to implement sec. 4 of the YOA was challenged as a violation of the principle of "equality under the law" guaranteed by sec. 15 of the *Charter*. In 1990 in *R. v S. (S.)*, the Supreme Court of Canada held that in Canada's federal system the discretion rested with the provincial government about whether to establish any of these programs. In another decision the Supreme Court also ruled that if provinces chose to establish alternative measures programs, they could develop their own criteria for eligibility that could be significantly narrower than those in other provinces.

At the same time *S.(S.)* was being dealt with, the Supreme Court gave its decision in *R. v. Askov* (1990), ruling that delays in the Ontario courts were denying accused persons—principally adults but also youths—the constitutionally guaranteed right to a trial within a reasonable time. The *Askov* decision placed great pressure on the Ontario government to deal with the problem of overcrowding in the court system and provided a strong impetus for moving the least serious cases out of the courts by making greater use of alternative measures programs. Accordingly, the Ontario government decided to join all other governments in Canada and establish alternative measures programs to relieve pressure on the courts. Hence, despite the Supreme Court of Canada decision in *S.(S.)*, the Ontario government developed some limited alternative measures programs to respond to the overcrowding in the courts

Even after deciding to adopt alternative measures, Ontario maintained the most restrictive diversion policies in Canada. Ontario was the only province to have alternative measures policies that could be used only when the police laid a charge and a youth appeared in court on one occasion, while other provinces allowed police to divert cases without laying a charge. Further, in Ontario the criteria to determine eligibility for alternative measures were narrow, generally limiting their use to property offences under $5000 where the youth had no prior record of offending (Ontario Ministry of the Attorney General, 1995). Ontario's criteria thus excluded some quite common non-violent offences, specifically break and enter. In most other provinces a youth charged with this offence could be con-

sidered for alternative measures. As a result of its narrow policy, Ontario had the lowest rates of use of alternative measures in Canada (Canadian Centre for Justice Statistics, 2000).

In contrast with Ontario, Quebec had the broadest criteria for the use of alternative measures, with the prosecutor having the discretion to send any charges to alternative measures and a requirement that all less serious cases were to be referred, usually on a pre-charge basis (Platt, 1995, p. 162). In Quebec, youths could be sent to alternative measures even with a prior record of offending. Due to this extensive use of alternative measures, Quebec had the lowest rate of youth court charging in Canada (Canadian Centre for Justice Statistics, 2001).

THE CONTEXT FOR INCREASING THE USE OF DIVERSION

During the 1990s, although levels of youth crime in Canada actually seemed to be slowly falling, or at worst had plateaued (Statistics Canada, 2002), there was, paradoxically, a dramatic increase in public concern about youth crime. Reflecting and perhaps fanning these flames, conservative politicians in federal opposition parties and some provincial governments demanded a "get tough" approach to youth crime. At the same time, academic critics and youth justice system professionals, including many judges (Doob, 2001), expressed concern that Canada was over-utilizing courts and custody under the *Young Offenders Act,* and that many cases should be diverted from the formal youth justice system.

The dominant rhetoric of the federal Liberal government at the time of the introduction of its *Strategy for Youth Justice Renewal* in 1998, which resulted in the enactment of the *Youth Criminal Justice Act* in 2002, was about the need "to deal more firmly and effectively with violent and repeat young offenders" (McLellan, 1998). Reflecting this concern, there are provisions in the new Act that facilitate the imposition of adult sentences and the publication of identifying information about serious violent offenders.

However, the most significant parts of the YCJA do not deal with the relatively small number of serious violent offenders, but rather with the large majority of offenders who commit non-violent offences or violent offences that do not involve serious injury. These are provisions that are intended to reduce the use of courts and to increase community-based responses to youth crime, while reducing Canada's "over-reliance on incarceration" for young offenders (YCJA, Preamble).

While the primary *legal response* to serious youthful offending should be through the court system, many youths can be "diverted" from the formal justice system and dealt with more informally, for example, through what the YCJA refers to as "extrajudicial measures" and "conferencing." The enactment of these provisions is a desirable development. Although there is a lack of research to conclusively establish the superiority of informal responses to youth crime in terms of reducing recidivism, it is clear that for a significant range of cases, informal responses are no worse than court-based responses for achieving accountability and protecting society. These approaches may also increase the engagement of victims and offenders in the justice system and perhaps even reduce recidivism. Informal responses certainly have the potential to be more expeditious and less expensive than the courts.

A major limitation of these YCJA provisions is that they are essentially permissive; they create no new legal rights for youths and impose no new obligations on governments. It is the responsibility of provincial and territorial governments to decide whether to allow police, prosecutors, and local program operators to implement these provisions. Further, there are legitimate concerns about the potential for these informal responses to abuse the rights of youths or ignore the needs of victims. There is need both for the monitoring of the implementation of these provisions and for research to determine how effective they are at reducing offending and meeting the needs of victims, offenders, and communities.

EXTRAJUDICIAL MEASURES UNDER THE *YOUTH CRIMINAL JUSTICE ACT*

The YCJA abandons the YOA terminology of "alternative measures" and adopts two new terms: "extrajudicial measures" and "extrajudicial sanctions." *Extrajudicial measures* are defined in sec. 2 of the YCJA as "measures other than judicial proceedings ... used to deal with a young person alleged to have committed an offence." Extrajudicial measures encompass all types of diversion, formal and informal, including the exercise of police discretion not to charge a youth.

Sections 4 and 5 of the YCJA set out general principles and objectives for the use of extrajudicial measures and are clearly intended to encourage their use by police, prosecutors, youth workers, and community groups. Section 2 of the Act also refers to "extrajudicial sanctions," which is the new term for what was called "alternative measures" under the YOA. *Extrajudicial sanctions* are one type of relatively formal extrajudicial measure. The operation of these pre-adjudication diversion schemes is governed by sections 10, 11, and 12 of the YCJA.

Section 4 of the YCJA sets out principles that govern the establishment of policies and programs about extrajudicial measures and are to be taken into account in making decisions about individual youth.

4 (a) ...extrajudicial measures are often the most appropriate and effective way to address youth crime;

(b) extrajudicial measures allow for effective and timely interventions focused on correcting offending behaviour;

(c) extrajudicial measures are presumed to be adequate to hold a young person accountable for his or her offending behaviour if the young person has committed a non-violent offence and has not previously been found guilty of an offence; and

(d) extrajudicial measures should be used if they are adequate to hold a young person accountable for his or her offending behaviour and, if the use of extrajudicial measures is consistent with the principles set out in this section, nothing in this Act precludes their use in respect of a young person who

(i) has previously been dealt with by the use of extrajudicial measures, or

(ii) has previously been found guilty of an offence.

Section 4(c) of the YCJA creates a presumption that police and prosecutors should not charge youths who have no prior record of offending and are believed to have committed non-violent offences. Section 4(d) makes clear that extrajudicial measures may also be appropriate for some youths with prior records of offending, depending on the nature of the current offence, the previous record, and the youth's circumstances. Further, extrajudicial measures may be appropriate for some cases involving minor violence, such as assaults in school that do not involve significant injury.

The fact that the YCJA permits the use of extrajudicial measures for youths with prior police involvement is significant. Taking into consideration the attitude of the victim and the youth, the seriousness and circumstances of the offence, and the likelihood of reoccurrence, in some cases it is appropriate to give a youth more than one opportunity to avoid court. It is not clear that youth court will provide a more effective or even a more punitive sanction than some form of extrajudicial measure. Indeed, an appearance in court is often a less engaging experience than participation in an extrajudicial sanctions program, although the long-term consequences of going to court may be more serious, especially if the youth acquires a significant record of offending.

Section 5 sets out criteria that should be considered by those establishing programs and policies for the use of extrajudicial measures. This section makes clear that notions of restorative justice are an important aspect of extrajudicial measures. While responses to youth offending outside the court system are intended to be informal, they should encourage youths to take responsibility for their acts, engage with their families and communities, and repair harm done to victims. Section 5 provides:

5. Extrajudicial measures should be designed to

(*a*) provide an effective and timely response to offending behaviour outside the bounds of judicial measures;

(*b*) encourage young persons to acknowledge and repair the harm caused to the victim and the community;

(*c*) encourage families of young persons—including extended families—and the community to become involved in the design and implementation of those measures;

(*d*) provide an opportunity for victims to participate in decisions related to the measures selected and to receive reparation; and

(*e*) respect the rights and freedoms of young persons and be proportionate to the seriousness of the offence.

While secs. 4 and 5 encourage the use of extrajudicial measures, they do not give youth a legal right to be dealt with outside the court system. The judicial precedents rendered under the YOA, which held that federal legislation that encourages use of informal responses to youth crime does not give any individual youth the legal right to be dealt with outside the court system, continue to apply under the YCJA. It is the police and prosecutors who decide whether a youth will be charged and taken to court, perhaps acting with the advice of probation officers or community agencies and taking account of the views of victims. Judges do not have the right to refer cases to extrajudicial measures. There is only narrow judicial power to dismiss charges that should have been dealt with by way of extrajudicial measures if there has been an "abuse of process."[2]

In addition to the narrow power to stay proceedings as an abuse of process, some judges, in appropriate cases, may suggest that the Crown prosecutor refer the youth to some form of extrajudicial measures. A judge might, for example, make this type of suggestion at a pretrial conference, which is a meeting held in many jurisdictions among prosecutor, defence counsel, and a judge, at which all involved typically resolve procedural issues and explore whether the entire case can be resolved without trial. This judicial power of "suggestion" for use of extrajudicial measures is not legally binding, but may be quite influential with some prosecutors. Finally, if there has been a failure by the prosecutor or police to deal with an appropriate case by means of extrajudicial measures, the judge might take account of this at the time of sentencing. This might, for example, result in a reprimand or an absolute discharge for a case that the judge thought should have been resolved by extrajudicial measures.

POLICE WARNINGS AND CAUTIONS: SECTIONS 6 & 7

In Canada, the police have the initial responsibility for investigating suspected offences and deciding whether to commence formal legal proceedings against a person believed to have committed a criminal offence. In most provinces, the police have the authority to commence the proceedings by appearing before a justice of the peace to swear an information (also referred to as "laying charges"). In some provinces, such as British Columbia, a Crown prosecutor[3] screens cases before police proceed to swear an information.

In all provinces, the police have a critical role in deciding whether to begin a process that could lead to a formal response to a suspected crime. A police officer may decide not to invoke the formal processes of court sanctions for adolescents who are apprehended for minor offences. The officer may decide that a youth should be dealt with informally by warning the youth about not committing further offences. This practice, commonly known as "police screening," was widely employed under the JDA, at a time when there were few formal programs for diversion from the juvenile court (see, for example, Gandy, 1970; Moyer, 1980). Police screening was especially common with delinquents under age 12, but it was used with juveniles of all ages. Under the JDA, some police forces kept records of "police cautions" so that they could determine when a youth had "run out of chances."

The practice of police screening reflects the belief that some cases do not warrant the time and effort of formal charging. It also reflects an understanding that the cautioning of a youth by a police officer can be an effective, low-cost way of holding the youth accountable and, in some cases, of arranging compensation for a victim. Further, the warning that future criminal acts will result in more serious consequences can have a significant deterrent impact on some youth.

It has been recognized that more extensive use of police screening would be appropriate in Canada. The YCJA makes explicit reference to police cautioning in an effort to encourage its use, as well as to provide some consistency and regulation to the practice. Sections 4 and 5 stress the importance of responding outside the court system to adolescent offenders, especially if they have no prior record of offending and the offence does not involve violence. Often a non-court police response is the most effective, most humane, and least expensive way of dealing with an adolescent who has made a mistake. In appropriate cases, the informal, relatively rapid response of a police officer—especially an officer with sensitivity and experience in dealing with youth—can have as much or more impact in terms of deterrence and accountability than a much delayed, often perfunctory appearance in youth court.

Unlike the YOA, which alluded to police screening only in vague terms, secs. 6 and 7 of the YCJA are specifically directed to the police. Section 6 states that, before taking steps to begin a formal court process against a youth, a police officer "*shall ... consider* whether it would be sufficient to warn the young person, administer a caution ... or refer the young person to a community-based program" [emphasis added]. In making a decision not to proceed to court, the officer should consider the seriousness of the offence, the prior record and attitude of the youth, and the views of the victim, as well as the policies of the specific police force.

While police officers have an obligation to consider whether to deal with a youth outside the court system, sec. 6(2) of the YCJA makes clear that this is a discretionary matter, specifying that the "failure of a police officer" to consider any form of extrajudicial measures "does not invalidate" any subsequent court proceedings and is not reviewable by a judge. However, if it appears that an officer has failed to consider some form of diversionary measures, the prosecutor may decide to divert the case.

When considering how to respond to a youth suspected of an offence, an officer may have a number of different options, depending on local resources and policies. The least intrusive response is for the officer who first comes in contact with the youth to personally warn the youth not to commit any further offences. The YCJA refers to both the police "warning" in sec. 6 and the police "caution" in sec. 7. There is no legal difference between a warning and a caution, but the caution is seen as a more formal response that might, for example, be administered at the police station by a senior officer or might be in a letter from the police to the youth and parents. Even so, a caution is still administered by the police without any need for charges to be laid and without any sanctions being imposed. The police warning is to be administered informally by the officer handling the case and may include the officer meeting with a youth's parents. The officer may discuss with the parents whether the offending behaviour is related to other problems that might be assisted by a social agency or doctor or whether the child's school might be able to provide help, leaving it for the parents to decide what help to seek. The officer might arrange for the youth to make a simple apology to a victim or to return stolen property.

Police forces generally now have policies that require a report of a police warning or caution to be filed, so that if there is a repetition of offending behaviour there may be a more intrusive response. There is understandably a desire for good records to be kept of prior police warnings, though in practice this may not always occur, particularly if a youth has been involved in cases served by different police forces. While this may result in some youths receiving "more chances than they deserve," the granting of second chances is not inconsistent with the YCJA.

Section 7 of the YCJA encourages provincial governments to have programs and policies for police cautioning, with the caution being administered by a specially trained officer who is sensitive to youth and aware of community resources. A caution may involve the police or prosecutor sending a "caution letter" to the youth and parents that warns of the consequences of further offending. The cautioning process may also involve a voluntary referral to further help from a social agency or community resource.

If the youth's behaviour or situation seems more serious, or there is a victim who expects or would benefit from some type of restitution or meeting with the offender, the youth may be referred by the police to a formal extrajudicial sanctions program. In most provinces the police can refer youths directly to such programs without charging the youth. In some provinces a referral to a pre-charge program can be made only by a Crown prosecutor after charges have been laid, although the views of the police officer handling the case are usually considered.

The value of the police warning and caution provisions of the YCJA for the handling of individual cases will be affected by the policies of local police forces and provincial governments, as well as by the training, knowledge, and sensitivity of individual officers. If the internal management systems of police forces focus on "charge rates," it is unlikely that there will be much screening or diversion, whereas if a police force has specially dedicated and trained officers whose mandate includes diversion and informal resolution of cases, and who are aware of community resources, it is likely that there will be extensive use of these informal responses to youth crime. While the enactment of the YCJA encourages many police forces in Canada to reconsider their approaches to youth crime and to expand their use of warnings and cautions, the new Act does not require such changes.

SUBSEQUENT USE OF A CAUTION OR WARNING: SECTION 9

Decisions by the police or a prosecutor to caution a youth or to refer a youth to a program of extrajudicial sanctions do not require any finding or formal admission of guilt by the youth. Therefore, sec. 9 of the YCJA provides that in the case where the police or prosecutor has cautioned a

youth or has referred a youth to extrajudicial sanctions, it cannot be used in any proceedings against the youth as proof of guilt in connection with that offence. In any event, if a case is resolved by a warning or caution or is referred to extrajudicial sanctions, it is rare for the case to be referred to court.

In any subsequent legal proceedings for a later offence, participation in a formal extrajudicial sanctions program is treated differently than having been warned or cautioned. Section 10(2)(e) requires that as a condition of participation in extrajudicial sanctions the youth must "accept responsibility" for the offence. If there is a subsequent finding of guilt for another offence in youth court, at the sentencing stage the court will usually be informed of the prior participation in extrajudicial sanctions (or alternative measures) in the two preceding years. Such participation is considered indicative of the failure of a less formal response to have an effect on offending behaviour and may be taken into account as an aggravating circumstance in sentencing.

Before deciding whether to caution a youth, make a referral to a program of extrajudicial sanctions, or send a case to court, a police officer will usually discuss the offending behaviour with the youth. The fact that the youth acknowledges the offending behaviour and expresses remorse could be a significant factor in deciding that a formal court response is not required. Section 10(4) of the YCJA provides that any statement made by a young person "as a condition of being dealt with by extrajudicial measures is inadmissible" against the youth in any civil or criminal proceedings. Further, unless the police officer fully advised the youth of his or her legal rights in accordance with the *Charter* and sec. 146 of the YCJA, which is unlikely to occur in a situation where a warning is being given, the statement would also be inadmissible on that ground.

The decision not to divert or screen a charge involves a significant exercise of police or prosecutorial discretion. There is a potential that this discretion may be exercised in a discriminatory fashion. Some research reveals that youth belonging to visible minorities are concerned that police are less likely to exercise their discretion not to charge when dealing with them (Warner et al., 1998). Beyond the issue of conscious or unconscious racial bias, there may be a tendency for officers to "give a break" to youths from more affluent neighbourhoods, thereby prejudicing youths from disadvantaged backgrounds. The exercise of police and prosecutorial discretion to screen or divert to extrajudicial sanctions should be guided by appropriate policies and training to ensure fair and effective application. Further, there should be adequate record keeping and information sharing to ensure that youths are not being repeatedly screened by different officers on different occasions.

YOUTH JUSTICE COMMITTEES: SECTION 18

To encourage the use of extrajudicial measures and community involvement in responding to youth crime, the YCJA has provisions authorizing conferences and youth justice committees. While both were available under the YOA, their use has increased with the enactment of the YCJA. The federal government is encouraging

this type of response to youth crime by providing educational materials as well as funding support for the operation and evaluation of model programs.

Under the YOA, sec. 69 allowed provincial governments to establish local volunteer youth justice committees "to assist ... in any aspect of the administration" of that Act or in any programs or services for young offenders. A significant number of these committees were established in different parts of Canada, in particular in Manitoba and in some Aboriginal communities. In each locality the committee had membership drawn from the community. These committees had a range of functions, such as monitoring and supporting the administration of the youth justice system, but their most common function was to administer "alternative measures programs." To emphasize the continuity in approach to youth justice committees, sec.165(4) of the YCJA provides that any youth justice committee established under the YOA is deemed to continue under the new Act.

Section 18 of the YCJA is similar to the youth justice committee provision in sec. 69 of the YOA, but has added a long list detailing possible functions for youth justice committees. The previous Act required that the members of these committees were to serve "without remuneration." While the members of these committees will continue to be drawn from the community, the YCJA does not require that all members serve voluntarily. This clarifies that in addition to volunteers, professionals who work for community agencies or schools or police officers may be members. It also allows for possible payment of a person serving in the role of coordinator.

Section 18(2) of the YCJA makes clear that youth justice committees may be asked to play a role in monitoring the implementation of the Act, advising federal and provincial governments about how to improve the youth justice system, and providing information to the public about the youth justice system. A youth justice committee may also be asked to play a role in coordinating the efforts of local child welfare agencies, social agencies, and schools in working with young offenders. Some youth justice committees are also involved in responding to offending by children under age 12, in conjunction with parents, police, and child welfare agencies.

YOUTH JUSTICE CONFERENCES: SECTIONS 19 AND 41

Sections 19 and 41 of the YCJA deal with conferences. The concept of the conference in the YCJA was at least partially inspired by the "family group conference," as developed in New Zealand. The conference is also based on the traditional practices of many Canadian Aboriginal communities for dealing with offending, and on the restorative justice model.

Section 2 of the Act defines a "conference" as "a group of persons who are convened to give advice" concerning a specific young person having difficulty with the law. This definition is broad, so that a conference may function and be used in a range of different ways. One example of the YCJA concept of the conference is an extrajudicial sanctions program that brings together an offender, family members, the victim[s] (where appropriate and willing to participate), victim[s]'s supporters, and community members who meet together to discuss the offence and develop a mutually acceptable plan. The "sentencing circle," which is judicially convened and primarily used with Aboriginal youths, is another example. Under sec. 19, the YCJA also allows for judges to call conferences to provide advice about whether to release a youth from detention pending trial, as well as advising at the time of sentencing or sentence review.

If a conference is presided over by a judge, a record of the proceedings should be kept and may be used by the judge for the purpose of making decisions about the youth. Although sec. 41 makes clear that the recommendation of a conference is not binding on the court, in practice judges are likely to follow the recommendations of a conference, since these recommendations reflect a consensus of the victim and members of the community. The conference may also have a restorative and conciliatory effect on the participants, and can serve an important role in providing the offender with an understanding of the consequences of his or her acts and in holding the offender accountable to the victim and society.

EXTRAJUDICIAL SANCTIONS UNDER THE *YOUTH CRIMINAL JUSTICE ACT*

The process for referring a youth to an extrajudicial sanctions program varies significantly from one jurisdiction to another, and sometimes between programs within the same province (Canadian Centre for Justice Statistics, 2000). Similar to the process for alternative measures under the

YOA, in some provinces a youth is referred to an extrajudicial sanctions program without charges being laid (called a "pre-charge program"), but in others, such as Ontario, charges are generally laid before a case can be sent to extrajudicial sanctions (i.e., a "post-charge program"). Some provinces use both pre- and post-charge programs.

In most pre-charge programs, the police refer youths directly to the program, perhaps after consultation with the Crown prosecutor's office, without commencing youth court proceedings. It is also possible to have a pre-charge program for which referrals are made by the Crown prosecutor after the screening of charges.

In post-charge programs, court proceedings are commenced and the youth is issued a summons or appearance notice for court. With post-charge programs, the youth will generally have a first appearance in court before the Crown prosecutor decides whether the youth should be referred to the program. If the case is referred to an extrajudicial sanctions program, the court case will be adjourned pending a decision about which sanction should be imposed. The charges will be dismissed by the court if the youth satisfactorily completes the program. Generally, the Crown prosecutor will arrange for formal dismissal of the charges without the youth reappearing. Post-charge programs are more cumbersome, but the benefit is that when extrajudicial sanctions are not completed, it is easier to bring a case to court if proceedings have already been commenced.

The initial decision about whether to divert a youth from the court system to an extrajudicial sanctions program is made by the police or prosecutor. Thus, the support of police and prosecutors is essential for the success of this type of program, and is more likely if they have an understanding of how the program operates and have a good relationship with the program administrators. Increasingly, police forces in Canada are becoming involved in various extrajudicial sanctions programs, which may be operated by officers with special training and interest in young offenders; even in these communities, the police who operate the program need to enlist the support of other officers and satisfy them that this is an appropriate way to hold youth accountable.

Section 10(2)(b) of the YCJA specifies that the person "who is considering whether to use [an] extrajudicial sanction [program]... [should be] satisfied that it would be appropriate, having regard to the needs of the young person and the interests of society." The making of this decision requires consideration of the threat posed to society by the youth's behaviour and circumstances and the effect of the offence on the victim.

The decision to refer is guided by provincial or local policy that regulates the exercise of discretion by the prosecutor or police. These policies typically specify that only certain offences are eligible for diversion. There is substantial variation across Canada in provincial policies and also in local attitudes and community programs. The introduction of the YCJA was accompanied by significant professional educational initiatives funded by the federal government, though there continue to be concerns about how police and prosecutors exercise their discretion in making "low visibility" decisions about diversion (Harris et al., 2004). Early reports indicate that significantly fewer cases are being sent to youth court under the new Act, though Ontario policies about the use of extrajudicial measures still remain among the most restrictive in Canada (Daly, 2004).

Extrajudicial Sanctions: Process and Practice

If a youth is referred to extrajudicial sanctions, the person or agency responsible for the program meets with the youth to ascertain what response is appropriate, and to ensure that the response is acceptable to the youth, as the youth must agree to the plan. In some localities the meeting is very informal, with just a youth worker and the young person present, although parents may also be included in such a meeting. Section 11 of the YCJA requires that parents must be notified, orally or in writing, of any extrajudicial sanction that has been imposed, but it is a common practice to involve parents in the process before decisions are made. However, unlike in youth court, where parents can be ordered to attend if their presence is necessary or would be in the best interests of their child (YCJA, sec. 27), the involvement of parents and victims in any extrajudicial sanctions program is voluntary. Normally, the meeting that takes place will result in the development of a plan that is recorded in a written agreement.

In some provinces, a common form of extrajudicial measure for minor offences, such as shoplifting, is to have the police or a community youth justice committee send a letter to the parents and youth that records the fact that the youth is believed to have committed an offence and warns the youth not to commit further offences,

leaving it to the parents to determine an appropriate response. In Manitoba, this is called a "parental action letter"; in Alberta and British Columbia, it is referred to as a "caution letter." The decision to impose no further sanctions will depend on the nature of the offence and may be influenced by the attitudes of the victim and the youth.

In some cases, it may be desirable to give the youth an opportunity to reflect on and acknowledge the offence by requiring the youth to write an essay or prepare a poster on the subject, although account should be taken of the youth's abilities in imposing any requirements for written work. Or it may be appropriate for the youth to do some community-service work or make a donation to a charity, impressing on the youth that offending behaviour affects the whole community. In cases where there has already been a suitable parental response to the offending behaviour, or some form of reparation has been made to the victim before the case comes to extrajudicial sanctions, no further response may be required after a meeting with the program operator.

Normally, extrajudicial sanctions are arranged with just one meeting between the youth and others involved in the process. More than one meeting is held if, for example, the participants feel that there is a need to gather more information, involve others, or consider their position. A plan may be arranged that will involve a reconvening of the group to monitor the youth's progress. In some localities, extrajudicial sanctions programs may make use of a range of responses that are not merely sanctions but also try to address the causes of a youth's offending behaviour.

Programs Aimed at the "Underlying Circumstances" of Offending Behaviour

While most youths who are sent to extra-judicial sanctions programs in Canada have not committed serious offences and are not likely to reoffend, there is a minority who may pose a future threat to society. If such youth do not have their needs addressed at this early stage, many may continue to commit crimes; however, it is difficult to predict which youth will reoffend. Extrajudicial sanctions programs that respond to the problems of youths at risk are consistent with sec. 3(1)(a)(ii) of the YCJA, which recognizes the importance of "addressing the circumstances underlying a young person's offending behaviour." This suggests that counselling or treatment conditions may be appropriate options for some youths referred to extrajudicial sanctions programs.

In some communities, programs are directed at certain types of offending behaviour, such as shoplifting. One option, commonly found in Quebec, may be to require a youth to attend a values development course directed at adolescents with offending problems. In some places, there may be a requirement for a community supervisor or mentor, or a referral may be made for some form of counselling. Such counselling might be provided by a therapist, doctor, or community agency; in an Aboriginal community, a youth may be required to enter into a relationship with a respected Elder as a mentor.

A response recommending therapy or counselling is premised on the belief that some offending behaviour is symptomatic of an emotional, social, behavioural, or substance-abuse problem. Furthermore, it is believed that responding in this manner could prevent further offending as well as being generally beneficial to the youth. In some provinces, this practice is not permitted. These provinces take a "non-interventionist approach," believing that a referral to counselling is too intrusive a response to the relatively minor charges that they deal with and should be imposed only by a court.[4] Even if policies preclude imposition of conditions of counselling, the staff or volunteers who meet with a youth may, in appropriate cases, make a referral to a youth or parents for further counselling, treatment, or support, explaining that this is a suggestion for help they may wish to obtain and is not a condition of participation.

Victim Involvement

Section 12 gives a victim the right to request and obtain information about how a youth who has been sent to an extrajudicial sanctions program has been dealt with. This is, however, a minimum requirement and, consistent with secs. 3 and 5 of the YCJA, many extrajudicial sanctions programs are trying to involve victims more actively in the process. It is important for victims to have a sense that justice has been done and, where appropriate, to have an opportunity to meet with offenders or receive some form of compensation for the harm that they have suffered (Pate & Peachey, 1988).

It is a common practice to notify the victim before sanctions are imposed and to invite input. Some extrajudicial sanctions programs are based on a conference model and place an emphasis on inviting the victim to a meeting with the youth, at which the offence is discussed and an appropriate response is developed. While these meetings can provide an important opportunity for victims to feel vindicated and for offenders to gain an appreciation of the effects of their conduct, special care should be taken to respect the needs and fears of victims. Victims should not be pressured into participating, and the meetings must be conducted with sensitivity to ensure that neither the victim nor the youth feels intimidated by the experience. If appropriate, extrajudicial sanctions may include some form of restitution, apology, or personal service by the youth to the victim, within a fair and realistic assessment of the youth's ability to make compensation.

Extrajudicial Sanctions in Aboriginal Communities

Many Aboriginal communities have established extrajudicial sanctions programs and youth justice committees that involve meetings with offenders and their family members, victims, and community members such as respected elders. This is consistent with Aboriginal philosophies of justice, which reflect restorative or reparative ideals and emphasize the importance of restoring relationships within the community.

Under the YOA, in some provinces the offence criteria for referral of Aboriginal youth to alternative measures were broader than for non-Aboriginal youth, recognizing that there are social, political, and constitutional reasons for dealing with Aboriginal youths outside of the conventional justice system, which has clearly failed to deal adequately with Aboriginal

offending. A wider offence jurisdiction for extrajudicial sanctions for Aboriginal youth under the YCJA may also be appropriate. Extrajudicial sanctions programs that give Aboriginal communities greater responsibility for their troubled adolescents have the potential for more effective healing-based, non-adversarial responses to youthful offending (Ross, 1996; Green, 1998).

ROLE AND RIGHTS OF YOUTHS

An extrajudicial sanctions program can offer a youth the opportunity for an expeditious, informal response to an alleged violation of the law. The youth and parents will generally feel less intimidated, and they are likely to participate more fully in discussions about the offence and their circumstances than in the more formal, adversarial court setting. So it is not surprising that research reveals that parents and youth are more likely to perceive themselves as having been treated fairly in a diversion program than in court (Morton & West, 1983). For the youth, diversion avoids the stigma of having a "youth court record." Parents may also encourage their child to choose extrajudicial sanctions, since there is no need to incur the expense of a lawyer and parents do not have to take time away from work or other activities to attend court. Thus, there can be considerable pressure on a youth to participate in extrajudicial sanctions. Furthermore, there is the potential for an intrusive response to a quite minor offence with extrajudicial sanctions, or even for participation by a youth who is not guilty of any offence. While the YCJA has provisions that are intended to minimize the risk of abusing the rights of a youth, there are fewer protections if a youth goes to an extrajudicial sanctions program than if the youth goes to court.

Extrajudicial sanctions programs are not designed to be "informal courts." Under sec.10(2)(e) of the YCJA, extrajudicial sanctions may be used "*only if* ... the young person accepts responsibility for the act ... that forms the basis of the offence that he or she is alleged to have committed" (emphasis added). Typically, this provision is satisfied at the meeting between the youth and program operator to develop a plan of extrajudicial sanctions. The youth will be asked to discuss the circumstances of the alleged offence, explaining the nature of his or her participation. Often a youth will make a full admission of guilt, but sec. 10(2)(e) technically does not require that the youth accept full legal guilt for the specific offence alleged; rather, it involves an acceptance of moral responsibility. Sometimes a youth may question some aspect of the specific charge or police report, but accept that he or she was in some way "responsible" for an illegal act. However, a youth who "denies his or her participation or involvement" or who expresses the wish to be dealt with in court cannot be dealt with by an extrajudicial sanctions program (sec. 10(3)). If this occurs, the program operator must refer the case to the Crown or police so that the matter can be dealt with in youth court.

Section 10(2)(d) requires that a youth be advised of the right to legal representation and given reasonable opportunity to consult with counsel before consenting to participate in extrajudicial sanctions. Most programs ensure that the youth accepts responsibility for the offence alleged, agrees to participate, and is aware of the right to consult a lawyer early in the process. However, unlike youths who are dealt with in court—for whom sec. 25 of the YCJA provides for access to legal representation if the youth cannot afford to pay a lawyer—there is no statutory provision for access to legal services for youths referred to extrajudicial sanctions. If the program is post-charge, the youth may, for example, have opportunity to meet briefly with duty counsel at youth court before the case is referred to extrajudicial sanctions. Some programs may arrange for duty counsel to be present to meet with the youth prior to the youth accepting responsibility and agreeing to participate, but in times of increasing fiscal restraint, it is difficult to obtain a commitment from legal aid authorities to fund this type of assistance. There are concerns that some youths may waive their legal rights, perhaps because of a "desire to get things over with" or because of parental pressure, without fully appreciating their position. This may happen even if a youth has not committed the act alleged or would have a valid defence to the allegations.

It would be desirable to ensure that all youths who are referred to extrajudicial sanctions have access to legal advice before waiving their right to go to court, especially since the youth's participation may be held against him or her if there were a later prosecution for another offence. However, given the less serious nature of the offences and the fact that only community-based sanctions can be imposed, the drafters of the YCJA (and the YOA) did not give youths referred to extrajudicial sanctions the statutory right to counsel.

CONSEQUENCES OF PARTICIPATION IN EXTRAJUDICIAL SANCTIONS

If a young person participates in extrajudicial sanctions and completes the plan agreed to, the case cannot proceed to court. If an extrajudicial sanctions plan is developed and agreed to but not completed, there may be another meeting between the youth and the program administrator to discuss problems that the youth may be having. The program administrator may then decide to refer the youth to the police or prosecutor, who may bring the case to court. Non-completion is most likely to result in referral to court if the offence was relatively serious and the non-completion was wilful and substantial. Under sec. 10(5)(b) the judge has discretion where there is partial completion of extrajudicial sanctions to either dismiss the charge or take account of the partially completed plan when sentencing the youth. The judge should consider how much of the plan was completed, the reasons why the agreement was not fully carried out, and whether the extrajudicial sanctions have had an impact on the youth.

Section 119(2)(a) of the YCJA provides for a two-year "period of access" for records relating to extrajudicial sanctions, running from the date that a youth consents to the specific sanction. During the two-year period of access, certain individuals, including the youth, the victim, and youth corrections or probation staff, can obtain access to the records of extrajudicial sanctions. If a youth is charged with and convicted of an offence within the two-year period, then sec. 40(2)(d)(iv) of the YCJA specifies that a pre-sentence report prepared to assist the judge in sentencing the youth for that offence shall include "the history of alternative measures under [the YOA]... or extrajudicial sanctions used to deal with the young person and the response of the young person to those measures or sanctions."

Some extrajudicial sanctions programs, especially those that are community-based, have a policy of actually destroying a youth's record of participation two years after the youth consented to participate. Program operators and government agencies are not technically obliged to destroy any records; however, after two years, no use may be made of any records kept in regard to an offence sent to extrajudicial sanctions, including photographs or fingerprints held by police forces. Also, after two years, assuming that there are no further offences, the Canadian Police Information Centre is obliged to destroy its records relating to the youth, including fingerprints and photographs.

CONCLUSION

Under the YOA, Canada's extensive reliance on court-based responses to youth offending was both expensive and associated with a high rate of youth custody. Diversion programs represent a socially useful and cost-effective response to many less serious situations of youth offending. The YCJA and related federal funding initiatives are intended to significantly increase the use of various diversionary measures, including police or prosecutorial screening and community-based extrajudicial programs. An expeditious, informal response is preferable to a delayed, formal court experience for many adolescents, parents, and victims. However, surprisingly little research exists on whether diversion actually reduces the risk of reoffending. Nonetheless, programs are most likely to be effective if they have trained competent staff, enough time to meet with victims and offenders before a conference is held, and monitoring and follow-up after a diversionary decision is made. There will always be a role for a formal court-based response for adolescents who commit serious offences or who are not responsive to informal intervention. The court system also has an important role in protecting legal rights. However, substantial scope exists in Canada for increased use of diversion programs, and the YCJA should encourage a significant increase in their use in the future.

References

Archibald, B. (1999). A comprehensive approach to restorative justice. In D. Stuart, et al. (Eds.), *Towards a clear and just criminal law: A criminal reports forum.* Toronto: Carswell.

Bazemore, G., & Walgrave, L. (Eds.). (1999). *Restorative juvenile justice: Repairing the harm of youth crime.* Monsey, NY: Criminal Justice Press/Willow Tree.

Braithwaite, J. (2000). Restorative justice and social justice. *Saskatchewan Law Review, 63,* 185.

Canadian Centre for Justice Statistics. (2000). Alternative measures in Canada 1998–99. *Juristat, 20*(6).

Canadian Centre for Justice Statistics. (2001). Youth court statistics 1999–2000. *Juristat, 21*(3).

Daly, K. (2001). Conferencing in Australia and New Zealand: Variations, research findings and prospects. In A. Morris & G. Maxwell (Eds.), *Restoring justice for juveniles: Conferencing, mediation and circles* (pp. 59–84). Oxford: Hart Publishing.

Daly, R. (2004, Mar. 28). Kids who hurt can also heal. *Toronto Star.*

Doob, A. N. (2001). *Youth court judges' views of the youth justice system: The results of a survey.* Toronto: Centre of Criminology, University of Toronto.

Gandy, J. M. (1970). The exercise of discretion by the police as a decision-making process in the disposition of juvenile offenders. *Osgoode Hall Law Journal, 8,* 329–339.

Green, R. (1998). *Justice in Aboriginal communities: Sentencing alternatives.* Saskatoon: Purich.

Harris, P., Weagant, B., Cole, D., & Weinper, F. (2004). Working in the trenches with the YCJA. *Canadian Journal of Criminology, 46*(3), 367–390.

Juvenile Delinquents Act, enacted as S.C. 1908, c. 40; subject to minor amendments over the years, finally as *Juvenile Delinquents Act,* R.S.C. 1970, c. J-3.

Kijewski, K. (1983). The effect of the decision to charge upon subsequent criminal behaviour. *Canadian Journal of Criminology, 25,* 201–207.

McLellan, A. (1998, May 12). Minister announces youth justice strategy. Accessed online at http://canada.justice.gc.ca/en/news/nr/1998/yoa.html.

Morris, A., & Maxwell, G. (2001). Restorative conferencing. In G. Bazemore & Schiff (Eds.), *Restorative community justice: Repairing harm and transforming communities* (pp. 173–197). Cincinnati: Anderson Publishing.

Morton, M., & West, G. (1983). An experiment in diversion by a citizen committee. In R. Corrado, M. LeBlanc, & J. Trepanier (Eds.), *Current issues in juvenile justice.* Toronto: Butterworths.

Moyer, S. (1980). *Diversion from the juvenile justice system and its impact on children: A review of the literature.* Ottawa: Department of Justice, 67–74.

Ontario. Ministry of the Attorney General. (1995). *Alternative measures program: Policy & procedures manual.* Toronto: Queen's Printer.

Ontario Social Development Council. (1988). *Young Offenders Act dispositions: Challenges and choices.* Toronto: Author.

Pate, K. J., & Peachey, D. E. (1988). Face-to-face: Victim–offender mediation under the *Young Offenders Act.* In J. Hudson, J. Hornick, & B. Burrows (Eds.). *Justice and the young offender in Canada.* Toronto: Wall and Thompson.

Platt, P. (1995). *Young offenders law in Canada.* 2nd ed. Toronto: Butterworths.

Prashaw, R. (2001). Restorative justice: Lessons in empathy and connecting people. *Canadian Journal of Community Mental Health, 20*(2), 23–27.

Ross, R. (1996). *Returning to the teachings: Exploring Aboriginal justice.* Toronto: Penguin.

Statistics Canada. (2002). Youth court statistics 2000–2001. *Juristat, 22*(3).

Stuart, D. (2001). *Canadian criminal law* (4th ed.). Toronto: Carswell.

Warner, J., Fischer, B., Albanes, R., & Anaitay, O. (1998). Marijuana, juveniles, and the police: What high-school students believe about detection and enforcement. *Canadian Journal of Criminology, 40*(4), 401–420.

Young Offenders Act, R.S.C. 1985, c. Y-1, enacted as S.C. 1980-81-82-83, c. 110, s. 3(1)(d).

Youth Criminal Justice Act (2002), royal assent February 19, 2002, in force April 1, 2003. YCJA, s. 3(1)(b)(ii).

Cases Cited

R. v. S.(S.), [1990] 2 S.C.R. 294.

R. v. Askov, [1990] 2 S.C.R. 1199.

R. v. O'Connor, [1995] 4 S.C.R. 441 at 457.

R. v. T.(V.), [1992] 1 S.C.R. 749

Notes

1. The term "restorative justice" is increasingly being used to characterize responses to offending that focus on restoring relationships of harmony between offenders and victim. These programs generally involve the victim, the offender, and family members in a process of discussion about the offence and its effects on the victim and the community, and the joint development of a plan to provide compensation to the victim and to help prevent recurrence of offending behaviour (see Archibald, 1999; Bazemore & Walgrave, 1999; Braithwaite, 2000; Prashaw, 2001).

2. While a youth justice court judge cannot direct a case to an extrajudicial sanctions program, there is a narrow residual discretion in any case for a judge to stay proceedings where compelling the accused to stand trial would contravene "the community's basic sense of decency and fair play and thereby … call into question the integrity of the [justice] system" (*R. v. O'Connor,* [1995] 4 S.C.R. 441 at 457). The abuse of process power is to be exercised only in the "clearest of cases" and might, for example, be invoked if there was evidence of discrimination or a lengthy delay in laying charges after a police investigation. There is also a doctrine known as *de minimis non curat lex* (about trifling things do not go to the law), which has occasionally

been invoked by Canadian judges to dismiss charges; as, for example, in drug cases where a small quantity of drugs are discovered. But it would appear that, since *R. v. T.(V.)*, [1992] 1 S.C.R. 749, this doctrine cannot be used in youth justice court to deal with cases that might have been diverted. See Stuart, D. *Canadian criminal law* (4th ed.). Toronto: Carswell, 2001, pp. 594–99.

3. The role of the Crown prosecutor will be discussed further in Chapter 10. However, section 3 of the YCJA gives prosecutors the power to administer cautions instead of starting or continuing judicial proceedings, and section 23 allows them to screen youth cases before charges are laid. It is up to provincial governments to decide whether to offer this option.

4. This is, for example, the official policy in Ontario. Counselling is not considered "an appropriate measure," although program workers provide "information about counseling and a [voluntary] referral might be appropriate as part of the negotiation process" (Ontario. Ministry of the Attorney General. *Alternative measures program: Policy & procedures manual*. Toronto: Queen's Printer, 1995, p. 15).

chapter ten

The Roles of Legal Professionals in Youth Court

Miriam Bloomenfeld*

Counsel, Criminal Law Policy Branch
Ontario Ministry of the Attorney General
and

David Cole

Judge, Ontario Court of Justice
Metro West Court, Toronto

INTRODUCTION

Many legal professionals participate in the adjudication of youth criminal cases. Police are the first point of entry for youth into the criminal justice system and make decisions regarding who is charged and for what. However, once a youth enters the system he or she is confronted with other legal professionals including Crown prosecutors, defence counsel, duty counsel, and judges. Their roles vis-à-vis the youth are dictated by law and policy, and the introduction of the *Youth Criminal Justice Act* (YCJA) will likely greatly impact on not only how youth are charged, but also how they ultimately will be processed by these professionals in the system. This chapter illustrates through a case example the roles of these legal professionals in youth criminal cases.

THE FACT PATTERN

Three Saturdays ago, 16-year-olds Peter H., Brian S., and Rick B. were at Peter's house, while his parents were at work. The youths broke into the liquor cabinet and drank most of a bottle of vodka. They realized they should replace the alcohol before its loss was discovered; rather than take the bus to the mall where the liquor store was located, they "borrowed"

* Counsel, Criminal Law Policy Branch, Ontario Ministry of the Attorney General. Ms. Bloomenfeld contributed exclusively to the portion describing the role of the Crown in youth prosecutions. The views expressed herein are those of the author alone and do not reflect the views of the Ontario Ministry of the Attorney General.

Peter's father's car to get there. Once they arrived at the mall, they split up. Within a few minutes, Peter was caught red-handed stealing a video game from a store in the mall. Following normal store policy, rather than having Peter charged with theft, mall security arranged for him to be prohibited from going to the mall for the next year, by serving him with a trespass notice. Meanwhile, Brian and Rick got caught at the liquor store using Peter's brother's identification to try to replace the alcohol they had drunk at the H. residence; as they were obviously drunk, the police simply summoned their parents to the mall, and their parents decided to ground them for the next two weeks.

The three met in the school cafeteria at lunchtime the following Monday. Peter was very angry about being caught, mostly because he thought that he had been "ratted out" by his classmate Buzzer L., who worked at the store and watched him take the video game. The youths decided it was time to "get" Buzzer. They agreed that Rick would scratch the word "rat" on the front of Buzzer's locker, while Peter and Brian would hide in a stairwell to lie in wait for Buzzer. When Buzzer came down the stairs to go toward his locker, Peter and Brian punched him several times; when he fell to the ground, Peter kicked him three times in the face, breaking his nose. Brian stole Buzzer's portable CD player, which had fallen to the ground during the fight. Vice-principal Margo MacKinnon heard the commotion and the youths were caught. Following the school's "zero tolerance for violence" protocol, the police were called; all three youths were arrested and taken to the station.

When Peter's parents were contacted, they told the police: "Given what he's being doing to this family for the last few days, he can sit and rot for all we care." Brian's and Rick's parents came to the station; the police told them that since all three youths were going to be charged with robbery and mischief (to Buzzer's locker) the police had no power to release them from the station.

The police told the parents that they would be recommending the Justice release their two sons on bail on strict conditions.

ROLE OF THE CROWN

Crown counsel play a unique role in the criminal justice system due in part to their position as "quasi-judicial officers," requiring a balance between their function as adversaries with their responsibility to exercise discretion as guardians of the public interest. Their complex role within the criminal justice system is aptly summarized in these two statements from the Supreme Court of Canada:

> It cannot be overemphasized that the purpose of a criminal prosecution is not to obtain a conviction; it is to lay before a jury what the Crown considers to be credible evidence relevant to what is alleged to be a crime. Counsel have a duty to see that all available legal proof of the facts is presented: it should be done firmly and pressed to its legitimate strength, but it must also be done fairly. The role of prosecutor excludes any notion of winning or losing; his function is a matter of public duty than which in civil life there can be none charged with greater personal responsibility. It is to be efficiently performed with an ingrained sense of the dignity, the seriousness and the justness of judicial proceedings.[1]...

[W]hile it is without question that the Crown performs a special function in ensuring that justice is served and cannot adopt a purely adversarial role towards the defence, [cites omitted] it is well recognized that the adversarial process is an important part of our judicial system and an accepted tool in our search for truth: see, for example, *R. v. Gruenke*, [1991] 3 S.C.R. 263 at 295, 67 C.C.C. (3d) 289 *per* L'Heureux-Dube J. Nor should it be assumed that the Crown cannot act as a strong advocate within this adversarial process. In that regard, it is both permissible and desirable that it vigorously pursue a legitimate result to the best of its ability. Indeed, this is a critical element of this country's criminal law mechanism: [cites omitted]. In this sense, within the boundaries outlined above, the Crown must be allowed to perform the function with which it has been entrusted; discretion in pursuing justice remains an important part of that function. [emphasis in original][2]

In the youth court context, the balancing of the dual aspects of the Crown's role is particularly challenging given young persons' reduced maturity and the potential impact that their involvement with the criminal justice system may have on the rest of their lives, as well as concerns regarding the long-term protection of the public. As the Preamble to the *Youth Criminal Justice Act* (YCJA – S.C. 2002, c. C-70) states, "Members of society share a responsibility to address the developmental challenges and needs of young persons and to guide them into adulthood." The Crown has a central role to play in discharging that responsibility in the context of criminal prosecutions.

Crown counsel's role extends far beyond the confines of the courtroom. Like judges and defence counsel, the in-court activities of Crown counsel in youth cases comprise only a fraction of their responsibilities. Crown counsel may be involved in a case from the pre-charge stage right through to post-sentence. Similarly, the types of activities that Crown counsel may perform in any given day vary broadly and may include giving advice to police, screening files, gathering information, negotiating plea resolutions, participating in pretrial conferences, interviewing witnesses, setting dates, legal research, and, of course, appearing in court. In Ontario,[3]

many key areas of prosecutorial discretion and decision-making are guided by Crown policy and practice memoranda. Thus, in conducting youth prosecutions, Crown counsel are responsive to legislative requirements, policy guidelines, and operational pressures.

In many ways, youth court requires even more out-of-court activity than ordinary, "adult" court. This distinction was true to some extent under the *Young Offenders Act* (YOA) but has been enhanced by the YCJA. This section provides a general account of some of the ways in which Ontario Crown counsel may be involved in youth court cases. This account is certainly not exhaustive and cannot reflect the wide diversity of the different jurisdictions within Ontario and across Canada. It may, however, provide some insight into the complexity of the Crown's role in youth cases.

The *Youth Criminal Justice Act*

The governing federal legislation for all criminal matters involving young persons aged 12 to 17 is the YCJA. The YCJA has the potential to have a profound impact on the way the criminal justice system deals with young persons. In response to criticisms of its predecessor, the YOA, it introduces many new principles, sentences, and procedural mechanisms and is considerably longer. To complicate matters further, some of the new features of the YCJA, such as certain types of sentencing alternatives, are optional depending on whether or how individual provinces wish to implement them. As a result, everyone involved in the criminal justice system, including judges, justices of the peace, Crown and defence counsel, police, probation officers, correctional officials, court staff, and the community are faced with the challenge of not only learning the new law, but also understanding how it has been implemented in different jurisdictions and adapting it to the realities of the current system. Some of the major changes and potential effects of the YCJA will be highlighted below as they relate to the role of the Crown in the progress of youth court cases.

Impact of *Youth Criminal Justice Act* Principles on the Role of the Crown

Many of the major changes in the YCJA stem not from new procedures or sentences but rather from an elaborate and comprehensive series of principles intended to govern the use of discretion and decision-making under the *Act*. In addition to being one of the few pieces of criminal legislation that has a preamble, the YCJA has a general Declaration of Principle (YCJA, sec. 3, see Appendix C) as well as specific principles intended to structure the use of discretion by criminal justice professionals in all major areas of decision-making, including extrajudicial measures (YCJA secs. 4, 5), sentencing (YCJA sec. 38), and custody and supervision (YCJA sec. 83). Many of these principles build upon and enhance ideas that emerged under the YOA.

Extrajudicial Measures and the Role of the Police

Crown counsel are often contacted by police for general or specific advice about legal issues arising during their investigations. In the youth context, police have special statutory obligations relating to taking statements from young persons and considering alternatives to laying charges. Prior to laying a charge, police must consider an "extrajudicial measure" as an alternative to commencing formal criminal proceedings. Specifically, the police must consider whether a young person could be held accountable for the alleged offence by no further action, a warning, a caution, or (with the young person's consent) a referral to a community program or agency that might assist the young person not to commit offences (YCJA, sec. 6(1)). The YCJA also provides for two more formal extrajudicial measures: a "police caution program" (YCJA, sec.7) and a "Crown caution program" (YCJA, sec. 8). Both of these programs are optional in that individual provincial governments can choose whether to implement them in their jurisdictions. Programs like these formalize the caution process, generally with a letter to the young person or a verbal caution. Ontario does not currently have either type of formal program. Many individual police services, however, have local caution programs or other forms of discretionary warning that serve the same purpose.

The philosophy of the YCJA is based, in part, on an assumption that out-of-court responses to youth crime are as effective—or in many cases, more effective—than formal court proceedings. Many of the principles set out in the Act reflect this assumption, and apply directly to a police officer's decision whether to lay a criminal charge

Logically, the new police obligation to contemplate an extrajudicial measure prior to laying a charge could reduce the number of charges that come into the Crown's office. If this happens, it is likely that there will be some shift in the number and/or types of charges that the Crown sees. For example, property offences may be dealt with via extrajudicial measures more often than in the past.

The Fact Pattern In the fact scenario above, police would consider extrajudicial measures for all three young persons. Because of the assault component of the robbery charge, none of the boys would qualify for the statutory presumption in favour of an extrajudicial measure (YCJA, sec. 4(c)). The alleged violence would not, however, disqualify the youths from pre-charge diversion. The potential to devise an extrajudicial measure that would hold these young persons accountable would be complicated by a number of factors, including the element of school bullying, the level of violence, Buzzer's injuries, the school's zero-violence protocols, and Peter's parents' frustration.

Bail Issues for Crown Counsel The Crown's position on bail depends on a complex constellation of factors drawn from the statutory requirements of the *Criminal Code* and the YCJA, as well as Ontario Crown policy.[4] The Crown's office receives the brief from the police and Crown counsel assess the case before taking a position with defence counsel and the court. A partial list of factors that play into that assessment includes the nature of the offence, the existence and nature of a criminal record, the impact of the offence on the victims, the strength of the case, the young person's personal history and circumstances, availability of supports

in the community, outstanding charges, and so on.

The YCJA modifies the *Criminal Code* bail provisions in three major ways:

- First, it introduces a restriction on pre-trial detention on the ground of "protection or safety of the public."[5] The YCJA contains a presumption against detention on this ground unless the young person has (a) committed a violent offence, (b) failed to comply with non-custodial sentences, or (c) committed an indictable offence for which an adult would be liable to imprisonment for a term of more than two years, and has a history that indicates a pattern of findings of guilt under the YCJA or the YOA (YCJA, sec. 29(2), sec. 38(1)(a)(b)(c)).

- Secondly, the YCJA sets out a new prohibition against detaining a young person prior to sentence as a substitute for appropriate child protection, mental health, or other social measures (YCJA, sec. 29(1)). This prohibition existed under the YOA but only in relation to the youth sentencing.

- Thirdly, the YCJA adds to the court's obligations by requiring an inquiry into the availability of a "responsible person" in cases where the young person might otherwise be detained. One of the alternatives to detention available in the YOA was the release of a young person into the care of a "responsible person." The YCJA promotes this option by adding a mandatory obligation that, prior to detaining a young person, the youth justice court or justice of the peace inquire as to the availability of a responsible person and whether the young person is willing to be placed in that person's care (YCJA, sec. 31(2)).

Crown decision-making regarding a young person's potential for judicial interim release and preparation for bail hearings must incorporate these new requirements. In practice, this may mean fewer and/or lengthier contested bail hearings.

The Fact Pattern Given that the alleged robbery is a violent offence, the statutory presumption against detention on the secondary ground does not apply in this case. Simply meeting one of the criteria for pretrial detention would not, however, prohibit the Crown from consenting to bail. Many offences demonstrating these criteria would lead to neither pretrial detention nor a custodial sentence. Crown counsel's position on bail would have to take into account, among other things, the effect of the offence on the victim and the young persons' return to school, the views of the parents, and the young persons' prior criminal histories, if any.

Charge Screening and Extrajudicial Sanctions Once the case file has been received from the police, the Crown "screens"[6] the case. Screening serves many essential functions in the Crown's management of criminal cases, including the determination of whether

- there is a reasonable prospect of a finding of guilt;
- assuming there is a reasonable prospect of a finding of guilt, it is in the public interest to discontinue the prosecution;
- the proper charge has been laid;
- the police investigation is complete and, if so, the fruits of the investigation are available to Crown and defence counsel;
- the Crown will be seeking a DNA databank order;

- appropriate statutory notices (if any) have been served;
- the circumstances of the offence require notification of the Children's Aid Society pursuant to sec. 72(1) of the *Child Family Services Act*;
- the young person is eligible for extrajudicial sanction;
- proper disclosure has been made to the accused young person;
- it is appropriate to make a preliminary estimate of the Crown's position on sentence.[7]
- this is an appropriate case in which to seek an adult sentence.[8]

The screening process will continue throughout the life of the case as new information is received by the Crown, but this initial assessment will often be essential in determining how a case will be dealt with.

In youth cases, one of the most significant decisions generally made at the screening stage is whether the case can be diverted from the court process by using an "extrajudicial sanction." An extrajudicial sanction is essentially a non-court response to an offence, used after a charge has been laid. Like the YOA before it, the YCJA gives each province a choice as to whether to establish an extrajudicial sanctions program (YCJA, 10(2)). Ontario does have such a program, carried over from the original "alternative measures" program established in 1988 under the YOA.[9]

In keeping with the YCJA's emphasis on principles, there are extensive statutory considerations that Crown counsel must factor into decisions regarding extrajudicial sanctions. The general principles set out in sec. 3, for example, contain many assertions that militate in favour of an extrajudicial sanction in appropriate cases. In addition, the specific principles and objectives applicable to extrajudicial measures also govern the decision to refer a case for extrajudicial sanction (YCJA, secs. 4 and 5). Finally, the YCJA sets out a number of procedural preconditions to the use of an extrajudicial sanction.

While most of the procedural requirements for an extrajudicial sanction are essentially identical to the YOA's alternative measures provisions, the YCJA introduces one significant addition: an extrajudicial sanction may be used to deal with an alleged offence only if the young person cannot be adequately dealt with by a warning, caution, or referral because of the seriousness of the offence, the nature and number of previous offences committed by the young person, or any other aggravating circumstances (YCJA, sec. 10(1)). This threshold for use of an extrajudicial sanction further entrenches the YCJA's principled preference for dealing with youth offences outside the formal court process wherever possible.

The Fact Pattern The fact scenario proposed above would trigger many of the principled considerations mandated by the YCJA. Although all three young persons are eligible for consideration for extrajudicial sanctions, Rick would be the best candidate for diversion given that his involvement in the offence was the most minimal. As part of the screening process, Crown counsel would assess whether there is any evidence linking Rick to the robbery charge. Depending on that assessment, Crown counsel may determine that there is no reasonable prospect of conviction against Rick on that charge. Alternatively, the Crown may decide that,

for public interest reasons, it is preferable in his case to proceed only on the mischief charge (for defacing Buzzer's locker).

If the Crown proceeded on reduced charges only, and Rick has no previous record, the statutory presumption in favour of an extrajudicial sanction for a non-violent offence would apply. Crown counsel would not be bound by the presumption, but would give an extrajudicial sanction serious consideration. Because of the school setting and the bullying elements of the offence, Crown counsel might consider the availability of specific, school-based programs of peer counselling or reconciliation. The ultimate decision as to what type of sanction might be appropriate would be made by the probation officer, who would meet with Rick and devise an extrajudicial sanction agreement.

Plea Resolutions and Youth Sentencing

Another significant purpose of Crown screening of case files is to determine what the Crown's position may be on sentence, with a view to potential resolution discussions.[10] The Ontario prosecution system has adopted a policy that encourages efforts to meet with defence counsel prior to the date of trial or preliminary hearing, to "discuss matters that will encourage the efficient use of limited resources including

(a) negotiation of guilty pleas to charges that have been screened, agreement as to the facts and law concerning such charges, and negotiation of the position of Crown counsel on sentence;

(b) the identification and narrowing of issues and attendant reduction in the number of witnesses required to attend court at a preliminary inquiry or trial through appropriate admissions by Crown and defence counsel; and

(c) any other matters that may affect the efficient disposition of the charges in a manner consistent with the proper administration of justice."[11]

Many factors play into the potential resolution of cases, including the circumstances of the offender and the offence, the impact of the offence on the victim and the strength of the Crown's case. Generally, if resolution discussions result in a guilty plea, the Crown's sentencing position will reflect the lower end of the applicable range or a plea to a reduced charge. The more lenient sentencing position often takes into account, among other things, the remorse indicated by an admission of guilt, the minimization of the trauma of testifying for the victim, and the preservation of court time and resources.

Early resolution of charges by way of extrajudicial sanction or guilty plea is particularly valuable in youth cases because of the statutorily entrenched principle that the passage of time has different, more serious consequences for young persons than for adults. The YCJA explicitly asserts that young persons have a different perception of time (sec. 3(1)(iv)). Common sense also dictates that consequences will generally be more meaningful for a young person if they are imposed closer in time to the commission of the offence. Not only will the link between the offending conduct and the sanction be more effectively reinforced, but the young person also will not have developed and grown to the point where the offence is a distant memory, committed by a younger self. A young person is often a profoundly different individual a year later than the one who committed the offence.

An early plea agreement will usually result either in a Crown undertaking to seek a particular sentence or range of sentence, or a joint submission by Crown and defence counsel. In either case, the matter will often be "pre-tried" before a judge, to determine whether the plea and sentence agreement is viable.[12] Case law has maintained that, while the administration of justice benefits from respecting joint submissions,[13] the court is never bound by them.

To further encourage the use of alternatives to custody, the YCJA contains new, non-custodial sentencing options, such as an "intensive support and supervision order" (YCJA, sec. 42(2)(l)) and a sentence ordering the young person to participate in a non-residential program (YCJA sec. 42(2)(m)). These are optional sentences in the sense that each province can choose whether to implement them, and their availability is circumscribed accordingly. Ontario does not currently offer intensive support and supervision programs or attendance programs as standalone sentences.

In support of the YCJA's promotion of rehabilitation and reintegration, each custodial sentence includes a period of supervision in the community. This is a departure from the YOA, which kept young persons in custody throughout the length of a custodial sentence. The ratio of custody to community supervision is, generally, two-thirds custody to one-third supervision.[14] For murder, attempted murder, manslaughter, and aggravated sexual assault, the division of custody and supervision is determined by the sentencing judge.[15] The Crown has the option, in limited circumstances, of seeking to extend the custodial portion of a custody and supervision sentence (YCJA, sec. 98, sec. 104). As well, if the young person breaches a term of the community supervision or commits a further offence, he or she could be remanded to custody for a portion or the entirety of the remainder of the sentence (YCJA, sec. 103, sec. 109).

A further complicating feature of sentencing proceedings under the YCJA is the option for the Crown to apply to have the offence judicially determined to be a "serious violent offence." A "judicial determination of serious violent offence" is a new provision introduced by the YCJA. After a finding of guilt, Crown counsel may ask the judge to determine that the offence is a "serious violent offence"; that is, an offence in which the young person caused or attempted to cause serious bodily harm (YCJA, sec. 42(9), sec. 2(1)). Such a judicial determination has no immediate consequences[16] for the young person, although it may become relevant in the future if the young person continues to commit serious violent offences. The question of whether a judicial determination of serious violent offence will be sought or imposed has, in some cases, been hotly contested.[17]

As currently drafted, the YCJA creates a presumption in favour of an adult sentence for a third, judicially determined serious violent offence if the offence is one for which an adult could be incarcerated for more than two years. The significance of serious violent offences in the adult sentence regime is uncertain, however, given the Quebec Court of Appeal's declaration that the adult sentence presumptions are unconstitutional (as discussed in Chapters 3 and 11). As well, a third judicial determination of serious violent offence could open the door to an "intensive rehabilitative custody and supervision sentence," pursuant to sec. 42(2)(r) and sec. 42(7). An intensive rehabilitative custody and supervision sentence, available in limited circumstances, provides for psychological treatment in a custodial setting.

The Fact Pattern In addition to the standard benefits of an early resolution, the young persons described in the hypothetical fact pattern present specific issues that make a quick disposition of the charges desirable. In particular, the fact that the offence took place in the school setting and constituted a form of bullying means that the future of Rick, Peter, and Brian's attendance at that school is jeopardized. The matter needs to be resolved in a way that will allow the three young persons to continue their education while protecting Buzzer and other students at the school from further fear or harassment. Finding a quick resolution that addresses these issues should be a high priority for everyone involved in the case.

The first issue that Crown and defence would have to resolve would likely be whether any of the three boys would receive a custodial sentence. If not resolved at this stage, the consideration of a custodial sentence would become a priority at a judicial pre-trial or sentencing hearing. In addition to the principles promoting restraint in the use of custody, the YCJA prohibits the imposition of a custodial sentence unless

(a) the young person has committed a violent offence;

(b) the young person has failed to comply with non-custodial sentences;

(c) the young person has committed an indictable offence for which an adult would be liable to imprisonment for a term of more than two years and has a history that indicates a pattern of findings of guilt under the YCJA or the YOA; or

(d) it is an exceptional case in which the young person has committed an indictable offence, in aggravating circumstances which would make a non-custodial sentence inconsistent with the YCJA's purpose and principles of sentencing (YCJA, sec. 39(1)).

Because he has no criminal record, it is likely that Rick would be ineligible for a custodial sentence should he be absolved of any responsibility for Buzzer's beating. Both Peter and Brian could, in theory, be liable to a custodial sentence because of the violence against Buzzer. However, because this is Brian's first offence and, in recognition of his lesser contribution to Buzzer's injuries, his counsel would have a good argument for a non-custodial sentence.

Peter's counsel would have more difficulty in persuading the Crown to support a non-custodial disposition. Peter was the ringleader and instigator of the attack on Buzzer. If he hadn't sought revenge against Buzzer for allegedly "ratting him out" for taking the videogame, the offence would not have occurred. Moreover, Peter's kicking Buzzer after he was down and breaking his nose may well amount to a "serious violent offence." It is likely that all parties would want to review a pre-sentence report[18] before taking a firm and final position on sentence. In addition, the Crown would want to seek input from Buzzer on the degree of his injuries and the impact of the offence, as well as to canvass the position of the school and Peter's parents.

Conferencing One of the novel features of the YCJA is the statutory introduction of "conferencing" as a procedural tool for facilitating decision-making. A "conference" is defined in sec. 2(1) as "a group of persons who are convened to give advice in accordance with section 19." Section 19 provides that "a youth justice court judge, the provincial director, a police officer, a justice of the peace, a prosecutor or a youth worker may convene or cause to be convened a conference for the purpose of making a decision required to be made" under the YCJA.

This provision arises from experience in many countries suggesting that the traditional punishment-oriented paradigm of criminal justice does not work well for all young people. Section 41 of the YCJA authorizes a youth justice court judge to convene a conference "for recommendations to the court on an appropriate youth sentence." Parliament has recognized that Canada's geographical, cultural, and ethnic diversity is such that a "one-size-fits-all" conferencing scheme would be inappropriate. Although some judges—particularly those who preside in or near Aboriginal communities—have been conducting (or stimulating) conferences for many years (cf. Green, 1998), there have to date been few types of *judicial* conferences other than those experiments known as "sentencing circles" or "family group conferences," mainly because the infrastructure necessary to support such "restorative justice" endeavours has not yet been developed in any substantial way.[19]

The YCJA does enable provinces to create rules to govern conferences called for by police, prosecutors, or provincial directors, but does not elaborate on what those rules might cover. To this point, Ontario has not propounded formal rules, but has created guidelines for these "non-judicial conferences." The intention of the guidelines is to set out basic principles that should be observed by all those convening, conducting, facilitating, or participating in conferences to ensure that the rights of the young person and the complainant as well as the integrity of the process are protected.

How and how often conferences will be used remains to be seen. Generally, it has been suggested that they might take one of two forms: either "case conferences," in which professionals meet with the young person and his or her family to discuss the best way to address the issues raised by the case; or "restorative conferences," in which the young person meets with community members, his or her family, and the complainant, if willing, to discuss the impact of the offence and ways to make amends. Potential advantages of conferences include the opportunity to bring together all of the relevant parties at one time, to generate ideas and come up with creative solutions, as well as the chance for the young person to confront the consequences of the offence and take responsibility. Challenges for Crown counsel asked to arrange, facilitate, or participate in conferences could include lack of resources, lack of expertise, conflicts with the Crown's traditional adversarial role, and the need to protect the rights of the young person and the complainant.

ROLE OF DEFENCE/DUTY COUNSEL

The *Canadian Charter of Rights and Freedoms*, the *Youth Criminal Justice Act*, and case law interpreting these statutes (and their predecessors) make it very clear that at all stages of the court process, as well as in the pre-court stages, young persons are to be given ample opportunity to take advantage of legal *advice* and *advocacy* before they may be sanctioned by any court process. [20]

In order to comply with these legal requirements, provincial and territorial justice ministries and legal aid plans have developed extensive and quite elaborate systems for the delivery of legal services to youths charged with offences. As these programs differ considerably across the country, we shall restrict ourselves to a very brief outline of Ontario's "mixed" system, which is reasonably typical.

Although a young person may make private arrangements to hire a lawyer as soon as he or she has been charged with an offence, the vast majority of young persons who appear in court in response to a charge being laid will not have done so by the time of their first appearance. Indeed, many young persons and their families may not realize that they can or should do so. The Ontario Legal Aid Plan has developed a system of "duty counsel" to advise and appear in court at a young person's first appearance (and often at several subsequent appearances).[21] They identify young persons who need advice by explaining to them (and their families) what is likely to happen on first appearance and usually address the court on the young person's behalf:

- If the charge is so serious that the young person has been detained in custody pending first appearance, duty counsel will go to the holding cells before court, advise the young person about his or her options, contact people who might agree to supervise[22] the accused's release on bail pending trial, examine and cross-examine witnesses at the bail hearing, and make arguments to the presiding justice as to why and under what conditions the young person might be released. In the fact scenario presented, duty counsel would likely appear for all three young persons; the bail hearings for Brian and Rick would likely be cases in which the Crown would agree that release on bail is appropriate. Given the fact that Peter is in more trouble, and given that his parents seem unwilling to assist him, securing a release on bail would likely be more difficult.

- If the charge is one where Crown counsel might be prepared to agree that the accused young person be diverted from the court process by performing an extrajudicial sanction (YCJA, secs. 4, 5, 8, and 10), duty counsel will meet with the young person, review the allegations, explain the various options available, secure the accused's informed agreement to enter the diversion program, negotiate with Crown counsel and the probation service over the terms of the proposed sanction, and speak in open court to the judge to explain the agreement. In the fact scenario presented, it might well be that the charge of mischief would be one about which duty counsel could approach Crown counsel to explore the possibility of diversion, especially the charge against Rick, the least involved young person.[23]

- If extrajudicial sanctions are not offered by the Crown, and the young person wishes to plead guilty to the charge, duty counsel (or privately retained counsel) may review the facts and the young person's understanding of the significance of a plea of guilty, advise the young person what is likely to happen should a plea be entered, obtain materials that may be used in mitigation of sentence, and present these (usually privately) to the Crown in support of a particular

sentence. Sometimes Crown counsel will agree on the terms of a sentence (a "joint submission"), sometimes not (an "open" submission). In either case, the judge pronounces the sentence after hearing submissions in open court.

Once the initial court appearance(s) have been completed, the young person has a series of decisions to make about what to do next. In most parts of Canada, duty counsel are not usually authorized to conduct trials on behalf of young persons who wish to dispute their guilt. A young person (or the family) in this position may either make his or her own arrangements to hire a lawyer or may apply to the Legal Aid Plan for a "certificate," which, if granted, may be taken to a lawyer of choice. Once the lawyer accepts the certificate, the Legal Aid Plan pays the fees.[24] If, after considering his or her position, the young person wishes to propose to the Crown that an extrajudicial sanction—or some other form of diversionary measure—be performed in lieu of the charge being further proceeded with, either duty counsel or counsel of choice (privately retained or acting under a legal aid certificate) may enter into negotiations with the Crown at any stage.

Under the *Juvenile Delinquents Act*, questions were consistently raised by judges and commentators as to whether a young person should or could be represented by a lawyer. Whereas the statutory recognition of a "due process" model for adjudication of youth cases under both the YOA and the YCJA has put many of these debates to rest, there still remain some difficult issues as to the appropriate role for lawyers representing young persons in Canadian courts. In essence, these seem to revolve around two recurrent themes: Who is the client? and What are the client's instructions to counsel? While space limitations preclude any detailed consideration of these themes (cf. Bala, 2003), suffice it to say that there may often be considerable tension between what the payers of legal services (the parents, institutional guardians, the state) may consider is best for the young person and what the accused wishes to instruct the lawyer to do. For example, parents may decide that they do not wish to spend money on a potential defence that they consider to be either unlikely to succeed or not in their child's best interests.

One new provision under the YCJA that may raise some ethical questions about the rights of young persons to legal representation authorizes provinces to set up schemes for "the recovery of costs of a young person's counsel from the young person or the parents of the young person" once the trial has been concluded (sec. 25(10)). This provision did not exist under the YOA; consequently, it is not currently known which provinces (presumably through their legal aid plans) intend to implement such cost-recovery schemes. Even if implemented, it is difficult to predict how aggressively they will be enforced. It is possible that parents who are aware that they may be pursued for the costs of representing their children will exert pressure to have their children plead guilty at a very early stage in the proceedings.

Another problem, particularly with very young persons, is that the instructions the lawyer receives from the client may make little sense, as the accused may be focused on issues that are not legally relevant (cf. Peterson-Badali &

Abramovitch, 1992; Peterson-Badali & Loegl, 1998). To take a simple example, in discussing what testimony an accused might give if he takes the stand, it is often exceedingly difficult to explain to an adult—let alone a 12-year-old—such concepts as the extremely limited admissibility of what he or she has heard "through the grapevine." Unfortunately, it is an all too common sight in youth court to see an accused demonstrating complete disinterest in the process while the court professionals are intensely involved in lengthy argument over some legally complex issue. In the fact situation presented, it might well be that counsel for Peter H. would have considerable difficulty explaining to his client that the fact that he considered Buzzer L. to have "ratted him out" did not provide him with a justification in law to take revenge in the way he did.

Finally, there are concerns generally in the legal literature about the power imbalance between defence (or duty) counsel and vulnerable and unsophisticated clients. Some of this current debate centres around whether defence counsel for young offenders should act in the role of legal advocate or guardian (Milne, Linden, & Kueneman, 1992). As legal advocates, counsel will provide a legal defence, functioning with youth in essentially the same manner as they would with adults; that is, advising them to remain silent, suggesting they not cooperate with the police, and trying to prevent a conviction. On the other hand, a guardian approach to representing young persons would involve looking out for what could be called their "best interests," with a greater focus on rehabilitative concerns, particularly during sentencing. However, as early as 1981, the

Law Society of Upper Canada in Ontario advised that, "there is no place for counsel representing a child … to argue what is in his opinion in the best interests of the child" (1981, cited in Bala, 2003). Nonetheless, it would appear that most defence counsel, when representing young persons, likely combine elements of both of these approaches to best address their clients' needs and requirements.

ROLE OF THE YOUTH COURT JUDGE

It will be clear from these descriptions of the roles of the police, Crowns, and duty/defence counsel that the youth court judge does not usually[25] become involved until much later in the process. It should also be kept in mind that, while some judges are selected—or, more likely, choose to preside in youth court—the role of the judge in youth court does not differ significantly from that of the judge in adult court. Indeed, in most court facilities where there is a mix of adult and youth cases, judges will usually rotate between adult and youth courts.

Presiding over Pretrial Meetings with Counsel

Although practices differ across the country, most court systems have developed mechanisms whereby Crown and defence counsel are encouraged to meet with a judge to discuss scheduling of more complex cases (judicial pretrials [JPTs]).[26] In the fact pattern presented, if all three accused signify that they intend to proceed to trial,[27] depending on the number of witnesses who will likely be called, this case might take one to four full court days to try. Given that court time is a precious and expensive commodity, a judge *other than the designated trial judge* would be assigned to conduct a JPT. Typically, these are quite informal procedures, where Crown and defence counsel meet in the JPT judge's office to talk about the case. While notes are taken, there usually is no court reporter present. The accused may be in the building available for consultation with counsel, but they are virtually always excluded from the JPT so that counsel and the judge may consult without concern that what they say may be misinterpreted.[28] Often, the police officer in charge of the case will be present to assist (brief) the Crown attorney.[29]

The JPT usually begins with Crown counsel giving the judge an overview of the case. Specific problems are then identified and reviewed. In the fact pattern, assume that Peter H. has not been granted bail (because his parents are not prepared to act as sureties, and no one else is available). Thus, every effort will be made to expedite the trial of all three young persons, because of concerns that Peter, who is presumed in law to be innocent (*Charter*, sec. 11(d)), should not spend a long time in custody awaiting the determination of his guilt or innocence (*Charter*, sec. 11(b); YCJA, secs. 3(1)(b)(iv) and (v)). In these circumstances, it might well be that statements of secondary witnesses (such as vice-principal MacKinnon) have not yet been taken, not because their evidence is unimportant, but because of resource constraints. In these circumstances, the JPT judge might set a timetable for the taking of her statement by the police and for its production to defence counsel.

Next, a series of commonly encountered issues will be discussed. For example, in the fact pattern, it would be likely that the police became aware of the bad blood between Peter and Buzzer from statements given to the police by the three accused when they were in the police station following their arrest. Parliament has long recognized the need to have special rules that police must follow in the taking of statements from young persons (YCJA, secs. 146–7). In several cases the Supreme Court of Canada has interpreted these provisions quite strictly and has refused to allow statements into evidence because the young person was deemed not to have been properly informed of his or her right to be silent in response to police questioning.[30] The reality is that because of budgetary constraints most police officers have not received proper training as to the special rules to be followed in taking statements from accused persons under 18. Thus, at the JPT there would likely be considerable probing as to whether the Crown would try to have the accused's inculpatory statements admitted into evidence on the trial. Obviously, if the Crown decided that he or she would not attempt to have the statements introduced as evidence, the trial would be considerably shortened. Judges who regularly conduct JPTs are usually selected to do so because they are quite interventionist, pushing the parties to take a hard look at whether they intend to "flog a dead horse" by taking up scarce (and expensive) court time for a result that is likely inevitable given the Supreme Court's rulings on point.

Toward the end of the JPT (or earlier if the parties signal that they are in attendance for that purpose), the judge may be asked his or her views on sentence should one or more of the accused be interested in considering abandoning their wish to continue to trial. This may take a number of forms. Crown and defence counsel may come in with a specific sentencing proposal, or they may disagree as to the sentence yet agree that the appropriate sentence is within a certain range or of a particular nature. In those cases, the judge will be asked if he or she is prepared to commit to the range or to the specific proposal. Further, the judge may volunteer, or be asked to indicate, what he or she would do, without any specific proposal from counsel.

The case law is quite clear that the judge conducting a trial of the particular accused should not usually agree in advance to commit him/herself to a particular sentence. This is based on the theory that to do so would be offensive to the notion of open justice, in the sense that the court proceeding would be seen as a rubber stamp for what has been worked out earlier in the judge's office. However, one of the main reasons JPT systems have been established is to facilitate the resolution of cases prior to trial, which is the main reason why the JPT is supervised by a judge other than the assigned trial judge. Thus, if the JPT judge agrees to commit him/herself to a range of sentence or a particular sentence, this is not considered offensive, particularly when it is kept in mind that neither Crown nor defence counsel are obligated to go along with what may have been agreed to at a JPT. What both parties get out of a judicial indication of what sentence will be imposed is certainty, in exchange for compromise.

Rick B. In the fact scenario, it is relatively simple for either counsel or judge (or both) to come up with a sentence proposal for Rick. First, there would be some discussion as to what charge(s) he might plead guilty to. If the Crown concedes that Rick's statement is inadmissible as evidence against him, it would likely be impossible for the Crown to prove that he either intended to join Peter and Brian in robbing Buzzer, or that he did anything to aid and abet them in the robbery. Rick's defence counsel would no doubt be aware of the law (and would likely know the "realpolitik" of the courthouse[31]) and would probably press for a withdrawal of the robbery and theft charges in exchange for a disposition relating only to the mischief charge.

Rick's counsel might take a hard line with respect to that charge, suggesting that since his client has spent a couple of days in custody already,[32] has probably been on a restrictive bail for some weeks or months, is a first-time offender, and may have been disciplined by the school (perhaps suspended and/or ordered to pay for the damage caused), the Crown should withdraw the charge. This is consistent with the provisions of the Declaration of Principle in sec. 3 of the YCJA (see Appendix C), which, in general terms, may be said to promote the principle of restraint in the invocation and application of the criminal law against young persons.

It is important to understand that the Crown is the gatekeeper in deciding whether to proceed with charges. Though the judge may provide his or her opinion in forceful terms—a certain amount of "leaning on" counsel is a very regular feature of JPTs—ultimately the Crown might decide that it is in the public interest to proceed against Rick on the mischief charge. If so, the charge would likely be "severed" from the charges against the other accused, and a new (and considerably shortened) trial set. More likely, for Buzzer to have the reassurance of a court

order that Rick not have any contact with him, Crown might propose that Rick plead guilty to the mischief charge but that he be given a "conditional discharge," the third lowest form of penalty—which, if the accused lives up to the conditions imposed, is deemed to lapse after a few years.[33] Defence counsel would also likely counter with an offer that Rick would enter into a "peace bond," a court order short of a finding of guilt, by which he would be "bound over" to keep the peace and be of good behaviour, and that he not have contact with Buzzer for a period of up to one year.

Brian S. It would also not be too difficult for experienced counsel and JPT judge to negotiate an agreed disposition for Brian. Since he is a principal in the robbery charge, Crown counsel would likely take a firm position that he should plead guilty to that charge. The difficulties for the Crown in proving Brian's participation in the robbery would not seem to be a problem here because vice-principal MacKinnon observed the beating.[34] However, Brian's defence counsel is not entirely without bargaining chips. Depending on instructions he or she might obtain from his or her client, there is a distinct possibility that the Crown might be more interested in having Brian "on side" as a witness against Peter than as an accused who cannot be compelled to go into the witness box to give evidence at his own trial. This possibility would probably not be initially raised at a JPT. More likely, it would have been discussed among Crown, police, and defence counsel in advance of the JPT, and the JPT judge would be asked to take the accused's cooperation with the authorities into account in sentencing. Indeed, if there is a possibility that threats may be made if an accused learns that a co-accused has "rolled over," a judge might be asked informally to conduct an unscheduled JPT, where this fact could be disclosed and a sentence that reflects his cooperation canvassed.

Given that the motivation for the beating was that Peter considered Buzzer to have "ratted him out," defence counsel would not likely get his client's agreement to roll over. Therefore, Brian's counsel would likely have to advise his/her client that he had two alternatives—either to sit back and force the Crown to prove its case, or to plead guilty and seek the lowest possible sentence.

Unlike in the United States and England, in Canada there is no formal (or usual) "discount" for a guilty plea. It is, however, generally accepted that there should normally be some substantial reduction in sentence. This is due to the fact that not only does the plea save the state the time and expense of a trial, but an admission of guilt is considered in case law as the commencement of the rehabilitation of the offender. Can Brian escape going to jail for this offence? Because he engaged in violence, the statutory bar against the imposition of custody in sec. 39 of the YCJA would not apply, and Brian could be sentenced to custody.

This certainly does not end the matter. The first issue is whether the parties at the JPT are aware that there is some "tariff"[35] for the offence. In the adult context, some provincial courts of appeal, which set sentencing policy for courts in that province, have indicated that there are tariffs for certain offences—sexual abuse in a position of trust and armed robberies of convenience stores being two examples. Other provincial courts of appeal are strongly resistant to the notion of a fixed tariff, preferring to make statements about what is a generally appropriate sentence for a certain type of case. Furthermore, there may be a local tariff generally agreed to by the judiciary in response to a perceived problem in their region—breaking into unoccupied summer cottages in rural areas often attracts much harsher penalties than a residential break and enter in an urban area.[36] Finally, the particular judge conducting a JPT will likely have a reputation—merited or otherwise—for having views as to the usual penalty to be imposed for certain types of offences. If they are experienced and conscientious, both counsel will likely know whether any of these tariffs exist, and, if so, what they are.

Next, counsel will review mitigating factors. In dealing with the offence, these might well include that Brian did not kick Buzzer when he was down, that his theft of the CD player was apparently spontaneous, and that the item was recovered in good condition. In terms of Brian himself, he is a first-time offender—his escapade of attempting to pretend he was old enough to buy alcohol would probably be known to the police and counsel, but would likely be discounted, both because it would be dismissed as a youthful prank and because no formal proceedings had been initiated by the police. Defence counsel would likely tell the Crown and the JPT judge informally about the family's views of how Brian has responded to being charged and being on bail; similarly, his performance at school and any steps he may have taken to seek counselling would be discussed. Crown counsel, through the police or through the victim services unit of the court, would likely seek out Buzzer's views of his attitude toward and fears of Brian.

If all of these factors check out positively, given the provisions of the YCJA, it is unlikely that Brian would be given a custodial sentence for this offence. More likely, he would be placed on probation (for up to three years) and ordered to perform some substantial hours of community service (YCJA, sec. 42(2)(i)), to take counselling for anger management (and perhaps alcohol abuse), not to possess any weapons, and to refrain from contact with Buzzer, Peter, and Rick.

Alternatively, there are several types of custodial orders that could be made. Because Brian's part in this offence did not involve "serious violen[ce]," a *deferred custody and supervision sentence* (DCSO) could be imposed. (See footnote 16 for more on the DCSO.)

Even if Brian receives a *custody and supervision order* (YCJA, sec. 42(2)(n)), the judge, as advised by counsel, must also consider whether the sentence is to be served in open or closed custody (or some combination of the two). Although there are some local variations, closed custody involves incarceration in a usually unpleasant, maximum-security environment. Depending on the part of the country where the offender is sentenced, open custody may vary from a forestry camp in an isolated area to a group home in a city. In order to promote an offender's rehabilitation, custodial authorities are directed under the YCJA to develop comprehensive assessment and treatment plans as soon as the offenders arrive at the facility to which they are sent. Reviews of whether an offender should be transferred to an-

other type of facility can occur regularly during the sentence. The last third of most custodial sentences is served in the community under supervision. Probation for up to three years may added on to the expiry of the custody and supervision order.

Peter H. Assuming that Peter does not wish to proceed to trial, and that he has instructed his lawyer to investigate "what I might get if I cop [plead] to this," it would likely be very difficult for counsel or the JPT judge to make any reasonable assessment of the sentence that should be imposed on the basis of the information available at the JPT. Peter presents some obvious ongoing difficulties, both because of his antecedents and because of his role in the offence—particularly the degree of violence involved in the assault.

There is also the possibility of a referral to a child welfare organization under sec. 35 of the YCJA, though strictly speaking this is not designed as a mechanism for obtaining information for sentencing purposes. This is a new power authorizing a judge to order that an offender be referred to a child welfare agency "to determine whether [he or she] is in need of child welfare services." Experience to date under the YCJA seems to suggest that this provision is mainly being used to receive reports about young persons who already have some involvement with child welfare agencies. Since Peter does not appear to have had previous involvement with such an agency, it would seem unlikely that such a referral would be made. On the surface it appears that because Peter's parents have given up on him he might be in need of child welfare services, which are mandated to offer their services to young persons over the age of 16. In reality, however, because of budgetary constraints, child welfare agencies tend to offer their services to older youth only in extreme circumstances, which Peter does not appear to meet.

Apart from the submissions of counsel, there are other ways a youth court judge can find out more information about an offender in order to determine the appropriate sentence:

- **Section 34 assessment:** A judge may order that the offender be assessed "by a qualified person" (typically a psychologist, psychiatrist, or other medical practitioner) for several purposes, including "making ... a youth sentence." In the factual scenario the judge might be invited (or decide on his or her own motion) to order an assessment on the basis that Peter "may be suffering from a physical or mental illness or disorder, a psychological disorder, an emotional disturbance, a learning disability or a mental disability." Unfortunately, resource constraints existing in most provinces are such that these assessments usually are ordered only in cases much more serious than that presented in the fact scenario. Peter may well fit into one or more of the listed criteria, but (1) there is little that is bizarre about his crime, and (2) his criminality is as yet insufficiently entrenched such that it is difficult to determine whether his recent offences are adolescent acting out or whether they mask more severe problems. A detailed written report, usually prepared by a multidisciplinary team of psychiatrists, psychologists, and social workers (with input from other sources such as family, school, and children's aid

services) is filed with the court, and is usually[37] distributed to all persons taking an interest in the case.

- **Pre-sentence report (PSR):** This is the most common type of report ordered by a youth court; it is virtually mandatory if the court is considering a custodial sentence (YCJA, secs. 39(6) and 40(1)(a)).[38] The court orders the provincial director—in practice, a probation officer—to interview the offender, the victim (if possible), and collateral sources (including parents, school authorities, and employers) with a view to examining

  - the age, maturity, character, behaviour and attitude of the young person and his or her willingness to make amends;

  - the young person's record (including previous diversions);

  - the availability and appropriateness of community services ... and the willingness of the young person to avail himself or herself of those services;

  - the young person's relationship with nuclear and extended family.

A pre-sentence report (which normally takes three to four weeks to prepare) is given to the young person, the young person's parents, counsel for the Crown and the defence, and to the judge, and usually contains recommendations regarding sentencing, to which the judge is not bound.

In addition to these types of sources of information, which will ultimately be filed in open court at the sentencing hearing, the judge may hear evidence, either provided informally (such as by letter or through the oral representations of counsel) or given under oath. The judge will then hear the positions of the lawyers, and will ask Peter if he has anything he wishes to say.[39]

There is little doubt that though sentencing is what judges do most frequently in any criminal court (Juristat, 2002), it remains the hardest part of the judge's role, particularly in a difficult case such as presented by Peter. Prior to 1996 there were very few guidelines for Canadian judges; while Parliament legislated maximum possible sentences (and a few minimum), broad judicial discretion was encouraged. However, with the advent of Bill C-41 (S.C. 1995, c.22, sec.6), Parliament introduced some legislative criteria that judges are supposed to consider in sentencing adults. The YCJA goes much further in fettering judges' sentencing discretion. Space limitations preclude us from developing this further; suffice it to say that in addition to various aspects of the Declaration of Principle that judges are required to consider, Parliament has virtually precluded the use of custody for many types of offences and offenders, except in the most egregious of circumstances (YCJA, secs. 3, 29, 38, 39). While anecdotal experience in the early months of the YCJA suggests that youth custody populations have declined quite considerably, whether the resources will be allocated to support meaningful alternatives to incarceration remains to be seen.

CONCLUSION

Each of the legal professionals involved in youth court have roles circumscribed by policy, law, and jurisprudence. As representatives of the state, Crown attorneys must balance their many roles both inside and outside the courtroom with respect to presenting the facts involved in youth cases and attempting to reach the most equitable result within the parameters of the YCJA. Defence or duty counsel must also attempt to balance their roles when representing young persons—both as guardians, keeping in mind the best interests of their client, as well as providing competent representation in their role as legal advocates. Finally, judges must also balance the many differing philosophies inherent to the YCJA when making sentencing decisions for young persons. They must take into account the arguments of the other legal professionals, and come to equitable decisions respecting the regulations as set out in law. While each represents differing interests and performs different functions with respect to young offenders, their roles have evolved with the advent of rights-based legislation under the YOA and will likely continue to do so under the YCJA.

References

Bala, N. (2003). *Youth criminal justice law.* Toronto: Irwin Law.

Boldt, E. D., Hursh, L. E., Jonson, S. D., & Taylor, M. (1983). Presentence reports and the incarceration of Natives. *Canadian Journal of Criminology, 25*(3), 269–76.

Green, R. G. (1998). *Justice in Aboriginal communities: Sentencing alternatives.* Saskatoon, SK: Purich Publishing.

Hagan, J. (1977). Criminal justice in rural and urban communities: A study of the bureaucratization of justice. *Social Forces, 55*(3) 597–612.

Juristat. (2002). Youth court statistics, 2001/02. *Juristat 23*(3).

Milne, H. A., Linden, R., & Kueneman, R. (1992). Advocate or legal guardian: The role of defence counsel in youth justice. In R. R. Corrado et al. (Eds.), *Juvenile justice in Canada: A theoretical and analytical assessment.* Toronto: Butterworths.

Peterson-Badali, M., & Abramovitch, R. (1992). Children's knowledge of the legal system: Are they competent to instruct counsel? *Canadian Journal of Criminology, 34,* 139–160.

Peterson-Badali, M., & Loegl, C. (1998). Young people's knowledge of the YOA and the youth justice system. *Canadian Journal of Criminology, 40,* 127–152.

Cases Cited

Boucher v. The Queen (1954), 110 C.C.C. 263 (S.C.C.) at 270.

R. v. Greunke (1991), 3 S.C.R. 263 at 295, 67 C.C.C. (3d) 289.

R. v. Cook (1998), 114 C.C.C. (3d) 481 (S.C.C.) at 489–490.

R. v. C.N.H. (2002), 170 C.C.C. (3d) 253 (Ont. C.A.).

R. v. H.A.M., [2003] M.J. No. 147 (Prov. Ct.).

R. v. T.K., [2003] O.J. No. 2877 (Ont. C.J.).

R. v. T.M, [September 18, 2003], unreported (Ont. C.J.).

R. v. M. (B.) [2003] S.J. Nos. 377 and 602.

R. v. I. (I.R.) (1993) 86 C.C.C. (3d) 289.

R. v. J. (1990) 59 C.C.C. (3d) 1.

R. v. D. (1996) 113 C.C.C. (3d) 56.

R. v. McDonnell (1997) 6 C.R. (5th) 231 (S.C.C.).

R. v. B.L.M., [2003] S.J. No. 870.

Notes

1. *Boucher v. The Queen* (1954), 110 C.C.C. 263 (S.C.C.) at 270.

2. *R. v. Cook* (1998), 114 C.C.C. (3d) 481 (S.C.C.) at 489–490.

3. Most of the provincial prosecution services across Canada have their own set of policy guidelines.

4. Crown Policy # B-1.

5. Section 515(10) of the *Criminal Code* sets out three criteria upon which persons may be detained pending sentence: (a) where detention is necessary to ensure the accused's attendance in court; where detention is necessary for the protection or safety of the public, including any victim or witness to the offence, having regard to all the circumstances including any substantial likelihood that the accused will, if released from custody, commit a criminal offence or interfere with the administration of justice; or (c) any other just cause being shown and, without limiting the generality of the foregoing, where the detention is necessary in order to maintain confidence in the administration of justice, having regard to all the circumstances, including the apparent strength of the prosecution's case, the gravity of the nature of the offence, the circumstances surrounding its commission, and the potential for a lengthy term of imprisonment.

6. In Ontario, many areas of prosecutorial discretion are the subject of policy guidelines or practice memoranda. Charge screening is

currently guided by a Practice Memorandum, dated October 1, 2002.

7. Crown Practice Memorandum on Charge Screening, PM [2002] No. 5, at p. 2 to p. 3.

8. Under the YOA, a young person aged 14 or older could potentially be transferred to adult court for trial, depending on the nature of the offence. For the offences of murder, attempted murder, manslaughter, or aggravated sexual assault, young persons aged 16 and 17 were presumptively transferred. The YCJA moves the determination of youth versus adult sentence from pretrial to post-finding of guilt, thereby eliminating the transfer hearing altogether, as youth will be informed before trial if the Crown will be seeking an adult sentence. A young person who is liable to an adult sentence has the option of electing to be tried in the Ontario Court of Justice or in the Superior Court of Justice, with or without a preliminary inquiry.

9. See Chapter 9 for an overview of events that occurred in the province of Ontario surrounding the provision of alternative measures.

10. Crown Practice Memorandum on Charge Screening, PM [2002] No. 5, p. 3, Crown Policy # R-1, Resolution Discussions.

11. Crown Policy # R-1, *supra*.

12. For a further discussion of judicial pretrials, see "Role of the Youth Court Judge," below.

13. See, for example, *R. v. C.N.H.* (2002), 170 C.C.C. (3d) 253 (Ont. C.A.).

14. Specifically, in imposing a custody and supervision sentence pursuant to sec. 42(2)(n) of the YCJA, the sentencing judge must advise the young person that "You are ordered to serve *(number of days or months to be served)* in custody, to be followed by *(one-half of the number of days or months stated above)*. See YCJA, sec. 42(5).

15. For first degree murder, the sentence maximums and the ratio of custody to supervision have different requirements; see secs. 42(2)(q) and (r).

16. The only potential immediate consequence of a judicial determination of serious violent offence is the young person's disqualification from a "deferred custody and supervision sentence (DCSO). A DCSO is analogous to a conditional sentence for adults. It is considered a custodial sentence but is served in the community under conditions. If the conditions are breached or the young person commits a further offence, the balance of the sentence may be served in custody. A young person who commits a "serious violent offence" is not eligible for a DCSO. At the time of writing, there is conflicting jurisprudence regarding whether a formal judicial determination of serious violent offence is required to prohibit the use of a DCSO: see *R. v. H.A.M.*, [2003] M.J. No. 147 (Prov. Ct.); *R. v. T.K.*, [2003] O.J. No. 2877 (Ont. C.J.); *R. v. T.M.*, [September 18, 2003], unreported (Ont. C.J.).

17. One of the threshold questions, for example, is whether a judicial determination of serious violent offence is available for an offence committed when the YOA was still in force. As well, the range of factual scenarios that might define "serious bodily harm" has yet to be determined.

18. A pre-sentence report is a report prepared by probation, ordered by the court to provide insight into the circumstances of the young person and the offence and to canvass potential services and facilities that might form part of the sentence. The contents of the pre-sentence report are specified in sec. 40(2) of the YCJA. Consideration of a pre-sentence report is mandatory if the court is contemplating a custodial sentence and discretionary in all other cases: YCJA, sec. 39(6), sec. 40(1).

19. In *R. v. M.(B.)*, [2003] S.J. Nos. 377 and 602, reversed on appeal in *R. v. B.L.M.*, [2003] S.J. No. 870. Turpel-Lafond J. provides an example of a youth justice court relying extensively on the conferencing process to explore the underlying causes of a young person's offences and potential ways to facilitate rehabilitation and reintegration.

20. *Charter* sec. 10(b). The most significant sections of the YCJA relating to the right to counsel are secs. 10(2)(c) and (d), 25, 26(6)(c), 32, 34(7)(a)(iii), 34(8), and 146(2)(b)(iii) and (iv).

21. The lawyers are either members of the private bar who agree to provide services at a set fee paid by the Plan or are salaried employees of the Legal Aid Plan.

22. The formal legal terms are to act as a "surety" or "responsible person."

23. Indeed, sec. 4(c) of the YCJA presumes that extrajudicial sanctions "are adequate to hold a young person accountable for his or her offending behaviour" if (a) the offence is characterized as non-violent, and (b) the young person has not previously been found guilty of an offence.

24. The failure of successive provincial governments all across Canada over the past two decades to make more than token increases to the legal aid tariff has meant that many senior lawyers will no longer accept clients under the Legal Aid Plan.

25. Youth court judges are authorized under the YCJA to conduct bail hearings. However, in most parts of the country, the vast majority of bail hearings are presided over by justices of the peace, rather than youth court judges.

26. Simple cases would not usually be the subject of a JPT.

27. Youth and adult criminal trials occur rarely, as most criminal charges are resolved by guilty pleas or the charges being dropped by the Crown before the case comes to trial (Bala, 2003, p. 363).

28. In the very rare case of an accused who insists on being present at a JPT, it will usually be held on the record in open court.

29. While the optics of the police meeting with a judge, in the absence of the accused, may seem to contradict our notions of open justice, experience demonstrates that the officer's presence is a practical necessity (particularly in complex cases) but yet is benign.

30. *R. v. I. (I.R.)* (1993) 86 C.C.C. (3d) 289; *R. v. J.* (1990) 59 C.C.C. (3d) 1; *R. v. D.* (1996) 113 C.C.C. (3d) 56.

31. Crown counsel might not be willing to risk judicial wrath by using up a lot of court time on such a speculative venture.

32. Even though Rick was likely held only overnight and most probably would have been released from custody at the courthouse—perhaps 16 hours in custody overall—the law is that any portion of a day spent in custody counts as a full day.

33. How long that will be depends on the length of the period of the discharge (up to three years) and on whether the charge was proceeded with by indictment or summarily (YCJA secs. 117–129).

34. Despite the lack of a detailed witness statement, a brief recital of what she saw would be contained in the overview of the case (called a "synopsis") written up by the investigating officer for the bail hearing.

35. Sometimes called "starting points." See *R. v. McDonnell* (1997) 6 C.R. (5th) 231 (S.C.C.).

36. For example, in Prince Edward Island there has for several years been a general tariff that virtually all first-time drunk drivers will be sent to jail.

37. The YCJA contains provisions by which the judge may order that some parties (including, in very rare circumstances, the accused) may not be permitted to see the report.

38. These reports are very powerful documents. Canadian and international research suggests that courts follow the recommendations contained in PSRs in about 85 percent of cases (Boldt et al., 1983; Hagan, 1977).

39. *Criminal Code* sec. 726 requires that the judge invite the offender to speak. The offender may decline to do so. The YCJA also mandates that youth participate in decisions that are made about them in court (sec. 3(1)(d)(i)).

chapter eleven

Sentencing under the *Youth Criminal Justice Act:* An Historical Perspective

*Anthony N. Doob**

Centre of Criminology
University of Toronto
and

Jane B. Sprott

Department of Sociology and Anthropology
University of Guelph

INTRODUCTION

Canadian youths have been sentenced by courts for committing offences under four different legal regimes since 1892, when Canada enacted its own *Criminal Code.* Prior to 1908, youths were sentenced under the same rules as then existed for adults. This does not mean that they received the same sentences as an adult would receive for the same offence; nor does it mean that a youth would necessarily serve time in the same prisons as adults (though in many instances in the nineteenth century, they did). Until the *Juvenile Delinquents Act* became law in 1908, there was no separate regime for handling youthful offenders—nor, therefore, was there any formal legal distinction between how a youth and an adult should be sentenced.

This chapter will trace the development during the past century of sentencing youths in Canada. It will suggest that the changes that have taken place—particularly since the 1980s—can be described along two dimensions. First, there has been a fundamental change in the purpose of sentencing as laid out in the legislation. Second, there has been a shift in the focus of control of sentencing from the judge to Parliament.

---

*© Jane B. Sprott and Anthony N. Doob

THE *JUVENILE DELINQUENTS ACT*

The 1908 *Juvenile Delinquents Act* (JDA) created a separate system for responding to young people who commit criminal acts. After 1908, "Where a child is adjudged to have committed a delinquency he shall be dealt with, not as an offender, but as one in a condition of delinquency and therefore requiring help and guidance and proper supervision" (JDA, sec. 3(2) see Appendix A). Proceedings were to be "as informal as the circumstances require" (sec. 17(1)), but in the end, "in the case of a child adjudged to be a juvenile delinquent the court may, in its discretion, take one or more of … several courses of action [set out in the Act] … as it may in its judgement deem proper in the circumstances in the case" (sec. 20(1)). The list of "courses of action" was not very long. It included dismissing the case or delaying it indefinitely, a fine ($25 maximum), various forms of supervision on probation, placing the youth in the care of a children's aid society, and placing the youth in a training school.

More importantly, in understanding the nature of sentencing under the JDA, the court could "at any time, before such juvenile delinquent has reached the age of 21 years and unless the court has otherwise ordered, cause … the delinquent to be brought before the court" (sec. 20(3)). If this were done, the sentence could be changed in a variety of ways. The formally stated guiding principle of the original sentence, or a re-sentencing hearing, was simple: "The action taken shall, in every case, be that which the court is of the opinion the child's own good and the best interest of the community require" (sec. 20(5)).

Further elaboration was provided later in the Act, where it was stated "that the care and custody and discipline of a juvenile delinquent shall approximate as nearly as may be that which should be given by his parents, and that as far as practicable every juvenile delinquent shall be treated, not as a criminal, but as a misdirected and misguided child, and one needing aid, encouragement, help and assistance" (sec. 38).

The JDA was clearly a child welfare–oriented law and remained Canada's juvenile delinquency legislation from 1908 to 1984. Under this law, almost any wrongdoing by a youth could constitute the offence of delinquency: the violation of a municipal by-law, a provincial offence, criminal offences such as theft or murder, and "sexual immorality or similar form of vice" all constituted "an offence to be known as a delinquency" and were dealt with, for sentencing purposes, as being legally the same in almost all instances. In other words, a seven-year-old riding a bicycle in a park in violation of local park rules and a 17-year-old murderer were both delinquents and were equally eligible, in law, to the same set of sanctions under the JDA. The exception to this statement was that indictable offences committed by those over age 14 were subject to possible transfer to adult court.

The welfare orientation of this law meant that the sentencing decisions made by the court were supposed to be in the best interest of the youth. Under the JDA, a delinquency was seen as a symptom of an underlying illness. The exact form of illness was not readily apparent from the offence, just as a fever is a symptom of many illnesses, some minor, some serious. Courts, it was argued, like doctors, had to have the full range of responses available to them and it was presumed that courts, like doctors, would make the decisions that would best serve the youth.

It was not, however, that simple. In the first place, the legislation was not—in law or in practice—completely oriented toward the interests of the child. As noted above, the court was supposed to do that which it thought was required for the child's own good and the good of the community (sec. 20(5)). Reconciling these interests proved to be difficult, especially in very serious offences where the community thought that the sentence should reflect the seriousness of the offence. Nonetheless, the overall orientation was clearly that the law was meant to be used as a tool to help "correct" the delinquent youth. It made sense, then, that the youth would be under the jurisdiction of the court until age 21. If it appeared that the treatment needed some modifications, the argument was, why not let the court make these modifications? The fact that a seven-year-old committing the offence of throwing a tennis ball in a park where such activities were prohibited could be subject to being brought back before the court until age 21 makes some sense if the purpose is to help the child, and if "serious delinquencies" like this could be symptoms of further underlying problems. This line of reasoning also assumes that the courts act solely in the interests of the youthful offender and that they know best how to "treat" a young person. These are, of course, debatable assumptions.

Similarly, under this logic it made sense for legal appeals to be restricted. Why would one need to appeal a sentence if the judge was already doing what was best for the youth? Hence, in order for an appeal from a juvenile court to even be heard, a superior court judge had to decide that there were special grounds to consider the appeal. A youth did not have any right to appeal a decision. In fact, the JDA required that "No leave to appeal shall be granted ... unless the judge or court granting such leave considers that in the particular circumstances of the case it is essential in the public interest or for the due administration of justice that such leave be granted" (sec. 37(2)).

It is not surprising, therefore, that sentences under the JDA did not reflect the seriousness of the offence. A study by Doob and Meen (1993) looked at the sentences being handed down in the Toronto courts in the dying days of the Act (1982–1984). There was at that time essentially *no* relationship between the seriousness of the offence and the sentence that was meted out by the court during the years 1982–84 in the Toronto courts that were studied. This finding is obviously not surprising. Under the JDA, the offence that a youth commits is simply the event that brings that youth to court. Once in court, the disposition of the court is meant to relate to the needs of the youth, not the event that brought the youth to court. There is, therefore, no particular reason to expect there to be a relationship between what the judge thought was in the best interests of the child and the seriousness of the event that brought the youth to court.

Sentencing Young Offenders Primarily on the Basis of Their Needs

An historical overview of sentencing is important, as concerns regarding the welfare of the young offender remain today. During the debates around the *Youth*

Criminal Justice Act (YCJA), one of the concerns—expressed repeatedly by those with a child-welfare orientation toward youth justice (many of whom come from Quebec)—was that the YCJA did not give sufficient weight to welfare concerns. In particular, it was pointed out by many such advocates that the Act would not permit long "treatment-oriented" sentences to be handed down to youths. The assumption was that some youths need long sentences to reap the benefits of a treatment program. Instead, as we will see, the YCJA requires that the length of a custodial sentence not be set by presumed or perceived welfare needs. A youth who was seen by the judge as needing a long treatment program in a custodial setting could not be sentenced to receive it if the offence that brought the youth to court was not serious enough to warrant a longer sentence. Indeed, some of those from Quebec who opposed the YCJA were, in particular, opposed to the provision that required the judge to take into account the length of time that a youth had spent in pretrial detention. The reason child welfare advocates opposed this section was simple: it could constrain the judge from imposing a sentence long enough for the youth to participate in a treatment program in custody.

Rehabilitation as a Sentencing Objective

There are a number of reasons for questioning whether rehabilitation should be the predominant principle in determining the sentencing of youths in Canada. Clearly, the idea is based in part on the theory that the courts can routinely identify the rehabilitative needs of youths—

or, indeed, whether they are even in need of rehabilitative programs. It is further premised on the notion that rehabilitation programs that have been proved to be successful are available for most or all youthful offenders and that youth will benefit from participation. A rehabilitative approach to sentencing would, one assumes, have some difficulty guiding those youths whose offending was minor and reflected normal adolescent behaviour (see Moffitt, 1993) rather than some underlying pathology. If the goal of sentencing is simply rehabilitation, then those youths not in need of it are left in the situation where a sentence is imposed without any principles. If one suggests that other principles (e.g., that the sentence should be proportional to the harm done) should be used in sentencing youths without treatment needs, then one is in the peculiar situation of implicitly suggesting that the harshness of a sentence should be determined by the treatment needs of one youth and by the offence for another youth. One suspects that such an approach would not be acceptable to many people in society. As Brodeur and Doob (2002) note, for most people—the youth specifically and society generally—a custodial sentence given for rehabilitative purposes alone is not likely to be seen as fair.

A rehabilitative approach to sentencing is almost certainly going to lead to youths who have committed similar (or identical) acts getting different sentences. Two youths with identical criminal records might arrive in court as co-accuseds with equal responsibilities for a minor crime. The youth who had no "needs" might get a non-custodial sentence befitting the minor nature of the crime. The youth with substantial needs (e.g., dysfunctional and alcoholic parents, doing poorly in school), who might be seen as benefiting from a custodial program, may get a relatively long custodial sentence in a genuine attempt to separate the youth from his or her parents and to provide adequate schooling. The problem, of course, is that no matter what is said about the underlying purpose of the two sentences, the sentence is an attempt to censure some behaviour. It would be reasonable, therefore, for all of those involved (including any members of the public) to assume that somehow the relative roles of the two youths were reflected in the sentence. In a very real sense, the child with the various needs (including the "need" for a better family) would receive additional punishment.

There is another ironic aspect of any attempt to sentence according to treatment needs: the youth who commits an offence may, in effect, jump to the head of the queue of those waiting for treatment. If a judge can *order* a youth to receive treatment immediately upon being sentenced, then other non-offending youths in the community would be placed as second-class citizens, having to wait for privileged offenders to receive their treatment. What would occur, then, would be the rather peculiar situation where offending youths are privileged with respect to access to treatment over non-offending youths. As Brodeur and Doob (2002) noted, "Is the judge whose job it is to sentence young offenders well placed to determine that the young person being sentenced for an offence is really the most needy young person in the community? Determining which needy young person is most in need is difficult. Those whose jobs it is to allocate child welfare or rehabilitative resources are likely to be better placed to be making these decisions" (p. 7). Similarly, judges are not well placed to decide who, among those in the correctional system (in the community or a custodial setting), are most in need of treatment resources. Judges, after all, see individual cases. Correctional officials have limited budgets for treatment programs and have to make difficult decisions on how best to use limited resources. Judges are not in the best position to allocate resources, as they lack the necessary information about available resources and are unfamiliar with the demands on those resources.

Even before the YCJA became law, the Quebec government argued that the new law was a violation of principles of fundamental justice in the *Charter of Rights and Freedoms* because the law did not allow "rehabilitation to be the dominant principle in the sentencing of youth offenders" (Anand & Bala, 2003, p. 402). Said differently, almost 20 years after Canada had moved away from a rehabilitation model of sentencing for youth, the Quebec government was asking the courts to reinstate the dominant approach to sentencing that had previously governed from 1908 until 1984. The Quebec government's attempt failed in the Quebec Court of Appeal, and the fundamental approach to sentencing contained in the YCJA survived the challenge. The point that is worth thinking about, however, is that the tendency to want to require the state to treat youths rather than punish them for their offences is still very much part of our culture. As will be shown later in this chapter, the YCJA combined these two approaches in an interesting—and often poorl understood—manner.

THE *YOUNG OFFENDERS ACT*

The *Young Offenders Act* (YOA), which came into effect in 1984, created fundamental changes in sentencing, some of which remain today in the YCJA. The *Young Offenders Act* continued one important symbolic provision of the *Juvenile Delinquents Act*. Sentences under the YOA were not called sentences: they were "dispositions." Hence, sec. 20(1) of the YOA lists the various dispositions that can be handed down, just as it refers to "pre-disposition reports" rather than pre-sentence reports. Clearly implied by this language is the theory that "dispositions" for youths are to be something that is different from "sentences"[1] for adults.

Perhaps the single most important break from the JDA is that all sentences under the YOA (using the language of the *Criminal Code* and the YCJA) were definite in length. Other than for murder, the maximum length of a sentence for a youth was either two or three years (depending on the offence). Equally important is the fact that a three-year sentence under the YOA meant that the youth was to be put in custody for three years. There were no parole or statutory release provisions in the Act, though for longer sentences a youth could request that a sentence be reviewed by a youth court judge and reduced if the judge thought it appropriate. Gone, therefore, were the indefinite sentences of the JDA and the provisions that allowed youths to be under the jurisdiction of the courts for years when they had committed only minor offences. The introduction of the YOA can be seen, in retrospect, as the beginning of an attempt to tame the youth court's tendency to intrude into the life of young people who offend. It was not, generally, entirely successful in this regard.

There were three major sets of amendments to the YOA during its 19-year life. In contrast, the JDA never received serious changes during its 76-year existence. For the most part, we will discuss the YOA as it existed when it was replaced by the YCJA.

The Declaration of Principle of the YOA (see Appendix B) had a few provisions related explicitly to sentencing. It is clear, however, that welfare considerations were still relevant to sentencing under this law. For example, the principles included the statement that youths have "special needs and require guidance and assistance" (sec. 3(1)(c)) and that the protection of society "is best served by rehabilitation, wherever possible, of young persons who commit offences, and rehabilitation is best achieved by addressing the needs and circumstances of a young person that are relevant to the young person's offending behaviour" (sec. 3(1)(c.1)). Finally, it suggests that "parents have responsibility for the care and supervision of their children, and, for that reason, young persons should be removed from parental supervision either partly or entirely only when measures that provide for continuing parental supervision are inappropriate" (sec. 3(1)(h)).

As noted by Trépanier (1989), there were hints in the YOA that the nature of the offence should be taken into account in determining the appropriate disposition. The maximum sentence under the YOA for offences other than murder was three years if an adult could be sentenced to life in prison; otherwise, it was two years. Youths who were sentenced in youth court for murder could receive a sentence of 10 years (first-degree murder) or seven years (second-degree murder). The YOA differentiated between offences that involved "serious personal injury" and all other offences by suggesting that for offences other than those involving serious personal injury, "a young person who commits an offence ... should be held accountable to the victim and to society through non-custodial dispositions whenever appropriate" (sec. 24(1.1)(b)). Finally, the YOA ordered the youth court to take into account the principle that "an order of custody shall not be used as a substitute for appropriate child protection, health and other social measures" (sec. 24(1.1)(a)).

Clearly, there was meant to be a change through this legislation in the way in which youths were sentenced. Changes did take place, but they were not entirely predictable. Earlier in this chapter it was noted that under the JDA, youth sentences in Toronto courts did not appear to be related to the nature of the offence (Doob & Meen, 1993). Sentences in these same courts were examined in exactly the same way in the first two years of the YOA. The changes were dramatic. First of all, custodial sentences were more likely to be handed down for all three categories of

offences that were examined (violent offences, property offences, and a residual category of administration of justice and other offences). More important in this context was the fact that the type of sentence handed down by the judge was more closely linked to the offence than it had been two years earlier. By the end of the decade (1989–90) there was an even stronger relationship between the offence type and the disposition. Proportionality in sentencing had entered Canada's youth justice system.

Sentencing under the *Young Offenders Act*

During the late 1980s, two events were occurring in many Canadian provinces. More youths were being sentenced to custody, and more of these youths were getting short sentences. The increase in the use of imprisonment for youths is clearly evident in Table 11.1, which shows the increase, during this period, in the use of custody in some (but not all) provinces.

What is equally important, however, is the fact that the increase in the use of custody occurred largely in the use of short sentences. The number and proportion of

TABLE 11.1	Proportion of Cases Receiving Custody					
	Newfoundland	**Québec**	**Manitoba**	**Saskatchewan**	**Alberta**	**British Columbia**
1984/5	14%	30%	14%	25%	10%	11%
1986/7	24%	30%	25%	23%	20%	21%
1988/9	21%	31%	28%	25%	18%	22%

Note: Data include only cases where the age of the offender was within the jurisdiction of the JDA in each province.

long sentences decreased in most of the six provinces that were examined (Table 11.2).

The size of the increase in the use of short sentences during this period was dramatic. In each of the six provinces that were examined, the increased use of short sentences was notable. In Alberta, for example, 25 percent of the custodial sentences were for three months or less in 1984/5. Four years later, this had increased to 66 percent.

What is equally true is that the proportion, and in many cases the *number*, of long sentences also decreased dramat-

ically. Even in the first days of the YOA, long sentences of custody were not a frequent occurrence. Nevertheless, there appeared to be a general decrease in the use of long custodial sentences.

One of the concerns expressed early on about the YOA was that it appeared to be responsible for an increased use of custody (Markwart & Corrado, 1989). The data indicate that at least some provinces were increasing the number of youths going to custody, but decreasing, on average, the amount of time that they spent there.

TABLE 11.2	Length of Custodial Sentences in the First Few Years of the YOA, Selected Provinces							
	3 months		4-12 months		13 months or greater		Total	
	%	Number	%	Number	%	Number	%	Number
Newfoundland								
1984/5	58%	103	34%	61	8%	15	100%	179
1986/7	63%	259	34%	139	3%	14	100%	412
1988/9	71%	202	28%	81	1%	3	100%	286
Québec								
1984/5	29%	491	54%	919	17%	290	100%	1700
1986/7	44%	902	50%	1032	5%	110	100%	2044
1988/9	51%	985	45%	861	4%	74	100%	1920
Manitoba								
1984/5	16%	82	62%	311	22%	110	100%	503
1986/7	44%	396	51%	463	6%	50	100%	909
1988/9	42%	418	53%	523	5%	45	100%	986
Saskatchewan								
1984/5	45%	97	50%	107	5%	10	100%	214
1986/7	55%	210	43%	164	2%	6	100%	380
1988/9	68%	332	29%	144	3%	14	100%	490
Alberta								
1984/5	25%	130	68%	355	8%	40	100%	525
1986/7	65%	621	34%	319	1%	10	100%	950
1988/9	66%	620	32%	302	1%	13	100%	935
British Columbia								
1984/5	44%	237	46%	249	9%	50	100%	536
1986/7	61%	722	36%	425	3%	35	100%	1182
1988/9	71%	821	26%	306	3%	29	100%	1156

Note: Data include only cases where the age of the offender was within the jurisdiction of the JDA in each province.

Identifying Problems with Sentencing under the *Young Offenders Act*

During the latter part of the 1980s, it seemed the seeds were sown for what would turn out to be some serious problems with sentencing under the YOA. In 1998, when it was announced that an entirely new Act to govern the handling of youths who offend was going to be introduced, the Minister of Justice highlighted three major problems with the sentencing of youths in Canada (Canada, Department of Justice, 1998). First, she noted that Canada had a very high rate of imprisonment of youths compared to most other countries, including the United States. Comparisons of this kind are difficult to make, but her assertion is supported by data (Sprott & Snyder, 1999, updated by Sprott for Doob & Cesaroni, 2004). Second, she noted that Canada does not differentiate adequately between serious (violent) offences and all other offences in the way in which it responds to youthful offenders. Third, she suggested that the response of the justice system did not reflect adequately the variability in severity of the offences committed by youth.

We have already seen that there was an enormous increase in the use of custody during the 1980s, and that many of these custodial sentences were short. By the end of the century, Canadian youth court judges appeared to be working on the assumption that a little bit of custody is good for many offenders.

Table 11.3 shows that more than three quarters of the custodial sentences handed down to young offenders in Canada were for three months or less. A third of them were for less than 30 days. Custody is an expensive punishment to impose on young people. In addition, it is a dramatic intrusion into a young person's life that can have very negative effects (see Cesaroni & Peterson-Badali, 2003; Doob & Cesaroni, 2004, Chapter 10). A sentence of a couple of weeks may not appear to be very intrusive. Nevertheless, when one considers the impact it could easily have on an already problematic school career, the sheer number of these custodial sentences raises significant questions.

More important, however, is the fact that custody—the most intrusive sentence available for anyone in Canada—is used largely for rather minor offences (Table 11.4). The data in Table 11.4 demonstrate

TABLE 11.3	Distribution of Sentence Lengths for Custodial Sentences (Secure and Open), Canada, 1999-2000	
Sentence length	Number of sentences	Percent
<1 month	7 857	33.8%
1-3 months	10 102	43.5%
4-6 months	3 808	16.4%
7-12 months	1 211	5.2%
13-24 months	2 19	0.9%
>24 months	18	0.08%
Total	232 15	100%

TABLE 11.4 Cases to Custody: Canada, P.E.I., Québec, Ontario, and Saskatchewan (1999-2000)

Most significant charge	Canada Number	%*	P.E.I. Number	%*	Québec Number	%*	Ontario Number	%*	Saskatchewan Number	%*
Theft under $5000	2005	9%	11	9%	242	10%	647	7%	185	9%
Possession of stolen property	1411	6%	5	4%	37	2%	628	7%	163	8%
Failure to appear	2579	11%	11	9%	123	5%	1116	12%	276	14%
Failure to comply with a disposition	5234	23%	38	29%	418	17%	1951	21%	321	16%
Subtotal	**11229**	**48%**	**65**	**50%**	**820**	**34%**	**4342**	**47%**	**945**	**47%**
Other thefts	1011	4%	11	9%	82	3%	388	4%	122	6%
Mischief/damage	726	3%	3	2%	40	2%	265	3%	87	4%
Break and enter	2853	12%	18	14%	377	16%	983	11%	283	14%
Minor assault	1521	7%	7	5%	134	6%	808	9%	98	5%
Total: Sum of eight offences	**17 340**	**75%**	**104**	**81%**	**1453**	**61%**	**6786**	**73%**	**1535**	**76%**
All cases	23 215	100%	129	100%	2400	100%	9 303	100%	2013	100%
Cases to custody per 1000 youths in the jurisdiction	9.48		10.4		4.4		10.2		20.5	

* Percentage of all custodial sentences that involved this offence as the most significant charge.

clearly that for Canada as a whole—as well as for the largest province (Ontario), the smallest province (Prince Edward Island), the province that uses custody least per capita (Quebec), and the province that uses custody most per capita (Saskatchewan)—custody is used for many relatively minor cases. Many of these minor offences may, of course, involve youths who have records of offending. However, given that a repeat offender has, of course, already been punished for the earlier offence, one can ask why a repeat offender is more deserving of harsh punishment than a first-time offender who has done exactly the same thing.

One other finding is evident in Table 11.4. Quebec, which uses custody less per capita than any other province (or territory), obviously also uses it more selectively. A somewhat lower proportion of Quebec custodial sentences are imposed in relatively minor cases. For example, in Ontario, 47 percent of the custodial sentences handed down in 1999–2000 were for one of four relatively minor offences: theft under $5000, possession of stolen property, failure to appear in count, or failure to comply with a disposition (typically, failure to comply with a probation order). In Quebec, only 34 percent of the custodial sentences were handed down for these minor offences. Quebec, it would appear, not only brings fewer cases into court than does Ontario, but also uses custody more selectively, preferring, presumably, to use it for the more serious offences.

Another quite different problem with sentencing under the YOA was that there was substantial evidence of disparity in sentencing. This is not particularly surprising. Although there were some provisions in the YOA that would appear to give guidance to judges in their sentencing decisions, judges had a great deal of latitude in deciding what to do. In one study (Doob & Beaulieu, 1992), for example, 43 youth court judges across Canada were given detailed written cases and asked how they would have sentenced each of four offenders. There were two important findings. First, judges varied dramatically in what they saw as the primary goal of sentencing a given offender. Second, the sentence that they said they would have handed down varied just as dramatically. For example, in one case a youth was described as having been found guilty of assault causing bodily harm. The range of sentences varied from secure custody to probation. For a case of a 15-year-old shoplifter with a criminal record, some of the judges would have placed him in custody, while one judge would have given him an absolute discharge.

Across provinces, there was evidence under the YOA of similar types of disparity. Whether one looks, overall, at the rate at which youths were sentenced to custody or the rate at which youths were sent to custody for particular offences, it is clear that for some offences the province in which the youth was being sentenced made a difference. The data in Table 11.5 clearly indicate these differences. Whereas close to 40 percent of the cases in Ontario resulted in custodial sentences, only about 27 to 28 percent of the Quebec and Alberta cases resulted in the youth being sent to custody. There was substantial variation for each of the offences that were examined.

TABLE 11.5	Proportion of Guilty Cases that are Sentenced to Custody for Selected Offences (Canada and the Four Largest Provinces, 1999-2000)

	All offences	Assault bodily harm	Minor assault	Break and enter	Theft over $5000	Theft under $5000
Canada	34.0%	30.4%	23.2%	38.6%	49.1%	22.2%
Québec	27.4%	24.2%	18.6%	3 1.9%	35.0%	20.1%
Ontario	39.8%	35.9%	27.9%	4 1.7%	5 1.0%	25.8%
Alberta	28.1%	18.9%	17.3%	38.1%	5 1.7%	17.9%
B.C.	33.7%	29.9%	15.3%	38.7%	47.9%	19.5%

Ironically, at the same time most of the public appeared to believe that sentences under the YOA were too lenient. Canadians have for decades believed that sentences for adult offenders are too lenient (see Doob & Roberts, 1988; Doob, 2000). However, it appears that more people view youth court sentences as being too lenient than hold this view for adult sentences. In one Ontario study (Doob, Sprott, Marinos, & Varma, 1998), 77 percent of respondents thought that adult court sentences were too lenient and 86 percent thought that youth court sentences were too lenient.

THE *YOUTH CRIMINAL JUSTICE ACT*

In May 1998, the Government of Canada indicated that rather than propose amendments to the YOA it was going to introduce a new replacement Act. The *Youth Criminal Justice Act* was first introduced into Parliament in March 1999 and became law on April 1, 2003. The new law was designed to accomplish a number of important goals, among them to reduce the use of custody and to ensure that sentences reflected the seriousness of the offence. It is a dramati-

cally different piece of legislation from the *Young Offenders Act* in many ways. One way in which it differs is that it has much more explicit principles that govern most decisions than did the YOA. Second, it is much more explicit than was the YOA in setting out the limitations on when a custodial sentence could be imposed. By setting out detailed principles of sentencing, it was hoped that the disparity in sentences across the country and the overuse of custody in many provinces could simultaneously be addressed.

Sentencing under the *Youth Criminal Justice Act*

Clearly there were problems to be addressed in how sentences had previously been administered. The sentencing provisions in the YCJA constituted some of the most significant changes in the new law. In the first place, protection of the public was described, in the Declaration of Principle (see Appendix C) as the *consequence* of certain approaches to youth crime. The youth justice system is described as being designed to prevent crime by addressing the underlying circumstances leading to offending, to rehabilitate young offenders, and to ensure that young offenders are subject to meaningful consequences "in order to promote the long-term protection of the public" (sec. 3(1)(a)). This is a dramatic shift for two reasons. If "protection of the public" is presumed to be a consequence rather than a goal in itself, the judge should be focusing on the actual principles of sentencing rather than trying to be a crime fighter. In effect, the YCJA frees the judge from responsibility for stopping crime. Second, the focus is on *long-term* protection rather than the kind of short-term protection one might get from a relatively short custodial sentence.

The sentencing provisions of the YCJA are important not only for what they say, but also for what they do not say. In contrast to the primarily rehabilitation-oriented *Juvenile Delinquents Act,* and the *Young Offenders Act,* which tended to endorse a range of different purposes, the *Youth Criminal Justice Act* states that

> The purpose of sentencing … is to hold a young person accountable for an offence through the imposition of just sanctions that have meaningful consequences for the young person and that promote his or her rehabilitation and reintegration into society, thereby contributing to the long-term protection of the public. (sec. 38(1))

Equally important, however, is that the YCJA contains a set of fairly explicit principles to be followed generally and, in particular, when a custodial sentence is being contemplated. These principles (in sec. 38) include the following:

- *The sentence cannot be harsher than the sentence that would be appropriate for a comparable adult for the same offence.* This is a much more explicit and

stronger version than existed in the YOA, which stated only that the youth sentence could not be harsher than the sentence an adult *could* get (i.e., the maximum sentence in the *Criminal Code*). The restriction in the YOA was largely meaningless, since maximum sentences for adults are typically much higher than the sentences actually handed down to adults.

- *The sentence must be proportionate to the seriousness of the offence and the degree of responsibility of the young person for that offence.* Note that this is an absolute. Proportionality is not to be "weighed" or "balanced" against some other factor (e.g., the perceived rehabilitation needs of the young person). It is a simple provision: proportionality governs sentence severity.

- *The judge must consider all reasonable non-custodial sanctions before considering imposing custody on the youth, and must pay particular attention to the circumstances of Aboriginal young persons when carrying out this responsibility.*

- *The judge must—within the limits set by the principle of proportionality—hand down a sentence that simultaneously*

  - is the most likely to rehabilitate the young person and reintegrate him or her into society, and

  - promotes a sense of responsibility in the young person, and

  - is the least restrictive sentence possible.

The "rehabilitation" component of this last clause (sec. 38(2)(e)(ii)) is crucial since it makes clear that in all cases the judge must consider the youth's rehabilitation and reintegration. However, this must be done *within the limits governed by proportionality* given the offence that the youth committed and the youth's level of responsibility for that offence. One way of understanding these considerations would be that the judge assesses the offence and, in effect, determines that the sentence should be at a certain level of severity. The judge then must craft a sentence that maximizes the likelihood of rehabilitation and reintegration, restricts the youth as little as possible, and promotes a sense of responsibility in the young person for the harm that he or she has done. Balancing these three considerations is, obviously, difficult. The most significant factor, though, is that the judge is not balancing or choosing between a proportional sentence and rehabilitation. Instead, the judge is required to hand down a sentence that is proportional and then is charged with the responsibility of ensuring that, within those constraints, the sentence is as rehabilitative as possible. It means, of course, that if there were a rehabilitative sentence that was more intrusive or severe than the youth deserved on the basis of the offence, that rehabilitative sentence would not be consistent with the law. Similarly, if a youth had committed a very serious offence, but it could be shown that the most rehabilitative sentence involved a short non-custodial sentence, that sentence too would not be appropriate.

Proportionality, of course, refers only to the *relative* harshness of the sentence in relation to the offence. It does little to tell the judge, on an absolute level, where a particular sentence should lie except in relation to other sentences. The YCJA does, therefore, go one step further: it places severe restrictions on the use of custody. A

custodial sentence cannot be imposed (sec. 39(1)) unless one of the following conditions holds:

- It is a violent offence.

- The youth has failed to comply with at least two previous non-custodial sentences.

- The youth has committed an indictable offence of a non-trivial sort (i.e., more serious than a minor property offence) and has at least two or three previous findings of guilt.

- There are exceptional circumstances (which the judge is required to identify explicitly) that would make a non-custodial sentence inconsistent with the purpose and principles of sentencing (including, of course, proportionality). If custody is given under this clause, the judge must explain not only why non-custodial sanctions were not appropriate, but also what was exceptional about this case.

Also indicated in this law, as was the case in the YOA, is that custody shall not be used "as a substitute for appropriate child protection, mental health, or other social measures" (sec. 39(5)).

It is noted in the Act that non-custodial sentences can be handed down repeatedly, even in cases where the youth has previously complied with that type of sentence. This has significance, as a study of sentences under the YOA demonstrates that when handing down sentences judges take into account not only the previous history of offending, but also the previous *sentences*. In effect, a sentence often "steps up" from the previous sentence. A study by Matarazzo, Carrington, and Hiscott

(2001) demonstrates that judges appeared to hold this "step" theory of sentencing under the YOA: sentences tended to be made more severe than the previous sentence regardless of what the youth was being sentenced for.

One of the most important aspects of the sentencing provisions of the YCJA is modestly stated in section 50: "Part XXIII (sentencing) of the *Criminal Code* does not apply in respect of proceedings under this Act except [for certain largely technical matters]." What is hidden behind this statement is that certain standard—and popular—purposes of sentencing, such as general and specific deterrence and incapacitation, have no place in the sentencing of youths under YCJA. In other words, by explicitly stating that Part XXIII of the *Criminal Code* (the part that, among other things, lists the principles that govern sentencing of adults) does not apply, the YCJA signals in yet another way that sentencing of youths is supposed to be governed by very different principles as compared to the sentencing of adults.

Probably the most controversial omission in the sentencing provisions with respect to sentencing principles is general deterrence. Youths who have offended are no longer to be used as resources to stop or deter other youths from committing offences. There is good reason for the decision to keep deterrence out of the YCJA: the empirical evidence demonstrates quite conclusively that harsher sentences do not act as deterrents to criminal activity (see Doob & Webster, 2003, for a recent review of this literature). In a similar vein, youths are not to be placed in custody in order to protect society from future behaviour (incapacitation). As we have made clear,

the sentence is meant to focus on what the youth did in the past. Within the constraints of a proportional sentence, attempts must be made to rehabilitate the youth. But youths are not to be punished to keep others from offending, nor are youths to be incapacitated solely because a prediction has been made that they will reoffend.

The YCJA also lists a number of new sanctions that may be made available to the judge. Since the administration of justice in Canada is a provincial responsibility, and provinces cannot be forced to provide all sanction choices for all cases, it is up to the provinces to decide whether such sanctions as intensive supervision on probation or a non-residential program (commonly known as an "attendance centre," sec. 42(2)(m)) should be available. There are other changes as well. For example, custodial orders have been modified and are now referred to as "custody and supervision orders" (42(2)). Such orders dictate that an offender would be expected to serve two-thirds of the order in a custodial setting and one-third of it on supervision in the community. If a youth is given a "custody and supervision order," the province is required to begin planning for reintegration as soon as the youth begins serving the custodial sentence. The conditions that are imposed on the youth serving the "supervision" portion of the custody and supervision order are set by provincial authorities rather than the sentencing judge. The theory behind this is that custodial staff are more likely to know, at the end of the period spent in custody, what is most useful for the youth.

For certain very serious cases (where the youth has been found guilty of murder, manslaughter, attempted murder, or aggravated sexual assault, or the youth's current offence has been found by the judge to be a "serious violent offence" and the youth has a record of having committed at least two prior serious violent offences), the youth can be given an "intensive rehabilitative custody and supervision order" (sec. 42(2)(r)). However, this is available only in the cases where the youth has some form of mental disorder and there is a plan that is likely to reduce the risk of future offending. Furthermore, the province must have an appropriate facility that offers such services and must also approve of the youth's participation. The best guess is that this provision will be imposed infrequently. In any case, it is governed by normal sentencing principles. In other words, once again the youth's psychological needs do not override proportionality considerations.

Transfers to Adult Court under the *Juvenile Delinquents Act* and the *Young Offenders Act*

Between 1908 and 2003, it was always theoretically possible for almost any case involving a young offender age 14 or older to be transferred to adult court. The transfer hearing took place early in the youth court process, before a youth had been found guilty of an offence. Often these hearings took weeks and sometimes months to complete. If an application were made under the YOA to transfer a case to adult court, the court had to "consider the interest of society, which includes the objectives of affording protection to the public and rehabilitation of the young person, and determine whether those objectives

can be reconciled by the youth being under the jurisdiction of the youth court" (sec. 16(1.1)). If the objectives could be reconciled, the youth would stay in youth court. If the court felt that the objectives could not be reconciled, the court was told that "protection of the public" was to be paramount and the case would go to adult court.

Numerous concerns (see, for example, Beaulieu, 1994) had been raised over the years about transfer hearings, not least of which was that the hearing, coming as it did before a finding of guilt, had an unrealistic aura to it since decisions had to be made without full information about the nature of the case. Judges, in effect, had to decide what should happen to a youth *if* that youth were found guilty.

In 1996, the law on the transfer of cases to adult court was changed. For youths 16 and 17 years old charged with any of four very serious violent offences (murder, manslaughter, attempted murder, and aggravated sexual assault), a youth would be "presumptively" transferred to adult court unless the youth successfully argued that the transfer should not take place. This "reverse onus" position put the responsibility on the young person to convince the court that his/her needs were best met in the youth system. The test (described above) as to whether a transfer should take place was the same as it had been. The change in the law had essentially no impact on the number of transfers that took place. Doob and Sprott (in press) estimate that at most about 10 to 20 percent of what would be presumptive cases were transferred to adult court, and this percentage did not change when the "presumptive transfer" law came into effect. In other words, announcing that youths would be presumptively transferred to adult court if they were charged with certain offences had no effect on the likelihood of an actual transfer taking place. Transfers have never been very prevalent in Canada. Out of the roughly 100 000 cases a year, fewer than 100 cases are typically transferred (see Figure 11.1).

ADULT SENTENCES UNDER THE *YOUTH CRIMINAL JUSTICE ACT*

The YCJA did away with transfers to adult court. After April 1, 2003, no case brought to youth court could be transferred to adult court. Instead, if proper notices were given early in the process by the Crown to the accused youth, the Crown could at the sentencing hearing request that a youth be given an adult sentence. Because youths subject to adult sentences would, in fact, be liable to imprisonment for five years or more, any youth at risk of receiving an

adult sentence would (because of *Charter of Rights and Freedoms* guarantees) be allowed to elect a jury trial (or a trial before a superior court judge). Technically, however, these judges would be sitting as youth court judges, and the jury trial, if there were one, would take place before a superior court judge sitting as a youth court judge. More importantly, the special protections available for youths would be in place throughout the court proceedings.

In addition, the YCJA maintained the list of offences that made youths presumptively eligible for transfer to adult court under the YOA (those found guilty of first- or second-degree murder, attempted murder, manslaughter, and aggravated sexual assault). However, they also added a fifth group: those who had twice previously been found (by previous youth court judges) to have committed "serious violent offences" (sec. 42(9)) and this time had also been found guilty of an offence that the judge declared to be a

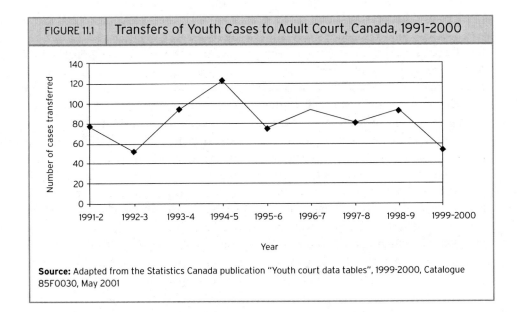

| FIGURE 11.1 | Transfers of Youth Cases to Adult Court, Canada, 1991-2000 |

Source: Adapted from the Statistics Canada publication "Youth court data tables", 1999-2000, Catalogue 85F0030, May 2001

serious violent offence. In addition, the legislation imposed the presumption of an adult sentence be lowered to age 14 rather than 16 (as it had been for presumptive transfers under the YOA). Provinces were given the freedom to raise that to age 16. Moreover, these "presumptions" became relevant only after the youth had been found guilty, not at the beginning of the process.

We would suggest it is likely that few cases will result in an adult sentence under the new legislation. The test under the YCJA as to whether a case should be sentenced as a youth or as an adult is an interesting one, in large part because it relates, once again, to the fundamental principles of the Act. As pointed out earlier in this chapter, the main factor governing the severity of a youth court sentence is proportionality: the sentence is to be proportional to the severity of the offence and the youth's responsibility for it. How, then, is a judge to decide whether a youth should receive an adult sentence? The answer is simple: proportionality. The youth court is to impose a youth sentence (i.e., a sentence that for offences other than murder has a maximum length of two or three years) when "it is of the opinion that a youth sentence imposed in accordance with the purposes and principles [of the YCJA itself and of sentencing in particular] would have *sufficient length* to hold the young person accountable for his or her offending behaviour" (sec. 72(1)(a), emphasis added). In other words, if the maximum length of a youth sentence (two or three years) is sufficiently long to allow a proportional sentence, a youth sentence shall be imposed. We have already noted (see Table 11.3) that there are very few

very long sentences (i.e., more than two years) being handed down in Canada. One might suspect, therefore, that few adult sentences will be imposed because few would be seen as necessary by the sentencing judge. A youth who receives an adult sentence is, for the most part, treated as an adult except for two things. First, the parole ineligibility periods for those found guilty of murder are considerably shorter for youths than for adults (5 to 7 years for youths age 14 to 15, and 7 to 10 years for a 16- to 17-year-old youth as compared to 10 to 25 years for an adult). Second, the placement of the youth into an adult or youth facility is a separate decision.

A youth given an adult sentence may be placed by the judge into a youth facility or an adult facility. Presumptively, a youth who is under 18 years old at the time of sentencing is to be placed in a youth facility; a youth over 18 is to be placed in an adult facility. This would occur unless the judge is satisfied "that to do so would not be in the best interests of the young person or would jeopardize the safety of others" (sec. 76(2)).

Before the YCJA became law, the Quebec government asked for a ruling from the Quebec Court of Appeal on the constitutionality of various of its provisions. That court decided that presumptive adult sentences for young people were, generally, unconstitutional. The Government of Canada decided not to challenge this decision, and instead indicated that it would introduce new legislation to bring the law in line with the Quebec Court of Appeal judgment. Hence this "presumptive adult sentence" provision—which one suspects from previous research (Doob & Sprott, in press) would have no impact—apparently no longer will exist. Those who opposed the presumptive adult sentence provisions of the Act are, undoubtedly, happy about this outcome; those who supported them are undoubtedly displeased with the Quebec Court of Appeal judgment and the decision of the Government of Canada to propose legislative change in line with the Quebec Court decision rather than appealing the decision to the Supreme Court of Canada. The empirical data suggest that emotional responses on both sides are rather misplaced. First of all, as is clear from Figure 11.1, in Canada we do not have a history of transferring many youths to adult court. Given that many of the youths who are transferred are not facing very serious offences (see Doob & Cesaroni, 2004), it is unlikely, we think, that many youths would under any circumstances be given adult sentences. Second, an adult sentence is not supposed to be imposed unless a youth sentence would be insufficient in length. Given that very few youth sentences approached the three-year maximum (see Table 11.3), it seems unlikely that judges will see the need for additionally harsh sentences. Thus it is hard to see how presumptive adult sentences would have had a large impact on the sentencing process when it is clear that the presumptive transfer of youths had little impact on the number of cases transferred to adult court (Doob & Sprott, in press).

The procedure for imposing an adult sentence rather than transferring a youth to adult court has obvious advantages. It comes into play only when the Crown has given notice that it will seek an adult sentence and the youth has been found guilty. In contrast, transfer hearings under the YOA, coming as they did before the youth

was found guilty, meant that there was the very real possibility that the youth would be subject to a public adult trial and then found not guilty, or guilty of a much less serious offence. The youth would, under these circumstances, still have suffered the effects of being named publicly as a defendant in adult court. Youths in youth court cannot be named. Under the YCJA, a youth cannot be identified until such time as an adult sentence is imposed.

CONCLUSION

The sentencing provisions of the *Youth Criminal Justice Act* clearly give much more guidance to judges on how sentencing should take place than did the comparable provisions of the *Young Offenders Act*. More interesting, perhaps, is the contrast with the sentencing provisions in the *Criminal Code* that govern the sentencing of adults. The *Criminal Code* provisions suggest that judges are supposed to choose one or more purposes that the sentence should serve (from a list that includes such standard purposes as denunciation, general and specific deterrence, incapacitation, and rehabilitation). Then judges are told that sentences must be proportional, though no guidance is given on how the purposes that are chosen are to be reconciled with the proportionality principle. The *Criminal Code*, like the *Young Offenders Act*, has admonitions to the sentencing judge not to use custodial sentences unless such sentences are necessary. However, the *Youth Criminal Justice Act* goes much further in listing criteria for the use of custody.

Not only are there more explicit principles of sentencing in the YCJA than we have experienced before in Canada, but these principles are expressed in much stronger language. We have already noted, for example, that the YCJA limits custodial sentences for youths to cases where one or more of a set of fairly explicit conditions are met. In contrast, the wording of the YOA suggested that "custody shall only be imposed when all available alternatives to custody that *are reasonable* in the circumstances have been *considered,*" and that in cases not involving serious violence non-custodial sentences should be imposed *"whenever appropriate"* (sec. 24(1.1), emphasis added). Language like "when-

ever appropriate" or "reasonable in the circumstances" does not appear to us to place many limits on the sentencing judge.

Clearly, with the YCJA, Parliament has implicitly declared that sentencing—and what happens to youthful offenders—is, and should be, a matter of public policy and that the broad guidelines that govern sentencing should be legislatively determined. It remains to be seen how this new Parliamentary control will work in practice and whether the move toward Parliamentary control of sentencing will spill over into the adult criminal justice system.

References

Anand, S., & Bala, N. (2003). The Quebec Court of Appeal *Youth Justice Reference:* Striking down the toughest part of the new Act. *Criminal Reports* (6th series), *10,* 397–418.

Beaulieu, L. A. (1994). Youth offences—Adult consequences. *Canadian Journal of Criminology, 36*(3), 329–342.

Brodeur, J.-P., & Doob, A. N. Locking up young offenders for their own good. A paper prepared for the Department of Justice, Canada (revised version, 2002).

Canada. Department of Justice. (1998). *A strategy for the renewal of youth justice.* Ottawa: Department of Justice Canada.

Canadian Centre for Justice Statistics. (2001). *Youth court data tables 1999–2000* (and various other years from 1990–1). Ottawa: Canadian Centre for Justice Statistics, Statistics Canada.

Cesaroni, C., & Peterson-Badali, M. (2003). Young offenders in custody: Risk and adjustment. *Criminal Justice and Behavior,* in press.

Doob, A. N. (2000). Transforming the punishment environment: Understanding public views of what should be accomplished at sentencing. *Canadian Journal of Criminology, 42*(3), 323–340.

Doob, A. N., & Beaulieu, A. L. (1992). Variation in the exercise of judicial discretion with young offenders. *Canadian Journal of Criminology, 34*(1), 35–50.

Doob, A. N., & Cesaroni, C. (2004). *Responding to youth crime in Canada.* Toronto: University of Toronto Press.

Doob, A. N., & Meen, J. (1993). An exploration of changes in dispositions for young offenders in Toronto. *Canadian Journal of Criminology, 35*(1), 19–29.

Doob, A. N., & Roberts, J. V. (1988). Public punitiveness and public knowledge of the facts: Some Canadian surveys. In N. Walker & M. Hough (Eds.), *Public attitudes to sentencing: Surveys from five countries.* Aldershot, England: Gower.

Doob, A. N., & Sprott, J. B. (in press). Changing models of youth justice in Canada. In M. Tonry & A. N. Doob (Eds.), *Youth crime and youth justice: Comparative and cross-national perspectives. Crime and justice: A review of research,* Volume 31. University of Chicago Press, 2004.

Doob, A. N., Sprott, J. B., Marinos, V., & Varma, K. N. (1998). *An exploration of Ontario residents' views of crime and the criminal justice system.* Toronto: Centre of Criminology, University of Toronto.

Doob, A. N., & Webster, C. M. (2003). Sentence severity and crime: Accepting the null hypothesis. In M. Tonry (Ed.), *Crime and justice: A review of research.* Volume 30. University of Chicago Press.

Markwart, A., & Corrado, R. R. (1989). Is the *Young Offenders Act* more punitive? In L. A. Beaulieu (Ed.), *Young offender dispositions: Perspectives on principles and practice.* Toronto: Wall and Thompson.

Matarazzo, A., Carrington, P.J., & Hiscott, D.R. (2001). The effect of prior youth court dispositions on current disposition: An applica-

tion of societal-reaction theory. *Journal of Quantitative Criminology, 17,* 169–200.

Moffitt, T. E. (1993). Adolescence-limited and life-course-persistent antisocial behavior: A developmental taxonomy. *Psychological Review, 100*(4), 674–701.

Sprott, J. B., & Snyder, H. N. (1999). Youth crime in the U.S. and Canada, 1991 to 1996. *Overcrowded Times, 10*(5), 1 & 12–19.

Trépanier, J. (1989). Principles and goals guiding the choice of dispositions under the *Young Offenders Act.* In L. Beaulieu (Ed.). *Young offender dispositions: Perspectives on principles and practice.* Toronto: Wall and Thompson.

Note

1. "Sentences" did not officially enter the language of youth justice until April 2003 with the implementation of the *Youth Criminal Justice Act.*

chapter twelve

Restorative Justice in Canadian Approaches to Youth Crime: Origins, Practices, and Retributive Frameworks

Liz Elliott

School of Criminology
Simon Fraser University

A young guy committed a number of break and enters and, along with his family, met with two of the [victim] families in a community conference. Among other things, they learned that the boy and his family have serious financial struggles. While doing follow up calls with one of the homeowners today, our facilitator relates that the husband wants to buy a turkey for the young guy and his family. This will be done tomorrow so they have it for Christmas dinner.

Not only does this boy have a far greater understanding of the impact of his decisions on others, the homeowners now see him as far more than "the little ^%*&" who took their sense of security. And they are far more than victims in the police report. These folks have redefined the rather ugly beginning of their relationship, beyond that of simply "victim" and "offender," and added some meat (as it were) to notions of "community."[1]

INTRODUCTION

This story of a community conference reflects a new approach to youth justice today in Canada. Youth justice itself has undergone significant changes since the 1800s, when children were incarcerated with adults in austere prisons and corporal punishments were the norm. However, the shift from strict punishments to dialogue and direct accountability marks a change in the rationality of youth justice, where responses to crime have evolved from the mere collective symbolic censure of punishments to inclusive problem-solving processes. The community conference described above is an example of restorative justice practice, a movement away from the courts and correctional system responses. The discourses of restorative justice are reflected in the direction taken by the new *Youth Criminal Justice Act* (S.C. 2002, c. C-7), which marks a shift in the approach to youth crime.

Youth crime itself involves more than just the expected vagaries of adolescent pursuits. While most youth crime is relatively minor in nature, some acts produce serious harms that call for community responses that go beyond the informal individual guidance offered by adult mentors. According to recent justice statistics for 2001, of the 51 952 guilty decisions on youth cases heard in Canada, 13 798 were for crimes of violence. Accounting, then, for about one-third of all youth offences, violent crime is an issue that must be addressed—although it is questionable that the old standards, punishment and detention, are empirically effective solutions. And it is important, also, to remember that 38 154 youths—two-thirds of the guilty cases in this study—were convicted of non-violent crimes such as property, driving, and drug offences (Statistics Canada, 2003).

In contrast to the exciting drama of television courtrooms, where criminal cases involving unusual acts of violence dominate the setting, are the mundane operations of Canadian provincial and family/youth courts. Much of what passes through our courts amounts to minor property offences and probation breaches. And increasingly—thanks to "zero-tolerance" and "three strikes and you're out" policies—there has been a tendency to criminalize behaviour that would otherwise be recognized as "children behaving like children." The idea that children should not be expected to act and think like adults is well reflected in criminal justice policy, primarily in the separation of youth from adults in the criminal justice processes, and the practice of handling children under 12 years of age through other social service measures.

In this chapter, some of these ideas are examined in greater depth through the paradigm of restorative justice, particularly as it evolves within the context of the retributive system. Key areas of discussion in restorative justice with youth will be examined, specifically its history, philosophy, and practice. This paradigm is then discussed in the context of the Canadian *Youth Criminal Justice Act* (April, 2003) and "community-based" restorative justice initiatives. The chapter ends with an overview of the role of victims and communities in current restorative justice practices, as well as discussion of the shifting concept of shame.

CANADIAN ORIGINS OF RESTORATIVE JUSTICE PRACTICES

Restorative justice has been described as a paradigm, a new way of thinking, a pattern of thinking, a program, and a process (Elliott, 2002). These variations are indicative of the range of understanding of restorative justice. Zehr's (1990) explanation of restorative justice reconstructs both notions of crime and justice:

> Crime is a violation of people and relationships. It creates obligations to make things right. Justice involves the victim, the offender, and the community in a search for solutions which promote repair, reconciliation, and reassurance. (p. 181)

In restorative justice, the focus of intervention is harm rather than crime per se, and the response is grounded in motives of repair or healing of people and relationships rather than the conviction and punishment of offenders.

A focus on harms rather than laws or rules redirects the intervention from authoritative structures such as the state or the school to real people, those who have been personally affected by the harm as victims, offenders, or other members of the community. In the retributive system, the people affected are used as a means to the ends demanded by case administration processes. Restorative justice treats the people affected as ends in themselves, ideally addressing the practical and personal needs of the primary parties as well as those of the community in which the harm occurred. These needs are positioned within a framework of relationships and interconnection, where obligations to make things right are mutually agreed upon through a process where the primary parties are supported and relationships between them are repaired to the extent possible. These obligations may extend to the larger community, where the capacity to address identified precipitating factors of the harm may require attention and strengthening (Elliott, 2002).

It is a common belief that restorative justice is a new trend, a "flavour of the month" in the calendar of criminal justice. In fact, basic principles and practices of restorative justice have long been practised in communities as a primary method of conflict resolution. In times past, conflicts—criminal or otherwise—were largely handled through negotiated restitution by kinship elders and community leaders in village assemblies (Cayley, 1998, p. 167). While the state had taken over the criminal law by the end of the twelfth century (Weitekamp, 1999, p. 89), restitution remained as a primary response to law breaking. Inquisitorial justice[2] emerged at the height of the Middle Ages early in the thirteenth century, but did not begin to dominate in organized societies until around 1750 (Bianchi, 1994, p. 16). Formally administered versions of justice such as those we recognize today were initiated by victims and were not affordable to most people until the early 1800s. While police functions enabled by appointed constables, night watchmen, and bailiffs were evident, formally organized police forces did not exist until the 1829 establishment of the Metropolitan London Police in England (Weaver, 1995, p. 50). In Canada, parallel developments were occurring but latterly, as crime occurring in the colonies was first managed informally, and then by an emerging system of courts as well as reformatories, industrial schools, and jails that were used to detain and punish those convicted of crimes.

Prior to colonization, community-based justice was simultaneously practised in Aboriginal communities as part of an overall holistic philosophy of life. In the Mohawk language, for example, the word "law" translates to "the way to live most nicely together" (Monture-Okanee, 1994, p. 227). Laws, in this instance, were about values that affirm and foster peaceful, co-operative interrelationships rather than being prohibitions about specific actions that might disturb otherwise peaceful communities. As Rupert Ross (1996), an Ontario Crown attorney with great interest in and experience with Aboriginal understandings of justice, explains:

> I frequently watch Aboriginal people shake their heads in disbelief at how often Western countries fall back on imposed "Codes of Minimum Behaviour" backed up by threat of punishment. The belief seems to be that unless the spirit of the individual is changed, such codes will only anger them by forcing them to do what they don't want to do in the first place. Then, once angered, they will try to beat the codes any way they can. Further, they will never go *beyond* the bare, legislated minimums. Most importantly, they are likely to take their anger out on precisely the people whom the codes were meant to protect, using ways that have not yet been legislated. Reliance on codes is therefore seen as never-ending, self-strangling, counterproductive and a great waste of time. The important issue is frame of mind—or spirit—as well as a focus on creating good relationships (pp. 90–91).

In Aboriginal justice traditions of the past and today, acts that generate harms create the need for healing of both individuals and communities. Further, Aboriginal healing processes "stress values like respect, sharing, humility and so forth" (Ross, 1996, p. 189). These processes involve whoever feels the desire to be present, and communities share in the responsibility to support individuals in their healing paths for the good of the whole.

CURRENT PRACTICES

Traditional Aboriginal teachings vary from culture to culture. Moreover, the idea that wrongdoers need teaching and healing is not always realized in Aboriginal communities today, which are variously burdened by the historical effects of residential schools, alcohol and drug abuse, discriminatory child welfare policies, poverty, and reserve life generally. Aboriginal people are still disproportionately represented in the formal criminal justice system, a reflection of discriminatory criminal justice and social welfare practices. Nonetheless, it is within this context that ideals of pre-colonization Aboriginal justice have recently begun to breathe life again.

Today, many Aboriginal communities have resurrected their traditional justice practices, in part or whole, often in conditions of extreme material and social deprivation. The well-known example of Hollow Water, Manitoba, marks one of the first modern revivals of Aboriginal justice practices. Beginning in 1984 with a discussion of community problems that particularly concerned youth, a team of mostly Aboriginal women from the community soon shifted the focus from the youth to the context of their homes, and specifically the behaviour of their parents. This began to unravel a series of revelations about family violence, abuse of alcohol and drugs, and sexual abuse (Ross, 1996). Processes of circle healing were offered as "healing contracts" for sex offenders,[3] in the place of more mainstream sentencing options that could involve incarceration (Cayley, 1998, pp. 192–196). Another example is Qwi:Qwelstom, the Aboriginal justice response of the Sto:lo nation in Chilliwack, British Columbia. Qwi:Qwelstom also runs parallel to the non-native justice system, using circle processes where the focus is on making things right through traditional teachings that apply to the people as a whole.

The first example in recent history of restorative justice practice in non-Aboriginal communities is found in the Kitchener-Waterloo area of Southern Ontario. In 1974 a probation officer approached a local Mennonite Central Committee to discuss a case involving two youths who had vandalized 22 properties. Together they, with others, worked with the two youths to bring them face-to-face with the people whose properties had been damaged. Restitution agreements were arranged and repayments followed soon after (Zehr, 1990). This pilot case launched what was to become known as the Victim Offender Reconciliation Program (VORP), which soon spawned similar projects in other Canadian communities with active Mennonite traditions. VORP processes involve the wrongdoer(s), the victim(s), and a trained community mediator in an encounter that is designed to involve all those affected, to facilitate greater understanding of the offence, and to come to a restitution agreement. However, this process was initially limited to first-time offenders who had committed relatively minor offences.

A community justice group in Langley, B.C., that evolved in 1982 as part of the VORP movement would later pilot another version of the program to address more serious offences that had generally been screened out of such processes. In the late 1980s, the Fraser Region Community Justice Initiatives Association (known as "CJI") began to offer vic-

tim–offender mediation to people affected by violent offences, particularly serious sexual assaults, robberies, and homicides. These mediations begin post-sentence, and may take months or years in preparation to ensure that both victims and offenders are prepared for an encounter. In the Victim Offender Mediation Program (VOMP), the facilitators work with the participants separately, bringing them to the point of a face-to-face encounter if the parties are agreeable. An evaluation of this program demonstrates the healing benefits of this restorative process: Unanimous support was noted from the victims and offenders in the 24 cases included in the evaluation (Roberts, 1995).

One restorative justice innovation that works alongside the formal criminal justice system is sentencing circles. Pioneered in recent years in northern communities such as the Yukon Territory (Stuart, 1996), Manitoba (Ross, 1996), and Saskatchewan (Green, 1998), sentencing circles are often held in Aboriginal communities, using formal court personnel and community members in informal settings such as community halls. Sentencing circles involve all interested members in a community to participate in deciding the most appropriate disposition for one of its members who has violated an accepted law. Described by one lawyer, "At its best, a sentencing circle is a physical manifestation of the principles of restorative justice while adhering to the stated principles of sentencing as articulated in the *Criminal Code* and interpreted in relevant case law" (Head, 2002). Circle sentencing is a "stocktaking and accountability exercise not only on the part of the offender but on the part of the community that produced the offender" (*R. v. Taylor,* 1996), and thus is considered to be more holistic than regular court processes.

Another common restorative justice process model is family group conferencing (FGC), which was imported to Canada from New Zealand via Australia in the mid-1990s. Based on Maori Aborigine traditions but adapted to suit legislative purposes, FGCs include the wrongdoer, his or her supporters (family, friends), the victim, victim supporters, social workers, and other interested parties. FGCs were originally used for both family welfare and youth criminal justice cases in New Zealand, and were legislated into that country's 1989 *Children, Young Persons and Their Families Act* (Hassall, 1996). This idea was then adopted and adapted by the Wagga Wagga police in New South Wales, Australia. A Royal Canadian Mounted Police (RCMP) detachment in Sparwood, British Columbia, was the first policing agency to experiment with FGCs in 1995. By 1996 the federal Department of Justice was researching the FGC experience in New Zealand and Australia (Chatterjee & Elliott, 2003). Currently, the RCMP advocates and offers training for its version of FGCs, called "community justice forums" (CJFs), which are directed primarily toward youth in conflict with the law.

Typically, a "conference" involves a number of activities surrounding an encounter between a victim and offender outside of the formal court process. Referrals are made by the police, courts, or other agencies to the restorative justice agency or practitioner, preferably in cases where the accused pleads guilty to charges or otherwise accepts responsibility for his or her harm-producing action, criminal

or otherwise. The conference facilitator then conducts a number of pre-conference meetings with the affected parties and their support people to ascertain the issues that are likely to arise in a group meeting and to determine whether a conference is even suitable for the case. If the case moves to a conference, the affected parties and their respective supporters meet in a circle with one or more neutral facilitators who "keep the circle," or safeguard the process. Participants generally respond to three main themes: What happened? How did what happened affect each person? and What can be done to repair the harm done? Attempts are made to build consensus in the development of the case outcomes, and follow-up meetings are held to confirm that the resolution plan is followed through.

TENETS OF RETRIBUTIVE JUSTICE AND THE IMPLICATIONS FOR RESTORATIVE JUSTICE

The concept of restorative justice has been interpreted in different ways by many authors, thus contributing to misconceptions about its philosophy, aims, and objectives. A key reason for frequent misunderstandings of restorative justice is the anachronistic use of restorative justice concepts in the context of the retributive system to which we are accustomed. One way to understand this is to revisit our conventional beliefs about law and justice, to consider their theoretical and philosophical foundations. Along the way, we encounter assumptions about ideas of human behaviour and social control that are often in contradiction to ideas emerging from a restorative justice framework. These assumptions of retributive justice must be reconsidered as we confront the promises of restorative justice in order to answer the question: "To what extent is a shift from judicial punishment to restorative justice, as the normal response to crime, feasible and desirable?" (Johnstone, 2002, p. 6).

Modern responses to acts of crime or rule-breaking are premised on two basic assumptions about human capacities that emerged in the last great shifts in thought, which began in the later half of the eighteenth century with the ages of "enlightenment" and "reason." At that time, philosophical discussions of justice began to conform to the demands of the new ways of thinking, where science began to dominate religious authority. Enlightened and rational thinkers, further, were also motivated by their observations of the sometimes barbaric and capricious punishments meted out by ecclesiastical and monarchical authorities in the name of God and the king. Governance by rule of law and democracy was seen as a progressive remedy to this situation. New emphasis was placed on the power of reason to ascertain truth, and criminal justice ideas of the conventional "reasonable man" were born, constituting the first basic assumption of human capacity. In criminal justice today, we are assumed to be reasonable people capable of making logical choices unless expert psychiatrists can convincingly demonstrate otherwise. Thus, we have the capacity to make reasoned choices about our behaviour and may be held responsible for these choices.

Retributive law and justice are also based on utilitarian beliefs about the "nature" of human behaviour. Underlying the criminal law is the "pleasure/pain" principle advanced in 1789 by Jeremy Bentham, who argued:

> It has been shown that the happiness of the individuals, of whom a community is composed, that is their pleasures and their security, is the end and the sole end which the legislator ought to have in view: the sole standard, in conformity to which each individual ought, as far as depends upon the legislator, to be *made* to fashion his behaviour. But whether it be this or any thing else that is to be *done*, there is nothing by which a man can be *made* to do it, but either pain or pleasure. (p. 24)

Thus, also imbedded in the retributive system is the second assumption that people's choices of behaviour may be controlled by simply resorting to measures that speak to the human tendency to pursue pleasure and avoid pain.

These two assumptions—that we are reasonable people capable of making reasonable choices and that in most instances we will tend to pursue pleasure and avoid pain—have remained more or less intact to the present. Criminal laws are accompanied by punishments, albeit in a range that affords judges the ability to accommodate mitigating and exacerbating circumstances. Indeed, punishment is the teeth that give the law its bite and is assumed to be a deterrent, both general and specific,[4] to the commission of crime. Consequently, following from this reasoning is the belief that disregard for the law is a product of the leniency of the corresponding punishments. Within this framework, the solution logically is then to "get tough" on crime and increase the severity of punishments. In a nutshell, this represents the "law and order" perspective on responding to crime, a commonly persuasive approach favoured by many politicians.

The threshold of "zero tolerance" as a line in the sand of criminal justice sanctions has had the further corollary effect of raising the scale of punishments in other institutions of society, most prominently schools. Institutional processes created to handle rule/law violations today seem burdened by a surfeit of minor acts, defying the legal maxim *"de minimus non curat lex"*—the law is not concerned with trifles. A good example is the failure of such policies in the agendas of school districts across North America. Faced with mounting ludicrous examples of school suspensions based on "trifles" such as horseplay in the snow, pointing chicken fingers at fellow classmates, and wearing scented hair gel (Cole, 2003), administrators and teachers have begun to explore other ways of handling social problems in the school. As stated by one Alberta teacher in a *Globe and Mail* article on the subject: "Zero tolerance sounds tough and decisive [but]... problems don't go away simply because you outlaw them" (in Cole, 2003).

Applied to the wider context of federal and provincial governance, this observation is a prescient one. The practice of attempting to solve social problems through criminal legislation is the backbone of any political party's platform and, often, performance when in power. Since political mandates fall in three- to five-year cycles, there is little incentive to develop, for example, crime prevention initiatives through social development that might require 10 to 20 years to yield results (Elliott, 2002). In this milieu, the temptation to conflate problem-solving with the creation of legislation is apparently irresistible (Campbell, 2000, pp. 346–348). Between 1994 and 1997, for ex-

ample, backbench Members of Parliament from all federal parties proposed 203 private members' bills, 52 of which advanced changes designed to "get tough on crime" (Gaucher & Elliott, 2001, p. 74). The issue remains whether it is realistic to assume that "outlawing" certain activities is equal to solving the problems these activities create.

Restorative justice, then, attempts to find expression against the backdrop of a retributive system that is predicated on the idea of the reasonable person who is simply controlled by pleasure and pain through laws and the threat of punishments and the notion that social problems are best solved by legislation or rule-making. Questions may be posed, however, as to the extent to which these assumptions are empirically sound. Is behaviour that supports "the greatest pleasure for the greatest number of people" meaningfully cultivated and supported through a system of laws and punishments? Are people really motivated to behave in the best interests of everyone, and by extension themselves, through avoidance of the pain inherent in punishment? Is punishment, the "deliberate infliction of harm," a good method by which to teach people how to live peacefully with each other in a civil society? Do we really solve problems merely by making laws or rules prohibiting certain acts? In other words, what do we really gain in tangible outcomes contributing to the safety and well being of people from the existing retributive system?

Perhaps the most cogent indicator of the difference between the retributive and restorative paradigms of justice is in the primary questions posed by each. The retributive system asks: Was a crime committed (evidence of law-breaking)? Who did it (guilty actor)? What do they deserve (punishment)? By contrast, the questions posed by a restorative approach are: Who was harmed? What are their needs? Whose obligations are these? In the retributive paradigm, the offender is centred, as is the question of his/her punishment; in the restorative lens, all those harmed (especially the primary victim) are centred, as is the question of healing. The retributive lens interprets the world of conflict as one of crimes and punishments, while restorative justice codes the same information in terms of harms and healing.

FROM CRIME AND PUNISHMENT TO HARMS AND HEALING

It has been established that the retributive system is based on a belief in the deterrent capacities of punishment in both preventing and responding to crime. The important question of the efficacy of punishment in achieving conformity to rules and laws, however, has been raised over the past few decades in psychology (Miller, 1983), sociology (Garland, 1990), philosophy (Cragg, 1992), and education (Kohn, 1999). Furthermore, the wisdom of using conformity to laws as a barometer of a healthy society is also questioned. Conformity on the basis of fear of externally imposed punishment has a limited sustainability compared to harmonious social relations on the basis of internally driven values. When offenders overcome their fear of the system, they may easily return to their harm-producing behaviour. Some use this as an argument for

tougher punishments—raising the fear threshold—in order to create more effective deterrents. We might question where this approach could take us—the state and offenders upping the ante to limits that eventually shock the common conscience.[5]

Therefore, it is disputable whether the resiliency of punishment is due to its efficiency in deterring crime. As far back as the late nineteenth century, Durkheim (1933, orig. 1893) argued:

[Punishment] does not serve, or does so quite secondarily, in correcting the culpable or in intimidating possible followers. From this point of view, its efficacy is justly doubtful and, in any case, mediocre. Its true function is to maintain social cohesion intact, while maintaining all its vitality in the common conscience. (p. 108)

Durkheim's point was that punishment is a poor tool for effecting safety and protecting society from specific offenders. Rather, punishment serves a more primary, symbolic, and cathartic purpose that counteracts the emotional reaction of the community to crime.

Nonetheless, the lack of emphasis on punishment found within the restorative paradigm has fostered much apprehension toward restorative justice within the retributive system. It is also a key reason why many restorative practices often become co-opted into producing punitive consequences for offenders that have no connection to the original harms committed. The tendency to seek "tough" punishments for various kinds of crimes has also marginalized the potential of restorative processes to handle many meaningful cases. Community service orders, for example, whether tangibly connected to the harm committed or not, are often perceived through the retributive lens as "lenient punishments." This perception then reinforces the use of restorative processes for relatively minor and even trivial acts that would otherwise not normally capture the attention of formal criminal justice responses in the first place,[6] and in turn widens the net of the criminal justice system itself.

By removing the focus from punishment, restorative justice is free to concentrate on harms and healing. Harms happen between people; thus, restorative justice is primarily concerned with relationships. Healing of individuals and relationships are seen as essential steps toward building inclusive and healthy communities. Victims, offenders, their supporters, and others work together to discuss what happened, how the event affected individuals, and what can be done (and by whom) to repair the harm. Processes that engage the community also provide an opportunity for people to actively reconnect with or define their individual and collective values and norms, enlivening what Durkheim referred to as the "common conscience."

Punishment is removed from consideration in Cohen's (1985) observations about trends in social control generally and criminal justice specifically. In its focus on harms and healing, restorative justice processes are consistent with what Cohen described as "moral pragmatism," which he offered as a "guiding criterion for evaluating 'community control' and other such forms of control" (p. 252). Cohen explains:

> The "moral" element affirms doing good and doing justice as values in themselves. By "doing good" I mean not just individual concern about private troubles but a commitment to the socialist reform of the public issues which cause these troubles. By "doing justice" I mean not equity or retribution but the sense of the rightness and fairness of punishment for the collective good. By "values in themselves" I mean that both utilitarian and strategic considerations should, where possible, be secondary to attaining these values for their own sake and whatever their other results ...
>
> The "pragmatic element" stands against all forms of premature theoretical and political closure, all quests for cognitive certainty which rule out certain solutions as being conceptually impure or politically inadmissible. If the guiding values of social intervention are made clear (justice, good or whatever else might be offered) then the only question is: what difference does this particular policy make? Each proffered solution must thus be weighed up in terms of its consistency or inconsistency with preferred values, the alternative solutions realistically available at the moment of choice, and the likelihood of the programme being able to realize (intentionally or otherwise) the desired goals with the minimum cost. (pp. 252–253)

Cohen's suggestion—including its reluctant acceptance of punishment for social censure purposes—sounds very much like the framework of a restorative justice "system." Crimes produce harms that demand both a moral and a pragmatic response. The responses themselves should be consistent with the professed values of the society, in both content and process. In a restorative justice context the word "healing" seems to cover these moral and pragmatic concerns through caring and practical support.

The question remains, however, as to how well restorative justice practices may be able to function and remain true to the philosophical tenets without suffering the time-honoured fate of being absorbed by the values of the existing retributive philosophy. As Thorsten Sellin commented many years ago, "beautiful theories have a way of turning into ugly practices" (in Cullen & Gilbert, 1982, p. 152). In the following sections of this chapter, this issue is examined through a consideration of Canada's newest youth crime legislation, the *Youth Criminal Justice Act.*

RESTORATIVE JUSTICE AND THE *YOUTH CRIMINAL JUSTICE ACT*

The *Youth Criminal Justice Act* (YCJA) replaced the *Young Offenders Act* (YOA), which was popularly seen by critics and media pundits as being ineffective and "too soft" on crimes committed by youth under the age of 18. This perception included the notions that youth were committing more crime, that crimes committed were more serious, and that youth in conflict with the law were "playing the system" based on their sophisticated understanding of the YOA. However, these perceptions have been challenged by various studies. A study using UCR data from 1977 to 1996 demonstrated that rates of police-reported youth crime had changed very little apart from one temporary peak in the early 1990s (Carrington, 1999). Another study examining youth violence found no evidence to support the idea that youth crime was becoming more violent (Doob & Sprott, 1998, 2004). Moreover, an examination of young people's knowledge of the YOA demonstrated no difference between youth and young offenders in their respective awareness of the dispositions of youth court records or even the age boundaries

encompassed by the YOA (Peterson-Badali and Koegl, 1998).

The YCJA does not appear to be a reactionary antidote to the concerns of the YOA's critics, however ill-founded these concerns may have been. Rather than conforming to expectations of "tough" versus "lenient" responses to youth crime, the notion of deterrence is not even mentioned in the YCJA. Indeed, a large impetus for the new legislation was based on the high rates of youth in custodial institutions and the need for an increased use of community-based sanctions. This transition from the incarceration strategies of previous youth justice intervention to restorative relationship healing (symbolized in the offering of the turkey in the conference story) is significant. The difference of significance between these two Acts, for the purposes of this chapter, lies in the mechanisms of response to youth crime. Specifically, the YCJA incorporates aspects of restorative justice ideals and processes in the form of "extrajudicial measures," to be used by police and Crown attorneys in lieu of the youth justice court system. Police officers have already begun to use these measures, particularly that which has been called "informal cautioning" in New Zealand and Australia. Also included in these measures are "extrajudicial sanctions," which were previously known as "alternative measures" under the YOA. Of particular resonance with restorative justice processes is the YCJA's provision under sec. 19 of a "conference," defined as a group of persons convened to provide advice in accordance with this section of the legislation.[7]

Under this legislation a conference can take many forms. It can be as informal as a police officer meeting with school officials to determine if charges should be laid. In other instances it may include a more formal, family group conference model where the primary affected parties and their supporters are brought together to discuss the situation and agree upon an outcome. The intent behind this aspect of the legislation is to allow any person who has the responsibility to make a decision in the youth justice system to be able to turn to others, professionals or otherwise, for input (Tustin & Lutes, 2002, p. 30). This is a new provision and it has been perceived as controversial, as the wording is vague and thus is open to individual interpretation. Each jurisdiction is expected to develop policies and guidelines for this process to ensure continuity. Furthermore, it is not clear how the costs associated with conferences will be addressed (a particularly contentious issue for municipalities that are being approached for funding by community justice organizations), whether youth have a right to legal representation at such conferences, or what the implications of insurance liability issues are in cases involving motor vehicles.

This terminology of "conference" within the law, while not directive of any specific kind of restorative justice process, is reflective of the well-known practice of family group conferencing (as discussed earlier) that originated in New Zealand in the 1980s, influenced in part by Maori Aborigine practices.[8] While many principles of the YCJA are consistent with the objectives of family group conferencing (or community justice forums) as practised in most countries, an important difference exists. Under the YCJA a conference is not a decision-making body.

The decision-maker, either the referring police agency or the courts, may or may not accept the advice or the recommendation of a conference, depending upon its consistency with the other principles of the YCJA such as proportionate accountability (Chatterjee & Elliott, 2003). The implications of this caveat have yet to be calculated, given that the Act was implemented only recently.

In its Declaration of Principle (sec. 3; see Appendix C), the YCJA differs from its predecessor (the YOA) in its attention to repairing of harm done (sec. 3(c)(ii)), the involvement of parents, extended family, community, and social or other agencies in the youth's reintegration (sec. 3(c)(iii)), and the role of victims (sec. 3(d)(ii)(iii)). While not making direct reference to restorative justice principles, the principles of the YCJA appear to generally conform to them. However, questions arise as to the potential of the Act's ability to be consistent with the restorative justice paradigm, particularly when the Act is located within a contextualizing retributive framework. For example, in what ways, if any, is the repair of harm done to victims and the community in a minor shoplifting charge realized through the consequence of 50 hours of community service dedicated to a cause unrelated to the offence? Are provisions available to include youth who may have no family support in extrajudicial processes, or are disadvantaged youth screened out from these possibilities by virtue of their lack of family or community relationships? And while the YCJA requires proceedings to treat victims with courtesy, compassion, and respect, and for them to be given an opportunity to participate and be heard— provisions that certainly conform to restorative justice values and principles—what are the actual implications of these provisions in a process that is still offender-focused?

Perhaps the fact that the term "restorative justice" itself does not appear in the YCJA, is indicative of the intended limits of the new Act. While specific concepts of the YCJA, such as repairing harm, victim inclusion, and the involvement of families and communities, are also apparent in restorative justice principles, the Act is intended to address criminal wrongdoing alone. Restorative justice is forward looking, attempting to discern harm prevention/reduction potential in social development strategies that typically include systems external to criminal justice such as those of education, social services, and community development. The YCJA is still backward focused, limiting its scope to the handling of specific cases of harms already committed.

The Fate of Victims in Restorative Justice within a Retributive Framework

In examining the hurdles encountered by others in attempting to implement restorative justice practices within a retributive justice framework, it is useful to return to the different, primary objectives of each paradigm. The mandate of the retributive system is to focus on crime and punishment of offenders, while the restorative philosophy is centred on harm and focused on the healing of all parties involved. A key juncture of difficulty, then, is the fate of crime victims in legislated restorative justice provisions that still adhere to an offender focus. In the current system,

victims are witnesses and the state assumes the role of the victim on behalf of society as a whole. While there are some defensible philosophical reasons for this, the practical implications are that victims' needs are secondary in deference to the retributive paradigm's higher-order requirement of addressing the crime and the offender. Restorative justice processes may offer a greater opportunity for victims to actively participate in the justice system, but their involvement is not central or even ultimately necessary in order to process the offender's case.

This point is demonstrated in several examples. A study of the well-established Thames Valley Police restorative cautioning initiative in the United Kingdom showed that in a sample of 334 cases in three pilot areas of the program in which there was an identifiable victim, 82 percent did not attend the restorative conference. More than 50 percent of victims interviewed noted that they were invited to the caution process but chose not to attend (Hill, 2002). In New South Wales, Australia, where restorative conferencing was introduced with the *Young Offenders Act 1997*, an evaluation study noted that victim participation was much higher, at 72.5 percent (Trimboli, 2000). The differences between these two may be explained by many variables such as whether the process was conducted by the police or government social workers, the severity of the offence, or general victim awareness of restorative processes. In Canada, a smaller sample of Aboriginal youth cases handled in family group conferences conducted in Winnipeg in the early 1990s demonstrated a low victim-participation rate of 12.5 percent, due to inability to locate victims to invite them to attend, inability of victims to travel distances to participate, or unwillingness of victims to become further involved (Longclaws, Galaway, & Barkwell, 1996).

Victim involvement in restorative conferencing is meant to be voluntary. However, victims often feel subtle pressures to participate that create discomfort for them and engender the fear of secondary victimization (Wemmers, 2002). Resistance to victim involvement has also been noted on the part of judges and the courts themselves, which may see the victim as another adversary rather than a client (Bazemore, 1998). Furthermore, such court paternalism has also been reflected in concerns about the "unknowns" in bringing together offenders and victims in restorative processes that are seen as not having the kinds of controls implicit in the retributive system (Bazemore, 1999).

Victim suspicions are not tempered by legislation that is created with their "interests" and restorative justice philosophy in mind. In Tasmania, for example, under the *Sentencing Act 1997*, the less than 50 percent rate of mandatory compensation orders made by judges for certain losses incurred by crime is seen as an example of a restorative justice rhetoric where victims "are political fodder to provide an illusion that something is being done for victims" (Warner & Gawlik, 2003, p. 73). There is also the perception that restorative justice processes are based on ideal circumstances, which rarely exist and in some communities are far from realized. Some Aboriginal women, for example, have registered deep concerns about the role of local politics and abuses of power in the use of restorative circle processes in isolated communities for the safety of victims (Stewart, Huntley, & Blaney, 2001).

These examples suggest that victims do not yet feel comfortable with or see their needs being met in an offender-focused "restorative justice" system. Indeed, there may be a sense that victims are used as a means to an end (correcting the offender), with benefits to them being seen as secondary to the processing of the offender's case. The YCJA, while providing for sensitivity to victims' needs in several provisions,[9] is still primarily concerned with addressing youth crime and the possible consequences for youth who are apprehended for violating the law. In spite of some encouraging provisions under the YCJA with respect to victims, the offender/punishment focus is central. The conferencing provision, as a response by the state to youth crimes in the YCJA, has the potential to be moderately restorative, as seen within the context of Van Ness and Strong's (2002) description of "the level of restorativeness to which the system aspires" (p. 234).

The Role of the Community in Restorative Justice within a Retributive Framework

Community groups may not be as restrained in how they develop restorative processes to meet their own needs. Less encumbered by the formal demands of institutional criminal justice where restorative justice is seen primarily as an "add-on" to the existing system (Elliott, 2003), restorative justice practices of community-based groups or organizations may well aspire to fully restorative ideals. Many examples exist of community organizations across Canada exploring restorative justice philosophy and practices. As the competencies and awareness of community practitioners develop, so does the potential for change in responding to social problems underpinning the symptoms of youth or adult crime. This raises the question of community capacity, and how to develop or harness resources needed to deal with both the individual and structural problems that contribute to the production of social harm. As the community is confronted with all of these issues—not just those that fall under the purview of criminal justice institutions—a holistic approach is possible simply because it is not circumscribed by specific institutional mandates.

The capacity of community-based restorative justice programs to aspire to fully restorative practices is not, however, without obstacles. Programs need referrals, and this requires the development and fostering of relationships with criminal justice institutions, schools, and the community at large. These relationships will encounter conflicts of their own, particularly regarding differences in philosophies about the role (if any) of punishment, in ascribing responsibility and defining accountability, and in the development of certain practices. If restorative justice is about healing, what are the fates of punishment and the concept of deterrence? How are accountability and responsibility to be recognized in informal, grassroots processes when referrals come from the police? How does a community agency develop processes that reflect and embody the values of restorative

justice *so that process is indeed product*? The answers to these questions belong to, and may differ among, the community groups that encounter them.

The use of community volunteers in facilitating restorative justice processes is an important measure in safeguarding against the usurping of community involvement by professional domination. In one of the first arguments for restorative justice, Christie (1977) notes that the lack of meaningful community engagement with criminal justice cases is due in large measure to the preponderance of "professional thieves" (pp. 3–5)—the lawyers, judges, treatment specialists, and so on who "steal conflicts" from the victim, offender, and community. The hidden casualty of the professionalization of criminal justice is the ability of individuals and communities to handle their own conflicts. The erosion of this ability to address most problems through civil rather than criminal processes has resulted in a society with what Judge Barry Stuart has described as a "911 mentality"[10]—the tendency of people to call in external, professionalized enforcement for most problems, including minor ones such as noise by-law violations or teenage loitering.

The participation of community volunteers in restorative justice practices thus has the potential to help rebuild the capacity to handle most conflicts in the fabric of the community itself, as each volunteer builds his or her own capacity to facilitate conflict resolution processes. More importantly, conflict processing is itself a highly communal act that, given the participation of community members, has the potential to help build or reconstruct community institutions necessary for crime prevention through social development (Crawford & Clear, 2003). Theoretically, as more and more people experience restorative processes to resolve conflict either as participants or facilitators, the inclination to resort to criminal justice professionals should diminish.

There are questions, however, regarding the suitable competencies of individual community volunteers. Conflicts are often traumatic for the immediate parties involved, and insensitivity and lack of awareness of the effects of trauma may result in the revictimization of participants by even well-meaning volunteers. Community-based restorative justice agencies that do not provide adequate training in trauma awareness and emotions sensitivity may offer programs run by volunteer facilitators who resort to a prescribed script, without the competencies to recognize or handle the effects of trauma on individuals throughout the process. Facilitators and other community members may still need to rely on professionals, particularly specialized counsellors, to handle the long-term individual healing remedies recommended by the participants in the restorative encounter itself.

Finally, there are important questions around the definition of "community," which is seen as an abstract explanatory concept much like "society." Common understandings of community as merely a geographical space (such as a neighbourhood) have led some to challenge the viability of restorative justice in large urban centres particularly, where this notion of community is seen as diluted by extensive population mobility. This has been countered with the explanation "community is not a place" but "a feeling, a perception of connectedness—personal connectedness both to other individual human beings and to a group" (McCold & Wachtel, 1998, p. 72). Our connectedness often comes through our interests—more generally family, work, hobbies, sports, and so on—that may include an incident in which particular people have a stake. If the essence of community is connectedness, then restorative justice can potentially build or repair relationships through processes that have this view of community as a foundation for practice.

The Role of Shame in Conferencing

One other area of concern and interest in restorative justice must be examined in considering its promises and potential pitfalls. This relates to popular conceptions of the role of shame, or "shaming," in restorative justice processes. A contentious issue among practitioners for many years, shaming has begun to lose its resonance as a highlighted feature of conferencing. However, given the appeal of shaming for facilitators who are more comfortable with a punitive model of justice, it remains a factor worth investigating.

One of the seminal works in restorative justice literature was Braithwaite's book on the role of shame in family group conferences (1989). His theory was originally conceived of as a contribution toward a general theory of crime:

> If the awareness that an act is criminal fundamentally changes the choices being made, then the key to a general explanation of crime lies in identifying variables that explain the capacity of some individuals and collectivities to resist, ignore, or

succumb to the institutionalized disapproval that goes with crime. ... This variable is shaming. Contrary to the claims of some labelling theorists, potent shaming directed at offenders is the essential necessary condition for low crime rates. (p. 4)

Braithwaite's work was used to explain the conferencing process, in which members of the community express how the harmful action affected each of them and offenders come to the recognition that they are part of a community they have offended. This is said to produce shame and to activate the offender's conscience, which is considered to be a more effective long-term crime-reduction strategy than are operant conditioning strategies such as punishment. Following the expression of shame is the reintegration of the offender into a welcoming community.

At least three concerns can be raised about the idea of shame in conferencing or other restorative processes. The first concern relates to the use of the word "shame" and its use as either a verb or a noun. To experience shame as one of nine major affects or emotions[11] is to use the term as a noun. If one outcome of a collective encounter regarding harm is that the perpetrator feels shame, the experience of shame is then self-produced. To consciously attempt to shame someone, however, is to employ the concept as a verb, as an action to be used against someone. Consequently, it puts the other participants in the conference in the position of engaging in harm themselves, in their roles as "shamers." Furthermore, having individuals relate the personal effects of harm as an exercise toward the shaming of an offender is to use the other participants as a means to an end, rather than to understand that the expression of each

person's own thoughts and emotions is important in itself.

The second concern relates to the idea of shaming as placing conference participants in the role of active agents in harmdoing. Shaming can also be seen as encouraging humiliation, which is itself a major cause of violence (Chatterjee & Elliott, 2003). Indeed, as one prison psychiatrist concludes, "The basic psychological motive of violent behaviour is the wish to eliminate the feeling of shame and humiliation" (Gilligan, 2001). The production of additional violence would hardly be a desired outcome of any process, much less a restorative one, and so shame (as a noun) must be handled with care and consideration by facilitators who have the ability to do so, rather than being encouraged and provoked by conference participants.

The last issue regarding the role of shame in conferencing concerns the misunderstanding of the group affect process itself. According to Nathanson (1997), affect is mutualized among community members so that positive affect is enhanced or maximized and negative affect is diminished or minimized. In this context, the positive potential of shaming is dubious, particularly if the idea is to maximize the negative affect of shame. As Nathanson explains:

> It has become increasingly clear that shame is reintegrative only when it takes place in an individual who had lived outside the interaffective life of the community until returned to it through a process like the Australian [family group conferencing] system..., and then experienced or recognized his or her chronic prior estrangement from empathic connection with the community as a blow that then produced

shame. The mutative force is empathy, not shame.

If the point of conferencing is to cultivate empathy rather than shame, the role of punishment is again questionable. The idea that conferencing is about shaming offenders has made restorative justice more palatable to those who hold strong beliefs about the significance of punishment in any justice process. The temptation to use shaming as part of a conferencing process, particularly with youth who are typically subjected to adult authority and admonition, is another manifestation of possible compromise of restorative practices within a retributive system.

CONCLUSION

The conflicts produced by attempts to integrate restorative justice within the retributive system will ideally result in opportunities to have deeper discussions about the purposes of criminal justice, rather than the mere dilution of another challenging idea. One salient issue of discussion on legislated conferencing or restorative justice generally is the incongruency of healing harm on the schedule of the court. In New South Wales, for example, youth justice conferences took twice as long on average to prepare for and facilitate than the statutory time periods allowed (Trimboli, 2000). Healing from trauma takes its own time and varies according to the individuals involved; a court can no more order a victim and offender to heal enough to safely participate in a restorative encounter by a certain date than it can order a cancer patient to heal on a schedule. This is a challenge for which there are no easy answers.

Restorative justice under the YCJA, despite its structural limitations and compromises, still offers greater potential for strengthening social development capacities and yielding greater crime prevention. The larger role for and participation of parents (Hillian & Reitsma-Street, 2003) in conferencing, for example, will help those youth who have families to support them. Research on restorative processes with youth demonstrates a positive impact on individuals generally (Schiff, 1999), although evaluation studies are themselves being challenged by practitioners grounded in restorative values. Perhaps more significantly, the enactment of the YCJA has sparked a vibrant dialogue between communities and the formal criminal justice system about the implications and potential of restorative justice, and perhaps even about justice itself.

References

Bazemore, G. (1999). Crime victims, restorative justice and the juvenile court: Exploring victim needs and involvement in the response to youth crime. *International Review of Victimology, 6,* 295–320.

Bazemore, G. (1998). Crime victims and restorative justice in juvenile courts: Judges as obstacle or leader? *Western Criminology Review, 1*(1). [Online].

Bentham, J. (1948, orig. 1789). *An introduction to the principles of morals and legislation.* New York: Hafner Press.

Bianchi, H. (1994). *Justice as sanctuary.* Bloomington, IN: University of Indiana Press.

Braithwaite, J. (1989). *Crime, shame and reintegration.* Cambridge, UK: Cambridge University Press.

Campbell, M. E. (2000). Politics and public servants: Observations on the current state of criminal law reform. *Canadian Journal of Criminology, 42*(3), 341–354.

Carrington, P. J. (1999). Trends in youth crime in Canada, 1977–1996. *Canadian Journal of Criminology, 41*(1), 1–32.

Cayley, D. (1998). *The expanding prison: The crisis in crime and punishment and the search for alternatives.* Toronto: House of Anansi Press.

Chatterjee, J., & Elliott, L. (2003). Restorative policing in Canada: The Royal Canadian Mounted Police, community justice forums, and the *Youth Criminal Justice Act. Journal of Police Practice and Research, 4*(4), 347–359.

Christie, N. (1977). Conflicts as property. *British Journal of Criminology, 17*(1), 1–15.

Cohen, S. (1985). *Visions of social control: Crime, punishment and classification.* New York: Basil Blackwell, Inc.

Cole, S. (2003, August 30). Saying no to zero tolerance. *The Globe and Mail.*

Cragg, W. (1992). *The practice of punishment: Towards a theory of restorative justice.* New York: Routledge.

Crawford, A., & Clear, T. (2003). Community justice: Transforming communities through restorative justice. In E. McLaughlin, R. Fergusson, G. Hughes, & L. Westmoreland, *Restorative justice: Critical issues.* Thousand Oaks, CA: Sage Publications.

Cullen, F. T., & Gilbert, K. E. (1982). *Re-affirming rehabilitation.* Cincinnati, OH: Anderson Publishing Company.

Doob, A. N., & Sprott, J. B. (1998). Is the "quality" of youth violence becoming more serious? *Canadian Journal of Criminology, 40*(2), 185–194.

Doob, A. N., & Sprott, J. B. (2004). Trends in youth crime in Canada. In K.M. Campbell (Ed.), *Understanding Youth Justice in Canada.* Toronto: Pearson Education.

Durkheim, E. (1933, orig. 1893). *The division of labor in society.* New York: The Free Press.

Elliott, L. (2002). *Con Game* and restorative justice: Inventing the truth about Canada's prisons. *Canadian Journal of Criminology, 44*(4), 459–474.

Elliott, L. (2003). From scales to circles: Restorative justice as peacemaking and social justice. In J. Roberts & M. Grossman (Eds.), *Criminal justice in Canada: A reader, second edition.* Scarborough, ON: Nelson Publishing.

Garland, D. (1990). *Punishment and modern society: A study in social theory.* Chicago: University of Chicago Press.

Gaucher, R., & Elliott, L. (2001). "Sister of Sam": The rise and fall of Bill C-205/220. *Windsor Yearbook of Access to Justice, 19,* 72–105.

Gilligan, J. (2001). *Preventing violence.* London, UK: Thames and Hudson.

Green, R. G. (1998). *Justice in Aboriginal communities: Sentencing alternatives.* Saskatoon, SK: Purich Publishing.

Hassall, I. (1996). Origin and development of family group conferences. In J. Hudson, A. Morris, G. Maxwell, & B. Galaway (Eds.), *Family group conferences: Perspectives on policy and practice,* pp. 17–36. Monsey, NY: The Criminal Justice Press.

Head, D. B. (2002, June). Sentencing circles: Ancient wisdom at work. *The Saskatchewan Advocate.*

Hill, R. F. A. (2002). Restorative justice and the absent victim: New data from the Thames Valley. *International Review of Victimology, 9,* 272–288.

Hillian, D., & Reitsma-Street, M. (2003). Parents and youth justice. *Canadian Journal of Criminology, 45*(1), 19–42.

Johnstone, G. (2002). *Restorative justice: Ideas, values, debates.* Portland, OR: Willan Publishing.

Kohn, A. (1999). *Punished by rewards: The trouble with gold stars, incentive plans, A's, praise, and other bribes.* Boston: Houghton Mifflin Company.

LaRocque, E. (1997). Re-examining culturally appropriate models in criminal justice applications. In. M. Asch (Ed.), *Aboriginal and treaty rights in Canada: Essays on law, equity and respect for differences* (pp. 75–96). Vancouver: UBC Press.

Longclaws, L., Galaway, B., & Barkwell, L. (1996). Piloting family group conferences for young Aboriginal offenders in Winnipeg, Canada. In J. Hudson, A. Morris, G. Maxwell, & B. Galaway (Eds.), *Family group conferences: Perspectives on policy and practice,* pp. 195–205. Monsey, NY: The Criminal Justice Press.

McCold, P., & Wachtel, B. (1998). Community is not a place: A new look at community justice initiatives. *Contemporary Justice Review, 1*(1), 71–86.

Miller, A. (1983). *For your own good: Hidden cruelty in child-rearing and the roots of violence.* Toronto: Collins Publishers.

Monture-Okanee, P. (1994). Thinking about Aboriginal justice: Myths and revolution. In R. Gosse, J. Youngblood Henderson, & R. Carter (Eds.), *Continuing Poundmaker & Riel's quest: Presentations made at a conference on Aboriginal peoples and justice,* pp. 222–232. Saskatoon, SK: Purich Publishing.

Nathanson, D. L. (1997). From empathy to community. In J. A. Winer (Ed.), *The Annual of Psychoanalysis, volume 25.* Chicago: The Chicago Institute for Psychoanalysis.

Nathanson, D. L. (1992). *Shame and pride: Affect, sex, and the birth of the self.* New York: Norton.

Peterson-Badali, M., & Koegl, C. J. (1998). Young people's knowledge of the *Young Offenders Act* and the youth justice system. *Canadian Journal of Criminology, 40*(2), 127–152.

Pfohl, S. (1994). *Images of deviance and social control: A sociological history.* 2nd ed. Toronto: McGraw-Hill, Inc.

Roberts, T. (1995). *Evaluation of the victim offender mediation project, Langley B.C.* Final Report for Solicitor General Canada.

Ross, Rupert. (1996) *Returning to the teachings: Exploring Aboriginal justice.* Toronto: Penguin Books.

Schiff, M. (1999). The impact of restorative interventions on juvenile offenders. In G. Bazemore & L. Walgrave (Eds.), *Restorative juvenile justice: Repairing the harm of youth crime,* pp. 327–356. Monsey, NY: Willow Tree Press.

Statistics Canada. (2003). *Cases in youth criminal court.* At http://www.statcan.ca. english/Pgdb/legal24a.htm.

Stewart, W., Huntley, A., & Blaney, F. (2001). *The implications of restorative justice for Aboriginal women and children survivors of violence: A comparative overview of five communities in British Columbia.* Ottawa: Law Commission of Canada [Online].

Stuart, B. (1996). Circle sentencing in Canada: A partnership of the community and the criminal justice system. *International Journal of Comparative and Applied Criminal Justice, 20*(2), 291–309.

Tomkins, Silvan S. (1962). *Affect imagery consciousness, Vol. I.* New York: Springer.

Tomkins, Silvan S. (1963). *Affect imagery consciousness, Vol. II.* New York: Springer.

Trimboli, L. (2000). *An evaluation of the NSW youth justice conferencing scheme.* Sydney: New South Wales Bureau of Crime Statistics and Research.

Tustin, L., & Lutes, R. E. (2002). *A guide to the Youth Criminal Justice Act.* Markham, ON: Butterworths.

Van Ness, D. W., & Strong, H. K. (2002). *Restoring justice* (2nd ed.). Cincinnati, OH: Anderson Publishing.

Warner, K., & Gawlik, J. (2003). Mandatory compensation orders for crime victims and the rhetoric of restorative justice. *The Australian and New Zealand Journal of Criminology, 36*(1). 60–76.

Weaver, J. C. (1995). *Crimes, constables, and courts: Order and transgression in a Canadian City, 1816–1970.* Montreal: McGill-Queen's University Press.

Weitekamp, E. (1999). The history of restorative justice. In G. Bazemore & L. Walgrave (Eds.), *Restorative juvenile justice: Repairing the harm of youth crime,* pp. 75–102. Monsey, NY: Willow Tree Press.

Wemmers, J.-A. (2002). Restorative justice for victims of crime: A victim-oriented approach to restorative justice. *International Review of Victimology, 9,* 43–59.

Zehr, H. (1990). *Changing lenses: A new focus for crime and justice.* Waterloo: Herald Press.

Case Cited

R. v. Taylor (1996), 122 C.C.C. (3d) 376 (Sask. C.A.).

Notes

1. Story relayed by Doug Borch, MSW, Coordinator, Children & Youth Services, Community & Neighbourhood Services, City of Calgary, Box 2100 Station M Mailcode 135, Calgary, Alberta T2P 2M5. www.calgarycommunityconferencing.com. Story found on www.sfu.ca/crj.

2. *Inquisitio* is Latin for "the search for evidence and guilt" (Bianchi, 1994, p. 16).

3. Some researchers question whether Aboriginal "traditions" were in fact part of the sentencing process in the Hollow Water case and decry the lenient sentence handed down (cf. LaRocque, 1997).

4. *General deterrence* refers to the notion that fear of sanctions will cause the public at large to avoid engaging in criminal behaviour, while *specific deterrence* is focused in the fear of sanctions in the punished offender. See Pfohl, 1994.

5. An example of the results of this punitive philosophy is found in the public revolt in Canada over the executions of minor property offenders in the 1800s, which began a social phenomenon that gradually resulted in the legal abolition of the death penalty in 1976.

6. An example of this came to be known in one restorative justice community as "the murder of Frosty," a case of a kicked-over snowman that was presented for diversion by a referring police officer. The group declined the referral.

7. Section 18 of the YCJA also permits for the convening of Youth Justice Committees, which are meant to encourage community involvement in youth justice. They differ from conferences as they have a broader mandate and may play a role in monitoring the implementation of the Act, advising governments on how to improve the system and provide public information about the workings of the youth justice system.

8. The impetus to use conferencing in New Zealand originated in state family welfare practices that were at odds with traditional Maori cultures. This expanded to youth criminal justice, resulting in changes to youth justice legislation in 1989. However, it is important to note that few of the Maori ways were retained as the practice was formalized into legislation, which is an indication of the hazards of wrenching culturally specific practices out of their holistic context and deploying them for other means.

9. YCJA, secs. 5, 12, 53(1), and 111.

10. Judge Stuart makes reference to this in the documentary "A Healing River—An Invitation to Explore Restorative Justice Values and Principles" (2004), Heartspeak Productions, Vancouver, B.C.

11. Affect theory has played a significant role in restorative justice practices, particularly in family group conferencing. Based on the work of Silvan Tompkins (1962, 1963), the affect of shame was further explored by Donald Nathanson (1992), whose work was influential in the development of a psychological explanation for the benefits of conferencing. Nathanson holds a different perspective on the role of shame in conferencing, however, than does Braithwaite.

chapter thirteen

Rehabilitation Revisited: The Changing Nature of "Intervention" in Juvenile Justice

Kathryn M. Campbell

Department of Criminology
University of Ottawa

A flourishing rehabilitative ideal requires both a belief in the malleability of human behavior, and a basic moral consensus about the appropriate directions of human change. (Allen, 1981)

INTRODUCTION

The concept of rehabilitation for both adult and young offenders has gone in and out of vogue over the course of the last century. The implications of rehabilitation for young offenders are particularly significant, as one rationale for having a separate system of justice for young persons is due in part to the belief that they are more likely to be amenable to interventions on their behalf. However, the provision of rehabilitative interventions for young persons has always been complicated, due in part to varying beliefs regarding the role and appropriateness of differing sanctions when dealing with young persons who violate the law. Rarely are the circumstances surrounding law breaking so straightforward that a sanction based on only one of the many philosophies, which include retribution, deterrence, incapacitation, and rehabilitation, is clear. Conflicting ideologies regarding the most apposite sanctions or dispositions have also been borne out through legislation for young persons over the past century. The orientation of a particular law, at a particular time, as well as the sanctions available through it, have reflected the difficulty of reconciling the many and variant philosophies toward dealing with young offenders.

With the inception of the first legislation in Canada aimed at juvenile delinquents at the beginning of the twentieth century, rehabilitation concerns were paramount and evident in the welfare orientation of the *Juvenile Delinquents Act.* Nevertheless, the indeterminate nature of sentencing under this law and the lack of due process resulted in much interprovincial variation and many youth spending years in custody for relatively minor offences. Replaced by the *Young Offenders Act* in 1984, the divergent philosophies inherent to approaches to youth criminality were laid bare, as the new statute embodied the conflicting notions of crime control, justice, and rehabilitation in its Declaration of Principle. The ambivalent nature and inconsistency of these approaches provided little overall guidance to judges in sentencing. The current youth justice legislation, the *Youth Criminal Justice Act,* is an attempt at a compromise. Reflecting this compromise, the rehabilitation of young persons as an objective of the law is given equal footing with crime prevention, by addressing the underlying causes of criminal behaviour and the long-term protection of the public through the provision of meaningful consequences for offences.

The term *rehabilitation* itself is complex and controversial and has been mired in contention. Ongoing debates have persisted for decades among criminologists regarding what constitutes rehabilitation, who should receive rehabilitative efforts, and whether or not rehabilitation has an effect on recidivism. The focus of this chapter will be to locate the practice of rehabilitation and reform within these discourses. In order to do so, the chapter will provide definitions for some of the controversial, and at times ambiguous, concepts used in discussions about rehabilitation. This will be followed by an overview of some facts relating to youth in custody, as well as some indications of the costs of custody and the numbers of youth subjected to intervention efforts. A historical and legal framework, presented next, is necessary to provide an understanding of how conceptions of the reform of young offenders have evolved, particularly as reflected through legislation. Specific critical issues related to intervention will then be examined, followed by some current program examples. The chapter concludes with some musings regarding ethical concerns around the provision of programs in the name of rehabilitation.

TERMS OF REFERENCE

Found within the literature around correctional treatment are a number of terms used, often interchangeably, when referring to both the policy and practice of rehabilitation. Therefore, in order to provide clarity, it is important to begin with some definitions. The term *rehabilitation* simply means to help a person to readapt to society, or to restore to a former position or rank (Collins English Dictionary, 1979). Generally, when referring to the term "treatment" under youth law this refers specifically to psychiatric, psychological, or medical treatment. In other words, such treatments are generally ministered by medical professionals and may involve the use of pharmacology. Finally, the word *intervention* is derived from the word *intervene* and means to take a decisive or intrusive role in order to modify or determine events or their outcome. This latter term has been found consistently in the research around rehabilitative efforts emerging from the province of Quebec.[1] For the purposes of this chapter, the terms "rehabilitation," "intervention," and "rehabilitative interventions" will be used to refer to those efforts on the behalf of governmental or non-governmental organizations to address youthful offending. Rehabilitative interventions may take many forms, such as crime prevention programs as well as institutional programs addressing specific behaviours (such as anger management or life skills) and programs offered through probation and parole services in the community. Such interventions may also include traditionally focused therapies (individual and group), educational efforts to address particular skill areas, and less structured, informal efforts aimed at providing guidance, assistance, and supervision.

FACTS ABOUT YOUTH CUSTODY

As a response to youth crime, rehabilitative interventions may take a variety of forms, can be provided by a number of individuals with varying qualifications, and are offered in several different arenas. Consequently, these services tend to vary with respect to costs. In terms of the tariff of sanctions for law-breaking behaviour, the most severe of these, secure custody, is also the most costly. The price of locking up a young person in a secure custody facility is approximately $126 000 per youth,

per year. Open custody facilities are somewhat less expensive at $93 000 per youth, per year.[2] Community-based programs cost considerably less. Multi-systemic therapy, which allows a young person to live at home with intensive family intervention and support, costs approximately $6000 to $7000 per youth (Leschied and Cunningham, 2001). This is somewhat more costly than other, less intensive community-based interventions. Finally, supervision on probation is the least costly, at approximately $600 to $700 per year (Bell, 2003, pp. 281–282).

As a sentencing option, custody is used less frequently than it has been in the past. Furthermore, given the many restrictions in the YCJA regarding the imposition of a custodial sentence, it is likely that this decline will continue. The most recently available statistics indicate that of the 84 592 cases processed by youth courts in Canada in 2002–2003, 13 810 resulted in a custodial sentence (Robinson, 2004). Of that number, 7276 (14%) received secure custody, whereas 6534 (13%) received open custody sentences. This is down from 34 percent receiving custodial sentences in 1999–2000 (Sudworth & deSouza, 2001) and 34 percent again in 2000–2001 (Statistics Canada, 2001). Furthermore, the majority of custodial sentences for this latest time period are relatively short: 55 percent were for terms of less than one month. What is interesting to note is that, in spite of the fact that the relative distribution of convicted youth cases by sentence type appeared stable between 1992–1993 and 2002–2003, the proportion of convicted cases sentenced to secure custody during that time increased slightly (from 12 to 14%). However, the average sentence length appears to be getting shorter (Robinson,

2004; Thomas, 2003). The average secure custody sentence in 1992–1993 was 94 days, while it dropped to 68 days in 2002–2003. This drop also been noted in the average length of stays in open custody as well; from 87 days in 1992–1993 to 66 days in 2002–2003. Moreover, the average probation sentence during this period appears to be increasing. In 1992–1993, the average term was 325 days, and in the 2001–2002 period it increased to 368 days (Thomas, 2003, p. 3). Thus, in the early part of this century, judges were handing down more secure custody sentences but fewer overall custodial sentences, although these sentences were of shorter duration than in the past.

Furthermore, the statistics indicate that secure custody sentences appear to be reserved mainly for the more violent offences. For example, in 2002–2003, 74 percent of homicide cases received a secure custody sentence, as did 64 percent of attempted murder cases, while only 25 percent of robbery cases resulted in a secure custody sentence (Robinson, 2004, p. 7). The use of custody as a sanction varies considerably across the country. In particular, secure custody ranged from 2 percent of cases in the province of Nova Scotia to 26 percent of cases in Newfoundland and Labrador. However, open custody rates also varied, with the highest in Nova Scotia at 31 percent to the lowest in Alberta at 6 percent (Robinson, 2004, p. 7).

HISTORICAL FRAMEWORK

Efforts to rehabilitate youth who commit crimes can be traced back to the reform movement of nineteenth-century North America. As discussed in Chapter 2, youth, at that time mainly working classes and recent immigrants, were subjected to the ministrations of various reformers, notably the child savers. Prior to the mid nineteenth century, the first efforts at dealing with young persons by the developing societies in the colonies involved treating them similarly to adults. Young persons were subjected to more or less the same deprivations and physical punishments as adults and were often housed in the same institutions. It was only in the latter half of the nineteenth century that efforts were directed at separating youth from adults for the purposes of punishment. These efforts—spearheaded by child savers, who believed that the morality of the poor and working classes had greatly influenced criminal behaviour—were motivated by a desire to protect children from what were believed to be the physical and moral dangers of an increasingly industrialized urban society (Mann, 2000). Children and young persons had become more visible as the influx of immigrants to urban centres followed by poverty and unemployment resulted in many youth living on the street and begging or stealing to survive. In this instance, child savers blamed parents for being immoral and unable or unwilling to control their children (Bell, 2003, p. 15).

It is within this context that the rehabilitative ideal emerged. Moving away from strictly punishing young offenders, the reform movement focused on the "individual, a widespread belief in the goodness of humanitarian sentiment, and above all, a belief in the ability of the state and professionals to reform individuals" (Bell, 2003, p. 16). Consequently, the placement of children and youth in adult facilities became problematic. Within the disciplines of penitentiary life, while allegedly motivated by notions of reform and rehabilitation, punishment was used most often to reinforce silence, labour, and obedience (Mann, 2000, p. 6). Resulting in part from the Brown Commission of 1848, which examined the conditions in the penitentiary at that time, institutions were developed for juveniles in Upper and Lower Canada (now Ontario and Quebec). The opening of these institutions signalled a movement away from treating all manner of "criminals" in the same way and toward a recognition that the needs of young persons could best be met under more humane conditions.

Reformatories, the first of which appeared in 1858, stressed education, vocational training, and religious instruction and were an attempt to provide the material conditions and guidance that were presumed to be lacking in the youth's home environment (Griffiths & Verdun-Jones, 1989; Schissel, 1993). While reformatories were initially reserved for youth convicted of crimes, "incorrigible" youth were later housed in reformatories and all children were treated, more or less, in the same fashion. While attempting rehabilitation, reformatories were also focused on crime prevention for children who by virtue of the fact that they had been neglected and impoverished were considered "potentially" criminal. Children were often given lengthy sentences in these specialized institutions, justified by the belief that only then could reformation be effected for the benefit of the child and society (Leon, 1977). However, there was little agreement as to the appropriateness of placing young offenders in such institu-

tions. For some, they were viewed as little more than prisons, where youth would be exposed to other delinquent youth and further criminalized; others argued that a long sentence in a reformatory was necessary to demonstrate public condemnation of criminal behaviour (Griffiths & Verdun-Jones, 1989, p. 502). Furthermore, while presenting a façade of altruism and philanthropy, reformatories (and later industrial schools) were mechanisms of social control, as the majority of their youth populations were comprised of the impoverished, the working classes, and recent immigrants.

As an alternative to reformatories, industrial schools were residential facilities where children could be committed for as long as proper for their "teaching and training." The first industrial school was established in 1887 and accepted children who were homeless, poor, begging, guilty of petty crime, or unable to be controlled by their parents (Leon, 1977, p. 79). With an emphasis on academic and vocational education, religious instruction, and work, they were meant to approximate as much as possible a family atmosphere. The family was now viewed as both the cause and potential cure of delinquency (Griffiths & Verdun-Jones, 1989, p. 594). While not without their own difficulties, industrial schools were favoured over reformatories, due in part to their attempts at establishing a more "family-like" environment through the cottage system, with incentives to earn remission or early release and a greater participation of women. While parents could request children be sent to industrial schools for an indeterminate period of time, they soon came to replace reformatories as the primary mechanism for controlling youth. These institutions, along with the developing system of probation, were the primary means of the reform of young persons in the late nineteenth and early twentieth centuries. Shortly thereafter was the creation of Canada's first juvenile court through the *Juvenile Delinquents Act* (JDA) in 1908.

LEGAL FRAMEWORK FOR INTERVENTION: YOUTH JUSTICE LEGISLATION OVER THE LAST CENTURY

Legislation for youth in conflict with the law in Canada has evolved considerably over the last hundred years. Beginning with the *Juvenile Delinquents Act,* and through the *Young Offenders Act* to the *Youth Criminal Justice Act,* each successive law has responded to social and political demands for change. Each law has also taken a different position on the place for rehabilitation. The following discussion outlines the philosophy of these laws with respect to rehabilitative interventions, as well as examining specific provisions aimed at guiding and assisting youth in conflict with the law.

Juvenile Delinquents Act: The "Best Interests of the Child"

The *Juvenile Delinquents Act,* Canada's first youth justice legislation, had a child-welfare, paternalistic orientation, focusing mainly on the rehabilitation of children and young persons. The JDA established juvenile courts, and under this law a juvenile delinquent was viewed as a mis-

guided and misdirected child in need of guidance and assistance. The definition of juvenile delinquent embraced both children involved with crime and those who were neglected and abused; rather, the "depraved and the deprived" (Havemann, 2000, p. 23). The welfare orientation of the JDA is consistent with the English common law principle of *parens patraie,* which gives the king the power to act as parent of the country or intervene in the family on behalf of the child's best interest (see Appendix A, section 38).

The primary emphasis under the JDA, through the system of probation and special court procedures and personnel, was on treatment, with minimal attention to accountability (Leon, 1977). Given that judges were guided by what they perceived to be the "best interests" of the child, children and youth sentenced under the JDA could likely receive lengthy terms of incarceration for seemingly quite minor offences. Furthermore, children and youth could be detained in these facilities until the age of majority: at that time, 21years. Such an approach, we have seen in Chapter 2, neglected the due-process rights of young persons and resulted in much interprovincial variation in sentencing.

The sole response to youthful offending under the JDA was one of concern for the young person's welfare and rehabilitation. This orientation, while an improvement over earlier harsher practices, was not without its complications. Primarily, the "best interests" doctrine allowed for a number of abuses, both physical and sexual, to occur in the name of rehabilitation in many youth facilities, which came to light only in later years (Bala, 2003). Furthermore, concerns surrounding the efficacy of interventions in youth facilities began to emerge in the 1970s, as high recidivism rates indicated that efforts to reform young persons were not particularly effective. Finally, a growing reform movement to recognize the rights of marginalized groups (women, gay and lesbian persons, youth, etc.) also influenced how young persons were treated under criminal law. With the introduction of the *Canadian Charter of Rights and Freedoms* in 1982, young persons' due-process rights were formally recognized and criminal legislation for youth had to necessarily follow. Additionally, collective discontent with this law culminated in its replacement by the *Young Offenders Act* in 1984.

Young Offenders Act: Declaration of Principle

The enactment of the *Young Offenders Act* in 1984 changed the nature of youth justice in Canada. In an attempt to address the limitations and shortcomings of its predecessor (the JDA), the YOA embraced the many conflicting philosophies regarding youthful offending in its Declaration of Principle (see Appendix B). As a social philosophy of law and in an effort to provide guidance to judges in sentencing, the Declaration of Principle contained provisions regarding the importance of crime prevention, societal protection, special needs and circumstances of youth, rehabilitation, limited accountability, and youth rights under the law. While moving away from the singular welfare orientation of the JDA, the YOA attempted to "balance" the many and varying approaches to youth justice. As we have seen, the YOA was not

particularly effective in this respect. Dissatisfaction with the YOA resulted in it being amended on three separate occasions, and it was ultimately replaced by the *Youth Criminal Justice Act* in less than 20 years, a legacy substantially less than the 76 years of the JDA.

Young Offenders Act: Sentencing

While the YOA had a strong rehabilitative focus, it also placed emphasis on accountability and protection of society. Shortly following its implementation, large numbers of young persons were sentenced to custody (Markwart & Corrado, 1989), which indicated more of a crime control/justice approach to sentencing, as did the introduction of determinate sentencing. However, given the myriad sentencing principles contained in the Declaration of Principle with no clear direction, judges were free to follow their own particular beliefs regarding the purpose of sentencing for young persons. Nonetheless, in 1991, Justice Latimer wrote for the Supreme Court of Canada in *Reference re. Young Offenders Act s. 2 (P.E.I.)*:

> It is clear ... that the *Young Offenders Act* does not generally recognize any proportionality between the gravity of the offence and the range of sanctions. It rather recognizes the special situation and the special needs of the young offender and gives to the judge special options that are not available for adults. It is still primarily oriented towards rehabilitation rather than punishment or neutralization. (as cited in Bala, 2003, p.100)

In a 1993 decision, *R. v. M.(J.J.)*, the Supreme Court of Canada further reinforced the importance of rehabilitation and reform in sentencing young persons (Anand, 2003, p. 947). *M.(J.J.)* was an

Aboriginal young person, convicted of three counts of break and enter and one breach of probation, who came from an abusive home environment. The Supreme Court affirmed his sentence of two years' open custody; while disproportionate to the gravity of his offence, this long sentence was considered acceptable given that the youth's home environment was recognized as a factor that needed to be considered when sentencing him. In this case, a more intrusive sanction, based on rehabilitation rather than proportionality, was allowed by the higher courts. Following from this decision, ostensibly courts could then justify longer custodial sentences based on concerns for the welfare needs of young persons. However, Parliament later responded to this by amending the YOA in 1995, when a section was introduced stating that custody "shall not be used as a substitute for appropriate child protection, health, and other social measures" (sec. 24(1.1)). Nevertheless, the wording of this section was sufficiently vague that a youth court justice could continue to give rehabilitative concerns great weight in sentencing decisions.

This orientation toward rehabilitation was not manifest in a straightforward manner in sentencing, given that there were other provisions at odds with this approach. The Declaration of Principle in the YOA emphasizes limited accountability, societal protection, and crime prevention, which are difficult to reconcile within a rehabilitative framework. Sentencing provisions as they existed under the YOA were also premised on the need to impose a determinate, fixed-length sentence based on the seriousness of the offence and the offender's past history of offending, and not necessarily on the rehabilitative needs of the young person. Leschied et al. (1992, p. 352) point to another premise under the original YOA that was incompatible with the provision of rehabilitation for young offenders: consent to treatment provisions.

Young Offenders Act: Consent to Treatment Order

From its inception until the final set of amendments in 1995, the YOA contained a treatment provision that could be ordered by a judge following a psychiatric/medical assessment. Section 20(1)(i) stated:

> subject to section 22, by order direct that the young person be detained for treatment, subject to such conditions as the court considers appropriate, in a hospital or other place where treatment is available, where a report has been made in respect of the young person pursuant to subsection 13(1) that recommends that the young person undergo treatment for a condition referred to in paragraph 13(1)(e).

Further to this, the law contained a provision (sec. 22(1)) regarding the necessity of obtaining the youth's consent to the treatment order, the consent of the treatment facility, as well as the consent of the youth's parents (although this was not deemed essential). At that time, the law recognized that "a young person may be suffering from a physical or mental illness or disorder, an emotional disturbance, a learning disability or mental retardation" (YOA, sec. 13(1)(e)) that would necessitate this form of intervention. The inclusion of the consent clause posed particular difficulties, as the treatment needs of young persons could be unmet if consent were withheld. In essence, this section embodied the conflicting philosophies of both welfare and justice inherent in this law; that is, a recognition of a disorder and a provision of treatment for that disorder, while allowing the young person to exercise his/her full rights by giving or withholding consent to treatment.

This provision was considered contentious (Leschied & Jaffe, 1991) and for a variety of reasons was later repealed in the 1995 amendments to the YOA. Practically, the treatment provision was rarely requested or ordered, perhaps in recognition that young persons in need of psychiatric or psychological treatment may not be in the best position to recognize the need for that treatment or provide their consent to it. The inclusion of the consent provision itself and the requirement of the young person's involvement reflects an assumption that youth possess the requisite capacity to consent, as well as an absence of a pathology that would hinder a consent decision. Moreover, under Canadian case law, in order to provide a legally valid consent, a full disclosure of the facts must have been provided to the youth, and the youth must give consent toward a specific act or set of acts (Landau, 1986). Additionally, consent would have to be given freely, without coercion, duress, or threats. In this instance, the youth must consent to a treatment that has a measurable duration, as well as a predictable outcome (Campbell, 1987). These criteria are far-reaching and there is some question as to whether in consent cases achieving all of these elements was ever possible. Following the repeal of this section of the law in 1995, judges were still able to order assessments for psychological or psychiatric treatment through provincial mental health legislation, absent consent considerations.

Young Offenders Act: Custody Under the YOA, youth court judges were responsible for deciding the level of custody that a youth would receive. Two levels of custody existed under the YOA—open custody and secure, or closed, custody—and provincial and territorial governments designated which facilities were considered open or secure. Open custody facilities could range from group homes and residential units to wilderness camps, whereas closed custody facilities often resembled smaller versions of adult jails and could be physically connected to adult facilities. Once a youth was sentenced to either open or secure custody, it was the provincial director of the province or territory who decided in which particular facility a youth would serve his/her sentence. Such a decision was based on the needs of the young person, the length of his/her sentence, and the availability of specific services. However, there was a judicial expectation under the YOA that open custody facilities would have a rehabilitative focus, and this was taken into account when sentencing (Bala, 2003, p. 462). Thus, sentencing a youth to open custody would result in that young person being subjected to educational and rehabilitative-type programming. On the other hand, a sentence to secure custody—where security concerns take precedence, as is common in adult facilities—was more often viewed as a punishment.

Immediately following enactment of the YOA, youth justice statistics evinced a noted increase in the numbers of youth in custody (Markwart & Corrado, 1989;

Leschied & Jaffe, 1991). Clearly, a custodial sentence is the highest tariff and the most severe punishment available to youth within the youth justice system. Youth custody facilities are generally quite harsh, sterile environments serving large numbers of young persons institutionalized for a variety of crimes. Some youth serving custodial sentences may be subjected to assault, abuse, and bullying, although it is rare (Green & Healy, 2003). Furthermore, in custodial facilities youth are surrounded by other delinquent youth, and are thus exposed to peers and role models who have engaged in much illegal activity, increasing opportunities for further delinquency. Finally, it is unlikely that any gains occurring in these often highly structured, highly supervised facilities are easily transferred to less structured, home environments.

Youth Criminal Justice Act: Preamble and Declaration of Principle

The current youth criminal justice law, the *Youth Criminal Justice Act* (YCJA) emphasizes, *inter alia,* the role for rehabilitation in sentencing of young offenders. In fact, the first references to rehabilitation and reintegration are found in the Preamble to the Act. The Preamble is intended to assist in determining the purpose and objectives of the YCJA, as well as in assisting in its interpretation (Bala, 2003, pp. 76–77). However, this emphasis on rehabilitation is considerably less than it was with the YOA, and the Act's considerations of the place for rehabilitation are tempered by the overriding concern for proportionality in sentencing. The YCJA

refers to rehabilitation in several places in its Declaration of Principle (see Appendix C). Specifically, one of the main intentions of the law, along with crime prevention and providing meaningful consequences to young offenders, is the need to rehabilitate young persons who commit offences and reintegrate them into society (sec. 3(1)(a)). In another section of the Declaration of Principle, where the need is emphasized for a system for young offenders that is separate from adults, rehabilitation[3] and reintegration are given significant consideration (sec 3(1)(b)(i)). Finally, the Declaration of Principle, in discussing sentencing or other measures that should be taken against youth who commit offences, emphasizes the need for meaningful consequences, within the context of a proportional sentence. It goes on to state that such measures must take into consideration the needs and level of development of the young person and should involve parents, family, community, and social or other agencies in the person's rehabilitation and reintegration (sec. 3(1)(c)(iii)).

Youth Criminal Justice Act: Sentencing The YCJA introduces both the purpose and principles of sentencing of young persons (sec. 38), and provides a clearer, more focused sentencing philosophy than the YOA (Bala, 2003, p. 403). The purpose of sentencing as stipulated in the YCJA (sec. 38(1)) is meant to

> … hold a young person accountable for an offence through the imposition of just sanctions that have meaningful consequences for the young person and that promote his or her rehabilitation and reintegration into society, thereby contributing to the long-term protection of the public.

This purpose has a variety of emphases, and it will be difficult for youth justice courts to accomplish all of these goals in sentencing young persons (Roberts & Bala, 2003, p. 403). Furthermore, the sentencing principles dictate that a youth sentence must not be harsher than an adult would receive in similar circumstances (sec. 38(2)(a)); there must be parity with other similar sentences in the region (sec. 38(2)(b)); and it must also be proportionate to the seriousness of the offence and the degree of responsibility of the young person (sec. 38(2)(c)). However, a youth court sentence is also meant to be the one most likely to rehabilitate the young person and reintegrate him or her back into society (sec. 38(2)(e)(ii)). Clearly, rehabilitation is expected to have greater weight in youth justice court sentencing than is expected in adult court (Roberts & Bala, 2003, p. 408). As discussed in Chapter 11, while proportionality is evidently the overriding concern with respect to sentence principles for young persons, it receives less emphasis in the YCJA than in the *Criminal Code,* thus leaving scope for rehabilitative concerns.

Under the YCJA, in light of the lessons learned from *R. v. M. (J.J),* as well as the emphasis on proportionality as central to sentencing, a youth cannot receive a custodial sentence that is disproportionately long due to his/her rehabilitative needs (Anand, 2003, p. 949). By rejecting the approach of the Supreme Court in this case, the YCJA goes further in emphasizing that youth custody should not be justified solely on social and child welfare concerns (Bala, 2003, p. 452). A sentence of this nature is in fact prohibited (YCJA, sec. 39(5)); however, a judge may refer a young person to a child welfare agency for assessment or invoke provincial mental health legislation to commit a youth to a mental health facility (sec. 35). Given the emphasis on proportionality in the YCJA, Roberts and Bala (2003) predict that "more tension between rehabilitation and proportionality will arise at the youth justice court level" (p. 408). Furthermore, they comment that rehabilitation is "subject to" proportionality considerations; thus youth court judges will make greater efforts in crafting sentences that have a rehabilitative effect while still respecting the constraints of proportionality (Roberts & Bala, 2003, p. 409). However, as Anand (2003) notes, it is also possible that youth can still receive a "rehabilitative discount" in terms of the length of a proportional sentence (Bala, 2003).

The place for rehabilitative concerns in sentencing has evolved considerably since the JDA. While rehabilitation was emphasized under the YOA, the lack of direction regarding the weight to be given to the various principles of sentencing resulted in much variation in youth court sentences. Under the YCJA, the sentencing principles provide clearer guidance to judges regarding the intentions of Parliament with respect to the sentencing of young offenders. The extent to which judges will respect these intentions remains to be seen. Anand (2003) indicates that "there is the real prospect that some judges will simply choose to ignore the requirements of the new legislative regime" (p. 957).

Youth Criminal Justice Act: Custody
The YCJA contains provisions regarding custody, and, similar to the YOA, much discretion is left up to the provinces

and the provincial directors in deciding which facility a youth will be placed in. While given the option of allowing the provincial director the opportunity to designate level of custody, all provinces have opted to leave this jurisdiction with the youth court judge. Sec. 85(1) specifies that in each province there must be "at least two levels of custody for young persons distinguished by the degree of restraint of the young persons in them." This is a movement away from the open and secure designation under the old law, and some have interpreted it as a movement toward the adult custody designation of minimum, medium, and maximum (Bala, 2003, p. 462). It is likely that most provinces will retain the open/secure designation given that existing facilities are set to accommodate youth in this manner. Furthermore, section 85(5) of the YCJA allows that custody designations must be the least restrictive, taking into account the seriousness and circumstances of the offence, the needs and circumstances of the young person, the safety of the young person in custody, the interests of society, matching programs to youth needs, and the likelihood of escape. The YCJA introduces some new custodial options for judges while retaining many of the old provisions as existed under the YOA.

1. ***Custody and supervision order (sec. 42(2)(n)):*** This provision is similar to custody under the YOA, but creates a mandatory period of supervision following custody as a means to address the lack of after-care available in the past for young persons released from custody. Custody orders now specify that the first two-thirds of a sentence be served in custody, with the last third being served in the community under supervision. Under the YOA, an 18-month custody sentence translated, in most cases, to 18 full

months in custody. However, under the YCJA, an 18-month custody sentence would translate into 12 months of custody, followed by six months on probation. The maximum length of custody is two years, or three years if the offence is one where life imprisonment could be imposed under the *Criminal Code* (Tustin & Lutes, 2002, p.69). A young person can be compelled to remain in custody for the length of the entire sentence if the court is convinced it is necessary for his or her protection and the protection of society.

2. ***Intensive rehabilitative custody and supervision order (sec. 42(2)(r)):*** This is a new sentencing option and is reserved for those youth aged 12 to 17 who have committed a presumptive offence and are suffering from a mental illness or disorder, a psychological disorder, or an emotional disturbance. In reality, this sentence is intended to be a treatment sentence (Tustin & Lutes, 2002, p. 70). The presumptive offences include first or second degree murder, attempted murder, manslaughter, aggravated sexual assault, or a third serious violent offence for which an adult is liable for a term of imprisonment for up to two years. The idea behind this sentence is to allow a young person who has committed a serious offence and is clearly suffering from some type of disorder to have access to treatment and intervention, most likely in a mental health facility. Also, the two-thirds custody, one-third community supervision split, applicable to most other sentences, does not apply in these cases to allow treatment facility officials to determine release decisions based on therapeutic progress.

    A further aspect of this sentence requires that an integrated plan of treatment and intensive community supervision be developed, and that the provincial director must determine that such a program is available and that a young person is willing to participate. While youth are not required to consent to the intensive rehabilitative custody order when placed in a facility under this order, they retain the right to give or withhold consent for drug or other medical treatment.[4] This sentence is similar to sec. 20(1)(i) under the YOA, discussed earlier. In cases where this sentence is ordered and it becomes clear that a youth is unmotivated to participate in treatment, the provincial director may apply to the court to have the youth's sentence converted to an ordinary sentence of custody and supervision (sec. 94(19)). This sentence is followed by community supervision, under strict legal control. The maximum length of this sentence is the same as for ordinary custody and supervision.

3. *Deferred custody and supervision order (sec. 42(2)(p)):* This new sentencing option entails a judge making an order for custody, respecting all the conditions and limitations of such an order, then deferring the custody portion and setting conditions under which the youth is to be supervised in the community. The conditions set by a youth court justice can include such things as keeping the peace, following a rehabilitative intervention, curfew, and so on. However, if the youth breaches any of the conditions, he or she may have to serve the remainder of his or her sentence in custody. This sentence is considered equivalent to a conditional sentence for an adult, is available to youth who have not committed a violent offence, and can cover a period of no longer than six months.

4. *Intermittent custody and supervision (sec. 47(2)):* When ordered, this sentence should not exceed 90 days; in essence, a judge orders that the custodial portion may be served intermittently (Tustin & Lutes, 2002, p. 74). While this sentencing option was available under the YOA, such sentences were rarely used. This type of sentence is intended to allow young persons to continue attending school or working and can be served on weekends.

5. *Youth serving adult sentences (secs. 61–82):* Under the YCJA, youth are still eligible to receive adult sentences, although the manner in which they are imposed now differs. Under the YOA, a youth who was guilty of committing a serious offence (e.g., murder, attempted murder, manslaughter, and aggravated sexual assault) and was aged 16–17 years would presumptively be sentenced as an adult, in adult court. In addition, youth would be subject to a transfer hearing prior to being found guilty of the offence. Under the YCJA, the Crown attorney must advise the court that he or she will be seeking an adult sentence, which can then be imposed in youth court under specific circumstances. The provisions now extend to youth aged 14 and up, and a fifth presumptive offence has been added (representing a third serious violent offence). As discussed in Chapters 3 and 11, the presumptive nature of the imposition of these adult sanctions has been successfully challenged by the Quebec Court of Appeal and will no longer apply. Thus, youth are still eligible to receive such sentences, although not presumptively. If a young person is convicted and awarded an adult sentence, he or she may serve a portion of it in a youth facility and later be moved to an adult provincial or federal facility.

COMMUNITY-BASED SENTENCES

Community-based interventions allow for young persons to remain at home while being supported by probation or parole officers or social workers. The YCJA recognizes the importance of community interventions with the implementation of two new sentencing options. Both of these sentences allow for the young person to be involved in programs that may contain therapeutic elements aimed at reducing the likelihood of reoffending (Bala, 2003, p. 435).

1. *Intensive support and supervision order (ISSP; sec. 42(2)(l)):* Considered a community-based alternative to custody (Tustin & Lutes, 2002, p. 69), this sentence allows for a higher level of more intense supervision to take place than does a probation order. Such an order may be in place for up to two years

and likely involves more frequent contact with probation services and more home visits. The provinces and territories retain the option of whether to offer this sentence, and it must be approved by the provincial director. Provincial community and social service ministries may offer this program, or it may be offered through community agencies on contract. It may also require attending a particular education or treatment program.

2. **Attendance centre order (sec. 42(2)(m)):** This is a new sentence and requires that a young person attend a non-residential community program that offers education or counselling, at the times and terms fixed by the court (Tustin & Lutes, 2002, p. 69). It is likely that programs will vary in availability and requirements, and a program cannot take up more than 240 hours over a six-month period.

CRITIQUES REGARDING INTERVENTION

While the intentions of Parliament, and ultimately statute, were and continue to be aimed in part at the provision of rehabilitation interventions for young persons who commit crimes, the reality as to what is actually provided for young persons may not be meeting these aims. Consequently, there are a variety of issues with respect to rehabilitation and intervention that demand critical examination. The first and most significant issue is concerned with the ongoing debates centred around program efficacy. A second area of interest relates to issues of race and class with respect to the implementation of intervention programs. The final area to be discussed has to do with ethical questions regarding the notion of treatment or rehabilitation as punishment.

Efficacy Debates

There are several basic concerns around offering programs for young persons who commit crimes that are of consequence. The first issue addresses the extent to which programs and services are actually offered to young persons, as dictated by federal statute and implemented by the provinces. Clearly, each province and territory has an obligation to offer rehabilitative services to young persons who commit crimes. However, some youth living in isolated communities must travel great distances not only to attend court but also to serve their sentences. This issue is particularly problematic for Aboriginal youth, as many live on reserves in remote parts of the country and are taken away from their home communities, families, and cultures to serve custody, which can have detrimental effects. Furthermore, the existence of many of the community-based provisions in the YCJA are dependent on not only the will of the provincial ministry but also the availability of funds. As Anand (2003) notes, "it seems likely that the only way that new non-custodial sentencing options will become available is if the provincial governments agree to pay for most of the costs associated with them" (p. 963).

The other, larger issue surrounding intervention relates to the intention of programs and rehabilitative interventions themselves—to what extent are they having an effect? In addressing this question it is also important to examine the issue of youth motivation to participate in rehabilitative programs. One argument for the provision of programs and interventions for young persons held in custodial facilities is that "something" is better than nothing. The provision of programs of intervention is also based on the notion that young persons will benefit from participation, along with the idea that the youth will be receptive and interested in participating in their own rehabilitation. This belief is somewhat suspect, given that many youth who enter the criminal justice system may be angry, uncooperative, and manipulative. Custodial sentences are generally fairly brief, and interventions are offered in environments that are often hostile and frightening for many young persons. This is not surprising given that youth are taken from familiar environments and initially locked up in sterile, jail-like facilities. It is questionable how much rehabilitation can be expected when a troubled youth is placed in custody alongside other troubled and offending youth (Green & Healy, 2003, p. 142). Given all of these circumstances, it is difficult for many youth to see any benefit in voluntarily participating in programs allegedly intended for their betterment.

A further area of concern regarding the provision of programs of intervention has to do with the lengthy debate in correctional circles regarding the efficacy of intervention programs for both youth and adults. This idea is based on the premise that intervention will have an effect on rates of recidivism, or reoffending. Since the time of reformatories and industrial schools of the late nineteenth and early twentieth centuries, concerted efforts have been aimed at providing programs of intervention aimed at curbing youth criminal activity. However, during the 1960s and 1970s this approach began to be questioned. This was due in part to an increased emphasis on the rights of marginalized persons, including youth, and in part to an emerging social science, particularly labelling theory and Marxist approaches that objected to rehabilitative interventions on principle. At that time, Martinson published his notable article on correctional treatment for youth and adults, where he concluded that basically "nothing works" (1974). While he later retracted his findings in 1979, Martinson's conclusions were embraced by both the conservative right, who believed rehabilitation was "soft" on criminals, and the liberal left, who supported the rights of prisoners to be free from interference. Rehabilitative interventions fell into disfavour at that time and have never quite recovered.

While many point to high rates of recidivism as evidence for the lack of efficacy surrounding rehabilitative interventions, a variety of research efforts over the years have attempted to ascertain what specific factors can and do have an effect on recidivism.[5] A number of factors have been suggested as to why many programs of intervention with youth in correctional facilities have little discernible effect (Feld, 1999, p. 281). Many programs are implemented without enough attention paid to methodology and may not be adhering to their stated conceptual or theoretical framework or even possess a sufficiently rigorous theoretical rationale that supports intervention. Moreover, outcome measures used to assess whether interventions are having an effect may not be sensitive or nuanced enough to measure the effect of the program of intervention. The individuals responsible for implementing the program may not subscribe to the rationale for the selected intervention and thus may not implement it properly—or may even sabotage the program, either overtly or covertly. Finally, the methods used to classify individuals for a particular program of intervention may have failed to do so properly, and a program intended for a specific type of problem or individual may not be reaching its intended target and thus have little or no effect.

In recent years, several meta-analyses have occurred that tend to demonstrate some efforts are having an effect. Meta-analyses involve analyzing the results of a series of similarly based studies through coding each study on a number of variables and combining and re-analyzing the data. They attempt to separate treatment effects from differences due to uncontrolled characteristics of the subjects or other limitations of research design (Logan & Gaes, 1993 in Feld, p. 281). Several meta-analyses since the 1970s have demonstrated positive results for some programs for juvenile offenders (Lipsey, 1992; 1999; Lipsey & Wilson, 1997). In an analysis of nearly 400 experimentally designed studies, Lipsey found that juveniles in treatment groups had recidivism rates that were approximately 10 percent lower than their untreated peers. However, some studies evidenced up to a 37-percent reduction in recidivism rates and similar improvements. Such programs tended to involve behaviour modification and address social and cognitive factors, problem-solving skills, and criminal or anti-social beliefs. They were aimed at increasing self-control, school achievement, and specific job skills. The results of these meta-analyses tend to concur: effective interventions for either youth or adults must target known predictors of crime or risk factors, should be behavioural in nature, should match the offender's learning style, and should be delivered to mainly higher-risk individuals (Andrews & Bonta, 1998; Andrews et al., 1990; Antonowicz & Ross, 1994; Cullen & Gendreau, 2000).

Issues of Culture and Race

The issues of culture, race, and gender[6] will have an impact not only on how rehabilitative interventions are offered, but also on how they are accepted by different individuals. Similar to prison populations, the racial and cultural makeup of youth custody facilities is quite diverse. One clear example is that Aboriginal youth are substantially overrepresented at every stage of processing in the criminal justice system, at arrest, detention, and custody (Hamilton & Sinclair, 1991). While this is most evident in the Prairie provinces in Canada, disproportionate numbers of black youth populate youth facilities in Montreal and Toronto, as do Asian youth on the west coast. The varied cultural backgrounds of these youth pose challenges for the provision of rehabilitative interventions. The "one-size-fits-all" philosophy of many youth custody facilities fails to take into account how both race and culture can impact on world views, social perspectives, and behavioural expectations. There is a growing recognition of the importance of considering race and culture in the provision of criminal justice interventions and the development and success of some efforts from the Aboriginal community attest to that fact (Fisher & Janetti, 1996).

Rehabilitation as Punishment

From a more radical viewpoint, rehabilitation is seen by some as an attempt by those in power to impose a repressive system of social control over vulnerable individuals. Such a critical perspective rejects what is considered a positivistic view of crime that focuses on individualistic terms, while ignoring greater social conditions of disadvantage. An orientation that accepts that rehabilitation has a place within corrections in fact understands delinquency in terms of individual and familial pathology (Havemann, 2000, p. 23). Thus, according to critics of the approach, rehabilitation becomes a further means of control and discrimination against largely powerless and marginalized young persons. What is challenged by this viewpoint is the notion that the offending behaviour stems from a defect in the personality of that person, who is considered amenable to change or rehabilitation within the youth custodial facility.

Many youth custodial facilities, similar to prisons, take youth away from their familial and social support systems. As we have seen with adult prisons, such facilities are not conducive to rehabilitation (Campbell, 2003). Rothman (1973) refers to the "noble lie" that prisons can serve rehabilitative purposes at all. From this perspective, then, rehabilitation is rejected outright, due in part to the relative powerlessness of the prisoner or young person to give or withhold consent to such efforts and the incongruous nature of the environment within which it is offered.

Is it possible to have a mitigated faith in rehabilitation per se, without ascribing to a purely positivist ideology? Perhaps the more important questions and answers lie in how we define rehabilitation and what our expectations are with respect to interventions for young persons who commit crimes. It is possible to believe that many youth are victims first and offenders second (Schissel, 1993). It is also possible to believe that we have a responsibility in Canadian society, which professes to care about issues of social justice, to provide young persons who commit crimes with the means to get past their troubles. This may translate into further research emphasis on more promising initiatives, which take place outside the walls of the institution and occur within the community, which look past questions of punishment, blame, and responsibility. The promise of some community-based initiatives offers some hope in this regard.

THE PROVISION OF INTERVENTION PROGRAMS

There is considerable variation in how programs of intervention are offered to young persons who commit crimes and are sentenced to periods of custody. Just as the YCJA provides the framework for the provision of such programs, each province and territory has the mandate for offering these services and it is likely that provincial politics will influence the number and types of programs offered. Nevertheless, there are a variety of programs that are offered generally to most youth who are serving custody, and there are specific programs that are aimed at targeting youth who have committed particular offences or offence-related behaviours. In general, all youth sentenced to custody have been subjected to a pre-sentence report, and are expected to participate in education, counselling, and recreation programs.

Assessment and Pre-sentence Reports

Most youth, prior to and upon entry to a youth custodial facility, are subjected to some form of assessment. This is done primarily to ascertain the particular strengths, weaknesses, and need areas of the young person and to help in deciding the most appropriate placement for him or her. The need for assessment prior to sentencing is based on the notion that a youth court judge must have adequate information on which to base decisions (Leschied & Wormith, 1997). In most cases, a formal assessment takes place in the form of a pre-sentence report, as is required by law prior before imposing a custodial sentence (YCJA, sec. 39(6)). As dictated by the YCJA (sec. 40), a pre-sentence report is quite extensive and contains a great deal of information related to the crime committed, the youth's family, school, and general functioning. It should contain information related to the youth's age, maturity, character, behaviour, and attitude, and his or her willingness to make amends. In addition, it should also contain any plans the youth has to change his or her conduct, and the availability and appropriateness of any community services for this young person. This type of report is generally prepared by a probation officer or a social worker and will include a recommendation regarding sentencing. Under the YCJA, a pre-sentence report is required to address the restriction on the use of custody in relation to the young person and explore the potential of community alternatives (Tustin & Lutes, 2003, p. 60). Further assessments are generally done following entrance to a youth custodial facility and later to assess progress and determine release.

Education

Education, as a form of intervention, has long been a part of most programming in youth custodial facilities. By law, youth must receive formal education until they are 16 years of age. However, many youth in custodial facilities possess learning, behavioural, and attentional problems (Loeber et al., 1998; Zimmerman et al., 1981) that have hindered their ability to function in traditional school environments. Thus, many facilities adapt their classrooms to provide low teacher/student ratios and allow students to learn at their own pace. While few institutions offer comprehensive vocational programs or work-study programs to youth, most demand that young persons take an active role in daily maintenance of the institution, specifically cleaning the facility. In most cases, this involves undertaking specific chores related to housekeeping and janitorial duties. Many youth correctional officials would argue that such activities provide youth the opportunity to develop good work habits (Bell, 2003, p. 303). However, the nature and extent of these demands are more often designed to meet institutional needs and not necessarily those of the young person.

Counselling

Aside from specific programs aimed to address particular need areas, as discussed below, most custodial facilities require that each youth follow his or her own treatment or intervention plan. Facilitated by a youth worker, social worker, or probation officer, and in conjunction with the young person and his/her family, the intervention plan will usually address issues related to school, to family, to the crime committed (if any), and to discharge planning. A youth's progress toward these issues will be monitored over the course of the sentence through family and individual sessions with his or her worker, with periodic written updates.

Recreation

Many youth facilities focus efforts on providing extensive recreational programs for youth in custody, based on the notion of therapeutic recreation. Specifically, it involves teaching youth how to better structure their free time to include positive recreational and/or leisure pursuits that foster healthier lifestyle choices (Coyl et al., 2001). Clearly, youth who learn how to occupy themselves during their leisure time are less likely to engage in criminal activity, as boredom and inactivity can lead to risk-taking behaviour. Recreational activities in youth custody facilities generally involve offering a variety of sports, fitness, and arts and crafts programs aimed at providing the opportunity to learn cooperative behaviour, to improve communication skills, and to gain the physical health benefits of increased activity. Some public-interest groups view the provision of such programs as bringing a "holiday camp" atmosphere to youth custody (Bell, 2003, p. 303). Consequently, in times of fiscal restraint, and as a result of public pressures, recreational programs are often the first to be eliminated.

PROGRAM EXAMPLES

In custodial facilities for young persons throughout Canada, a variety of different programs exist aimed at specific need areas. Contrary to the provision of intervention programs for adult federal offenders, which are fairly uniform across the country, provincial jurisdiction for young offenders dictates that each province has the power to designate the nature and type of programs offered in its facilities. While there are far too many programs to be discussed here, some of the more widely used programs will be noted.

Cognitive-Behavioural Interventions: Aggression Replacement Training

In recent years, cognitive behavioural approaches to intervention with both adults and youths who commit crimes have garnered a great deal of attention. Loosely based on social learning theory, which is premised on the notion that all behaviour is learned, cognitive approaches focus on and target the thought processes related to decisions to react in anti-social ways, and they teach new means of controlling behaviour. Cognitive skills training is often accompanied with problem-solving training, social skills training, and pro-social modelling with positive reinforcement of non-criminal behaviour or attitudes (Lipton, et al., 2002). One method that has been widely used with young persons is aggression replacement training (ART), which includes many cognitive behavioural strategies (Goldstein, Glick, & Gibbs, 1998).

Aggression replacement training is comprised of three specific skill areas:

skillstreaming, anger control training, and moral reasoning training. *Skillstreaming,* intended to enhance pro-social skills, involves instructional procedures where appropriate behaviours are modelled. Through role-play youth are given feedback, followed by opportunities to practise these skills in real-life situations. The second component, *anger control training,* teaches young persons the skills necessary to reduce anger and aggression through self-control. It provides the opportunity for youth to learn the triggers of their own anger, recognize the physiological cues of anger arousal, and learn anger "reducers" and "reminders" to defuse their internal triggers. Finally, the skills learned in skillstreaming are used in these anger situations, followed by self-evaluation strategies. The third aspect to ART is called *moral reasoning training,* which involves exposing youth to a series of moral dilemmas in a group context and is aimed at advancing the young person's moral reasoning to a higher level (Goldstein, Glick, & Gibbs, 1998, pp. 33–35). Together, the three components of ART are meant to provide youth the opportunity to learn more reasoned means of dealing with anger-provoking situations.

Substance-Abuse Programs

Substance-abuse programs are offered in many facilities, as substance abuse is considered a major risk factor for chronic/persistent young offenders. It is important that substance-abuse programs be developmentally significant, intensive, system-based, and include relapse prevention. However, the research around the efficacy of substance-abuse programs is mixed. One problem with such programs is that they fail to adequately address the family,

school, and community problems strongly associated with drug use for adolescents (Howell, 2003, p. 140).

Sex-Offender Programs

When young persons commit sex-related offences, it raises questions about the notion of risk. These types of offences are among the most vilified in society, and the media and public often demand punitive responses to such behaviour. Nonetheless, adolescent sex offenders are often victimized emotionally, psychologically, and sexually, and some will repeat earlier victimization experiences (Ryan & Lane, 1991). Treatment strategies include a combination of cognitive interventions, anger management, social skills training, alcohol and substance-abuse programs, victim empathy, and age-appropriate development of socially acceptable sexual behaviour.

Boot Camps

Boot camps are a form of secure custody under the YCJA and are a politically popular response to youth crime in the United States. They represent a militaristic, discipline-oriented form of intervention that emphasizes personal responsibility. While most are consistently punishment-oriented, some boot camps offer educational and recreational programs as well. Boot camps have been established in three provinces in Canada in recent years, although Project Turnaround, in Barrie, Ontario, recently closed. The impulsive nature of much youth crime and the inability of many youth to understand the consequences of their behaviour demonstrate how a boot camp philosophy toward intervention will have little overall impact on youth crime. Furthermore, recent Canadian research on the efficacy of a program such as Project Turnaround indicates the "generalized failure of Ontario's boot camp to show positive effects on youth" (Centre of Criminology, 2001). An extensive U.S. study has indicated that there are no differences in recidivism rates of boot camp participants when compared with others in more traditional facilities (Mackenzie et al., 2001).

COMMUNITY-BASED INITIATIVES

As discussed earlier, community-based sentences provide youth the opportunity to remain in the community while serving their sentences, with the support of professionals. Recent research indicates that such initiatives have a greater effect than do those offered in institutional settings. In their meta-analysis of 117 studies of young offenders treated outside of institutional settings, Lipsey and Wilson (1997) found that such interventions reduce recidivism to about half the rate it would have been without treatment. Intensive community supervision or intensive supervised probation programs use a variety of methods to monitor youth who are living in the community, but have direct contact with parole or community workers. Two programs that have garnered attention in recent years are multi-systemic therapy and restorative justice initiatives.

Multi-Systemic Therapy

Multi-systemic therapy (MST) is aimed at chronic or serious offenders and attempts to influence the major criminogenic risk factors through the application of intervention strategies in a multi-modal fashion. It is described as follows:

MST is a home-based, family-based, present-oriented therapeutic intervention using family strengths to attenuate risk factors and improve family relations, peer relations, and school performance. MST aims to reduce criminal offending by targeting the multiple causes of anti-social behavior and empowering parents to maintain the gains made in treatment. (Leschied & Cunningham, 1998)

MST adopts a social-ecological approach to anti-social behaviour; this perspective of criminal conduct believes that it has multiple causes and that interventions must address these many sources to be effective. The causes emanate from the youth him/herself, but also from the family, peers, school environment, and neighbourhood. Thus, the focus is considered to be more effective when undertaken in the community: the MST therapist works with the family in the home or school, and is available 24 hours a day. This approach by nature is highly individualized and flexible to meet each youth's individual needs. The ultimate goal is to empower the family to take responsibility for continuing and contributing to treatment. At the family level, MST therapists attempt to help caregivers open lines of communication and develop caregiver skills, and encourage them to engage in mutually desired activities with their children (Huey et al., 2000, p. 452). With respect to peer interaction, MST focuses on increasing the youth's association with pro-social peers. However, the application criteria limit the types of youth who can participate in MST, and it is available only to those youths who have at least one involved parent or caregiver in their life. The program is not considered appropriate for sex offenders or those who have substance abuse problems without criminal activity. While the initial results of a large Canadian study appeared encouraging (Leschied & Cunningham, 1998), later research has indicated no long-term treatment effects (Cunningham, 2002). Given that there may be a variety of reasons for the lack of effect, further study of such intensive community-based programming is needed.

Restorative Justice Programs

Restorative justice initiatives are being used more and more frequently with young persons who violate the law, particularly in cases of minor offending. These initiatives can take many forms, such as circle sentencing, victim offender mediation, and conferencing. Most often they occur in the community, but have also been "added on" to other more traditional forms of intervention as a means to restore harms done. As discussed in Chapter 12, these initiatives find a place in the YCJA in the form of conferences (sec. 19). Borrowing from the practice of family group conferences in New Zealand and Australia, a conference occurs following an admission of guilt or responsibility on the part of the young person and involves the victim, the victim's supporters, the offender and his/her supporters, as well as a facilitator. The objective of conferences is to find an agreed-upon means to the heal harms that occurred through the commission of the offence.

As a form of intervention, restorative justice programs offer an interesting alternative to traditional means of processing through the criminal justice system. Primarily, they are the sole means of rehabilitative intervention that engages the

victim on anything more than a superficial level. The victim, broadly defined, and the community have a large role to play in restorative justice practices. The victim is given the opportunity to be heard, to participate in the process of "doing justice." In contrast to the adversarial, retributive system, restorative justice is not concerned with meting out punishment, but rather restoring harms done and healing relationships among victims, offenders, and the community.

CONCLUSION

The provision of rehabilitative interventions in youth custodial settings is fraught with challenges. Historically, Canadian legislation to deal with youth who commit crimes began with a welfare orientation and has evolved to a more complex philosophy that emphasizes crime prevention, meaningful consequences, and rehabilitation and reintegration. The place for rehabilitation has evolved considerably as well, as has the practice and purpose of intervention for youth who commit crimes. The *Youth Criminal Justice Act*, while limiting the use of custody, also provides the opportunity for a variety of less invasive interventions to occur in the community. While some recent research is beginning to demonstrate that efforts at rehabilitation have demonstrated some effects, it is also important to question if society has the right to impose particular interventions on individuals against their will. Given that rehabilitative services are provided in the context of a court disposition (Leschied & Wormith, 1997, p. 246), true voluntary participation is not possible. It is very difficult for young persons to have faith and trust in professionals whom they view as working for the "system"; this in turn impacts on a youth's progress in a program of intervention.

Clearly, there are some young persons who have committed serious, violent crimes whom we have failed as a society, who require placement for a time in custodial facilities. Fortunately, these youth are in the minority. Unfortunately, in the past we have tended to use custody for far too many youths who are not in need of such intensive interventions. As Green and Healy (2003) note, the criminal justice system has become a "default" system, a fallback when other systems, such as social service and mental health, are unable to deal with a youth's problems (p. 76). The greater emphasis on the use of community-based sanctions under the YCJA holds much promise. However, it must also be matched by enthusiasm on the part of youth court justices to limit custodial sanctions in sentencing and by provincial governments to provide adequate funding for such community-based initiatives to take place.

References

Allen, F. A. (1981). *The decline of the rehabilitative ideal: Penal policy and social purpose.* New Haven, CT: Yale University Press.

Anand, S. (2003). Crafting youth sentences: The roles of rehabilitation, proportionality, restraint, restorative justice and race under the *Youth Criminal Justice Act. Alberta Law Review, 40*(4), 943–963.

Andrews, D. A., & Bonta, J. (1998). *The psychology of criminal conduct* (2nd ed.). Cincinnati, OH: Anderson

Andrews, D. A., Zinger, I., Hoge, R. D., Bonta, J., Gendreau, P., & Cullen, F. T. (1990). Does correctional treatment work? A clinically relevant and psychologically informed meta-analysis. *Criminology, 28,* 369–404.

Antonowicz, D., & Ross, R. (1994). Essential components of successful rehabilitation programs for offenders. *International Journal of Offender Therapy and Comparative Criminology, 38,* 97–104.

Bala, N. (2003). *Youth criminal justice law.* Toronto: Irwin Law.

Bell, S. (2003). *Young offenders and juvenile justice: A century after the fact* (2nd ed.). Scarborough, ON: Thomson Nelson.

Bourdoin, C. M., Henggeler, S. W., Blaske, D. M., & Stein, R. J. (1990). Multisystemic treatment of adolescent sexual offenders. *International Journal of Offender Therapy and Comparative Criminology, 34,* 105–113.

Bourdoin, C. M., Mann, B. J., Cone, L. T., Henggeler, S. M., Fucci, B. R., Balske, D. M., & Williams, R. A. (1995). Multisystemic treatment of serious juvenile offenders: Long-term prevention of criminality and violence. *Journal of Consulting and Clinical Psychology, 63,* 569–578.

Campbell, K. M. (1987). *Consent to treatment order.* Unpublished paper, McGill University, Faculty of Law.

Campbell, K. M. (2003). Rehabilitation. *Encyclopedia of Corrections and Prisons.* Thousand Oaks, CA: Sage Publications.

Centre of Criminology (2001). *4:1 Criminological highlights.* Toronto: Centre of Criminology, University of Toronto.

Collins English Dictionary. (1979). *Collins dictionary of the English language.* Glasgow, Scotland: William Collins Sons & Co. Ltd.

Coyl, C., Kinney, W. B., Riley, B., & Shank, J. (2001). *Benefits of therapeutic recreation: A consensus view.* Ravensdale, WA: Idyll Arbor Publishing.

Cullen, F.T., & Gendreau, P. (2000). Assessing correctional rehabilitation: Policy, practice, and prospects. In J. Horney (Ed.), *Criminal justice 2000: Vol. 3. Policies, processes and decisions of the criminal justice system*, pp. 109–175. Washington, DC: National Institute of Justice.

Cunningham, A. (2002). *One step forward: Lessons learned from a randomized study of multisystemic therapy in Canada.* Centre for Children and Families in the Justice System of the London Family Court Clinic. Online at http://www.lfcc.on.ca.

Feld, B. C. (1999). *Bad kids: Race and the transformation of the juvenile court.* NY: Oxford University Press.

Fisher, L., & Janetti, H. (1996). Aboriginal youth in the criminal justice system. In J. Winterdyk (Ed.), *Issues and perspectives on young offenders in Canada.* Toronto: Harcourt, Brace and Company.

Goldstein, A. P., Glick, B., & Gibbs, J. C. (1998). *Aggression replacement training: A comprehensive intervention for aggressive youth.* Champaign, IL: Research Press.

Green, R. G., & Healy, K. F. (2003). *Tough on kids: Rethinking approaches to youth justice.* Saskatoon, SK: Purich Publishing Ltd.

Griffiths, C. T., & Verdun-Jones, S. N. (1989). *Canadian criminal justice.* Toronto: Butterworths.

Hamilton, A. C., & Sinclair, C. M. (1991). *Report of the Aboriginal Justice Inquiry of Manitoba. Volume 1: The system and Aboriginal people.* Winnipeg, MB: Queen's Printer.

Havemann, P. (2000). From child saving to child blaming: The political economy of the YOA. In R. M. Mann (Ed.), *Juvenile crime and delinquency: A turn of the century reader*, pp. 19–43. Toronto: Canadian Scholars' Press Inc.

Howell, J. C. (2003). *Preventing and reducing juvenile delinquency: A comprehensive framework.* Thousand Oaks, CA: Sage Publications.

Huey, S. J., Henggeler, S. W., Brondino, M. J., & Pickrel, S. G. (2000). Mechanisms of change in multisystemic therapy: Reducing delinquent behaviour through therapist adherence and improved family and peer functioning. *Journal of Consulting and Clinical Psychology, 68*(3), 451–467.

Landau, B. (1986). The rights of minors to consent to treatment and to residential care. In B. Landau (Ed.), *Children's rights in the practice of family law.* Toronto: Carswell.

Leon, J. S. (1977). The development of Canadian juvenile justice: A background for reform. *Osgoode Hall Law Journal, 15*, 71–106.

Leschied, A. W., & Cunningham, A. (1998). *Clinical trials of multi-systemic therapy with high risk Phase I young offenders, 1997–2001.* Year end report 1997–1998. London, ON: The Family Court Clinic.

Leschied, A. W., & Cunningham, A. (2001). Seeking effective intervention for serious young offenders: Interim results of a 4-year randomized study of multi-systemic therapy in Ontario, Canada. Centre for Children and Families in the Justice System of the London Family Court Clinic. Online at http://www.lfcc.on.ca.

Leschied, A. W., & Jaffe, P. (1991). Dispositions as indicators of conflicting social purposes under the JDA and the YOA. In A. Leschied, P. Jaffe, & W. Willis (Eds.), *The Young Offenders Act: A revolution in Canadian juvenile justice.* Toronto: Wall and Thompson.

Leschied, A. W., Jaffe, P. G., Andrews, D., & Gendreau, P. (1992). Treatment issues and young offenders: An empirically derived vision of juvenile justice policy. In R. R. Corrado, N. Bala, R. Linden, & M. Le Blanc (Eds.), *Juvenile justice in Canada: A theoretical and analytical assessment*, pp. 347–366. Toronto: Butterworths.

Leschied, A. W., & Wormith, J. S. (1997). Assessment of young offenders and treatment of correctional clines. In D. R. Evans (Ed.), *The law, standards of practice and ethics in the practice of psychology*, pp. 233–258. Toronto: Emond Montgomery Publications Ltd.

Lipsey, M. W. (1992). Juvenile delinquency treatment: A meta-analytic inquiry into the variability of effects. In T. D. Cook, H. Cooper, D. S. Cordray, H. Hartman, L.V. Heges, R. J. Light, et al. (Eds.), *Meta-analysis for explanation*, pp. 83–127. New York: Russell Sage Foundation.

Lipsey, M. W. (1999). Can rehabilitative programs reduce the recidivism of juvenile offenders? An inquiry into the effectiveness of practical programs. *Virginia Journal of Social Policy and the Law, 6,* 611–641.

Lipsey, D. S., & Wilson D. B. (1997). *Effective intervention for serious juvenile offenders: A synthesis of research.* Vanderbilt Institute for Public Policy Studies. Nashville, TN.

Lipton, D. S., Pearson, F. S., Cleland, C. M., & Yee, D. (2002). The effectiveness of cognitive-behavioral treatment methods on offender recidivism: Meta-analytic outcomes from the CDATE project. In J. McGuire (Ed.), *Offender rehabilitation and treatment: Effective programmes and policies to reduce re-offending,* pp. 79–112. Chichester, UK: John Wiley & Sons, Ltd.

Loeber, R., Farrington, D. P., Stouthamer-Loeber, M., & Van Kammen, W. B. (1998). *Antisocial behaviour and mental health problems.* Mahwah, NJ: Lawrence Erlbaum.

MacKenzie, D., Gover, A., Armstrong, G., & Mitchell, O. (2001, August). *A national study comparing the environments of boot camps with traditional facilities for juvenile offenders.* Online: National Criminal Justice Reference Centre http://www.ncjrs.org/txtfiles1/nij/187680.txt.

Mann, R. M. (2000). Struggles for youth justice and justice for youth: A Canadian example. In R. M. Mann (Ed.), *Juvenile crime and delinquency: A turn of the century reader,* pp. 3–18. Toronto: Canadian Scholars' Press Inc.

Markwart, A., & Corrado, R. (1989). Is the *Young Offenders Act* more punitive? In L. Beaulieu, (Ed.), *Young offender dispositions: Perspectives on principles and practice.* Toronto: Wall and Thompson.

Martinson, R. (1974). What works? Questions and answers about prison reform. *Public Interest, 35,* 22–54.

Martinson, R. (1979). New findings, new views: A note of caution regarding sentencing reform. *Hofstra Law Review, 7,* 242–258.

Roberts, J. V., & Bala, N. (2003). Understanding sentencing under the *Youth Criminal Justice Act. Alberta Law Review, 41*(2), 395–423.

Robinson, P. (2004). Youth court statistics, 2002/03. *Juristat, 24*(2).

Rothman, D. (1973). Decarcerating prisoners and patients. *Civil Liberties Review, 1,* 8–30.

Ryan, G., & Lane, S. (1991). *Juvenile sex offending: Causes, consequences and corrections.* Lexington, MA: Lexington Books.

Schissel, B. (1993). *Social dimensions of Canadian youth justice.* Don Mills, ON: Oxford University Press.

Statistics Canada. (2001). *Graphical overview of the criminal justice indicators, 2000–2001.* Ottawa: Minister of Industry.

Sudworth, M., & deSouza, P. (2001). Youth court statistics, 1999/2000. *Juristat, 21*(3).

Thomas, J. (2003). Youth court statistics, 2001/2002. *Juristat, 23*(3).

Tustin, L., & Lutes, R. E. (2002). *A guide to the Youth Criminal Justice Act.* Toronto: Butterworths Canada Ltd.

Zimmerman, J., Rich, W., Keilitz, I., & Broder, P. (1981). Some observations on the link between learning disabilities and juvenile delinquency. *Journal of Criminal Justice, 9,* 1–17.

Cases Cited

Reference re Young Offenders Act s. 2 (P.E.I.), [1991] 1 S.C.R. 252, 62 C.C.C. (3d) 385 at 398.

R. v. M.(J.J.) (1993), 81 C.C.C. (3d) 487 (S.C.C.).

Notes

1. The province of Québec deals with the majority of young who commit crimes quite differently than the rest of the country. It has the lowest numbers of youth in custody, it diverts more youth to extrajudicial sanctions, and there is historically a stronger emphasis on clinical and rehabilitative, as opposed to punitive, approaches to youth justice (Green & Healy, 2003, p. 187).

2. These figures are estimates for Phase I youth (12- to 15-year-olds) in the province of Ontario based on a per diem cost of $255/day for open custody and $345/day for closed custody (Leschied & Cunningham, 2001). The costs for Phase II youth (16- to 17-year-olds) is $279.85 per day or $102 000 per year, and does not include capital costs and overhead expenses. Ontario long held a jurisdictional split between Phase I and Phase II youth, with different ministries responsible for allocation of different services for each group. These two groups have now been subsumed under the Minister of Children and Youth Services.

3. While rehabilitation is also emphasized as a sentencing objective for adults, along with denunciation, deterrence, incapacitation, and reparation (*Criminal Code* sec. 718),

proportionality is referred to as the more general "fundamental principle" of adult sentencing (Roberts & Bala, 2003, p. 407).

4. Such treatments can be imposed on young persons involuntarily only if their lack of capacity to consent has been established under provincial child welfare or mental health legislation (Bala, 2003, p. 487).

5. Recidivism, or reoffending, is not necessarily the best measure of whether a program of intervention is having an effect. Recidivism measures when a person is caught engaging in criminal activity, and many people who reoffend are simply never caught. Furthermore, gains from rehabilitative programs may occur in other areas, such as social functioning or problem solving, that are unrelated to criminal activity and cannot be assessed through rates of recidivism. Finally, it is possible that programs were not implemented properly in the first instance, and it may not be realistic to expect that they will have an impact on recidivism.

6. The issue of gender and the provision of programs to young girls who commit crimes and are sentenced to custody is discussed at length in Chapter 14.

chapter fourteen

Understanding Girls' Delinquency: Looking Beyond Their Behaviour

Sibylle Artz

School of Child and Youth Care
University of Victoria

Diana Nicholson

School of Child and Youth Care
University of Victoria

Carmen Rodriguez

School of Child and Youth Care
University of Victoria

INTRODUCTION

In order to understand the phenomenon of delinquent and criminal behaviour among girls in Canada, it is important to examine how our juvenile justice system interprets, labels, and responds to girls' delinquency and also the extent to which our efforts to intervene and alter their behaviour are effective. This chapter begins with a review of Canada's responses to girls' offending behaviour, especially our willingness to incarcerate female youth. Next, official statistics are examined to provide a sense of the extent of the problem, including the difficulty associated with trying to develop a clear and accurate picture of girls' offending behaviour. Gender differences in the pathways to delinquency and violence are then discussed, as well as the influences of the justice system on girls and the issues that relate to working with delinquent girls. The chapter concludes with promising interventions for working more effectively with delinquent girls in Canada.

CANADA'S RESPONSES TO YOUTHFUL OFFENDING

Canada is known internationally for having one of the "harshest regimes for young offenders in the Western world" (Mallea, 1999, p. 3). Our custodial facilities are filled primarily with marginalized youth, among them the disabled, Aboriginal, poorly educated, and poverty-ridden (Green & Healy, 2003), who often receive much harsher sentences than adults. Thus, while adults are eligible for time off for good behaviour, automatic consideration for probation after serving one-third of their sentence, and statutory release after serving two-thirds of their sentence, youth are not. Therefore, as Mallea (1999) states, "a two-year sentence for a young offender is more or less the equivalent of a six-year sentence for an adult" (p. 4), despite the fact that the public thinks that sentences for youth are too lenient.[1]

International comparisons, although difficult to make because most countries report aggregates of their prison population that combine youth and adult offenders, show that Canada creates more space to incarcerate youth than many other developed countries. On the assumption that the number of youth prisons that exist in a country is generally correlated with the number of youth serving time in custody, Figure 14.1 serves to illustrate this point by comparing the number of youth prison facilities per 100 000 youth across six Western industrialized countries.

Further, while Canada has a far lower proportion of violent crime among youth than the United States, Canadian youth are incarcerated at a higher rate. One source suggests that we lock up almost twice as many youth per 100 000 population as does the United States (Society for Children and Youth of British Columbia, 2001). The Department of Justice Canada (2003) provides in Figure 14.2 a graphical representation of the comparison between custodial dispositions for youth in Canada and the U.S.

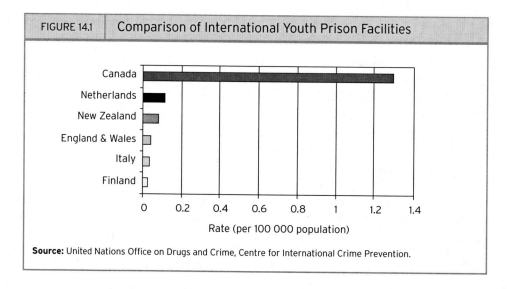

| FIGURE 14.1 | Comparison of International Youth Prison Facilities |

Source: United Nations Office on Drugs and Crime, Centre for International Crime Prevention.

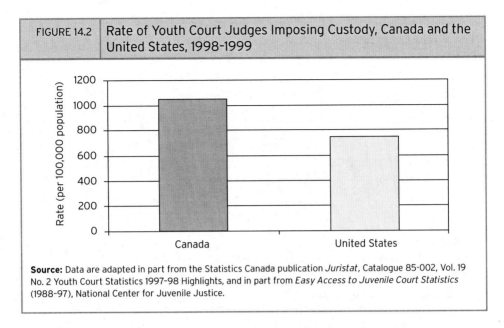

FIGURE 14.2   Rate of Youth Court Judges Imposing Custody, Canada and the United States, 1998-1999

Source: Data are adapted in part from the Statistics Canada publication *Juristat*, Catalogue 85-002, Vol. 19 No. 2 Youth Court Statistics 1997-98 Highlights, and in part from *Easy Access to Juvenile Court Statistics* (1988-97), National Center for Juvenile Justice.

Given Canada's record on incarceration, many experts in youth justice are calling for increased alternatives to custody for both female and male young offenders (Bala, 2001; Corrado, Odgers, & Cohen, 2000; Garbarino, 1999; Kowalski & Caputo, 2001; Reitsma-Street, 2001). Up until recently, only two provinces in Canada—Quebec and New Brunswick—were taking steps toward decarceration of youth (Mallea, 1999), despite the fact that among incarcerated youth, only about 10 percent require custody to protect society (Corrado, Odgers, & Cohen, 2000). The *Youth Criminal Justice Act* (*YCJA* S.C. 2002, c. C-70) contains provisions specifically aimed at reducing the numbers of young persons in custody and restricting custody to only the most serious offences (*YCJA*, sec. 39(1)), as well as attempting to reduce the number of youth incarcerated for breaches (Green & Healy, 2003). Only time will tell whether these provisions will result in significant change.

UNDERSTANDING GIRLS' DELINQUENT AND CRIMINAL BEHAVIOUR

Aside from incarcerating youth at a noticeably higher rate, our response to youthful offending also differs depending on the gender of the perpetrator. Reitsma-Street (2001) has highlighted our propensity to criminalize girls more frequently than boys for "breaching court orders" for minor infractions such as breaking curfew or running away from home. Figure 14.3 represents the proportion of girls charged with "failing to comply" with court orders (i.e., breaching probation orders that include curfew, staying at home) in relation to total charges levelled against Canadian girls. As shown, in 1995–1996 "failure to comply" comprised more than a quarter of all charges against girls.

The increase in charging girls with minor offences has been noted in the literature (Sprott & Doob, 2003), as has our

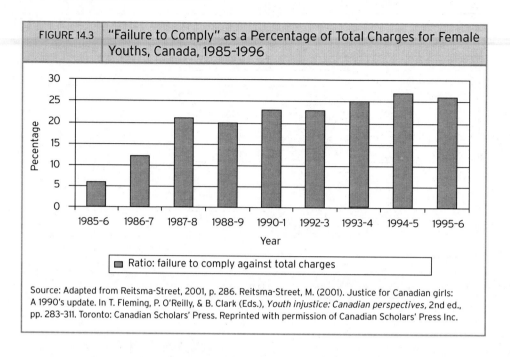

FIGURE 14.3 "Failure to Comply" as a Percentage of Total Charges for Female Youths, Canada, 1985-1996

Source: Adapted from Reitsma-Street, 2001, p. 286. Reitsma-Street, M. (2001). Justice for Canadian girls: A 1990's update. In T. Fleming, P. O'Reilly, & B. Clark (Eds.), *Youth injustice: Canadian perspectives,* 2nd ed., pp. 283–311. Toronto: Canadian Scholars' Press. Reprinted with permission of Canadian Scholars' Press Inc.

willingness to criminalize girls for minor offences as a means to protect them from self-destructive behaviours such as gravitating toward drug involvement and/or the sex trade (Corrado, Odgers, & Cohen, 2001). Girls are frequently incarcerated for what is perceived to be their own good, rather than for committing additional crimes. Such paternalism is further reflected in the data provided in Figure 14.4, which show for the period 1997–2001 how frequently "breaches" are used to keep girls in line.

Despite our willingness to incarcerate girls for breaches and minor offences, in Canada the number of charges laid against boys continues to be three to four times greater than the number against girls. In 1998–1999, self-reported delinquency among 12-to 15-year-old Canadian adolescents shows that one female for every six males engages in property-related delin-

quency, while two females for every nine males engage in violent forms of delinquency (Canadian Centre for Justice Statistics, 2003). Males and females enter into deviant and delinquent behaviour at a similar age: 15.5 years for males (Sinclair & Boe, 1998), and 15 years for females (Dell & Boe, 1998), but Canadian statistics show that males engage in deviant and delinquent behaviour in greater numbers and persist for a longer period of time. Thus, males represent 80 percent of convictions in youth court, while females account for only 20 percent of convictions (Canadian Centre for Justice Statistics, 2000).

In actual numbers, 77 704 boys compared to 24 609 girls were charged with criminal offences throughout Canada during 2001 (Statistics Canada, 2002). Boys' greater persistence in deviant and delinquent behaviour is reflected by rates of chronic recidivism. Among adult chronic

FIGURE 14.4	"Failure to Comply"* as a Percentage of Total *Criminal Code* Offences, Canada, 1997–2001

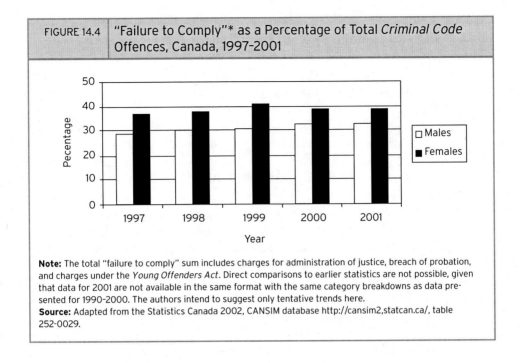

Note: The total "failure to comply" sum includes charges for administration of justice, breach of probation, and charges under the *Young Offenders Act*. Direct comparisons to earlier statistics are not possible, given that data for 2001 are not available in the same format with the same category breakdowns as data presented for 1990–2000. The authors intend to suggest only tentative trends here.
Source: Adapted from the Statistics Canada 2002, CANSIM database http://cansim2,statcan.ca/, table 252-0029.

recidivists, 93 percent are men and 7 percent are women (Ministry of the Attorney General, 2000). While offending continues to rise beyond 15 years of age for boys (Canadian Centre for Justice Statistics, 2000), youthful offending peaks for girls at around 15 and then declines. Although this age trend has persisted for many years, little is known about what might be occurring for girls that prompts them to commit more offences at this age and fewer when they are 16 or older.

Additionally, despite consistently lower comparative incidence rates for girls, there have been frequent media reports that especially aggressive behaviour among girls is skyrocketing (for an in-depth discussion, see Chesney-Lind & Pasko, 2004a). However, caution must be exercised when interpreting increases in crime rates for girls because girls have a small number of

charges to begin with and therefore a small increase in that number leads to a large percentage increase; a percentage increase that may be numerically correct, but inflates the actual value of the numbers (B.C. Police Services Branch, 1998). For example, in 1992 one adolescent female in Canada was charged with homicide, and in 1993 four young females were charged with this offence (Statistics Canada, 2002). If we choose to report only the *percentage rate* of increase of homicide committed by young females in Canada, this would be a 300-percent increase—a value that is technically true while vastly overstating what has occurred.

Thus, percentage increases in girls' aggression generally give an inflated sense of girls' aggression. Nonetheless, the *actual number* of Canadian girls engaging in delinquent and violent behaviour has, in fact, increased at different points over the past 20 years. Recently, there was an increase in girls' criminal involvement in the mid 1990s. Figure 14.5 shows overall charges for adolescent females in Canada from 1996–2001.

Certainly, some of the increase in actual numbers of charges can be accounted for by population increases. Over time, the *rate* of violence and delinquency may remain the same, but because our population is increasing, the number of reported crimes has also increased. To obtain an accurate reflection of any "real" increase, it is important to look at statistics that report incidence as a percentage of the total population. Figure 14.6 illustrates that a slightly different picture emerges when examining overall charge rates for adolescent females in Canada when expressed as a proportion of the total adolescent population. In Figure 14.6, girls committed the most crimes (all *Criminal Code* offences) in 1996, then engaged in increasingly less criminal activity through 1999. The number of crimes committed

by girls has risen again in the last few years, although it has not reached the high point of the mid 1990s.

Included in this aggregate category of "all *Criminal Code* offences" are property offences, crimes against the person, drug offences, administrative offences, and offences under the *Young Offenders Act*. In order to understand more about girls' aggressive and violent behaviour, it is important to pull out violent crimes from the aggregate category of total *Criminal Code* offences. The data on violent crimes separated out from total *Criminal Code* offences are provided in Figure 14.7, and present a more disturbing picture: one in which girls' use of violence does appear to be on the increase.

So what exactly is going on? Is there some truth behind publicly expressed concerns and fears about girls' aggressive behaviour? While these questions cannot be answered quickly or easily, a number of Canadian researchers are actively exploring them.

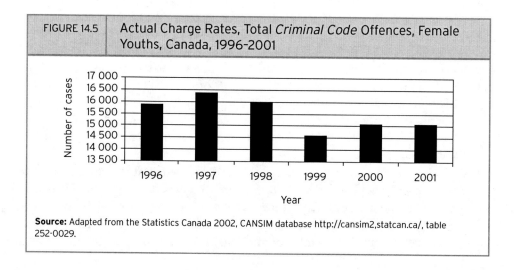

| FIGURE 14.5 | Actual Charge Rates, Total *Criminal Code* Offences, Female Youths, Canada, 1996–2001 |

Source: Adapted from the Statistics Canada 2002, CANSIM database http://cansim2,statcan.ca/, table 252-0029.

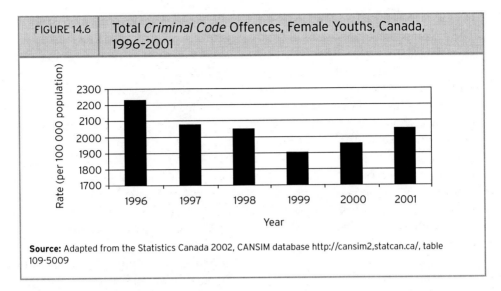

FIGURE 14.6   Total *Criminal Code* Offences, Female Youths, Canada, 1996-2001

Source: Adapted from the Statistics Canada 2002, CANSIM database http://cansim2,statcan.ca/, table 109-5009

SOME EXPLANATIONS FOR THE INCREASES IN GIRLS' USE OF AGGRESSION

A growing body of research indicates that increases in girls' involvement in delinquency and crime may be due to increased reporting of schoolyard fights, crackdowns on bullying behaviour (DeKeseredy, 2000) and zero-tolerance policies (Sprott & Doob, 2003). This suggests that the same aggressive behaviours previously viewed by educators, parents, and police as unfortunate or bad, but not criminal, are now being reported and used as the basis for charges.

Very recently, Sprott and Doob (2003; see also 2004) have stressed caution when interpreting reports of increased numbers

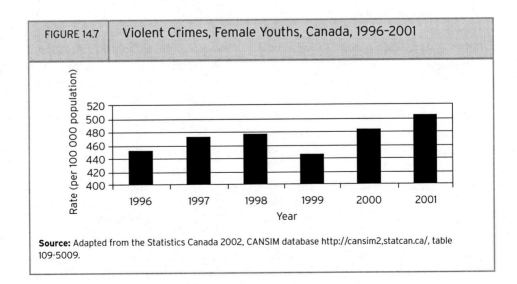

FIGURE 14.7   Violent Crimes, Female Youths, Canada, 1996-2001

Source: Adapted from the Statistics Canada 2002, CANSIM database http://cansim2,statcan.ca/, table 109-5009.

of girls' cases being heard in youth court. Their examination of nine years of youth court data (1991–2000) suggests that it is misleading to believe that girls are committing crimes in increasing numbers. They found that boys are being found guilty of fewer property offences, and because offences committed by girls have remained relatively stable over time, the proportion of cases involving girls has risen but only in relation to the total number of cases heard in youth court. Other explanations are found in investigating the gendered pathways to delinquency and violence and will be discussed next.

GENDER DIFFERENCES IN THE PATHWAYS TO DELINQUENCY AND VIOLENCE

Research shows that girls become involved in delinquent and violent behaviour for different reasons than boys. For example, Artz (1998; in press) emphasizes the role of stereotypical gender relations that subordinate and objectify females as the basis for much of adolescent female-on-female aggression. Katz (2000) notes that "both minority and white women's violent behaviour is best predicted by the experience of sexual discrimination" (p. 36). Chesney-Lind and Okamoto (2001) and Katz (2000) note a clear link between trauma, victimization, and girls' delinquency, and Means (2002) found that others' research (cf. Acoca & Austin, 1996; Acoca & Dedel, 1998) and her own consistently identified physical, sexual, and emotional abuse of girls as the first step on the path to delinquency and later criminality. Lanctôt, Émond, and LeBlanc (in press), in examining a Quebec sample of

adjudicated female youth, underscore the influence of situational factors such as maternal poverty in prompting aggressive behaviour.

Further, research—especially that which focuses on gender differences in aggression and violence and on the need for gender-sensitive intervention with young people who are in conflict with the law—suggests that a much better grasp of the different pathways for girls and boys into deviant and delinquent behaviour is needed (cf., American Bar Association & National Bar Association, 2001; Artz, Blais, & Nicholson, 2000; Chesney-Lind & Shelden, 1998; Means, 2002; Moretti & Odgers, in press). As these researchers point out, given that girls who enter the justice system are more often the victims of physical, psychological, and especially sexual abuse, the programs and setting offered them must take these difficult and often debilitating experiences into account. As well, girls and boys have different developmental needs and trajectories and require different forms of support and intervention for active positive development (Beyer, 1998, 1999; Canada, 1998; Garbarino, 1999; Gilbert, 2000; Gilligan, 1982; Miller, 1976; Pipher, 1994; Plummer, 1999; Pollack, 1998). However, gender continues to be absent in some discussions of youth justice in Canada (for example, in Green & Healy, 2003).

Artz, Blais, and Nicholson (2000) report that girls usually commit crimes in the company of peers and are often initiated into lawbreaking by older boyfriends, while boys appear to be initiated more often by family members (fathers and older brothers). Researchers in New Zealand suggest that girls' older appearance at an early age can stimulate older peers and the girls themselves to believe they are old enough to join in prohibited activities (Moffit, Caspi, Rutter, & Silva, 2001). Although generally a history of abuse—and especially a history of sexual abuse—is often seen to be central to girls' engaging in deviant, delinquent, and criminal behaviour, no single factor can predict such behaviour, and more often than not a number of systemic (i.e., family, community, and social contexts) and individual (i.e., personal) factors come into play (Leschied et al., 2000). Factors that contribute to girls' delinquency and aggression are known to include (summarized from Artz & Nicholson, 2002; in press[2]):

- problematic family dynamics and parental relationships, especially when these involve parental and sibling conflict and violence, parental rejection, low parental support, parental separation, and difficult mother–daughter interactions that result in low maternal attachment;

- gender-based oppression and abuse, especially the sexual objectification and sexual abuse of females, and the acceptance of patriarchal control and the need to attract the male gaze and male approbation;

- mental health and personality factors including depression, low self-esteem, conduct disorder, suicidal ideation and suicidal behaviour, and atypical physiological responses to stress;

- school difficulties, including low achievement, low school attachment, and dropping out of school;

- the alleviation of boredom and attention-seeking grounded in a need to be noticed, included, stimulated, and valued;

- the abuse of and chronic use of alcohol and drugs by the parents of delinquent and aggressive girls and by the girls themselves;

- connections to delinquent peers, especially older males; and

- negative self-representations, particularly the belief that others see them in negative ways.

Single-factor explanations fall short of predicting delinquent behaviour, and similarly no single path to delinquency is known to exist either for girls or for boys. For example, in their discussion on the etiology of aggression in females, Hoffman, Cummings, and Leschied (under review) note that, "female aggression does not begin with a single isolated event, but rather stems from a progression of traumatizing factors that build over time" (p. 3). As well, in thinking about girls (and, for that matter, boys), it is important to be conscious of the fact that within-sex differences also exist. Lanctôt, Émond, and Le Blanc (in press) stress that previous approaches in research and intervention that treat delinquent females as a homogenous group have done little to further our knowledge about delinquent females. These authors emphasize the need to better understand within-group difference among girls as a basis for prevention and intervention. Katz (2000) concurs and provides well-documented evidence that white and African American girls who engage in delinquency, while often sharing a history of sexual abuse and sexual discrimination, also differ in how a variety of problematic life experiences (e.g., peer group involvement, neighbourhood disorganization, physical abuse, fear, alienation, family size) affect their involvement in delinquency.

Before turning to consider best practices in working with delinquent girls, it is important to note that any inquiry into girls' delinquency must also take into account sexist attitudes that influence responses to their lawbreaking. For example, when girls break the law, their first encounter is usually with police who may well still be harbouring patriarchal attitudes. Police, like many others in our society, experience concern and sometimes outrage when they encounter girls who do not reflect the moral purity that is expected of their gender and respond to girls based on these feelings (Canadian Association of Elizabeth Fry Societies, n.d.). Reitsma-Street (in press) and others (Walkerdine, Lucey, & Melody, 2001) support the belief that adults within the justice system wield tremendous power to determine not only what is legal, but also what is feminine. When girls engage in delinquent behaviour, they are seen as acting like boys and judged to be aberrations of femininity (Chesney-Lind & Shelden, 1998). Pate (2002) reports examples of justice system workers' intolerance of girls' displays of assertiveness, confidence, and leadership, behaviours deemed to be out of character for girls. Others attest to a longstanding propensity to treat girls more paternalistically and harshly than boys, especially for minor illegal behaviours that are viewed as "unfeminine" (Geller, 1987; Parent, 1986; Reitsma-Street, 1989).

Parents are also implicated in sexist responses to girls' offending behaviour, and have been documented as high referral sources for girls charged with breaking the law. When asked why they turn their daughters in to police, they report an unwillingness to break with traditional gender expectations for girls' behaviour because they fear that their daughters are becoming societal misfits (Chesney-Lind & Pasko, 2004b).

THE CHALLENGES OF WORKING WITH DELINQUENT AND AGGRESSIVE GIRLS

Although the literature is clear that many girls in custody come with a history of having experienced severe physical, emotional, and sexual abuse, such abuse does not necessarily end with their entry into the justice system. Acoca (1999), in examining the conditions experienced by girls in custody in the United States, reports that staff use foul and demeaning language in dealing with girls and that inmates are the victims of inappropriate touching, pushing, hitting, and isolation by staff and fellow prisoners. She also found that administrative policies and rules that dictated the use of only prison-issued clothing for inmates resulted in girls being deprived of clean clothing. Additionally, Acoca (1999) reports that strip searches conducted in the presence of adult male staff are routine and perpetuate an atmosphere of disrespect toward girls that is clearly harmful to their well-being.

In research conducted in British Columbia by Artz et al. (2000),[3] it was found that youth custody workers were interested and willing to examine their own assumptions and practices and were actively searching for new ways to work with incarcerated girls and boys. However, when these workers participated in the research, development, and delivery of professional development programs aimed at improving their practice, they pointed to a variety of systemic and individual barriers that impede their efforts to move beyond meeting the very basic needs of youth in custody. These barriers included such things as low staffing and inadequate facilities, as well as a lack of understanding about gender differences and insufficient gender-specific programs. These workers also identified conflicting beliefs about the purposes of custody and minimal opportunities for communication, collaboration, and collegial support.

In addition to beliefs that boys were seen as easier to work with than girls, staff described distinct perceptions of gender differences in the troublesome behaviour exhibited by incarcerated youth. The ways in which they perceived boys and girls are summarized in Table 14.1 (adapted from Artz, Blais, & Nicholson, 2000).

According to the descriptors provided in Table 14.1, girls appear to be using strategies that are more emotional, subtle, complex, and relational than those used by boys. This so-called problem behaviour has been duly noted and examined by a

TABLE 14.1	Custody Workers' Perceptions of Gender Differences in the Problematic Behaviours of Incarcerated Youth
Boys	**Girls**
form more enduring cliques than girls	establish a new pecking order with each new girl in a group
are driven by anger and fear	are driven by strong emotions, especially anger and vindictiveness, and are more "nasty" than boys
use others to do their dirty work	involve others more in doing their dirty work and get more power by using others to do their dirty work
will not beat up "aggressive" girls because of repercussions, but will use/employ a girl to victimize another girl	victimize boys verbally (put downs) and with tone of voice, facial expressions
victimize and bully girls sexually	base their "hierarchy of power" on physical attractiveness and the ability to attract the male gaze, which leads to the ability to marshal a following that has the capacity to inflict physical harm or, if big and strong rather than beautiful, base their power on their reputation to personally inflict harm and to be just as strong as the boys
base their "hierarchy of power" on physical size and strength	
intimidate/victimize by controlling access to food and video games	use subtle non-verbal gestures, threatening and demeaning notes, and shunning and exclusion to exert dominance
are more overt in their use of aggression and violence	use threats of physical beatings to maintain "ownership" of certain boys
seem to enjoy watching girls victimize other girls, especially if the victimization is sexual	are more subtle and covert than boys in their victimization of others
have fights with other boys and move on	use males to do physical fighting for them
	plan out their violence more elaborately and include more people
	also victimize and bully other girls sexually
	hold grudges and follow through with vendettas over long time periods

number of researchers (Craig & Pepler, 1997; Crick & Grotpeter, 1996; Jones, 1998; Merten, 1997; Tremblay, 2000). Such behaviour has been cited by Alder (1997) as the reason why many workers consider boys to be more "open and honest" than girls, who are considered more "hysterical and manipulative" (p. 21). This behaviour has been identified as the main source of the often-expressed sentiment among those who work with girls that they are much harder to work with than boys (Baines & Alder, 1996; Kersten, 1990; Hudson, 1989), and as the reason why many of those working in the juvenile justice system prefer working with boys (Chesney-Lind & Okamoto, 2001; Okamoto, 2002). Moreover, these researchers have also noted that behaviours exhibited by boys (for example, employing hierarchies of power, using sexual intimidation against girls, working in cliques, getting others to do one's dirty work) are seen as "so much worse" when exhibited by girls. Such conceptions are clearly a manifestation of the enduring problems inherent in gender politics and patriarchal constructions of what is acceptable behaviour in girls and boys. When girls appear to be acting in ways that are complicit in their own oppression (i.e., the adoption of male-based use of force and the sexual victimization of other girls as central to establishing their hierarchies of power), their behaviours should be read not as "worse" but as indicative of the degree of oppression to which they have been subjected. These issues of oppression persist when moving from the dominant culture to the experiences of minority youth in custody, and are writ large in the experiences of Aboriginal youth, especially Aboriginal girls in conflict with the law.

ABORIGINAL FEMALE YOUTH IN CANADA

A report from the Ministry of the Solicitor General (La Prairie et al., 1996) shows that Aboriginal people have the highest arrest, incarceration, and crime rates of any group in Canada. Two factors considered key to understanding this overrepresentation of Aboriginal people in correctional institutions are (a) the fact that more Aboriginal people fall into the socially and economically vulnerable and marginalized groups involved in the criminal justice system, and (b) an overreliance on the use of imprisonment. Figure 14.8, which shows the violent crime rates for female youth across Canada's provinces and territories, illustrates that those provinces and territories that have the highest proportion of Canada's Aboriginal population (western provinces and northern territories) also have the highest rates of violent crime among female youth.

Whether living on- or off-reserve, Aboriginal people contend with meagre living conditions, poverty, and socio-economic deprivation. Further, cultural conflict (i.e., conflict in behavioural norms of divergent cultural groups), racism, absence of culturally adequate correctional programs, and the maintenance of obsolete practices within the justice system (i.e., the absence of alternative programs such as restitution or restorative justice) are all variables that contribute to the disproportionate representation of Aboriginal people involved with the justice system in Canada (Broadhurst, 1996; Jiwani, 1997; Li, 2000; Shaw, 1991). As Jiwani (1997) states,

> Violence occurs when people are dispossessed of their lands, disbarred from practicing their traditions, forced into

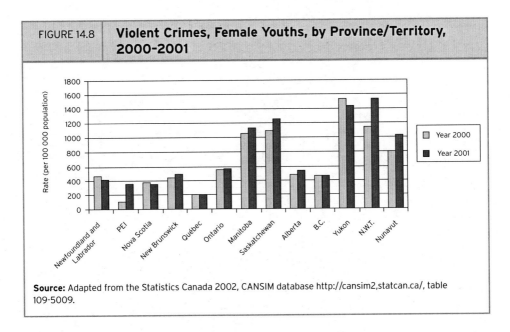

| FIGURE 14.8 | **Violent Crimes, Female Youths, by Province/Territory, 2000-2001** |

Source: Adapted from the Statistics Canada 2002, CANSIM database http://cansim2,statcan.ca/, table 109-5009.

contained areas, divested of their property, treated in a discriminatory fashion … and forced into situations where they have little choice.… (p. 4)

Various reports (Boe, 2000; Correctional Service of Canada, 2000; Canada, Department of Justice, 2002; La Prairie et al., 1996) confirm that the involvement in criminal activity of most Aboriginal offenders reflects social rather than criminal problems. Consequently, attempts to reduce Aboriginal overrepresentation in crime and incarceration will need to consider the economic, political, emotional, and social factors that contribute to their imbalanced presence within the justice system.

RACIALIZED JUSTICE

Cultural racism, sexism, and poverty can be considered forms of violence that intersect in the lives of Aboriginal women, women of colour, and immigrant and refugee women from racialized communities (Bannerji, 1987; Jiwani, Gorkoff, Vardy-Dell, & Normandeau, 1999; Ng, 1994). Members of these groups are often perceived as having an inherent tendency toward criminal behaviour and dishonesty, and as being violence prone (Indra, 1979; van Dijk, 1993). Young Aboriginal females, like others who become involved in crime and delinquency, experience multiple challenges within their life worlds, including the challenge of attempting to adapt to mainstream Canadian society while also attempting to develop within their traditional culture. Figure 14.9 depicts the extent of some of the challenges they face within family life in comparison to non-Aboriginal females. Here, Aboriginal and non-Aboriginal females are only equally likely to be exposed to mental illness and parents with a criminal record. Aboriginal females are more

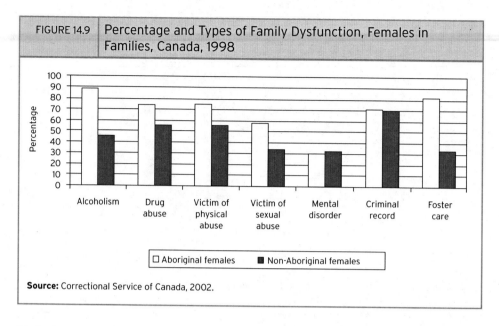

FIGURE 14.9 Percentage and Types of Family Dysfunction, Females in Families, Canada, 1998

Source: Correctional Service of Canada, 2002.

likely than non-Aboriginal females to experience all other forms of dysfunction in their families.

Chesney-Lind and Okamoto (2001) argue that girls' behaviour is framed differently based on their ethnicity. They cite the U.S. example that when African American girls were compared with white girls on the same socially problematic behaviours, African American girls were described as making inappropriate "lifestyle" choices and held responsible for those choices, while white girls were excused for their behaviour as their actions were interpreted as the result of low self-esteem and abandonment and therefore, strictly speaking, not their fault. Given this differential assessment of responsibility, Chesney-Lind and Okamoto suggest that assignment decisions about incarceration versus treatment seem to be made on the basis of colour, with higher proportions of African American and Latina girls sent to custody while more white girls are sent to treatment facilities.

According to La Prairie et al. (1996), differential processing based on cultural conflict and racial discrimination continues to contribute to the overrepresentation of Aboriginal youth in the criminal justice system. Racism, in its different manifestations (personal, systemic, and/or ideological or cultural) operates in the policing, judiciary, and penal systems (Satzewich, 1998). Some examples of systemic problems found in the judicial system include the underrepresentation of Aboriginal people in the police force and the fact that almost all judges are white and less than one percent of lawyers are Aboriginal people (Satzewich, 1998).

Moreover, it is important to recognize that the Canadian justice system is based on values such as retribution and blame; values that are foreign to Aboriginal people as they are removed from traditional aboriginal justice systems. Language barriers and socio-economic difficulties might further impede a fair hearing or trial (Satzewich, 1998). As well, evidence suggests that these racist issues persist when Aboriginal people enter the penal system. One example found in the Report of the Commission on Systemic Racism in the Criminal Justice System in Ontario (1995) demonstrated that prisoners were being prevented from possessing artifacts essential to their ceremonial and spiritual practices. Given the racialized nature of Canadian justice and social systems, the importance of culturally sensitive understandings of delinquency and crime can therefore not be overstated. Thus, when working with delinquent girls, it is necessary to include a well-articulated grasp of culture, along with an understanding of gender.

WORKING WITH DELINQUENT GIRLS

Respecting Culture

Approaches and practices that are culturally meaningful, suitable, sensitive, and culturally centred should be put in place for Aboriginal and other minority-group members in custody. For example, treatment strategies need to be holistic in order to address the entire complex of interrelated problems and needs of Aboriginal offenders (Reppucci, Fried, & Schmidt, 2002). As La Prairie et al. (1996) emphasize, interventions must reflect and incorporate Aboriginal traditions and culture, such as the use of sweat-lodges, healing circles, and smudging, to stand a better chance of meeting the needs of Aboriginal offenders, both young and old. As well, Hyde and La Prairie (1987) suggest that expanding the Aboriginal representation within the judiciary system can lead to a greater understanding of Aboriginal values and traditions and can influence the par-

ticipation of Aboriginal people in court in a positive manner, thus improving relations between criminal justice authorities and Aboriginal peoples.

As well, even though Canadians as a society are more concerned about individuality than collectivity, Kingwell (2000), Rosenberg (2000), and Currie (2000) strongly advocate for a community approach to responding to Aboriginal youth in the justice system. They stress that the system must find ways of involving diverse communities either by creating community-based models and programs and/or by creating partnerships between the government and marginalized communities. Hyde and La Prairie (1987) found that crimes committed by Aboriginal people are very different from crimes committed by non-Aboriginals: Aboriginals commit more violent and social disorder offences than non-Aboriginals, but commit far fewer property offences and almost no crimes for profit (i.e., drug trafficking, fraud, and armed robberies) when compared with non-Aboriginal people.

A community-wide focus that addresses and sustains compassionate relationships is also recommended as the best way to meet the needs of Aboriginal female offenders (Green & Healy, 2003). Programming and treatment for Aboriginal females must include cultural parenting traditions, community ways of life, peer-support networking, and, ultimately, the development of an indigenous law system founded on family and kinship relations rather than on "relationships of force" (Youngblood Henderson, in Green & Healy, 2003, p. 102). Any approach that takes into account the experiences of minority groups must grasp and struggle with the implications of centuries of oppression and marginalization and assist people in assuming their legitimate place within society.

Acknowledging Gender

In her review of 23 gender-specific programs for girls operating in the United States, Means (2002) states that one solution to working effectively with girls is to "stop squeezing girls into a justice system designed for boys. Rather, design specific programming based on the experiences of girls" (p. 5). She also recommends following the suggestions provided by Chesney-Lind and Brown (1999) and Bloom and Covington (2001), which state that effective programs for incarcerated girls and women must combine a culturally sensitive approach that supports them in all facets of their lives. For example, counselling and interventions that address girls' multiple needs, including assistance with recovery from sexual abuse and violence, need to be combined with educational and occupational support and involvement with well-functioning role models and the chance to live in non-chaotic communities.

Means (2002) notes that gender-specific programming does more than merely focus on girls; it "takes into account the developmental needs of girls at adolescence, a critical stage of gender identity formation. It nurtures and reinforces "femaleness" as a positive identity with natural strengths" (p. 19). Means also notes that there is no one program or approach that can be expected to work for all girls in all places, and recommends instead a process for developing interventions that fit local needs. Such a process is founded upon a clear understanding of local systems and local data and includes broad representation from, and coordination among, girl-serving agencies, juvenile justice practitioners, and the police.

Chesney-Lind and Okamoto (2001), in examining the relationships between patterns in girls' delinquency and gender responsive interventions, found that in designing programs for girls, their greater emotionality; their gender-specific developmental and therapeutic needs, especially their needs for supported recovery from trauma and abuse; and their ability to elicit strong gender-based behavioural and emotional responses from workers need to be considered. Chesney-Lind and Okamoto also noted girls' positive responses to cognitive behavioural interventions and interventions that were aimed at teaching their parents how to better communicate and parent them, and they pointed to the positive potential for the use of dialectical behaviour therapy (DBT) (see Trupin et al., 1999) with severely emotionally and behaviourally disturbed girls, especially those with diagnosed borderline personality disorder (a disorder that is not uncommon among delinquent and violent girls: cf. Lescheid et al., 2000). DBT combines validation, problem-solving, and group training in psycho-social skills and seems promising for those girls in custody suffering from mental health issues.

Also promising is the participatory staff development approach designed by Artz, Blais, and Nicholson (2000; 2001) and the youth custody workers who worked with them. In order to create a gender-sensitive approach to working with youth in custody, researchers, line staff, and supervisors worked together to develop a professional development training curriculum. The training modules that were developed blended a mix of theoretical knowledge about gender, culture, normative and atypical adolescent development, learning and communication styles, conflict resolution, and crisis intervention with practical group and role play activities for implementing the theoretical knowledge. The process of co-creating the curriculum was based on building buy-in and personal investment among all concerned. Much like what Means (2002) suggests as best practice, the emphasis was on process, broad representation, and inclusion, with special attention paid to the specific needs of workers and youth who encounter each other every day. Extensive consultation with all involved took place prior to implementation.

What has yet to take place is a systematic evaluation of the effects of this kind of staff development on youth, especially girls, in custody. It has been noted that so little research on gender-specific interventions has been conducted that it is too early to speak definitively about what does and does not work (Chesney-Lind and Okamoto, 2001; Means, 2002).

In Canada, girls' programs tend to be borrowed from interventions that were not expressly designed to be gender specific or culturally sensitive. Research on programming for girls who use aggression and violence is still sparse. Hoffman, Cummings, and Leschied (under review) emphasize the importance of premising research with girls on designs that compare girls to girls, in order to avoid making boys' behaviour the "gold standard" for adolescent behaviour. In their intervention program, which focused on educating girls about the negative effects of gender

socialization and about the impact of various forms of aggression, Hoffman et al. were able to demonstrate decreases in aggression and anti-social beliefs. Harder to change were negative attitudes toward females generally, which appeared connected to viewing other girls as competitors.

The competitive basis for social interdependence among girls is one area that seems to be central to the entrenchment of behavioural patterns that justify violence and is strongly implicated in holding in place a moral position that rationalizes the use of aggression and violence against others (see Artz, in press, in Moretti, Odgers, & Jackson and in Pepler, Madsen, Webster, & Levene, 2004, for an in-depth discussion). Perhaps explicit work aimed at changing girls' grasp of their social interdependencies (i.e., moving away from seeing the world as a place where they are engaged in a zero-sum game of survival that pits them against mostly other girls, to seeing a world in which they can experience trust and collaboration) could be added to the approach suggested by Hoffman et al. (under review).

CONCLUSION

In working toward more effectively and positively dealing with girls' participation in delinquency and crime, progress must occur in a number of areas. Primarily, it is important to understand that girls' involvement in delinquency and crime arises out of a complex set of psycho-social conditions that seem to draw in most of all those who are marginalized (psychologically and/or socially), and especially those girls who suffer from sexual abuse in its many forms. Also significant is an appreciation that while some similar factors appear to contribute to both girls' and boys' participation in delinquency and crime, differences also persist. Ongoing work on strain theory (see, for example, Broidy & Agnew, 1997; Katz, 2000) promises to help us with this as it takes into account the differential strains (stresses, challenges, forms of oppression, and marginalization) that girls and boys experience, along with taking into account the different experiences of minority groups, especially people of colour. General strain theory and revised strain theory appear to leave room for an understanding of different life courses and standpoints and, with that, an understanding that pathways to delinquency and crime emerge in psychological and sociocultural contexts that offer different strains and stresses to different people. Since no single pathway to delinquency and crime exists, our theories about delinquency and crime must provide explanations that adequately consider multifaceted human experiences and must be able to accurately reflect the within- and between-group differences in females and males and in different cultural and ethnic groups.

Much has to be done to reduce the use of incarceration in Canada, especially with girls—who, more than boys, seem to be placed into custody as a means of controlling non-criminal behaviour. The *Youth Criminal Justice Act* appears to support the notion that incarceration should be used only for violent and serious crime, and according to Green and Healy (2003) its implementation may result in

- greater use of diversionary alternatives, such as warnings, cautions, and referrals;

- ability of a judge, police officer, youth worker, prosecutor, or justice of the peace to call a case conference to discuss what needs to be done with a particular youth;

- increased use of restorative justice;

- move to more integrated, holistic, and cooperative approaches to justice that involve interagency and interdisciplinary responses; and

- sentencing of youth that does not result in punishment greater than would be given to an adult convicted for the same offence committed under similar circumstances.

Although the potential for positive change exists with the YCJA, how this Act will be interpreted and applied remains to be seen.

An additional challenge for Canadian youth justice workers (researchers, theorists, policy makers, and direct practitioners alike) at all levels is the need to adequately respond to all minority groups in our country, and the special responsibility to redress the shameful history of our treatment of First Nations people. The overrepresentation of First Nations youth and adults in our criminal justice system and in every category of social need in our society speaks loudly to centuries of oppression that must be addressed. Theories about delinquency and crime need to take into account the social construction of the conditions of crime. Policies and prevention and intervention strategies must be flexible enough to be tailored to individual needs, but must not ignore the firmly established systemic abuses that create fertile conditions for the oppressed group's participation in deviancy and crime as the only logical response under the circumstances.

We value individual rights and choices, but need to do far more about addressing structural inequities along gender, race, and class lines, inequities that contribute directly to delinquency and crime. The life worlds of girls who participate in delinquency and crime, especially those who carry these behaviours over into adulthood, reveal that the majority of women engaged in crime belong to social groups long recognized as marginalized and disadvantaged. It is important to counter the potential to react with shock to girls' involvement in delinquency and crime and confront notions that girls who do so are "so much worse" than boys. The involvement of any group in delinquency and crime is surely a signal that the social conditions that give rise to such behaviour are operative in their life worlds. Any rise in crime rates, rather than triggering outrage against a particular group, should trigger outrage against a collective willingness to allow a rise in the conditions that create these crime potentials.

References

Acoca, L. (1999). Investing in girls: A 21st century strategy. [electronic version] *Juvenile Justice, VI* (I). Washington, DC: Office of Juvenile Justice and Delinquency Prevention. Retrieved March 25, 2003 from: http://www.ncjrs.org/html/ojjdp/jjjournal1099/invest1.html.

Acoca, L., & Austin, J. (1996). *The crisis: Women in prison.* Report submitted to the Charles E. Culpeper Foundation. San Francisco, CA: National Council on Crime and Delinquency.

Acoca, L., & Dedel, K. (1998). *No place to hide: Understanding and meeting the needs of girls in the California Juvenile Justice System.* San Francisco, CA: National Council on Crime and Delinquency.

Alder, C. (1997). *"Passionate and willful" girls: confronting practice.* Paper presented to the Annual Meeting of the Academy of Criminal Justices Sciences. Louisville, KY.

American Bar Association & National Bar Association. (2001). *Justice by gender: The lack of appropriate prevention, diversion and treatment alternatives for girls in the justice system.* Report jointly issued by the American Bar Association and the National Bar Association, Washington, DC, May 1, 2001.

Artz, S. (1998). *Sex, power and the violent school girl.* Toronto: Trifolium.

Artz, S. (in press). Revisiting the moral domain: Using social interdependence theory to understand adolescent girls' perspectives on the use of violence. In M. Moretti, C. Odgers, & M. Jackson (Eds.), *Girls and aggression: Contributing factors and intervention principles.* Boston, MA: Kluwer Academic Publishers.

Artz, S., Blais, M., & Nicholson, D. (2000). *Developing girls' custody units: Phase I report.* Unpublished report to Justice Canada, Youth Justice, under Order No. 45000117788.

Artz, S., & Nicholson, D. (in press). *Understanding aggressive girls in Canada: A literature review.* Greensboro, NC: ERIC-CASS.

Artz, S., & Nicholson, D. (2002). *Aggressive girls: Overview paper.* Ottawa: Health Canada, National Clearinghouse on Family Violence.

B.C. Police Services Branch. (1998). *B.C. Crime Trends.* Victoria, BC: Ministry of the Attorney General.

Baines, M., & Alder, C. (1996). Are girls more difficult to work with? Youth workers' perspectives in juvenile justice and related areas. *Crime & Delinquency, 42*(3), 467–485.

Bala, N. (2001). *Brief on the proposed new Youth Criminal Justice Act (Bill C-7)*, presented to the Senate Legal and Constitutional Affairs Committee, October 24, 2001. [electronic version] Retrieved November 25, 2002 from http://qsilver.queensu.ca/law/papers/jcjabrief-oct2001.htm.

Bannerji, H. (1987). Introducing racism: Towards an anti-racist feminism. In Y. Jiwani, K. D'Aoust, S. Grewal, B. Bunjun, H. Kaur & T. Conley (Eds.), *Intersecting inequalities: Immigrant women of colour, violence & health care.* [electronic version]. Retrieved November 14, 2003 from http://www.harbour.sfu.ca/freda/articles/hlth.htm.

Beyer, M. (1998, Summer). Mental health care for children in correction. *Children's Legal Rights Journal.*

Beyer, M. (1999). Recognizing the child in the delinquent. *Kentucky Children's Rights Journal, 7* (1).

Bloom, B., & Covington, S. (2001). *Effective gender-responsive interventions in juvenile justice: Addressing the lives of delinquent girls.* Paper presented at the 2001 Annual Meeting of the American Society of Criminology. Atlanta, Georgia, November 7–10, 2001.

Boe, R. (2000). *Aboriginal inmates: Demographic trends and projections.* [electronic version]. Forum on Corrections Research, Vol. 12, 1, Research Branch, Correctional Service of Canada. Retrieved November 13, 2003 from http://www.csc-scc.gc.ca/text/pblct/forum/v12n1/indexe.shtml.

Broadhurst, R. G. (1996). Aboriginality and crime in Australia: Estimates of differential risk of penal involvement and explanations of Aboriginal crime. In C. La Prairie, P. Mun, B. Steinke, E. Buller, & S. McCue (Eds.), *Examining aboriginal corrections in Canada.* [electronic version]. Ministry of the Solicitor General. Retrieved November 14, 2003 from http://www.sgc.gc.ca/publications/abor_corrections/199614_e.pdf.

Broidy, L., & Agnew, R. (1997). Gender and crime: A general strain theory perspective. *Journal of Research in Crime and Delinquency, 34*(3),

275–306. Reprinted with permission in M. Chesney-Lind & L. Pasko (Eds.) (2004) *Girls women and crime* (pp. 3–23). Thousand Oaks, CA: Sage Publications Inc.

Canada. Department of Justice. (2002). *A one-day snapshot of Aboriginal youth in custody across Canada.* Bittle, S., Quann, N., Hattem, T., & Muise, D. (Eds.), Youth Justice Research, Research and Statistics Division. Retrieved November 11, 2003 from http://canada.justice.gc.ca/en/ps/rs/rep/snapshot.pdf.

Canada. Department of Justice. (2003). *Youth Criminal Justice Act explained.* Retrieved October 29, 2003 from http:canada.justice.gc.ca/en/ps/yj/repository/4refrenc/03figres/4030002a.html.

Canada, G. (1998). *Reaching up for manhood: Transforming the lives of boys in America.* Boston, MA: Beacon Press.

Canadian Association of Elizabeth Fry Societies. (n.d.). *Labelling young women as violent: Vilification of the most vulnerable.* Ottawa: Author.

Canadian Centre for Justice Statistics. (2000). *Sentencing young offenders in Canada, 1998/99.* Cat. No. 85-002-XPE2000007. Ottawa: Statistics Canada.

Canadian Centre for Justice Statistics. (2003). *An examination of sex differences in delinquency.* Crime and Justice research paper series. Ottawa: Statistics Canada and the Department of Justice Canada.

Chesney-Lind, M., Artz, S., & Nicholson, D. (2002). Girls' delinquency and violence: Making the case for gender-responsive programming. In L. Rapp-Paglicci, A. Roberts, & J. Wodarski (Eds.), *Handbook of violence* (pp. 190–214). New York, NY: Longman.

Chesney-Lind, M., & Brown, M. (1999). Girls and violence: An overview. In D. J. Flannery & C.R. Huff (Eds.), *Youth violence: Prevention, intervention, and social policy* (pp. 171–199). Washington, DC: American Psychiatric Press.

Chesney-Lind, M., & Pasko, L. (Eds.). (2004a). *Girls women and crime.* Thousand Oaks, CA: Sage Publications Inc.

Chesney-Lind, M., & Pasko, L. (Eds.). (2004b). *The female offender: Girls women and crime,* 2nd ed. Thousand Oaks, CA: Sage Publications.

Chesney-Lind, M., & Okamoto, S. (2001). Gender matters: Patterns in girls' delinquency and gender responsive programming. *Journal of Forensic Psychology Practice, 1*(3), 1–28.

Chesney-Lind, M., & Shelden, R. (1998). *Girls, delinquency and juvenile justice.* (2nd ed.). Belmont, CA: West/Wadsworth.

Corrado, R., Odgers, C., & Cohen, I. (2000, April). The incarceration of female young offenders: Protection for whom? *Canadian Journal of Criminology 42*(2), 189–207.

Correctional Service of Canada. (2000). A profile of Aboriginal offenders in federal facilities and serving time in the community. [electronic version] In S. Trevethan, J. P. Moore, & C. Rastin, (Eds.). *Forum on Corrections Research, 14*(3). Retrieved November 11, 2003 from www.csc-scc.gc.ca/text/pblct/forum/v14n3/index_e.shtml.

Correctional Service of Canada. (2002). A needs profile of serious and/or violent Aboriginal youth in prison. In R. Corrado, & I. Cohen (Eds.), *Forum on Corrections Research, 14*(3). Retrieved November 11, 2003 from www. csc-scc.gc.ca/text/pblct/forum/v14n3/v14n3a7e.pdf.

Craig, W., & Pepler, D. (1997). A developmental perspective on conduct disorder. In C. Essau & F. Peterman (Eds.), *Developmental psychopathology: Epidemiology, diagnosis, and treatment* (pp. 97–140). Amsterdam: Harwood.

Crick, N., & Grotpeter, J. (1996). Children's treatment by peers: Victims of relational and overt aggression. *Development and Psychopathology, 8*(2), 367–380.

Currie, A. (2000). Some aspects of access to justice in Canada. Research and Statistics Division, Department of Justice Canada. In M. Rosenberg (Ed.), *Expanding horizons: Rethinking access to justice in Canada.* Proceedings of a Symposium Organized By the Department of Justice Canada. Retrieved November 13, 2003 from http://canada.justice.gc.ca/en/ps/rs/rep/ehorizons-e.pdf.

DeKeseredy, W. (2000). *Women, crime and the Canadian criminal justice system.* Cincinnati, OH: Anderson.

Dell, C., & Boe, R. (1998). *Female young offenders in Canada: Revised edition.* [electronic version] Ottawa: Correctional Service of Canada. Retrieved February 3, 2003 from http://www.csc-scc.gc.ca/text/rsrch/reports/r80/r80e_e.shtml.

Garbarino, J. (1999). *Lost boys: Why our sons turn violent and how we can save them.* New York, NY: Free Press.

Geller, G. (1987). Young women in conflict with the law. In E. Adelberg & C. Currie (Eds.), *Too few to count.* Vancouver, BC: Press Gang.

Gilbert, S. (2000). *A field guide to boys and girls.* New York, NY: HarperCollins.

Gilligan, C. (1982). *In a different voice: Psychological theory and women's development.* Cambridge, MA: Harvard University Press.

Green, R., & Healy, K. (2003). *Tough on kids: Rethinking approaches to youth justice.* Saskatoon, SK: Purich.

Hoffman, S., Cummings, A., & Lescheid, A. (under review). Treating aggression in high-risk adolescent girls. *Canadian Journal of Counselling.*

Hudson, A. (1989). Troublesome girls: Towards alternative definitions and policies. In M. Cain (Ed.), *Growing up good: Policing the behavior of girls in Europe.* London: Sage.

Hyde, M., & LaPrairie, C. (1987). Amerindian police crime prevention. Working paper prepared for the Solicitor General of Canada. In *Report of the Aboriginal Justice Inquiry of Manitoba, Aboriginal Justice Implementation Commission.* [electronic version]. November 1999 Vol. 1, The Justice System and Aboriginal People. [electronic version]. Retrieved November 11, 2003 from http://www.ajic.mb.ca/volume.html.

Indra, M. D. (1979). South Asian stereotypes in the Vancouver Press. In Y. Jiwani (Ed.),

Culture, violence, and inequality. Keynote speech at the March 1997 workshop: Violence against Women: Meeting the cross-cultural challenge. [electronic version]. Retrieved November 12, 2003 from http://www.harbour.sfu.ca/freda/articles/culture.htm.

Jiwani, Y. (1997). *Culture, violence, and inequality.* Keynote speech at the March 1997 workshop: Violence against women: Meeting the cross-cultural challenge. [electronic version]. Retrieved November 12, 2003 from http://www.harbour.sfu.ca/freda/articles/culture.htm.

Jiwani, Y., Gorkoff, K., Vardy-Dell, G., & Normandeau, S. (1999). *Violence prevention and the girl child.* [electronic version]. London: The Alliance of Five Research Centres on Violence. Retrieved November 12, 2003 from http://www.harbour.sfu.ca/freda/reports/gc.htm.

Jones, C. (1998). *New-age bullies use cyberspace to harass peers.* www.theage.com.au/daily/981006/news/news15.html.

Katz, R. (2000). Explaining girls' and women's crime and desistance in the context of their victimization experiences. *Violence Against Women, 6*(6), 633–660, reprinted with permission in M. Chesney-Lind & L. Pasko (Eds.), (2004). *Girls Women and Crime* (pp. 24–41). Thousand Oaks, CA: Sage Publications Inc.

Kersten, J. (1990). A gender-specific look at patterns of violence in juvenile institutions: Or are girls really "more difficult to handle"? *International Journal of Sociology of the Law, 18*, 473–493.

Kingwell, M. (2000). Citizen access to justice: Issues and trends for 2000 and after. In M. Rosenberg (Ed.), *Expanding horizons: Rethinking access to justice in Canada.* Proceedings of a Symposium Organized by the Department of Justice Canada. [electronic version]. Retrieved November 13, 2003 from http://www.harbour.sfu.ca/freda/reports/gc.htm.

Kowalski, M., & Caputo, T. (2001). Recidivism in youth court: An examination of the impact of age, gender, and prior record. In T. Fleming, P. O'Reilly, & B. Clark (Eds.), *Youth injustice: Canadian perspectives* (2nd ed.). (pp. 483–510). Toronto: Canadian Scholars' Press.

Lanctôt, N., Émond, C., & LeBlanc, M. (in press). Adjudicated females' participation in violence from adolescence to adulthood: Results from a longitudinal study. In M. Moretti, C. Odgers, & M. Jackson (Eds.), *Girls and aggression: Contributing factors and intervention principles.* Boston: Kluwer.

La Prairie, C., Mun, P., Steinke, B., Buller, E., & McCue, S. (1996). *Examining aboriginal corrections in Canada.* [electronic version]. Ministry of the Solicitor General. Retrieved November 13, 2003 from http://www.sgc.gc.ca/publications/abor_corrections/199614_e.pdf.

Leschied, A., Cummings, A., Van Brunschot, M., Cunningham, A., & Saunders, A. (2000). *Female adolescent aggression: A review of the literature and the correlates of aggression* (User Report No. 2000-04). Ottawa: Solicitor General Canada.

Li, P. (2000). *Cultural diversity in Canada: The social construction of racial differences.* [electronic version]. Strategic Issues Series. Research and Statistics Division. Retrieved November 12, 2003 from http://canada.justice.gc.ca/en/ps/rs/rep/RP2002-8.pdf.

Mallea, P. (1999). *Getting tough on kids: Young offenders and the "law and order" agenda.* Winnipeg: Canadian Centre for Policy Alternatives.

Means, R. (2002). *Decreasing the raise (sic) in female delinquency through gender specific program (sic) and proactive police involvement.* Unpublished Report. Department of Interdisciplinary Technology as part of School of Police Staff and Command Program, Eastern Michigan University, Michigan, USA.

Merten, D. (1997). The meaning of meanness: Popularity, competition and conflict among junior high school girls. *Sociology of Education, 70*, 175–191.

Miller, J. B. (1976). *Toward a new psychology of women.* Boston: Beacon Press.

Ministry of Attorney General. (2000). *Recidivism in the B.C. offender population.* Management Report No. 2000:0173. Victoria, BC: Province of British Columbia.

Moffit, T., Caspi, A., Rutter, M., & Silva, P. (2001). *Sex differences in antisocial behaviour: Conduct disorder, delinquency, and violence in the Dunedin Longitudinal Study.* Cambridge: Cambridge University Press.

Moretti, M., & Odgers, C. (in press). Aggressive and violent girls: Prevalence, profiles and contributing factors, In Corrado, R., Roesch, R., & Hart, S. (Eds.). *Multi-problem and violent youth: A foundation for comparative research.* Amsterdam: IOS Press.

Moretti, M., Odgers, C., & Jackson, M. (Eds.) (in press). *Girls and aggression: Contributing factors and intervention principles.* Boston: Kluwer.

Ng, R. (1994). Sexism and racism in the university: Analyzing personal experience. In Y. Jiwani (Ed.), *Culture, violence, and inequality.* Keynote speech at the March 1997 workshop: Violence against women: Meeting the cross-cultural challenge. [electronic version]. Retrieved November 12, 2003 from http://www.harbour.sfu.ca/freda/articles/culture.htm.

Okamoto, S. (2002). The challenges of male practitioners working with female youth clients. *Child and Youth Care Forum, 31*(4), 257–268.

Parent, C. (1986). Actualités et bibliographies: La protection chevalresque ou les representations masculines du traitement des femmes dans la justice pénale. *Déviance et Société, 10*(2), 147–175.

Pate, K. (2002). *Women and girls in prison: Canada's alternative to equality and justice.* Paper presented to the Winnipeg Women's Legal Education and Action Fund, October 24, 2002. Retrieved January 29, 2004 from http://www.elizabethfy.ca/confernc/leaf/1.htm.

Pepler, D., Madsen, K., Webster, C., & Levene, E. (Eds.) (2004). *Development and treatment of girlhood aggression.* Hillsdale, NJ: Lawrence Erlbaum.

Pipher, M. (1994). *Reviving Ophelia: Saving the selves of adolescent girls.* New York, NY: Grosset/Putnam.

Plummer, D. (1999). *One of the boys: Masculinity, homophobia and modern manhood.* New York, NY: Harrington Park Press.

Pollack, W. (1998). *Real boys: Rescuing our sons from the myths of boyhood.* New York, NY: Henry Holt.

Reitsma-Street, M. (1989). More control than care: A critique of historical and contemporary laws for delinquency and neglect of children in Ontario. *Canadian Journal of Women and the Law, 3*(2), 510–530.

Reitsma-Street, M. (2001). Justice for Canadian girls: A 1990's update. In T. Fleming, P. O'Reilly, & B. Clark (Eds.). *Youth injustice: Canadian perspectives* (2nd ed.), (pp. 283–311). Toronto: Canadian Scholars' Press.

Reitsma-Street, M. (in press). Connecting policies, girls, and violence. In M. Moretti, C. Odgers, & M. Jackson (Eds.) *Girls and aggression: Contributing factors and intervention principles.* Boston: Kluwer.

Report of the Commission on Systemic Racism in the Ontario Criminal Justice System (1995). *In Racism in the justice system.* [electronic version]. Toronto: Queen's Printer for Ontario. Retrieved November 18, 2003 from http://www.crr.ca/EN/MediaCentre/FactSheets/eMedCen_FacShtRacismInJusticeSys.htm.

Reppucci, N. D., Fried, C. S., & Schmidt, M. G. (2002). Youth violence: Risk and protective factors. In R. Corrado & I. Cohen (Eds.), *A needs profile of serious and/or violent aboriginal youth in custody.* [electronic version]. Forum on Corrections Research, 14(3), Retrieved November 13, 2003 from http://www.csc-scc.gc.ca/text/pblct/forum/v14n3/index_e.shtml.

Rosenberg, M. (Ed.). (2000). *Expanding horizons: Rethinking access to justice in Canada.* Proceedings of a Symposium Organized by the Department of Justice Canada. [electronic version]. Retrieved November 13, 2003 from http://www.harbour.sfu.ca/freda/reports/gc.htm.

Satzewich, V. (1998). *Racism and social inequality in Canada: Concepts, controversies and strategies of resistance.* Toronto: Thompson Educational Publishing Inc.

Shaw, M. (1991). *Survey of federally sentenced women: Report to the task force on federally sentenced women on the prison survey.* [electronic version]. Ottawa: Solicitor General Canada. Retrieved November 14, 2003 from http://canada.justice.gc.ca/en/ps/rs/rep/RP2002-8.pdf.

Sinclair, R., & Boe, R. (1998). *Male young offenders in Canada: Recent trends.* [electronic version] Ottawa: Correctional Service of Canada. Retrieved February 3, 2003 from http://www.csc-scc.gc.ca/text/rsrch/briefs/b22/b22e_e.shtml.

The Society for Children and Youth of British Columbia. (2001). Youth Justice—Position Statement 5. Retrieved October 29, 2003 from http://www.scyofbc.ca/advocacy/youth_justice.html.

Sprott, J., & Doob, A. (2004). Trends in youth crime in Canada. In K.M. Campbell (Ed.), *Understanding Youth Justice in Canada.* Toronto: Pearson Education Canada.

Sprott, J., & Doob, A. (2003, January). It's all in the denominator: Trends in the processing of girls in Canada's youth courts. *Canadian Journal of Criminology and Criminal Justice,* 73–80.

Statistics Canada (2002). *Adults and youths charged by offence category and sex, provinces and territories, 1996–2001* [electronic version]. Ottawa: Statistics Canada. Retrieved February

4, 2003 from http://www.statcan.ca/english/freepub/82-221XIE/01002/tables/html/22142.htm.

Tremblay, R. (2000). The origins of youth violence. *Isuma, 1*(2), 19–24.

Trupin, E., Stewart, D., Boesky, L., McClurg, B., Beach, B., Hormann, S., & Baltrusis, R. (1999, February). *Evaluation of a dialectical behavior therapy with incarcerate female juvenile offenders.* Paper presented at the 11th annual research conference A system of care for children's mental health: Expanding the research base, Tampa, FL.

United Nations. (2001). *Seventh United Nations survey of crime trends and operations of criminal justice systems, covering the period 1998–2000.* Retrieved October 20, 2003 from http://www.unodc.org/pdf/crime/seventh_survey/7pv.pdf.

van Dijk, T. A. (1993). Elite discourse and racism. *Sage series on race and ethnic relations, 6.* New York, NY: Sage.

Walkerdine, V., Lucey, H., & Melody, J. (2001). *Growing up girl: Psychosocial explorations of gender and class.* Houndmills, Basingstoke, Hampshire: Palgrave.

Notes

1. However, provisions under the *Youth Criminal Justice Act (YCJA)* have introduced new regulations regarding custody and supervision so that youth will now serve two-thirds of their sentence in custody, with one served on community supervision (sec. 42(2)(n)).

2. See Artz and Nicholson, 2002, and Artz and Nicholson, in press, for a review of this literature.

3. This research was funded by Justice Canada.

chapter fifteen

Aboriginal Youth and the Criminal Justice System

*Larry N. Chartrand**

Faculty of Law
University of Ottawa

INTRODUCTION

For Aboriginal peoples, the failure of the punitive/deterrence model of criminal justice comes as no surprise. Aboriginal societies have generally not subscribed to the punishment model of crime control, as they have valued a different approach to dealing with anti-social behaviour within their communities. It is an approach that places healing, teaching, and guidance as the preferred means to achieving peaceful communities. It is an approach that has much in common with the contemporary rehabilitation and restorative approaches to justice.

To the extent that the recent *Youth Criminal Justice Act* (YCJA) reflects a restorative approach, there is an increased opportunity for Aboriginal justice perspectives to be accommodated. If these opportunities are realized, it is likely they will have a positive impact on reducing Aboriginal youth crime and victimization in Canada. There are aspects of the YCJA, such as justice committees, justice conferences, Aboriginality awareness, medical assessment processes, and probation modification powers, that encouragingly affect rehabilitation efforts and therefore indirectly address the overrepresentation of Aboriginal youth in custody.

The first part of this chapter will be a review of Aboriginal youth over-involvement in the criminal justice system, involving a comparison of Aboriginal and Canadian justice concepts and processes, particularly in relation to sentencing. The mismatch between Aboriginal expectations and mainstream expectations is one part of the reason for

*The author would like to thank the Research and Statistics Division and the Policy Centre for Victim Issues of the Department of Justice Canada in allowing portions of this chapter, which was based on research conducted for the Department, to be published.

Aboriginal overrepresentation in the criminal justice system. It is part of the larger experience of cultural dislocation due to the negative impact of colonization and racism on current social and economic circumstances. This review will then lead into a discussion of how holistic healing approaches to youth crime offer a more humane means of dealing with this problem.

The last section of this chapter will examine the specific mechanisms within the new YCJA to determine how well they can accommodate Aboriginal perspectives and processes. While the YCJA offers much promise, there are significant barriers to implementing positive change found in both the lack of provincial resources to fully implement the spirit of the YCJA and the attitudinal resistance to the paradigm shift that the Act requires. Even if these barriers are overcome, the YCJA is still largely a criminal justice response to Aboriginal youth social adjustment problems. Rehabilitation is only one of the options promoted by the Act, as proportional accountability (i.e., punishment) remains an important and integral part. Although custody is to be used sparingly, it is still a significant part of the tools available. Aboriginal healing responses to crime must still largely find their expression in the gaps and gullies of the discretion built into the system.

GENERAL DEMOGRAPHICS OF ABORIGINAL YOUTH IN CANADA

In the 2001 census, 976 305 people identified themselves as Aboriginal (Statistics Canada, 2003).[1] This represents 3.3 per-

cent of the Canadian population and a jump of 22 percent since the 1996 census. It is not surprising, then, that more than a third of Aboriginal youth are under 14 years old as of 2001. The Aboriginal population is fast-growing, is much younger than the general population, and has twice the birth rate of the non-Aboriginal population (Silver & Mallet, 2002). In Saskatchewan, the median age of an Aboriginal person is 18.5 years, compared to the median age of 38.8 years for a non-Aboriginal person, a difference of more than 20 years (Senate of Canada, 2003).[2] In Manitoba, 37.7 percent of the Aboriginal population is below the age of 15, compared to 20.1 percent of the non-Aboriginal population (Silver & Mallet, 2002).

Thus, not only are there likely cultural differences between Aboriginal and non-Aboriginal people, there are also generational differences. One population is getting older (the one with the political power and resources); the other is getting younger (the one without political power and resources). According to a recent study by the Canadian Council on Social Development, Aboriginal people were more than twice as likely to live in poverty as non-Aboriginal people (Canadian Council, 2000). More specifically, half of Aboriginal youth living in cities lived below the low-income cut-off (Senate of Canada, 2003).

Almost half of Aboriginal people live in urban centres, with a significant number in the Prairie cities. The highest proportions are found in Winnipeg (8%) and Saskatoon (9%) (Senate of Canada, 2003). In some parts of Winnipeg, (the north end and inner city), the Aboriginal population is as high as 20 percent of the population;

such a high concentration is not found in any other part of Canada (Canada & Manitoba, 2002). Moreover, one in four children are six years or younger in this area (Silver & Mallet, 2002).

CHARACTERISTICS OF ABORIGINAL YOUTH CRIME AND VICTIMIZATION

In 1999 in Canada, Aboriginal youth accounted for nearly one-quarter of youth admissions to custody, yet they represent only 7 percent of youth aged 12 to 17 (Statistics Canada, 2001). The overrepresentation is most pronounced in the Prairies, British Columbia, and Ontario. In Manitoba, for example, 75 percent of sentenced custody admissions were identified as Aboriginal youth even though only 16 percent of Manitoba's youth population is Aboriginal. Such rates of disproportionate incarceration of Aboriginal youth in custody present a major crisis within the Aboriginal community (Statistics Canada, 2001). In one study, it was found that, statistically, Aboriginal youth had a better chance of going to jail than graduating from high school (Saskatchewan, 1992). Based on these rates, Green and Healy (2001) have predicted that this crisis will grow unless drastic changes are forthcoming:

> If the current high number of Aboriginal youth already in custody were to increase at the same rate as the over-all Aboriginal population, the resulting effect would be crippling, both within the youth justice system and Canadian society as a whole. (p. 91)

In March of 2002, a snapshot of Aboriginal youth in custody across Canada found that the typical Aboriginal youth was a status Indian male between 16 and 17 years of age who was guilty of a property-related offence. A majority lived and committed the offence in an urban area (Canada, Department of Justice, 2003).

Not only is the Aboriginal population overrepresented in terms of groups of offenders, it is overrepresented among victims as well. Thirty-five percent of Aboriginal people report being a victim of crime, compared to 26 percent of non-Aboriginal people (Statistics Canada, 2001). In terms of violent crime, Aboriginal people are three times more likely to be victims than non-Aboriginal people (Statistics Canada, 2001). Furthermore, Aboriginal violence occurs predominantly in Aboriginal communities, and the majority of the victims of Aboriginal offenders are Aboriginal themselves (Canada, Department of Justice, 2000).

Although victimization of Aboriginal people is much higher than that of non-Aboriginal people, statistics show that it is Aboriginal women and children who largely bear the burden of victimization (Health Canada, 1996). There is also some evidence that youth victimization is a serious problem in Aboriginal communities (Kingsley & Mark, 2000). However, there is no comprehensive survey of Aboriginal youth victimization in Canada; nor does the *Statistics Canada Profile* (2001) provide a breakdown by age or address the issue of youth victimization. This omission may be partly explained by the fact that much of the literature categorizes victimization of Aboriginal youth and women within the category of family violence. For example, there is a considerable amount of literature that examines the staggering problem of Aboriginal child abuse within the framework of family violence. For example, one study by Dumont-Smith and Sioui-Labelle (1991) found that 40 percent of children in some northern communities were victims of family violence.

A great deal of the literature on Aboriginal youth victimization is examined within the framework of family and domestic violence because of the very high prevalence of such victimization in this context (Royal Commission on Aboriginal Peoples, 1996b). Recent studies continue to support the conclusions of older research that domestic violence is epidemic in Aboriginal communities. For example, a study conducted by La Prairie (1995) regarding Aboriginal victimization and family violence experienced in a number of urban centres in Canada showed disturbingly high rates of domestic violence. Important findings revealed that 74 percent of the respondents experienced family violence, and 49 percent experienced child sexual abuse. Perhaps one of the most important findings that La Prairie makes is that the experience of family victimization is linked to subsequent victimization and criminal activity in later life. The more severe the child abuse, the more likely the child will become involved in juvenile delinquency, particularly males. Moreover, such male children are at a significantly higher risk to repeat the cycle of violence toward their future partners (McGillivary & Comaskey, 1996).

The link between childhood victimization and the perpetuation of a cycle of violence became painfully obvious in the work of Absolon and Winchester (1994) for the Royal Commission on Aboriginal

Peoples (RCAP). The authors also discuss how Aboriginal identity can be a factor in exacerbating the inability to cope with victimization. Absolon and Winchester prepared a report that identified various themes and issues from urban learning circles. In particular many of the participants talked about their "survival" of the residential schools and the child welfare system. They reported:

> Although not all people who went through foster care or adoption had terrible experiences, in most cases their Aboriginal identity suffered because the majority of them were placed in non-Aboriginal homes where their identity was either overtly humiliated, consciously denied or simply overlooked through ignorance. Only one woman, from the Saskatoon circle, told about how her adoptive parents always acknowledged her Aboriginal identity, always told her to be proud, and admitted their own ignorance and inability to tell her more about it, though they supported her efforts to learn. At the other end of the spectrum were stories about multiple foster homes, shaming of anything Aboriginal and all forms of abuse. The men in the inmate's circle were testimony to this pattern as most were the children of residential school students and were graduates of the child welfare system. These men expressed the anger and rage of their victimization with great frankness.

Thus, there are unique issues connected to society's negative attitudes about Aboriginal identity that may contribute to increased pathological responses, including the perpetuation of violence as learned behaviour.

All of these deprivations will likely have an effect on development and in many cases may manifest in violence and aggression toward the self and/or others. One example is a study by Kingsley and

Mark (2000) that documents the experience of Aboriginal children and youth involved in the sex trade.[3] It supports the conclusions of other research that Aboriginal children and youth represent a disproportionate percentage of commercially sexually exploited youth in Canada, and that in some western cities:

> In some communities, the visible sex trade is 90% Aboriginal ... While Aboriginal people make up only two to three per cent of Canada's population, in many places they form the majority of sex trade workers. In Winnipeg, for example, virtually all street-involved youth are Aboriginal. (pp. 8–12)

Kingsley and Mark identified several factors that contribute to an Aboriginal youth entering the sex trade and simultaneously create barriers to their exit. Aboriginal-specific barriers included the high risk of Aboriginal youth to escape dysfunctional families and their having no visible support or place to turn for help. They speak of a lack of role models and elders and of racism and how it contributes to low self-esteem, which was one of the largest influencing factors in their lives. Both Kingsley and Mark (2000) and Elliott (1997) underline the fact that historical, cultural, and economic factors experienced by Aboriginal children and youth are different and unique and that these "factors limit the application of non-Aboriginal research, programs, and policy to Aboriginal youth-at-risk" (Kingsley & Mark 2000, p. 42).

In terms of "solutions," Kingsley and Mark found that the youth in their study regarded cultural connection as important in any healing strategy. They state:

> The theme of finding strength and power from their Aboriginal heritage was of fundamental importance to almost all youth who participated in the consultations.... Cultural connection for these youth can take a variety of forms, including sweat lodges, pow wows, fasting, artwork and oral traditions. The vast majority of the youth expressed interest in having access to a Native center which would both help them exit the sex trade and guide them on their healing path. (p. 66-67)

FETAL ALCOHOL SPECTRUM DISORDER AND ABORIGINAL YOUTH CRIME

One area that has been the subject of increased attention with respect to the involvement of Aboriginal youth in criminal activity, is that of fetal alcohol spectrum disorder (FASD). FASD is an organic brain disorder that occurs in a fetus who is exposed to a certain amount of alcohol (Conry & Fast, 2000). Although the disorder may affect anyone in society, it is of great concern to the Aboriginal community, due in part to research that indicates a significant overrepresentation of Aboriginal people with FASD (Masotti et. al., 2003).

Studies have found that the prevalence of individuals with FASD within the Aboriginal community is estimated to range from 25 to 200 per 1000 births, whereas the prevalence rate for the general Canadian population is said to vary from 1 to 10 per 1000 births (Masotti et al., 2003, p. 1). In a study of offenders sentenced in the criminal justice system over a 12-year period by Chartrand and Forbes-Chilibeck (2003), 42 reported cases were identified in which the offender being sentenced had a diagnosis of FASD or suspected FASD.[4] Of the 42 cases, 31were confirmed to be Aboriginal offenders, 3 were non-Aboriginal, and 6 were unknown. These data are consistent with judicial impressions as explained by one judge in the Yukon:

> In the Yukon, estimates suggest that at least half of the offenders through our courts are mentally challenged as a consequence of FAS (fetal alcohol syndrome), FAE (fetal alcohol effects) or early life trauma. Many have been to jail so often, they have become institutionalized…. These are the people who fill our jails. (*R. v. Elias*, 2001)

Furthermore, of the 42 cases reviewed by the Chartrand and Forbes-Chillibeck study, 21 were youth offenders under the age of 19 years. This suggests that youth offenders are significantly overrepresented in the reported cases of sentencing involving offenders with FASD. This situation is clearly problematic, given that these youth are being sentenced for crimes that involve compromised abilities to control their own behaviour because of their disability. A study by Streissguth et al. (1996) confirms that those with FASD have an increased likelihood to be in trouble with the law; she found that, of 415 individuals with FASD in British Columbia, 60 percent aged 12 and over had. Thus, the justice system is sentencing and incarcerating individuals undeserving of the label "criminal." Consequently, Green and Healy (2003) ask obvious questions: "Why aren't these young people in the care of child protection or mental health professionals? Why are they squarely within the confines of the youth justice system?" (p. 70).

Offenders with FASD have an organic brain disorder that puts them at risk of behaving inappropriately and thereby increase their likelihood to commit crime. Thus, while they are in need of treatment as opposed to punishment, many courts are frustrated and at a loss as to what to do because of the lack of therapeutic services available (*R. v. C.J.M.*, 2000). The words of Judge Trueman in *C.J.M.* are illustrative of this frustration:

> In all cases of brain injury, however caused, permanent or otherwise, there exists the proven advantage of early intervention, to maximize social skills and shape behaviour. To incarcerate an individual in a prison setting that fails to recognize FAS, and fails to accommodate those with the disability, is to further the development of socially maladaptive behaviours that occur from forcing those with compromised mental functions to respond daily in a hostile environment. This is not only detrimental to them, but to the rest of society when they are ultimately released. (para. 82)

Judges have few options but to incarcerate these offenders as there are no other appropriate therapeutic options available for them (Chartrand & Forbes-Chillibeck, 2003).

Research in this area shows that individuals with FASD are also highly vulnerable to victimization. In one study, evidence for high rates of neglect (86%), physical abuse (52%), and sexual abuse (35%) were found in the histories of those with FASD (Boland, et al., 1998). FASD individuals are at greater risk of being victimized and are also more likely to be in conflict with the law. And, since Aboriginal peoples are disproportionately affected by FASD, this increases the already high risk of Aboriginal offenders becoming victims within the criminal justice system. Yet, there is no research that examines the extent of victimization of Aboriginal people with FASD. This is a significant gap in the research given the extent of victimization by those most vulnerable in Aboriginal communities and the extent of this disability in the Aboriginal community.

UNDERSTANDING THE CAUSES OF ABORIGINAL YOUTH CRIMINAL INVOLVEMENT

There is ample authority to indicate that the impact of colonization is the most significant factor behind the circumstances that now contribute to Aboriginal peoples' overrepresentation in the criminal justice system as both offenders and victims (RCAP, 1996a). Many studies demonstrate how current social and economic factors that result in greater risk of criminal activity can trace their roots to colonization and the negative impact it has had on existing individual and collective well-being. The following extract from the Royal Commission on Aboriginal Peoples explains this connection:

> [M]any factors contribute to weakening the fabric of a society and loosening the bonds of relationships and self-regulated behaviour: social change that is rapid or beyond the control of a society; family breakdown, which interferes with the nurturing and socialization of children; poverty and economic marginalization, which restrict opportunities for youth and contribute to a loss of hope; loss of respect for the wisdom of Aboriginal people's culture; and learned patterns of self-defeating or self-destructive behaviour passed on from one generation to another (pp. 62–63).

The "cultural trauma" that colonization has caused is the predominant explanation for the prevalence of Aboriginal criminal activity and victimization, as has been documented by the majority of researchers, including several Aboriginal justice inquiries (Manitoba, 1991; Alberta, 1991; Saskatchewan, 1992). Further, Ross (1996) corroborates these conclusions and provides an insightful summation of the impact of colonization and how individuals are affected today:

> [R]esidential schools were not the solitary cause of social breakdown amongst Aboriginal people. Rather, they were the closing punctuation mark in a loud, long declaration saying that nothing Aboriginal could possibly be of value to anyone. That message had been delivered in almost every way imaginable, and it touched every aspect of traditional social organization. Nothing was exempt, whether it was spiritual beliefs and practices, child-raising techniques, pharmacology, psychology, dispute resolution, decision-making, clan organization or community governance.... And what happens when you are told, from every direction and in every way, that you and all your people have no value to anyone, no purpose to your lives, no positive impact on the world around you? No one can stand believing those things of themselves.... At some point people brought to this position stand up and demand to be noticed, to be recognized as being alive, as having influence and *power*. And the easiest way to assert power, to prove that you exist, is to demonstrate power over people who are weaker still, primarily by making them do things they don't want to do. The more those things shame and diminish the weaker person, the more the abuser feels, within the twisted logic of victimization, that they have been empowered and restored themselves. (pp. 46, 48)

This is the socio-political and personal reality of Aboriginal youth. Green and Healy (2003) have argued that youth crime is primarily the result of social conditions. Unfortunately, the criminal justice system is far too often used to solve problems that could be better dealt with by other systems in society, such as child protection, mental health, and social services. It is not uncommon, for example, that a youth's criminal offence is directly related to alcohol or drug use, only to "observe that there is no treatment available now or in the future, and to conclude that this youth should therefore remain in custody until something is available" (p. 75). The criminal justice system is a very expensive default for addressing the effects of social, cultural, and economic marginalization of Aboriginal youth in our society.

A significant proportion of charges against Aboriginal youth involve lifestyle offences (system-generated offences against the administration of justice, such as breach of probation). In Saskatchewan, nearly 40 percent of all youth cases heard included at least one offence against the administration of justice (Green and Healy, 2003). What this means, in effect, is that youth are being charged for failing to comply with parole or probation conditions that "relate to their home life, and whose breach was directly affected by a myriad of social problems faced in that household" (p. 79). Ironically, many of the probation-order conditions are designed to be "treatment"-oriented. In other words, the judge is imposing conditions such as a curfew, residence requirements, school or employment attendance, abstention from alcohol and drugs, all of which are designed to guide the youth toward more pro-social behaviours. Yet, these breaches often form the basis of new charges that, in turn, are added to their record, a factor that is routinely used to justify harsher penalties and fuel the cycle of incarceration even where the original offence would not have resulted in custody (Green and Healy, 2003). In many cases, the original breach is a function of family dysfunction and involves factors beyond the youth's control. While police and prosecutors can use their discretion to not charge for breach of probation, in many cases they have no choice, as other social services resources are nonexistent or hard to access. Hence, remand and custody become the fallback social safety net.

When the impact of social factors results in greater involvement in the criminal justice system than would otherwise be the case, and the circumstances that gave rise to such social factors of poverty and social marginalization are attributed to the continuing effects of colonization, the result is systemic discrimination of Aboriginal youth in the criminal justice system. Various Aboriginal justice inquiries have studied the issue of systemic discrimination in the criminal justice system, and the literature in this area is extensive.[5] However, in spite of many comprehensive recommendations for change, the system remains largely the same.

The existing system does not address, and is inherently incapable of addressing, the underlying causes of Aboriginal criminality (RCAP, 1996a). Sending offenders to jail only makes them better criminals and more bitter and angry when they return to the community (CHCH Position Paper, 1993, referred to in Ross, 1994). Aboriginal alternatives to the existing justice system have, in part, been motivated by this failure of the existing system to "heal" offenders.

ABORIGINAL ALTERNATIVE JUSTICE PROCESSES

The objective of Aboriginal justice initiatives is to provide alternatives that are culturally relevant and beneficial to both the offender and the community. Some criticisms of these processes include the threat of re-victimization of victims, particularly women and youth, and the danger of reinforcing inequitable power relations within the community. Nevertheless, with certain precautions, alternative processes have been shown to be effective in addressing the concerns of Aboriginal women and youth.

Benefits of Aboriginal Alternative Justice Processes

Over the years, courts and legislatures have responded to the overrepresentation of Aboriginal offenders by recognizing the value of Aboriginal approaches to justice and incorporating an understanding of the long-term effects of colonization in dealing with such offenders. This recognition has translated into various reforms.

In addition to some limited legislative reforms, there are important changes that are being implemented throughout Canada in various Aboriginal communities that are designed to deliver justice in a culturally relevant and meaningful way. Several Aboriginal communities have put into practice various alternative justice initiatives aimed at making justice more meaningful, effective, and relevant to the lives of community members (Clairmont & Linden, 1998). These developments are often described as important in furthering Aboriginal self-government and as more culturally relevant and effective systems (RCAP, 1996c), in part due to the holistic approach to healing the offender. This approach differs fundamentally in theory and world view from the mainstream retributive system of criminal justice (Dumont, 1993; Koshan, 1998). The following section is a brief description and comparison of some of the key principles of Aboriginal traditional justice with mainstream justice processes.

Aboriginal Justice Traditions It is, of course, impossible to describe one conceptual framework of justice that is applicable to all Aboriginal peoples in Canada. However, it has been accepted by academics and the authors of various inquiries into the impact of the criminal justice system on Aboriginal peoples that there are some common fundamental values that have widespread acceptance among many, if not most, of the Aboriginal peoples in Canada (Manitoba, 1991).

Holistic Understanding This principle stems from the idea that all things, animate and inanimate, are interconnected. As such, actions or omissions will have far-reaching implications in countless ways, some obvious and others not, which underscore the healing approach to resolving anti-social behaviour. By contrast, from this perspective it is considered simplistic and a violation of nature to deal with criminal behaviour by examining only the act itself and suggesting that the act determines the appropriate response. The act is a product of the actions of an individual who has been influenced by a host of other factors, some more obvious than others. It is unethical to ignore these factors, for they are integral to the act itself. More importantly, these factors are unique to the individual. Healing the cause must, by necessity, focus on the individual and not simply the act.

Inclusive Decision Making Related to the principle of holistic interconnectedness is the principle of inclusion in decision-making. When an Aboriginal community is involved in dispute resolution, it is understood that everyone has a right/obligation to voice his/her opinion on the matter. This principle is consistent with the realization that it is impossible to know in advance the effect of an offender's actions on others. The decision-makers will weigh among themselves the value of the intervention. Likewise, the decision-makers are also not pre-determined and include anyone who has expressed an opinion on the matter, and consensus must be reached regarding the proper resolution.[6]

Violation/Crime Viewed as "Sickness" Another principle that is widely accepted in many Aboriginal societies is the idea that violation of community norms or standards of behaviour is not viewed as inherently "bad," warranting punishment. Rather, the violation is seen more as a "sickness" that needs to be addressed and healed, while the individual is perceived as separate in identity from the sickness. The inquiry is about how the sickness can be cured and not about the meting out of a punishment proportional to the violation committed. Nor is there an attempt to ensure that the "solution" is similar to past cases where similar violations occurred; rather, attempts are made to heal the harms done. In Aboriginal society there is a recognition that the underlying causes of the sickness, or the reasons why a violation occurred, may be different, although the visible manifestation or violation of a community norm may be the same. In other words, two individuals may commit the same crime but for entirely different reasons. The focus of inquiry is on the reasons for the violation and not on the violation itself.

The principles outlined above have informed and guided many traditional Aboriginal justice systems. Although the effects of assimilation have prevented Aboriginal peoples from relying exclusively on their traditional laws and systems, the underlying values that informed these systems have remained largely intact within many Aboriginal societies. They continue to find expression in contemporary processes of community decision making, although at times they are often compromised by the imposition of Western systems of justice. Where there is discretion within the process and where the community has a meaningful role to play in the exercise of such discretion, these principles will invariably emerge to guide the process.

Canadian Justice Traditions In contrast to Aboriginal justice concepts, the mainstream Western-based model of justice is more concerned with the punishment of wrongdoers than with addressing the underlying causes of offending behaviour. Thus, the focus of inquiry, in this instance, is limited to the circumstances of the offence and what the appropriate sentence ought to be according to the nature of the violation itself. There is a lack of concern or interest in uncovering the root causes of the wrongful behaviour, whereas under the Aboriginal model there is a greater depth of inquiry into the reasons motivating the wrongful behaviour.

Likewise, the breadth of inquiry in the Canadian model of justice is limited to those actors who are relevant to the inquiry, and is rather narrowly defined to the question of whether the wrongful behaviour actually occurred. The preoccupation with the act itself tends to limit the "voices" that are considered relevant to the inquiry. Furthermore, complex rules of evidence have been developed to limit the inquiry. In the Aboriginal model, the breadth of inquiry is more extensive, as the relevance of someone's input is measured only by the willingness of the person to speak on the matter. Such input may address the specific act, or it may go beyond the circumstances surrounding the offence. In the case of a young person, an inquiry may touch on matters related to the offender's childhood, the role of the parents or community in the youth's life, or the degree to which the youth identifies with the culture of the First Nation.

Criticisms of Aboriginal Alternatives

Not all Aboriginal justice initiatives function in the same manner. Some run the risk of not addressing the needs of the more vulnerable persons within Aboriginal communities—or worse aggravating and compromising such persons, particularly women and children, who are often the victims of violent crime and sexual abuse. Ross (1996) argues that reforms calling for Aboriginal "community courts," which are essentially a mirror image of the existing process, have been discredited to the extent that they "continue to promise identical failures, the secrets of abuse will remain, and the illness will continue to spread from one generation to the next" (p. 203). Furthermore, where communi-

ties adopt circle sentencing[7] as the only aspect of Aboriginal justice reform—while the existing criminal process remains largely intact with no comprehensive healing plan or a lack of community commitment—the process may merely continue to perpetuate existing patriarchal power imbalances in the community (Drummond, 1997; Crnkovich, 1996).

Furthermore, the system may continue to abuse vulnerable groups within a community, such as Aboriginal women and youth.

> It has been questioned whether victims are truly free to participate, or must bow to community pressure and the lack of meaningful alternatives. The prevalence of violence against women and children and the internalization of dominant attitudes may test whether healing is a viable option today. (Koshan, 1998, p. 42)

Nahanee (1995) has maintained that allowing Aboriginal offenders to benefit from a healing approach that inevitably results in more lenient sentences violates the human rights of the Aboriginal women who have been victimized. Moreover, such use of culture as a defence is offensive to Aboriginal women. Koshan (1998) explains:

> Aboriginal women perceive as too lenient, and indeed racist, the "culturally sensitive" sentencing of Aboriginal men convicted of crimes of violence. Sentences which allow a violent offender to remain in his community are seen as imposing very serious risks for survivors and potential victims of such crimes, emphasizing rehabilitation at the expense of community safety. Political and judicial support for community sentencing combined with the apathy or outright tolerance of some Aboriginal community leaders and elders towards violence against women may exacerbate these risks. (pp. 40–41)

In spite of these concerns, it would be wrong to assume that all Aboriginal justice alternatives are problematic due to beliefs that they are perpetuating women's and youths' inequality and fail to truly address their needs as victims in male-dominated Aboriginal communities. Policy-makers must be aware that there are significant differences in the quality of various Aboriginal justice alternatives and that there are, of course, examples of programs that take into account the perspective of victims in addressing violence against women and children, such as some existing comprehensive Aboriginal healing programs.[8]

THE PROMISE OF THE *YOUTH CRIMINAL JUSTICE ACT*
Declaration of Principle and Sentencing

Although the *Criminal Code* expressly recognizes the principle of "rehabilitation" as a valid objective in sentencing, it is regarded as secondary when sentencing offenders. The *Criminal Code* makes it clear that the objectives of denunciation and deterrence, through appropriate levels of punishment, are to be given primacy over the objective of "rehabilitation." In comparison, the YCJA appears to place greater emphasis on rehabilitation. The Act contains several fundamental principles in its Declaration of Principle (see Appendix C) that are meant to provide overarching guidance in how youth are dealt with by the criminal justice system. Moreover, the principles expressly identify the need to address the circumstances underlying a young person's offending behaviour and indicate that the system is intended to rehabilitate young

persons and reintegrate them into society (secs. 3(1)(a) and (b)). The emphasis on rehabilitation and reintegration is also reflected in the sentencing principles of the YCJA. Section 3 38(1) states that the purpose of sentencing a youth is to "hold a young person accountable for an offence through the imposition of just sanctions that have a meaningful consequence for the young person and that promote his or her rehabilitation and reintegration into society, thereby contributing to the long term-term protection of the public."

Nevertheless, punishment, although not expressly stated as such, still appears to be a primary objective of the YCJA. The YCJA makes mention of the concept of "fair and proportionate accountability" (secs. 3(1)(b)(ii) and 3(1)(c)). Section 38(2)(e) states that section 38(1), which emphasizes the promotion of accountability through meaningful consequences and rehabilitation and reintegration, is subject to section 38(2)(c), which requires that sentences must still be "proportionate to the seriousness of the offence," indicating that more serious crimes must be accorded more serious sanctions. While it appears that the YCJA is fundamentally based on a punishment (i.e., proportionate) model of justice, it does mandate that incarceration truly be the penalty of last resort. There are several provisions that require that all other options other than incarceration be seriously considered, especially in the case of Aboriginal youth offenders (secs. 38 and 39).

This emphasis on proportionate accountability (punishment) over rehabilitation is a fundamental point of departure between Aboriginal concepts of justice and Canadian concepts of justice. In the Aboriginal model, the extent to which punishment is a factor in determining the outcome of an offender's case is of secondary importance to the goal of healing and rehabilitation of the offender. Furthermore, for some Aboriginal communities, the more serious the behaviour, the more attention is paid by the community to determine a solution to address the causes of the behaviour, whereas in less serious cases, fewer community resources are directed at the problem.[9] This approach to dealing with offending behaviour is largely contrary to the current structure of the *Criminal Code,* and the YCJA, Under the Canadian system, the less serious the crime (often measured by the degree of violence), the more appropriate are sentencing alternatives that allow for rehabilitation and healing to take place over sentencing choices involving incarceration. Instead, the response to more serious crimes appears to be punishment and retribution. Thus, the overall structure of the *Criminal Code,* and to a lesser degree the YCJA, is counterintuitive to Aboriginal traditional cultural approaches.

To some extent, this incompatibility between Aboriginal and Canadian objectives in sentencing is addressed by the inclusion of sec. 718.2(e) of the *Criminal Code.* It states:

> A court that imposes a sentence shall also take into consideration … all available sanctions other than imprisonment that are reasonable in the circumstances … for all offenders, *with particular attention to the circumstances of aboriginal offenders.* (emphasis added)

The Supreme Court of Canada, in the landmark *Gladue* case, has affirmed that this provision recognizes the primacy given to rehabilitation as a sentencing objective in the Aboriginal model of justice (*R. v. Gladue,* 1999). For example, Justice Iacobucci recently remarked in the *R. v. Wells* decision that the "requirement to pay 'particular attention to the circumstances of aboriginal offenders' recognizes that most traditional aboriginal conceptions of sentencing hold restorative justice to be the primary objective" (*R. v. Wells,* 2000, para. 37). In addition, the Supreme Court of Canada stated in *Gladue* that sec. 718.2(e) was to take into account the unique and systemic background factors of Aboriginal offenders. The court stated:

> [T]he logical meaning to be derived from the special reference to the circumstances of aboriginal offenders, juxtaposed as it is against a general direction to consider "the circumstances' for all offenders, is that sentencing judges should pay particular attention to the circumstances of aboriginal offenders *because those circumstances are unique,* and different from those of non-aboriginal offenders. (*R. v. Gladue,* 1999, para. 37)

Similarly, the circumstances experienced by adult Aboriginal offenders covered in section 718.2(e) also justify special treatment for Aboriginal young offenders. Prior to its enactment, the YCJA was criticized for not including a provision to consider the special circumstances of Aboriginal young offenders. Subsequently, Parliament responded by adding a similar provision to the YCJA that has significant implications for Aboriginal youth. Specifically, with respect to considering sanctions other than custody, sec. 38(2)(d) states:

> All available sanctions other that custody that are reasonable in the circumstances should be considered for all young persons, with particular attention to the circumstances of aboriginal young persons.

Whereas the *Gladue* decision provided the Supreme Court of Canada with the opportunity to define the meaning of the Aboriginal-specific direction in sec. 718.2(e) of the *Criminal Code,* it is likely that this interpretation will no doubt be relevant to how sec. 38(2)(d) will be interpreted for Aboriginal youth. Bala (2003) has indicated that the purpose of including this section in the YCJA was Parliament's recognition of the unique circumstances that Aboriginal youth face. Furthermore, its inclusion reflects the recognition that the status quo has proven "ineffective in dealing with Aboriginal offenders who have the highest rates of recidivism" (p. 52).[9]

Importantly, and unlike the *Criminal Code,* reference to Aboriginal people is also stated in the Declaration of Principles of the YCJA (see Appendix C). Section 3(1)(c)(iv) requires that the measures taken against young persons who commit offences should take into account not only gender, ethnic, cultural, and linguistic differences, but also respond to the "needs of aboriginal young persons." This could logically include the need of Aboriginal youth to be able to access their culture and practise their traditions. It may allow for an Aboriginal youth, as an integral part of his or her community, to be dealt with by the justice system in accordance with Aboriginal values and beliefs. It may also include the recognition that Aboriginal youth are particularly vulnerable to breach of probation conditions due to their social and economic circumstances (Green & Healy, 2003).

Notably, however, the requirement that courts take into account the unique needs of Aboriginal youth is subject to the proviso "within the limits of fair and proportionate accountability" (sec. 3(1)(c)). There are two ways of interpreting this proviso. One is to suggest that it applies to the limited-comparison basis of sentences given to Aboriginal youth with other Aboriginal youth. In other words, as long as Aboriginal youth measures are proportionate to those given to other Aboriginal youth in similar circumstances, the proviso is satisfied. However, another interpretation could mean that Aboriginal youth measures are to be compared to all other youth, and that a measure for an Aboriginal youth cannot be disproportionate to the norm as measured by this standard. It is likely that the first option of interpretation is the more appropriate one, as the second option could very well defeat the overall purpose of singling out Aboriginal youth for special consideration in the first place.

Youth Justice Committees and Conferences

In addition to the sentencing provisions and the Declaration of Principle, there are other provisions in the YCJA that add additional legislative support to recognizing Aboriginal alternatives to justice, particularly sentencing circles and diversion programs. For example, youth justice committees and conferences can be convened to recommend appropriate measures at various stages along the process (YCJA, secs. 18 and 19). Aboriginal communities could likely take advantage of these provisions and could provide some degree of input into the process by incorporating Aboriginal values of justice into the decision-making process. In particular, sec. 19 authorizes "conferences" to be conducted at several stages of the criminal process and can be initiated by various justice personnel. The provision reads as follows:

19(1) A youth justice court judge, the provincial director, a police officer, a justice of the peace, a prosecutor or a youth worker may convene or cause to be convened a conference for the purpose of making a decision required to be made under this Act.

(2) The mandate of a conference may be, among other things, to give advice on appropriate extrajudicial measures, conditions for judicial interim release, sentences, including the review of sentences, and reintegration plans.

In addition to the above provisions, the YCJA specifically addresses the holding of conferences for the purpose of providing advice to the judge on sentencing. Section 41 of the Act states:

When a youth justice court finds a young person guilty of an offence, the court may convene or cause to be convened a conference under section 19 for recommendations to the court on an appropriate youth sentence.

The youth justice conferences authorized under sec. 19 and sec. 41 could be viewed by Aboriginal communities as an endorsement of circle decision-making processes that have been used in the past with the discretion of the judge. Many of the existing Aboriginal youth justice committees that operated under sec. 69 of the *Young Offenders Act* could simply be continued under sec. 18 of the YCJA.

Furthermore, such committees would then have the mandate to promote and hold conferences and/or recommend extrajudicial measures that are more consistent with traditional Aboriginal processes of dispute resolution (sec. 18). Because there is very little statutory direction in the YCJA in terms of how conferences under sec. 19 will be integrated into the process, much discretion will remain with the court and various justice personnel. The opportunities to increase the input of interested parties and community members in the resolution of an Aboriginal youth caught in the system are considerable and consistent with the Aboriginal cultural values of inclusiveness identified earlier.

Conferences are mandated to provide input at different stages of the justice process, including finding alternatives to the regular process, interim release, and release from custody. At present, Aboriginal communities have been involved primarily in diversion decisions and in sentencing decisions, with little or no involvement at the interim release stage of the process. Thus, powers provided by sec. 19 can be seen as an endorsement for Aboriginal communities to become involved at an even earlier stage of the process, and perhaps even prior to charges being laid.

Extrajudicial Measures and Extrajudicial Sanctions

There are several other ways the YCJA allows for early involvement of the community to divert matters. Provisions exist in sections 4 and 5 for having an offender comply with extrajudicial measures if the offence is non-violent and the youth has admitted responsibility for the act. Further, sec. 5(c) encourages families and communities to become involved in the design and implementation of extrajudicial measures, thus allowing the opportunity for community involvement. This provides legislative recognition to Aboriginal youth diversion programs that are already in existence.

Aboriginal Youth Suffering from Fetal Alcohol Spectrum Disorder

In terms of Aboriginal youth who have FASD, the YCJA does contain provisions that address the unique issues they face. For example, sec. 34(1) gives a youth justice court the authority to have a young offender assessed by a qualified person where the court believes that the youth is suffering from a mental illness or disorder. While such a provision existed under the YOA (sec.13), at that time such assessments were used primarily for sentencing purposes. Under the YCJA, the use of these assessments has been expanded to pretrial detention hearings and can be ordered by the court at any time for a variety of purposes (Tustin & Lutes, 2003). The YCJA also allows judges, under sec. 42(2)(l), to order a young person into an "intensive support and supervision program." However, this option is dependent on the availability of such programs and approval of the province through the office of the Provincial Director. In one case in Saskatchewan involving a youth offender with FASD, the judge thought that an intensive supervision order would have been ideal (*R. v. M.B.*, 2003a). However, at the time of the decision (May 2003), the province of Saskatchewan had not implemented or approved the use of "intensive supervision orders" under sec. 42(2)(l).

Case Illustration

The case of *R. v. M.B.* is particularly illustrative of the difficulties in implementing various aspects of the YCJA. In this case, Judge Turpel-Lafond demonstrated sensitivity to the experience of Aboriginal youth by reinforcing the provision of community-based dispositions under the YCJA. The facts of the case involved a youth gang leader who instigated and committed two armed robberies in Saskatoon. The defence counsel and the Crown presented a joint submission on sentencing to the judge, asking for incarceration of two years. Normally judges do not interfere with joint submissions, as the court routine and the number of cases that must be "processed" hinders opportunities to inquire into the circumstances of any one case beyond basic superficialities. However, Judge Turpel-Lafond, after reviewing the YCJA legislation, realized that the "assembly-line fashion in which youth matters are processed in the Provincial Court of Saskatchewan may not be consistent with the principles which guide the Court in light of the YCJA" (p. 281). Judge Turpel-Lafond decided that the "deal" presented by counsel did not reflect the principles of sentencing in sec. 38 of the YCJA, and suspected that the youth may have FASD. The Court refused to deal with the offender summarily and instead reviewed the pre-sentence file and ordered an assessment under sec. 34, which concluded that the accused did suffer from FASD. This in turn led to a desire to have more information on the youth and to evaluate whether a program could be designed that would truly address the needs of the youth and the protection of society. The judge ordered two conferences under sec. 19 and 41 of the YCJA. She saw the conferences as a tool to obtain more information on the reasons for the offending behaviour and to seek the best measures to rehabilitate the youth.

The judge found that the circle conference was very valuable in revealing alternatives to custody that were not previously explored by counsel or the youth worker. It was only through the circle conference that it was discovered the youth had an uncle and an aunt in another town who were able and willing to provide the necessary care and supervision he needed. Consequently, the judge ordered probation for 18 months with several conditions that involved his living with his aunt and uncle. Judge Turpel-Lafond observed that this type of sentence for armed robberies would normally be considered an unusual case. However, given that the YCJA requires courts to approach matters in a new light, Judge Turpel-Lafond explains:

> The YCJA, through the conferencing provisions, and its guiding principles, encourages those administering the Act to "prevent crime by addressing the circumstances underlying a young person's offending behaviour" (s.3(1)(a)(i)). This requires a very different approach than has been taken in the past to young people, and especially in the context of Aboriginal inner-city youth in Saskatoon, an effort to bring them to a position of active participation in defining their life's circumstances and choices. Accountability must be emphasized but this is only meaningful if the Court truly engages with the youth and

his or her family, in tandem with victims and others impacted by crime, to look at their circumstances. (p. 301)

The result for M.B. was extraordinary. The Court, with its overwhelming caseload and lack of resources and supports, will not normally be able to live up to the expectations of the YCJA. It is worth quoting at length the opinion of Judge Turpel-Lafond:

> The Court is on its own in attempting to implement this legislation and conduct conferences without adequate or meaningful supports from government. Compounding this is the fact that no additional resources have been assigned to support the additional work required by legislation to look at the circumstances underlying a young person's offending behaviour. In the case at bar, the Court used its chambers days to deal with this youth. This was an exceptional case and the approach described here, which is an attempt to implement this legislation in Saskatoon, is not workable with a procession of over 35,000 appearances by youth in the Youth Court at this court point in a year. Court time, space, and coordination are all required if the conferencing provisions of the YCJA are to be fully implemented. Without these supports and planning for implementation, the assembly line approach will continue.... (p. 296, 312)

Although Judge Turpel-Lafond has limited her comments to Saskatchewan, clearly her observations have equal validity in other jurisdictions in Canada.

Unfortunately, intervention in this case did not end here. What is disheartening about the case is that a couple of months later, the "alternative identified" by the court of having M.B. live with his uncle and aunt soon dissolved as M.B.'s grandfather was diagnosed with cancer and his aunt and uncle had to take care of him as well. Because they were unable to care for both M.B. and the grandfather, M.B. left to stay with his sister in Saskatoon. In reviewing the probation order, Judge Turpel-Lafond noted that there were no resources available for this youth (M.B. 2003b).

> The Court can only conclude that the situation is bleak. In recognizing this, it would appear that the Court has come up against the greatest obstacle faced in implementing the principles and procedures of the new Youth Criminal Justice Act—a lack of resources for youth like M.(B.) who suffer from FASD and come from traumatic backgrounds. (M. (B.), 2003b para. 31)

In fact, the decision in *R.v. M.B.* was overturned by the Saskatchewan Court of Appeal on October 9, 2003. The Court substituted a sentence of 22 months' custody with no reasons given as of the date of writing. It is possible that the Court of Appeal must have been influenced by the disproportionality of the original sentence given the nature of the crime. If so, it sends a very discouraging message that not much has changed and that the references to Aboriginal youths' needs and unique circumstances have little practical effect.

CONCLUSION

As stated earlier, overrepresentation of Aboriginal youths as both offenders and victims in the criminal justice system appears to be the result of colonization and resultant social and economic marginalization. In many cases, Aboriginal youth are caught in a system that only exacerbates their disadvantage. Despite the improvements that exist in the YCJA to increase and validate Aboriginal input, it is still criminal legislation and such a system will likely have little overall impact in addressing the underlying causes of Aboriginal youth crime. More fundamental reforms are needed in social supports and community interventions that empower the community and can lead to the long-term well being of Aboriginal communities and their youth.

One such reform is the development of comprehensive healing approaches that not only address the immediate needs of the offenders and victims, but also can lead indirectly to overall community well being. Through the process of community involvement in Aboriginal youth justice initiatives, the community will naturally benefit from increased positive social interaction and collaboration.

Through its flexibility, the YCJA has much to offer Aboriginal youths and communities with respect to incorporating comprehensive Aboriginal youth healing processes. Diversion from the criminal system to a healing process is possible, as well as allowing for significant input at the sentencing stage depending on the preferences and needs of the Aboriginal community and the youth involved. The first *M.(B.)* case from Saskatchewan offered much hope *if* the resources and time had been in place to provide real alternatives to incarceration. Much will depend on the extent to which the provinces and the public embrace the rehabilitation and community-based principles contained in the YCJA. However, at the end of the day—and given the recent Court of Appeal decision of *M.(B.)*—not much appears to have changed under the new YCJA. However, it is still early and it may take time for attitudes to change and resources to be redirected. For Aboriginal youth, fundamental changes in approaches to youth justice are desperately needed.

References

Alberta. (1991). *Task force on the criminal justice system and its impact on the Indian and Metis peoples of Alberta.* Edmonton, AB: Government of Alberta.

Absolon, K., & Winchester, T. (1994). *Cultural identity for urban Aboriginal peoples: Learning circles synthesis report.* In Royal Commission on Aboriginal Peoples. (1996) *Seven Generations* CD-ROM. Ottawa: Libraxus.

Bala, N. (2003). *Youth criminal justice law.* Toronto: Irwin Law.

Boland, F. J., Burrill, R., Duwyn, M., & Karp, J. (1998). *Fetal alcohol syndrome: Implications for correctional service.* Online at http://canada.gc.ca/.

Canada. Department of Justice. (2000). *Restorative justice in Canada: A consultation paper.* Retrieved from http://canada.justice.gc.ca/en/ps/voc/rjpap.html.

Canada. Department of Justice. (2003). *One-day snapshot of Aboriginal youth in custody across Canada.* Ottawa: Justice Canada.

Canada, HRDC, & Manitoba, Aboriginal Affairs Secretariat. (2002). *Aboriginal people in Manitoba, 2000.* Winnipeg: Government of Canada and Manitoba.

Canadian Council on Social Development. (2000). *Urban poverty in Canada: A statistical profile.* Ottawa: Author.

Chartrand, L. N., & Forbes-Chilibeck, E. (2003). The sentencing of offenders with fetal alcohol syndrome. *Health Law Journal, 11* (forthcoming).

Clairmont, D., & Linden, R. (1998). *Developing and evaluating justice projects in Aboriginal communities: A review of the literature.* Ottawa: Aboriginal Corrections Policy Unit, Solicitor General of Canada.

Crnkovich, M. (1996). A sentencing circle. *Journal of Legal Pluralism and Unoffical Law, 36,* 159–181.

Conry, J., & Fast, D. (2000). *Fetal alcohol syndrome and the criminal justice system.* Vancouver: British Columbia Fetal Alcohol Syndrome Resource Society.

Drummond, S. (1997). *Incorporating the familiar.* Montreal: McGill University Press.

Dumont, J. (1993). Justice and Aboriginal people. In Royal Commission on Aboriginal Peoples (Ed.), *Aboriginal peoples and the justice system: Report of the national round table on Aboriginal justice issues* (pp. 42–85). Ottawa: Canada Communication Group.

Dumont-Smith, C., & Sioui-Labelle, P. (1991). *National family violence survey: Phase I.* Ottawa: Indian and Inuit Nurses Association of Canada.

Elliott, D. (1997). *Social and health-care pilot project for sex trade workers: Interim report.* Retrieved June 17, 2002, from http://www.city.kamloops.bc.ca/planning/pdf/shop.pdf.

Green, R. (1998). *Justice in aboriginal communities: Sentencing alternatives.* Saskatoon, SK: Purich Publishing.

Green, G., & Healy, K. (2003). *Tough on Kids.* Saskatoon, SK: Purich Publishing.

Health Canada. (1996). *Family violence in Aboriginal communities: An Aboriginal perspective.* Ottawa: Health Canada & National Clearinghouse on Family Violence.

Kingsley, C., & Mark, M. (2000). *Sacred lives: Canadian aboriginal children & youth speak out about sexual exploitation: Save the Children Canada.* Retrieved June 19, 2002, from http://dsp-psd.communication.gc.ca/Collection/RH34-12-2000E.pdf.

Koshan, J. (1998). Aboriginal women, justice and the *Charter:* Bridging the divide. *University of British Columbia Law Review, 32,* 23–54.

La Prairie, C. (1995). *Seen but not heard: Native people in the inner city.* Ottawa: Minister of Public Works and Government Services.

Manitoba. (1991). *Report of the Aboriginal justice inquiry of Manitoba.* Winnipeg, MB: Government of Manitoba.

Masotti, P., Szala-Meneok, K., Selby, P., Ranford, J., & Van Koughnett, A. (2003). Urban FASD interventions: Bridging the gap between Aboriginal women and primary care physicians. *Journal of FAS International,* 1–8.

Matthews, C.J. & Lewis, L. (1995). *Racism in the criminal justice system: A bibliography.* Toronto, ON: Centre of Criminology, University of Toronto.

McGillivary, A., & Comaskey, B. (1996). *Intimate violence, Aboriginal women and justice system response: A Winnipeg study.* Winnipeg, MB: Research Council on Family Violence and Violence against Women.

Nahanee, T. (1995). *Marriage as an Instrument of Oppression in Aboriginal Communities.* (Unpublished Keynote Address to the National Association of Women and the Law's 11th Biennial Conference, St. John's, Nfld., May 13, 1995).

Ross, R. (1994). Duelling paradigms? Western criminal justice versus Aboriginal community healing. In R. Gosse (Ed.), *Continuing Poundmaker and Riel's quest.* Saskatoon, SK: Purich Publishing.

Ross, R. (1996). *Returning to the teachings: Exploring Aboriginal justice.* Saskatoon, SK: Penguin Books.

Royal Commission on Aboriginal Peoples. (1996a). *Bridging the cultural divide. A report on aboriginal people and criminal justice in Canada.* Ottawa: Supply and Services Canada.

Royal Commission on Aboriginal Peoples. (1996b). *Report of the Royal Commission on Aboriginal Peoples: Gathering strength* (Vol. 3). Ottawa: Supply and Services Canada.

Royal Commission on Aboriginal Peoples. (1996c). *People to people, nation to nation: Highlights from the Report of the Royal Commission on Aboriginal Peoples.* Ottawa: Supply and Services Canada.

Ryan, J.(1993). *Final report: Traditional Dene justice project, Lac La Martre, NWT.* Lac La Martre, NWT: Lac La Martre Band Council, Dene Cultural Institute and Arctic Institute of North America.

Saskatchewan. (1992). *Report of the Indian Justice Review Committee.* Saskatoon, SK: Government of Saskatchewan.

Silver, J., & Mallet, K. (2002). *Aboriginal education in Winnipeg inner city high schools.* Winnipeg: Canada Centre for Policy Alternatives.

Standing Senate Committee on Aboriginal Peoples. (2003). *Urban Aboriginal youth: An action plan for change.* Ottawa: Senate of Canada.

Statistics Canada. (2001). *Aboriginal peoples in Canada: Canadian Centre for Justice Statistics Profile Series.* Ottawa: Minister of Industry.

Statistics Canada. (2003). *Aboriginal identity population, 2001 counts, for Canada, provinces and territories.* Ottawa: Statistics Canada. Online at http://www12.statcan.ca/english/census01/products/highlight/Aboriginal/Page.cfm?Lang=E&Geo=PR&View=1a&Code=0&Table=2&StartRec=1&Sort=4&B1=Distribution01&B2=Total.

Streissguth, A. P., Barr, H. M., Kogan, J., & Bookstein, F. L. (1996). *Understanding the occurrence of secondary disabilities in clients with fetal alcohol syndrome (FAS) and fetal alcohol effects (FAE).* Ottawa: Centers for Disease Control and Prevention, [unpublished].

Tustin, L., & Lutes, R. E. (2003). *A guide to the Youth Criminal Justice Act.* Toronto: Butterworths.

Cases Cited

R. v. Elias, [2001] Y.J. No. 45, 2001 YKTC 501 (C. J. Barry Stuart).

R. v. C.J.M., [2000] B.C.J. No. 2714 (Prov. Ct.) (QL) (J. Trueman).

R. v. Moses (1992), 71 C.C.C. (3rd) 347 (C. J. Barry Stuart). *R. v. Wells*, 2000 S.C.C. 10.

R. v. Gladue, [1999] 1 S.C.R. 688, (1999), 133 C.C.C. (3d) 385 (S.C.).

R. v. M. (B.) [2003a] 3 C.N.L.R. 277, (Sask. Prov. Ct.) (Turpel-Lafond)

R. v. M. (B.) [2003b] S.J. No. 602, (Sask. Prov. Ct.) (Turpel-Lafond)

R. v. Wells [2001] S.C.R. 201

Notes

1. Of this population, 62 percent identified as North American Indian, 30 percent identified as Métis, and 5 percent identified as Inuit (Statistics Canada, 2003).

2. Standing Senate Committee on Aboriginal Peoples, *Urban Aboriginal Youth: An Action Plan for Change* (Ottawa: Senate of Canada, 2003) at 8–15.

3. This study is a model study of direct youth participation research. Aboriginal youth were directly involved in consultations and focus groups from 22 communities across the country. Their input dictated the direction of the study as their combined voices resulted in six themes that became the framework of the study and the focus of recommendations.

4. Cases decided by judges are "reported" in law reports where the editor of the law report considers the case to have some precedential value. There is no scientific methodology used for determining the cases to be reported. However, since cases are reported for reasons other than those related to the prevalence of FASD, one can have some assurance that they are roughly representative of the population that has been sentenced by the Canadian justice system.

5. For a relevant bibliography on racism in the criminal justice system, including references to Aboriginal peoples, see Mathews and Lewis (1995).

6. One must be cautious to not overgeneralize, since not all Aboriginal peoples necessarily employed the consensus decision-making model, and those who did may not have used it for all infractions of community standards. For example, the Dogrib tribe of the Dene people used circle decision-making involving all the senior men and women of the community only in serious cases and dealt with less serious cases by way of predetermined procedures and "solutions" (cf., Ryan, et al., 1993).

7. Circle sentencing differs from the adversarial approach, where lawyers representing the Crown and the offender argue their cases before an independent, neutral third party. In the circle process, there are more participants (including the victim, community elders, police, parole officers, etc.) who sit in a circle and reach a consensus as to what is the best course of action for dealing with the offender. Typically, the approach tries to further rehabilitation and healing options rather than punishment. For such a process to work, the community must be actively involved (Green, 1998).

8. A widely known example of such a comprehensive healing approach is the Hollow Water Community Healing Program.

9. In the case of *R. v. Moses* (1992), Judge Stuart argues that where an Aboriginal offender has a serious criminal record and has committed a serious crime, additional effort and resources in determining a sentence by circle consensus decision-making are required. This approach allows the community to better address the underlying causes that result in the offender repeatedly confronting the criminal justice system.

10. Judge Turpel-Lafond in a recent Saskatchewan case has affirmed that the rationale behind sec. 718.2(e) of the *Criminal Code* applies to the YCJA provision as well (*R v. M.B.*, 2003a).

chapter sixteen

Voices of Youth

*Compiled by Kathryn M. Campbell**

INTRODUCTION

A great deal of research undertaken in the field of criminology and criminal justice, as it relates to the experience of incarceration, tends to concentrate on the system itself, including more abstract analyses of its role, function, processes, and deficits. All too often, the voices of those subjected to criminal justice interventions are silent. In recent years, however, a few experiential analyses, from the perspective of the subject of criminal justice interventions, have emerged. These analyses are uniquely situated to provide insights into the world of the prison, its many deprivations, and the challenge of survival. The writings of Roger Caron (2002), Jimmy Boyle (1984), and Julius Melnitzer (1995) are examples of phenomenological writings on the experience of incarceration. However, very little has been written from the perspective of *young* persons, their experiences and understanding of incarceration and the effects on them of being processed through the system. While some work does exist that describes how youth interpret varying aspects of their exposure to the criminal justice system (cf. Artz, 2000; Lane et al., 2002), these works tend to situate the youth's experience within other frameworks of analysis.

   In order to convey how young persons understand and interpret their involvement in the criminal justice system, interviews with young persons in conflict with the law were undertaken. Thus, the objective of this chapter is simply to present the experiences and perspectives of these young persons, in their own words. The following are transcripts of interviews with two young offenders. Each has been involved with the social service and criminal justice systems in his or her home province and has served time in open and secure custodial facilities.

---

* As much as possible, transcripts have been left intact with editing done only for clarity and for length. Any and all identifying information has been changed to protect the young person's privacy and respect confidentiality.

JAMES

James is an 18-year-old, black male student. At the time of the interview he was serving a six-month intensive probation sentence under the *Young Offenders Act*. This had followed three months of regular probation and three months of a closed custody sentence for robbery.

> I was a normal kid, you know, I was doing what I had to, going to school. I lived with my mother and my little brother. My relationship with my mum, it was all right at first, and I guess, as I got older, I started to change, she changed a little bit too. I wanted to be out more, longer, I didn't want to study. I started to get into drugs those times, around 16. Just weed at first, it got me a bit lazy, I didn't feel like doing anything no more. My mom acted on that, cause she seen it and it was bothering her, so she thought what was best was to like, put me in a group home or something, to try to change me.

Experiences with the Social Service/Child Protection System

Group Homes It began with a little argument I had with [mom], and she told me I had to leave and I took off. It was really from there. The argument was with my sister, and it was always kiddie stuff, like the TV or something like that. My mom got the wrong idea, she thought that I hit her to get the TV or something like that, so she started screaming at me, and I started screaming at her and we both started screaming at each other, so I just walked out. The cops came and they asked me if everything was all right. I told them the whole story, you know, this happened with my mom. So they took me to the station. They called my mom, they asked her

a couple of questions I didn't hear. Then they asked her if she wanted me to come back. She didn't want me to come back at the time. They held me there till they found a placement, actually within the same day or something. They took me to a group home. It was different. It was all right. Actually they were good there. And I went to court after that, so then I got placed there for like six months. I wasn't charged [criminally], it was child protection, that's how it started. I stayed there; I did everything; I did good. At first, when I got there, I didn't really want to talk to my mom because of all that. Then she came to see me a couple of times, it was all right. We started talking a bit.

After six months, I went back home. Everything was fine. I wasn't going to school and then I got placed again. I think I gave up on everything. I said, forget everything, you know. I stopped doing most everything that I was doing good, like being involved in sports and all that stuff. I just stopped. It was mostly things that was happening with my mom. She put me through group home and all that stuff. I was looking at all the bad. I was only out for four or five months.

I remember I came here [second group home], I think it was the same stuff with my mother, house rules and stuff. The same six months, like every winter, I got locked up. It was all fine here [second group home]. I just kept to myself at first, you know. Talking to people here and there. I was cool with the staff. I was going to school. I didn't really hang out with nobody period, at the group home, school, outside, nothing, period. I just like to stay alone. I don't really like to talk with other people or nothing. I never got into [real] trouble, went to school straight. I got in trouble with school you know, but it was all … like getting kicked out of classes too much, getting suspended and stuff like that. Like, I would just misbehave. Days when I feel miserable I would just misbehave. Or like, the teacher, I don't feel like working, you know and obviously in a class you're supposed to be working. I don't feel like doing it so I just walk out or something, anything not to be in class.

Experiences in the Youth Justice System

Criminal Charge Before my six months was up, was when I first got my charge. I was going to the alternative school, the first couple of months I was doing good there and stuff then I started to slip up a little bit.… It was a "taxing" [robbery] charge. Me and a couple of friends, we went after school and we taxed some kids at the other school. We asked the kid for money and he said he didn't have. With taxing, I don't know what other people do, but the kid told me he doesn't want to give [money], you'd get roughed up. You just grab him and chuck him against the wall or something. Just get him scared: "Cough it up or you take it yourself," you know. In the situation with me there was no contact or nothing with the victim. So we asked him for his card, and he gave us the card (bank card). But we never used it, we just shot it away. I came back to the group home and nobody knew about it, you know, nobody knew about nothing. It was one kid from the group home I did it with.

That taxing thing, these guys, they weren't really my friends. I just met them when I came to the group home because we were going to the same school. So it was like, I'll take the bus with them and we did stupid stuff. The other guy, the kid I was with, we didn't really say nothing. That wasn't even our intention. We were just going, walking, going to catch the bus. This kid,

my friend told me, he'd seen this kid pull out money and he's checking it. But I don't really believe that. I think he just told me that just to get me okay, you know. But the truth is our intentions weren't really to rob that kid. We were just going home and the guy said that and then he went up to the kid and I just followed. Mostly I was just there. The most I did was probably just make the kid get scared or something. But I didn't even do nothing, like no contact. Nothing. Just by being there, standing there with the other guy. The other guy, he was like up right in his face. Looked like he was going to grab him, you know. So the kid's looking at him and he's looking at me.

I ran away from the group home about two or three weeks after that. I just left. I stayed at my friend's house. I was on the run for awhile, like four months, then I went to my mom's house. I was there for a couple of days, whatever, then the cops came and stuff. My mom says she didn't call them, but like till this day, I don't know. When they took me at my house, [the cops] treated me good you know, like they didn't rough me up or nothing. They told me, "OK, we're going to the car now." They put the handcuffs on me in the house. Then we went down the stairs. When they brought me out, that's when I took off. Then they caught me and then they put cuffs on my ankles, so I couldn't run and stuff. They told me they were bringing me in because I was on AWOL [absent without leave]. I had charges on me, which were the taxing and another incident when I was living at my house, a broken window. So, whatever, they said I had some charges and stuff. I was arrested because of that. That's why I took off, you know. They caught me and they brought me to the station. They held me there for a couple of hours, then they brought me to detention. They told me I have rights, I could call a lawyer, stuff like that. I called my lawyer.

They asked me if I wanted to call my mom too, so I called her. They were asking me about the window charge; they were asking me about that. They made me sign some statements and stuff. That charge got dismissed, but the taxing charge, I went to court for. There were four or five taxing charges, but it only happened once. I don't know, but I guess it was the same people that did the other ones, they thought I was with them. They never caught me so, they thought that I had got away or something. When they told me that I had four or five charges, I was like "What?"

Detention When I got there I was mostly blanked out. Like I was in my own little world, you know. I just got there and I went straight to my room. I didn't even look around, nothing. I just stayed in my own little world. I didn't feel the need to be there, I didn't want to hear nobody say nothing, I didn't want to hear nothing. I went to court the next day. I was there for awhile, the charges came up three months after. For three months I stayed there. It was boring and I wanted to get out of there. They kept me in, I think my mom had something to do with it you know.

The first couple of times my mom called I didn't want to talk to her. At first I was like, no, no. Then, after, I started to talk to her. The way I am is if I'm mad, at anything, anything period, like I'm mad at everything, basically. I'm not mad for like two hours or nothing. I'm mad for like a whole week. It's in my head for like that whole week. I didn't even want to talk to her because of that.

Because I knew, when I first got into the group homes and stuff, I knew it was never going to stop. Every time we came out, we would say, "Oh yeah, we're going to work on this, we're going to work on that." But for the first few months, everything's good

and then after that, it just goes back to the same old, same old arguing every day and stuff, you know. I was mad at that too.

It was pretty easy in Detention. I got along with the staff. It wasn't rough. I wouldn't say that. Some days I made it rough. It would start out with, like one of the staff getting on my back. And then I would just push it further. A staff would give me an early night [a punishment to go to bed early] for being in my room one minute late. He would give me an early night for the next day. Then I'd get mad at that, then I'd start making noise. I'd bang on the door or I'd just keep knocking at night, every time I'd go the bathroom. You just bother them. Just let them know, at least. That's the only thing I coulda done.

What was worst was just being there. Being told when to go to bed. Being told you can't watch this at this time. There wasn't really nothing bad about it too much, it was just being controlled by someone else, that you don't even know.

Court Well the first two court dates were dismissed or something like that. Postponement. When I actually went to court for it, first I pleaded not guilty because I wasn't guilty. I wanted to know where these other four [charges] came from. My lawyer did some checking and he told me that they put my name in it because the people that did it, the public or whatever, they gave the description. The description by the victims fit me. He said they had also strong proof or something like that. So I was like, okay. The next time I go down I must plead guilty. Now I told him I was going to plead guilty.

It kept getting postponed and postponed. At the end of it I probably would have ended up doing, you know, the [same] time. Probably would have end up doing less time, if I'd have pled guilty a while ago. So I decided, forget all this chasing, chasing. Just give me my time. So I pled guilty and he gave me six months, but he gave me three months in custody and the rest on probation, intensive probation, community supervision.

I was surprised. I thought I was going to get out on probation or something. I was kind of upset to hear that. Because I never had that before [secure custody]. So when my lawyer told me, I could get probation, I was more hoping for that. He added three months, it wasn't too bad. I coulda got more. I coulda got worse. Like Centre X or something. I never went there. But from what people tell me, it's worse. It's cause it's more like a jail. It's more like a real young jail. Detention's like a hotel or something. Compared to what it really should be, Detention's like nothing. It's like a day camp. Cause you just go there, you just do your school, you do the chores and stuff. As long as you do what you're ordered, that's all basically you have to do. Centre X you have the real jail time. Mostly you're in your room. You barely get free time and stuff, you know. At Detention it's like it's free time till the point you don't even want free time no more.

The judge, he was pretty cool, you know. He looked at me a couple of times to see how I'm looking or how I'm gonna act. He said something to me but it was nothing really like, to me or towards me. It was more he had to ask me something. He was pretty good. Because from what I understand or from what I see, is that I could have got more time than that. Cause it was four things, it wasn't just one charge. So I coulda got way more than that because, I think the other kid that got caught, he got, what was it, nine months closed custody or something like that.

Probation After I left [Detention] I went home, to my mom. I was on supervision, community supervision. I'm home but I'm

supervised. I have curfew and stuff. I wasn't allowed back on the Avenue A, that's where [the robbery] happened.

The parole officer, he'd come to my house. I had to go see him twice a week. Either he'll come or I'll go. Every day at six. I didn't like it, but I was just happy to be out. I didn't care what they say as long as they say, okay I can go home, okay I'll do it. That was perfect. No problems at all. Then the intensive probation started. Which is what I'm on now. It's like a little bit more stricter. I have to do the same thing; beep the parole officer's pager at six. Every day at six o'clock. I come here [office] only once a week. I don't usually come here, they come to my house.

Since I came back, things are better. I think it's cause, I think my mom gave up, you know. When I came out I was turning 18, so I don't think she really wanted to put me through all those things again. Cause it wouldn't be the youth system, you know, it would be adult after that. So I don't think she wanted to put me through that. I think she just kinda forgot about it. Some of the stuff, she just let it slip a little bit. I know I've changed in some ways but to me, the way I think, I'm just doing what I have to do.

School I found myself a new school. I'm not in the regular high school. There's a program, 16 plus program. I'm in that. It's all right. It's like a work-study program that we're doing. It's like three days we're in school and two days we're working in a factory. It's like baby stuff, Pampers and stuff like that. Pack boxes, shipping and receiving. It's easy. I like physical work, so I picked it. We get a reference or a job similar to that or something at the end. At least we have experience. In other schools, there's a lot more kids. There's all different types of teachers, so all have different moods. I couldn't get along with that. At my school there's only a couple of kids, like eight kids. There's one teacher. That's it. So it's levelled out a bit, you know. At least I know her personality and we only have her so I know how she is. Other schools it's like I didn't know the other people. It was too much different personalities and stuff, who I couldn't agree with.

Friends/Peers–Gangs I've never been a victim of a crime. I was just being picked on, something like that. Not taxing wise, but like, different colours and shit. Gangs. There's red and blue, you know. Red is for Bloods, blue for the Crips … but my colour was red.

When I decided to call myself a Blood? When I was turning 16, like 15 and a half.

A lot of people know. Cause I don't hide nothing, man. I walk with my bandanas all the time; to school, to everything.

What does it mean? For me, I didn't become a member just because I have enemies that are blue or cause I want to be recognized or nothing. Me, I did it cause I consider them as family. To me, I never got along with my mom. I don't know my dad. My brother, he's too small. I have two sisters, but they're older. They moved on and stuff. I stopped talking to a lot of people cause of different reasons. Like troublemakers and stuff, I stopped talking to them. Then I joined the Bloods or whatever cause I see them as family, you know. I don't consider them friends. I don't like friends. I don't have friends. Now, all I have is family. I don't believe in friends no more. Cause there's always something with friends. Jealousy or something. If I'm gonna know you and you're gonna be cool with me then you might as well be family. You help me I help you, that's it. 'Cause whenever I'm with them, it's like, we don't go look for trouble. We just stay and chill in one pipe. If the trouble comes, then we handle it or whatever. We don't go out looking for trouble, get loud and drinking

on the street. You know, stuff like that. We don't do that stuff. We just stay calm. In the summertime we just go to the parks and chill out there, that's all we do. 'Cause a lot of us we have dogs and stuff. We just go to the park to let them run around, let them play with each other. We stay there, play basketball, that's all we do.

If a Crips shows up there'd be a beef, no doubt. There'll be beef for sure. 'Cause it's not allowed. There's places we can't go and there's places they can't go. So it's like, if they end up there, they know they shouldn't have been there. So something's gonna happen. Most of the people that we have problems with were usually Crips and stuff. Plus where we live is known as a Blood area.

You can get killed, very easily. Like there's certain parts [of town] that I can't go at all. You know Y neighbourhood? I can't go there at all. I'll be dead. First step, anyone of them see me, I'll be dead. Like dead, dead, dead, dead. That's like the biggest part of the Crips, I think. That's like the biggest Crip area. I can't even pass through. There are those places too, that's pure Bloods. Crips cannot go at all. Can't be seen, period. I might as well just dig my own grave.

Everybody's the boss in my group. I think it's that, most of the people who are in my crew, we're just like red. That's the colour, we's just red. And then we just happen to see eye to eye on the same things.

To be a Blood you gotta know us or you gotta talk to us. We gotta know who you are first. We don't just take in anybody. We don't want all different types of little kids or little people that just wanna be cool. Women, it's not that they're not allowed. Cause we have the girls, the Blood girls. We have them but we don't really let them get into all of this stuff cause it's not really for them. I don't see it as a girl thing. If a guy has a problem with a girl, okay, go deal with your business. But I don't see it as a girl gang. Getting together and fighting other gangs.

You can't be younger than 16. Cause then we feel responsible. I wouldn't want my little brother to go out there and start joining the gangs and stuff. And then if something happened to him, what's my mom going to say? So that's how I see it. When other kids come up to me, they're like, "You're a Blood, dah, dah, dah. Can I do your thing?" I'm like, "No, you can't. 'Cause you're still young. What's your mom going to say if something happens to you one day? What am I going to do? You're part of me. We're all responsible for everybody. It's not just your mom, guys, it's us too, you know." That's why I consider them as family. Cause it isn't everybody just doing things for themselves. Doing things for you, your parents, everybody, you're family.

We have all the Asians. It's mostly Asians and blacks, that's all. There's no white guys though. Only Asians and blacks. The Crips, they're black, white, Spanish. It's mostly Spanish and black. In my town there's a lot of Spanish and black, a couple of whites here and there, you know. The majority of Crips, as I see it, is a lot of Spanish and blacks.

We smoke sometimes, just weed, that's it. We drink sometimes, yeah. I don't really go nowhere. I just like to stay at home. I just like to chill. I don't like to chill where there could be problems or cops. That's why I just go to the park. So it's like if anything I can just go home. If the cops come, okay I'm going home. Cause my home is right next to the park.

There's no meetings and stuff. Nah, there's none of that. You just say what's up. If you want to chill, you call and you say what's up. The most we'll do is fight. That's the law that we'll break the most. Fight. Less than

doing some robbery, some criminal acts, you know. That's like the farthest we'll go, is fight. Like a gang fight, that's the farthest.

Yeah, I had a lot [of fights]. Mostly it's by myself, though. Usually like when I'm going somewhere by myself and I wear my colours other places, that I don't usually go and they'd approach me. They be like, "Yo what's happening, you know it's blue around here". I'll tell them straight up, "I don't care. I'm from across town. I don't care. I'm passing through. If you guys are gonna do something, do something. If not, let me go." Usually they'll wanna do something. And then whatever happens, happens. I have to, my back's against the wall. I gotta do what I gotta do. Only a couple of times it was more than one [guy]. But it was nothing I couldn't really handle. It's usually just colours. Colours, blocks, disrespecting families. That's how it would start. It would start like disrespect over another member … It depends on the mood, you know.

I'm sure my mom knows. But ever since I've been wearing red, she doesn't really pay attention. She asked me a couple of times, Oh well, you're a blah, you're a this or this. I'm like, yeah, come on. You see the colours, nothing but red in my house, so. But she doesn't really pay attention. She'll just tell me, be careful, you know. Yeah, yeah, I know.

Because, to tell you the truth, though, the real Bloods and Crips, they're from L.A. That's where it started. Those are the real Bloods and Crips. All this criminal stuff and all this stuff that you guys heard before about Bloods and Crips, that's mostly them. That's where it came from. The truth is though, everybody else is mostly like wannabes or something. Everybody just wannabe like them. Cause they see them do it, then they wanna do it too. That's mostly it though. In L.A., if you were to ask a Crip the same question, he'll tell you something else. Cause they do it different. Here people do it different. Down there is more serious. They really die for this, really. No matter what, let's say there were like 50 Crips and one Blood, they would really die for it. Here people say that, but when it comes down to it, they don't really know. Cause they don't live it. So they get scared or they chicken out. They're like whoa, I didn't want this to get serious.

Yeah, we have weapons. We have knives. Some have guns and stuff. Yeah, I have knives. All types. I usually walk with my knife. Not now, because my probation stuff. But before this, before I was on intensive probation. I was walking around all the time because I couldn't trust nobody. You couldn't trust because we all live in the same place. It's only a street that's separating us, not even like a block or nothing. It's just a street that's separating the blue from the red. We could walk freely. I don't need to carry my weapons cause a lot of them know me.

To tell you the truth, there's a lot of times I could use my knives but me, I'm not a weapon type person. I'll buy a knife. I'll buy any type of weapon but it doesn't really mean I'm gonna use it. Before, I used to buy knives galore. I had over 10, 15 knives. But none of them were ever used. Every time I fight I could be the first to pull it out and do that, but I never do. It never comes to my head. Once I'm fighting all I want to do is fight. It never comes to my head to think, oh I have a knife on me. It's funny; I've never actually used it. I have it, yeah, just in case. Like I had a knife pulled on me but it wasn't like… It was close to me but it wasn't like he was going to stab me. He pulled it out to make me back off. But I didn't. I could have been dead that day. It was over a different district.

John, the leader of my probation team, the head boss, he knows about the Bloods, he told me. He was like, "You gotta watch that, cause the cops is watching you too." But they can't really say anything. Cause they could tell me to stop, but I'm not. It's up to me. It's not against my probation to wear red, you know. They could give me good advice. I'll take it, but I'm gonna still do what I still do. We made a commitment, once we all, we knew who we all were. I'll say 30, we were 30, we all met. The first time that we all formed, that we all met, like once you join you can't leave. You can't leave unless you have a really good reason. You can't just pick up and leave because you're scared that you're moving to a Crip town and they might kill you or something like that. It's family.

We take it very seriously, you know. Because if it wasn't then it would all be a joke. Like everybody would be wearing red and blue. That's why I consider them family. It's not like any people just say, "Yo you're gonna be …, we're going to be Black Panthers today," you know. Nah, it's more than that. It's deeper than that. It's deeper than the colour.

JEWEL

Jewel is a 17-year-old female of mixed race. At the time of the interview she was a student and under the jurisdiction of both the *Young Offenders Act* and provincial child welfare legislation. Jewel was serving an 18-month term of probation, with a residency condition for her to abide in a group home until her eighteenth birthday. This followed a sentence of eight months' secure custody and four months' open custody for assault.

Basically I remember everything at the age of five, six. Five, six, my grandfather died, my mom's father. That's when my mom went downhill, she was very close to her father. He passed away; she started doing lots of coke. That continued for a very long time. My mom was very inadequate and she had drug abuse [problems]. I figured things out. I was very smart for my age and I learned stuff that I shouldn't have learned at the age of six. Like, the smell of drugs, for instance. Hash or pot, I knew the difference between them. I just didn't know exactly what it was but I knew it was something. Freebasing also has a certain odour to it and I knew the smells and what they would do. But I just didn't know the proper names to it. My dad was very blunt about everything. He just didn't care if I was there or not. My mom more or less tried to stay in her room, which she constantly did. She would always be high all the time on coke, at least 23 hours out of 24. So basically at that age I felt like I had to take care of myself and my mom. Cause I didn't know what was going on. She was just always sleeping, all the time and whatever. So I was just like, okay, mommy's sick. I felt emotionally, mentally all by myself. Most of the time there was an okay amount of food for a little kid because my parents, they did drugs so they didn't really bother eating. My mom did not work, my father did. In a way I kind of liked it because if I wanted something, I always got it when they were high and I learnt how to manipulate that when I was a kid. Other than that it was just like very lonely.

Me and my father were close at one point. But he was also stoned, heavily drug addict[ed]. He would do everything and anything he could get his hands on and my mom just did hash, weed, and coke. My dad was always out. He would come home after work and I'd always ask to go out. If he felt like it, he took me out. My dad, the times that he was around, taught me a lot

of stuff. How to survive on the street, hustling, stuff like that. He taught me how to B&E [break and enter]; how to get money. For an example, we used to go to clubs and he used to sit me on a pool table and play pool for money. He wouldn't take me out when I was six, I mean [only] when I got more older. We used to play basketball for money. There was a lot of street fights and stuff like that. He taught me stuff like that ... criminalization wise.

Experiences with the Social Service/Child Protection System

First off, my dad's sister took me when I was eight. I left so my parents could clean up themselves. I just didn't really have it too easy there. At my aunt's, I was getting abused by my cousin beating on me. She was 13 at the time and I was 8. Every time we used to walk the dog she used to always kick me in my shins in the same spot to the point where I used to have bruises, without exaggeration. And she used to threaten me a lot. She used to tell me how she was going to take the dog's leash and tie it around my neck and kick me off the hills. My little cousin upstairs, he was young. He seen it one time [the beating] and he went to go tell my aunt. I remember that day. I was taking a shower and my aunt comes in and she's screaming and I got so scared. I didn't know what she was yelling at and I just started to sit there and cry. I thought she was yelling at me for something. All of a sudden she was like, "Why didn't you tell me? When you finish your shower, get your ass out here." And I just started crying and because I know how my aunt is and I didn't want her to get in trouble. She's still my cousin, I still loved her. I found out that my aunt punched my cousin in the head and told her to leave. So my cousin was sitting outside crying. That was just really bad.

Then after school, I left. I went back home. I stayed with my mom until my ninth birthday. I was first placed in the system when I was nine, that's when I got taken off of her. My mom and I were at a friend's house. She wanted me to take off my Rollerblades and I said no. She was like, "I don't want you falling" and "I'm like, "I'm not going to fall." So she tried to come and take them off me and I kicked her with them. She started getting mad. She was like, I'm calling your social worker and you're going to be out of my house. And her friend started swearing at her a lot. Saying things like, "Ah you fucking bitch, how can you kick your daughter out of your house, you're not a good mother…." So he left and I found out afterwards that he's the one who called social services on us. And I got taken off of her. I didn't understand much of what the hell was going on. And then all of a sudden I'm plopped in front of this woman. She was like, "Hi, I'm your new foster mother." And I'm like, "Do I have to call you mother?" She's like, "No." And I'm like, "Good." Pretty shitty. I was the youngest. I got picked on, pretty much by her daughter, the foster mom's daughter. And then I used to get name called by the boys that was there and stuff like that.

Less than a year after that my aunt took me, another aunt. Actually she's not really even my aunt, she's my cousin. She's like a second mom to me, basically, my godmother. She's been my legal guardian. My mom had no choice. She was inadequate anyway, so it's not as if, "I don't want her living with her." So basically I just call her mom or aunty, you know what I mean. I lived with her for about five years. A lot of

shit went down. I was very troubled. Always I kept to myself. I started taking drugs. I tried almost everything. The drugs I've never tried was crack. I never sniffed anything. I never did no needles. I never did PCP, LSD, stuff like that. There's just certain drugs I refused to touch because of seeing my parents grow up [on drugs]. Basically I did drugs because I wanted to. There's no other thing about that. My mom, actually, took it pretty hard when she found out that I was doing drugs. She was like, "It's all my fault." I'm like, "No, first off, you're not the one who twisted my arm and said I had to do it." It's just I wanted to see what it was like, experimenting, stuff like that. I left my aunt's place at 14 because I was in drug rehab for a year and a half.

For the first six months of rehab, I was just, yeah, yeah, whatever, bullshit. Come up at the bus stop and you know, do some drugs, whatever. And then I realized how much it was really hurting my aunt. And then I just stopped and looked at myself. Shit, I don't want to end up like my parents. So I said, "Yeah, I want to start taking this seriously." And for about a year I took it seriously and it worked out. And then after that I was back at my aunt's. I used to do a lot of stuff to my aunt. I used to steal from her, stuff like that, you know money, food, anything. Just cause it was there. I liked it, it caught my eye, I took it.

There was a time period where my dad just left my mom. My mom had my brother but it was not the same father. They continued living together and even during the pregnancy my dad still tried to help out my mom a bit. And he knew it wasn't his. So he tried helping her out but she had another boyfriend. I did not like this man and I still don't. I was very confused; I didn't know what I wanted. I wanted to live with my mom because I knew I could manipulate her and get what I wanted from her. But I didn't want to live with her because I needed a parent, more or less, you know what I mean. So that's why if people was to ever ask me, "How's your parents?" I don't have parents, you know what I mean? Never had parents. My mom and dad is a mom and dad by name but...my aunt I would say, more or less, is my parent.

My dad, there was a point in time where he would only pop in maybe once or twice a year. And he got me a teddy bear. It was Christmas. My aunt and her daughter wanted to show me what it feels like to be robbed from and stealing and stuff like that. She wanted to demonstrate how it is. I took the gift that my dad gave to me very closely because I didn't see him as much as I used to. So I said you're not getting my teddy bear. She says "Yes, I'm going to take your teddy bear just to show you how it feels to take something without asking for it." She was basically trying to teach me something. My aunt, I love her dearly and I would never, no matter how mad I get at her or what I would ever happen to say to her, I would never lay a hand on my aunt. Never, never, never, never. Me and my aunt got into an argument and we were yelling back and forth at each other. We were like standing closely, yelling at each other. And her daughter got involved and her daughter started like pushing me, nudging type of thing. And I told her to stay out of it. And she was like, "Don't talk to my mother like that." I'm like, "Listen, it has nothing to involve you, you need to move." She kept nudging me. I told her, "Stop it." And I seen her coming towards me again and I thought she was going to nudge me again and I tripped out. I have a tendency to pass out when I get really pissed off. I blacked out. And I remember I grabbed her, I had her in a headlock and I was punching her.

And then after that, my aunt was hitting me on my head. She was like, "Stop it, stop it. Jenny's turning blue, she can't breathe, stop, stop." But I wasn't really paying attention, so everything was just like blurry-ish. I let go of Jenny and crawled to my bed, I was staying in the corner of it and I was just rocking back and forth. Jenny lost her glasses and they were broken and then she started to get mad and she took a broom and she started hitting me with it. The broom broke; it broke and cut her. My aunt grabbed her daughter. She was like, "Jenny, listen, you need to calm down, you know." Cause my cousin has heart problems. So she left my room and I got out and I wanted to walk away but she started back up at me. Anyways, we got into a big fight, verbally this time. The ambulance came and they checked up on my cousin, to make sure she was okay.

My aunt has three kids. The oldest was the daughter, and she has two sons. That evening the two sons came home and I got into a fight with her oldest son. He grabbed me and he threw me to the wall and I started swinging at him. Because he said, "Don't ever touch my sister..." He's grabbing on me, fuck, whatever. So I started swinging at him. I got out of his grip. I didn't want to hit my cousin because he has cerebral palsy, seizures and stuff. And if he was to get hit he could have another seizure. So I didn't really want to hit him. My aunt's boyfriend at the time, jumped on me to put me to the floor to calm me down. I started swinging at him. I'm like, "Get off me." And my cousin, the youngest son, grabbed me and took me outside. He's like, "Listen, what's wrong with you"? I just started breaking down and I just started crying. And I'm like, "Fuck you know, everybody's on me man." We had a big long conversation and after that, ever since that evening I was quote, bad tempered, and I wasn't trusted around anybody. My aunt was taking care of her father at the time. She's like, "Well, I don't want you with my father just in case he does something to piss you off and you go after him." And it was just like little comments like that, back and forth, which really started to piss me off. One day it just got so bad that I said "Fuck it," and I grabbed all my stuff, told her I was leaving for school, closed the door. She was like, "Okay, goodbye, have a good day." I closed the door and I walked over to my mom's with all my stuff. I dropped off all my stuff and I said, "Fuck it, I'm never going back there. I'm going to school, good bye." And I left and I went to school and I talked to the counsellor at school. I'm like, I'm not going back to my house. And I explained to them why. And then after that my social worker came down and I got placed to a group home.

I was there for about five months. I got into an argument with the staff.... I got into another argument so I ran away. I left for a month. I was just back and forth between friends. Sometimes I wouldn't even bother eating. I don't even know how but I just immuned myself to it. There would be like a week or so that I just wouldn't really bother eating. I would pick at stuff. Or buy chips here and there, stuff like that. I got charged for my crime in July.

Criminal Charge An assault of a police officer was the main charge. I was walking my friend home and on my way back this cop stopped me. It was about three o'clock in the morning. That's when I was on the run. I was dressed up. I had a skirt, whatever. And he started asking me questions and stuff so I gave him false identification and I left the scene. And after that I was up the other street and two guys were like following me. So I turned, and as I got to the corner of another street I

seen the same cop who stopped me the first time. So he started chasing me and I ran. And then after that I stopped running and he grabbed me from behind and then cause I have a thing that if I get grabbed from my neck or grabbed from behind and I don't know who the person is I have this tendency of just like, spazzing. And I had a hammer in sleeve for my own protection, cause me and my friend came back from a club and I was dressed up and the cop came up behind me and I used the hammer on him.

I really don't know what happened to him, because from some people I heard he was in the hospital for six months. Some people said he just had a little tiny concussion. I didn't really know cause no one told me first hand. Everyone told me second hand or third hand so I never really knew exactly the damage that was done to him.

Basically in my mind, all I wanted to do was go home and something was in my way of stopping it and so I just blacked out. That's what happened and then after that I was in the alleyway and the other cop was like trying to sit on me to calm me down or what ever. These other cops seen and they called backup and then other cops came along. I got restrained. I got an asthma attack from being restrained. I got handcuffed and I had a Velcro strap around my feet. Then I was in the back of the cop car and I couldn't breathe and so I had an asthma attack. And they called the ambulance and everything like that and I was in the hospital for a while. And then an investigator obviously knew my true identification and that was that.

After that I went to Detention and from Detention I went to Girls' secure unit. I was there for a month before I arrived in court. That's when I got my sentence. Because basically if I do something wrong,

I say I did it wrong. And I'm not going to say, oh well no, when they have all kinds of evidence obviously, you know. I do stupid things; I'm not that stupid. It was supposed to be for a year in total, with 18 months probation. The probation would start when I got to open unit. It didn't really work out my way. I got eight months closed custody, and I was there a month before I got sentenced but it didn't count. So I was there for nine months and then I went to open custody. I was supposed to be in open custody for four months. I went back to court after my four months and they told me they were transferring me back for my own protection—child welfare—I was there for a year and a half. They don't trust me. And then they told me that they have a feeling that I would end up to my old ways again. They always ended up with some kind of excuse not to let me go. My [custody] sentence is over, I still have probation until March. In May or June I'll be out on my own.

Family Relationships Now Basically, I would more or less say that everything I've been through, I don't really feel bad for myself. My mom, I still talk with my mom. She would sometimes just sit there and she would cry and she'd say, "I'm sorry for what I put you through." And I'm like, "Listen, if you wouldn't have done what you've done and if I wouldn't have gone to do what I did, I wouldn't be as a strong person as I am today." Basically I just learnt. I learned who I was and what I want to become and basically what I don't want to be. She's still the same.

My dad, I see my dad once in a while. He hangs around a park a lot. He hangs around with the bums. I don't know if he has a place or not, but I still see him and I say hi and stuff. I sit there and talk with him for like an hour. He's doing a lot better. He told me that he quit most of the drugs that he was doing. He just stays to weed, hash, and his drinking. And I believe him in a way because basically my dad was always very honest. My dad never hid anything from me.

My brother came along when I was ten. My brother's in a foster home right now. He is eight. We're ten years apart. He was in a foster home at the age of three. The same foster home that he's in now. He was there for about five years. I keep in contact with him. Me and his foster mom are very close. I like her a lot. She's very down to earth. 'Cause, like, my brother is my life. From 10 to 14 I was very, very suicidal. I just didn't care about anything and it finally clicked in to me that I have a little man to take care of, type of thing. During the time when he was born, I would come over all the time to see him at my mom's. It got to the point where my mom used to call him my son. Cause I used to take care of him all the time, it got to the point where he used to call me mommy. When he was sick I would bring him to the doctor. He was something that I could actually look forward to. I took that very seriously.

School At school, I used to get picked on a lot, 'cause I was also very active when I was a kid. Always running around getting bruised, my clothes always dirty. Because drug addicts, they're not the cleanest, so I used to get picked on because of how my clothes looked. Or just because I was small and stuff like that. But that was when I was younger and then I grew up a little bit more, and I learnt how to start talking for myself. And then after that everything started clearing up.

School, I never liked school. I still don't like school. But they're things that you don't like that you gotta do. I did my classes but I just passed or teachers may just have passed me because they liked me, you know. I should have been finished school last year. It's just that, with my classes, cause I wasn't their certain age, they stuck me in grade 7/8's when I was supposed to be doing grade 9 work. So I would get kicked out all the time cause I am also ADHD [attention deficit hyperactivity disorder]. I can't sit in one place, and if something's too easy I finish it quickly and I want something else to do. I get bored very quickly. And I would always get kicked out, so I failed my grade 9. Now I'm at an alternative school and I just want my grade 10 French and my math so I can go to trade school, auto mechanics. In trades, you need grade 10.

Friends I have a few very close friends. During my AWOL's [on the run] I thought friends were certain friends and I found out they weren't friends. But basically now, if I looked at it, they were just like drug acquaintances. I don't like girls. I have like maybe two, three friends, that I actually consider a friend, that are girls. Other than that they're all just acquaintances. I always grew up with guys. I was always like tomboy-ish. Running around all tough, type of thing. One of my best friends, I was best friends with him for five years; he helped me through a lot.

When I went to Girls' secure unit, I met one girl and she wrote poetry. She could come up with a two-page poem about her life in five minutes. It just came out like that. And I'm like, "Aw shit, that's cool. Teach me how to write." She's like, "I can't teach you how to write. Basically you write down how you feel but make it rhyme." So I tried and I'm like, "This sounds like shit compared yours, but listen to it anyways." She's like, "It's okay, it's okay." And ever since then I started writing. I wrote poetry for classes, like my English classes. I wrote fairy tales. A lot of stories and stuff like that. I like creative writing a lot and I have a lot of poetry actually. I have two notebooks full and I'm working on a third one.

Drugs and Alcohol I drink once in a while but not constantly. It will not be every day. It'll basically be when I feel to, type of thing. I'm bored, let's go have a drink or something. But I don't let it control me. It's not consistently all the time. Drugs, basically it's "been there done that." It's boring now, I'm past that stage. Move on, you know what I mean? I stopped for about six months and then got to a period where I started up. It was a very short time and then after that I said, "It's boring." And that was it. That was when I was on my AWOL. Then after that I was locked up so I couldn't get to it. Ever since then, I got bored of it.

Social Workers I didn't like any of them. There was one I had for four and half years, almost five years and I didn't like him at all. I only started to actually trust him near the five years. Then after that I found I had to be transferred because I was no longer under child welfare, which made me really mad. While I was in Girls' secure unit alone I had four different [workers]. So I was like, "You know what, forget it." I never liked social workers or anything like that just because of the fact that it's a stranger, coming in my life, telling me what to do. And telling me what they think is good for me when they don't know me from Adam. And that, especially now, pisses me off because I could tell you all kinds of stuff, what happened to me, but certain people have a tendency of getting a certain image about me which I'm far from being that image. I'm not like that anymore and there's still like people that say, "Oh, well, you know she did this and she did that, so she must be like her parents, or something." And that just really pissed me off. I always had that impression that that's what they always thought about me. Or if I would say something to them, they would always interpret it wrong. I always felt they tried to invade my personal space and I didn't like it. Oh, they could try but basically you can't succeed unless I let you.

Experience in the Youth Justice System Custody

Lawyers/Judges/Police My relationship with my lawyer? Basically it's like, "Hi, I'm your lawyer." Okay, this is what I did and get me out of it or get me less time. It wasn't, "I'll call you tomorrow and get coffee." My family court lawyer, I was just too young to say anything. "You want to go home with your mommy?" "No." "Okay." That was just that. So she said whatever, for me not to go. My criminal lawyer, I couldn't say really much. She asked me, "Are you guilty"? And I said, "Yeah." And she was like, "Oh, okay." And I guess she just said, "She's guilty, that's it."

One judge I had for awhile, I think his name is Judge Smith or something like that. Some man, I would always somehow be in front of him. I never remembered him but he would always remember me. He was like, "Oh I remember you, you're back here again." I just never paid attention. The last time I went to court, for my criminal charge, he would talk to me. He was like, "Listen, I'm talking to you now. You really got to start smartening up, cause next time it may not be as nice." And I'm like, "I know." And he asked me a few questions and I talked to him.

[The police] treated me very mean [after the assault]. I wasn't expecting like caviar after I just attacked one of them. They were very freaking rough. I blacked out. It's like I knew it, but didn't know it. It's like not paying attention to anything. Basically I'm a very determined kid. When I want to do something, I do it. I wanted to go home

and that's where I wanted to go. That's the only thing that I was pretty much thinking about. It was like, I want to go home and all of a sudden I have the feeling I'm being attacked. He wasn't really trying to attack me but he was trying to arrest me. But he grabbed me from behind and I was like, whoa.

I would say the worst thing that I ever had to go through was when I first went to lock-up. Just the fact of staying in a little room—it's about the size of a little bathroom. This room is like a little jail cell, literally. Sit there and having to hear that door lock and you can't come out whenever you want. You just have to sit there in your bed by yourself and have to think about what you've done. Even if you're not trying to think about it, the flashbacks still go there. Lock-up is not very much of a punishment. Life alone is a punishment. No matter what you do and if you regret it, I think that's your main punishment right there. Just the fact that you have to go to sleep with that on your mind every day, every night.

Remembering what you did, that's just the biggest punishment on its own. I took a lot of shit hard. That's also why for the longest time I was suicidal. Every time I used to do something stupid I used to take it out on myself a lot. To the point where I'm like, "Oh fuck, I can't take this." I never cut myself but I used to self-mutilate in different ways. I used to grow nails and every time I used to get mad I used to either hit my head on walls or just sit there and start scratching up my arms or my legs and rip out my hair. I tried OD-ing [overdosing] on pills. I tried OD-ing on alcohol with pills. I tried suffocating myself. I tried so much shit. Every once in a while I say I'm fed up with life, but I don't take it to extremes anymore. I just write it all down. If I wouldn't have gone to lock-up and I wouldn't have found myself. Since lock-up I had a different perspective on a lot of things and am more of a person than anything. I still don't take no shit from nobody and I still have an anger problem, so they claim. But I wouldn't say anger problem, I would just basically tell you what I'm feeling. If you don't like it, too bad for you, because I already said what I had to say. I'm more verbal than physical. I've learnt how to say how I feel. I learnt how to express it and if I don't say it verbally I write it. I don't stuff anything down anymore.

I had a lot of arguments with staff. They would say something and they would be so quick to say go to the back room [time-out room] or you're getting sent off. And I'm like, "Listen, do you have any kids?" And for the ones who would tell me no, boy, I would just ram into them. I'm like, "Listen." And I would tell them exactly how it feels. "Obviously you don't know exactly how it feels because, first off, you don't have kids and second off, you're not the one who has to be locked up in a little room." Or, "You're not the one who has to be locked up period and you see other kids visiting with their parents and your parents never show up" and shit like that. There's a few people that I met along the way that were okay, that I actually liked. They didn't act like they had the freaking rulebook shoved up their ass. Basically, they treated us how they wanted to be treated. Some of them had kids of their own and obviously wouldn't do half of the shit that they had to do to us, to their own kids.

I'm getting my own apartment. I was actually job searching today. Getting myself a job, I'm going to get my own apartment and live a happy little humble home by myself.

CONCLUSION

The purpose of this chapter is not to analyze the content of the young persons' interviews, nor to provide interpretations of them within particular frameworks of analysis. Rather, the interviews are presented for their own sake: to convey an overview of the experiences and perspectives of two young persons who have been in conflict with the law and who have also been subjected to social service interventions. At the time of interview, both James and Jewel were still involved with the system and still under jurisdiction of the youth justice court. Their stories remind us that each young person, each "case," in the criminal justice system has his or her own personal history, his or her own, often tragic, life circumstances. Thus, while it is essential to examine how youth law and youth justice systems have been developed, understood, administered, and researched, it is equally important to not lose sight of those who are most affected by youth justice: the young persons themselves.

The focus of this edited collection has been to provide a framework for understanding youth justice in Canada: both how responses to youth crime have evolved historically, and how youth justice is currently practised. The various contributors to this collection have outlined the intentions of policy and law, the manner in which they are applied, and the manner in which we respond to youth criminality. This last chapter stands in stark contrast to the others by presenting the voices of two young persons who describe their own trajectories through the youth justice and social service systems. What is significant about these testimonies is that they provide a window into the truth about youth justice that only the youth themselves can convey: the realities of pain, loss, frustration, confusion, strength, growth, and even transformation. The words of these young people underline the importance of listening to youth and of learning from their experiences. Those researching and working in the youth justice system in Canada can only benefit from allowing youth the opportunity to be heard and making use of these experiences to inform both policy and law.

References

Artz, S. (2000). Jenny's story. In R. M. Mann, *Juvenile crime and delinquency: A turn of the century reader,* pp. 245–266. Toronto: Canadian Scholars' Press.

Boyle, J. (1984). *Pain of confinement: Prison diaries.* Dufour Editions.

Caron, R. (2002). *Go boy: This is the true story of life behind bars.* Toronto: White Knight Publications.

Lane, J., Lanza-Kaduce, L., Frazier, C. E., & Bishop, D. M. (2002). Adult versus juvenile sanctions: Voices of incarcerated youth. *Criminology,* 48(3), 431–455.

Melnitzer, J. (1995). *Maximum, medium, minimum.* Toronto: Key Porter Books.

APPENDIX A Juvenile Delinquents Act

CHAPTER J-3

An Act respecting juvenile delinquents

Short title 1. This Act may be cited as the *Juvenile Delinquents Act*, R.S., c. 160, s 1.

Definitions 2. (1) In this Act

"child"   "child" means any boy or girl apparently or actually under the age of sixteen years, or such other age as may be directed in any province pursuant to subsection (2);

"court"   "court" or "juvenile court" means any court duly established under
"juvenile court"   any provincial statute for the purpose of dealing with juvenile delinquents, or specially authorized by provincial statute, the Governor in Council, or the lieutenant governor in council, to deal with juvenile delinquents;

"court of appeal"   "court of appeal" has the same meaning as it has in the *Criminal Code*;

"guardian"   "guardian" includes any person who has in law or in fact custody or control of any child;

"industrial   "industrial school" means any industrial school or juvenile reformatory
school"   or other reformative institution or refuge for children duly approved by provincial statute or by the lieutenant governor in council in any province, and includes such an institution in a province other than that in which the committal is made, when such institution is otherwise available;

"judge"   "judge" means the judge of a juvenile court seized of the case, or the justice, specially authorized by federal or provincial authority to deal with juvenile delinquents, seized of the case;

"justice"   "justice" except in section 5 has the same meaning as it has in the *Criminal Code*;

"juvenile   "juvenile delinquent" means any child who violates any provision of the
delinquent"   *Criminal Code* or of any federal or provincial statute, or of any by-law or ordinance of any municipality, or who is guilty of sexual immorality or any similar form of vice, or who is liable by reason of any other act to be committed to an industrial school or juvenile reformatory under any federal or provincial statute;

"magistrate"   "magistrate", except in subsections 13(1) and (4), and except in section 14, means two or more justices of the peace and also a police magistrate, a stipendiary magistrate and any other person having the power or authority of two or more justices of the peace;

"probation   "probation officer" means any probation officer for juvenile delin-
officer"   quents duly appointed under any provincial statute or this Act;

"superintendent"   "superintendent" means a superintendent of neglected children, or of neglected and delinquent children, or a superintendent or director of child welfare, or a commissioner of the Bureau of Child Protection, or, in general, any officer, whatever is his designation, who is appointed by any provincial government to have the general charge or supervision of work in the province dealing with delinquent children, and also the lawful deputy of such officer;

"supreme court judge"

"supreme court judge" means

(a) in the Province of Ontario, a judge of the Supreme Court of Ontario;

(b) in the Province of Quebec, a judge of the Superior Court;

(c) in the Province of Nova Scotia, a judge of the Supreme Court of Nova Scotia;

(d) in the Province of New Brunswick, a judge of the Supreme Court of New Brunswick;

(e) in the Province of British Columbia, a judge of the Supreme Court of British Columbia;

(f) in the Province of Prince Edward Island, a judge of the Supreme Court of Prince Edward Island;

(g) in the Province of Manitoba, a judge of the Court of Queen's Bench;

(h) in the Province of Saskatchewan, a judge of the Court of Queen's Bench;

(i) in the Province of Alberta, a judge of the Supreme Court of Alberta;

(j) in the Province of Newfoundland, a judge of the Supreme Court of Newfoundland; and

(k) in the Yukon Territory, a judge of the Territorial Court of the Yukon Territory.

Alteration of definition "child"

(2) The Governor in Council may from time to time by proclamation

(a) direct that in any province the expression "child" in this Act means any boy or girl apparently or actually under the age of eighteen years, and any such proclamation may apply either to boys only or to girls only or to both boys and girls, and

(b) revoke any direction made with respect to any province by a proclamation under this section, and thereupon the expression "child" in this Act in that province means any boy or girl apparently or actually under the age of sixteen years. R.S., c. 160, s. 2.

Delinquency

3. (1) The commission by a child of any of the acts enumerated in the definition "juvenile delinquent" in subsection 2(1), constitutes an offence to be known as a delinquency, and shall be dealt with as hereinafter provided.

How child dealt with

(2) Where a child is adjudged to have committed a delinquency he shall be dealt with, not as an offender, but as one in a condition of delinquency and therefore requiring help and guidance and proper supervision. R.S., c. 160, s. 3.

Court's jurisdiction	**4.** Except as provided in section 9, the juvenile court has exclusive jurisdiction in cases of delinquency including cases where, after the committing of the delinquency, the child has passed the age limit mentioned in the definition "child" in subsection 2(1). R.S., c. 160, s. 4.

Summary trials

5. (1) Except as hereinafter provided, prosecutions and trials under this Act shall be summary and shall, *mutatis mutandis*, be governed by the provisions of the *Criminal Code* relating to summary convictions in so far as such provisions are applicable, whether or not the act constituting the offence charged would be in the case of an adult triable summarily, except that

(a) the provisions relating to appeals do not apply to any proceeding in a juvenile court, and

(b) the provisions prescribing a time limit for making a complaint or laying an information in respect of offences punishable on summary conviction where no time is specially limited for making any complaint or laying any information in the Act or law relating to the particular case, do not apply to any such proceeding against an adult, except when an adult is dealt with under section 4 of this Act.

Time for commencement

(2) The provisions of the *Criminal Code* prescribing a time limit for the commencement of prosecutions for offences against the *Criminal Code* apply, *mutatis mutandis*, to all proceedings in the juvenile court.

"Justice"

(3) Whenever in such provisions the expression "justice" occurs, it shall be taken in the application of such provisions to proceedings under this Act to mean "judge of the juvenile court, or justice specially authorized by federal or provincial authority to deal with juvenile delinquents". R.S., c. 160, s. 5.

Powers of judge

6. (1) Every judge of a juvenile court in the exercise of his jurisdiction as such has all the powers of a magistrate.

Idem

(2) In addition to those expressly mentioned in this Act, the juvenile court judge has all the powers and duties, with respect to juvenile offenders, vested in, or imposed on a judge, stipendiary magistrate, justice or justices, by or under the *Prisons and Reformatories Act*.

Discretion of court

(3) The discretion of the juvenile court judge as to the term for which a juvenile delinquent may be committed is not affected by this section. R.S., c. 160, s. 6.

Appointment of deputy judge

7. (1) The judge of a juvenile court may with the approval of the attorney general of the province in which such court is situated appoint a deputy judge, who has all the powers and authority of a judge of a juvenile court in case of the absence or illness or other disability of such judge.

Tenure of office

(2) A deputy judge so appointed holds office during pleasure and is removable at any time by the attorney general or by the judge, with the approval of the attorney general, without cause.

Resignation

(3) The resignation of a deputy judge may be accepted by either the judge by whom he was appointed, or the attorney general. R.S., c. 160, s. 7.

All cases to go to juvenile court	**8.**	**(1)**	When any child is arrested, with or without a warrant, such child shall, instead of being taken before a justice, be taken before the juvenile court; and, if a child is taken before a justice, upon a summons or under a warrant or for any other reason, it is the duty of the justice to transfer the case to the juvenile court, and of the officer having the child in charge to take the child before that court, and in any such case the juvenile court shall hear and dispose of the case in the same manner as if the child had been brought before it upon information originally laid therein.
Exception		**(2)**	Subsection (1) does not apply to any justice who is a judge of the juvenile court or who has power to act as such under any Act in force in the province. R.S., c. 160, s. 8.
Exceptional procedure when offence is indictable	**9.**	**(1)**	Where the act complained of is, under the provisions of the *Criminal Code* or otherwise, an indictable offence, and the accused child is apparently or actually over the age of fourteen years, the court may, in its discretion, order the child to be proceeded against by indictment in the ordinary courts in accordance with the provisions of the *Criminal Code* in that behalf; but such course shall in no case be followed unless the court is of the opinion that the good of the child and the interest of the community demand it.
Order may be rescinded		**(2)**	The court may, in its discretion, at any time before any proceeding has been initiated against the child in the ordinary criminal courts, rescind an order so made. R.S., c. 160, s. 9.
Notices to parents	**10.**	**(1)**	Due notice of the hearing of any charge of delinquency shall be served on the parent or parents or the guardian of the child, or if there is neither parent nor guardian, or if the residence of the parent or parents or guardian is unknown, then on some near relative, if any, living in the city, town or county, whose whereabouts is known, and any person so served has the right to be present at the hearing.
Service of notice		**(2)**	The judge may give directions as to the persons to be served under this section, and such directions are conclusive as to the sufficiency of any notice given in accordance therewith. R.S., c. 160, s. 10.
Powers of clerk	**11.**	**(1)**	The clerk of every juvenile court has power *ex officio* to administer oaths and also, in the absence of the judge and deputy judge, to adjourn any hearing for a definite period not to exceed ten days.
Duties of clerk		**(2)**	It is the duty of the clerk of the juvenile court to notify the probation officer or the chief probation officer, in advance, when any child is to be brought before the court for trial. R.S., c. 160, s. 11.
Private trials	**12.**	**(1)**	The trials of children shall take place without publicity and separately and apart from the trials of other accused persons, and at suitable times to be designated and appointed for that purpose.
Place of trials		**(2)**	Such trials may be held in the private office of the judge or in some other private room in the court house or municipal building, or in the detention home, or if no such room or place is available, then in the ordinary court room, but when held in the ordinary court room an interval of half an hour shall be allowed to elapse between the close of the trial or examination of any adult and the beginning of the trial of a child.

Names not to be published or identity of child indicated	**(3)**	No report of a delinquency committed, or said to have been committed, by a child, or of the trial or other disposition of a charge against a child, or of a charge against an adult brought in the juvenile court under section 33 or under section 35, in which the name of the child or of the child's parent or guardian or of any school or institution that the child is alleged to have been attending or of which the child is alleged to have been an inmate is disclosed, or in which the identity of the child is otherwise indicated, shall without the special leave of the court, be published in any newspaper or other publication.
Application to newspapers	**(4)**	Subsection (3) applies to all newspapers and other publications published anywhere in Canada, whether or not this Act is otherwise in force in the place of publication. R.S., c. 160, s. 12.
Detention home	**13. (1)**	No child, pending a hearing under this Act, shall be held in confinement in any county or other gaol or other place in which adults are or may be imprisoned, but shall be detained at a detention home or shelter used exclusively for children or under other charge approved of by the judge or, in his absence, by the sheriff, or, in the absence of both the judge and the sheriff, by the mayor or other chief magistrate of the city, town, county or place.
Penalty	**(2)**	Any officer or person violating subsection (1) is liable on summary conviction before a juvenile court or a magistrate to a fine not exceeding one hundred dollars, or to imprisonment not exceeding thirty days, or to both.
Exception	**(3)**	This section does not apply to a child as to whom an order has been made pursuant to section 9.
Idem	**(4)**	This section does not apply to a child apparently over the age of fourteen years who, in the opinion of the judge, or, in his absence, of the sheriff, or, in the absence of both the judge and the sheriff, of the mayor or other chief magistrate of the city, town, county or place, cannot safely be confined in any place other than a gaol or lock-up. R.S., c. 160, s. 13.
Where there is no detention home	**14. (1)**	Where a warrant has issued for the arrest of a child, or where a child has been arrested without a warrant, in a county or district in which there is no detention home used exclusively for children, no incarceration of the child shall be made or had unless in the opinion of the judge of the court, or, in his absence, of the sheriff, or, in the absence of both the judge and the sheriff, of the mayor or other chief magistrate of the city, town, county or place, such course is necessary in order to insure the attendance of such child in court.
Promise to attend may be accepted	**(2)**	In order to avoid, if possible, such incarceration, the verbal or written promise of the person served with notice of the proceedings as aforesaid, or of any other proper person, to be responsible for the presence of such child when required, may be accepted; and in case the child fails to appear, at such time or times as the court requires, the person or persons assuming responsibility as aforesaid, shall be deemed guilty of contempt of court, unless in the opinion of the court there is reasonable cause for such failure to appear. R.S., c. 160, s. 14.

Bail may be accepted	15.	Pending the hearing of a charge of delinquency the court may accept bail for the appearance of the child charged at the trial as in the case of other accused persons. R.S., c. 160, s. 15.
Court may adjourn or postpone hearing	16.	The court may postpone or adjourn the hearing of a charge of delinquency for such period or periods as the court may deem advisable, or may postpone or adjourn the hearing *sine die*. R.S., c. 160, s. 16.
Proceedings may be informal	17. (1)	Proceedings under this Act with respect to a child, including the trial and disposition of the case, may be as informal as the circumstances will permit, consistent with a due regard for a proper administration of justice.
Not affected by irregularities	(2)	No adjudication or other action of a juvenile court with respect to a child shall be quashed or set aside because of any informality or irregularity where it appears that the disposition of the case was in the best interests of the child.
Service of process in another jurisdiction	(3)	Except as provided in subsection (5), if a person, whether a child or an adult, against whom any warrant has issued out of a juvenile court cannot be found within the jurisdiction of the juvenile court out of which the warrant was so issued, but is or is suspected to be in any other part of Canada, any judge or deputy judge of a juvenile court within whose jurisdiction such person is or is suspected to be, or if there is no juvenile court having jurisdiction in such place, then any justice within whose jurisdiction such person is or is suspected to be, upon proof being made on oath or affirmation of the handwriting of the juvenile court judge or other officer who issued the warrant, shall make an endorsement on the warrant, signed with his name, authorizing the execution thereof within his jurisdiction.
Authority to arrest	(4)	Such endorsement is sufficient authority to the person bringing such warrant, and to all other persons to whom the warrant was originally directed, and also to all probation officers, constables and other peace officers of the juvenile court or of the territorial division where the warrant has been so endorsed, to execute the warrant therein and to carry the person against whom the warrant was issued when apprehended, before the juvenile court out of which the warrant issued.
Child outside of jurisdiction	(5)	Where a child who has been before a juvenile court and is still under the surveillance of such court has been caused by the court to be placed in a foster home outside of the jurisdiction of such court or has been committed by the court to the care or custody of a probation officer or other suitable person or to an industrial school, outside of the jurisdiction of such court, the court may take any action with respect to such child that it could take were the child within the jurisdiction of such court, and for any such purpose any warrant or other process issued with respect to such child may be executed or served in any place in Canada outside of the jurisdiction of such court without the necessity of complying with subsection (3). R.S., c. 160, s. 17.
Seal not required	18.	It is not necessary to its validity that any seal should be attached or affixed to any information, summons, warrant, conviction order or other process or document filed, issued or entered in any proceeding had or taken under this Act. R.S., c. 160, s. 18.

Child's oath may be dispensed with

19. (1) When in a proceeding before a juvenile court a child of tender years who is called as a witness does not, in opinion of the judge, understand the nature of an oath, the evidence of such child may be received, though not given under oath, if in the opinion of the judge the child is possessed of sufficient intelligence to justify the reception of the evidence and understands the duty of speaking the truth.

Corroborative evidence

(2) No person shall be convicted upon the evidence of a child of tender years not under oath unless such evidence is corroborated in some material respect. R.S., c. 160, s. 19.

Release on probation

20. (1) In the case of a child adjudged to be a juvenile delinquent the court may, in its discretion, take either one or more of the several courses of action hereinafter in this section set out, as it may in its judgment deem proper in the circumstances of the case:

(a) suspend final disposition;

(b) adjourn the hearing or disposition of the case from time to time for any definite or indefinite period;

(c) impose a fine not exceeding twenty-five dollars, which may be paid in periodical amounts or otherwise;

(d) commit the child to the care or custody of a probation officer or of any other suitable person;

(e) allow the child to remain in its home, subject to the visitation of a probation officer, such child to report to the court or to the probation officer as often as may be required;

(f) cause the child to be placed in a suitable family home as a foster home, subject to the friendly supervision of a probation officer and the further order of the court;

(g) impose upon the delinquent such further or other conditions as may be deemed advisable;

(h) commit the child to the charge of any children's aid society, duly organized under an Act of the legislature of the province and approved by the lieutenant governor in council, or, in any municipality in which there is no children's aid society, to the charge of the superintendent, if there is one; or

(i) commit the child to an industrial school duly approved by the lieutenant governor in council.

Support of child

(2) In every such case it is within the power of the court to make an order upon the parent or parents of the child, or upon the municipality to which the child belongs, to contribute to the child's support such sum as the court may determine, and where such order is made upon the municipality, the municipality may from time to time recover from the parent or parents any sum or sums paid by it pursuant to such order.

Return of juvenile delinquent to court

(3) Where a child has been adjudged to be a juvenile delinquent and whether or not such child has been dealt with in any of the ways provided for in subsection (1), the court may at any time, before such juvenile delinquent has reached the age of twenty-one years and unless the court has otherwise ordered, cause by notice, summons, or warrant, the delinquent to be brought before the court, and the court may then

take any action provided for in subsection (1), or may make an order with respect to such child under section 9, or may discharge the child on parole or release the child from detention, but in a province in which there is a superintendent, no child shall be released by the judge from an industrial school without a report from such superintendent recommending such release, and where an order is made by a court releasing a juvenile delinquent from an industrial school or transferring such delinquent from an industrial school to a foster home or from one foster home to another under this subsection, it is not necessary for such delinquent to be before the court at the time that such order is made.

Evidence on hearing

(4) When a child is returned to the court, as provided in subsection (3), the court may deal with the case on the report of the probation officer or other person in whose care such child has been placed, or of the secretary of a children's aid society, or of the superintendent, or of the superintendent of the industrial school to which the child has been committed, without the necessity of hearing any further or other evidence.

Child's own good

(5) The action taken shall, in every case, be that which the court is of opinion the child's own good and the best interests of the community require. R.S., c. 160, s. 20.

May be dealt with under provincial law

21. (1) Whenever an order has been made under section 20 committing a child to a children's aid society, or to a superintendent, or to an industrial school, if so ordered by the provincial secretary, the child may thereafter be dealt with under the laws of the province in the same manner in all respects as if an order has been lawfully made in respect of a proceeding instituted under authority of a statute of the province; and from and after the date of the issuing of such order except for new offences, the child shall not be further dealt with by the court under this Act.

Order in advance

(2) The order of the provincial secretary may be made in advance and to apply to all cases of commitment mentioned in this section. R.S., c. 160, s. 21.

Parent or guardian may be ordered to pay fine, damages or costs

22. (1) Where a child is adjudged to have been guilty of an offence and the court is of the opinion that the case would be best met by the imposition of a fine, damages or costs, whether with or without restitution or any other action, the court may, if satisfied that the parent or guardian has conduced to the commission of the offence by neglecting to exercise due care of the child or otherwise, order that the fine, damages or costs awarded be paid by the parent or guardian of the child, instead of by the child.

Limit of amount

(2) Where a fine is imposed and ordered to be paid by the parent or guardian, the limit of amount imposed by subsection 20(1) does not apply, but shall in no case exceed the amount fixed for a similar offence under the *Criminal Code*.

Recovery of amount

(3) Where, under the provisions of this section or of section 20, a sum of money is ordered to be paid, the court may adjudge, either by the order respecting the payment of such sum or by an order made sub-

sequently, that the money shall be recoverable by distress and sale of the goods and chattels of the party and in default of such distress by imprisonment, and the amount is so recoverable or is recoverable in the same manner as a fine imposed under any provision of the *Criminal Code* is recoverable, or is recoverable as provided in any Act of the legislature of the province making provision for the recovery of fines.

Parent or guardian to be heard

(4) No order shall be made under this section without giving the parent or guardian an opportunity of being heard; but a parent or guardian who has been duly served with notice of the hearing pursuant to section 10 shall be deemed to have had such opportunity, notwithstanding the fact that he has failed to attend the hearing.

Appeal

(5) A parent or guardian has the same right of appeal from an order made under this section as if the order had been made on the conviction of the parent or guardian.

Additional action

(6) Any action taken under this section may be additional to any action taken under section 20. R.S., c. 160, s. 22.

Religion of child to be respected

23. (1) No Protestant child dealt with under this Act shall be committed to the care of any Roman Catholic children's aid society or be placed in any Roman Catholic family as his foster home; nor shall any Roman Catholic child dealt with under this Act be committed to the care of any Protestant children's aid society, or be placed in any Protestant family as his foster home; but this section does not apply to the placing of children in a temporary home or shelter for children, established under the authority of a statute of the province, or, in a municipality where there is but one children's aid society, to such children's aid society.

Order to enforce preceding provision

(2) If a Protestant child is committed to the care of a Roman Catholic children's aid society or placed in a Roman Catholic family as his foster home or if the Roman Catholic child is committed to the care of a Protestant children's aid society or placed in a Protestant family as his foster home, contrary to this section, the court shall, on the application of any person in that behalf, make an order providing for the proper commitment or placing of the child pursuant to subsection (1).

Children of religious faith other than Protestant or Roman Catholic

(3) No child of a religious faith other than the Protestant or Roman Catholic shall be committed to the care of either a Protestant or Roman Catholic children's aid society or be placed in any Protestant or Roman Catholic family as his foster home unless there is within the municipality no children's aid society or no suitable family of the same religious faith as that professed by the child or by his family, and, if there is no children's aid society or suitable family of such faith to which the care of such child can properly be given, the disposition of such child is in the discretion of the court. R.S., c. 160, s. 23.

Children not allowed to be in court

24. (1) No child, other than an infant in arms, shall be permitted to be present in court during the trial of any person charged with an offence or during any proceedings preliminary thereto, and if so present the child shall be ordered to be removed unless he is the person charged with the alleged offence, or unless the child's presence is required, as a witness or otherwise, for the purposes of justice.

Exception	(2)	This section does not apply to messengers, clerks and other persons required to attend at any court for the purposes connected with their employment. R.S., c. 160, s. 24.

Children under twelve

25. It is not lawful to commit a juvenile delinquent apparently under the age of twelve years to any industrial school, unless and until an attempt has been made to reform such child in his own home or in a foster home or in the charge of a children's aid society, or a superintendent, and unless the court finds that the best interests of the child and the welfare of the community require such commitment. R.S., c. 160, s. 25.

Children to be separated from adults

26. (1) No juvenile delinquent shall, under any circumstances, upon or after conviction, be sentenced to or incarcerated in any penitentiary, or county or other gaol, or police station, or any other place in which adults are or may be imprisoned.

Exception

(2) This section does not apply to a child who has been proceeded against under section 9. R.S., c. 160, s. 26.

Juvenile court committee

27. (1) here shall be in connection with the juvenile court a committee of citizens, serving without remuneration, to be known as the "juvenile court committee".

Juvenile court committee *ex officio*

(2) Where there is a children's aid society in a city or town in which this Act is in force, the committee of such society or a sub-committee thereof shall be the juvenile court committee; and where there is both a Protestant and a Roman Catholic children's aid society then the committee of the Protestant children's aid society or a sub-committee thereof shall be the juvenile court committee as regards Protestant children, and the committee of the Roman Catholic children's aid society or a sub-committee thereof shall be the juvenile court committee as regards Roman Catholic children.

Appointment by court

(3) Where there is no children's aid society in a city or town in which this Act is in force, the court may, and, upon a petition signed by fifty residents of the municipality in question, shall appoint three or more persons to be the juvenile court committee with respect to Protestant children, and three or more other persons to be the juvenile court committee with respect to Roman Catholic children; and the persons so appointed may in their discretion sit as one joint committee.

When child of religious faith other than Protestant or Roman Catholic

(4) In the case of a child of a religious faith other than Protestant or Roman Catholic, the court shall appoint three or more suitable persons to be the juvenile court committee as regards such child, such persons to be of the same religious faith as the child if there are such suitable persons resident within the municipality willing to act, and if in the opinion of the court they are desirable persons to be such committee. R.S., c. 160, s. 27.

Duties of committee

28. (1) It is the duty of the juvenile court committee to meet as often as may be necessary and consult with the probation officers with regard to juvenile delinquents, to offer, through the probation officers and otherwise, advice to the court as to the best mode of dealing with such delinquents, and, generally, to facilitate by every means in its power, the reformation of juvenile delinquents.

Representatives may be present	**(2)** Representatives of the juvenile court committee, who are members of that committee, may be present at any session of the juvenile court.
Certain cases reserved for judge	**(3)** No deputy judge shall hear and determine any case that a juvenile court committee desires should be reserved for hearing and determination by the judge of the juvenile court. R.S., c. 160, s. 28.
Court may appoint probation officer	**29.** Where no probation officer has been appointed under provincial authority and remuneration for a probation officer has been provided by municipal grant, public subscription or otherwise, the court shall, with the concurrence of the juvenile court committee, appoint one or more suitable persons as probation officers. R.S., c. 160, s. 29.
Powers of a probation officer	**30.** Every probation officer duly appointed under this Act or of any provincial statute has in the discharge of his or her duties as such probation officer all the powers of a constable, and shall be protected from civil actions for anything done in *bona fide* exercise of the powers conferred by this Act. R.S., c. 160, s. 30.
Duties of probation officer	**31.** It is the duty of a probation officer **(a)** to make such investigation as may be required by the court; **(b)** to be present in court in order to represent the interests of the child when the case is heard; **(c)** to furnish to the court such information and assistance as may be required; and **(d)** to take such charge of any child, before or after trial, as may be directed by the court. R.S., c. 160, s. 31.
Probation officers under control of judge	**32.** Every probation officer, however appointed, is under the control and subject to the directions of the judge of the court with which such probation officer is connected, for all purposes of this Act. R.S., c. 160, s. 32.
Adults liable who contribute to delinquency	**33.** **(1)** Any person, whether the parent or guardian of the child or not, who, knowingly or wilfully, **(a)** aids, causes, abets or connives at the commission by a child of a delinquency, or **(b)** does any act producing, promoting, or contributing to a child's being or becoming a juvenile delinquent or likely to make any child a juvenile delinquent, is liable on summary conviction before a juvenile court or a magistrate to a fine not exceeding five hundred dollars or to imprisonment for a period not exceeding two years, or to both.
Liability of parents and guardians	**(2)** Any person who, being the parent or guardian of the child and being able to do so, knowingly neglects to do that which would directly tend to prevent the child being or becoming a juvenile delinquent or to remove the conditions that render or are likely to render the child a juvenile delinquent is liable on summary conviction before a juvenile court or a magistrate to a fine not exceeding five hundred dollars or to imprisonment for a period not exceeding two years, or to both.
Adjournment	**(3)** The court or magistrate may postpone or adjourn the hearing of a charge under this section for such periods as the court may deem advisable or may postpone or adjourn the hearing *sine die* and may impose conditions upon any person found guilty under this section and suspend sentence subject to those conditions, and on proof at any time that those conditions have been violated may pass sentence on such person.

No defence if child does not become delinquent	(4)	It is not a valid defence to a prosecution under this section either that the child is of too tender years to understand or appreciate the nature or effect of the conduct of the accused, or that notwithstanding the conduct of the accused the child did not in fact become a juvenile delinquent.
Limitation	(5)	Notwithstanding anything to the contrary in section 5 or in the provisions of the *Criminal Code* referred to in paragraph 5(1)*(b)*, any prosecution for an offence under this section may be commenced within one year from the time when the offence is alleged to have been committed. R.S., c. 160, s. 33.
Penalty for inducing, etc. child to leave home, etc.	34.	Any person who induces or attempts to induce any child to leave any detention home, industrial school, foster home or any other institution or place where such child has been placed under this Act or who removes or attempts to remove such child therefrom, without the authority of the court, or who, when a child has unlawfully left the custody of an institution or foster home knowingly harbours or conceals such child without notice of the child's whereabouts to the court or to the institution or to the local police authorities, is guilty of an offence and is liable upon summary conviction before a juvenile court or before a magistrate to a fine not exceeding one hundred dollars or to imprisonment for a period not exceeding one year, or to both. R.S., c. 160, s. 34.
No preliminary hearing	35. (1)	Prosecutions against adults for offences against any provisions of the *Criminal Code* in respect of a child may be brought in the juvenile court without the necessity of a preliminary hearing before a justice, and may be summarily disposed of where the offence is triable summarily, or otherwise dealt with as in the case of a preliminary hearing before a justice.
Application of *Criminal Code*	(2)	All provisions of the *Criminal Code* not inconsistent with this Act that would apply to similar proceedings if brought before a justice apply to prosecutions brought before the juvenile court under this section. R.S., c. 160, s. 35.
Contempt of court	36. (1)	Every juvenile court has such and like powers and authority to preserve order in court during the sittings thereof and by the like ways and means as now by law are or may be exercised and used in like cases and for the like purposes by any court in Canada and by the judges thereof, during the sittings thereof.
Enforcing of process	(2)	Every judge of a juvenile court, whenever any resistance is offered to the execution of any summons, warrant of execution or other process issued by him, may enforce the due execution of the process by the means provided by the law for enforcing the execution of the process of other courts in like cases. R.S., c. 160, s. 36.
Appeals by special leave	37. (1)	A supreme court judge may, in his discretion, on special grounds, grant special leave to appeal from any decision of the juvenile court or a magistrate; in any case where such leave is granted the procedure upon appeal shall be such as is provided in the case of a conviction on indictment, and the provisions of the *Criminal Code* relating to appeals from conviction on indictment *mutatis mutandis* apply to such appeal, save that the appeal shall be to a supreme court judge instead of

to the court of appeal, with a further right of appeal to the court of appeal by special leave of that court.

When leave to appeal may be granted

(2) No leave to appeal shall be granted under this section unless the judge or court granting such leave considers that in the particular circumstances of the case it is essential in the public interest or for the due administration of justice that such leave be granted.

Application for leave to appeal

(3) Application for leave to appeal under this section shall be made within ten days of the making of the conviction or order complained of, or within such further time, not exceeding an additional twenty days, as a supreme court judge may see fit to fix, either before or after the expiration of the said ten days. R.S., c. 160, s. 37.

Act to be liberally construed

38. This Act shall be liberally construed in order that its purpose may be carried out, namely, that the care and custody and discipline of a juvenile delinquent shall approximate as nearly as may be that which should be given by his parents, and that as far as practicable every juvenile delinquent shall be treated, not as criminal, but as a misdirected and misguided child, and one needing aid, encouragement, help and assistance. R.S., c. 160, s. 38.

Not to affect provincial statutes

39. Nothing in this Act shall be construed as having the effect of repealing or overriding any provision of any provincial statute intended for the protection or benefit of children; and when a juvenile delinquent, who has not been guilty of an act that is under the provisions of the *Criminal Code* an indictable offence, comes within the provisions of a provincial statute, he may be dealt with either under such statute or under this Act as may be deemed to be in the best interests of the child. R.S., c. 160, s. 39.

Repeal of former law

40. Whenever and so soon as this Act goes into force in any province, city, town, or other portion of a province, every provision of the *Criminal Code* or of any other Act of the Parliament of Canada inconsistent with the provisions of this Act, stands repealed as regards such province, city, town, or other portion of a province. R.S., c. 160, s. 40.

Sections in force in Canada

41. Subsections 12(4) and 17(3) and (5), and section 34 shall be in force in all parts of Canada, whether this Act is otherwise in force or not. R.S., c. 160, s. 41.

When Act shall be enforced

42. Subject to section 41, this Act may be put in force in any province, or in any portion of a province, by proclamation, after the passing of an Act by the legislature of any province providing for the establishment of juvenile courts, or designating any existing courts as juvenile courts, and of detention homes for children. R.S., c. 160, s. 42.

Any city or town may ask for this law

43. (1) Subject to section 41, this Act may be put in force in any city, town, or other portion of a province, by proclamation, notwithstanding that the provincial legislature has not passed an Act such as referred to in section 42, if the Governor in Council is satisfied that proper facilities for the due carrying out of the provisions of this Act have been provided in such city, town, or other portion of a province, by the municipal council thereof or otherwise.

Special appointment of judge

(2) The Governor in Council may designate a superior court or county court judge or a justice, having jurisdiction in the city, town, or other portion of a province, in which the Act is so put in force, to act as

juvenile court judge for such city, town, or other portion of a province, and the judge or justice so designated or appointed has and shall exercise in such city, town, or other portion of a province, all the powers by this Act conferred on the juvenile court. R.S., c. 160, s. 43.

Enforcement of Act

44. This Act shall go into force only when and as proclamations declaring it in force in any province, city, town or other portion of the province are issued and published in the *Canada Gazette*. R.S., c. 160, s. 44.

Operation of Act

45. Notwithstanding section 44, this Act shall be in force in every part of Canada in which the *Juvenile Delinquents Act*, chapter 108 of the Revised Statutes of Canada, 1927, was in force on the 14th day of June 1929. R.S., c. 160, s. 45.

R.S.C. 1970, c. J.3.

APPENDIX B Young Offenders Act

DECLARATION OF PRINCIPLE

Policy for Canada
with respect to
young offenders

3. (1) It is hereby recognized and declared that

  (a) crime prevention is essential to the long-term protection of society and requires addressing the underlying causes of crime by young persons and developing multi-disciplinary approaches to identifying and effectively responding to children and young persons at risk of committing offending behaviour in the future;

  (*a.1*) while young persons should not in all instances be held accountable in the same manner or suffer the same consequences for their behaviour as adults, young persons who commit offences should nonetheless bear responsibility for their contraventions;

  (b) society must, although it has the responsibility to take reasonable measures to prevent criminal conduct by young persons, be afforded the necessary protection from illegal behaviour;

  (c) young persons who commit offences require supervision, discipline and control, but, because of their state of dependency and level of development and maturity, they also have special needs and require guidance and assistance;

  (*c.1*) the protection of society, which is a primary objective of the criminal law applicable to youth, is best served by rehabilitation, wherever possible, of young persons who commit offences, and rehabilitation is best achieved by addressing the needs and circumstances of a young person that are relevant to the young person's offending behaviour;

  (d) where it is not inconsistent with the protection of society, taking no measures or taking measures other than judicial proceedings under this Act should be considered for dealing with young persons who have committed offences;

  (e) young persons have rights and freedoms in their own right, including those stated in the *Canadian Charter of Rights and Freedoms* or in the *Canadian Bill of Rights*, and in particular a right to be heard in the course of, and to participate in, the processes that lead to decisions that affect them, and young persons should have special guarantees of their rights and freedoms;

  (f) in the application of this Act, the rights and freedoms of young persons include a right to the least possible interference with freedom that is consistent with the protection of society, having regard to the needs of young persons and the interests of their families;

(g) young persons have the right, in every instance where they have rights or freedoms that may be affected by this Act, to be informed as to what those rights and freedoms are; and

(h) parents have responsibility for the care and supervision of their children, and, for that reason, young persons should be removed from parental supervision either partly or entirely only when measures that provide for continuing parental supervision are inappropriate.

Act to be liberally construed

(2) This Act shall be liberally construed to the end that young persons will be dealt with in accordance with the principles set out in subsection (1).

R.S., 1985, c. Y-1, s. 3; 1995, c. 19, s. 1.

APPENDIX C *Youth Criminal Justice Act*

DECLARATION OF PRINCIPLE

Policy for Canada with respect to young persons

3. (1) The following principles apply in this Act:

  (a) the youth criminal justice system is intended to

    (i) prevent crime by addressing the circumstances underlying a young person's offending behaviour,

    (ii) rehabilitate young persons who commit offences and reintegrate them into society, and

    (iii) ensure that a young person is subject to meaningful consequences for his or her offence in order to promote the long-term protection of the public;

  (b) the criminal justice system for young persons must be separate from that of adults and emphasize the following:

    (i) rehabilitation and reintegration,

    (ii) fair and proportionate accountability that is consistent with the greater dependency of young persons and their reduced level of maturity,

    (iii) enhanced procedural protection to ensure that young persons are treated fairly and that their rights, including their right to privacy, are protected,

    (iv) timely intervention that reinforces the link between the offending behaviour and its consequences, and

    (v) the promptness and speed with which persons responsible for enforcing this Act must act, given young persons' perception of time;

  (c) within the limits of fair and proportionate accountability, the measures taken against young persons who commit offences should

    (i) reinforce respect for societal values,

    (ii) encourage the repair of harm done to victims and the community,

    (iii) be meaningful for the individual young person given his or her needs and level of development and, where appropriate, involve the parents, the extended family, the community and social or other agencies in the young person's rehabilitation and reintegration, and

    (iv) respect gender, ethnic, cultural and linguistic differences and respond to the needs of aboriginal young persons and of young persons with special requirements; and

  (d) special considerations apply in respect of proceedings against young persons and, in particular,

(i) young persons have rights and freedoms in their own right, such as a right to be heard in the course of and to participate in the processes, other than the decision to prosecute, that lead to decisions that affect them, and young persons have special guarantees of their rights and freedoms,

(ii) victims should be treated with courtesy, compassion and respect for their dignity and privacy and should suffer the minimum degree of inconvenience as a result of their involvement with the youth criminal justice system,

(iii) victims should be provided with information about the proceedings and given an opportunity to participate and be heard, and

(iv) parents should be informed of measures or proceedings involving their children and encouraged to support them in addressing their offending behaviour.

Act to be liberally construed

(2) This Act shall be liberally construed so as to ensure that young persons are dealt with in accordance with the principles set out in subsection (1).

S.C. 2002, c. 1.

Index